Weimar and the Vatican
1919-1933

Weimar and the Vatican

1919-1933

German-Vatican Diplomatic Relations in the Interwar Years

STEWART A. STEHLIN

Princeton University Press
Princeton, New Jersey

Copyright © 1983 by Princeton University Press
Published by Princeton University Press, 41 William Street,
Princeton, New Jersey 08540
In the United Kingdom:
Princeton University Press, Guildford, Surrey

Library of Congress Cataloging in Publication Data will be
found on the last printed page of this book

ISBN 0-691-05399-5

Publication of this book has been aided by the Whitney Darrow
Publication Reserve Fund of Princeton University Press

This book has been composed in Linotron Janson
Clothbound editions of Princeton University Press books
are printed on acid-free paper, and binding materials are
chosen for strength and durability. Paperbacks, although satisfactory
for personal collections, are not usually suitable for library rebinding.

Printed in the United States of America by Princeton University Press
Princeton, New Jersey

To
My Mother,
My Teachers,
and
My Friends

PREFACE

The years after World War I were important years for Germany—a period in which the Reich, having lost the war, had to accommodate itself to a new republican form of government, solve enormous socio-economic problems, and reestablish working relations with the other governments of Europe. The importance of Germany's relations to states such as England, France, and the Soviet Union are immediately apparent and have already been the subject of much study. What has not been sufficiently investigated is the importance of Germany's re-lations to the Holy See and the significance of these relations both for Germany's internal and external policy and for interwar European diplomacy in general.

The Vatican has always been an enigma. Its veil of secrecy and its ban on use of its archival material from the twentieth century have prompted the belief in the Vatican's ability to exert powerful pressure behind the scenes as well as a readiness to believe any rumor about the influence—nefarious or otherwise—of the Pope and the Curia. As one observer of the Holy See put it, many governments heard what they already believed about the Vatican and later on corroborated it by believing what they then heard. Nevertheless, the Vatican's influ-ence and prestige had undeniably increased steadily in the twentieth century, and many have recognized the Pontiff himself as a spokesman for Christians and for all men. Within the last few years the world has seen a pope accorded an invitation to speak at the United Nations on world issues, acknowledged by the Anglican Archbishop of Can-terbury as prime spokesman for Christendom, become instrumental in averting armed conflict in Poland, and sent wishes for a speedy recov-ery, after an assassination attempt, by world leaders from the entire political spectrum, including those of the Soviet Union. The Pope may not have the military divisions about which Stalin so sarcastically asked,[1] but he has become a "force," an influence in diplomatic as well as in internal affairs, if only to the extent that social, educational, religious, and moral issues bear on politics. Countries, then, if they

---

[1] In 1935, French Premier Pierre Laval asked Joseph Stalin to remove restrictions on Catholics in Russia in order to conciliate the Pope, he is to have replied: "The Pope! How many divisions has *he* got?" Winston S. Churchill, *The gathering storm* (Cambridge, Mass., 1948), p. 135.

cannot have God on their side, at least would like to have the Pope there.

A study of Germany's relations with the Vatican not only gives us an insight into aspects of Weimar foreign policy, into the close interrelation of foreign and domestic problems, and the role which Rome played in German affairs, but also offers us a glimpse, in this case study, of how the Curia conducts its own foreign policy. All too often one hears intellectuals and journalists as well as the general public ask why Rome remained silent on a given issue, why the Papacy took so long to act. By examining the degree to which both Rome and Berlin could maneuver diplomatically, we can see some of the many considerations in the decision-making process which Rome followed and, by analogy, can seek to understand Vatican diplomacy in general.

I undertook this study after noticing that students in German history courses, although familiar with the relations of the Church and the Vatican to the Nazis, about which already much has been written, knew or could find little on the period prior to the concordat of 1933, particularly as to the important role which Berlin perceived that the Vatican could play in German affairs. They already were aware that Hitler had signed a treaty with the Vatican in 1933 but knew little of the history or context of these negotiations or that 1933 was merely the culmination of work done in the preceding thirteen years. Once the history of German-Vatican negotiations in the Weimar period is examined, the entire concordat problem can be understood better as an important aspect of twentieth-century German history, not limited in its significance merely to the Nazi era. Moreover, students in this country have little awareness of the delicate issues which church-state relations created in the overall political situation in a religiously divided country such as Germany, which depended on coalition governments for its existence. Again the period under consideration here provides a good example of the important role which Berlin and Rome played in the diplomatic considerations of each other and illustrates the interconnection of many aspects of Germany's domestic and foreign policy as they related to the Vatican.

I have arranged the material for this study in a chronological-topical format. I have tried to keep to a minimum the technical discussion of ecclesiastical administration and the legal aspects of the concordats. Nevertheless, some mention of these subjects is both inevitable and necessary. Because of the interrelation of the many aspects of this complicated story there is, at times, some duplication of facts in the narrative but only when it seemed necessary to supply the reader with important information. Besides discussing Rome's diplomacy after 1919 and the role which the Reich played in it, I have sought to portray in the first chapters how Germany worked to have the Holy See aid the Germans in securing their political borders, regaining lost territory, solving their economic problems, and maintaining peace and unity within the country against any centrifugal or particularist forces. For its help Rome hoped to gain concessions in the field of church-state relations. The course of these negotiations, which occurred simultaneously with those in the international arena, is narrated in the last chapter.

Since Vatican archives are closed for the period covered by this work, I have relied largely on material in diocesan repositories and public and private archives in Germany, England, France, Italy, Belgium, Poland, and Austria, as well as on interviews with many of the people who had been active during this period. The great number of sources available to the scholar, including copies of documents from Rome in other repositories, allows us to evaluate the situation despite the lack of direct access to material in the archives of the Holy See. Moreover, the Vatican Secretariat of State was then run by a small staff headed from 1914 until 1930 by Cardinal Pietro Gasparri and thereafter by Cardinal Eugenio Pacelli. Decisions were made in close consultation with other members of the Sacred College and with the Pontiff himself, who closely supervised the conduct of the Vatican's policy. The Cardinal Secretary of State then handled the day-to-day business—meetings with the diplomats, representing the Curia in general—while the Pope usually addressed himself to larger issues. The Pontiff and his Secretary formed, so to speak, a team. Although Gasparri and Pacelli generally signed diplomatic correspondence and appear more frequently in this work than does the Pope himself, this is not to imply that the Pontiff had no part in the decision making, but rather that the Cardinal was his spokesman, the Aaron to the Pope's Moses.

The research and writing of this work were done during released time from my teaching duties, with the aid of a Guggenheim and a Senior Fulbright Fellowship, and during summers and sabbatical leaves granted by New York University. Moreover, I was fortunate to have had aid from the American Council of Learned Societies, the American Philosophical Society, the Andrew W. Mellon Foundation, and the New York University Humanities Research Fund to help to defray expenses during the various stages of my research and writing. I wish to acknowledge my gratitude for the help and consideration given me by the staffs of New York University's Bobst Library and of all the archives which I used and mention in my bibliography, especially those of the Bavarian *Geheimes Staatsarchiv* and the German Foreign Office Archives, and to all those listed who gave me valuable information and granted me interviews. In addition I would like to pay tribute to the late Professors Hajo Holborn and Ernst Deuerlein, whose advice and encouragement were of immense value in focusing the direction of my research in the initial stages of this work. I am also indebted to Professors Karl Otmar von Aretin, Philip Cannistraro, J. Victor Conzemius, Renzo De Felice, Guenter Lewy, Rudolf Lill, Rudolf Morsey, Konrad Repgen, Herbert Weichmann; His Excellency Bishop Wincenty Urban; Charles Burns, Dieter Golombek, Robert Graham, S.J., Wilhelm Klein, S.J., Angelo Martini, S.J., Johannes Schauff, Ludwig Volk, S.J., among many others, all of whom gave me of their time and knowledge which I greatly appreciate.

Thanks are also due to all my friends, colleagues, and students who have read and given suggestions for improving the manuscript, especially Daniel Abels, Carole K. Fink, Brian P. Hotaling, Darline G. Levy, Mary Nolan, Brenda Parnes, Eugene D. Richie, Gerard W. Sheridan, Robert R. Tomes, and Roger Whitney.

I would also like to register my thanks and appreciation to R. Miriam Brokaw of Princeton University Press for her sympathetic help and support during all stages in the production of this book.

Finally I would like to acknowledge my debt of gratitude to my mother, who patiently typed the drafts of this manuscript.

New York, New York
January, 1983.

CONTENTS

LIST OF ILLUSTRATIONS

All photos courtesy of United Press International, Inc., New York City, unless otherwise stated

ABBREVIATIONS FREQUENTLY USED IN THE FOOTNOTES

AA	Germany, German Foreign Office (Auswärtiges Amt)
AAS	Vatican, *Acta Apostolicae Sedis*
AFO	Austria, Austrian Foreign Office
AN	France, Archives Nationales
AW	Poland, Wrocław (Breslau), Archiwum Archidiecezjalne
BA	Germany, Bundesarchiv
BelgFO	Belgium, Belgian Foreign Office
BFM	Germany, Bavaria, Bavarian Foreign Ministry
BFO	Great Britain, British Foreign Office
BRV	Germany, German Foreign Office, Botschaftsakten Rom-Vatikan, laufende Nummer
BSTA	Germany, Bayerisches Hauptstaatsarchiv, Allgemeines Staatsarchiv
Cologne, Marx.	Germany, Historisches Archiv der Stadt Köln, Nachlass Marx
FFO	France, French Foreign Office (Ministère des Affaires Étrangères)
Ges. Päpstl. Stuhl	Germany, GSTA, Gesandtschaft Päpstlicher Stuhl
GSTA	Germany, Bayerisches Hauptstaatsarchiv, Geheimes Staatsarchiv
HHSTA	Austria, Oesterreichisches Staatsarchiv, Abt. Haus-Hof- und Staatsarchiv
PGSTA	Germany, Geheimes Staatsarchiv Preussischer Kulturbesitz

POLITICAL PARTY ABBREVIATIONS

DDP	Deutsche Demokratische Partei (German Democratic Party)
DNVP	Deutschnationale Volkspartei (German National People's Party, Nationalists)

DVP   Deutsche Volkspartei (German People's Party)
KPD   Kommunistische Partei Deutschlands (Communist Party of
          Germany)
NSDAP   Nationalsozialistische Deutsche Arbeiterpartei (National
          Socialist German Workers' Party)
SPD   Sozialdemokratische Partei Deutschlands (Social Demo-
          cratic Party of Germany)

Weimar and the Vatican
1919-1933

INTRODUCTION

In 1919 Europe had just emerged from a war more destructive of human life and material than any previous conflict. The transformation of the economy, society, government, and ideology universally induced by the events of World War I made people aware that conditions had changed, that life would never again be the same, that a restoration—even an ostensible restoration—would not occur, as it had in 1815. Out of the shambles of European order and society each country sought to retain or regain a position of power or respect. Each opportunity on the diplomatic chessboard was not to be overlooked. The situation seemed to transmute Clausewitz's famous dictum—"war is the continuation of politics by other means"—into the proposition that peace is the extension of war by other means. In 1919, with all things in flux, new openings could be made, old alliances renewed, and diplomatic fortunes won overnight.

Two such governments which grasped the significance of the moment were Germany and the Vatican. Germany, defeated and disgraced, threatened with harsh peace terms, needed every ally whose word carried weight. The Papacy, immured within the Vatican walls since 1870, waiting for an opportunity again to play an important role in the affairs of Europe, scrutinized every diplomatic event in the hope that a new situation might improve its position. In 1919 a new opportunity opened up for the Vatican to reassert itself, a new chance for a republican Germany to regain some of its lost property and prestige. It was at this juncture in time that the diplomatic goals of these two governments coincided in many points of general policy. During the four years of hostilities the attitude of both the Reich and the Vatican changed toward one another as each increasingly regarded the other as an important factor in its diplomatic considerations and as many of the problems which were to concern the two governments in the postwar era began to emerge. The wartime experience of the diplomatic polarization of Europe, of having to win international support for its position, showed Germany the need for closer ties and cooperation with the Vatican. On the other hand, the war had proved to the Vatican that it still could command respect from the European powers, that its voice could still be heard in diplomatic circles.

The mechanism for the conduct of normal diplomatic affairs—the bilateral exchange of representatives by two governments—however, had not been fully developed between the Papacy and the Reich. Whereas individual German states had ministers at the Vatican, none spoke for the entire Reich; and, conversely, the Pontiff's nuncio in Munich had official jurisdiction only within Bavaria. The weakness of this underdeveloped diplomatic staffing became increasingly evident to Germany's policy planning during the war, and the importance of the Vatican for Germany's diplomacy continued to be made evident during the Weimar period.

The German states had long recognized the need for a representative at the Papal Court. Austria had had a permanent mission there for centuries, Prussia since 1747, and Bavaria since 1803. Nuncios represented the Vatican in Vienna and Munich but not in Berlin, where Protestant hostility was too great to allow a Papal delegate to take up residence. The question had been raised during the reign of Friedrich Wilhelm III without success. In the 1860's Otto von Bismarck was already convinced that regular diplomatic relations with a nuncio in Berlin might be a better method of safeguarding the rights of the State in its relations with the Church than by maintaining the Catholic department in the Ministry of Education and Religious Affairs (*Kultusministerium*). Not only the Prussian monarch, however, but also the liberals and many Protestant conservatives opposed this move. In 1887, Bismarck, in a letter to the Prussian Minister at the Vatican, Kurd von Schlözer, noted his failure to persuade Kaiser Wilhelm I to allow the nunciature in Munich to extend its jurisdiction to all of Germany as the Vatican had suggested. Periodically thereafter the Roman Curia inquired about the possibility of establishing a nunciature for all Germany. In 1893, Leo XIII personally brought the subject to the attention of German Ambassador to the Italian Government in Rome, Bernhard von Bülow, explaining how such a nuncio could serve as a moderating influence on the Catholic Center Party, which had until then caused the Chancellor trouble in the Reichstag. These overtures notwithstanding, the complexion of Vatican-Reich relations remained unchanged during the Imperial period; Prussia and Bavaria were represented in Rome by diplomatic legations while Rome was represented in Germany only through its nuncio in Munich.[1]

[1] Germany, Auswärtiges Amt, Politisches Archiv (hereafter cited as AA), IA, Preussen 2 Nr. 2, Vol. 2, memorandum of the Foreign Office, September 27, 1909. Ernst Deuerlein, *Das Reichskonkordat* (Düsseldorf, 1956), p. 2. Bismarck had publicly expressed his views on German-Vatican relations in a speech in the Prussian House of Deputies, stating that a nunciature would be more useful than the secretary for Catholic affairs in the Prussian Ministry of Education and Religious Affairs. Again, much later, on July 31, 1892 in a speech in Jena the Chancellor, now retired, noted: "We would be more easily done with our Catholic Question if we had a nunciature to deal with. . . ." Otto von Bismarck, *Die politischen Reden des Fürsten Bismarck*, ed., Horst Kohl (Stuttgart, 1893),

When hostilities broke out in 1914, the Vatican found itself in a very serious predicament. Both sides asked for its blessing or at least its sympathy for their course of action in the war. The Papacy, which considered itself an impartial arbiter, feared the prospect of being forced to choose between the warring coalitions, both of which contained large Catholic populations. A prolonged occupation of Catholic Belgium by the Reich, or for that matter any extension of Protestant Germany's influence, hardly promoted Rome's interest. Nor would Rome applaud an overwhelming Allied victory in 1914. France, though the "oldest daughter of the Church," in the shadow cast by the Dreyfus Affair, had passed the law for the separation of Church and State and had broken off diplomatic relations with the Vatican in the decade before the war. Great Britain, a Protestant land, at that moment was undergoing renewed troubles with Catholic Ireland. Russia, the champion of Orthodoxy and oppressor of Catholic Poland, was not particularly disposed toward the Vatican. A Russian victory in the east could cause even more difficulty for the Poles and hinder the Balkan Catholics in their relations with Rome.[2] Moreover, the Vatican found little comfort in a possible defeat of Austria-Hungary, since this country represented the one great Catholic power in Europe. As early as January 1915, Bülow, once more Ambassador to the Italian Government at the Quirinal, informed the Chancellor of the Curia's fear for the Danubian monarchy and its wish for the perpetuation of Vienna's great-power status. Thus concerned over the Dual Monarchy's fate, dreading victory by the Italian lay state, which would surely affect the Vatican's situation, the Curia was bound to oppose the war which could bring about all these contingencies.[3]

A European war threatened not only the international position of the Papacy but also its financial stability, for wartime measures could easily cut it off from its sources of income. Only the unilateral Treaty of Guarantees, which the Italian Government promulgated in 1871 when it occupied Rome, guaranteed the independence of the Papacy, though it had never been tested. The war now catapulted many questions to the forefront. Would the Pope be allowed to receive money and representatives from states at war with Italy, the Curia wondered.

Vol. 5, p. 237. 23rd Session of the Prussian House of Deputies, January 30, 1972. Joseph Roth, "Zur Vorgeschichte der Berliner Nuntiatur," in *Reich und Reichsfeinde* (Hamburg, 1943), Vol. 4, pp. 215-236. Deuerlein, *Reichskonkordat*, p. 2.

[2] George La Piana, "The political heritage of Pius XII," *Foreign Affairs*, XVIII (1940), 486. *Augsburger Postzeitung*, April 15, 1919.

[3] AA, IA, Päpstl. Stuhl 7, Vol. 3, Bülow (Rome-Quirinal) to Bethmann-Hollweg, January 6, 1915. W. W. Gottlieb, *Studies in secret diplomacy during the First World War* (London, 1957), p. 373.

Such questions as these, discussed in Church circles, made it imperative from a diplomatic standpoint for the Vatican to avert war and to reconcile the adversaries, and, if that could not be done, at least to remain publicly as strictly neutral as possible.

Germany, on the other hand, was most anxious to see its position justified in the eyes of the neutrals. In fact, when the United States abandoned neutrality in favor of active participation in the war in 1917, the Vatican became even more important in German planning.[4] From the beginning of the war Berlin had repeatedly sent messages to its ministers in Rome to make certain that the Allied Powers did not gain the full confidence of the Papacy.

But in 1915, upon being granted concessions at the Treaty of London by the Allies, Italy entered the war against the Central Powers.[5] After that, the representatives of the Central Powers at the Vatican found it increasingly difficult to carry on their functions in Rome; the Quirinal made accusations of espionage against them, restricted their movements, and even confiscated some of their property. Finally, in May the Austrian, Bavarian, and Prussian ministers, along with their staffs, left Rome and crossed the border into Switzerland, where in Lugano they continued to function as best they could away from the government to which they were accredited. Germany realized that this departure considerably weakened its position and feared that the Allies would further strengthen their hold on this important neutral power. Reports from Lugano constantly registered concern that the Pope was falling under the influence of the Western Powers and that the Curia, composed predominantly of Italians, was showing sympathy with the Allied cause.[6]

Within Germany and Austria-Hungary there was widespread unhappiness with what was perceived as Papal discrimination, especially when in the 1916 Consistory Pope Benedict XV would elevate three French prelates to the rank of cardinal without appointing any from the Central Powers. The influential Center Party leader, Matthias Erzberger, feared that the appointment of the new cardinals, which increased the number of French members of the Sacred College to a modern-day high (eight), would be interpreted in both Germany and

---

[4] For current discussion on the matter, see Reinhard R. Doerries, "Imperial Berlin and Washington: new light on Germany's foreign policy and America's entry into World War I," *Central European History*, XI (1978), 23-49.

[5] Carl Bergmann, *Der Weg der Reparation* (Frankfurt a.M., 1926), p. 97f. Gottlieb, Part 2: Italy among the Great Powers.

[6] AA, IA, Päpstl. Stuhl 3 Nr. 1, Vol. 18, Mühlberg to Bethmann-Hollweg, November 11, 1916. AA, IA, Päpstl. Stuhl 3 Nr. 2, Vol. 21, Mühlberg to Bethmann-Hollweg, November 14, 1916.

other countries as an indication that the Vatican was leaning toward the Allied Powers. He wrote to his confidant at the Papal Court, Msgr. Rudolf von Gerlach, urgently asking him to point out to the Pope the political gravity of the move and warned that the Vatican would lose favor among the German population.[7] Prussian Minister to the Vatican Otto von Mühlberg also inquired of Curial officials about the matter and was informed by Cardinal Secretary of State Pietro Gasparri that the new French cardinals were merely replacing those who had died since the last consistory. Moreover, he told the German envoy that as soon as circumstances permitted after the war, the Vatican would also name the Prince-Bishop of Breslau and the Archbishop of Prague to the Sacred College.[8] The normal replacement of deceased princes of the Church and the circumstances of war which would have made it difficult for members of the hierarchy from the Central Powers to come to Rome to receive the red hat had apparently given France a favored position in the Consistory. The Vatican reassured Germany and Austria-Hungary that it had acted within the bounds of normal ecclesiastical procedure under wartime conditions, but the episode illustrates the Central Powers' eagerness to maintain their representation in the College of Cardinals and the importance on which they placed having their views adequately represented in Rome.

The pressures of European conflict placed a great burden on the Pontiff. Benedict, born into a respected Ligurian family in 1854, had seen both pastoral and diplomatic service and had ascended the Papal throne at the very onset of the war. Though small in stature and rather frail in appearance, his assured actions and his energetic capacity for work confirmed the strength of his will. The situation had not looked promising for Benedict after his hasty and curtailed coronation in the limited space of the Sistine Chapel on September 6, 1914. From the first the Pontiff held to a policy which he adhered to until his death. Only two days after his coronation he exhorted Catholics to pray for the end of the war and urged the rulers to put a stop to the bloodshed and to make peace. In his first encyclical *Ad beatissima* on November 1, 1914 he continued with the same idea: "We beseech princes and rulers that they not delay to bring back to their people the life-giving blessings of peace. . . . If their rights have been violated, they can certainly find other ways and means of obtaining a remedy." In the allocution to the cardinals of January 22, 1915 he defined the theme

---

[7] AA, IA, Preussen 2 Nr. 2a, Vol. 9, Erzberger to Gerlach, November 11, 1916. For a defense of the Pope's position see *Germania*, "Die neuen Kardinäle," November 12, 1916.

[8] AA, IA, Päpstl. Stuhl 3 Nr. 2, Vol. 21, Gasparri to Mühlberg, November 22, 1916. Bertram was actually made cardinal in 1916, but it was not announced till 1919.

further. If he was not allowed to hasten the end of this war, at least he would do all he could to lessen its woes. For the belligerents to invoke the Papacy to side with them would be neither right nor useful to peace. Instead, the Holy See had to remain above the fray, above the level of nations. Thus many of the Pope's statements were couched in general terms which avoided specific issues which the war had raised. He did not, for example, speak out on the question of war guilt or the acts of one side or the other in its conduct of the war. But his refusal to take sides, in his opinion, was necessary in order to make his voice heard on humanitarian issues, against the sufferings of all parties, and in favor of ending the hostilities. The Holy Father spoke out tirelessly to encourage both sides to compromise, and his further allocutions during 1915 and 1916 continued this theme of peace (July 28, 1915, December 4, 1916).[9]

The Papacy, in order to show its concern for all people, including those in Central Europe now cut off from direct contact with Rome, worked on three levels—religious, humanitarian, and, finally, political. On the religious level the Pope constantly expressed paternal concern and the wish for reconciliation, ordering by Pontifical decree prayers in the entire Catholic world for that purpose. Although all people could not unite in this pious hope, the fact remains that during this period of hostilities the Papacy by means of its supranational position offered the ecclesiastical means to bring the opposing sides closer together, proclaiming the message of reconciliation which Christian nations should heed. More successful were Vatican efforts for the victims of war. It aided in such things as the exchange of prisoners, the repatriation of certain groups of interned civilians, the hospitalization of the wounded in Switzerland, supervision of prisoners of war, and distribution of packages to the prisoners. *La Civiltà Cattolica*, the Jesuit organ in Rome and semi-official spokesman for the Vatican, chronicled much of this work in its issues of 1918.[10]

In addition to speeches and later the famous peace note of August

[9] Great Britain, Foreign Office, Public Record Office (hereafter cited as BFO), 371/7671/5302, De Salis (Vatican) to Curzon, British Foreign Secretary, October 25, 1922, pp. 4-5. Karl Mirbt, *Das Konkordatsproblem der Gegenwart* (Berlin, 1927), p. 8. Vatican, *Acta Apostolicae Sedis* (hereafter cited as *AAS*), VII (1915), 365-377; VIII (1916), 465-469. For a discussion of the Papal neutrality, see Hubert Jedin and John P. Dolan, eds., *The Church in the modern age* (New York, 1981), pp. 35-39.

[10] *La Civiltà Cattolica*, 1918. Germany, Bayerisches Hauptstaatsarchiv, Geheimes Staatsarchiv (hereafter cited as GSTA), MA 104064, Ritter to Bavarian Foreign Ministry (hereafter cited as BFM), February 7, 1919. Gottlieb, pp. 370-371. An enumeration of the Vatican's charitable activities to relieve wartime and post-war suffering is given in the *Bayerischer Kurier* "Der Vatikan und deutsche Kriegsnöte 1914-1922," August 2, 1924. Jedin, pp. 38-39.

I, 1917, the Papacy expressed its desire for peace on the political level by setting the wheels of Vatican diplomacy moving to influence the combatants to come to a compromise. The results of all these efforts was the emergence of the Pontiff—the "Prisoner of the Vatican" since 1871 whom several governments had treated as a political *quantité négligeable* during the war—from his long isolation. His voice was raised on world issues and his position enhanced. Both sides sought the Vatican's sympathy in a war where every bit of support was needed.[11]

During the hostilities the British Government had already surprised the world by sending an envoy to the Holy See. In 1915 the Dutch Prime Minister P. Cort van der Linden supported in Parliament the idea of sending a representative to Rome, basing his endorsement not on reasons of domestic policy but on the Pope's international political importance. "This is reality," he declared. "One can regret this, but nothing can change the facts. There is no more important political center which can exert influence in the interests of peace than the Papacy. We must work with it and therefore the legation is necessary."[12]

Although Great Britain, along with the other Entente Powers, had agreed in the Treaty of London (1915) to Italy's demand to exclude the Vatican from the eventual peace negotiations, London also emphasized the value it placed on its contacts with the Holy See by raising its representative at the Vatican to the rank of minister extraordinary and plenipotentiary in 1916. The Vatican by its own peace initiatives in 1917 was moved more into the center of the international spotlight, and newly formed states, such as Finland and Estonia, although largely Protestant, sought the Holy See's immediate recognition. Further acknowledgment of the importance of the Papacy and of the efforts of the Pope in world affairs was graphically displayed following the cessation of hostilities on January 4, 1919, when President Woodrow Wilson paid an unprecedented visit to the Vatican. In December 1918, Benedict had issued an encyclical in which he welcomed the future peace negotiations, ordered prayers for the conference's success, and expressed the belief that a lasting peace would surely be greeted everywhere in the Catholic world with joy.

The Pontiff's statements on peace no doubt brought joy especially to German Catholics, whose underpinnings were badly shaken during the war years. Many Catholics in the Reich underwent a transformation during this period from loyalty to the Wilhelmine system in 1914, through a more liberal parliamentary system in 1917-1918, to final

[11] GSTA, MA 104064, Ritter to BFM, February 7, 1919.
[12] AA, PO II, PO 2 Nr. 2 Vat., Vol. 1, memorandum of Meyer-Rodehüser, June 12, 1929.

acceptance of the republic in 1919. Of the 65 million inhabitants of the German Reich in 1910, 23.8 million were Catholics who were underrepresented in the upper classes or in important positions in the government. Of 90 Prussian ministers and state secretaries between 1888 and 1914 only four were Catholics, of the Imperial state secretaries during this time only two were Catholics. Among the academicians the Catholics were also poorly represented.[13] As one analyst stated it, in the last years of the Empire, German Catholicism presented itself as a pyramid with the industrial worker and the small peasants as the broad base with a relatively large layer consisting of the new middle class, then many fewer people in the strata representing the economic entrepreneur and academic officials, and finally a very small number of people, the Catholic nobility, at the very top.[14]

In 1914 the Catholics suffered from an inferiority complex within the establishment. Yet, like most Germans, they had accepted the justice of the German cause and had attempted to show that they, as one of the former *Reichsfeinde* (enemies of the Reich) of the *Kulturkampf* days, could be just as loyal as their Protestant brethren. Many hoped that their loyalty would be rewarded with a greater role in the nation's councils. Many German Catholics in 1914 saw the interests of their government and their religion coinciding. A victory for Germany and Austria-Hungary, with a combined population of 65 million Catholics as opposed to 45 million Protestants and 6 million of other confessions, would certainly benefit the Church. Still more obviously, a victory of the Central Powers would liberate Catholic Poland from Orthodox Russia. Numerous brochures, articles, and statements in official documents mentioned that the position of the Vatican could be improved in the world, and that Germany could help by closer cooperation with Rome, implying a need for closer diplomatic ties.[15]

But during the war years within the Catholic political party, the Center, a new type of politician was gaining prominence, as personified by Erzberger, who sought to introduce a strong element of pragmatic thinking into Catholic internal policy, in partnership with Social Democrats and liberals, while yet retaining close ties with the Vatican—ties which would aid Germany, the Vatican, and German Catholicism. Erzberger, like others in Germany, began to question the

---

[13] Heinrich Lutz, "Die deutschen Katholiken in und nach dem ersten Weltkrieg," *Hochland*, LV (1962-1963), 194.

[14] Hans Müller, "Der deutsche Katholizismus 1918/19," *Geschichte in Wissenschaft und Unterricht*, XVII (1966), 522. See also C. Bauer, *Deutscher Katholizismus, Entwicklungslinien und Profile* (Frankfurt a.M., 1964).

[15] Lutz, "Deutsche Katholiken," 198-199. See also Stewart A. Stehlin, "Germany and a proposed Vatican state, 1915-1917," *Catholic Historical Review*, LX (1974), 406ff.

government's wartime policy, particularly after late 1915, when the failure of military action to accomplish the intended objectives became evident. He knew that the German war aims included annexation of large areas in the west, for example, but through his contacts with Vatican sources he also knew that Benedict was most explicit in his demand for a total restoration of Belgian sovereignty. Yet another two years of bloodshed were needed before Erzberger and a majority of his party came to realize that an annexationist policy would not serve Germany's ends.[16]

The transformation of the Center's thinking derived in large part from Erzberger's ability to argue persuasively that the government's war aims were wrong, that the Imperial political systems were not working correctly,[17] that peace as the Pope had proposed would be to the Reich's best interest, and that the two governments should enter into closer relations. Thus, as the Center agonized over and reappraised its attitude both to the conduct of war and to the policies of the government, more Center members as well as officials of the Foreign Office urged that the Reich's diplomatic position be strengthened by permitting the Vatican to establish a mission in the German capital. They reasoned that the moral and diplomatic weight of neutral powers could help to influence world opinion in favor of the German cause. Now, with the Vatican speaking out in favor of mediation, and again attempting to take part in international affairs, the need for closer ties with the Vatican became increasingly obvious to German diplomats.

In 1917 *Germania*, the Center Party newspaper, featured several articles calling for converting the Bavarian nunciature into a Reich nunciature, since stronger ties with Rome would benefit Germany's international position. The new nuncio, Giuseppe Aversa, writing to Erzberger to inquire into the Imperial Government's attitude to such a move, told him in confidence that should Berlin show interest, Rome would certainly support the suggestion. But the possibility of such a step, despite its significance for Germany's foreign relations, was made extremely difficult by internal complications which reflected the political complexities in the structure of the Empire.[18] Aversa had touched a sensitive nerve in the German body-politic—the problem of the rights

---

[16] Lutz, "Deutsche Katholiken," 201 and see Klaus Epstein, *Matthias Erzberger and the dilemma of German democracy* (Princeton, 1959), chs. 5-8, and John K. Zeender, "The German Center Party during World War I: an internal study," *Catholic Historical Review*, XLII (1957), 441-468.

[17] See Lutz, "Deutsche Katholiken," 198-207. Stehlin, 411ff.

[18] AA, IA, Preussen 2 Nr. 5, Vol. 2, Aversa to Erzberger, February 28, 1917. See for example *Germania*, February 10, 1917.

and prerogatives of the individual German states (*Länder*). Although Erzberger favored and worked to further closer German-Vatican ties, he also understood the complexities of Reich-*Länder* relations. He replied that, under the circumstances, establishing diplomatic relations between the two governments by accrediting the nuncio in Munich to the Reich Government in Berlin was not feasible, for several reasons: shifting the locus of Vatican influence within Germany from Munich to Berlin would offend the Bavarian monarch; accrediting one envoy to both Berlin and Munich would prove a logistical impossibility, as the same person could not handle the business in both cities simultaneously, and, finally, the Kaiser would probably not agree to allow a diplomat at present accredited to a state within the Reich to become subsequently accredited to the Reich or to Prussia since he would view this as placing the Empire in a secondary position.[19]

The Bavarian Minister-President Count Georg von Hertling, aware of Aversa's overtures to Erzberger, concurred with Erzberger's opinion that establishing the nunciature in Berlin would not be opportune. He recalled the fears of the Center Party in the nineteenth century that a nuncio in Berlin would interfere in internal affairs either by forcing Papal views upon the party or by becoming a tool of the government which could use him in influencing the party to accept government policies. As the famous Bishop of Mainz, Wilhelm Emmanuel Ketteler, had once phrased it: "St. Hedwig's was too close to the Royal Palace."[20] Moreover, continued Hertling, Bavaria prided itself on being the leading Catholic power within the Reich—a position which the establishment of a nunciature in Berlin would considerably weaken.[21] The problem which the war period already foreshadowed for Weimar was that Vatican ties, considered a benefit for German foreign affairs, were also regarded as a disruptive force in German internal affairs. The Vatican naturally also urged closer relations. Many German Catholics, especially in Prussia, felt their interests could better be served by a Papal representative in the Reich capital rather than in Munich. Nevertheless, while urging Berlin to agree to this move, Rome was also careful not to injure its connections to Bavaria.

The Vatican had already informed the Bavarians that, despite the emergence of the question of the nunciature, it would do nothing without consulting the Munich Government, and inasmuch as the Vatican hoped to avoid any misunderstandings between Bavaria and Prussia, the ne-

[19] AA, IA, Preussen 2 Nr. 5, Vol. 2, Aversa to Erzberger, February 28, 1917; Erzberger to Aversa, March 2, 1917.

[20] Ketteler was referring to the Catholic cathedral in Berlin, which was indeed not far from the Royal Palace.

[21] GSTA, Ges. Päpstl. Stuhl 949, Hertling to Erzberger, March 12, 1917.

gotiations would begin only after the conclusion of the war. This satisfied Munich for the time being, but the Bavarian Minister in Rome, Otto von Ritter, warned his superiors to watch the situation vigilantly so as not to be outmaneuvered by the Prussians.[22]

Negotiations during wartime never went further, and Msgr. Aversa, who might have played an important role and whom German officials suspected of coveting the position for himself, died suddenly in April 1917. Already one year before, Rome had sent word to Count Hertling that Benedict realized the importance of the Munich nunciature for all Germany and the impending difficulties for the Reich once hostilities had ended. Therefore the Vatican intended to send to Munich after the war a man of first-class abilities, the Under Secretary of State (and future Pope) Msgr. Eugenio Pacelli.[23]

Aversa's death prompted Rome to name Pacelli to the position sooner than originally planned. The speed with which the Vatican made the new appointment in April underscored the importance which the Curia placed in having the post filled and its desire to avert any possible campaign in the German press against an Italian nuncio. This was made all the easier since Bavarian officials knew Pacelli through his position in the Secretariat of State and considered him a *persona gratissima* for the Munich nunciature. Vatican circles, on the other hand, also showed great satisfaction with the selection of Pacelli, since it was generally felt in those trying days, when filling vacant diplomatic posts was a difficult task, that Pacelli, though Italian, was best equipped to carry out the duties with ability, dignity, and impartiality. A tall, gaunt man with the look of an ascetic, Pacelli came from a minor Roman noble family and had entered the Vatican diplomatic service at twenty-five, after having already earned three doctorates. Having risen fast in the Vatican service, at forty-one he was now appointed to this difficult post in Munich. German observers in 1917 commented to the Foreign Office on the new Papal diplomat's lack of experience in the foreign service and compared him to Aversa, who had lived abroad for many years while Pacelli, except for a few tourist trips, had remained in Italy. "His strengths up until now," noted one report, "lay primarily in the orderly way in which he has carried out assignments entrusted to him whereby he has showed a juridical acumen, admired even by his colleagues, which was coupled with a Machiavellian manner of doing things." His outward manner, the observers commented, made one think more of a civil servant than a diplomat. While his comportment paled in comparison with Aversa's cosmopol-

[22] GSTA, Ges. Päpstl. Stuhl 949, Ritter to Hertling, April 11, 1916.
[23] GSTA, Ges. Päpstl. Stuhl 949, Ritter to Hertling, April 16, 1916.

1. Nuncio Eugenio Pacelli distributing gift parcels to Allied soldiers who are German prisoners during the closing year of the war

itan style, he did possess a complete and detailed knowledge of Benedict's plans and intentions, since in his position as Under Secretary of State he had been intimately associated with both the Secretary of State and the Pontiff. Pacelli was, in the final analysis, able to negotiate more speedily without requiring detailed instructions for every step.[24] After a meeting between Pacelli and Mühlberg in 1916, the Prussian Minister had already appraised him as follows:

> He is a gifted prelate, well versed in history and canon law, skilled with words, and quick at repartee in discussions. Zealous and inspired by the powers and importance of the Church, he will accordingly seek to strengthen and increase its influence. Pacelli has shown himself to be friendly towards Germany. During the various struggles which we had to endure with the Curia during the time of Pius X, he sought to work in a fair and accommodating manner, as far as his strict subordination to his superiors allowed.[25]

[24] AA, IA, Päpstl. Stuhl 4, Vol. 10, Romberg, Stockhammern, Bercham (Bern) to Bethmann-Hollweg, April 29, 1917.
[25] AA, IA, Päpstl. Stuhl 4, Vol. 10, Mühlberg to Bethmann-Hollweg, September 21, 1916.

In 1917, Mühlberg, after having spoken to Pacelli, who visited the Prussian diplomat in Lugano on his way to Munich, reported that the Nuncio, besides paying his respects to Church and State officials in the Bavarian capital, would also journey to Berlin to introduce himself to Reich Chancellor Theobald von Bethmann-Hollweg and make himself known to the members of the Foreign Office—a departure from practice. Reich officials, aware that the Vatican might use the opportunity of the new Nuncio's visit to raise the question again of Papal representation in Berlin, did not wish in the interests of Germany's foreign policy to overlook such initiatives. Mühlberg stressed to Bethmann-Hollweg, in light of his favorable impression of Pacelli, that it was no longer necessary to recommend that the Nuncio be warmly received, as "he is a man with a future. The Curia will not simply read his reports but will give them serious consideration."[26] Nevertheless, before departing for Berlin Pacelli took the precaution of fully briefing Hertling about the purpose of his trip.[27]

While in Berlin in June 1917 Pacelli visited the Chancellor and the Foreign Office Secretary, Arthur von Zimmermann, and performed such diplomatic amenities as laying a wreath with the Papal colors at the grave of Wilhelm I. Zimmermann explained to the Bavarian Minister in Berlin, Count Hugo von Lerchenfeld, that the visit was not political in nature but was merely to introduce the new Vatican diplomat to the officials in Berlin. Zimmermann assured Lerchenfeld that nothing had been discussed about a nunciature and that when the matter should arise Bavaria's wishes would naturally be considered. However, Zimmermann did state that the diplomatic events in the preceding years had made it clear to German officials that after the cessation of hostilities a Papal representative in Berlin was virtually a necessity. All of these discussions made the Bavarians uneasy. Lerchenfeld further noted that Pacelli had generally made a very good impression on everyone with whom he came in contact.[28]

The Nuncio, acting on general instructions from Benedict, took advantage of his meetings with the Chancellor and also with the Kaiser in June to discuss and evaluate the prospects of peace and whether the Vatican could be of use in a mediatory role. Popes already had acted as arbiters in earlier decades; Bismarck had asked Leo XIII to arbitrate between Spain and Germany over the Caroline Islands dispute in 1885, and Nicholas II had hoped that the Pope would support with his moral authority his proposal for the Hague Peace Conference in 1899.

---

[26] AA, IA, Päpstl. Stuhl 4, Vol. 10, Mühlberg to Bethmann-Hollweg, May 22, 1917.
[27] GSTA, MA 976, Pacelli to Hertling, June 19, 1917.
[28] GSTA, MA 976, Lerchenfeld to Lössl (BFM), June 28, 1917.

Now in 1917 the Pontiff sought to make use of this authority in an even more difficult act of mediation.[29]

Expressions of war weariness had appeared in all the belligerent countries, and the strains of the war had clearly begun to show. In Austria-Hungary, particularly, feuding between component parts of the Empire, food shortages, nationalistic unrest, and military defeats led many Austrian leaders to believe that an immediate peace was the only way to stave off Austria-Hungary's demise. The Vatican too desired to prevent the dissolution of the Dual Monarchy. Moreover, as Austria-Hungary weakened, the importance of seeing Germany retain some degree of strength became increasingly important to the Vatican. The Papacy remained publicly neutral, but practical considerations also convinced Rome to interpret neutrality as the maintenance of a balance between the Powers, by neither overtly favoring one over another nor allowing one to gain predominance. Therefore, a number of reasons coalesced to make Benedict decide that the moment was both timely and opportune for the Curia to initiate a peace proposal: its desire to prevent the total collapse of the Central Powers, thus creating an imbalance in Europe, the opportunity to play a role in international affairs, and the fear that the Socialists, then meeting in Stockholm, were about to seize the initiative and to offer their own peace plan.

On August 1, 1917 the Pontiff sent an appeal to the warring parties to come to some solution to the conflict. He called attention to the deterioration of economic conditions in all belligerent countries and expressed his concern over the social unrest which was likely to follow the end of hostilities. His note also referred to some of the subjects later to be touched on in Wilson's Fourteen Points: disarmament, an international court of arbitration, economic cooperation, and the freedom of the seas. He made mention of reparation and called for the complete restitution of occupied territories, in particular the evacuation of Belgium and northern France by Germany, and of the German colonies by the Allies. Finally, he pleaded for equity in adjusting territorial matters in Poland, in the Balkans, between Germany and France, and between Italy and Austria.

In the west the leaders and the press in general reacted coolly to the note, believing that it might be an enemy-inspired diplomatic maneuver. The general feeling of the press in Germany to the Pope's efforts was not favorable except in Catholic newspapers. The overwhelmingly Protestant Pan-Germans as well as the right wing of the

---

[29] Wolfgang Steglich, ed., *Der Friedensappell Papst Benedikts XV. . . . .* (Wiesbaden, 1970), ch. 3; Steglich does detailed work in clarifying the situation. GSTA, MA 976, Ritter to BFM, July 27, 1917. Jedin, pp. 39-47.

National Liberal and Progressive Parties accused the Pontiff of having allowed himself to be used by the Western Powers. The military regarded the plan as connected with the political offensive in the Reichstag which supported a moderate peace without forced territorial acquisitions. Those in favor of annexation, such as many Rhenish industrialists, were appalled by the Papal plan. Some asked why the Pope made such a proposal at that moment if it were not that one of the Allied Powers was becoming militarily exhausted. Other opponents gave the issue a religious character by asking why Protestant Germany, in the year of the 400th anniversary of the Reformation, should accept a peace negotiated by the Catholic leader.[30]

Neither the Allies nor Germany, however, were ready or in a critical enough military position to be entirely in favor of returning to the *status quo ante bellum*, as the plan suggested. The German High Command, for example, had every reason to be optimistic, since the failure of the Kerensky Government to carry out its military offensive in the summer of 1917 indicated the imminent collapse of Russia's war effort, which in turn would allow Germany to concentrate her forces to win in the west. Thus, in response to the note, the Allies replied that before negotiating they had to know what German war aims were, especially in regard to Belgium. The Germans, however, were not prepared at that moment to make concessions on Belgium as long as there was a possibility that it could be retained. Despite the Nuncio's repeated requests for a declaration on Belgium, Chancellor Georg Michaelis informed Pacelli in vague terms that he could not "issue a decisive declaration of policy" at that time. With that inadequate answer from the Reich, which the Allies would not accept as a basis of peace talks, the Papal efforts came to naught.[31]

Although the Papal initiative had been motivated by specific diplomatic considerations, it also demonstrated Benedict's sensitivity to the quickening disintegration of Europe. The text of the August 1 message revealed his concern for the broader aspects of the problem: "Must the civilized world become nothing but a field of death? And Europe, so glorious and flourishing, is she [sic], as though carried away by a universal madness, to rush into the abyss and aid in her own suicide?"[32] The efforts made by the Papacy to act as mediator here her-

---

[30] AA, IA, WK 2, Vol. 2, Presseberichte Nr. 32, August 17, 1917. Hans Gatzke, *Germany's drive to the west* (Baltimore, 1950), pp. 221-222. Fritz Fischer, *Germany's aims in the First World War* (New York, 1967), pp. 417-418, 433. Arno Mayer, *Political origins of the new diplomacy* (New Haven, 1959), p. 230.

[31] Mayer, *Political origins*, pp. 229-235. Gatzke, *Germany's Drive*, pp. 219-225, 232-234. Fischer, pp. 416-420.

[32] Mayer, *Political origins*, p. 281.

alded its intention to once more play a role in international affairs and actively concern itself with Europe's problems. Several months later Pacelli, who wrote to Hertling expressing Rome's clear disappointment with the Reich's answers to the Papal peace note, now rejected the Papacy's responsibility for the failure to find a formula for peace. At the same time Pacelli, still interested in improving the cause of peace and noting that Hertling was journeying to Berlin, requested him to do what he could to bring about peace negotiations, especially with regard to Belgium.[33]

During the last year of the war, and perhaps because they feared that their refusal to accept Papal mediation and renounce Belgium had weakened their position, German officials were very uneasy lest the Pope support the Allied Powers. The Allies had been exerting pressure on the Vatican to support their cause or at least condemn the actions of the Central Powers. Papal neutrality was not enough; active alliance with the Western Powers had been demanded, particularly by the French. The Allied press met Papal insistence on its neutrality with accusations of the Vatican's partiality for the Central Powers.[34] Nevertheless, by 1918 increasingly nervous about the deteriorating military situation, the Foreign Office gave serious consideration to the rumor that Benedict, convinced of the Central Powers' inability to win, might be ready to back the Allies. Ritter, however, saw no evidence of this. Conceding that at times the Pontiff seemed to lean slightly toward the Western Powers at one moment or another, the Bavarian envoy nevertheless explained that Benedict, under the weight of Allied pressure, had only meant to placate them temporarily while adhering to his policy of neutrality and maintaining the diplomatic equilibrium. This, however, was not serious, for whenever the Central Powers had asked for a hearing to present the German side of an issue, Ritter said, they had always been well received. The Bavarian Minister therefore expected the Papacy to maintain its policy of public neutrality throughout the war, for, as he said, there was only one way for the Papacy to protect itself during a wartime situation—in general to stand above it—and this he felt was what Benedict was doing.[35]

[33] GSTA, MA 976, Pacelli to Hertling, October 1, 1917.

[34] GSTA, Ges. Päpstl. Stuhl 959, Ritter to AA, April 25, 1918 and Stehlin, 410ff. AA, Bostschaftsakten Rom-Vatikan (hereafter cited as BRV), Lfd. Nr. 60, Vol. 5, Mühlberg to AA, April 7, 1918. The Germans, on the other hand, were constantly concerned with their image at the Vatican lest the Allies force the Vatican to come out against the Central Powers. In addition to the regular diplomatic channels, Germany continually sent messages via private individuals to defend its position. Erzberger was very instrumental in pleading the German cause throughout the war. See Epstein, pp. 149ff., or, for example, Hertling's private letter to Benedict defending the use of submarine warfare, GSTA, MA 976, Hertling to Benedict, February 17, 1917.

[35] GSTA, MA 976, Ritter to BFM, January 29, 1918.

The amiable working relations, despite the war, were further emphasized a few months later when Mühlberg reported that in the course of a conversation with Pacelli the Nuncio voluntarily offered the opinion that relations between Germany and the Vatican were very good since Germany asked for nothing beyond the limits of the neutrality and impartiality that the Pope had set for himself. The Entente Powers, conversely, demanded a clear and explicit declaration of Vatican support, which they hoped to extract by pressure.[36] Berlin could thus console itself with the realization that the Western Powers had equally failed to win outright Vatican support. At any rate, the Reich derived comfort from the fact that the German case was still being fairly listened to in Rome.

In August 1914 Germany, possessing a formidable army with superior equipment and supply services, had had expectations of speedily winning the war. But plans had soon faded. After September the fighting settled down into trenches, and the battle line moved but little. In the east, Germany and its Allies had been more successful, securing the dissolution of the Russian army and occupying huge amounts of land, especially after the Treaty of Brest-Litovsk (March 1918).[37] But even at the height of its expansion in the east, the Reich was unable to win a clear advantage in the west. Despite General Erich von Ludendorff's spring and summer offensives, the Allies had checked the German advance. The military had overestimated Germany's chances for victory. At home, the Reichstag had already passed a resolution in July 1917 in favor of a peace of understanding without forced territorial annexations, and growing popular unrest indicated dissatisfaction with both the conduct and effects of the war. By 1918 the naval blockade imposed on Germany by the Allies was felt in shortages of both foodstuffs and vital war materials; the German people and the armies in the west were already exhausted; and Germany's ally, the Austro-Hungarian Empire, was showing increasing signs of breakup. In contrast, after the entry of the United States in 1917, the Allies had been strengthened by the arrival of fresh troops from across the Atlantic.

The failure of the German military offensive in 1918 and the continued success of the Allies in the west, together with the news of the

---

[36] AA, IA, Päpstl. Stuhl 15, Vol. 8, Mühlberg to Hertling, April 7, 1918. Both sides in the conflict accused the Pope of supporting the other. Gustave Hervé, a Right nationalist journalist close to French Premier Georges Clemenceau, demanded that the Allies depose Benedict, declare the Holy See vacant, and force a new election. His candidate would have been Cardinal Désiré Mercier of Malines, Belgium. *Neue Preussische Zeitung*, May 7, 1918.

[37] The Vatican had not opposed the Central Powers' expansion to the east since this was expected to weaken the Orthodox Church and further the eastward spread of the Roman faith. Gottlieb, p. 373.

surrender of Germany's ally Bulgaria in September, convinced the German High Command that Germany had spent its strength and could not continue the war. In October, the German Government began negotiations with the Allies for a cessation of hostilities on the basis of Wilson's Fourteen Points. On October 15, 1918, *L'Osservatore Romano*, the official newspaper of the Holy See, noted the Papacy's satisfaction with Germany's willingness to discuss peace terms at this time and hoped that this would finally lead to the end of hostilities.[38] The expressions of hopeful expectation, however, carried in the Vatican newspaper on October 23, that the Kaiser himself might soon introduce reform in order to quell popular unrest and prevent Germany from following Russia's example, were not to be fulfilled.[39] The rapid succession of events in Germany—the Kaiser's abdication on November 9, the collapse of the monarchy, and the outbreak of the revolution—ended all thoughts that political transformation would be limited to an extension of the franchise, some liberalizing measures, or a cabinet change. On November 11, 1918, civilian representatives of the new republican government of the Reich signed the armistice at Compiègne, thus ending the hostilities which had wracked Europe for four long years.

The war had finally come to an end; all the diplomatic efforts of both the Vatican and Germany were in vain or cast into doubt. Rome had been unhappy with the war for both humanitarian and practical reasons; a total victory by either side would not have been to its advantage. With America's entry into the war and the Allied determination to continue the struggle, the Curia realized that Germany could not win the war and therefore had to be helped in obtaining a reasonable peace. The Papacy tried to remain neutral, i.e., not officially siding with either camp, but it also tried to effect a balance and saw its role in terms of *neutralizing* the unequal power of one side over the other. The Germans, however, up until March 1918 still hoping for a *Siegfrieden* (peace by victory), welcomed Rome's diplomatic efforts and charitable help, but were basically pursuing a military victory. Thus the Vatican had reaped a good deal of Allied resentment for its endeavors and not a good deal of German appreciation. Nevertheless, a precedent had been set. The new emerging political constellation in Europe had created a situation in which the Vatican perceived the necessity of lending its aid to Germany. The Reich, on the other hand, although not having availed itself of the Papacy's services in 1917, was made aware of its potential value for German interests,

[38] *L'Osservatore Romano* cited in Friedrich Ritter von Lama, *Papst und Kurie in ihrer Politik nach dem Weltkrieg* (Illertissen, 1925), pp. 2-3.

[39] Lama, p. 3.

especially when military means had failed or had been discredited. Thus the attitude of both governments toward each other had changed, and they now regarded one another as more important in their policy considerations than before. Although the war had not facilitated better relations between the Vatican and the Reich, it had quite definitely emphasized their importance.

The many changes which had occurred in Europe during the war years—the collapse of empires, the creation of new states, the revolutionary uprisings, the fantastic expenditure in manpower and material—made it difficult even for statesmen to see clearly the direction in which Europe might be heading. One thing, however, was certain: from out of the war years the Papacy emerged, so to speak, out of its silence. In order to speak on humanitarian issues from a greater position of strength, to bargain for better conditions for the Church, and to pursue its own foreign policy goals, Rome perceived a need and an opportunity to voice its opinion on international issues, extend its diplomatic ties, and gain some influence in the structuring of the new Europe and determining the fate of Central Europe. Its peace efforts and charitable acts for the needy had lent it a prestige and respect that it had lacked for several decades and had strengthened its diplomatic position. Germany, on the other hand, had seen its dreams and empire disappear. The conflict had made it realize its lack of strong allies and external support. In such a situation, far worse than before 1914, the aid of a respected, neutral power became even more imperative, and the inadequacies of German-Vatican diplomatic representation became all the more obvious. The awareness of the problems facing both governments in 1919 only reinforced the wartime experience, convincing both sides that closer diplomatic ties could benefit both. Already a good basis existed upon which to work. Except for the British legation which was established at the Vatican in late 1914, only Germany and Austria-Hungary of the Great Powers were represented at the Papal Court. With these connections still intact, it now remained for the diplomats of both states to improve their contacts and to cope with the difficulties now facing them at the beginning of 1919.

CHAPTER I

1919: New World, New Government, New Problems

The armistice signed on November 11, 1918, brought a close to the hostilities which had transformed the map of Europe and caused the collapse of well-established state systems, including Bismarck's Empire. Continental governments, weakened and some near bankruptcy from the exactions made by the war, now had to meet to formulate guidelines for the new, emerging Europe and to redefine the diplomatic structure which had been called into question by Germany's defeat. The economic life of Europe was dislocated as it had not been for centuries, and haste was made to call a peace conference in order to settle the issues and return the world to a more stable condition. Moreover, the fear of revolution was ever present in the minds of the European rulers, who, anxious about the upsurge of Bolshevik activity after 1917, now sought to contain the doctrines preached by Vladimir Ilyich Lenin and other revolutionary Marxists from spreading in the west.

The end of the war came as a welcome relief to a Germany stunned by military defeat and wearied by wartime demands. During 1919 the Republic had many difficulties to face—revolts from the left in Berlin, secession in the Rhineland and Bavaria, economic unrest, a treaty to be signed with the Allies, and preparations to create the new governmental structure for the Reich. In February a coalition to run the country was formed by the middle or moderate parties, the Social Democrats, the Democrats, and the Catholic Center. These coalition members, having been in opposition during the Imperial period, now continued to rule until August 1923, with the exception of five months in 1921 when the Socialists left the cabinet. Yet despite the many issues confronting the government, Germany's industrial, technical, and population resources were largely intact, its presence as a power, albeit defeated, was still recognized as such; many of the old institutional pillars of Imperial society—the army, the diplomatic corps, the law courts, and the Church—continued to function, with their representatives maintaining positions of importance as before.[1] Thus the Republic had to formulate a policy to deal with its problems while taking into consideration the realities of the uncertain post-war situation, the political philosophies of the new ruling parties, as well as those societal attitudes and institutions such as the Catholic Church which had been retained from the past.

The Vatican also joyfully greeted the war's end. Having raised its voice once more in world affairs, having asserted its humanitarian concern for all parties in the conflict, without being forced to choose publicly between the warring sides, it hoped for a lasting peace and a diplomatic role for the Papacy in Europe. Now in 1919 Rome too had to face a new situation: to come to grips with a world whose outlines had not yet taken shape.

In the late nineteenth century Papal diplomacy had been concerned with the question of territoriality and of the Papal possessions in Italy. The Pontiff had also begun to speak on the question of social legislation and the relations of ruler and citizen. Leo XIII treated the subject broadly in his writings, but it had become a major concern for his successors. With the destruction of the old order in 1918 and the rise of national feeling in old as well as in newly created states, the Papacy became increasingly concerned with its role in the post-war world. It was naturally anxious to preserve both its neutral status on the international level and the rights of the Church in every country. This made the search for a new and viable *modus vivendi* between states and a harmonious working relationship between Church and State within each country an increasingly important matter.[2] However, by the end of the war conditions had changed in Europe so drastically that the relations between the Vatican and individual European states had also been greatly transformed. Republican Germany, for example, in large part diplomatically isolated, and the Vatican, seeking to reassert itself in world affairs, had to reexamine their relationship to one another to find the areas of common concern and to determine if and how they could be of help to each other. This was to be the task which both faced in 1919.

The areas of mutual interest which Rome and Berlin now had to consider, such as moderating Allied demands, the new international balance of power, the fate of the German missions overseas, the spread of Bolshevism, and the regulation of church-state relations, will be discussed later on in this chapter. There was, however, a basic prob-

[1] Gerhard L. Weinberg, "The defeat of Germany in 1918 and the European balance of power," *Central European History*, II (1969), 260.
[2] Joseph Moody, ed., *Church and society* (New York, 1953), p. 77.

lem which the Vatican and Germany also had to deal with immediately before any meaningful cooperation could occur: that of regularizing diplomatic relations between the two governments. Should Germany continue to have a representative in Rome, and, if so, in what capacity—as representative of Germany or Prussia? Should the Bavarian mission, which had been retained in 1871 as a concession to Munich, be continued or abolished? This was a sensitive issue which dealt with Bavaria's historic rights—a subject which had to be handled very carefully in 1919, when Berlin was seeking to have the new constitution provide a more centralized form of government for Germany. On the other hand, there was also the question of a nuncio to Germany—should he reside in Munich, or, if accredited to the Reich, in Berlin? A representative of the Pope in the German capital would surely arouse the suspicion of many Protestants, who would tend to regard him as the center of Catholic proselytization.

Nevertheless, Germany had to face and quickly solve the problem of establishing relations, since it was basic to two other concerns, external and internal. Since German delegates were meeting representatives of the Allies in 1919 to discuss and receive the peace conditions, the Reich naturally sought to influence any power or government, such as the Vatican, which in turn could conceivably play a role in the outcome of the decisions to be made at Versailles. The borderlands of Germany, for example those areas which Germany might lose, contained a large Catholic population. The Reich's ability to plead its case in Rome for retaining these lands would be easier and probably more effective once Germany had full diplomatic ties to the Holy See. In addition, relations with the Vatican would have some bearing on the internal problems created by the collapse of the monarchy. A new constitution had to be written and the position of the Church in the new State defined. All of these interconnected problems had to be confronted concurrently at a time when Germany was slowly sorting out the strands of its future during the chaotic early days of the postwar period.

In 1919 the proponents of full diplomatic relations between Rome and the Vatican became more vocal. The Catholic Center Party had now become a pillar of the new government, and such prominent leaders as Erzberger and the trade union leader Johannes Giesberts had become members of the cabinet. The party endorsed a policy which called for freedom for the Church, state support for confessional schools, and a concordat to regularize church-state relations. In conformity with these goals the Center strongly advocated closer ties with Rome and used its position as an integral part of the ruling coalition to urge its political partners into supporting such a policy. The

Center, however, did not have too difficult a struggle on this matter, for most Germans—the leading politicians practically without exception—saw the maintenance and strengthening of diplomatic ties with the Vatican as politically useful. Only some of the more extreme Protestants, such as the spokesman for the strongly anti-Catholic Evangelical League (*Bund*), voiced some doubt about establishing the embassy.[3]

The matter was discussed in the National Assembly on several occasions. On February 28, 1919, Center Deputy Peter Spahn had raised the issue and called it ridiculous that Germany had no representative at the Vatican.[4] In July, Spahn, while mentioning the importance of Papal influence in the world, now stressed that German Catholics, comprising one third of the nation's population, were demanding that a German ambassador be sent to the Vatican.[5] Foreign Minister Hermann Müller, a Socialist, speaking before a legislative committee on September 27, 1919 and making the cabinet's position plain, stated that Papal representation in Germany was necessary for the good of both internal and external German policy. One month later, in full session of the National Assembly, the Center representatives again urged the legislature to establish a German embassy, stressing that the relations with the Vatican were too important a matter to be left to the individual states, especially in view of the fact that large Catholic populations lived in the contested border areas.[6] In addition, the German Curial official (later Cardinal) Franz Ehrle had written an article to show the importance of establishing an all-German mission in Rome, and by the summer of 1919 the German press overwhelmingly supported such an embassy.[7] Moreover, to show the Vatican's interest in establishing relations with Germany, on April 2 Benedict had sent a personal handwritten letter to President Friedrich Ebert, expressing, what was for the Vatican very cordial sentiments for the new Socialist-led government. The Pontiff complimented the Socialist President of the new Republic, calling him a distinguished, honorable man and expressed the hope "that the existing relations between the Holy See and the German Reich should not only remain unchanged but should become even closer."[8] There was no general disagreement about re-

---

[3] Deuerlein, *Reichskonkordat*, pp. 13-15.

[4] *Ibid.*, p. 7.

[5] Germany, Reichstag, *Stenographische Berichte über die Verhandlungen des Reichstages* (Berlin, 1920), Vol. 328, p. 2079. 69th Session, July 29, 1919. Hereafter cited as Germany, Reichstag.

[6] Deuerlein, *Reichskonkordat*, pp. 13-15. Germany, Reichstag, Vol. 330, pp. 3366, 3386. 106th Session, October 23, 1919.

[7] Deuerlein, *Reichskonkordat*, p. 7.

[8] *Ibid.*, p. 8.

taining German representation in Rome; rather the problem was the form that this representation was to take.

In September 1919 the Reich Cabinet decided upon opening a German embassy accredited to the Holy See. However, the difficulty unfortunately lay in Bavaria's position. Munich had the closest and most complete ties with Rome, but this situation in turn now created complications for full diplomatic representation between the Reich Government and Rome. The revolutionary Eisner Government in Munich, taking power in November 1918, had immediately requested Ritter to stay on in his post. The Bavarians believed that their state, with a predominantly Catholic population, could best deal with the Curia by retaining its own representative in Rome. Closing the legation would be a blow to Bavaria's historical tradition of independence and role as spokesman for Catholic Germany. A German ambassador would no doubt be Protestant and hence, Munich believed, would not understand the Bavarian situation. Thus, despite Germany's need for a Reich embassy, Munich saw no practical reason to give up its own legation.[9]

Bavaria, proud of its long tradition of relations with the Vatican and of its influence at the Papal Court, quite naturally was reluctant to make any concessions in one of the few areas in which it still believed it had retained some influence. This issue of the legation was in many ways magnified, for it exemplified the opposing tendencies of particularism and centralism in Germany which had been causing tension since the founding of the Empire in the nineteenth century. Bavaria, as a middle-size German state, had seen its power and influence diminish in 1871 when it became part of the German Reich. As compensation it was granted certain privileges, such as the rights to administer its own telegraph, railroad, and postal systems; to be exempt from certain federal taxes; and to retain its own ministry of war, general staff, and several diplomatic missions. Many of these privileges the new Republic had eliminated or curtailed, and the Bavarians were now trying to salvage what little independence of action they had. Munich desired Bavaria's continued participation in the *corpus germanicum* as well as its retention of some autonomy and a distinctly Bavarian outlook on politics, society, and life.

---

[9] When Count Zech, Prussian Minister in Munich, went to see Archbishop Michael von Faulhaber in January 1920 to persuade him to give up the demands for Bavaria's separate diplomatic ties with Rome, Faulhaber remained unmoved and replied that in its nunciature and in its concordat Bavaria had an entirely different legal basis than did the rest of Germany; that it had an entirely different ecclesiastical historical tradition. Germany, Munich, Erzbischöfliches Archiv, 1352, Faulhaber to Ritter, February 16, 1920.

2. Baron Otto von Ritter, Bavarian Minister to
the Holy See

Throughout 1919 the Bavarians had shown increased concern lest,
with the formation of a new governmental structure for Germany,
they might be requested or forced to close their legation. Baron Otto
von Ritter, the Bavarian Minister at the Vatican and a member of the
diplomatic corps for over twenty years, had served at the legation in
Rome since 1909, one of the few diplomats from the Imperial era who
continued at his post throughout the entire Weimar period. High Curial officials rewarded his long service at the Vatican with their trust
and confidence, and his colleagues regarded him as one whose word
could carry influence at the Papal Court. He was one of the few people
who later could boast of a friendship with Pacelli which had continued

for over thirty years. All three Popes to whom he was accredited as well as their secretaries of state esteemed him highly.[10] Ritter had urged Bavaria in early 1919 to maintain its ties with Rome lest the Allies outmaneuver the Reich. This undoubtedly reflected his concern about the abolition of his own position, and he thus argued with more than altruistic logic. The enemy, he felt, had understood better than the Germans the value of using the authority, aid, and mediation of the Vatican for its own domestic and foreign policy purposes. The Allies had established legations in Rome in order to maintain constant personal communication with the Curia, while diplomats of the Central Powers had been forced to leave Rome for the duration of the war.

The Vatican, continued the Bavarian, basically did not engage in extensive written correspondence with other powers. Out of perhaps excessive caution it preferred direct personal contact. If a newcomer to Rome did not win the confidence of the Curial officials, then maintenance of meaningful diplomatic contact became very difficult. The Bavarian staff was known and trusted by Vatican officials and could work more effectively in explaining the situation in Germany than could any new ministers, who would first have to familiarize themselves with the situation in Rome. Should the legation be withdrawn or subsumed under a Reich embassy, the difficulty which a new representative would experience, especially from a predominantly Protestant country, would wipe out all the good which the Bavarian representative had won for German Catholics. Lastly, Ritter speculated that an official separation of Church and State in Germany, as was even at that moment being discussed in the National Assembly in Weimar, would only increase the importance of this diplomatic contact, since the separation of Church and State, as history had shown, did not diminish the influence of the Pope on the Catholic population but many times had even increased it. By maintaining the legation and close ties to Rome, the State could ensure that the concerns of the Church could be channeled to coincide or at least not oppose those of the State.[11] Given all these circumstances, Ritter stressed the importance of maintaining the Bavarian mission at the Vatican and not reorganizing the structure of Germany's diplomatic representation.

Prussia, on the other hand, the other German state which had a mission at the Vatican before the war, initially had not raised any objections to closing its legation since the German embassy, which would replace it, would be reporting to Berlin, and the Prussian Gov-

[10] Georg Franz-Willing, *Die bayerische Vatikangesandtschaft, 1803-1934* (Munich, 1965), p. 93.
[11] GSTA, Ges. Päpstl. Stuhl 963, Ritter to BFM, March 14, 1919.

ernment believed it could easily make its wishes known in the capital, where both the Prussian and German governments were located. When the actual discussions to establish the embassy began in 1919, however, Prussia declared its willingness to give up her legation only on condition that Bavaria do so also; otherwise Prussia, which in absolute numbers had more Catholics living within its borders than Bavaria,[12] would also insist upon retaining its minister in Rome. Clearly it was not practical for Germany to maintain three separate missions in Rome, nor could the Reich afford to anger either of its two largest member states, which were conscious of their traditions and rights. Therefore the Foreign Office postponed its budgetary requisitions for the embassy until the difficulties could be solved.[13]

The controversy over Bavaria's position led to a minor press war between north and south German newspapers during the month of October. Bavarian Minister-President Johannes Hoffmann seemed to understand the difficulties which Munich was causing the German Foreign Office, but, as he informed Count Julius von Zech, Prussian Minister (after 1921 Representative of the Reich Government) to Munich, opinion in Bavaria was running high in favor of maintaining the mission, and he could not oppose it. Zech also doubted the Bavarians' readiness to concede the point. He believed that the powerful Center Party in Bavaria would be less likely to alter its position, especially after the Pope, perhaps not fully perceiving the political difficulties that two Papal representatives might cause, had announced, in a letter to the Bavarian bishops, the Curia's intention to reconfirm the nunciature in Munich. Bavaria would naturally desire reciprocal representation in Rome. If Munich renounced its mission at the Vatican, the Bavarian public would conclude that the anti-clerical forces in Protestant Prussia which wanted to increase the power of the Central Government and to diminish Bavaria's position had forced Munich to concede. If such a view became prevalent, said Zech, it would strengthen particularist sentiment in the south and hinder cooperation between the various areas of Germany in the crucial first years after the war. Zech recommended a compromise with Munich to clear away the impediments hindering the new German Republic from functioning properly.[14]

[12] Prussia's population in 1910—Catholics, 14,581,829; Lutherans, 24,830,547. Bavaria's population in 1910—Catholics, 4,863,251; Lutherans, 1,942,658. Germany, Statistisches Amt, *Statistisches Jahrbuch für das Deutsche Reich, 1914* (Berlin, 1914), p. 9. Hereafter cited as Germany, *Statistisches Jahrbuch*.

[13] GSTA, Ges. Päpstl. Stuhl 965, excerpt from the report of the Bavarian legation in Berlin to the BFM, October 8, 1919.

[14] AA, IA, Bayern 58 Geheim, Zech to AA, October 17, 1919.

The matter also acquired a legal dimension. The Weimar Constitution was promulgated on August 11, and under Article 78 all questions of foreign policy and relations with foreign states were reserved to the jurisdiction of the Reich Government. This could be interpreted as meaning that now Bavaria could not constitutionally maintain its Vatican mission without Berlin's express permission. Munich countered by asserting that the Vatican was not a foreign state, and therefore the clause did not pertain in this instance. In order to break the stalemate and reach a compromise, Foreign Minister Müller had proposed that in exchange for the withdrawal of the Bavarian legation Munich be granted the right to nominate someone for the post of German ambassador.[15]

The delay in clarifying the issue had already lasted almost a year. The legations of both Bavaria and Prussia continued to function with unclear status, and the announcement of a German embassy, which had appeared imminent, had not taken place. Speed was necessary, as Zech suggested, for it would be unwise for the sake of future negotiations to give the impression to the Curia that the new Central Government was weak, that the nation was not united, or that the individual states could apply pressure on the Reich Government to obtain their desires.[16] Zech also quite rightly pointed out that the concession Berlin offered to Munich was not practical since Berlin would assume only *de jure* control over the embassy while Munich would have it *de facto*. The Center Party, he indicated, would gain control again at some time in Bavaria. The Bavarian wing of this Party strongly advocated Bavarian particularism, and a Center-led government could, through its power to nominate the ambassador, directly influence the Vatican on its behalf. If the Vatican showed support for the government, this would only strengthen the Center's political control in Bavaria. The Reich Government would no longer be master of its own policy at a post which, as Zech saw it, could evolve into one of the most important political centers in the coming era. A veto exerted by Berlin would not alter the situation, since Munich had the right to present other names should the first candidate prove unacceptable. Berlin's use of this veto right, then, would solve nothing but would only exacerbate new conflicts between north and south.[17]

Prussia was willing to concede its rights to the Reich, no doubt confident that its interest would also be served by the Reich Government, but Bavaria was unwilling to renounce any of its historical,

[15] Germany, Bundesarchiv (hereafter cited as BA), R 43 I, Vol. 159, cabinet minutes, October 22, 1919, p. 7. *Deutsche Allgemeine Zeitung*, October 28, 1919.
[16] AA, IA, Bayern 58, Vol. 3, Zech to AA, October 26, 1919.
[17] AA, IA, Preussen Nr. 6i, Vol. 2, Zech to AA, October 29, 1919.

particularist rights. By the end of October the *Reichsrat*, the upper house of the German legislature, had still not given official approval for establishing an embassy because the status of the Bavarian and Prussian missions had not been clarified or approved by the respective state legislatures. The Bavarians were highly critical of Prussia's apparent altruism, since, as Ritter said, it was willing to close its legation inasmuch as with a German embassy it would appear again only under another name. Inevitably each party began to discern wider implications in its opponent's actions. Munich suspected that Berlin's pressure to close the legations was all part of a wider scheme to reduce Bavaria, the second largest state, to political impotence in Berlin's drive to form a strongly centralized state.[18] The Reich and Prussians, however, viewed the obstinacy of the Bavarians as an effort to resist the new centralizing tendencies which the founders of Weimar believed were necessary to help Germany out of its weakened condition, and as an attempt by Munich to conduct its own policy which in turn could dominate German policy in Catholic matters.

Political consideration no doubt also formed part of the Prussian Cabinet's thinking. A coalition of the same parties (Socialist, Center, and Democrat) which governed the Reich also ruled in Prussia. In contrast, Bavaria had just experienced a revolutionary government which was more to the left than the Central Government, while the new, conservative Catholic Bavarian People's Party, more to the right than Berlin, had also shown itself quite strong in *Landtag* elections. Should Bavaria win the right to nominate Reich officials, it would be the case of the tail wagging the dog. Appointments made by Bavaria, or any other state, would in all likelihood be more conservative or radical, depending on what group controlled the state government, than Prussia's moderate coalition preferred.

As a consequence, in November the Prussian Government, while informing the Reich Government that in the interests of national unity it was bowing to the Central Government's wish and closing its legation, made it clear that should Bavaria be given the right to nominate the ambassador, then Prussia would demand similar privileges in other posts. Generalizing from this case, Prussia noted that various German states were also pressing for special favors from the Central Government. Prussia warned that this system of concessions endangered the entire Republic, arguing that if all were not handled equitably, then

---

[18] GSTA, MA 103505, Ritter to BFM, October 30, 1919. For a discussion of Prussia's relations to the Reich Government and the reactions of the southern states to the Reich's centralizing tendencies, see Enno Eimers, *Das Verhältnis von Preussen und Reich in den ersten Jahren der Weimarer Republik (1918-1923)*, (Berlin, 1969), especially Part B, vii.

Prussia, as the largest *Land* (state), would demand to be treated as the most favored state.[19] The Vatican issue was clearly causing disagreement within government circles and was exposing some of the fragility of the relations between the Reich Government and the *Länder*.

The fact that the Germans intended to escalate their diplomatic activities at the Vatican also concerned both France and Italy. The French viewed the fact that a German ambassador might soon be sent to the Vatican as an indication of the important role which Catholics and the Center Party now played in the new Weimar coalition, and, by extension, feared that it portended a growing cooperation between the Curia and Berlin, which could work against French interests in the post-war world. Italian Prime Minister Francesco Nitti also expressed concern for similar reasons about the new German initiative and stated his intention to dissuade the Vatican from accepting a German ambassador.[20]

The Vatican, in keeping with its position of neutrality or balance among the international powers, was most anxious for ties with Germany. However, its position was also difficult and somewhat ambiguous as to the type of representation it desired. The Pope had already expressed his wish to reestablish a nunciature in Munich and had welcomed Bavaria's intention to retain its legation. Naturally in areas with large Catholic populations, where the Vatican was eager to renegotiate a concordat, it was to its advantage to have accredited representatives work out the details. In addition, direct diplomatic relations with a Catholic area, such as Bavaria, would not have to take into consideration the larger Protestant population which dealings with Germany as a whole would have to do. The Vatican did not want to provoke any internal dissension within Germany. Yet it had also made clear to German representatives still in Rome its desire for Germany's continuation as a strong power in Central Europe. Establishing full diplomatic relations with the Reich would enhance Vatican prestige and influence over all of Germany, including areas for which no legation had previously existed. What would have most pleased the Vatican was both retaining the Bavarian legation and establishing relations with the Central Government, with keeping its traditional means of diplomacy functioning in areas of Germany where the Church had special interests and at the same time accommodating or even capitalizing on the new post-war circumstances to extend its contacts.[21]

[19] BA, R 43 I, Vol. 159, Hirsch, Prussian Minister-President, to the Reich Government, November 11, 1919.

[20] France, Ministère des Affaires Étrangères, Archives et Documentation (hereafter cited as FFO), Allemagne 370, Barrère (Rome-Quirinal) to FFO, December 16, 1919.

[21] GSTA, Ges. Päpstl. Stuhl 965, Ritter to BFM, December 3, 1919.

In December it appeared that a compromise had been worked out by which Bavaria would agree to close its legation on condition that the German ambassador report not only to the German Foreign Office but also to Munich, since this would indicate Bavaria's special status and its importance in Catholic affairs.[22] In January the agreement between Bavaria and Berlin was drawn up, and the Central Government urged the Curia to instruct Nuncio Pacelli and Archbishop Michael von Faulhaber of Munich to use their influence to support the settlement.[23]

Interestingly enough the final decision in what was essentially an internal German affair dealing with the powers of the Central and state governments did not come about through any action by either the Bavarian or the Reich Government, but occurred only after the Holy See made its wishes clear. The Vatican had hoped to expand its diplomatic connections within Germany, not consolidate them. In fact, Faulhaber, perhaps reflecting Rome's thinking, had seen no reason why relations with Munich and Berlin could not exist simultaneously.[24] As long as negotiations were in progress, Rome refrained from explicit statements. When the provisions of the agreement calling for the closing of the Bavarian legation were announced, then the Papacy let it be known that it was very unhappy since the legation was needed to deal with Church affairs particular to Bavaria. The Vatican feared that without a Bavarian legation in Rome a hostile government in Munich might at some future time request the closing of the nunciature. In early 1920 Cardinal Secretary of State Gasparri made clear to both Bavarian and Prussian diplomats his impression that he believed that the Bavarians had agreed to closing the legation only under pressure from Berlin, and he told the Prussian Minister that as much as he welcomed relations with the Reich he would rather see the situation remain a *status quo ante bellum*, that is, with a Bavarian and Prussian minister in attendance, than have the Bavarian mission close altogether. He stressed that political consideration had not motivated his opinion, but that the interests of the Church in Bavaria had. The Vatican strongly endorsed the political unity of Germany, but in cul-

[22] AA, IA, Päpstl. Stuhl 15, Vol. 9, Zech to AA, December 19, 1919.

[23] AA, IA, Päpstl. Stuhl 4, Vol. 10, Foreign Minister Müller to Prussian legation at the Vatican, January 16, 1920. French reports claimed that Berlin had originally also intended to have the Munich nunciature closed and simply transferred to Berlin. But it encountered the categorical resistance of Archbishop Faulhaber, supported by all of his clergy, later the opposition of Gasparri, and finally an absolute veto from the Pope himself. FFO, Allemagne 370, report of a French agent, May 3, 1920.

[24] AA, IA, Preussen 2 Nr. 5, Vol. 2, Boltano Tremezzo to Grünau (AA), November 17, 1920.

tural and religious affairs the Curia wanted to maintain the traditional method of dealing with individual states.[25]

The Pope appeared displeased that negotiations had dragged on for a year and that the proposed settlement seemed potentially detrimental to the Church. Therefore the Vatican finally made its wishes known. The Cardinal Secretary of State in early February informed the Prussian Minister that "it was the urgent wish" of the Holy See for the Bavarian legation to be retained, and, despite all argument to the contrary, Rome believed that Bavarian religious matters could not properly be represented by a Reich minister in Rome.[26]

On February 6, 1920, Nuncio Pacelli stiffened Bavaria's opposition to the Berlin compromise by officially delivering a Papal promemoria to the government in Munich, explicitly stating that the Vatican would like to see a Reich embassy and a Bavarian legation in Rome and nunciatures in both Munich and Berlin. If this were not possible, then the Curia preferred the *status quo ante*. Because of its reservations, the Vatican in any event intended to maintain its nunciature in Munich. To show that it was prepared to lend its support to any who opposed the compromise, Pacelli presented the Vatican's position not only to the government but also to the Bavarian People's Party (BVP), the Bavarian ally of the Center Party, and the party whose support was crucial for approval of the agreement with Berlin.[27] Concerned over the earnestness with which the Vatican reacted, and aware of the other diplomatic considerations weighing on the government, Ritter had recommended all along to Munich and Berlin that it would be better to retain the mission than irritate the Curia at a time when the Germans, including the Bavarians, had every reason to maintain its good wishes and support "for all sorts of matters."[28] In other words, foreign policy requirements were to take precedence over domestic considerations. The Bavarian Minister's advice was finally heeded. In view of the energetic position taken by the Vatican and with further negotiations spurred on by the Reich Government, Prussia eventually dropped its objections to the retention of the Bavarian mission at the Vatican and agreed to the establishment of a Reich embassy on the condition that

[25] This is still the Vatican's policy today. In dealing with individual German states (*Länder*) of the German Federal Republic, the Vatican has a series of treaties and agreements, including concordats with Bavaria and Lower Saxony.

[26] AA, IA, Bayern 58, Vol. 3, Bergen to AA, February 6, 1920.

[27] AA, IA, Bayern 58, Vol. 3, Zech to AA, February 7, 1920. The Bavarian wing of the Center Party had broken away from the parent group shortly after the founding of the Weimar Republic and formed the new Bavarian People's Party.

[28] AA, IA, Bayern 58, Vol. 3, Ritter to BFM, February 2, 1920.

the Prussian Government be allowed to deal with matters pertaining to Prussian church affairs and the Holy See.[29]

At the beginning of 1920 the technicalities appeared to have been finally settled, and the Reich Government took up official relations with the Holy See, appointing an ambassador to the Papal Court and making preparations for the arrival of a nuncio in Berlin. Consequently, the Bavarian legation at the Vatican as well as the Papal nunciature in Munich were reconfirmed, and the Nuncio, Pacelli, was named and accredited to the Central Government. All governments concerned hoped that relations could now proceed more normally.[30] The protracted negotiations over the forms of diplomatic representation not only affected German-Vatican relations but also highlighted the relations among the states within the new republic. The dispute had shown the residual fear which the south Germans, especially the Bavarians, had that the Prussians would overshadow them, a fear that their interests would not truly be represented when presented in an overall policy for the Reich.

Particularism was still a factor to be reckoned with in Germany, and here was a test case of its strength against the Central Government: a battle to test the strength of the Berlin of 1919, and the length to which it could go in imposing its will over the entire land, a battle to measure how far the *Länder* could go in gaining or maintaining states rights. Particularism was an issue which was not settled here but continued throughout Weimar, for it indicated that, despite a belief in central government, Berlin had to compromise in order to conciliate the states, especially when the new republic was just being established. Moreover, things had changed since 1871, when the Reich, as a predominantly Protestant state, was unwilling to establish relations with the Papacy. Now in 1919, with the Catholic Center Party a key support for the new Reich administration and with a general feeling

[29] GSTA, MA 102627, Preger (National Assembly, Weimar) to BFM, February 17, 1920. Franz-Willing, p. 168. An indication of Berlin's attitude toward the Munich nunciature was Berlin's recommendation in the new penal code to provide police protection under Article 104 for the Berlin but not the Munich nunciature. Bernard Zittel, "Die Vertretung des Heiligen Stuhles in München 1785-1934," in *Der Mönch im Wappen* (Munich, 1960), p. 489.

[30] The Germans had done well in their appointments, as admitted even by foreign diplomats. The British Minister to the Holy See had high praise for the German envoys. "Germany, who [sic] was represented by Herr von Bergen as Ambassador and Baron Ritter as Bavarian Minister, a strong combination of the Protestant north and the Catholic south, has certainly not neglected the interests of this post. . . . The governments of the Central Powers have deemed it advisable to strengthen, if anything, their representation since the war; a flattering attention accentuating the importance of the post and as such appreciated by the Holy See." BFO, 371/8886/5333, Russell (Vatican) to Curzon, February 28, 1923.

in government circles that the Papacy was too important in world affairs to allow Germany to go unrepresented, the old belief that Germanism was synonymous with Protestantism was being replaced by a more conciliatory and pragmatic attitude toward the relations of religion to diplomacy. Some compromise had to be made if only out of sheer necessity.[31]

The negotiations also illustrate Vatican thinking and tactics in dealing with foreign states. The Holy See quite clearly desired to maintain relations with Catholic states such as Bavaria, where it believed its policies and interests would probably receive a more sympathetic hearing than in states with religiously mixed populations, such as Prussia or the Reich as a whole. Yet diplomatic relations with the new Germany were also desirable since they would facilitate church-state relations over a much larger area than just Bavaria. The Vatican remained discreet in its negotiations, preferring to let the Germans work out the matter as an internal affair. Only after it became apparent that the Bavarians were on the point of renouncing their mission did the Vatican make clear that this was not to its liking. Germany's willingness to comply and reach a solution agreeable to its member states and to the Vatican also demonstrates the importance which the Vatican held for the Berlin Government. Moreover, the maintenance of two German missions in Rome was not necessarily regarded negatively by the Berlin Government. Once the areas of competence for the respective missions were defined, there was much to be said for having two representatives who could report information and exert influence in Germany's behalf to counterbalance that of other Powers. The Bavarian Minister in Rome summed up Germany's thinking and stressed the value of a second German mission:

> The Vatican lays great weight on maintaining official relations based on mutual, sincere trust, with Germany in general as well as with Bavaria in particular. I believe that it lies not only in the interest of Germany's internal but also her foreign policy to cultivate and utilize the disposition and atmosphere now prevailing at the Vatican on one hand because we can otherwise count on so little sympathy in the world and on the other because the authority of the Holy See in general has risen since the war. Moveover we should avoid anything which could prejudice the good will of the Pope against us.[32]

It is easy to understand the urgency with which Germany wished to establish relations with the Vatican in 1918-1919 when one consid-

---

[31] Georges Goyau, "Sur l'horizon du Vatican," *Revue des deux mondes*, Année 92 (1922), Part 1, 762.

[32] GSTA, MA 104064, Ritter to BFM, January 24, 1920.

ers the myriad of problems, both internal and external, facing Berlin while these negotiations were going on. The Curia could be of assistance to the new Republic in its dealings with other nations, especially the Allies, or it could be a potential enemy should it support the forces opposed to Germany. During the war years the Papacy had maintained its neutrality, speaking out for a just peace and intervening on humanitarian grounds against acts perpetrated by the armies of both the Central and Allied Powers against the civilian population.[33] The fact that the Curia was accused by factions on both sides of favoring the opposing group is perhaps the strongest argument that it did try to retain a balance in its dealings with both sides.[34]

After the war Germany had reason to increase its activities in Rome if for no other reason than to counteract Allied diplomacy. In recent years Germany's opponents had expanded their connections and influence at the Papal Court. In addition to Belgium, which already maintained full diplomatic relations since the pre-war days, Great Britain had established a legation there in 1914; the Italians were quietly negotiating with the Vatican for closer contacts; and the French Government, while not officially maintaining relations with the Holy See, regularly conveyed its attitudes and exchanged opinions with Vatican officials through the members of its hierarchy, who made frequent visits to Rome during the war years. Moreover, in April 1918 the Papacy had appointed a nuncio to Poland, no doubt the first step toward establishing full relations with this country; but in any event it gave the Vatican an observer on the scene to listen to the Polish viewpoint on matters concerning the new Slavic state.[35] All of these diplomatic overtures were exceedingly dangerous for German foreign policy since each of the states had been either at war with Germany or had some grounds for a territorial dispute with the Reich. The Germans, on the other hand, had no representative in Rome until December 1919, when the Bavarian and Prussian legations returned from their exile in Lugano, Switzerland.

Another basis for German anxiety and uncertainty about the Vatican was concern not only over what influence the other Powers were exerting on the Curia but over what policy, despite its neutrality, Rome deemed best in its own interests. The Vatican had never been

[33] AA, IA, Päpstl. Stuhl 15, Vol. 9, extract of letter of Cardinal Gasparri to Pacelli attached to note of Zech to AA, March 29, 1919.

[34] See Stehlin, 418ff. *Augsburger Postzeitung*, April 15, 1919.

[35] GSTA, MA 104442, Ritter to BFM, November 20, 1918. GSTA, MA 99877, memorandum of Fr. Cölestin Schweighofer, Papal Consultor, May 24, 1919. GSTA, MA 104446, Ritter to BFM, June 17, 1919. GSTA, Ges. Päpstl. Stuhl 959, Ritter to BFM, April 21, 1918.

pleased with Protestant Prussia's strong influence within the Reich since 1871 and was naturally concerned in 1919 to learn of Prussia's role in the new centralized state lest it block or obscure Vatican influence in southern Germany.[36] Although the idea was not pursued as a counter-move to Prussia's influence, the Vatican had initially suggested to foreign diplomats that the Allied Powers establish legations with the various German states.[37] Such suggestions only reinforced the belief in German government circles that the Vatican might support German separatist movements or closer ties between Catholic southern Germans and Austria.[38] Vatican support, official or unofficial, could have considerable influence among the Catholic population and could certainly weaken the nascent Republic's central government. Once more a reason was given for the urgency to exert a countervailing influence in Rome in these critical years.

Berlin realized that it was not only imperative to court the Vatican for negative reasons—to ward off the progress which Allied diplomacy might make—but also that the support of the Curia could be of great positive value in attaining German diplomatic objectives, especially in matters where both governments shared similar concerns. One obvious issue in which Rome could be of assistance was in helping to decide the future of German religious missions abroad. Like all Christian countries Germany had sent missionaries in the nineteenth century to all parts of the world to found hospitals, establish schools, and convert the non-Christians. Over time the value of mission holdings, funded largely by money from the homeland, had grown and represented considerable financial investments for the parent institutions. Also, the number of people who had used the mission facilities had steadily increased from year to year.[39]

The importance to Germany of such missions was obvious. Since many of the leaders of this colonial world had been educated according to German standards, spoke German, or had received health care there, Berlin had hoped that these people would retain a friendly attitude toward the Reich. Now in 1919 all this was threatened by the victors'

[36] GSTA, Ges. Päpstl. Stuhl 963, Ritter to BFM, January 18, 1919. *L'Osservatore Romano*, January 12, 1919. Hereafter cited as *Osservatore*.

[37] British diplomats reported that Pacelli sent word to French officials urging France to send diplomatic representatives to Munich and other state capitals in order to counteract Berlin's predominance. BFO, 371/3790/5403, Acton (Zurich) to BFO, June 7, 1919.

[38] AA, IA, Preussen 2 Nr. 5, Vol. 2, Zech to AA, December 26, 1919. AA, IA, Päpstl. Stuhl 1, Vol. 11, Saenger (Prague) to AA, December 15, 1919.

[39] For tabulations of the activities of the missions, see: H. A. Krose, ed., *Kirchliches Handbuch für das Katholische Deutschland* (Freiburg i.B., 1919), Vol. 8 (1918/19), pp. 148-169.

proposals not only to deprive Germany of all its former colonies, but also to expel all German missionaries, including some 2,000 Catholic priests, brothers, and sisters from the colonial areas and to place the property under control of local Christians—though not necessarily the denomination which held it previously. For Germany this would mean a potential loss of influence and goods in the colonial territories as well as in the Holy Land, where a number of the religious orders maintained establishments. It would mean a loss of prestige for Germany, a nation which prided itself on asserting that it had done its share in helping to civilize the world. Berlin regarded it as an unjust act against many German nationals who had spent their lives abroad, as well as a breach of the agreement of 1885 concerning the Congo, which specified that missionaries even in time of war were to be regarded as neutrals. The Allied proposal also disturbed the Vatican because of the setback it would inflict on Catholic missionary efforts and the potential loss of Catholic property to other groups. Besides the injustice of the matter, such a move would mean that many of the missions would then remain unmanned, and the ensuing chaos would interrupt the Christianizing work which these missions were providing. Even if the missions remained in the hands of a local Christian board of directors, many of the members could be anti-German or anti-Catholic and thus block the work which had been accomplished by the German missionaries.[40] Both governments, then, not long after the cessation of hostilities found a basis of common interest where they could immediately cooperate with one another.

In March 1919 the German bishops called the attention of the Holy See to the fact that the Allies intended to remove all German influence and control over their missions by inserting clauses to that effect in the peace treaty, and requested the Vatican to help prevent these measures. The Curia thereupon sided with Germany on this issue and published a series of articles in the *Osservatore* which argued for retention of the German missions, stating that the missionaries were church officers and the missions themselves were property belonging to the Congregation for the Propagation of the Faith, not to German nationals.[41] Besides its newspaper campaign in June, the Vatican sent Archbishop Bonaventura Cerretti, Secretary for Extraordinary Ecclesiastical Affairs, or Under Secretary of State, to Paris to ensure that the Vatican's position on the Catholic missions was placed before the Peace Conference, and, in an indirect way, to represent German interests in this matter. The conference, especially after Wilson had been won

[40] *Augsburger Postzeitung*, June 7, 1919. *Kölnische Volkszeitung*, June 10, 1919.
[41] Walter H. Peters, *The life of Benedict XV* (Milwaukee, 1959), p. 169.

over by Cerretti's arguments, revised the pertinent clauses and granted freedom for all Catholic missions to continue their work.[42] On July 1 Benedict cabled his thanks to the White House for the President's support of the Vatican's stand.[43] Thus the Holy See had been able to use its influence to work in the interests of both governments in the international arena, an area where Germany still lacked influence.

The specter of Bolshevism also deeply concerned both the Reich and the Curia in 1919. The Spartacist revolt in Berlin in January 1919 and further Communist uprisings in Berlin, Munich, and other cities in succeeding months made Ebert's Government fear for the security of the new Republic.[44] Socialism, with its emphasis on the materialist aspects of life, was a movement which had already clashed with the Church during the nineteenth century. With great uneasiness the Pope now observed how Socialism in its most virulently atheistic, Bolshevist form had taken possession of Russia in 1917 and how it systematically was attempting to stamp out religion by closing churches, forbidding worship, and oppressing the clergy. The promise of world revolution was beginning to attain actuality. By 1919, in addition to the Communist uprisings in areas of Germany, Soviet governments, albeit short-lived, had succeeded in gaining control in some places such as Hungary and even in Bavaria. Lenin expected that Germany would soon follow Russia's lead, and the Pope feared the same. On January 16, 1919 an article appeared in the *Osservatore* about both Russian and German Bolshevism, warning that the dangers of Communism could spread from Russia to engulf Germany.[45] If Germany fell to the Bolsheviks, Central and even Western Europe might be inundated by atheistic Communism. Moreover, considering the uncertain political situation in the Germany of 1919, there was no reason to be sure that the course of politics in that country might not turn radically to the left. In fact, Pope Benedict XV had directed his nuncio in Warsaw, Achille Ratti, the future Pius XI, to keep careful watch on the activities in Russia and to report what the refugees were telling him about Soviet plans. Pacelli, the future Pius XII and now Nuncio to Bavaria, had himself experienced the chaos of the revolution in Munich in April-May 1919. He had been personally threatened when revolutionaries had broken into the nunciature in late 1918, and fear

[42] *Ibid.*, p. 170.

[43] Joseph P. Tumulty, *Woodrow Wilson as I know him* (New York, 1921), p. 482. Peters, p. 171.

[44] For details about the West's fear of Bolshevism, see Arno J. Mayer, *Politics and diplomacy of peacemaking* (New York, 1967). For the manner in which Germany exploited this fear to its advantage, see p. 10f.

[45] *Osservatore*, January 16, 1919.

for his life had in fact caused the Curia to order Pacelli to leave Munich for a while and travel to Switzerland.[46] Reports of the unstable conditions throughout the area made the Vatican believe that Central Europe was tottering on the brink of a political collapse which would lead to a Communist takeover. Germany had to be retained in the western Christian camp as a potentially strong and stable area; it had to serve as a bulwark against further advances from the east. In the eyes of Vatican officials everything was to be utilized to support the forces of law and order and to prevent further erosion of the political situation. Thus here was a matter of common concern where the Reich and the Vatican could work together, for both sincerely wished to halt the spread of Communism. But, in addition, Germany could make use of this issue, as it often did in the following years, to play upon Rome's fears in order to win its support in reducing Allied demands and restrictions on the Reich. Not only should the Vatican support Germany in protesting harsh and unfair demands which would cause international bitterness and delay a restoration of peace, but it should help by ensuring that the Reich remain economically, politically, and militarily viable in order to protect Europe and its institutions.

The Curia viewed a moderate peace, however, as not only imperative to Europe's welfare but also advantageous to the Vatican's own diplomatic position. One way to maintain Papal independence was to ensure that no state was dominant in Europe. The memories of Napoleon's subjugation of the Papacy a brief hundred years before was still very vivid for the Vatican. If Germany did not remain a viable power in Europe, the ensuing diplomatic imbalance might open the door not only to Bolshevism but also to French or Allied control of Europe, allowing no leeway for Vatican diplomacy to maneuver. After the armistice the Allies were in a strong position, and on the continent France appeared predominant. The Vatican was laboring under the same illusion as most governments that France had taken over the role of pre-World War I Germany and had the economic and political potential for becoming the leading force on the continent. Therefore the Vatican deemed it necessary to continue some support to Germany in order to help re-create the balance and allow Rome to maintain some diplomatic effectiveness. The aid, however, was not to be perceived at the conference table but rather in the Pontiff's ability to influence European governments indirectly in light of the new prestige and respect which he had gained during the war.

The Pope had originally desired to be included in negotiations for

---

[46] The Germans were greatly disturbed lest this incident discredit them in Vatican circles. AA, IA, Bayern 59, Vol. 6, the chargé d'affaires (Bern) to AA, January 4, 1919.

the post-war world, but once the provisions of the secret Treaty of London of April 26, 1915, became known, by which the Allies promised Italy not to invite the Vatican to the peace table, Benedict XV had to content himself with exerting influence from afar. But the Pope's determined statement of neutrality, his refusal to take sides, his offers of mediation, his peace proposals, had by 1919 raised the stature of the Papacy in the opinion of many governments which had forgotten its existence behind the walls of the Vatican.[47] Benedict had lifted his voice, in what he considered his duty as a religious leader to admonish the nations to moderate their positions and to work for an agreement by compromise. In numerous statements and allocutions during and immediately after the war he reiterated his conviction that the rights of all peoples had to be considered in rebuilding Europe, that nations did not die. The Pontiff firmly opposed any arbitrarily dictated peace, for the Holy See could scarcely approve a settlement which imposed great losses or humiliation on any large group of Catholics. He therefore urged, not a vindictive peace, but a just one which would leave Germany its self-respect. This was the tone of Papal pronouncements immediately after the armistice.[48]

The Curia made it clear in 1919 that it was against any League of Nations which favored the "Anglo-Saxon-French constellation" to the disadvantage of the Central Powers in both the political and economic spheres, since such a disproportionate arrangement would be not only unfair but also endanger Vatican interests.[49] Benedict appeared to feel under pressure from the Allies, especially France, and he welcomed the return of the German missions to Rome, which would then serve as a diplomatic counterweight for him. The Pontiff resisted all French urgings to delay the return of the Germans, for he had had enough restrictions placed on him during the war. Now he wanted access to all nations and a certainty of sufficient German strength to provide a proper balance in European affairs.[50]

[47] BFO, 371/7671/5302, De Salis to Curzon, October 25, 1922, pp. 4-5, 12. The prestige of the Vatican had risen considerably during the war, and all major powers by the early 1920's were renewing or taking up diplomatic relations with Rome. As French Premier Alexandre Millerand commented in 1920, after France began the process of reestablishing relations with the Vatican, Protestants, Orthodox as well as Catholics, republics and monarchies, states with concordats and those seeking them, were all in agreement that their own interests required diplomatic relations with the Vatican. What they recognized was that the Vatican was a government whose connections were worldwide. Friedrich Engel-Janosi, *Vom Chaos zur Katastrophe* (Vienna, 1971), p. 13. Sisley Huddleston, *Those Europeans* (New York, 1924), p. 323.

[48] Editorials in the *Osservatore* had made it plain that the Pontiff would play no part in a peace which stressed *vae victis* (woe to the vanquished). Peters, p. 169.

[49] AA, IA, Päpstl. Stuhl 1, Vol. 11, Federn (AA) to AA, September 4, 1919.

[50] AA, IA, Bayern 60, Vol. 2, Ritter to AA, November 11, 1919.

In early 1919 articles began to appear in the *Ossèrvatore* about the grave problems facing Western civilization, counseling moderation of the Allied demands so that a stability could once more be established in Europe to fend off Bolshevism, which might spread farther than just Germany. Excessive demands, at the Peace Conference, stated the *Osservatore*, could create an atmosphere of hate leading to further war. As the Bavarian Minister observed, the specter of Bolshevism hung over the Paris proceedings, and so much had been rumored about the chaos which it brought with it that even the Vatican, which had weathered so many storms, was now filled with concern about this new phenomenon.[51]

Rome also expressed these views to the Allied Powers. In March, Viscount John Francis De Salis, British Minister at the Vatican, reported that Cardinal Gasparri had written to him stating that

> unless a peace which Germans can accept and which is not humiliating for them is shortly reached, Germany will become a Bolshevik ally and imitator of Russia. In view of the supreme interests of civilization and of European peace the Holy See considered it their [sic] duty to hasten to give warning to Great Britain and through her to other powers of the Entente urging the conclusion of a speedy and suitable peace.[52]

While expressing the same thoughts to the Belgian Ambassador, Gasparri elaborated further that the revolution and unrest in Germany were caused by the hardships for the populace following the armistice. In order to avoid exposing Germany to further political dangers, the Cardinal recommended that the naval blockade that the Allies had imposed on Germany during the war be lifted, and the final peace terms not involve excessive territorial demands nor disproportionate reparations.[53]

On June 22, Gasparri went a step further in supporting more mod-

[51] GSTA, Ges. Päpstl. Stuhl 963, Ritter to BFM, February 17, 1919. *Osservatore*, February 25, 1919, "Ogni indugio e pericolo!" (Every delay is dangerous!) *Osservatore*, April 5, 1919. GSTA, Ges. Päpstl. Stuhl 964, Ritter to BFM, April 8, 1919.

[52] BFO, 371/3776/5403, De Salis to BFO, March 8, 1919.

[53] Belgium, Ministère des Affaires Étrangères, Services des Archives (hereafter cited as BelgFO), St. Siège 1919-1922, van den Heuvel (Vatican) to Hymans, Belgian Foreign Minister, March 8, 1919. The cease-fire terms provided for the blockade to remain in force but that the victors should consider provisioning the German population during the armistice period. The Allies asked the Reich to employ its own ships in transporting the foodstuffs. The German High Command refused to do this, presumably regarding the ships as war potential or a bargaining point at the peace conference. In March 1919 Berlin finally agreed to use its ships, and supplies began to arrive in German ports. The Germans blamed the Allies, but the High Command and the government in Berlin were essentially responsible for the privation experienced by the German public.

erate peace conditions. In a memorandum to the British Government he stated his awareness of German consent to the peace treaty with certain reservations, including their refusal to accept the guilt for the war or to agree to have the Kaiser and other German leaders placed on trial. The Holy See urgently requested the Allies to concede to the German objections, for the interests of a speedy and fair peace required such a compromise. The memorandum then proceeded to explain Rome's view of why a trial of the Kaiser would be unjust: he alone was not responsible, and the tribunal would consist of judges from the accusing states, thus violating impartiality. Could the court, asked Gasparri, determine the long-range causes of the war without studying all the diplomatic documents, and were the Allied ministries then willing to open their archives to such a court? To demand that Holland give up the Kaiser, who had fled there in 1918, would also negate the right of asylum. If the court did not pronounce a sentence, lack of action would be seen as an exoneration of the Kaiser; if it did, it would be viewed, especially in Germany, as an act of revenge and without sanctions, since there was no precedent for such a trial.[54]

Similar considerations were also mentioned for the military leaders. On July 1 in his cable to President Wilson thanking him for his support of the Church's position on the German missions, Benedict requested another favor:

> We desire to express to you our sincere gratitude and at the same time we urge Your Excellency to be good enough to employ your great influence, also, in order to prevent the action, which according to the Peace Treaty with Germany it is desired to bring against the Kaiser and the highly placed German commanders. This action could only render more bitter national hatred and postpone for a long time that pacification of souls for which all nations long. Furthermore, this trial, if the rules of justice are to be observed, would meet insurmountable difficulties. . . .

On August 15, Wilson replied to Benedict by thanking him for his words and the clarity of their exposition and promised to bear in mind the Pontiff's thoughts in the negotiations ahead.[55]

Several months later Gasparri returned to this subject while speaking to the British representative in Rome. The diplomat reported:

> The Holy See, the Cardinal said, had always thought desirable that for two reasons the proceedings against the Kaiser should be aban-

---

[54] BFO, 371/4271/5392, Gasparri to Gaisford (Vatican), June 22, 1919. A similar argument was made in the *Osservatore*, June 25, 1919.

[55] Peters, p. 171. Tumulty, pp. 482-483.

doned. In the first place, these proceedings and a subsequent sentence would accentuate and prolong national hatreds . . . , place England in a disagreeable position and at the same time shake the throne not only of England but of every other monarchical State.

The Cardinal's comments exhibited two aspects of Papal policy: concern for the general peace with an agreement tempered by practical considerations. Similarly Gasparri expressed hope that the proceedings against the military would be dropped since they would also cause ill will by forcing Germany to deliver its own citizens to foreigners for trial. Moreover, he added, "the handing over of the guilty could not take place without grave danger of a revolutionary movement of a militarist-Bolshevik character which would certainly reach the whole of Europe." The Holy See trusted that, in view of these facts, England as well as France would not insist on the trials.[56] Although many other considerations besides Papal urgings caused the delegates in Paris to drop the idea of a trial for the Kaiser and other Germans (the Dutch refusal to turn him over, decreasing interest among the Allies to undertake the prosecution), Papal intervention had no doubt played a role in their decision, and had certainly been of great aid in preserving the missions for Germany and the Church. In all Vatican initiatives the Germans were quick to note its aid to them and to apprehend that the Vatican might be of even more use later on.[57]

One German politician who had readily perceived the Vatican's potential diplomatic value for Germany was the Center leader Matthias Erzberger. During the war he had made certain that the Pope was kept informed of Germany's position on all matters of wartime policy. He had acted frequently as liaison between the Berlin Government and the Holy See and had strongly urged establishment of a Vatican state to ensure Papal independence from Allied, especially Italian, control. Erzberger had sought to demonstrate the loyalty of German Catholics to the Holy See by sending money which had been collected in Germany for the Pope, whose sources of revenue in Central Europe had been severed during the period of hostilities.[58] In the immediate post-war period Erzberger still sent long memoranda to the Vatican explaining Germany's policies. He hoped for some Vatican support for Germany, for Rome to send instructions to the clergy in the Allied countries to work for moderating the peace terms and the reparation

[56] BFO, 371/4272/5397, De Salis to Curzon, January 26, 1920.

[57] GSTA, Ges. Päpstl. Stuhl 965, Ritter to AA, July 4, 1919. H.W.V. Temperley, ed., *A history of the Peace Conference of Paris* (London, 1920), Vol. 2, pp. 304, 307, 358, 375.

[58] Epstein, pp. 102-103. Stehlin, 406-407.

demands. By supplying the Papacy with information about dire conditions in Germany he desired to heighten the Pontiff's fear of anarchy. The French, in fact, had learned that Erzberger and the Berlin Government were supplying information to the Vatican via the Apostolic legation in Bern and that the Germans had suggested to Curial officials that Rome lend its support to such causes as a Catholic Irish state in order to weaken Great Britain and to lobby and encourage those delegates in Paris endorsing Wilson's Fourteen Points as a basis of peace rather than the more severe demands of the French.[59] Erzberger also kept in close touch with Pacelli in Munich, who also passed on information to the Vatican.[60] As one French observer perceived it, Germany was conducting a policy to gain the Holy See's support at any price:

> Rome, with all the moral authority which belongs to it, with the special influence which it can exert on all those souls attached to the ideals of social order. . . , seems to it [Germany] in its own way like the most stable rock in the midst of current and future storms. It would like to tie its future to that of Rome which it sees as full of promise and serene certitude. It is naturally afraid of seeing the Entente Powers, particularly France, vying with it for first place in an alliance with the most effective moral authority in the world.[61]

Although the instances where Berlin and Rome could cooperate in attaining their foreign policy goals were sufficient grounds for Berlin to seek the Curia's support, there was also a further reason for the Reich to concern itself with the Vatican's position, for it affected not only diplomatic problems but also internal and constitutional matters and the daily lives of many German citizens as well. Rome was most anxious to clarify the legal position of the Church, which had been placed in question after the collapse of the monarchy. Berlin, sensing Vatican interest in establishing a good relationship with the new government, found another reason to begin discussions with Rome, since a regularization of church-state relations could not only assist in stabilizing the situation within the country but also be of aid in some crucial diplomatic situations.

The collapse of the monarchy had shocked many Germans who had come to believe in and depend on the durability of the Imperial system. This was especially difficult for many Catholics who were at-

[59] FFO, Allemagne 370, memorandum on the relations of Germany and the Vatican, January 23, 1919.

[60] *Ibid.*, March 2, 1919.

[61] FFO, Allemagne 370, note from the Office of the Commander in Chief of the Allied Armies-Administrators of the Rhenish Territories, April 28, 1919.

tached to the monarchical principle. There was no real republican tradition in the political sense of the word among the Catholics, nor had the revolutionary events in 1918-1919 created one.[62] For the Vatican as well as for the Church hierarchy it meant dealing with an administration not based on tradition but a government which could be altered according to the wishes of the people and whose leaders were many times influenced by beliefs such as Liberalism or Socialism, whose philosophical foundations were often inimical to or which at least differed with those of the Church. The underpinnings of the social and political order had been altered, and the moorings to which, at least in the political sphere, the Church had tied itself had been loosed; the Church had nothing to attach itself to in the unsettled time after the war had ceased. In the Baltic areas the returning soldiers and *Freikorps* groups were pillaging. Workers' and soldiers' councils had been set up from Bavaria to the Baltic, and in Munich a revolutionary dictatorship had been formed under Kurt Eisner. The Spartacists had attempted *Putsche* in several German cities, and the Reich looked as if it might dissolve into anarchy.

The Pope was concerned with conditions in Germany not only because of the international implications of the situation and the threat of Bolshevism but also because of his concern for the Church in Germany per se and, as pastor of his flock, for the plight of the German people. Shortly after the armistice he had expressed his concern by his encyclical of December 1918 and by his speech at Christmas to the cardinals, stating that he hoped for a lasting and just peace and that he had ordered prayers for that purpose. While stressing his impartiality the Pope again pleaded for mild and just peace terms for Germany.[63] He spoke against the blockade and stressed the misery of the innocent civilian population and undertook to see what steps could be taken to stave off the hunger threatening Germany. On July 15, 1919, he sent a message of encouragement to the German bishops, expressing his support for them and their flocks, and urged the prelates to work to heal the damages of war as quickly as possible.[64]

While the Pontiff demonstrated his pastoral concern for the social and spiritual well-being of the Germans, a new constitution was being written at Weimar which would establish a new political basis for unity in the Reich, a new relation between the government and the religious organizations within Germany, and which would remove many of the restrictions on the Church remaining from the Imperial period.

[62] Heinrich Lutz, *Demokratie im Zwielicht* (Munich, 1963), p. 67.

[63] GSTA, Ges. Päpstl. Stuhl 963, Ritter to BFM, February 7, 1919.

[64] Joseph Schmidlin, *Papstgeschichte der neuesten Zeit* (Munich, 1936-1939), Vol. 3, p. 280. *AAS*, XI (1919), 305f.

While Rome regarded some of these developments favorably, other tendencies and viewpoints represented at the Constitutional Assembly worried the Vatican. It was not only the misery and anarchy which was concerning the Holy Father and the bishops but also some of the legislation being enacted at Weimar by the National Assembly and by the individual state governments.

Throughout the chaotic months of late 1918 and early 1919 the National Assembly was meeting in the little Thuringian city of Weimar and formulating a constitution which reflected the interests and philosophies of most delegates in favor of instituting a liberal democracy based on popular representation. For many liberals and Socialists, freedom and democratic principles, however, meant a separation of Church and State, a restriction of religion to a private sphere where it would not influence political affairs nor receive financial aid from the State for its institutions or programs. More concretely, if the Reich Government or the individual states declared a formal separation of Church and State, this might mean there would be neither religious education provided in the schools nor State support for training of religious instructors. Education had always been a prime concern of the Church, which had insisted on the rights of Catholic parents to obtain a Christian education for their children. In the opinion of the Vatican it was the Church's duty to assure the souls entrusted to its care an education according to the beliefs of the Church.

Already in November 1918 Prussia and Bavaria, both in the hands of Socialist majorities and the two largest German states which had agreements with the Catholic Church regarding church-state relations, announced their intention of separating Church and State, and there were indications that other states were also inclining in that direction.[65] The announcements caused great concern in Catholic circles. Cardinal Felix Hartmann of Cologne, speaking for the Prussian episcopate, addressed several protests to the Prussian Government, declaring that such an act violated existing laws, deprived the Church of its rights, and denounced the goal of de-Christianizing the schools. The Church had an obligation to ensure a Christian education for the children, he reiterated, and the bishops could not be influenced by circumstances or by public opinion but only the truth as they saw it.[66] A pastoral letter to Catholics followed, warning against such an act and stating that the Church might now be deprived of the legal guarantees to its position which had been obtained in the nineteenth cen-

[65] GSTA, MA 104492, May (Stuttgart) to BFM, December 10, 1918.

[66] Germany, Geheimes Staatsarchiv Preussischer Kulturbesitz (hereafter cited as PGSTA), Rep 90, P.11.1.1., Vol 9, Hartmann to Prussian Government, November 19, December 2, 16, 1918.

tury and of agreements which regulated the obligations of both parties, if thus arbitrarily set aside. The bishops also reaffirmed that the Church provided a morality for society and argued that a state existing in a society without religion would only weaken the social fiber. They, therefore, requested the laity's assistance in protesting this injustice.[67] The Pontiff supported these efforts in a letter to the Prussian episcopate, expressing his consternation over events, and endorsed the actions of the bishops to preserve the rights which they had secured during the nineteenth century. He singled out especially the importance of maintaining religion in the schools, which, he believed, was the basic pillar in the education of true Christians and good citizens.[68]

In Bavaria, government actions provoked similar ecclesiastical measures. On January 3, 1919, the Bavarian Minister to the Vatican was instructed to inform Munich of the Vatican's displeasure with measures to impede religious education in the Bavarian schools,[69] and in his Lenten remarks Archbishop Faulhaber warned against their dangers.[70] The bishops wished to dissuade the government from unilaterally abrogating the Concordat of 1817 between Bavaria and the Vatican; only bilateral agreement, the bishops insisted, could effect a change in their relationship.[71] The Bavarian episcopate found further encouragement for their position in Benedict's announced intention of September 22 to retain the nunciature in Munich and to support their stand on the school question.[72]

In Weimar the National Assembly had been debating the religious issue, and Articles 135-138 of the Constitution proposed granting German citizens freedom of worship, and the right of the churches to administer their own affairs, but did not make specific the relations between the Church and the State. The discussions became heated, the Right and Center opposing the articles, since the legal rights of religious bodies and the relations between Church and State had not been clearly defined. The Democrats and Socialists, however, united and voted for passage.[73] This only partially resolved the religious question. In December, several months after the adoption of the Constitution, the bishops of Germany felt constrained to write to the Reich Government about the matter. While acknowledging that freedom of

---

[67] *Kölnische Volkszeitung*, December 24, 1918.

[68] *Ibid.*, December 28, 1918.

[69] GSTA, Ges. Päpstl. Stuhl 962, Ritter to BFM, January 3, 1919.

[70] *Bayerischer Kurier*, March 10, 1919.

[71] Germany, Bamberg, Archiv des Erzbistums Bamberg (hereafter cited as Germany, Bamberg), Akten der Erzbischöfe, Nr. 39, 2, Faulhaber to Archbishop Jakobus Hauck, June 19, 1919.

[72] *Bayerischer Kurier*, October 12, 1919.

[73] *Kölnische Volkszeitung*, April 8, 1919.

conscience had been guaranteed and that the Constitution allowed the Church latitude in many areas, the bishops pointed out that there were also legal areas where their rights had neither been defined nor assured, such as in the matter of the Church's rights over education and the consequences of a unilateral suspension by the State of its financial responsibilities to the Church. The bishops stated, however, their hope for friendly cooperation between the leaders of both Church and State. The Chancellor answered that the framers of the Constitution had striven to preserve the rights of the Church and also hoped for cooperation between both institutions. Despite the exchange of communiqués, the aftermath of the constitutional deliberations left both sides aware that much still remained to be accomplished before a resumption of normal church-state relations took place.[74]

The matter of swearing oaths also concerned the Church. Prior to 1919, oaths had been taken upon a Bible or by invoking the name of God. The Weimar Constitution was also to eliminate this practice. For pious Christians this indicated a further secularization of society and raised the question of the validity of the oath, which now lacked divine witness. For these Christians this was again only one more indication of the weakening of religion as a factor in society and the increasing secularized tone of the new republican government. In more practical terms the new Constitution also raised the question of support for the Church. Would the State contribute anything to the salaries of the clergy or to the upkeep of the buildings, recognizing in religion a pillar of the social order, or would the Church be cut off to go its own way? Would the Church be permitted to supervise education, as it had in Bavaria, if the law were interpreted to mean that religion had absolutely no place in educational matters which were controlled by the State? Conversely, prior to 1918 the State had some rights in the nomination of bishops. Although the Constitution granted religious bodies the right to control their own affairs, under certain circumstances, in border dioceses, for example, would not the State seek to be consulted on the choice of the spiritual leaders? What influence, the Church asked, would a democratic and oftentimes non-religious administration try to obtain in episcopal appointments, and would it be in the best interests of the Church to have Socialists and free-thinkers advising in these selections?

Until 1918 the Papal Bull *De Salute Animarum* of 1821 in Prussia and the Concordat of 1817 in Bavaria had regulated these matters to the general satisfaction of both parties. But in 1919 the uncertainty of

---

[74] AA, IA, Päpstl. Stuhl 15, Vol. 9, bishops to the Reich Government, December 17, 1919; Reich Chancellor to bishops, December 1919, *sine dato*. Articles to which the Center had objections were Articles 10, 137, 138, 143-149. See also ch. 7.

exactly which rights the Church did have made the Holy See want to renegotiate the entire question of church-state relations with the Central Government or any state government which showed an interest.[75] This attitude was supported by a detailed letter to Pacelli from the Bavarian bishops specifying the changes which the new situation had brought about, discussing problems concerning the State's right to nominate a bishop, the nomination of the cathedral chapter, religious education, the theological professorships at universities, and the property and financial rights of the Church. The bishops concluded by urging the Holy See to help regulate the situation.[76]

As the provisions of the Constitution indicated, the German lawmakers had not intended a total break between Church and State, as had occurred in France in 1905. Nevertheless, the situation had been altered, necessitating a new *modus vivendi*. German officials also felt pressure to readjust the situation, for the new Central and state governments did not need the added difficulty of dealing with a hierarchy which was inimical to the civil authorities. Unity within the State demanded a speedy resolution to the problem. Also, in spite of the temptation for the civil government to seek to gain new advantages at the negotiating table, other considerations came into play. Ritter warned the government to reach a speedy settlement and not to make things too difficult, for Germany needed Vatican help in the international arena. Also, should the civil government opt for complete separation of Church and State and totally divorce itself from any influence on the Church, the Vatican, with pressure from the Entente Powers, might appoint pro-Allied prelates in border-area dioceses. Perhaps, mused Ritter, it would still be better to keep a link with the Church and thereby ensure the appointment of bishops sympathetic to the Republic.[77] Berlin and Munich could therefore ponder how best to handle the problem of Church and State. One thing, however, was certain: the Vatican was now determined to clarify the situation and to rework its treaties with German states, since the Reich Constitution had unilaterally altered the legal situation in Germany but had not sufficiently clarified the guarantees and rights of the Church which Rome desired.

Politically, the Center Party had represented Catholic interests in Imperial Germany. In 1919 Erzberger sought to convince the Vatican that it was to the Church's interests for the Center to join the Weimar Government to take advantage of the new political situation and assure

[75] PGSTA, Rep 90, P.11.1.1., Vol. 9, Pacelli to Zech, December 24, 1919.

[76] Bamberg, Akten der Erzbishöfe, Nr. 39, 2, Bavarian episcopate to Pacelli, December 12, 1919.

[77] GSTA, Ges. Päpstl. Stuhl 965, Ritter to BFM, November 17, 1919.

Catholics of a voice in the government.[78] Although the bishops had already spoken out against any concessions being made on the role of the Church in society or the schools,[79] and despite the unclear status of the Church to the State, or perhaps precisely because of it, the Center Party had entered the government in the hopes of capitalizing on the changed situation and of working out a new set of ground rules by which Church and State could coexist and the Catholic layman could realize his commitments to his civil and religious authorities.

The Papacy also favored a speedy conclusion of a new agreement with Germany on these relations. The war had presented the Roman Church with a peculiar situation. In 1914, although its prestige was growing and its moral influence was again beginning to be recognized by world powers, the Church's presence was still largely felt through the hierarchies in nations with Catholic populations. The Holy See had few representatives accredited to the civil governments, envoys who could speak for Rome and seek to gain a legal position for the Church and to protest the rights of its members. The Church, then, not only had to be a spiritual force but had to increase its contacts with state governments in order to carry out that spiritual mission. The upheaval of 1919 presented an opportunity to start from the ground level up, to enter into diplomatic relations with other states, and to regularize church-state relations by means of concordats. The Holy See sought systematically to sign concordats with civil governments which would legally guarantee rights to the Church that would eliminate episcopal elections and centralize appointment procedures in the hands of the Curia, without secular interference wherever possible. Such treaties also granted juridical recognition to ecclesiastical institutions and frequently required the State to contribute to the clergy's salary. During the interwar period no fewer than forty states signed such agreements. With the concordats the Papacy was able to open the gates for contact with foreign governments which had slammed shut in 1870 and which Versailles had not assisted in opening for Rome. In this sense the concordats were not only to preserve Church rights within a given country but to formalize a working relationship between the Vatican and the other governments to solve problems in religious areas and those pertaining to internal and foreign affairs.[80]

Benedict was thus anxious to come to terms with the Germans.

[78] Epstein, p. 288. For the reorientations of the Center in the Reich and Prussia, see Herbert Hömig, *Das preussische Zentrum in der Weimarer Republik* (Mainz, 1979), p. 35ff.
[79] AA, BRV 1047, Vol. 1, Müller (Bern) to AA, November 17, 1919.
[80] J. van den Heuvel, "Benoît XV," *Revue Générale*, CVII (1922), 274. La Piana, 488-489. Nazareno Padellaro, *Portrait of Pius XII*, trans., Michael Derrick (New York, 1957), pp. 44-47.

Nuncio Pacelli, who echoed this sentiment, took the first step, beginning with the largely Catholic state of Bavaria, when on January 20, 1920 he handed Minister-President Hoffmann a note informing him that the Vatican desired to regulate anew the relations between the south German state and the Holy See by a treaty.[81] Count Zech had also been informed by Pacelli that if the desire for a nunciature in Berlin were received in Rome in any form, even a semi-official form, as far as he had been told, the nunciature would be established.[82]

On the Reich level contacts remained cordial. Ebert had paid Rome, as well as the Catholics of Germany, the courtesy of expressly informing the Pope of his selection as Reich President by the National Assembly on February 11. In turn, on April 2, Benedict, as already mentioned, congratulated and wished him success in his new position, and furthermore took the opportunity to call for closer relations between the two governments.[83] In August a meeting was arranged between Pacelli and President Ebert in Munich. The meeting went well, and each party impressed the other. During the conversation Ebert explained Germany's internal problems and the difficulties caused by the treaty's demands. He assured the Nuncio that the Reich Government was not hostile to the Church, that in the new Germany it would be free from any restrictions in carrying out its pastoral duties, and that Berlin was interested in reaching an accord with it. Regarded from a political standpoint, Ebert was reminding Pacelli of his agreement with his Center coalition partners which had been part of the basis for their entering the government. But by giving these assurances to the Vatican he was also seeking to interest the Papacy in Germany's diplomatic struggle and gaining its moral and political help to sustain the new government within Germany. This conference, then, was not merely a protocol visit but actually marked the beginning of the relations between the Vatican and the Weimar Government.

The meeting bore fruit when four weeks later, on September 27, the Reich Government announced its intention of establishing a German embassy at the Vatican. Foreign Minister Müller justified the move because of Germany's need for good relations with the Vatican, to deal with the many weighty internal and external questions facing it.[84] Soon thereafter Pacelli traveled to Berlin to meet other Reich officials. Although the negotiations were complicated and, as has been

[81] Deuerlein, *Reichskonkordat*, p. 10.

[82] AA, IA, Päpstl. Stuhl 15, Vol. 9, Prittwitz (Rome-Quirinal) to AA, December 4, 1919.

[83] Schmidlin, Vol. 3, p. 279. Deuerlein, *Reichskonkordat*, p. 7.

[84] Ernst Deuerlein, "Die erste Begegnung zwischen Reichspräsident Ebert und Nuntius Pacelli," *Münchener Theologische Zeitschrift*, XVIII (1966-1967), 159.

explained earlier in this chapter, would result in both a German and a Bavarian representative in Rome and, for the time being, a nuncio only in Munich, the initiation of discussions clearly indicated an interconnection of foreign and internal policy motives for the parties in discussing a concordat and the question of diplomatic relations between both governments.

Another example of a subject which the Vatican believed should be regulated by a concordat and which the Reich viewed as having very important implications for its foreign and domestic policy was the question of diocesan boundaries. After the war much of the land in the east and west which Germany was to lose to the Allies was inhabited predominantly by Catholics.[85] Were these areas to remain under German ordinaries or, if not, were the clergy at least to be trained in Germany, thus giving Germany a modicum of influence over the areas? Within the boundaries of the new Reich were the dioceses to conform to political borders or should some of them be redrawn? By the Versailles Treaty Germany lost such areas as Alsace-Lorraine to France and the larger part of Posen and West Prussia to Poland, with another section of West Prussia going to form the new state of Danzig. The total population of the lost territories was 5,517,270, of which 3,625,682

[85] Population of territory separated from Germany in 1919 (1910 census figures)

Prussia	Catholic	Protestant
Province of Posen	1,422,238	646,580
Province of West Prussia	882,695	789,081
Community of Reichstal	7,784	6,521
District of Kalscher	36,577	1,462
District of Eupen	25,151	655
District of Malmédy	17,464	219
Saar	482,140	202,678
Total population lost	2,874,049	1,647,196
Upper Silesia	1,779,494	175,079
	4,653,543	1,822,275

In 1910 the population of Catholics and Protestants in Prussia was:

		Catholic	Protestant
		14,581,829	24,830,547
		4,653,543	1,822,275
In 1920 (before the plebiscites)	-	9,928,286	23,008,272
If one considers Alsace-Lorraine with a population of			
	-	1,610,500	412,274
Germany in 1910 had	-	23,821,453	40,275,467
a) Loss of Alsace-Lorraine		1,610,500	412,274
		22,210,953	39,863,193
b) Loss to Prussia		4,653,543	1,822,275
Germany in 1920 had	-	17,557,410	38,040,918

Figures taken from Krose, Vols. 3 (1910/11), 6 (1916/17), 8 (1918/19), and report in AA, BRV, Abstimmungsgebiet Ost-West Preussen, Vol. 1 on statistics.

were Catholics. Statistically 32.6 percent were Lutheran, 65.7 percent Catholic and 1.2 percent Jewish and .5 percent others—almost the very reverse of the total confessional percentages in the former Reich, where Protestants amounted to about 63 percent of the population. In the remaining German territory, including the plebiscite areas, 64.3 percent of the population was Lutheran and 34.0 percent was Catholic. If areas such as Eupen-Malmédy, Upper Silesia, or the Saar (Saarland) were lost, the Catholic population of Germany would drop still further.[86] It was again in the interests of the government to strengthen German Catholics in the plebiscite areas, and the first steps here would be a settlement of the diocesan borders and the jurisdictional authority of the German Catholic episcopate. If the separated or plebiscite areas remained ecclesiastically attached to their traditional dioceses or ecclesiastical provinces, German influence could be maintained, at least on a religious or cultural level. If the areas were already separated from the Reich, provisions for religious links between German minorities in other countries and German dioceses would also be of diplomatic value in maintaining the population's awareness of its *Deutschtum*. Again, a concordat could provide for all these concerns.

Already in November the Prussian Minister in Rome, Diego von Bergen, was warning of Warsaw's attempts to use propaganda to influence the Vatican to support the Polish claims to diocesan border changes in the east. Bergen urged that more German diplomatic efforts be made to counter these claims and that more Germans be appointed to important Curial congregations to bolster German influence.[87] The concern was sufficient to have the Prussian Government in November order Bergen to return from Lugano to Rome as soon as possible to deal directly with the danger to the threatened dioceses.[88] Berlin had learned that France was exerting pressure in the Rhineland in favor of a pro-French Rhenish state and was urging Rome to separate the Saar from the dioceses of Trier and Speyer. In addition to requesting the bishops of the affected dioceses to instruct their clergy to use their influence with the laity in urging them to remain loyal to the Reich, Germany also energetically protested in Rome against such a move. The Vatican's official position was to make no changes as long as the national boundaries of a country were not fixed by international treaty.[89] Pacelli told Prussian Minister Zech that eventually

---

[86] Krose, Vol. 8 (1918/19), pp. 347, 354-356.

[87] AA, IA, Bayern 53, Vol. 12, Bergen to AA, November 13, 1919.

[88] AA, IA, Päpstl. Stuhl 15, Vol. 9, AA to Bavarian legation in Lugano, November 30, 1919.

[89] Germany, Paderborn, Archivstelle beim Erzbischöflichen Generalvikariat, XXII, 1, Naumann (AA) to Bishop Karl Joseph Schulte, May 27, 1919. See also Walter A.

the diocesan borders would be adjusted to the national borders and a German prelate, for example, would not be able to retain jurisdiction over Polish territory. No doubt to apply pressure on Berlin to sign a treaty with Rome, Pacelli added that the Vatican eschewed such unilateral changes, preferring to effect them only after consultation with Prussia and Germany, ideally during negotiations for a concordat.[90] But since the relations between the State and Church had not begun to be renegotiated there was yet another reason for speed.

Setting the Republic on a democratic course, solving the economic problems, and retaining the unity of the Reich were only some of the many critical issues facing Germany at the same time, and the government could not avoid the task of attempting to sort out and unravel the complex and often related difficulties with which it had to deal. Berlin had to reach an accommodation on the question of schools and religion and on the relations of Church and State in the new Republic, since both the Vatican as well as the Catholics of Germany expected something to be done to regularize relations, especially in Prussia and Bavaria, where some form of agreement had already existed. Moreover, with the Center Party now in the government of the Reich, its members were urging the cabinet to take action; since they were loyal and important supporters of the new government, they could not be ignored. But notwithstanding the hard bargaining which a concordat promised, the Reich needed Vatican aid in its relations with the other nations. Too uncompromising a position on internal affairs threatened to jeopardize important diplomatic policy decisions.

1919, the year of Versailles and the founding of the Republic, had also proved the Vatican's importance to Germany. Rome was a potential source of aid or influence not only in international but also in domestic affairs. It had therefore been crucial to solve the problem of diplomatic representation. By 1920 the Vatican and Germany had taken the first step and regularized their relations, thus opening up the channels for a dialogue on the pressing issues which were of concern to both governments.

McDougall, *France's Rhineland diplomacy, 1914-1924* (Princeton, 1978), pp. 85-96. AA, IA, Bayern 53, Vol. 12, Becker, Prussian Minister of Education and Religious Affairs to Prussian Minister-President, November 4, 1919, and Bergen to AA, December 10, 1919. GSTA, MA 101072, Ritter to BFM, August 29, 1919.

[90] AA, IA, Preussen 2 Nr. 2n, Vol. 5, Zech to Prussian Cabinet, November 27, 1919.

CHAPTER II

Defining the Needs, Securing the Ties
1920-1922

In his historic meeting with Pacelli, Ebert had stressed Germany's diplomatic needs. The Reich President hoped to interest the Holy See in the Reich's political and economic plight. For Germany, diplomatic and economic problems were more pressing at the moment than were those dealing with Church and State. The essential value of the Vatican for Germany was its role as an intermediary representing German interests in world affairs, and in the crucial months after Versailles the possibilities to aid Germany were considerable. Berlin noted that the number of apostolic nunciatures accredited to foreign states had also increased in the preceding decade. Before the war there had been four (Munich, Madrid, Vienna, and Brussels), but by 1920 eleven existed,[1] and more were in the process of being established. As the Germans quickly realized, if the Pontiff could be persuaded to intervene in favor of the Reich, his fast-growing diplomatic network would be of immense use, especially in his efforts to exert a conciliating influence for peace among the nations.[2]

The Pontiff had already done more than merely issue protests against wartime activities. Already by 1920 Benedict had helped by making appeals for and personally providing food, clothing, and other gifts for the deprived in Europe; had made numerous pleas for the return of war prisoners; and had spoken out against Versailles Article 227, which would have condemned the Kaiser and leading German officials as war criminals. By February 1920 the Pope had given 2,918,453 lire in aid to the starving children in Central Europe.[3] Since the actual and potential importance of the Papacy was obvious to the new Weimar Government and since all internal disputes about the nature of German accreditation in Rome had been settled, Germany could now work with the Curia at the highest diplomatic level. Therefore, with

[1] The seven additional nunciatures were: Berlin, Lisbon, Warsaw, Prague, Budapest, Belgrade, and Bern.

[2] GSTA, MA 104444, Ritter to BFM, July 30, 1920.

[3] *Bayerischer Kurier*, February 16, 1920. Michael von Faulhaber, *Deutsches Ehrgefühl und Katholisches Gewissen* (Munich, 1925), pp. 28-29.

evident satisfaction to the Foreign Office, Diego von Bergen, former Prussian Minister to the Vatican, delivered his credentials to the Holy See as first Ambassador of the German Republic on April 30, 1920. Although a Protestant, Bergen, who claimed partial Spanish ancestry, was more familiar with the Mediterranean temperament than the average Prussian and was well liked by his Latin colleagues.[4] As requested by the Vatican, the Bavarian legation continued to function, but the Prussian legation was closed and replaced by a German embassy with the former Prussian Minister filling the post as the first ambassador. In offering his credentials, Bergen presented a letter from President Ebert to the Pontiff, in which the President praised the Pontiff for his paternal interest in Germany during the war years, his striving for peace, and his effort on behalf of prisoners of war. Benedict, equally cordial to the Socialist head of state, expressed his satisfaction with the resumption of Germany's representation at the Papal Court.[5]

In addition to the Ambassador himself, the staff consisted of a mere handful of co-workers. One year later the Foreign Office prevailed upon the diocese of Breslau to release one of its clerics, Msgr. Rudolf Steinmann, from his duties in Germany to serve as embassy consultor, or specialist for religious affairs, to deal with ecclesiastical problems for which the diplomats had not been trained. This appointment was especially important since Bergen, as well as half of the German staff, was Protestant, and the German diplomats here needed someone well versed in Catholic doctrine upon whom they could rely for advice.[6] Berlin had made a wise choice in selecting Bergen. He had already served as councillor and later minister of the Prussian legation to the Vatican, and was a *persona grata* with Vatican officials. Cardinal Adolf Bertram of Breslau, in being asked about the requirements for a diplomatic position in Rome, had said that one cannot be qualified overnight. Knowledge of the intricacies of Vatican policy could best be gained by someone who had spent a long time studying and working in Rome.[7] The Reich Government apparently understood and shared this opinion when appointing its diplomats to the Vatican. Bergen had

---

[4] In addition to being twice approached in 1926 by politicians inquiring whether he might wish to become German Foreign Minister in a new cabinet, he was also asked by the government to take over the Paris embassy. He expressed disinterest in both of these posts, citing health reasons, but he most probably had no desire to assume either of these more demanding and difficult positions.

[5] AA, PO II, PO 10 Vat., Vol. 1, Ebert to Benedict XV, April 16, 1920.

[6] AA, PO II, PO 10 Vat., Vol. 1, Haniel (AA) to Bertram, February 15, 1921. *Germania*, December 12, 1921.

[7] AA, IA, Päpstl. Stuhl 3 Nr. 2, Vol. 23, Bertram to Becker (Prussian Ministry of Education and Religious Affairs), February 15, 1920.

won support for his own appointment not only from his superiors in the Foreign Office but also from the powerful Center politician Erzberger, who praised Bergen for his qualities as a diplomat, his experience at the Vatican, and his fine rapport with Vatican colleagues.[8] Berlin believed that Bergen would be the best person to serve German interests, and would be acceptable to German Catholics and to Curial officials.

The new appointment was not greeted with enthusiasm by the French or their allies the Poles. The Germans had scored a diplomatic point, since by speedily naming an ambassador to the Vatican they had diverted attention from the French, who were loudly publicizing their intentions soon to resume relations with the Vatican, but had made no appointment yet.[9] The French feared that the Germans would use this new position to influence the Papacy to the disadvantage of France, and Paris had exerted pressure in Rome to hinder the establishment of relations between Germany and the Vatican.[10] Although the Italians were also unhappy with the new embassy, they deferred making any statements to that effect after the Vatican made plain its desire to conduct full-scale diplomatic relations with the Germans. But the French had particular reason to worry, since *ipso facto* the intent of the Germans was to extend their influence in Rome, and the French were alarmed lest the Germans gain a diplomatic advantage over them.

Conversely, the Germans knew that any French initiatives in Rome would not be to the Reich's interests. They had experienced the disadvantages of a lack of representation during the war years and knew that the Allied Powers, such as the French, intended to increase their pressure on the Curia by strengthening their diplomatic contacts with Rome. The advantages for France in having a representative at the Papal Court were being debated in the French Chamber of Deputies during that year. Remarks made by French politicians about the support which the Vatican could lend to French policy caused the Germans much uneasiness; one example was the statement by one deputy that a French diplomat at the Vatican would help France to influence the selection of pro-French bishops for the dioceses in the occupied Rhineland.[11] One year later, during the debate over the resumption of ties in the French Senate, proponents of the measure openly used the argument that Germany drew support in the Saar by portraying France

[8] Karl Dietrich Erdmann *et al.*, eds., *Akten der Reichskanzlei: Kabinett Scheidemann* (Boppard a.R., 1971), p. 128, note 10.

[9] BFO, 371/3851/5403, De Salis to Curzon, May 23, 1920.

[10] FFO, Allemagne 370, Barrère (Rome-Quirinal) to FFO, January 4, 1920.

[11] AA, PO II, PO 3 Vat., Frankreich, Vol. 1, memorandum of Fleischer (Prussian Ministry of Ed. and Relig. Affairs), January 17, 1921.

as an anti-religious nation. The presence of a French ambassador in Rome would defuse this German weapon, and the appointment would also have a profound impact on the population of the occupied Rhineland. French Premier Aristide Briand further endorsed this proposal, speaking in its favor.[12] The critical nature of the post-Versailles settlement had thus only intensified the international scramble to woo and gain predominance at the Vatican.

Berlin was convinced that inadequate German representation, diplomatic and ecclesiastical, in Rome would leave the field clear for French influence and cause the Vatican to hesitate in supporting the Reich where it might easily do so. In the Consistory of 1916 no new German bishops had received the cardinal's red hat. In 1919, with the death of Cardinal Hartmann of Cologne, only one German cardinal remained—Prince-Bishop Adolf Bertram of Breslau—in comparison to eight French cardinals and two Polish ones. Both Bergen and Ritter had not failed to mention this to Gasparri during 1920, and both churchmen and laymen alike exerted pressure to persuade the Pope that to correct any impression of Rome's favoritism for the Allies, he should now tangibly indicate the Vatican's goodwill toward the former Central Powers. The Archbishop of Cologne was a logical choice for the cardinal's hat, since the spiritual leader of this major diocese in the Rhineland was traditionally named to the Sacred College. Another candidate would be Archbishop Faulhaber of Munich. The Austrian Curial Cardinal Andreas Frühwirth, former Papal envoy in Munich, and Nuncio Pacelli were of this opinion and had sought to win Benedict to their view. For the Bavarians, Faulhaber's nomination to the College of Cardinals would also be a gain since it would place Bavaria in a stronger position within the Reich, especially during the controversy over administrative centralization. Ritter, in conversation with Benedict, mentioned that Bavaria was entitled to a sign of recognition, whereupon Benedict replied, "Yes, if the Bavarians remain what they were." The Pope's remark reflected his concern over Bavaria's internal situation. Negotiations for a concordat were underway, yet the anti-religious educational policies of the Socialists in 1919 had caused the Papacy to await developments.[13]

But one year later, in 1921, after things had settled down somewhat in Germany—when the revolutionary tide receded, the Socialists in Munich replaced by a middle-class, more conservative cabinet, and the republican government functioning in Berlin—Benedict named Archbishops Faulhaber of Munich and Karl Joseph Schulte of Cologne

---

[12] GSTA, MA 106157, transcript of proceedings in the French Senate and *Le Temps*, Nr. 22050, December 17, 1921 and Nr. 22051, December 18, 1921.

[13] GSTA, MA 104322, Ritter to BFM, June 14, 1920.

to the Sacred College, thus demonstrating the Vatican's regard for German concerns about representation. The see of Cologne by tradition usually had a cardinal as archbishop but not Munich. The French representative in the Bavarian capital, speaking to Pacelli, questioned the Bavarian's appointment. Faulhaber, answered the Nuncio, by virtue of his personal record, his activity within his diocese, and the high regard in which both Catholics and non-Catholics alike held him, had merited the award. The Nuncio added, however, that he was more a Bavarian than a German and thought the French would find him conciliatory to French interests. Likewise, in view of the solicitude with which Archbishop Schulte had worked for the care of French wounded prisoners during the war, the Nuncio doubted that France would find any difficulty with the other new cardinal.[14]

For the Germans, however, Faulhaber's elevation to the Sacred College was greeted as a sign of Papal esteem for Germany and especially for Bavaria in its time of trouble. Indeed, while in Rome for the consistory, the two new German princes of the Church used the opportunity for personal conversations with Curial members and other cardinals and made a very favorable impression on Vatican officials. As Ritter commented, cardinals can be more influential and work more effectively than the most conscientious of bishops. Faulhaber had delivered a speech in Rome, in Italian and without notes, which Curial officials had noted, and Gasparri had spoken well of him to Ritter, declaring, "Your Archbishop has won a great deal of respect since I first knew him. He is a truly worthy prince of the Church who distinguishes himself by his balanced speech." The two prelates also met with the English Cardinal Francis Bourne, who was known to have close contacts with British leaders, to discuss the world situation and the position of the Church. Finally, much to German satisfaction, both cardinals were named members of several Curial congregations.[15]

Berlin did not fail to use the influence of the German episcopate to aid the Reich. Bertram had already petitioned Gasparri in 1919 to assist Germany in preventing the trial of the Kaiser, military officers, and civil officials. The bishops had also been asked by the government to prepare an official statement protesting these actions.[16] On February 10, State Secretary Edgar von Haniel wrote Bertram requesting that the hierarchy exert pressure on the Holy See to protest the extradition proceedings. The Reich official appealed to the bishops to write

[14] FFO, Allemagne 367, Dard (Munich) to FFO, February 21, 1921.
[15] GSTA, MA 104474, Ritter to BFM, March 19 and 21, 1921.
[16] Poland, Wrocław (Breslau), Archiwum Archidiecezjalne (hereafter cited as AW), 1A 25v, 30, draft of protest and explanation of Bertram, February 7, 1920.

as soon as possible, for it was a patriotic necessity.[17] The Vatican's espousal of Germany's cause and the ensuing moderation of the Allied demands no doubt were a source of satisfaction to Berlin and demonstrated not only the Holy See's value for Germany but also the importance of keeping Rome informed of Germany's position. Thus in 1921 the Finance Committee of the Bavarian *Landtag* made no secret of including 20,000 marks in the budget of the Bavarian Ministry of Foreign Affairs, to go to Cardinal Faulhaber with the purpose of assisting the Cardinal's efforts in influencing the Vatican. The government recognized the Cardinal's ability by virtue of his position of directly presenting the German position when foreign relations were discussed before the College of Cardinals.[18]

In addition to obtaining proper diplomatic representation and maintaining an adequate number of cardinals to offset those from countries such as France or its ally Poland, Berlin also made efforts to ensure the naming of enough Germans to lower Vatican bureaucratic positions. The situation in 1919 was not good, since the expulsion of Germans and Austrians from Rome during the war opened many of the posts that the Germans had held in the Vatican hierarchy to other nationals. This in turn meant that in this diplomatic quota system the Germans were not proportionally represented in the policy-making congregations or committees of the Vatican and could not adequately present the Reich's viewpoint correctly or counter any anti-German arguments put forward by other countries. During the first years of the Republic, Berlin frequently raised the subject of German representation in Rome with Curial officials. After the war, for example, although Italian, French, and English judges (*uditori*) sat on the Rota, or the highest court for Church affairs, Germany had none. Appointment to the court brought prestige to both the individual and to his country, and the position was an influential one, for the Rota's decisions at times affected more than just ecclesiastical interests. Germany was therefore most concerned that a German successor to Msgr. Franz X. Heiner, who had died during the war, be appointed as soon as possible. The Reich had no legal right to request the selection of a German, yet the Foreign Office believed that the Vatican, seeking to maintain a balance in Europe, would give very serious consideration to Germany's request.[19] Already in October 1919 Ritter had written to Faulhaber:

[17] AW, 1A 25v, 30, Haniel to Bertram, February 10, 1920.

[18] BFO, 371/5974/5283, Leeds (Munich) to Foreign Secretary, August 6, 1921. Although British officials in London commented that with the inflationary value of the mark the sum was very small, the fact that it had been included in the Bavarian Government's budget indicated the value placed on maintaining Vatican support.

[19] AA, IA, Päpstl. Stuhl 3 Nr. 2, Vol. 23, Ritter to BFM, February 14, 1920.

Now more than ever we need qualified clerics here in Rome who can worthily and usefully represent German interests. We must now concentrate on the academic and religious sectors in order to get ahead since in all areas we are so severely restricted. One important international post where we have been left freedom of movement is the Vatican. Therefore on to Rome![20]

Meanwhile the French had also been building bridges to the Vatican which only reinforced German belief in the need for speed in strengthening contacts with the Holy See. The French hierarchy had been urging Rome for some time to proclaim Joan of Arc a saint. In May 1920, at a time when France and the Vatican were preparing to resume diplomatic relations, the Pontiff decided, as a gesture of goodwill and reconciliation, to canonize her. The Church's purpose was to emphasize the religious character of the Maid of Orleans, her faithfulness to God's promptings, and the Christian virtues of her life. While not disputing the Vatican's right to choose whomever it considered worthy of sainthood, the Reich viewed the proceedings as proof of strong Gallic influence in Rome. In Berlin's opinion Paris had been successful in advocating the cause of one who had also embodied the virtues of patriotism against a foreign invader. The Germans feared that France would use the canonization for political purposes and as a propaganda weapon against the Reich by indicating that the Vatican's praise for Joan and France in the Middle Ages was an indirect condemnation for the Kaiser and Germany in the twentieth century. The German analysis of the situation was that the canonization of this particular saint precisely two years after the war would not strengthen the cause of world peace but only aggravate the enmity between the former warring nations. In what was an impolitic overreaction the German and Bavarian ministers refused to attend the canonization ceremonies and accomplished little else but call attention to their displeasure with what the Church had done.[21]

The enmity which existed between Germany and France did, however, affect all levels of society and reached up into the levels of the higher clergy as well. From April through June 1921 an exchange of letters took place between Cardinal Louis Dubois of Paris and Cardinal Schulte of Cologne in which Dubois appealed to Schulte to recognize France's just claims for reparations. The correspondence continued with mutual recriminations about the political overtones of their charitable work and their efforts on behalf of war prisoners. The matter surfaced when Dubois' letter of April 17 was made public by the

[20] Germany, Munich, Erzbischöfliches Archiv, 1352, Ritter to Faulhaber, October 21, 1919.
[21] GSTA, MA 104322, Ritter to BFM, May 26, 1920.

3. Benedict XV being borne from the Vatican
to his throne in St. Peter's for the canonization
of Joan of Arc, May 1920

Paris-based Havas News Agency before Schulte had an opportunity
to reply.[22] Always extremely sensitive to public controversies between
prelates which had nationalistic overtones, the Vatican found the situation very unpleasant. Although the French Government, mindful
of possible damage to its Vatican ties, assured Rome that Paris had in
no way supported Cardinal Dubois' letter to the Cardinal of Cologne,[23] the Vatican was still concerned, for it had to be very circumspect in its moves lest they be interpreted by one side or the other as
approval. But for Germany the fact that two of the Church's highest
prelates were publicly taking sides on the issue indicated the depth of
the enmity between the two nations which entered even into the College of Cardinals. Despite the precept of brotherly love, ranking
churchmen were taking national positions, thus underscoring the Vatican's potential importance as a mediator in such situations.

In the fall of 1920 further signs had appeared of Paris' ostensible

[22] AA, PO II, PO 20 Vat., Köln, Vol. 1, Dubois-Schulte correspondence, April 17,
May 11, May 24, June 5, 1921.
[23] AA, PO II, PO 20 Vat., Köln, Vol. 1, Bergen to AA, July 21, 1921.

drive to increase its influence at the Holy See. The French Chamber, then finishing the debate on the resumption of diplomatic relations with the Papacy, was being attentively watched by Germany. During the proceedings of November 23 the Socialist deputy Joseph Paul Boncour observed that the French Right supported the Catholic elements in Central Europe and argued that diplomatic relations with Rome could gain influence for France among south German Catholics.[24] Reporting on an article in *The Daily Telegraph*, the French Ambassador to Great Britain had also previously alluded to the possibility of Vatican and French cooperation in influencing the clergy in southern and western Germany to work for a separation of Catholic Germany from Prussian influence should an advantageous moment occur.[25] Thus, when in 1921 the Quai d'Orsay, or French Foreign Office, announced that, after a break in relations of seventeen years, France was resuming its ties to the Vatican and appointing Charles Jonnart, a distinguished and much respected senator, to the Rome post, the German Foreign Office felt well justified in its decision to strengthen its position at the Vatican if only for negative reasons—to block French influence on the Curia.

The Reich, however, did not assign such great significance to its relations with the Vatican solely to counter Allied influence in the Curia. It hoped that a close working relation, once diplomatic relations were established, would also help Germany marshal Vatican support for Berlin's position on every major issue as it appeared on the diplomatic scene. But in order to cultivate and retain these good relations Germany had to tread carefully in areas where Rome showed particular concern. Some of the diplomatic initiatives taken by the Vatican in Germany's behalf during the war had ramifications for the postwar situation which, if not handled correctly by Germany, would endanger any further German influence at the Papal Court. Tensions were to develop over these matters in 1920-1921, causing the Foreign Office some anxious moments.

The Vatican had always attached great importance to secrecy in its diplomatic dealings. A source of its effectiveness had been the assurance that it carried out negotiations without press leaks, virtually impressing the seal of the confessional upon them. Exposure of its activities would naturally damage Vatican effectiveness, destroy the trust nations placed in it, and impede the conduct of discussions or quiet mediation best conducted beyond the glare of public view. In the

[24] AA, PO II, PO 3 Vat., Frankreich, Vol. 1, Wedel (Paris) to AA, November 25, 1920.

[25] FFO, Allemagne 370, Cambon (Vatican) to Millerand, French Premier, March 16, 1920. *The Daily Telegraph*, March 16, 1920.

immediate post-war years the Vatican voiced uneasiness over possible disclosures about its role in World War I, about the Vatican peace initiative in 1917, and its efforts to prevent the trial of the Kaiser and the assignation of guilt to Germany. But with the cessation of hostilities and the ensuing Reichstag inquiry into their cause, the announcement that Germany would publish an unprecendented collection of diplomatic documents, *Die Grosse Politik*, alerted Curial officials and German diplomats to a situation which could potentially strain relations between the two governments. Berlin's propensity to "tell all" and the indiscreet statements of leaders such as Kaiser Wilhelm or Chancellor Bernhard von Bülow had gotten Germany into difficulties for two decades, invariably with friends as much as with enemies.

In May 1920 Bergen cabled Berlin that reports concerning Germany's plan to publish documents about the 1917 peace overtures were causing the Vatican Secretariat of State to fear that the texts would compromise Papal diplomats and the Secretariat itself. The Curia had no desire to have the whole question of its peace moves brought up again, since some critics of Rome had viewed the Papal peace offer as a clear sign of Rome's partiality for the Central Powers and of its efforts to save them from defeat. A renewed discussion on this topic in 1920 might prejudice any efforts that the Vatican now made on behalf of the Reich for the reduction in the demands of Versailles.[26] Berlin assured the Ambassador, however, that it had planned nothing of the sort at the moment but if it had, the Reich would consult the Vatican before proceeding.[27]

Nevertheless, in July Pacelli again raised the matter, stating that an exhaustive documentation of the peace proposals served no purpose since surely nothing more could be learned than what had already been published. The Vatican undoubtedly found it ironic that the country largely responsible for dooming the Papal peace initiative because of its failure to respond positively to Benedict's appeal was now pressing to have the negotiations, including the Vatican's role, made public. The Nuncio's comments amounted to a diplomatic way of expressing Vatican displeasure. In August Gasparri wrote to Bergen, reviewing all the Vatican had done in 1917 and stressing that Rome did not consider it necessary or opportune to publish further material dealing with the case. Once more the Foreign Office assured the Vatican that it had communicated this request to the Reichstag Investigating Committee in May, which had agreed not to bring up the ques-

---

[26] AA, microfilm series T-120, roll 1999, serial 4057H, frame E066456, Bergen to AA, May 20, 1920. For an extensive discussion of the Papal peace moves, see Steglich; Mayer, *Political origins*, p. 229ff.

[27] AA, T-120, 4057H/E066457, Boyé (AA) to Bergen, May 30, 1920.

tion without prior consultation with the nunciature. In any event, should the Papal peace move be brought up, the Foreign Office representative at the committee hearing had been already instructed once more to remind the committee of the Papal request.[28] The Foreign Office was fully aware of the importance of not allowing disclosures of the past to mar the expectations for the future. It was simply best to leave certain sensitive matters out of the realm of public discussion. Since the Curia lay great stress on carrying out its business in secret, whoever desired its support had to honor this viewpoint and be mindful of the Vatican's feelings on this issue. Bergen had had this matter brought to his attention by several important Vatican officials as well as by Gasparri himself, who specifically objected to Papal activities being made a subject of parliamentary investigation.

The Vatican's displeasure with Germany only increased in the following months when Philipp Scheidemann, former Reich Chancellor and leading Socialist, published a brochure *Papst, Kaiser, und Sozialdemokratie in ihren Friedensbemühungen im Sommer 1917*, which dealt with the Papal peace overtures and apparently contained a selection of official documents. Scheidemann insisted that these documents had not been supplied from government files but had come from "another source." Despite government efforts, publication could not be stopped, for Scheidemann had already distributed galley proofs to foreign correspondents. The Foreign Office expressed its deepest regrets to the Curia and explained that the disarray and chaos during the revolutionary period had permitted the possibility of indiscretions.[29] Foreign Minister Walter Simons also sought to assuage Rome's displeasure with Berlin by personally giving his assurance that despite his best efforts nothing could be done to block the distribution of Scheidemann's publication, as the government could not forbid it.[30] The controversy over the role of the Vatican in 1917 had meanwhile extended into the newspapers when Erzberger and former Chancellor Konstantin Fehrenbach both entered into the fray, each giving his views of the Vatican's involvement in the matter.[31]

The discussion in the press and the possibility of documents still being used by the Investigating Committee, as Bergen noted in several dispatches, continued to disturb Gasparri throughout 1921. In September the Ambassador related how the Cardinal continually remarked, "I can no longer work with your government. Even with the

[28] AA, T-120, 4057H/E066460-461, -466, -467, -468, Zech to AA, July 15, 1920; Haniel to Zech, August 6, 1920; Gasparri to Bergen, August 31, 1920.

[29] AA, T-120, 4057H/E066473, Haniel to Bergen, April 22, 1921.

[30] AA, BRV 69, Vol. 1, Simons to Bergen, April 28, 1921.

[31] See Epstein, ch. 14.

best of intentions I can no longer help you in the future." With great difficulty Bergen proceeded to pacify him, and the Cardinal finally agreed to retract his statement on the condition that all future German indiscretions be prevented. Bergen of course feared that if documents were used in the Investigation Committee, the Vatican would take it as an indication of Germany's disregard of Rome's wishes.[32]

When the committee took up the issue, the Papal moves were discussed. The Foreign Office, however, did everything possible to ensure that the sessions were not public on days when matters deemed confidential by the Vatican were examined, and it requested the press to give minimal attention to the committee's proceedings.[33] Domestic pressure and the desire to maintain a parliamentary balance by making concessions to political party demands had caused the government to permit a Reichstag committee to see the documents without fully comprehending the impact that this action would have on current diplomacy. It had, however, seriously endangered further German-Vatican cooperation. As late as 1922 Bergen still sent notes to the Foreign Office indicating the need to placate the Vatican, pleading that in view of Vatican support of Germany in the current reparation negotiations such disclosures should be made only if absolutely necessary and then only after settlement of the reparations question. Domestic considerations had to be subordinated, in this instance, to the needs of foreign policy. A reappraisal or objective solution of past problems could not be made when it might jeopardize current negotiations.[34]

Moreover, even Reichstag deputies asserted that the Pope had not done enough for Germany, and government officials, especially from the Foreign Office, had to defend the Pontiff against such attacks.[35] What were irritations to the Vatican were problems for the Foreign Office, which had to explain to Reichstag committees, journalists, and other sectors of society why the Vatican was to be handled very gently precisely at that moment and which at the same time had to make excuses and apologies to the Vatican for any affront emanating from Germany. This was the predicament the Foreign Office found itself in: trying to placate a foreign power which it was convinced Germany needed, and trying to allow the Reichstag committee to carry out its functions without appearing arbitrarily to block it or explaining too much about current diplomatic initiatives.

[32] AA, T-120, 4057H/E066511-513, Bergen to Haniel, September 24, 1921.
[33] AA, T-120, 4057H/E066514-515, Haniel to Bergen, November 7, 8, 1921.
[34] AA, T-120, 4057H/E066556-557, E066559, Bergen to AA, December 14, 23, 1922.
[35] Germany, Reichstag, 86th Session, March 16, 1921, Vol. 348, p. 3033. See also Vols. 348-349, 352, 359, 361.

The Curia had very pointedly informed the German Ambassador on numerous occasions in 1921 of Benedict's expectation that these indiscretions would end. It would be impossible, lamented Gasparri, to aid the Reich if a few days later all the negotiations and conversations appeared in the newspapers or if a few weeks later a debate occurred over the issue in a parliamentary committee meeting. The Cardinal claimed that the goal of the 1917 proposal had been to find a formula for peace which would also have helped the Central Powers. The desired results had not been obtained, but a discussion of the entire affair by the Germans would now only create greater difficulties for the Papacy among the Allies who already accused Benedict of being pro-German.[36]

A similar incident threatened again to becloud German-Vatican relations in 1922. Here again the international politics of Germany were marred by braggadocio. Advance rumors of statements in the Kaiser's memoirs, soon to be published, indicated that Wilhelm was asserting that the Papal peace initiative had been inspired by the Kaiser himself on the basis of his meeting in 1917 with Pacelli at General Headquarters in Kreuznach. The Vatican denied this and endeavored to have this statement corrected before the book was published so that Pacelli would not have to make an official rebuttal and enter into a controversy about the validity of the memoirs. Gasparri appeared even willing to have the Vatican assume the costs of correcting the galleys to avoid the conflict. The Cardinal had also asked for German government aid in the matter, but since part of the story had already been released to the press, it could do little, and so Pacelli was instructed to deny Wilhelm's statement. The matter, however, failed to create as serious a problem as originally feared, since the French press immediately treated the memoirs as unreliable in general, thus creating a climate in which the Vatican could maneuver. Gasparri could now allay his concern of renewed French accusations of the Vatican's partiality during the war years.[37] Nevertheless, this incident again displayed the Vatican's sensitivity in such situations.

Another source of tension between Rome and Berlin was the criticism which some German politicians and journalists leveled against Benedict's position during the war. Annoyed with the manner in which the Allies had treated Germany, newspapers struck out against so-called friends and neutrals and asked if they indeed had been of aid to the Reich. Articles appeared in the press throughout 1920-1921 in

[36] AA, T-120, 4057H/E066519-520, Bergen to AA, January 6, 1922.
[37] GSTA, MA 104066, Ritter to BFM, October 6, 13, 1922.

such leading conservative or nationalist liberal-oriented papers as *Der Reichsbote, Kreuzzeitung*, and *Tägliche Rundschau*, criticizing the Pontiff for his purported anti-German stand during the war. The Foreign Office tried to terminate these articles, and the Catholic press made extra efforts to contradict these opinions and to stress the Papacy's accomplishments and efforts for Germany during and after the war.[38]

The reason for the Curia's hyper-sensitivity was that precisely during the period that Germany was discussing publishing documents about Papal peace overtures in Reichstag committees and individuals were criticizing its wartime role, the Vatican had again begun lending its support to Germany's position. One of the complex problems in which Germany hoped the Holy See would be of assistance was reparations. Versailles had ascribed responsibility for the damages and losses incurred by the Allies and their nationals to Germany and its allies, and it obliged Germany to offer compensation. The Reich was to make deliveries in kind and to surrender 20 billion gold marks as an initial payment until the Reparations Commission determined the final bill by May 1, 1921. Of the major powers, France, having experienced the ravages of war on its own soil and troubled with its own fiscal problems, believed it necessary to receive payments from Germany in order to reconstruct its economy. England, more dependent on trade for its financial stability, was more inclined to moderate its demands and give Germany time to rebuild so that normal trade conditions could recommence. Although there was debate in German Government and industrial circles about what method to use in avoiding what they considered unjust and unreasonable exactions, all political parties, including the Socialists, felt the Allied demands failed to consider economic realities and were impossible to fulfill. In Berlin's opinion, the West had to be convinced that the German economy would be crippled by these insensate payments and that all Europe would suffer.[39] Therefore Germany's strategy was to keep the amount to be paid as low as possible and to plead that a large reparations debt would so harm the German economy that it would render the Reich incapable of meeting any further financial obligations. Berlin also believed that the passage of time since Versailles would work to its benefit. The Reich hoped that the Western Powers, particularly England, would grow impatient when they did not receive the payments they had been counting on and which Germany maintained were difficult

[38] *Kölnische Volkszeitung*, "Zu den jüngsten Angriffen auf den Heiligen Stuhl," September 18, 1920.

[39] A description of how the reparations question affected inter-party negotiations over economic policy and fiscal reform can be found in Charles S. Maier, *Recasting bourgeois Europe* (Princeton, 1975), pp. 243-304.

to make, and would then be more willing to moderate their original demands.[40]

Rome was also convinced that the reparation provisions were preventing Germany from regaining economic stability, without which there could be no equilibrium in Europe or improvement in international relations. As early as 1919 the Germans were pleased to observe the Pope's unhappiness with the negotiations taking place at Versailles. Even before the provisions of the 1915 London Treaty, which at Italy's insistence excluded the Holy See from participating in the peace proceedings, became known, the *Osservatore* had carried articles announcing Benedict's refusal to take part in a settlement based on unduly harsh treatment of the vanquished. Thus in June 1919 Gasparri gave the following statement to the press:

> It had been repeatedly stated that the Holy See was making efforts to obtain a seat at the conference, but the truth is nothing further from our thoughts. Monsignor Cerretti, who is now in Paris, was merely entrusted by the Holy Father with the task of trying to save flourishing German missions in Africa and Australia.[41]

Disappointment at being excluded from the conference no doubt colored the Vatican's thinking about the utility and effectiveness of the Versailles Treaty. By diplomatic as well as other public and private channels Rome expressed its displeasure with the severity of the treaty, the impossibility of carrying out its reparation clauses, and the dangerous consequences it could have for all Europe.

In conversation about Versailles with the Austrian Minister, the noted historian Ludwig Pastor, Gasparri said, "We now count ourselves as lucky not to have been invited and not to have participated in this work which will result not in one but in ten wars." While deploring the imposed peace, the first in history, as he hyperbolically stated, in which the name of God had been completely excluded from the treaties, he was pleased to note that at least Italian Prime Minister Nitti had had the courage to call for revision of the peace treaties.[42] It was a clear declaration of the Vatican's preference for a change in the

---

[40] See also ch. 5, p. 217ff. for the reparations problem. For discussion of the reparations issue, see Marc Trachtenberg, *Reparation in world politics* (New York, 1980), especially chs. 3, 5, 6; Sally Marks, *The illusion of peace* (New York, 1976), pp. 38-49 and "The myths of reparations," *Central European History*, XI (1978), 231-255; Stephen Schuker, *The end of French predominance in Europe* (Chapel Hill, 1976), pp. 14-28; Maier, ch. 4; Peter Krüger, "Das Reparationsproblem der Weimarer Republik in fragwürdiger Sicht," *Vierteljahrshefte für Zeitgeschichte*, XXIX (1981), 21-47.

[41] *The Catholic Bulletin*, June 21, 1919, p. 1 quoted in Peters, p. 169.

[42] Ludwig von Pastor, *Tagebücher, Briefe, Erinnerungen*, ed., Wilhelm Wühr (Heidelberg, 1950), letter to his wife, March 12, 1920, pp. 680-681.

peace arrangements. Gasparri also informed Bergen in April 1920 of his delight at British Prime Minister David Lloyd George's meeting with Nitti before the arrival of French Premier Alexandre Millerand at the San Remo Conference. This meeting, he hoped, would allow the moderates to clarify and unify their position on the reparation issue before they met with the French representatives. The German minister had presented Gasparri with information regarding the German viewpoint, and Faulhaber presented the case to Pacelli, who immediately relayed it to Nitti. Since the Germans were not invited to San Remo, their position would not be represented. The Reich appreciated Gasparri's action and clearly viewed it as an indication of Vatican willingness to assist Germany.[43]

Several months later, in July, the Germans were invited to a conference at Spa to discuss a plan for reparation payments. Before the opening of the meeting, the *Osservatore* again stated Rome's negative opinion of the treaty's stipulations. It questioned whether the treaty's demands would not overtax Germany's economic capacity. The demands of Versailles, continued the newspaper article, had caused untold suffering not only to the defeated nations but also to France, Italy, and the neutral states. This situation required concessions on both sides. Although the Curia now viewed optimistically the decision for all concerned parties to meet and discuss mutual problems, the *Osservatore* also warned that the Allied demands for payment were still unrealistic. Should the threatened military action be undertaken by the Western Powers to obtain these demands, the *Osservatore* continued, the peace effort would be set back to its starting point. In July 1920 Gasparri spoke to the Bavarian envoy about the Spa Conference and expressed his great displeasure at the Allies' unwillingness to permit Germany to retain its former military forces even for purposes of maintaining law and order within its own borders. He voiced concern about this point since the Allied position would make it impossible for the Reich to withstand the Bolshevik menace, which he believed was approaching steadily since the last defeat of Polish troops by Soviet forces that summer. In Gasparri's opinion Germany's military strength should be increased rather than decreased.[44] In August, on the anniversary of the Papal Peace Note of 1917, the *Osservatore* again stressed its opinion that the situation would have been better had the Powers heeded the Papal appeal.[45]

[43] AA, PO II, PO 2 Vat., Vol. 1, Bergen to AA, April 17, 1920. Germany, Speyer, Bischöfliches Hausarchiv, AXV 21, Faulhaber to Bishop of Speyer, April 20, 1920.

[44] GSTA, Ges. Päpstl. Stuhl 976, Ritter to BFM, July 8, 1920. See also *Osservatore* in 1919-1920.

[45] *Osservatore*, August 1, 1920. GSTA, Ges. Päpstl. Stuhl 976, Ritter to BFM, August 21, 1920.

In the fall of 1920 the Pontiff warmly received the first German pilgrims arriving in Rome since the war, which Berlin interpreted as another indication of Benedict's favorable disposition toward Germany. In December 1920 the German Ambassador thanked the Pope for his gift of cash and some 2,000 woolen children's suits to alleviate the hunger and privation in Germany during the Allied blockade in the winter of 1918-1919. Bergen also expressed his gratitude on behalf of German prisoners of war, 2,100 of whom had recently been returned home from Allied territory, and now requested the case of the prisoners still in French camps be taken up—which the Pope promised to do. While on the subject of Germany's difficulties, the Pope brought up the matter of some of the Versailles demands, such as the mandatory transfer of 800,000 German dairy cows to Allied countries. This he found entirely unjust and uncharitable, stating his intention to speak out on that point.[46]

Taking a cue from comments such as the Pontiff's, Ritter had written Munich recommending that diplomats as well as private individuals inform the Curia of the German viewpoint and of the terrible economic, financial, and social conditions in the Reich, lest Vatican officials think that the diplomatic reports were government-inspired and colored. Respected politicians as well as high churchmen would be of value in this work, which was most effective when verbally delivered rather than presented in a mere written report. As examples of people engaged in such work, Ritter cited Count Hans von Praschma of Silesia and Baron Engelbert von Kercherinck from Westphalia, men active in political life and familiar with the German economy, who had spent time in Rome during 1920 to meet with Curial officials in order to explain the impending dire consequences for all Europe if Germany failed to recoup economically. Count von Kercherinck, for example, informed the Vatican about conditions in the Ruhr area and argued that the threat of Bolshevism in the region was not a mental fantasy of some insincere or hysterical people but was real and consisted of armed and well-organized groups of revolutionaries located not only in the Rhineland but in other areas of Germany which possessed the potential of fomenting a revolt at any moment. Aware of the Curia's dread of Communism, Count Praschma vividly described the economic hardship which the loss of the rich Silesian territory had caused Germany and took care to point out the rich potential for Bolshevik propaganda there, due to the prevailing ethnic and economic unrest. The Silesian Count speculated on the inability of Poland to withstand the Red Army's advance into Silesia if it broke through at

[46] AA, PO II, PO 2 Vat., Vol. 1, Bergen to AA, December 6, 1920.

Warsaw, the current theater of hostilities.[47] Thus, visiting Church dignitaries as well as private citizens supported the official diplomatic representatives in Rome in portraying the economic plight of the Reich, stressing the problems that it caused the Church and warning of the spread of Bolshevism, all of which was certain to create anxiety among the Church leaders.

It was not surprising then that articles appeared in the *Osservatore*, advocating fewer restrictions on Germany and supporting the retention of the *Einwohnerwehr*, or German local militia, in order to maintain law and order despite Allied intentions to disband it.[48] Moreover on several occasions Gasparri employed diplomatic channels to urge the British and French to allow the retention of the Bavarian *Einwohnerwehr*. The Germans had reason for satisfaction with their efforts to influence the Vatican in view of Gasparri's support for the local militia and his opposition to the reparation demands. In fact, Foreign Office Councillor Schlüter informed his superiors that he had continually heard from numerous prelates returning from Rome that both the Holy Father and the Secretary of State seemed to have been influenced by the German arguments and were working for a revised settlement rather than the one imposed at Versailles.[49]

The negotiations and disagreements among the Allies over a reparations figure continued on into 1921: the French, Belgians, and Italians generally holding out for a high figure; the British, eager to restore pre-war trade with Germany, opting for lower sums. In February 1921 at the London Conference Germany and the Allies again failed to reach agreement over a schedule of payments, and the Western Powers applied sanctions against the Reich by occupying Düsseldorf, Duisberg, and Ruhrort in order to force an agreement. Disappointed by the lack of success at London and aware that the Reparations Commission would soon announce the final payment figure, Berlin took the gamble on an appeal to the United States to intervene.[50] Since the Reich, as the defeated power, was not in a position to deal equally with the Allied nations, in early 1921 it requested the Vatican to help Germany decrease the reparations payments which it owed to the

[47] GSTA, MA 104450, Ritter to BFM, July 10, 1920. The Prussian Cabinet, after consultations with the Ministry of Education and Religious Affairs and Cardinal Bertram, granted 50,000 marks out of propaganda funds to help to finance the Count's trip. AA, PO II, PO 2 Vat., Vol. 1, memorandum of Delbrück (AA), April 21, 1920; Praschma to Delbrück, April 23, 1920.

[48] GSTA, Ges. Päpstl. Stuhl 976, Ritter to BFM, July 8, 1920; MA 104455, Ritter to BFM, January 25, 1921.

[49] AA, PO II, PO 2 Vat., Vol. 1, excerpts from the travel report of Councillor Schlüter, November 24, 1920.

[50] Maier, p. 245.

Powers and to present its request for intervention to the United States. In Germany's eyes America was of all the victorious powers, the least likely to exact the "pound of flesh" or make excessive demands on the Reich. Germany, still technically in a state of war, the U.S. Senate having refused to ratify the Versailles Treaty, could not deal directly with Washington.

The Vatican was willing to undertake such an intermediary role after it observed that the attempts to regularize European finances and international relations at London had been ineffective, that sanctions had been applied, and that neither side seemed prepared to retreat. Mediation by a neutral seemed necessary. Many observers also believed that the United States should be brought into the discussions, since it was also the Allies' creditor. Some diplomats therefore hoped, as did Gasparri, that in the ensuing conversations they might link Allied debts with the reparations question and thereby solve both problems simultaneously.[51]

In March 1921 the Vatican cabled American President Warren G. Harding for his help in regularizing European relations. After receiving Harding's reply that he might be willing to help, Rome had the Apostolic Delegate in Washington, Giovanni Bonzano, speak to Republican Senator Joseph McCormick, known for his pro-German sympathies, requesting him to contact other American politicians to see what could be done. McCormick told the Papal emissary, however, that America would probably accept the role of mediator only if Germany stated what it was prepared to pay. Relaying this information to the Germans that an announced fixed sum would be a *prova importante di buona fede*, Gasparri suggested to Bergen that Germany should indicate its willingness to pay reparations to the sum of 50 billion gold marks. Payments, he felt would be arranged so that Germany would assume the Allied debts to America for which the Reich would offer its harbors, mines, customs duties, and railroads as guarantees of payment. Further details could be then worked out later.[52] Gasparri informed Ritter in March of his entry into the mediation with the hope that it would lead the way to European peace.[53] Late that month, Bergen met with Foreign Minister Simons, vacationing in Lugano at the time, to discuss their answer to the Vatican which it could relay to the United States. On the 26th Simons had already written to his staff in Berlin, stating, "I am personally of the opinion that all hesi-

[51] Erdmann, *Kabinett Fehrenbach*, p. xliii.

[52] AA, RM 5 Secr., Vol. 1, Bergen to AA, March 25, 1921. Erdmann, *Kabinett Fehrenbach*, p. 612, note to document Nr. 220. AA, RM 5 Secr., Vol. 1 contains most documents of the deliberations.

[53] GSTA, Ges. Päpstl. Stuhl 980, Ritter to BFM, March 18, 1921.

tations have to be put aside when we see here the possibility perhaps in this way to obtain a general settlement of the problem and to be delivered from the hands of the band of oppressors which surrounds us."[54]

On March 30 Bergen cabled Berlin that Harding had received Bonzano, who had informed the President of the Pope's great desire to have the United States assist in ending the "painful European conflict." Harding reiterated his interest in the plan; Bergen therefore urged that a warm reply be given and a conciliatory attitude adopted to demonstrate good faith and Germany's willingness to negotiate.[55] Berlin hastened to comply with Gasparri's suggested approach. The treaty had required Germany to make reparation according to its capabilities. The exact degree to which Germany could pay, however, was a matter of dispute between the Reich and the Allies. The Reich therefore informed Gasparri that it agreed that its obligation should not be more than 50 billion marks, but should this sum not be acceptable to the Allies then the Germans would recommend creating an impartial commission under American leadership to work out a plan of payment. In addition, Berlin declared itself ready to assume a loan to be used in paying reparations and also to provide some payment in kind and in services in place of cash. Should the loan be insufficient to cover the reparation subventions payment, Germany was prepared to assume some of the Allied debts to the United States, insofar as it was capable of doing so. Finally, for every credit granted to Germany the government stood ready to provide security for the loans.[56] This, Germany believed, was a reasonable and concrete offer on which to begin negotiating a settlement of the reparations question as a whole.

The discussions, however, never went further. On April 14 the *Germania*, which had heard of the Vatican's dealings, prematurely published the news of a neutral power's undertaking mediation in Germany's behalf. Immediately other papers picked up the story naming the Vatican as the power involved. Several days later French Premier Briand protested the Vatican's role in carrying Germany's message to the United States. Fearing that exposure of its activities could be misconstrued and possibly damage French-Vatican affairs when France

[54] Erdmann, *Kabinett Fehrenbach*, p. 613, note 3.

[55] AA, RM 5 Secr., Vol. 1, Bergen to AA, March 30, 1921.

[56] AA, RM 5 Secr., Vol. 1, AA to German Embassy (Vatican), April 12, 1921. Erdmann, *Kabinett Fehrenbach*, AA to Albert, State Secretary of the Reich Chancellery, March 27, 1921, pp. 613-614, note 5.

was about to resume relations with the Vatican, Gasparri declined to continue his activities.[57]

Understandably the Vatican was very conscious of its exposed position, and predictably the French press pointed to this most vulnerable point. *Le Temps* of April 18 wrote about the Vatican's recent mediatory activities and connected them with the recent revelation about the Papal peace move of 1917. "We do not know if the report will be denied in Rome," the newspaper commented, "but it turns out that the German newspapers are just publishing some details about the role of the Holy See in 1917. The situation thus presents some topical interest for these revelations."[58]

In answer to inquiries in the Reichstag about the mediation of a foreign power in Germany's behalf, Foreign Minister Simons related that the Reich Government had turned for help to the United States in the hopes of finding a solution to the financial problem. Moreover he admitted that another power had been asked to intervene with Washington but that an indiscretion on the part of German newspapers had caused the diplomatic initiatives to founder. The Minister bitterly commented that he had learned from reliable sources that because of these articles the "power" had lost interest in acting as intermediary.[59] In self-defense the *Osservatore* on April 24 denied the Vatican's involvement, but added, if it had been true, what then? The German request was to ask America to help settle a serious international dispute. In the absence of direct diplomatic relations between Germany and the United States, it was natural to ask a third power for assistance. The mere act of transmitting the note requesting mediation, as the *Osservatore* reasoned, would then in no way hurt the Allies.[60]

[57] Erdmann, *Kabinett Fehrenbach*, pp. 613-614, note 5. For possible explanations of how *Germania* received the information see Erdmann, *ibid.* For mutual recriminations between Erzberger and Fehrenbach over the matter, see *Germania*, May 28 and June 1, 1921. After the Vatican withdrew its offer to mediate, Germany then approached the United States directly. *Ibid.* AA, RM 5 Secr., Vol. 1, memorandum of Simons, April 20, 1921. Simons informed the American Commissioner in Berlin, Ellis Dresel, that as a consequence of premature publicity a neutral power which had been invited to transmit a message to America had failed to act, and the Reich Cabinet had now decided to send it through the U.S. Commission if it would accept it. United States, Dept. of State, *Papers relating to the foreign relations of the United States, 1921* (Washington, D.C., 1936), Vol. 2, pp. 40-41, Dresel (Berlin) to Secretary of State, April 20, 1921; for German appeals to the United States, see p. 36ff.

[58] BelgFO, St. Siège 1919-22, Beyens (Vatican) to Foreign Minister Jaspar, April 26, 1921.

[59] Germany, Reichstag, 96th Session, April 26, 1921, Vol. 349, p. 3417.

[60] BFO, 371/6026, De Salis to BFO, April 26, 1921. *Osservatore*, April 24, 1921.

Undoubtedly the Vatican had shown goodwill toward Germany in these negotiations, for it coincided with its own endeavors to restore Europe to working order. Germany's apologies to the Holy See were profuse, and the Foreign Office offered its deep regrets that the Holy See had been embarrassed by such a premature disclosure. Once again indiscretions of a parliamentary or journalistic nature on Germany's part had strained the goodwill of its friends and marred its own initiatives. Bergen had many an anxious moment in trying to explain away the reasons for the *faux pas*. If the Curia had not had its own reasons for continuing its policy of reconciliation, the German diplomatic efforts to win the Vatican over to its side would surely have had even greater difficulties.

On April 27 the Reparations Commission, having accepted a Belgian compromise between the English and the French positions, rendered its decision that Germany should pay a total 132 billion gold marks. Despite arguments from the Right not to give in to the Allies' ultimatum, the Berlin Government accepted the schedule of payments, raising the money needed for the first installment by borrowing in London. The new Chancellor, Joseph Wirth, a peaceful yet sincere nationalist, embarked on what he termed a policy of fulfillment to try to meet Allied terms and thereby demonstrate the impossibility of fulfulling them. Yet he was not adept or accomplished enough to convince either the many skeptics among the Allies, especially the French, that Germany was fully prepared to cooperate with the West or the Rightists at home that the policy offered a viable solution to Germany's problems. It resulted, however, with Wirth's resignation in November 1922, in helping to pave the way for the next cabinet of Wilhelm Cuno to adopt an all-or-nothing policy of passive resistance after France invaded the Ruhr in 1923.[61]

During the critical months in 1921, however, when these decisions about the final reparations figure were being made and in spite of the recent German diplomatic and press indiscretions, Vatican policy remained unchanged: Germany had to be supported not only for its own sake but for the good of Europe. The enormity of the reparation demands and the vigor with which the French pursued them caused Gasparri and other Europeans at that time to look no further for the causes of Germany's economic plight than the explanations offered by the Reich. Many leaders accepted, in varying degrees, the German argument that it was the Allied demands which were causing inflation, driving the mark downward, impeding growth and trade, and hindering a return to normalcy. Inflation as a technical problem was little

[61] See ch. 5.

4. Chancellor Joseph Wirth walking through
the park in Berlin with his dog, March 1922

understood at that time by the so-called experts, and in the confused
and tense international atmosphere it was easy to point to the obvious
and view France's reparation policy as the main difficulty in restoring
economic stability to Europe. Aware that there were disagreements
among the Allies about requiring full payment and that England was
inclined to moderation, Gasparri pursued his policy of supporting
Germany in seeking less stringent exactions.[62]

In the summer of 1921 the Vatican once more had a nuncio in Paris.
In September the new Papal delegate, Cerretti, informed officials of
the German Embassy that one of the priorities for his new mission
was to exert a moderating influence on French policy. German diplomats in Paris also anticipated that the Nuncio's presence would im-

[62] See ch. 5 for German responsibility for the inflation, p. 217ff.

prove Franco-German relations and explained to him that Germany's need to retain the Ruhr and Upper Silesia amounted to a question of economic existence. France's support for Polish claims in Upper Silesia, said the Germans, not only went against the principle of justice but would have unforeseeable economic consequences. Cerretti agreed to the necessity for Germany to retain its industrial areas to remain capable of making payments.[63]

In November, when the Reich Postal Minister Johannes Giesberts passed through Rome, he called on both the Pope and Cardinal Gasparri. The Pontiff still indicated his interest in Germany, particularly on hearing descriptions of the fall in value of the mark due to the inflation and its possible consequences for the European economy. From this conversation with the Pontiff, Giesberts derived the impression that the leading Vatican officials could be counted as friends of the Reich who would speak out in favor of reduction of the reparation payments. Gasparri's explanation of the Pontiff's regret at having failed to mediate successfully in April further buttressed this opinion. Gasparri persisted in believing that Germany could find a solution to the reparations question by working through the United States. The Secretary had instructed the Apostolic Delegate in Washington to suggest to Harding during the sessions of the upcoming Washington Conference in November that he attend to the European situation as well as to that of the Pacific. One day later the Cardinal indicated to Bergen that he understood that the recent journalistic indiscretion was not the government's fault and told the Ambassador of the Vatican's willingness to intercede again with the United States on Germany's behalf if the occasion presented itself. But by now Germany was in direct contact with Washington over the issue, and Berlin no longer required the Curia's good offices.[64] Nevertheless, the Germans were very pleased with the Cardinal's statements indicating that the press leaks earlier in the year had not severely damaged relations with Rome, as manifested by Curial willingness to be of further assistance to the Reich.[65]

Although the Vatican continued to seek a solution to the economic problem by mediating on behalf of Germany and lending its support to Berlin's efforts to reverse the reparation payments during the 1920's, an event had occurred in early 1922 which at first caused Germany to fear the loss of Rome's support. On January 22, 1922, after a short

---

[63] AA, PO II, PO 8 Vat., Vol. 1, Mayer (Paris) to AA, September 3, 1921.

[64] The United States had informed Berlin that, while not willing to mediate the reparations issue, it would be more than glad to pass on any German comments or suggestions to the Allies.

[65] GSTA, Ges. Päpstl. Stuhl 980, Ritter to BFM, November 17, 1921. AA, PO II, PO 2 Vat., Vol. 1, Bergen to AA, November 17, 1921.

illness Benedict XV died unexpectedly. No guarantee existed that his successor would continue his policies of pursuing a solution to world peace with such urgency, or regarding Germany's position as crucial to Europe. Bergen viewed the situation perhaps too pessimistically when, conceding how hard the Vatican had already worked to aid the Reich, he now asked what the future would bring: "For Germany his [Benedict's] death signifies a great loss, since among the Cardinals—with the exception of Gasparri to some degree—I know of none who would want to bring the same understanding, goodwill, and attention to our current critical needs and concerns, to our particularly complicated situation, as Benedict."[66]

Benedict had held the Church together during the trying war years, and had walked the narrow tightrope of neutrality, having been accused by both sides of partiality to the other. He had been able to maneuver the Vatican through this storm, and by raising his voice in constant pleas for world peace and reconciliation he had increased the esteem for and influence of the Vatican in the eyes of the world. Bergen, as did Germany, had special cause to lament the passing of Benedict, since his policies had been of aid to the Reich, on both a humanitarian and diplomatic level. German diplomats mourned the loss of this leader who always had sympathetically listened to their troubles.

Shortly after Benedict's death Ritter and Bergen met with the Austrian Minister, Pastor, to discuss the candidates for the vacant Papal throne. They were unanimous in regarding Gasparri as the candidate most acceptable to the former Central Powers. Ritter and Bergen both felt that Cardinal Achille Ratti of Milan, another possible candidate, would not be satisfactory, since during his service as nuncio to Poland he had been regarded as having been anti-German. Pastor, who had known Ratti for years, believed that the German opinion was really well founded.[67] Despite German misapprehension, when the white smoke signifying the election of a Pope appeared above the Sistine Chapel on February 6, 1922 it signaled that the Archbishop of Milan had been chosen. Achille Ratti, who assumed the name of Pius XI, had been prefect of the Ambrosian Library in Milan and later of the Vatican Library and was known as a scholar. In 1918 he had been sent to Poland as apostolic visitor and named nuncio in the following year. In 1921 he became Archbishop of Milan, only one year before his elevation to the throne of Peter. A short, well-built man, with a

[66] AA, PO II, PO 11 Nr. 1 Vat., Vol. 1, Bergen to AA, January 23, 1922.

[67] Austria, Oesterreichisches Staatsarchiv, Abt. Haus-Hof-und Staatsarchiv (hereafter cited as HHSTA), NPA, 87, Pastor to AFO, January 24, 1922. For Ratti's work as nuncio in Poland, see ch. 3.

robust physical constitution, he gained some reputation for mountain climbing in his earlier days. Amiable in conversation, he passed from one major European language to another with ease. He also was known for his shrewdness and a tenacity of purpose which could border on stubbornness. While coming from simple stock and disliking everything aristocratic as *troppo elegante*, he nurtured a distrust for political democracy and had little or no sympathy for Catholic democratic movements, preferring all his life to deal with strong rulers like himself. In October 1919, after his appointment as nuncio, he was consecrated bishop not in St. Peter's but in the cathedral of Warsaw by members of the Polish hierarchy. "In this way," as he told the latter, "I became to some extent just one of yourselves." It was a symbolic move not lost on the Poles—or for that matter on the Germans—who were uneasy that his interest in Poland might lead him now as Pope to pursue an anti-German policy. While in Warsaw he also had seen the Red Army approach the Polish capital, a fact which undoubtedly left an indelible mark on his thinking and underlined his fear of Bolshevism. All agreed that he was a difficult and exacting chief, as hard on himself as on others—obstinate and inflexible in his opinions—yet respected, admired, and served loyally by his staff.[68]

Although details concerning the Conclave were not disclosed, apparently Ratti was able to allay the German cardinals' objections to him. Before the election Cardinal Schulte of Cologne had not concealed his doubts about Ratti, not on the grounds of the Italian's personality or character, but because of his possible pro-Polish leanings and his lack of experience in political and diplomatic affairs. But during the Conclave the German Cardinal had the opportunity to speak at length with Ratti, at whose request the conversation was conducted in German, and he came away with such an improved impression of the new Pope that he could "completely assure" Bergen there would be no change in the Vatican's attitude toward the Reich. Press opinion in Poland, England, and France was generally pleased with the choice of Pius, whom they portrayed as a friend of Poland.[69] The Pope, however, had taken pains to express his interest in Germany and his friendly feelings for the Reich to the German cardinals during the Conclave and to deny any overt pro-Polish sympathy. Moreover, Cardinal Bertram had openly expressed his high regard for and belief in the impartiality of the new Pope. Nevertheless the Curia and German

[68] Daniel A. Binchy, *Church and state in fascist Italy* (London, 1941), pp. 73, 76-81. Carlo Falconi, *The popes in the twentieth century*, trans., Muriel Grindrod (Boston, 1957), p. 153ff.

[69] AA, PO II, PO 11 Nr. 1 Vat., Vol. 1, Schoen (Warsaw) to AA, February 11, Sthamer (London) to AA, February 11 and Mayer (Paris) to AA, February 7, 1922.

5. Pius XI addressing the crowds in St. Peter's Square shortly after his election, February 1922

diplomats in Rome were concerned that a lingering suspicion about Ratti's anti-German sympathies might cause anti-Vatican statements to be made in either German Government or public circles, which in turn would damage relations between both governments and perhaps cause a cooling of Papal interest in initiating any diplomatic moves on the Reich's behalf. Bergen therefore requested the Foreign Office in Berlin to exert influence upon the press to report favorably about Pius' election and to await his policies with an open mind.[70]

In February Cardinal Schulte also wrote to the Chancellor expressing similar ideas, stating that Pius was *at least* as pro-German as Benedict had been, and for the press to call the Pontiff, who had studied German culture and who knew the language and customs of Germany better than any pontiff in the last three hundred years, anti-German was ridiculous. Chancellor Wirth assured Schulte that Berlin had confidence in Pius and had taken steps to influence public opinion in favor of the Pope and had requested the press to forgo making any accusations against his impartiality. As an example of the government's ef-

[70] AA, PO II, PO 11 Nr. 1 Vat., Vol. 1, Bergen to AA, February 8, 1922. GSTA, MA 104439, Ritter to BFM, February 12, 1922, Schmidlin, Vol. 4, p. 156.

forts the Chancellor cited articles appearing in the influential *Deutsche Allgemeine Zeitung* in February, as well as in other newspapers, which in fact favored the new Pope. Moreover, Wirth called attention to numerous complimentary articles which praised Pius' objectivity during the plebiscite in East Prussia when he was serving in Poland.[71]

Although the German press was not hostile to the new Pope and generally refrained from dire warnings or accusations based on Pius' activities as nuncio in Poland, articles in the papers in early 1922 asked the question generally in the minds of German citizens and government officials, of whether Pius would follow Benedict's strategy for international reconciliation which benefited Germany.[72] By the end of 1922 it appeared that he had, since he continued the policy of his predecessor on the matter of reparations, as Papal statements during the economic conferences and public pronouncements about the necessity for reconciliation based on a viable system of payments all affirmed. The most obvious indication of continuity in diplomatic policy was Pius' immediate reappointment of Cardinal Gasparri as Secretary of State. Gasparri had been the Germans' preferred candidate for the Papal throne, and in the coming years Pius was expected to draw upon the Cardinal's long experience in diplomatic affairs to help draft policy.

Gasparri, the son of Umbrian peasants, was a specialist in canon law whose brilliance as a student had caught the eye of his superiors. After some work abroad as apostolic delegate in South America he was named Secretary of the Congregation of Extraordinary Ecclesiastical Affairs in 1902. During the next fourteen years he supervised the compiling of the *Codex Juris Canonici*, the official law code of the Church until the 1980's. Benedict had already appointed him Cardinal Secretary of State in 1914, and he had conducted the complicated foreign affairs of the Vatican both during the war years and the period immediately thereafter with a firm grasp of both the broad sweep and the details of international affairs.[73] The singular honor which Pius conferred upon him in asking him to retain his post demonstrated the esteem in which he was held. His efforts toward reconciliation in Europe, his apprehensions about the economic policies of the Allies toward Germany, and his fears of Bolshevik advances coincided with the thinking and course of action which the new Pope desired to pursue, and his appointment was a most reassuring sign to the Germans. The events of 1922 did not indicate a major change in Papal policy

---

[71] BA, R 43 I, Vol. 159, Schulte to Wirth, February 9, 1922; Wirth to Schulte, March 8, 1922.

[72] *Frankfurter Zeitung*, "Die Bedeutung der Wahl Pius XI," February 11, 1922.

[73] Binchy, p. 93.

toward Germany; it would remain the Reich's task to supply the Vatican with information and statistics to ensure that this opinion and policy continued.

Prior to the Genoa Conference in July 1922 Cardinal Gasparri demonstrated that his thoughts on the world situation had not altered, for he once more returned to his suggestion for alleviating Europe's economic woes. The Cardinal considered the meeting of great importance because Germany had been invited to take part. The first step to obtain a total European settlement, Gasparri maintained, was a solution to the economic problem, and he placed great hope in Lloyd George's ability to carry this point. Even without revising the treaties, the conference could find a solution by linking German reparations to Allied war debts. Germany was being asked to pay reparations over a period of many years. During this time the Reich would be saddled with an army of occupation in part of its territories and control commissions, all of which would further hinder both Germany's and Europe's economic development. If, however, all parties involved agreed to permit Germany to assume the Allied war debts to America in exchange for reparations, on a scale which Gasparri had worked out and which he believed realistic and equitable, a settlement to everyone's benefit could be reached. America would receive its money, the Allied Powers would be able to rebuild their economies without large debts siphoning off money, and Germany would be relieved of all control commissions. America would even gain, since Germany, more solvent than many of America's present debtors, could offer securities (ports, railways, mines, etc.) which others would not be willing to give, thus clearing the air of the enmity and hate created by the long years of negotiations over payment.[74] Rome, it seemed, was making efforts to formulate a plan to ease Germany's reparations burden, and the Cardinal was looking ahead to ensure the revival of the European economy as soon as possible without long-drawn-out payments, occupation forces, and controls over Germany. To emphasize this point the *Osservatore* of April 8 went out of its way to ask for divine blessings for the Genoa Conference and recommended that, though specific reparation sums were not to be discussed at the meeting, the delegates explore ways in which the vanquished could absolve their debts as soon as possible.[75]

The Americans, however, while not attending the conference, showed no interest in linking war debts and reparations.[76] Germany was already having difficulties in controlling its inflation and keeping up its

[74] BFO, 371/7425/5308, De Salis to BFO, April 6, 1922.

[75] GSTA, MA 104092, Ritter to BFM, April 8, 1922. *Osservatore*, April 8, 1922.

[76] See Denise Artaud, *La question des dettes interalliées et la reconstruction de l'Europe (1917-1929)* (Paris/Lille, 1978), especially Vol. 1. Maier, p. 287.

payments. In January Berlin had asked for and obtained a partial moratorium from the Allies. If the Cardinal's suggestion were adopted, it would be even less likely that America would receive prompt payment. The French were also unhappy about the Cardinal's plan and heatedly denounced the Vatican proposal as pro-German, which in turn only confirmed Berlin's opinion that France desired to ruin Germany financially. Nevertheless, Gasparri continued to hope that he could convince the Powers of the reasonableness of his suggestion and about a reconciliation of the nations. Lack of success, he feared, would subject Europe to a worse catastrophe than the last war. In that case Germany's ability to withstand a Bolshevik onslaught would then be questionable.[77] The Pontiff expressed similar thoughts in an open letter to Gasparri on April 29.[78] The Vatican this time was very careful lest any step be interpreted as being too pro-German. As a consequence, when the German Foreign Office inquired whether Reich Chancellor Wirth might visit the Pontiff while in Italy for the conference, the Vatican replied that although the Pope would like to see the Chancellor, he should avoid paying his respects at the Vatican so as to forestall accusations about the visit which might endanger the Pope's plans for reconciliation.[79]

On May 11, Msgr. Giuseppe Pizzardo, Under Secretary of the Congregation of Extraordinary Ecclesiastical Affairs in the Secretariat of State, delivered a Vatican recommendation for solving the financial problem to the British delegation, with the request that Lloyd George exert all means to carry it out. The Pontiff suggested that Germany initially pay 30 billion marks upon which interest was to be paid and which would be guaranteed by its harbors, custom duties, etc., and that as soon as this guarantee was given, all occupation troops and Allied commissions on German soil be removed.[80] Gasparri agreed to act as go-between and transmit any German proposals to Lloyd George in the hopes of speeding the negotiations.[81]

During the early months of 1922 the Germans readily supplied the Vatican with various information concerning the Reich's ability to pay, a sign of the Foreign Office's conviction that the Vatican was working in Germany's behalf, and consequently the Foreign Office sent the Curia words of encouragement and promptings to continue its efforts. In late July, after Gasparri denied that he directed his efforts toward fixing a specific final reparations figure and affirmed his desire only to

[77] GSTA, MA 104092, Ritter to BFM, April 29, 1922.
[78] *Osservatore*, April 29, 1922.
[79] GSTA, MA 104092, Ritter to BFM, May 1, 1922.
[80] AA, BRV 125, Vol. 2, Steinmann (Vatican) to Maltzan (AA), June 17, 1922.
[81] AA, BRV 125, Vol. 3, Bergen to Simson (AA), July 18, 1922.

keep the sum within Germany's capacity to pay, he conceded the difficulty of establishing Germany's exact financial resources. Bergen then reminded him of the possibility of establishing an impartial commission to determine the figure. Knowing the English to be more accommodating on reparations than the French, the German Minister urged the Cardinal to renew his efforts to interest Lloyd George in this suggestion. When Gasparri hesitated until he had more information about the entire economic picture, Bergen gave Gasparri an Italian edition of John Maynard Keynes' revisionist work *The Economic Consequences of the Peace*.[82]

At the same time German diplomats continued to relay to the Curia the warnings emanating from Berlin of dire economic consequences since nothing constructive had come of the Genoa Conference, and touched upon all the points which might disturb the Curia, including the fact that in April Germany had signed a treaty with Bolshevik Russia at Rapallo. Already anxious about the advance of Communism, this German overture to the east most probably reinforced Gasparri's theory that Germany neither could nor should be pushed beyond its economic limits. On July 25 the Foreign Office had Bergen again inform the Cardinal of the seriousness of Germany's financial and economic plight. Despite the partial moratorium, the mark continued to fall, and the Reich would scarcely be in a position to resume any monetary payments. If the situation worsened, remuneration in kind would also have to cease. The consequence of all this would be that Germany as well as Austria would require foreign assistance to feed their populations—an unstable condition which undoubtedly would release social revolutionary forces. The Reich Chancellor therefore appealed to the Holy See to make this situation clear to the Allies and to express the need for a total moratorium in reparation payments.[83] Bergen also wrote to Zech in Munich, asking him to convey the same message to Pacelli, who in turn would pass it on to Gasparri, and to mention the possibility of revolutionary consequences for all Europe if the reparations problem were not solved.[84] In other words, the Germans were making certain that the Vatican would learn of the gravity of the situation from all sides and in the name of the Reich Chancellor himself.

The seriousness of the German arguments impressed Gasparri, for they merely confirmed his own analysis. He instructed the Nuncio in Paris, the Apostolic Delegate in Washington, and Cardinal Francis Bourne of Westminster, who had a fine rapport with Lloyd George,

[82] AA, BRV 125, Vol. 3, Bergen to AA, July 25, 1922.
[83] AA, BRV 125, Vol. 3, Haniel to German Embassy (Vatican), July 25, 1922.
[84] AA, BRV 125, Vol. 3, Bergen to Zech, July 27, 1922.

to determine what they could do to moderate Allied demands.[85] Thus, as Bergen contentedly remarked, "our wishes have been fulfilled on the part of the Holy See with a willingness for which we can be thankful."[86]

In early August Cardinal Bourne informed the Vatican of Lloyd George's general agreement with Rome's suggestions about the reparations problem, and he encouraged the Holy See to urge Belgium's support for moderation. Gasparri thereupon instructed the Nuncio in Belgium to seek out the Belgian monarch "even if he were outside the capital" in order to explain the seriousness of Germany's situation and its request for a total moratorium of cash payments then being discussed in London. The Nuncio was also ordered to inform him of the Reich Chancellor's desire for Papal intercession, and to request him to have Belgian representatives be as accommodating as possible. The importance which Rome placed on these negotiations was underlined by the fact that Gasparri had seriously considered taking the unusual step of himself writing to Lloyd George and sending Cerretti on a special mission to London, but he ultimately decided to work through normal channels.[87]

The Vatican policy soon received further encouragement from England and Belgium. Several days after Gasparri had sent out his diplomatic feelers, Bourne reported that Lloyd George had agreed to listen to the Pontiff's suggestion and, at the English request, Berlin was sending to London Carl Bergmann, a specialist in economic affairs. Bergmann was to be ready for consultation should the British Foreign Office request it. The Nuncio to Belgium reported that the King was also sympathetic to the Pontiff's request and promised to pass it on to the Belgian representative in London.[88] Gasparri thereupon sent a text of his proposal for reparations to be published in *The Times* under the name of Italian Senator Cesare Silj, brother of Cardinal Augusto Silj. He had already unofficially sent a revised version to Belgian and French officials, but here his plans ran into snags. The representatives of these nations informed him that they could not agree to his suggestions, which they regarded as far too pro-German. No settlement which merely cancelled the financial obligations of these nations to the United States and failed to take into account these nations' need of capital would be acceptable. Both states insisted on first receiving some hard

[85] AA, BRV 125, Vol. 3, Bergen to AA, July 28, 1922.

[86] AA, RM 70, Vol. 1, Bergen to AA, August 7, 1922.

[87] AA, BRV 125, Vol. 3, Bergen to AA, August 8, 1922.

[88] AA, BRV 125, Vol. 3, Simson to German Embassy (Vatican), August 10, 1922; Bergen to AA, August 11, 14, 1922.

currency payment; only then would they discuss Germany's assumption of their debts to the United States.[89]

Despite all the overtures made by the Vatican, nothing concrete had been accomplished by the end of the year with regard to a settlement. Disappointed by Allied replies, in the fall Gasparri expressed pessimism that anything would come of the negotiations at the conference table unless America took part. Nevertheless the Vatican continued to pursue its efforts by requesting exact information from Germany about its financial and economic situation.[90] Throughout the exchange of notes Germany reiterated its statement that Allied demands were too high and repeatedly supplied Rome with documentation of the Reich's poor economic situation which justified its counteroffers for a lower amount of reparations.[91] The Cardinal Secretary also discussed his proposal with American financier J. P. Morgan. Morgan's presence in Rome in late October prompted the German Embassy to suggest that Gasparri meet with the American. Arrangements for this meeting were made via the Embassy to the Quirinal and the American Embassy.[92] Several days later Morgan paid a call at the Vatican. Gasparri hoped to persuade France to regard the question as purely financial and to interest the United States in taking part in the discussions, but the possibility for a solution as desired by Gasparri was very slim. Morgan pointed out to the Cardinal that the stumbling block would be France. Now, with the fall of Lloyd George in October 1922, Raymond Poincaré and his hard-line policy toward Germany had gained added strength in the Allied camp, and America was not indicating any inclination to intervene in the matter.[93] Two weeks later Morgan, after discussion on the matter with other French and British officials, wrote from London that France would simply not agree to such a proposal. Despite this negative reply to his aspirations, the Cardinal doggedly sought other means to convince the Allies. He sent a message through his

[89] AA, BRV 126, Vol. 4, Meyer (Vatican) to Simson, September 8, 1922.

[90] AA, BRV 125, Vol. 3, Bergen to AA, August 18, 1922; Meyer to AA, October 13, 1922, and Bergen to AA, December 18, 1922.

[91] AA, BRV 128, Vol. 6, Bergen to AA, December 23, 1922. While on a trip to Rome to discuss the Saar question, Msgr. Ludwig Kaas of the Trier diocese had been asked by the Reich Chancellor to raise the issue of reparations once more. In prior conversations with Pacelli, Kaas had learned of Rome's work to obtain a workable sum for Germany and how the Curia was exerting indirect influence in Washington, London, Brussels, and at the Quirinal in Rome. While meeting with Gasparri and the Pope, Kaas indicated the urgency of solving the question by tying the problem of military occupation and the economic distress of the civilian population to the reparations question, thus giving an added impetus for the Church to seek a solution. AA, PO II, PO 24 Vat., Vol. 7, German Embassy (Vatican) to AA, December 26, 1922.

[92] AA, BRV 125, Vol. 3, Meyer to AA, October 25, 1922.

[93] AA, RM 70, Vol. 1, Meyer to AA, October 28, 1922.

contacts to Italian Prime Minister Benito Mussolini, requesting that Italy energetically support the Cardinal's proposal at the upcoming Brussels Conference.[94]

By early 1923, however, the Cardinal reluctantly realized that his hopes for a settlement were not to be realized, and Europe was to endure more years of protracted negotiations. His goal had been to "depoliticize the reparations," to center the question entirely on financial matters which would exclude sanctions, and this in turn would then lead to the withdrawal of the occupation forces and stability for Central Europe. The Vatican had used all its means—newspaper, diplomatic channels, direct and indirect—to bring about a solution. The Pontiff assured Bergen that the Curia had pursued all possible leads, including further notes to the British and Belgians, and assuringly stated that even if the success they had desired had not been achieved, in time the repeated advice of the Vatican in favor of moderation would have its effect especially on Belgium.[95] Perhaps nothing more could have been done during these first years after Versailles to moderate the treaty conditions to arrive at a settlement, but Germany had had the benefit of the Vatican, which energetically threw its weight into the affair at a time when Germany could not easily or persuasively carry its message to the Allies. Berlin was able to pass on its suggestions and state its case, knowing that the many points in its argument would reach the Allied capitals via Vatican channels.

Germany had reason for satisfaction with the development of its relations with the Vatican since the war, for on the international level Vatican and German policy frequently coincided, and cooperation had become possible and indeed desirable. But, in addition to international affairs, one aspect of their relations that dealt with German internal political affairs was also considered very important by both parties. Just as Bergen's appointment as German ambassador symbolically indicated Germany's new relationship with the Vatican and its hopes to influence Papal policy in favor of Germany, the Papal appointment of a nuncio to the Reich Government underlined the Vatican's great interest in the regulation of the Church's affairs within Germany itself. The necessity of appointing a Reich ambassador to the Holy See had been made plain by Germany's need for allies in international affairs.

[94] AA, BRV 127, Vol. 5, Meyer to AA, November 10, 1922. In the initial contact which took place between the Vatican and the representative of Italy's new Prime Minister, one of the first promises of the new Italian leader was to do all in his power to solve the reparations question. AA, BRV 127, Vol. 5, German Embassy (Vatican) to AA, November 9, 1922.

[95] AA, BRV 125, Vol. 3, Bergen to AA, August 18, 1922; Meyer to AA, October 13, 1922.

The appointment of a nuncio to Germany touched more directly on domestic matters. A Vatican representative accredited to Berlin affected Catholic-Protestant relations as well as Bavarian-Reich relations—the problem of federalism versus centralization. Despite all diplomatic overtures before 1918 no nunciature had been established in Berlin because of a combination of Protestant opposition, Reich fears of offending Bavaria which desired to retain the Munich nunciature, and the opposition of the Hohenzollerns, who had no wish to see the nuncio become doyen of the diplomatic corps, as was his due according to diplomatic protocol, since this would place him on a level with the ruling German princes.[96] Before the war Cardinal Georg von Kopp of Breslau, whose diocese included the Reich capital, opposed it since he himself preferred to have all business between Berlin and Rome pass through his hands. Members of the Center Party, disinclined to have a Papal representative observing them in Berlin, also opposed it. Now, as Pastor observed, Kopp was dead, the Center was part of the Reich Government, the government had other concerns and needs, and the political influence of extreme Protestant groups had sharply diminished.[97]

The Belgians as well as other diplomatic observers regarded the establishment of the Berlin nunciature as a victory for the Reich, since by sending a representative to the Reich capital the Vatican underlined its support or endorsement for German unity. This meant a setback for French efforts to weaken Berlin's influence in southern Germany.[98] The French were also displeased, since the nuncio automatically became doyen of the diplomatic corps in Berlin, superseding the representative of any other state which, like France, had hopes of at some time obtaining this position for its own representative.[99] On June 30 Pacelli delivered his credentials to President Ebert and stated that he had been appointed to Berlin in order to help to regulate anew the relations between Church and State in accordance with the new situation and present-day exigencies, and he pledged himself to work to cultivate relations which would protect the interests of German Catholics and the welfare of the State. President Ebert, who welcomed the establishment of the nunciature, assured the Papal envoy of the Reich's cooperation.[100]

[96] Zittel, p. 463. For background to the establishment of the nunciature, see Roth, pp. 216-236.

[97] Pastor, letter to his wife, May 22, 1920, pp. 686-687.

[98] BelgFO, Allemagne 2, Kerckove (Vatican) to Foreign Minister Hymans, May 3, 1920.

[99] *Kölnische Volkszeitung*, May 16, 1920.

[100] Lama, pp. 93-94. The Vatican again indicated its desire for good relations with

Although now fully accredited to Berlin, Pacelli at first still preferred to keep his permanent residence in Munich, for he had already begun negotiations for a Bavarian concordat and did not want to leave until completion of the work. The Bavarians, anxious to keep Pacelli in Munich, feared that the Vatican desired to conclude a Reich concordat, and they did not wish to see the individual status of Bavaria subsumed into a treaty dealing with all areas of Germany as a whole. In fact, the Bavarians even argued that Pacelli should remain and first complete a concordat for Bavaria, since using this treaty as a model Berlin would then find it easier to negotiate its own concordat with Rome.[101] The Nuncio was now in the enviable position of having both Berlin and Munich vie for his presence.

Berlin understood Pacelli's wish to shuttle between Munich and Berlin. The Nuncio's request was typical of his exacting nature and desire to supervise all details himself. Although unwilling to leave Munich until completion of the treaty with Bavaria, he was also unprepared to appoint a delegate to represent him in Berlin since he doubted anyone understood how to conduct negotiations as he would wish. Someone unacquainted with the Berlin routine might fall under the influence of politicians or officials whose advice would counter that of the Vatican. Pacelli therefore retained both posts and regarded the "short distance" between Berlin and Munich as presenting no problems for him in traveling back and forth.[102] Control of Vatican affairs in both cities was to remain solely in his hands, and the official date for Pacelli to take up permanent residence in the Reich capital and the naming of a successor for him in Munich were left undetermined.

Pacelli had returned in June from one of his visits to Berlin quite content. He told his old friend Count Zech, the Prussian Minister in Munich, that he had been well received by everyone from President Ebert to the Chancellor and cabinet ministers and was confident in his ability to work with them in settling problems. He had also met with Allied diplomats, who had questioned him at length about his opinions of the internal situation in Germany to which Pacelli, with his great knowledge and attention to detail, gave thorough and explicit answers. Zech was certain that the Nuncio had been helpful in ex-

---

Germany when in April 1951, after World War II, the Papal Nuncio, as doyen of the diplomatic corps, delivered his credentials to Theodor Heuss, President of the German Federal Republic, and presented the foreign diplomats accredited to the Bonn Government to the President. He reminded Heuss that after the capitulation in 1945 the Pope was the first to recognize the distinction between the German people and the Nazi regime. Heuss greeted this accreditation as a milestone in Bonn's reintegration into the family of nations. *Rhein-Echo*, April 5, 1951.

[101] GSTA, MA 100009, Ritter to BFM, May 21, 1920.

[102] AA, PO II, PO 9 Vat., Vol. 1, memorandum of Haniel (AA), June 2, 1920.

plaining Germany's position and influencing the various diplomats in Germany's behalf. Because of his strong personality, impressive grasp of conditions in Germany, and high moral standing, Pacelli would, with time, exert influence upon the diplomatic corps in Berlin which would be to Germany's benefit. At first, as Zech noted, Pacelli had not seemed anxious to spend any length of time in the Reich capital, but after several visits to Berlin he perceived the greater diplomatic opportunities which the city offered and was now looking forward to the challenge which his duties there offered him.[103] Zech's comments about the Nuncio's abilities seemed justified, for Pacelli had matured and learned much from his diplomatic experiences since his first days in Munich during the war. In the shortest time Pacelli soon won for himself a unique position in diplomatic circles in Berlin, not only because of his position as doyen of the diplomatic corps but also because of his outgoing, imposing personality, his wit and social grace, and his well-informed opinions. The palace he occupied in the Rauch-strasse soon became a center of ecclesiastical and diplomatic activity, and the scene of important meetings and discussions. The influence which he began to exert even beyond Catholic circles testified to his effectiveness as a diplomat.[104] The role Pacelli was assuming exactly accorded with the Reich Government's initial aspirations. In a cabinet meeting in 1920 the ministers pointed out that the establishment of the nunciature was propitious not only for church-state relations but also for fostering contacts on an international level. The most important task of the Nuncio, in this regard, was to reconcile peoples and nations. His house was the ideal place for the resumption of informal discussions between German officials and foreign diplomats, all of which would be very valuable for the Reich.[105] But all this yet lay in the future, and Pacelli had still to demonstrate the purpose and value of a Papal representative in the German capital.

Several pressing matters dealing with internal situations in Germany awaited the Nuncio. The mutual rights and obligations of Church and State which existed before 1914 became null and void in the new republican era. It was now to the advantage of both sides to rethink their positions and to negotiate a new agreement. The government had indicated its willingness to do so, for this would lessen religious conflict within the country as well as hopefully gain some diplomatic credit for Weimar in the eyes of the Vatican. Pacelli, in surveying the

---

[103] PGSTA, Rep. 90, P.11.1.1., Vol. 10, Zech to AA, July 12, 1920.

[104] Ludwig Kaas, "Eugen Pacelli, erster Apostolischer Nuntius beim Deutschen Reich," *Gesammelte Reden* (Berlin, 1930), pp. 20-21 in Roth, p. 236.

[105] BA, R 43 I, Vol. 159, minutes of Reich Cabinet meeting, undated (probably July 1920), p. 45.

situation upon his arrival in Berlin, made no secret of his desire to have the Allies grant some concessions to Berlin so that it could consolidate the position of the Republic and institute the constitutional and legislative measures needed to bring stability to Germany. The new Constitution was not unfavorable to the interests of the Church, and Pacelli had on occasion even stated to the French Ambassador that he believed the new government was more solicitous of the rights of the Church than the fallen dynasties, despite their claims of attachment to the church and altar.[106]

The selection of a new archbishop for Cologne, occurring at the same time as Pacelli's accreditation to Berlin, had posed a problem which only underlined the need for defining the position of the Church and its relation to State in the new Germany, and the need for the Nuncio to devote his full energies to situations which affected both Germany's internal and external affairs. In 1919 Cardinal Felix Hartmann, one of the most respected prelates in all Germany, had died. Cologne, along with Breslau and Munich, was one of the most influential sees in Germany, and its bishop exerted an influence far beyond the borders of his diocese. The new prelate would be most influential in forming Church policy, especially in the post-war period, when the Church was growing and accommodating itself to the new government and society. In addition, since much of the archdiocese, as well as parts of the dioceses of Trier, Limburg, and Münster (all grouped within the ecclesiastical province of the metropolitan see at Cologne), were occupied by Allied troops, it was very important for Berlin to have someone appointed who enjoyed the confidence and support of the Berlin Government, someone with patriotic leanings.

The French, on the other hand, were also aware of this situation and realized the opportunity of supporting someone who might lend his ecclesiastical support to French interests in the Rhineland. French officials in the occupied area forwarded a report to Paris, advising that the future archbishop not be someone pro-Prussian or an adversary of Rhenish autonomy. The question of Rhenish autonomy formed part of a larger struggle of provincial decentralization versus a centralized German state, and for this fight all French forces had to be utilized to support autonomy. "The influence of an archbishop of Cologne, the veritable primate of the Rhine," continued the report, "would not be negligible for this work of grouping [the forces] preparatory to a perhaps decisive battle."[107] The French Ambassador to the Vatican wrote Paris, warning of Bergen's active lobbying at the Vatican for a pro-

---

[106] FFO, Allemagne 370, Laurent (Berlin) to FFO, June 19, 1921.
[107] FFO, Allemagne 367, report of a French agent, January 5, 1920.

Prussian prelate, and expressed the belief that selection of a new bishop was as critical for French as for German policy.[108]

The problem of episcopal selection, however, was not only made difficult by diplomatic considerations but was further complicated by the lack of guidelines for the election of the new archbishop. The Papal Bull of 1821, *De Salute Animarum*, had specified the rules for the election of bishops in Prussia. But the events of 1919 had brought the validity of this document into question. The Vatican now desired to use the opportunity to renegotiate a treaty with the Prussian Government and eliminate the privilege of some diocesan chapters, such as at Cologne, of electing their bishops and the government's right to approve the candidate. The chapter of the cathedral in Cologne, on the other hand, insisted on maintaining the right to elect Hartmann's successor. Berlin backed the position of Cologne's clergy to hold the election in the traditional manner, since the chapter would likely elect a nationally oriented prelate whom Prussia would then confirm. To concede the issue would create a precedent and cause Berlin to lose its influence in the appointment of bishops most important for German policies. Moreover, to concede now would also weaken the Reich's negotiating position later on when the question of regularizing church-state relations came up.

Little time, however, remained to await the outcome of what would be long negotiations between Church and State; the vacant see and political and ecclesiastical considerations necessitated a speedy decision. The German Church lacked the guidance of Cologne's archbishop, and Berlin feared that Paris would use the time advantageously, to influence either the Vatican or the chapter to select someone more acceptable to France's position. Because of the seriousness of the circumstances, the unreliability of the mails to and from Rome, and with the German representatives to the Vatican still in Switzerland, most of the negotiation was conducted through Nuncio Pacelli, whose task was to observe, consult with officials in Cologne and Berlin, and make recommendations to Rome. Already in late 1919 and early 1920, Pacelli had met with members of the government as well as with the chapter in Cologne. A compromise, worked out in 1920, indicated a grasp of reality shared by both negotiating parties and their awareness of the potential for protracted negotiations to hinder the functioning of the Church and secular government in this new era. As a gesture of goodwill, the Vatican allowed the chapter to select the new archbishop, as had been its prerogative, with the proviso that this would not be a precedent for future elections. In this way the Vatican was

---

[108] FFO, Allemagne 367, Laurent to FFO, January 14, 1920.

still permitted a free hand to negotiate a church-state treaty in the future. Pacelli and the Prussian Government agreed upon Bishop Karl Joseph Schulte of Paderborn as the new archbishop—a man loyal to Germany, yet one who impressed France by his work during the hostilities for French prisoners of war in Germany. A candidate had been selected who met German requirements, while still not being an ardent chauvinist whose nomination would have aggravated French-Vatican relations. Pacelli then persuaded the cathedral chapter of the value of electing Bishop Schulte, which it did on January 15.[109]

He was installed immediately so that he could take up the pressing work facing the leader of the most important diocese in western Germany. Neither side had conceded anything which would compromise their positions in further negotiations, and a major vacancy in the hierarchy had been filled without too much delay. Pacelli's handling of the situation seemed equitable and brought him credit again as a negotiator, but the Cologne affair only emphasized to Pacelli, the Vatican, and Berlin alike, that the situation was only provisional, that other situations such as this would inevitably occur, and that a new regulation of church-state relations in Prussia as well as in Bavaria was an urgent matter.

Another internal issue to which the Vatican had to direct its immediate attention was that of the separatist movement. Now that the link to the past had been broken by the war, the question was raised in both Bavaria and the Rhineland as to whether these areas should become independent of the Reich. While not movements of mass support, they were nevertheless naturally of concern to Berlin lest they become so. French support of separatist activities, which aimed at weakening the Reich, complicated the matter. English officials reported the activity of the French legation in Munich in encouraging such sentiments and urged the establishment of a British consulate general in Munich, purposely to help counter French influence. Arguing in favor of separation, the French pointed out that England was powerless on the continent and unable to obstruct French policy, including possible control of the Ruhr. If this were to happen, Bavaria would then become economically dependent on France, which would be able to control the amount of coal that the south German state received. Conversely, understanding with France would give Bavaria the benefit of connections with a strong Allied Power.[110] In addition, some reports sent to Paris by French agents gave France reason to believe that Pacelli might also be sympathetic to separatism.[111] In Jan-

---

[109] GSTA, MA 104492, Ritter to BFM, January 24, 1920.

[110] BFO, 371/4798, Kilmarnock (Berlin) to BFO, September 29, 1920. For French intentions concerning southern Germany see Mayer, *Politics and diplomacy*, p. 89.

[111] FFO, Allemagne 367, Tirard to French Premier Leygues, November 3, 1920.

uary 1920 Faulhaber's strong stand for the retention of a Bavarian nunciature gave even Zech the feeling that the prelate had become convinced of the advantages to the Church of separating Bavaria from the Reich.[112]

The Vatican undoubtedly could have gained advantages for the Church in working with an all-Catholic state such as Bavaria, but encouraging such moves would weaken Germany and thereby create the imbalance in Europe—either by opening the door to French dominance or Bolshevik encroachments—which the Curia feared. If, however, a concordat securing Church rights in Bavaria could be worked out (negotiations were then underway), the Church could have its position secured internally and not weaken Germany externally by supporting separatism. Pacelli already indicated the Vatican's position in January 1920. Several days after his return from a visit to Berlin, a member of the Bavarian People's Party (BVP) talked to him about the differences separating the newly formed Bavarian party and the Center Party and spoke in favor of a complete separation of Bavaria from the Reich, which he deemed in the interests of Bavaria and the Church. Pacelli sharply disagreed and answered that what he had seen and heard in Berlin assured him that the Reich Government could work with the Church.[113] The value to the Church of dealing not only with Munich but also with the Central Government in Berlin, which represented not only the Bavarians but also other large groups of Catholics such as in the Rhineland and Silesia, was obvious to the Papal diplomat.

In Rome during the same month, when the Bavarian People's Party announced its formal separation from the German Center Party, Gasparri called in the Bavarian Minister to learn if this was a move to separate Bavaria from Germany. He feared Bavarian dissatisfaction with the centralizing tendencies of the Weimar Government and that some of its economic policies would induce the party toward separatism. When assured that it was only a tactical maneuver, Gasparri reiterated his stand that the splitting of the Reich would impede European diplomatic equilibrium.[114] Despite French influence, Gasparri was not inclined to foster what he believed might lead to civil war in Germany by supporting separation or the formation of a South Ger-

---

[112] AA, IA, Bayern 60, Vol. 2, Zech to AA, January 15, 1920. There were also articles, mostly in north German newspapers, accusing the Vatican of supporting a separation of Catholic Germany from the Protestant north, but accusations or suspicions by the press were also commonly present in any period where a separatist movement was seeking support. In 1928, for example, articles appeared in the French press stating that the Vatican was supporting the autonomist movement in Alsace-Lorraine against France! GSTA, MA 104442, Ritter to BFM, June 1, 1928.

[113] AA, IA, Päpstl. Stuhl 4, Vol. 10, Zech to AA, January 12, 1920.

[114] GSTA, MA 104064, Ritter to BFM, February 7, 1920.

man state. Besides, if such a state were formed to include Austria, it would probably awaken South Tyrolean interest in joining, which would then cause difficulties for the Vatican with Italy. If the Vatican chose to be pro-separatist, it would then effectively limit its influence in the rest of the Reich, where it was now obtaining a more predominant place than it ever had before. A strong Germany would also be a base against Bolshevism.[115] If it threw its weight toward decentralization of the Reich, the Church's position might tip the balance or make it immeasurably more difficult for Berlin to control the situation. Instead, advised by Pacelli and in line with its overall policy, the Vatican decided that separatism was not to its advantage and chose a "hands off" policy for what it considered an internal affair. By reacting negatively to the situation, it once more positively aligned its policy with that of the Reich.

Moreover, one other factor was involved. Since the war, Italo-Vatican relations had warmed considerably and direct, although unofficial, contact between the Nitti Government and the Holy See ensued. In April the Italian Ambassador to Germany, Giacomo De Martino, while in Rome, paid a call on Cerretti, who was at that time Secretary for Extraordinary Ecclesiastical Affairs in the Secretariat of State, to inquire about the Vatican's attitude toward Germany, and particularly the Curia's attitude toward separatism. Cerretti assured him of the Vatican's insistence on the restoration of Germany to the family of nations and the reconstitution of its economic life, and in no way would support a weakening of its central government. De Martino, who expressed his satisfaction, noted that it coincided with the policy pursued by Italy. His unprecedented visit to the Vatican indicated the importance which Italy attached to the Vatican's opinion in this matter.[116] Italy had made it clear that a separate Bavaria or a greater German-Catholic state which encompassed Bavaria and parts of the former Austro-Hungarian Empire was not to its liking. Here was a point in common between the two Rome governments. With these considerations in mind, the Vatican spelled out to French representatives that any expectation on Paris' part of Church support for separatism would be disappointed.[117] Pacelli's task was to hammer out a new concordat for Bavaria and to initiate proceedings for regulating the

---

[115] AA, BRV 137, Vol. 15, Nadolny (Stockholm) to AA, July 19, 1923.

[116] AA, PO II, PO 2 Vat., Vol. 1, Office of Delbrück (AA) to Zech, April 22, 1920. For a discussion of increasing Italo-Vatican cooperation in the 1920's, see Peter C. Kent, *The pope and the duce* (New York, 1981), pp. 17-43.

[117] AA, IA, Päpstl. Stuhl 15, Vol. 9, Bergen to AA, February 11, 1920. Bergen mentions that Gasparri also sent communications to Nitti suggesting Italian support for Germany at the various international conferences.

situation in the rest of Germany for which the Vatican would in turn endorse the Central Government. Pacelli's assumption of his duties in Berlin further demonstrated the Vatican's commitment to a strong Germany. Upon several occasions Pacelli had expressed his sentiments on the importance of a united Germany, and his activities in working for better church-state relations supported this. No doubt his relaying of these opinions to Rome on the basis of his on-the-spot observations confirmed the Vatican's position on the matter.

In early 1920 Pacelli went to Rome for consultations regarding the guidelines for the intended discussions on church-state relations in Germany. Wherever he could, he sought to convince officials of the value of maintaining and extending relations with the Reich and its individual states, for in this new era the German authorities appeared to him willing to aid or to support the Church in reaching some of its objectives. He also informed the Vatican of the economic difficulties encountered by the average German, and disputed the French assertion that "things aren't that bad" as to warrant the Papacy's sympathy. The German and Bavarian ministers in Rome had been attempting all along to stress the seriousness of Germany's plight, and both appreciated Pacelli's support, which they were sure had been given serious consideration by his superiors. Moreover, the Nuncio's actual presence in Rome at that time helped tremendously, since he could now verbally describe and elaborate on the conditions in Germany rather than merely send written reports.[118]

Another immediate matter in which Pacelli proved instrumental in influencing Vatican policy in Germany's behalf was the question of the local militia (*Einwohnerwehr*). According to Versailles, Germany was to be demilitarized, including this local defense force. In some areas of Germany, especially in Bavaria, the militia historically had the right to carry arms. If the Allies now forbade this, the populace would have another cause for resentment against the peace settlement. More important, abolition of the *Einwohnerwehr*, which in practice served as a police force, would weaken the fledgling government in its ability to withstand a coup or revolt. Pacelli had personally witnessed the revolution in Munich in 1919 and knew the threat that it could pose to a militarily weak administration. He also was aware of the attachment that the Bavarians had for their militia, whose dissolution would cause discontent, to the exclusion of any practical benefit to the Allies. In April 1920 he wired the Holy See, stressing the importance that the militia held for the security of the state and requested the Pope to make diplomatic overtures to the Allied Powers, especially Italy, to

---

[118] GSTA, MA 100009, Ritter to BFM, April 6, 1920.

withdraw their objections to the *Einwohnerwehr*. Pacelli's report and request confirmed Gasparri's own judgment that after the recent unrest in western and central Germany any future disturbance of the stability in Central Europe would surely open the door to the Communists. He therefore energetically entreated Italian Prime Minister Nitti to mention the importance and positive value of the militia not only for Germany but for all Europe. He also requested Nitti at the upcoming conference at San Remo to explain to the Allies, especially France, the dangers of overexaggerating German militarism.[119] His arguments were used at the meeting, and his efforts bore fruit, for the question of disarming the *Einwohnerwehr* was put off at the conference, and the militia was not dissolved for the time being.

The Vatican, accustomed to dealing with monarchies, would perhaps have preferred to see this form of government maintained in most states of Europe. Pacelli, like Faulhaber, was in fact known to be monarchically inclined. But the Curia was far too circumspect to allow its predilections to interfere in the internal affairs of a country like Germany, once the new government had been established, or to endanger the position of the Church, which was actually improving under the Republic. Rather, it sought to work out a *modus vivendi* with the new state, capitalizing on the opportunities presented by the new situation. Despite temptations Rome had resisted the idea of endorsing a "divide and conquer" policy in Germany, but rather had supported Berlin so as to create a strong state in Central Europe, since this was also to Rome's overall diplomatic interests. Once the Berlin nunciature had been created and a German ambassador accredited to the Holy See, the mechanisms to strengthen the ties between Rome and the Reich were established, and negotiations for a church-state agreement, which the post-war situation required and which Rome was most anxious to have signed, could proceed.[120]

At the very inception of the Republic, German officials perceived that the Vatican was and could be of further assistance to Germany in international affairs. Although deeply divided over domestic problems, practically all Germans, regardless of party or social class, endorsed the aim of revising the Versailles Treaty. On this matter they presented a much more united front than did the Western Allies. German leaders differed only on the method of obtaining their goal—by demonstrating, through "fulfillment," the injustice and inefficacy of

[119] GSTA, MA 99515, minutes of Bavarian Cabinet meeting, April 17, 1920, p. 7; MA 104477, Ritter to BFM, April 16, 1920.
[120] Lama, pp. 94, 199.

the treaty or by obstructing its implementation.[121] Since Versailles, German foreign policy had been almost obsessively preoccupied with obtaining modification of the treaty's provisions; Germany's efforts on all international control committees to win Britain to its side, its vague efforts at economic *détente* with France to frighten Britain, and its settling of differences with Russia at Rapallo (1922) to give the Reich more maneuverability vis-à-vis the West, had all been aimed at winning diplomatic leverage to obtain some concessions on important matters such as reparations and border rectifications. The Foreign Office therefore utilized every means to mobilize international opinion through organizations such as the League of Nations, the unions, the International Labor Organization, and of course the Catholic Church. Thus, its relations with Rome dealt in large part with seeking the Vatican's aid in obtaining some changes in the treaty. In this sense, Germany's ties to Rome can be viewed as part of the larger context of German policy and seen as another method with which the Reich pursued its revisionist diplomacy.

In domestic affairs, with a policy which sought to unify the state and legally to redefine relationships which could provide a basis of stability for the new Weimar society, Berlin officials were quick to realize the value of concluding a concordat. Here again internal and external policy coincided. The border territories of the Reich greatly concerned the government, since these areas were now occupied, alive with separatist tendencies encouraged by foreign powers, or subject to plebiscites which might go against the Reich. These areas in both the east and the west were also strongly Catholic. Therefore, Berlin saw clearly the need to ensure the Vatican's support of Germany's claims and policies regarding these regions. In addition, the signing of a concordat recognizing the jurisdiction of the German episcopate in these territories and demarcating diocesan boundaries would serve a dual purpose for Germany—help to solve its diplomatic border problems and regulate a pressing internal matter. In November 1921 the Pope had invited nations to negotiate with the Vatican. For Germany this meant not only to negotiate a concordat but also to protect its eastern and western borders by ecclesiastical means.

[121] Hans Gatzke, ed., *European diplomacy between two wars, 1919-1939* (Chicago, 1972), p. 7. Despite the growth of world opinion, especially in Anglo-Saxon countries, that Germany had some justifiable grievances against the treaty, the ultimate significance of German revisionism for European peace is still debated. In the 1920's and 1930's German revisionist policy resulted in a series of adjustments in the treaty, but some scholars, Hans Gatzke, for example, argues that it was a major cause of the interwar instability. Gatzke, *European diplomacy*, pp. 7-12.

101

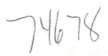

CHAPTER III

The Borders East
1920-1928

The land to Germany's east had been historically an area into which Germans dreamed of expanding—where, during the *Drang nach Osten* from the tenth century on, Teutonic Knights, Hanseatic merchants, and German colonists had moved; where in the eighteenth century Habsburgs and Hohenzollerns had assisted in dismembering the Kingdom of Poland. But after 1919 history reversed itself, and Slavic states were created or arose from the distant past to lay claim to territory occupied by the German and Austro-Hungarian Empires. The eastern borders of Germany from the Baltic to Silesia were now being pushed westward, and populations, land, and vital industrial material were being taken by the new Polish, Czechoslovak, and Lithuanian states. Faced with these and the possibility of even further losses through plebiscites, the Reich Government sought wherever possible to influence voters in these areas and to maintain contact with the German population in the former German territories. These efforts were based on the hope that Berlin's concern for the ethnic Germans and its support for a German identity would someday yield dividends in border rectifications based upon self-determination. Once more, Berlin sought to accomplish this goal by persuading the Church that, in addition to the justice of Germany's claims, the Vatican's practical interests coincided with those of the Reich.

The territory in the east of most concern to Berlin immediately after the war was Upper Silesia. The industrial and general economic value of the area created bitter competition between Germans and Poles for its control and caused Berlin and Warsaw to give the problem utmost attention. This territory of some 4,000 square miles and a population of approximately 1,900,000 was ethnically divided between Germans, who were mostly in the north, and Poles in the extreme southeast, whereas the middle of the province was a triangular area of mixed population which contained many factories and mines. This area was second only to the Ruhr in industrial importance, in 1913 producing

21 percent of the Reich's coal.[1] The Versailles Treaty, in its original form, had proposed to grant, without consulting the inhabitants, the greater part of Upper Silesia to Poland. In response to German protests, supported by Great Britain, the Allies decided to hold a plebiscite here sometime in 1920-1921, on a date to be decided by the Powers.

After the treaty went into effect, in January 1920 an Inter-Allied Plebiscite Commission took control of this region. The forces of the Commission consisted of British, Italian, and French soldiers, but most of the troops as well as the administrative personnel were French, and the French member of the Commission served as its chairman. The appointment of General Henri Le Rond, one of France's leading experts for Polish affairs at Versailles, to serve as its representative on the Commission amply demonstrates the vital importance that France placed on the outcome of the plebiscite.[2] In this overwhelmingly Catholic area, with a population reputedly very attached to its clergy, the ethnic division also came into play. The Church was therefore a critical factor in all calculations relating to the plebiscite.

Both Germany and Poland realized the critical role which the Church could play in influencing the election here since many of the clergy believed it was their duty and right to instruct their flocks on the proper manner in which to vote.[3] Upper Silesia came under the ecclesiastical jurisdiction of the Prince-Bishop of Breslau, Cardinal Bertram, who, like most of the higher clergy, was German and thus was naturally expected to be sympathetic to the Reich. Some of the lower clergy, however, were Polish and would be inclined to heed the appeals of the new Polish state for unification with the Polish fatherland.[4] Clearly the plebiscite would present difficulties for the Church and divide the clergy as well as the laity.

The diocese of Breslau, encompassing the Reich capital itself, was one of the richest and largest in Germany, stretching from the Baltic to Upper Silesia. Moreover, Bertram, a leading Biblical scholar and effective administrator, knowledgeable in Romanesque art, law, and

---

[1] Gregory Campbell, "The struggle for Upper Silesia, 1919-1922," *Journal of Modern History*, XLII (1970), 361.

[2] For an account of the political events in Silesia and the Commission activities, see Sarah Wambaugh, *Plebiscites since the world war* (Washington, D.C., 1933), Vol. 1, ch. 6. Hereafter cited as Wambaugh, *Plebiscites*.

[3] Campbell, 364, 367.

[4] It is difficult to obtain statistics on the ethnic background of the population since, when asked for their linguistic preference, they declared themselves bilingual. As regards the clergy, some estimates, including French, stated that approximately 20-25 percent could be called pro-Polish. BFO, 371/4821/5279, Loraine (Warsaw) to Curzon, December 2, 1920. FFO, Allemagne 370, Doulcet to FFO, December 5, 1920.

educational policies in Germany, also served as chairman of the Fulda Bishops' Conference, the synodal organization for the Reich (except Bavaria), which afforded him influence beyond the borders of his own diocese.[5] As ordinary of Upper Silesia, the Cardinal was not anxious to have this area, part of the Breslau diocese since the eighteenth century, in Polish hands, since this would probably mean the transferral of ecclesiastical jurisdiction to a Polish prelate.[6] Moreover, much land belonging to the diocese, primarily forests in the area of Wartensleben, had been assigned to Poland and Czechoslovakia. The income for the diocese from these lands had ceased. Bertram calculated that the loss of revenue from the Polish lands alone already amounted to 150,000 marks, creating a potential financial deficit, for the money was used to defray the normal diocesan expenses. Bertram had thus sought the aid of his government in negotiating with foreign states so that Breslau could retain these lands or receive compensation for them.[7] He naturally did not want to see further losses to his diocese now with the plebiscite. In this instance the interests of the Reich Government and the local ordinary corresponded exactly.

In March 1919 Bertram wrote a letter to the president of the Inter-Allied Commission, offering his reasons why the separation should not take place. In the Middle Ages the area had consisted of several principalities, was then part of the kingdom of Bohemia, and later passed with that crown to the Austrian Habsburgs in 1526, coming finally after the Seven Years' War in 1763 to Prussia. "Indefatigable German labor" had developed the mineral wealth and industry in the last 150 years. Loss of the collieries of Upper Silesia, he argued, would ruin the welfare and industry of the Reich. Since many of his flock spoke Polish, Bertram conceded that the language should be granted equal status in the schools and public life along with German, but he believed that the area could not do without German culture and technical knowledge. Transfer to Poland would not profit the populace, most of whom desired to remain with Germany but had been agitated by agents coming from Poland.[8] One week later the Cardinal wrote a similar letter to the Pope, seeking his aid in saving this section of Breslau's diocese for Germany. Besides employing the same arguments that he had made to the Commission, the Cardinal now went into greater detail about the economic hardship which the loss of Si-

---

[5] Georg Schreiber, *Zwischen Demokratie und Diktatur* (Münster, 1949), pp. 40-41.

[6] Because of territorial changes along the German-Polish border in 1945, the problem of ecclesiastical jurisdictions again became acute. See note 115, p. 153.

[7] AA, PO II, PO 24 Vat., Vol. 1, memorandum of AA, December 5, 1920.

[8] AW, 1A 25t, 8, letter of Bertram to the president of the Inter-Allied Commission, March 4, 1919.

lesia's coal would mean to Germany, and explained that the cession of Upper Silesia and the Catholic areas along Germany's eastern border would not only weaken the diocese of Breslau but also diminsh Catholic influence in Germany as a whole.[9] Bertram was trying to point out to the Vatican that although the Allies, especially France, might favor the territorial transfer to Poland, the Church's interests would not be served by adding a Catholic area to an already predominantly Catholic state. Instead, by keeping the political and ecclesiastical boundaries as they were, the influence of Breslau's bishop could be sustained within the Reich and the religious balance within Germany could be continued. Two months later, Bertram requested the Pontiff to intercede with the Allies on behalf of Germany for a reduction of the treaty obligations, not only for what concerned Breslau but for all Germany since the burdens imposed on Germany—the transfer of territory and goods—would cause economic disaster and were too great for the Reich to bear.[10] As a churchman and a German, Bertram was asking Rome to intervene.

The new Polish state, having established relations with the Vatican, soon opened the struggle for Upper Silesia on the ecclesiastical front. In August 1919 Warsaw requested that until the final political decision about Allied-occupied Upper Silesia was made, the entire area should be removed from the ecclesiastical jurisdiction of Breslau and placed under the impartial supervision of an apostolic vicar. The Polish Government cited historical precedent for this and hoped that the presence of such an administrator would lessen clerical partisanship. Warsaw also requested the sending of apostolic vicars to all areas in East and West Prussia, where plebiscites were being held. These areas affected the dioceses of Culm and Ermland. Moreover, for these posts in plebiscite areas, the Poles also suggested candidates whom they claimed were highly regarded by the clergy of the territory.[11]

Concerned over this Polish move, Bertram hoped the Vatican would not entertain such a step, for he knew that it would embitter the Berlin Government against Rome and that it would be viewed in the Reich as a move by the Curia favoring Poland. Culm's bishop, Augustinus Rosentreter, also upset about the dangers to his authority which such appointments would pose, urged Bertram as the leading prelate in eastern Germany, to speak out against the Polish demands.[12] Bertram, however, had already penned a long letter to Pacelli, stating how he had striven for peaceful relations between the Polish and the German

---

[9] AW, 1A 25t, 8, Bertram to Pope, March 12, 1919.
[10] AW, 1A 25u, 30, Bertram to Erzberger, May 18, 1919.
[11] AW, 1A 25t, 8, Pacelli to Bertram, August 26, 1919.
[12] AW, 1A 25t, 8, Rosentreter to Bertram, September 9, 1919.

faithful, how he had shown concern for the Poles, and how he had guided his flock with care so as not to incite nationalist passions in such a difficult situation. He stood opposed to the appointment of apostolic vicars, since this would undermine normal episcopal authority. Echoing Rosentreter's fears, he warned Pacelli that the German Government would regard the appointment as a move in favor of Poland and might suspect from the evidence that a now weakened Germany was being considered *"une quantité négligeable"* by the Vatican. Such a conclusion on the part of Berlin would only create new problems for the episcopate in its relations with the State and for Catholic deputies working with the government. In addition, Bertram elaborated for the Nuncio the enormous administrative difficulties which would occur in separating parts of the diocese from the bishop's control.[13]

The matter might have initially been regarded as a purely ecclesiastical affair concerning diocesan borders, but the Prussian Government had also been keeping close watch over the situation. In October the government intervened, thereby bringing the political aspect of the problem into sharper focus. Carl Becker, Secretary of State in the Prussian Ministry of Education and Religious Affairs, writing to Prussian Minister-President Paul Hirsch, called attention to Polish attempts to gain appointments for apostolic vicars who would then virtually eliminate the local ordinary's jurisdiction. In Becker's opinion such moves lacked ecclesiastical justification and could be considered only purely political. Since any territorial alterations in the dioceses in Prussia would alter the provisions in the Papal Bull *De Salute Animarum* (1821) to which Prussia had agreed, any changes without consultation with Prussia would be considered an unfriendly act. He therefore had the Prussian Minister at the Vatican make this clear to the Curia.[14] Bergen undertook to inform Vatican officials of the German viewpoint but also wanted to strengthen his position by having more German clerics and laymen come to Rome to discuss the German situation. "The officials here," he wrote, "are favorably disposed toward us; nevertheless the Curia is poorly informed about the events in Germany and is still partly influenced by news from the enemy camp. . . ."[15]

In December, Bertram was in Rome to discuss the matter. The Vatican meanwhile had explained the difficulty to the Poles for the Curia to appoint the candidates suggested by them as apostolic vicars and advised that the Polish Minister to the Vatican hold discussions

[13] AW, 1A 25t, 8, Bertram to Pacelli, September 1, 1919.

[14] AW, 1A 25t, 8, Becker to Prussian Minister-President, October 29, 1919.

[15] AA, IA, Preussen 2 Nr. 2a, Vol. 9, Bergen to AA, January 16, 1920.

with Bertram himself to learn if some arrangement could be made. After conversations between the Cardinal and Poland's representative in Rome, Józef Kowalski, and with the Polish Cardinal Edmond Dalbor, Bertram believed that, by making slight concessions with regard to his jurisdictional rights, he had settled the matter in a way which would block the appointment of apostolic vicars. If any of the clergy had complaints against the bishop on political grounds or desired to take action against any of his clergy because of their political activities, he promised he would then contact Achille Ratti, then Apostolic Nuncio to Poland, in an attempt to solve the problem by the mediation of the Vatican representative.[16] But Warsaw, after studying the proposals worked out by Bertram and Kowalski, countered again with a proposal aimed at weakening German influence in the area. According to the new Polish suggestion, the territories of Upper Silesia and other sections of Prussia where plebiscites were to be held would be placed under a high commissioner for ecclesiastical affairs nominated by the Holy See, who would be Ratti himself. Ratti's task would be to ensure a free plebiscite vote without intervention from the clergy. In order to safeguard against the erosion of the local ordinary's authority, any action taken by the commissioner would be effective only after consultation with the bishop, and any complaints about lack of clerical impartiality made either to the ordinary or to Ratti would be brought to the attention of the other party.[17]

Since the meeting in Rome between Bertram and Kowalski in January and the Polish counterproposals, the Germans had also taken steps to block the Polish request. Representatives of the Prussian Ministry of Education and Religious Affairs and the German Foreign Office journeyed to Breslau to confer with Bertram and to support his opposition to the transfer of some of his jurisdictional powers to Nuncio Ratti. Bertram had already made clear to Gasparri in a detailed Latin missal that *"modiste et solemniter"* (humbly and solemnly) he rejected the new suggestion of the Polish Government, since it would make the authority of the local bishop only an *"umbra ridicula"* (ridiculous shadow). Moreover, the transfer of the entire administration for an area of more than one million Catholics to the Nuncio, who had none of the necessary documents at hand nor a staff to administer the territory, would be practically unmanageable. Such a decision by the Holy See, argued Breslau's bishop, would only weaken his authority and strengthen Polish propaganda efforts for the separation. Bertram

[16] AA, IA, Preussen 2 Nr. 2a, Vol. 9, Haenisch (Pruss. Min. of Ed. and Relig. Affairs) to Prussian Cabinet, January 27, 1920. AW, 1A 25t, 8, Bertram to Gasparri, December 16, 1919.

[17] AW, 1A 250, 28, Kowalski (Vatican) to Gasparri, February 4, 1920.

defended his record as a fair administrator by reminding the Secretary of State that even Kowalski had conceded that he had always guided his flock in a just and impartial manner.[18]

While Bertram stressed the ecclesiastical aspect of the problem, the Foreign Office meanwhile instructed Bergen in Rome to raise the legal issues involved. If Upper Silesia were removed from the jurisdiction of Breslau's bishop, even temporarily, it would be a breach of the agreement between Church and State of 1821, which regulated diocesan borders and which, according to the specific statement of Nuncio Pacelli in Munich, still remained in effect. Such a move the Germans could only view as pro-Polish. Not only did Germany question the legality of the move, but they used perhaps the strongest diplomatic threat which they could muster against the Vatican. Berlin also warned that such a move would merely delay and complicate the incipient negotiations for a regulation of church-state relations in Germany.[19] Not only could it cause bitterness and loss of confidence in the Vatican's goodwill to Germany but it could also give the supporters of the concordat increased difficulties in passing it in the legislature.

The Polish demand created a serious problem for the Vatican. In the immediate post-war years a growing tension between Germany and Poland had developed, and the issue of border revision now threatened to force the Vatican to choose sides between two states. On the other hand, Germany's territorial integrity was important for the Vatican's policy of religious balance within Germany and diplomatic balance on the European stage. On the other hand, the Poles had been loyal to the Papacy against all adversity for centuries, and the Pope had already taken their part against Prussia and Prussia's discriminatory *Polenpolitik* in the nineteenth century. To desert them now when they had become an independent state would appear ungrateful and possibly damage the Vatican's influence with the government of the new state.[20] Despite the arguments of both sides, the Vatican decided upon a middle course. Mindful of the need for impartiality, it appointed Ratti to the post of religious commissioner for the plebiscite areas, which met with the approval of Poland and the Allies. To please Germany, Rome specified that until the plebiscite Ratti would reside most of the time in Upper Silesia rather than in Warsaw so that he not be unduly influenced by the Poles.[21]

---

[18] AA, IA, Preussen 2 Nr. 2a, Vol. 9, memorandum of Horstmann (AA), March 9, 1920. AW, 1A 250, 28, Bertram to Gasparri, February 25, 1920.

[19] AA, IA, Preussen 2 Nr. 2a, Vol. 9, memorandum of Haniel (AA), April 16, 1920.

[20] Maximilian Claar, "Die Aussenpolitik des Vatikans seit den Lateranverträgen," *Zeitschrift für Politik*, XXI (1930-1931), 804.

[21] In 1920, Msgr. Lorenzo Schioppa was named ecclesiastical commissioner for the

Ratti, who up until 1918 had been a librarian and scholar, had become Nuncio to Poland only two years before his new appointment in Upper Silesia. His additional duties in the plebiscite area indicated the high regard that the Curia had for him and for the manner in which he had carried out the difficult tasks of overseeing and helping to regularize relations between the Curia and the new Polish state. The British representative in Upper Silesia, Colonel H.F.P. Percival, as well as the British Foreign Office, at first saw no value in Ratti's new appointment since it would be open to exactly the same objection as had been made against maintaining the authority of Breslau's ordinary; i.e., it granted control to an outside ecclesiastic who was unfamiliar with the immediate situation in Silesia. But the British representative at the Vatican, Viscount De Salis, argued that the choice was an excellent one. The Vatican, he said, believed that a native Silesian who was impartial would be difficult to find, and Ratti prior to his appointment to Warsaw in 1918 had no connections to the new state. Since there was no objection on personal grounds, the Curia believed him a good choice. De Salis emphasized "that the Holy See have themselves [sic] every reason for guarding against reproach of partiality in a political question of this sort." Given the need for a moderating hand in the period before the plebiscite, the British made no objection to the Papal move and even favored it, while the French, who had no representative at the Vatican in early 1920, had been content to let Britain represent the Allies at the Vatican in this matter.[22] Thus armed with the backing of Poland and the Allies, the Vatican appointed Ratti to the post. Ratti realized the problems involved in such a double assignment and would have personally preferred the appointment of a commissioner from a neutral country such as Holland, or at least to have shared the post with Nuncio Pacelli so that no criticism of partiality could be made. Gasparri, however, considered this unnecessary,[23] for he was confident of Ratti's ability to be fair in the months remaining before the vote.

Germany was initially unhappy over Rome's decision. Gasparri

Teschen plebiscite area—which also belonged to the Breslau diocese. Rome informed him that, although he had full jurisdictional powers here, he was to coordinate his activities with Bertram. He dutifully informed Bertram of his assignment and the policies and work he intended to concern himself with. AW, 1A 250, 28, Schioppa to Bertram, July 11, 1920.

[22] BFO, 371/4301/5415, 371/4302/5397, BFO to Percival, February 23, 1920; Percival to BFO, March 1, 1920; De Salis to BFO, March 11, 1920. AW, 1A 250, 28, Gasparri to Bertram, March 22, 1920.

[23] AW, 1A 250, 35, statement of Cardinal Cerretti in the *The Milwaukee Sentinel*, January 19, 1930 and Angelo Novelli, *Pio XI* (Milan, 1923), p. 156, cited in memorandum "Die römische Kurie und Oberschlesien," by Friedrich Ritter von Lama, p. 3.

therefore tried to soothe German feelings by immediately assuring Bertram of Ratti's instructions to carry out his assignment in close consultation with Breslau's Cardinal. Since, as the Secretary of State emphasized, the Commissioner was appointed to ensure clerical impartiality during the preparations for the plebiscite, he was to have no episcopal jurisdiction nor interfere with normal diocesan affairs.[24] Berlin remained skeptical as to whether Rome's optimism was justified and whether in practice the Commissioner would not limit Bertram's authority, which in turn would hurt the Reich's chances of influencing the plebiscite through the local hierarchy. Nevertheless the Vatican was too important in Berlin's diplomatic plans for there to be any thought of angering the Curia by a display of vigorous protest over the decision. Instead Berlin tried to make the best of it by renewed efforts in pleading Germany's cause, which had now developed into a twofold strategy to convince Rome that it was in the best interests of the Church that the territory remain with Germany and that the authority of the local ordinaries remain intact.

As Ratti was being appointed, Berlin continued to send documentary material to Rome via Bergen, to dispatch Silesian aristocrats such as Count Praschma to Rome, and to encourage the hierarchy to send more German clergy to the Holy City to present its case. At the same time, efforts were made to win Ratti himself for the German viewpoint. The task of influencing the new Religious Commissioner was left primarily to Breslau's Cardinal. In April, Bertram wrote to Ratti concerning the plight of Breslau's diocese and requested him to pass the information on to Rome. Bertram pointed out that once the Catholic parts of the provinces of Posen and West Prussia had been separated from the Reich, as had occurred after Versailles, eastern Germany had almost become a diaspora area for Catholics; Protestantism, which has always been stronger in the eastern section of Germany than in the western or southern areas, would totally dominate the territory. If, then, Upper Silesia with more than one million Catholics went too, this would decrease the strength and size of Breslau's diocese to such an extent that it would be catastrophic for eastern German Catholicism, for Catholic voting strength in the local state and national legislatures, and for the financial stability of this important diocese. He again appealed to the Vatican to help to rectify this situation or prevent further loss.[25]

In Rome, Bergen and the Silesian nobleman Praschma were also explaining to Vatican officials about the significance of the loss of the

[24] AA, PO II, PO 24 Vat., Vol. 1, Bergen to AA, April 16, 1920.
[25] AW, 1A 250, 28, Bertram to Ratti, April 11, 1920.

area for Germany. By the end of May some grounds for encouragement developed. Praschma had had an audience with the Pope and had described in detail the significance of the border changes and the Silesian situation for the Catholic Church in Prussia and Germany. The Pontiff, according to Praschma, appeared deeply moved by this explanation and promised to support any measures which might be suggested to aid in resolving the problem in Silesia. He along with Ratti definitely favored having the plebiscite vote take place very soon so that there would be less opportunity for political influences coming from either German or Polish sources outside the region. The Pontiff also stated that he favored counting the votes *en bloc*, for the entire area, rather than by communes, as specified in the treaty, so as to maintain the unity of the region. The Germans in Rome once more requested that data about Polish influence in Upper Silesia be sent by Berlin as soon as possible so that it could be presented to the Secretary of State. Praschma felt that German diplomats, aided by such statistical and factual reports, would then reinforce the good impression already made and eventually win the Holy See's support for Germany's viewpoint.[26]

Berlin decided against massive propaganda within Silesia, where it considered a majority of the populace pro-German, who would vote in favor of remaining part of the Reich. Moreover, Berlin relied heavily on the advice of Prince Hermann von Hatzfeldt, the German Commissioner for the plebiscite area, who stressed that the Church's attitude was crucial for the vote. As opposed to other disputed territories, such as Eupen-Malmédy, where the outcome was less certain, in Silesia Germany had every hope of winning. It all depended on whether the clergy was more pro-Polish or pro-German. Until the summer of 1920 there had been no marked moves within the area for an ecclesiastical separation of the territory from Breslau. Hatzfeldt, therefore, did not regard it as opportune to organize any German rallies or demonstrations to protest political transfer of the area to Poland, since this might awaken anti-German sentiments and encourage counterdemonstrations. Without the participation and approval of the Bishop any such rally would be ill-timed, for Bertram was against any demonstration which might create further tension in the area and cause the curtailment of his ecclesiastical jurisdiction.[27]

Meanwhile the Vatican Commissioner had already begun to take up his new duties. On June 13 Ratti issued a letter reminding all Silesians as Catholics "to endeavor to understand the position of the other side

[26] AA, PO II, PO 24 Vat., Vol. 1, Praschma and Bergen to AA, May 31, 1920.
[27] AA, PO II, PO 24 Vat., Vol. 1, Hatzfeldt to AA, July 1, 1921.

and to remember that, Poles or Germans, they were all Catholics and the Holy Father considered all of them to be his children." The letter most probably had little effect in changing anyone's mind, but it did indicate the Curia's attempt to be fair.[28] Nevertheless the Nuncio's presence in the plebiscite area began to be viewed as a potential plus factor for both sides. The French Chargé at the Vatican, Jean Doulcet, believed Ratti pro-Polish and that his reports would be of use to the Polish, Belgian, and French missions in Rome in countering Berlin's influence.[29] The Germans hoped that a commissioner in the area would realize the importance of retaining Breslau's rights if he were impartial, which they had no real grounds to doubt, and would assist the German mission in Rome. Bergen sustained this analysis by stating that in the first few weeks after taking up his duties Ratti had not acted in any way contrary to German interests.[30]

The problem of the jurisdictional rights of the local ordinary and the relation of the Church to the plebiscite decision developed into a heated political and diplomatic issue. In June, Bertram requested permission from the Inter-Allied Commission to travel into Upper Silesia to consecrate a church and to confirm a group of children. The authorities denied his request. Given the circumstances of the upcoming plebiscite, they believed it would be better if the Cardinal remained away, for his presence might lead to demonstrations in favor of Germany. Bertram wrote the Nuncio asking for his assistance, but Ratti replied in July that despite his intercession with the Commission nothing could be done and that he, Ratti, as well as the Holy Father now recommended a policy of *quieta non movere.*[31]

Bertram was hurt and frustrated by the refusal and the implication that he had not been impartial and too closely identified with the German cause and that his presence in Silesia on purely pastoral matters would cause pro-German demonstrations. Bertram again wrote to Ratti indicating that the "very devoted tone" which the Nuncio took in dealing with the Inter-Allied Commission could be received only most unhappily in German circles. At the same time he justified his conduct as leader of his flock. True, he explained, as early as 1919 he had made it clear that he would deplore the separation of Upper Silesia from Germany with its population and valuable mineral wealth. No one would understand if he, the bishop of the area and a German, had said otherwise. Yet he had also allowed freedom of choice in the coming election for laity and clergy alike and specifically ordered the

[28] Francis Sugrue, *Popes in the modern world* (New York, 1961), p. 172.
[29] FFO, Pologne 58, Doulcet to FFO, April 21, 1920.
[30] AA, PO II, PO 24 Vat., Vol. 1, Bergen to AA, June 10, 1920.
[31] AW, 1A 250, 28, Ratti to Bertram, July 12, 1920.

clergy to refrain from political activities in the churches or in their pastoral work, and to show moderation, love, and concern for all persons regardless of their viewpoints. Well aware of his episcopal responsibilities and the reality of the situation created by the Versailles Treaty, he had published these guidelines in a proclamation that he had sent to his clergy on June 24, 1919. Bertram also rejected the suggestion which had been made to him after the Commission had denied him entry that Ratti represent him in his episcopal functions in Upper Silesia. This would result in exactly the situation he wished to prevent—the diminution of the ordinary's legitimate rights—and would encourage people to believe that the area was to be separated from Breslau. The suggestion alone, he stated, "had given cause for most unpleasant rumors and interpretations on the Polish side."[32] Obviously he was insulted and angered by the questioning of his impartiality, the erosion of his control over his diocese, and the curtailment of his right to minister to his people on political grounds. Perhaps even worse, in his opinion, the Nuncio was not supporting him more energetically.

On July 12 he turned to the German Foreign Office for support, requesting Berlin to protest to Rome on his behalf about the Nuncio's acceptance of an invitation by the Polish clergy to visit two pilgrimage centers in Upper Silesia, which Bertram feared would be portrayed by the Poles as an indication of Ratti's support for Warsaw and would only embitter the Germans against Rome. He believed that Ratti meant well but was not fully aware of all the implications of his actions in the complicated situation. He desired the Vatican to caution him, but since the matter had taken on more political than religious overtones, he preferred to have Berlin take up the matter with the Holy See. Meanwhile, Hatzfeldt in Upper Silesia had also raised Bertram's case with the Inter-Allied Commission as an example of discrimination against the Cardinal as a German national. He consulted the president of the Commission, French General Le Rond, and Ratti himself and was unsuccessful in receiving a favorable reply from either. The Nuncio informed him that

> it is best if, during a time of extreme tension, he not come to Upper Silesia; in fact his trip to Upper Silesia would give cause for German nationalist demonstrations. The Pope has said that spiritual matters which could afford delay could be put off until after the plebiscite. In pressing matters his nuncio could look after the situation.

[32] AW, 1A 250, 28, Bertram to AA, July 12, 1920; Bertram to Prussian Minister of Education and Religious Affairs, July 18, 1920.

The lack of success with the Commission, and Ratti's reason for not doing more confirmed Bertram's fears. It indicated an erosion of his authority, causing resentment in Berlin and remonstrances at the Vatican. Berlin reported Ratti's comments to the Curia and requested that Rome instruct the Nuncio not to interfere in the duties of the Bishop and to confirm, now as before, that Bertram was entitled to carry out all of his ecclesiastical functions in Upper Silesia.[33]

The German feeling of indignation was not directed at first against Ratti himself but arose from a suspicion that his position as nuncio to Warsaw, his believed sympathy for the Poles, and the support and affection which the Poles extended him were being employed by Warsaw and Paris as a counterbalance in Upper Silesia to the German Bertram. Berlin feared that some of Ratti's less than prudent statements of affinity for the Poles or his willingness to cooperate with the Allied authorities could be misinterpreted. For example, upon arriving to take up his duties in Upper Silesia, Ratti had called himself the "humble colleague" (*umile collaboratore*) of the members of the Inter-Allied Commission, dominated by the French. This phrase, to anyone unfamiliar with the Italian language and its polite and courtly diplomatic expression, sounded very accommodating and worked upon the emotions of many Germans in an already excitable situation and resulted in a distrust and disappointment on the part of many of the German-speaking population of the region toward the Papal delegate. This in turn caused Ratti to lean more heavily on Polish sources for his information. The attitude on the part of the Germans was understandable but unfortunate, for, as was later proved, German suspicions of his pro-Polish attitude were exaggerated. In fact, the Germans afterward learned that, when the plan for the partition of Silesia was presented, Ratti supported the border suggested by the Italian member of the Commission, General Alberto De Marinis, which would have assigned the entire industrial sector to Germany. But Ratti's initial moves to keep all sides content and prevent unrest did not dissipate German uneasiness and caused many Silesians to react coldly or with reserve toward him.[34]

On July 20 Bergen received a formal statement from the Pope confirming the authority of the Breslau ordinary, announcing that Ratti would be cautioned about his statements, and promising that the Vatican would undertake measures to see that Bertram received permis-

---

[33] AA, BRV 404, Vol. 1, memorandum, "Papst Pius XI als hoherkirchlicher Kommissar für die Abstimmungen Oberschlesien," arrival date February 28, 1922, pp. 2, 5.
[34] *Ibid.*

sion to visit the area.[35] Ratti, as even Bertram observed, meant well, but he was new at his post and new to diplomatic work in general. In his attempt to be impartial he had failed to realize that his cooperation with the Commission had caused the Germans to raise the counter-protest that unwittingly he was discriminating against them and by not supporting Bertram he was indirectly rendering aid to the Poles. It was the direct protest on legal and political grounds by the German Government which caused the Vatican to caution Ratti about his diplomacy. Mindful of the concordat proceedings about to take place in Germany, supplied with German arguments about the situation, Rome had perhaps a better overview of what constituted impartiality. It never wavered in allowing the ordinary to fulfill his normal ecclesiastical functions. The crisis over Ratti's actions passed by; however, to the suspicious Germans, the incident proved once more the importance of vigilance in ecclesiastical politics for the sake of national interests, the need for sympathetic churchmen in Rome, and the necessity that Ratti, still Nuncio to Poland as well as Commissioner in Silesia, be watched closely lest he view all matters through a Polish optic.

The situation was developing not only on diplomatic and ecclesiastic levels. Tensions had been mounting in Upper Silesia throughout 1920, and skirmishes between Germans and Poles had been reported throughout the year. Both Ratti and Bertram had agreed on the great danger of an armed conflict. Their analysis was correct. On August 18, 1920 a revolt urged by Polish agitators began, and bands of Poles roamed through the province, upsetting civil administration, disarming the local German police force, and dislocating all vestiges of local German control. The Commission was able to restore authority in the area only by autumn. On August 31 Bertram had issued a plea to his flock in both German and Polish to restore order and to keep aware of Christian principles. Meanwhile, Polish language newspapers such as the *Gazeta Opolska* in Oppeln and the *Sztandar Polski* of Gleiwitz carried articles questioning the Nuncio's reluctance to assume a more determined anti-German stand and Ratti's failure to inquire more fully from pro-Polish partisans about their opinions on the situation.[36] Both sides were attacking the Nuncio's neutrality. Ratti in good conscience, however, felt that he did not wish to risk further outbreaks of violence nor to show partiality either by paying undue heed to Polish complaints or by urging Bertram to enter the area.

[35] AW, 1A 250, 29, Behrendt (AA) to Prussian Minister of Ed. and Relig. Affairs, September 14, 1920. FFO, Pologne 58, Le Rond to FFO, December 5, 1920.

[36] AW, 1A 250, 35, *Gazeta Opolska*, Nr. 217, October 9, 1920; *Sztandar Polski*, Nr. 237, October 14, 1920 in memorandum of Friedrich Ritter von Lama, "Die römische Kurie und Oberschlesien," pp. 13-14.

Despite Ratti's attempt at impartiality, German feelings of lack of confidence in the Nuncio continued to increase, and Prince Hatzfeldt echoed them in his reports to the Foreign Office. On October 5, a meeting between German and Polish Upper Silesian priests took place in Beuthen with the purpose of moderating rancor or excessive nationalistic sentiment among the clergy. The Germans requested that no clergyman be permitted to deliver a public speech in a parish without approval of the local pastor lest a clerical visitor undermine the local priest's authority. But since many of the pastors in the area were German, the Poles believed there would be little chance of many Polish visitors receiving this permission. No consensus could be reached. Instead the Polish contingent declared openly that the clergy's attitude would greatly influence the plebiscite result; therefore they were not willing to renounce the right to bring in priests from outside the diocese to speak in Catholic parishes. In other words, political issues were going to be won by religious means. Hatzfeldt confirmed the presence of a large number of foreign priests, particularly members of Polish religious orders, in the area. When presented with these facts, the only action the Nuncio took was to promise that if a priest was found in the area without permission of the bishop and for political purposes, his permission to celebrate Mass would be withdrawn. This might be serious ecclesiastical punishment, complained Hatzfeldt, but it did not take into account the political realities of the situation. Ratti, who was overworked, had had to return frequently to Warsaw to attend to matters there and had not been present in Silesia enough to keep abreast of all the developments. The Prince formally requested that Germany ask the Vatican to forbid these priests from entering the area and promised further to supply the names of these clergymen as soon as possible. He ended his report by remarking that more than thirty years before Leo XIII had told him: "The Poles are used to putting religion in the service of politics," and that he believed that the present situation seemed to lend credence to the former Pope's statement.[37]

Hatzfeldt's judgment of Ratti, implying disinterest or lack of sympathy for impartiality, was perhaps too severe. The Nuncio was absent from the plebiscite area during the month when the very existence of the Polish state was in doubt and the Soviet army was advancing on Warsaw. The Nuncio courageously remained at his post in the capital despite the departure of many other diplomats. Had Warsaw fallen, then the Upper Silesian plebiscite might have been superfluous. Under the circumstances the Nuncio could not have been expected to consider his Silesian assignment more important than his work in the

---

[37] AA, PO II, PO 24 Vat., Vol. 1, Hatzfeldt to AA, October 7, 1920.

Polish capital—yet no allowance was made for the existing situation nor was there even mention of it in the German reports.

Besides the arguments of German diplomats in Rome, another method for the Reich to counter any possible adverse impressions relayed to the Vatican by Ratti was through the office of Nuncio Pacelli in Germany. Bertram was not slow in sending Pacelli detailed accounts of the difficulties in his diocese, along with documents about the conditions there and requests for Vatican support for his position. The French too recognized Pacelli as an important source of information forwarded to Curial officials, who regarded his opinion highly. But just as the Germans suspected Ratti of being pro-Polish, the French believed Pacelli to be strongly pro-German. In fact, the French Foreign Minister warned his diplomats that they must speak to him only with extreme caution. The Nuncio had frankly stated to the French representative in Bavaria his attitude about Upper Silesia and candidly hoped to see Germany win there, since a transfer of the area to Polish control would diminish the Center Party in the Reichstag by the loss of its Silesian members. From such statements the French concluded that Pacelli was stressing the importance of Vatican support for the Reich in his reports to the Curia and would be of little help to them in settling the problems of Germany's eastern border or, for that matter, in assisting to detach areas from the Reich on the left bank of the Rhine.[38] But in addition to the reasons for German retention of the area put forth by Bertram about his legal rights and those of Pacelli about the loss of Center influence in the Reich, after the Russo-Polish conflict of 1920 the Germans introduced a third argument. If Upper Silesia became Polish and there was a renewal of the recent Soviet-Polish fighting, the Soviets would surely seek to occupy, and, if they won, retain this industrial area, and this would result in a loss of a million Catholics to Bolshevism.[39] German officials raised this danger directly to the Curial prelates and also with Pacelli, who probably supported the validity of their analysis as he passed it on to Rome. It was undoubtedly taken quite seriously, given the Vatican's fear of Communism.

On October 13 Bertram received word from Gasparri once more reconfirming his jurisdiction in the area. Having studied the case, the Vatican explained that the Poles had assumed that Ratti had more authority than he had been granted. Statements made to this effect were in error, such as a comment made by the Polish Prime Minister to the Polish member of the Inter-Allied Commission on October 11

[38] FFO, Rive Gauche du Rhin 103, Foreign Minister to Doulcet, January 12, 1921.
[39] Campbell, 371.

indicating that Ratti was ecclesiastically responsible for the territory, and newspaper reports indicating that Bertram no longer had ecclesiastical jurisdiction over Upper Silesia but that authority had been transferred to the Nuncio. Wojciech Korfanty, leader of the pro-Polish insurgents, had succeeded in having articles placed in the Silesian papers inaccurately announcing that Gasparri had given Ratti permission to exercise jurisdiction over Upper Silesia and to take any ecclesiastical measures, including the naming and transferring of priests, which he considered necessary for assuring a fair plebiscite.[40] Naturally such statements caused confusion among the Catholics—both clergy and laity—in the area.

The Secretary of State now corrected these interpretations and explained how they had possibly begun. Most probably, continued Gasparri, the misunderstanding was at first due to the fact that the political officials were unaware of the terminology of canon law in reading the Curial instructions to the Nuncio, and later the press picked up the story and elaborated on it. However, Ratti, said Gasparri, was carrying out his mission as requested, and the Cardinal Secretary of State asked for Bertram's understanding in the matter and requested that he not judge Ratti by newspaper accounts or erroneous reports.[41] Gasparri's reply was a tacit concession that Ratti had perhaps not fully understood the political importance of all his actions and had gone a little too far in allowing Poland to make propagandistic capital out of his statements and actions. At the same time it was the Vatican's method of keeping an even hand in the situation. The German newspapers printed parts of Gasparri's reply in an effort to clarify this ecclesiastical misunderstanding, but ironically its publication was also a piece of political fuel which could now be used to support the German side.

One week later Gasparri also informed Berlin that Rome supported Bertram's condemnation of violence in Upper Silesia and the manner in which Bertram was handling the situation. In addition, the Cardinal Secretary of State promised to remind Kowalski that the purpose of Bertram's trip there was to deal with spiritual matters in an area where he still retained full episcopal power. Moreover, the Vatican would use its influence with the Inter-Allied Commission to obtain a travel pass for the Cardinal.[42] On the basis of Gasparri's public statements and what they learned in conversation with diplomats, French officials believed that Rome had made a policy decision, probably instructing

[40] AW, 1A 250, 35, memorandum of Lama, p. 13ff.

[41] AW, 1A 250, 29, Gasparri to Bertram, October 13, 1920.

[42] AW, 1A 250, 29, Gasparri to Simons (AA), October 20, 1920; Simons to Bertram, October 29, 1920.

Ratti to obtain satisfaction for Breslau's Cardinal and for the German viewpoint. General Le Rond felt that Ratti had become less sympathetic to the French-Polish position. In November Ratti informed the Commission of the Vatican's categorical recognition of the rights of the Bishop over the territory, which in turn *ipso facto* acknowledged his right of entry.[43]

The reports of Pacelli and the German mission in Rome had without doubt influenced Gasparri's decision, but the statements made by Polish officials, such as the one of October 11 overstating the role which Ratti was to play in Upper Silesia, apparently caused the Vatican promptly to define the rights of Cardinal Bertram and to indicate that Rome was not expressly in favor of or partial to Poland. Therefore, Ratti received instructions to request formally of the Inter-Allied Commission that Bertram be allowed to visit Upper Silesia. Gasparri's statement was interpreted as meaning that the Vatican clearly did not share the viewpoint of Le Rond or of Ratti that Bertram's presence would be inflammatory and detrimental to peace and stability.[44] The Vatican had ruled in favor of the ordinary, which, according to canon law, was legally the correct thing to do, but because of the involvement of the politicians and the press it appeared as if the Vatican now had decided in favor of the Reich.

Despite the concessions won in October, Bertram was not able to make his visitation to Upper Silesia, and the Germans continued to voice lack of confidence in Ratti. In early November Hatzfeldt wrote to Berlin that Bertram and Ratti were by no means closer in their views about the Cardinal's rights than before, and the Prince felt it was even impossible to talk to the Nuncio about the matter. "A second conversation strengthened my opinion that we will never find the slightest support from this man. He is a typical diplomat of the Middle Ages, . . . he holds a monologue—even with the Cardinal—and in every sentence there is a 'but.' For example: 'Certainly it is my duty to support the Cardinal's jurisdiction, but if the Inter-Allied Commission says his entry [into the area] would cause disturbances, and it must maintain law and order, what should I do then?' " Hatzfeldt also entertained the idea of requesting Ratti's recall but thought that the proceedings would take too long to be of use. He added that perhaps it might be worth suggesting that the Curia appoint a special representative to the Commission for Upper Silesia—a suggestion that was

[43] FFO, Pologne 58, Le Rond to FFO, December 5, 1920.
[44] AW, 1A 250, 30, Haniel to Prussian Minister of Ed. and Relig. Affairs, November 2, 1920.

later followed.[45] A memorandum of the Foreign Office in November echoed the disappointment with Ratti. Theoretically both the Nuncio and the Curia acknowledged Bertram's jurisdiction, but since the Commission had not granted him permission to enter, the Foreign Office had come to believe that the Nuncio was not providing sufficient representation for the Cardinal. Berlin feared that the Silesian populace would view the restrictions on Bertram as a sign of Germany's inability to undertake any strong diplomatic action and as an indication that the Curia was partial to Poland, one of the winners at Versailles.[46]

By mid-November the situation had reached an impasse. The Commission, under pressure from Germany and the Vatican to permit Bertram to enter the area, while not expressly refusing, hesitated to grant the request unless it was assured the visit would not disturb the peace. Korfanty, agitator and head of a group of extremely pro-Polish Silesians, had been campaigning against the German Government and had been masterfully making use of the loyalty of the Poles to the Catholic Church with such slogans as "Being Catholic means being Polish."[47] He had also launched a protest movement against the Cardinal, whom he claimed was a German nationalist using his intended visit to the area for political ends. Korfanty's forces threatened demonstrations should the Cardinal arrive. The German Foreign Office conceded that, although it believed Ratti personally pro-Polish, he had tried to reach a settlement agreeable to both sides. But now, with the threat of demonstrations and violence, Ratti would have more grounds for not pressing the Cardinal's cause more vigorously. To complicate the issue further the Foreign Office noted that the German element in the area, fearing and annoyed by the pro-Polish, anti-Bertram activities of Korfanty and the Poles, was making the mistake of turning to the other extreme—proclaiming the nationalistic and political value of the Cardinal's trip, even soliciting the aid of German non-Catholics by using this argument. This, in turn, the Poles used to support their argument and incite further violence and disorders.[48]

The matter might have gone on with protests and counterprotests from Church and government authorities until the plebiscite, had not other events given the affair a curious turn and deepened the bitterness over the situation. Violence had become endemic in the area by autumn 1920. In addition to a propaganda campaign, both sides engaged

[45] AA, PO II, PO 24 Vat., Vol. 1, Hatzfeldt to AA, November 8, 1920. Campbell, 369.

[46] AA, PO II, PO 24 Vat., Vol. 1, memorandum of AA, November 13, 1920.

[47] Campbell, 368.

[48] AA, PO II, PO 24 Vat., Vol. 1, Delbrück (AA) to Simson, January 12, 1921.

in demonstrations, street fights, and shootings. In September, Germany had made a formal request to the Commission to close the border to Upper Silesia from Poland since Polish fighters as well as quantities of ammunition were coming into the area. Moreover, Germany declared that the French troops in Silesia were shutting their eyes to these incursions. Bergen was instructed to give full information to the Vatican on this matter and to seek its support.[49] On October 21 Bertram had written to Pacelli deploring the violence and chaos in the plebiscite area and condemning the work of outside agitators. Although not extolling the Germans as guiltless, the Cardinal found the Poles to be in general more fanatical and prepared to go to violent means to reach their goals. He stated that Polish agitators were constantly undermining the authority of the Breslau ordinary by continually telling the people that spiritual authority in the area rested with the Nuncio and that this arrangement had the approval of the Holy Father. Given the circumstances, Bertram concluded that the Nuncio's statements lacked sufficient strength to maintain the Vatican's impartiality here. Therefore, he proposed to issue another pastoral letter to ensure that the clergy refrain from politics. To make certain that no misunderstanding occurred this time in the lines of communication with Rome, Bertram requested that Pacelli submit an outline of his statement to Gasparri for the Curia's approval before he issued it.[50]

Bertram's resolve was further bolstered by petitions from his clergy, who reported that the influx of non-diocesan priests had grown larger. The clergy, especially in Silesia, had always been regarded by the faithful as advisors in political as well as religious affairs. Most of the diocese and clergy had observed the Bishop's instructions of June 1919 which permitted both clergy and laity complete freedom of choice in the upcoming election but forbade the use of Church functions as an occasion to raise this question. Nevertheless, some of the clergy had disagreed with the Bishop's orders and regarded the plebiscite question as having religious or at least ecclesiastical ramifications and in conscience spoke out on the matter from the pulpit. The action of these priests resulted in dissension in various parishes between pro-Polish and pro-German factions and animosity against the priest and against the Church whose representative he was. In some cases, seeing the damage which this question was causing the Church, some diocesan priests had ceased to discuss the question altogether. But now it

[49] Erdmann, *Kabinett Fehrenbach*, joint session of Reich and Prussian Cabinets, September 6, 1920, pp. 158-159.

[50] AW, 1A 250, 29, Bertram to Pacelli, October 21, 1920; Pacelli to Bertram, November 2, 1920.

appeared that many visiting priests from Poland were taking the opportunity to preach or to discuss the plebiscite issue and to urge separation from the Reich. One letter to Bertram from several pastors, for example, presented a list of twenty-eight names and the place of origin of the non-diocesan priests working in the area and stated that this was by no means all of them. There was no evidence that local church authorities had called them in. Many came for a few days and then moved on to other parishes. They spoke on political matters, yet wore their priestly habit in order to make a favorable impression on the laity and give credence to the belief that the plebiscite was also a religious matter and that the Church endorsed Poland. They did not say Mass or hear confessions; when asked why, they answered that because of their pro-Polish stance the Bishop had not permitted them to do so, thus causing the laity to resent Bertram's alleged action and to suspect him of using his office to support the pro-German faction. The simple folk did not differentiate between diocesan and non-diocesan priests, between ecclesiastic duties and private activities of the clergy; they saw only the priest in front of them and accepted his statements as ecclesiastically mandated. Some Breslau priests suspected that Polish prelates were granting priests leaves of absence to work in Upper Silesia. The pastors therefore called their Cardinal's attention to this matter and requested that he take measures to stop this agitation.[51]

In view of the unrest Bertram issued his episcopal edict on November 25, stating that because of the numerous complaints and disorders, "after careful negotiations with the Holy Apostolic See" by virtue of his authority and with the approval of the Holy See, all clergy of whatever nationality in the plebiscite area were expressly forbidden to participate in political demonstrations or to hold political speeches without permission of the competent Church authorities; all non-diocesan clergy were forbidden from political activities with or without consent of the parish priest under penalty of suspension. Bertram added that "the fact that the Holy See has authorized me in a special rescript drawn up on its own initiative, ... is striking proof of the importance which the highest authority of the Church attaches to this injunction."[52]

Bertram's prohibition could be viewed as a method of ensuring his control over his diocese and as a means of demonstrating the Church's impartiality by preventing priests of either ethnic group from engaging

---

[51] AW, 1A 250, 29, Pastors Tylla, Kubis, *et alii* to Bertram, arrived on November 4, 1920.

[52] BFO, 371/4822, Verordnungen des Fürstbischöflichen General-Vikariat-Amtes zu Breslau, Nr. 682, November 25, 1920.

in politics. The reaction in the Polish *Sejm*, or Parliament, was to view it in just the opposite manner, to see only the practical results of his move. Since approximately seventy-five percent of the parish priests in the province were German, the Poles naturally regarded the Cardinal's order as a handicap to their activities in the weeks before the vote and as a deliberate attempt to downgrade the Polish cause.[53] The *Sejm* introduced motions to try to block the implementation of the edict and to pressure Rome into separating Upper Silesia from the diocese of Breslau immediately. There were even threats of breaking diplomatic relations with the Vatican unless the Curia complied. Numerous organizations and clubs throughout Poland protested the edict, and the Polish hierarchy as a group also sent a strong condemnatory letter to the Vatican. On this question all political parties were united. Overnight Ratti had become unpopular—he was accused of not having used all in his power to protect Polish interests in Rome. As an article in Warsaw's *Kurjer Poranny* stated, the fear was growing that the Vatican had now opted for Germany, thus shattering Polish political hopes. Suddenly long-dormant suspicions, many of which had been disproved, reappeared—Benedict was never really friendly to Poland, Germany contributed more to Peter's Pence and consequently received more favors, etc. Circumstantial evidence was then cited from specific events during both the wartime and post-war periods to substantiate these assumptions.

In order to urge the Vatican to reconsider its view, the Prince-Bishop of Cracow, Adam Sapieha, and the Armenian-rite Archbishop of Lwów (Lemberg) departed for Rome.[54] The Polish Government had already protested against the edict by sending messages to the Nuncio, the Inter-Allied Commission, and the Polish Minister at the Vatican. One could have said until then that Ratti's actions had angered only the Germans. Yet all this was forgotten by December 1920, and the Poles now accused him of not having presented the Polish position forcefully enough with the Curia so as to block Bertram's moves.[55] Only Ratti himself, in an ironical mood, expressed belief that the Vatican's policy of supporting the local ordinary and remaining neutral by keeping the clergy out of political embroilment had been correct and that he also had been impartial—that he was there in Upper Silesia to represent Church interests, not to identify himself with any party. As he commented, "When only the Germans were against me, I did not know whether I was on the right track, but when the Poles

[53] BFO, 371/4821/5279, Loraine (Warsaw) to Curzon, December 2, 1920.

[54] AA, PO II, PO 24 Vat., Vol. 1, Dirksen (Warsaw) to AA, December 14, 1920.

[55] AA, PO II, PO 24 Vat., Vol. 1, Dirksen to AA, December 1, 4, 1920.

also expressed their feelings against me, I was certain I was doing the right thing."[56]

Now the Germans had to ensure that pressure on the Vatican did not result in a reversal of Bertram's edict. The Cardinal requested the Foreign Office to take steps to protest the Polish tactics against him. He personally did not desire to engage in a press polemic with the Polish hierarchy but felt himself attacked, first by inaccuracies which accused him of acting without the support of the Vatican and second by statements that his edict was a political move directed solely against the Poles. He explained in emphatic terms to Berlin that he had sent a sketch of his proposed statement to Rome via Pacelli and had received explicit approval. His censure of political activities by clerics applied to Germans as well as to Poles. His jurisdiction had been confirmed for the area, the diocesan borders were still intact in accordance with the Papal Bull of 1821; consequently, in good conscience he maintained that he had been perfectly within his rights to issue such a proclamation. Finally, with a sign of exasperation, he requested the German representative at the Vatican respectfully to remind Gasparri that in matters dealing with Upper Silesia and the plebiscite Rome should not rely solely on reports from its Nuncio in Poland but should also seek the opinion of Nuncio Pacelli.[57] Bertram no doubt felt that on the basis of developments so far the Vatican was generally inclined to realize the validity of the Breslau and German position and had merely to continue receiving the correct information in order to make just decisions.

Caught between its attempt at impartiality, its endorsement of Breslau's claims, which unavoidably indicated support for Germany, and the bitter resentment of the Poles, the Vatican took steps to calm the situation in December 1920 by removing Upper Silesia from Ratti's jurisdiction and appointing Msgr. Giovanni Ogno Serra, attaché at the Vatican nunciature in Vienna, to the post of special Papal representative to the area. Three months later Ratti was relieved of his duties in Poland as well. Benedict, after reviewing the activities of his Nuncio, found no grounds for the accusation of partiality. But perhaps in removing him from his post here the Pontiff was to some degree agreeing with the German view that Ratti, because of circumstances and his inexperience, had not been the ideal person for the post. During the last months of Ratti's mission to Poland his popularity had seriously declined, primarily because of the events in Upper Silesia, where he was blamed for not having blocked Bertram's decree. Most proba-

---

[56] Sugrue, p. 173.

[57] AA, PO II, PO 24 Vat., Vol. 1, memorandum of AA, December 5, 1920.

bly the incident was as much responsible for his recall from his War-saw post and his appointment as Archbishop of Milan in March 1921 as the fact that the see had become vacant.[58] The French speculated that the reason for the action which the Vatican had taken all during the crisis in Upper Silesia was that the Curia at first saw its interests best served by favoring Poland and so appointed its Nuncio to War-saw to supervise the plebiscite region too. When it learned, however, that the great majority of the clergy sympathized with Germany (French sources stated 80 percent), that the agitation was causing disturbances and division within the local church, and that Polish misunderstand-ings about the role of the Nuncio were interfering with good relations between Warsaw and Rome, the Vatican began to rethink its strat-egy.[59]

While the French conjectures were in large degree correct and had played a role in Curia thinking, there were other reasons for the Vat-ican move in December. True, Poland, a new and Catholic state, was applying pressure on the Curia. The Vatican, also aware that France supported Poland, was in the process of resuming diplomatic relations with Paris and consequently remained circumspect lest a false step wreck the negotiations. But, on the other hand, the Germans also had been pressuring Rome for some time with their demands. Since Ber-tram still had not received permission to enter the plebiscite area, Bergen had been instructed in late November once more to remon-strate and seek the action which the Vatican had promised. Since Rome had affirmed Bertram's rights, Bergen concluded that the reason for difficulties was the original Vatican error of appointing Ratti, an inexperienced diplomat, rather than Pacelli to oversee this perplexing situation. When Under Secretary of State Cerretti promised Bergen that Ratti would be given more specific statements on how to conduct himself and ordered to press once more for Bertram's entry permit, the Ambassador expressed doubt that Ratti would be more effective than before, and suggested that he be recalled. Cerretti rejected this request inasmuch as the Nuncio's work in Poland as a whole had been satisfactory and did not justify this reprimand. After many interviews and discussions with the aid of other German representatives in Rome, Bergen was able to persuade the Vatican that since Ratti was not *persona grata* at the moment in either Warsaw or Berlin, it should ap-point someone of lower rank, such as Msgr. Ogno Serra, to take up the position in Upper Silesia and report directly to the Vatican. Ber-gen had also informed Berlin that the possibility of eventually remov-

[58] Binchy, p. 77. Schmidlin, Vol. 4, p. 15.
[59] FFO, Allemagne 370, Doulcet to FFO, December 5, 1920.

ing Ratti from Warsaw was good, for the see of Milan would soon be vacant, and he intended to suggest the Nuncio for the post.[60]

In addition, Gasparri himself was having grave doubts about extending undue support to Polish claims, for he expressed misgivings about Poland's recent expansionist policies then embittering its relations with all of its neighbors. The Cardinal Secretary feared that an overly aggressive Poland by means of unwise policies might cause its own destruction, and all that this Catholic state had accomplished in the past few years would go for naught. Gasparri had consulted Warsaw on many occasions since 1918 about what he considered were unwise, ultra-nationalistic, expansionist policies that led Poland into territorial disputes with Russia, Czechoslovakia, Lithuania, and Germany. Thus he feared that the unrest in Silesia was part of this aggressive strategy which had won endorsement in Warsaw and which would only hinder good relations between the Reich and Poland. In his opinion, Poland could exist only with the support of its eastern or western neighbors. No help could be expected from Soviet Russia; therefore it seemed all the more senseless to him for Warsaw willfully to destroy the bridges to the west and damage the Reich in its most sensitive areas. Moreover, in assessing the European situation, he became convinced that Russia and Germany eventually would regain strength and would then engage in a continuing anti-Polish drive to regain the territory that they had lost to Poland, at which time Warsaw would have cause to regret its Upper Silesian policy. The Cardinal ended his brief diplomatic analysis with the prophetic words, "Poland will have to pay dearly for this if Germany recovers again."[61] The Cardinal's farsighted views again exemplified his perception of the future structure of power in Europe and Germany's position in it.

The storm which broke over Bertram's proclamation had caused Rome to calm the tense situation by creating the new post for Ogno Serra in Upper Silesia and by having him immediately issue a statement similar to Bertram's to the clergy by authority of the Holy See. It, however, forbade all political activities to the clergy, secular or religious, diocesan or visiting, so that no one could say that the edict would be of advantage to the Germans. In addition, the Holy See reaffirmed its support of Bertram despite Poland's demand for removal of Upper Silesia from the Breslau diocese, but in exchange Gasparri requested Bertram to defer his trip into the area.[62]

---

[60] AA, PO II, PO 24 Vat., Vol. 1, Bergen to AA, December 9, 1920. Ratti in fact did become Archbishop of Milan in June 1921.

[61] GSTA, MA 104446, Ritter to BFM, May 13, 1921. Engel-Janosi, *Chaos*, pp. 38-39. HHSTA, 87, Pastor to AFO, May 6, 1921.

[62] AW, 1A 250, 30, Gasparri to Bertram, December 8, 1920.

Behind the scenes, however, Gasparri, while basically supporting the German position, also reprimanded the German Cardinal on the handling of the situation. The phrasing of the November pastoral letter, said the Secretary, had harmed Germany's chances in the election, since it was now being used by Polish propagandists as proof that the local ecclesiastical administrators were biased and that Polish-speaking Catholics could be treated fairly only by the Polish hierarchy. The difficulty created over the edict, continued Gasparri, was a case study of what occurs when the lines of communication between the local ordinary and the Holy See break down. Church discipline had not been strictly observed. Rome had preferred to wait and see how the situation continued to develop before the Church made any statement. Bertram, however, decided to act and had gained Rome's agreement in principle to the outline for the edict. But, in Gasparri's opinion, Bertram unnecessarily stated that he had Papal authorization for his proclamation, and this in turn caused various repercussions for Vatican policy, as he pointed out from the pile of telegrams he had on his desk. Bertram's right to issue the statement was uncontested, but a prudent omission of mention of the Holy See would have permitted the Vatican to protect him against Polish accusations. It was now impossible to do anything more since Rome as well as Bertram was attacked. For Gasparri to make any further move to support Breslau or any German position would certainly confirm Poland's suspicions. The Reich had recently asked the Vatican for aid in convincing the Powers to grant the right to vote to all non-resident Silesians and in getting the plebiscite postponed so that these outvoters could have time to return for the balloting. Gasparri made a point of telling Bergen that because of Bertram's unwise statement, this request would now have to be refused. If Berlin needed the help of an international power it would have to seek such support from Great Britain. Now strict parity would be enforced—any exception in favor of one group, said the Secretary, would require an exception made for the other.[63]

In the seesaw maneuvers to gain Papal support, diplomats viewed the Vatican's move as a concession for Germany in removing Ratti but a victory for Poland in appointing Ogno Serra—in other words, as Gasparri had pointed out, a strict parity or concession to both sides. The French believed this to be the significance of the new appointment. The Quai d'Orsay acknowledged that the clergy would play a crucial role in the outcome of the election and that now Bertram's pro-German influence had been weakened by the Holy See's appointment

---

[63] AA, PO II, PO 24 Vat., Vol. 1, Bergen to AA, December 11, 1920. Campbell, 371.

of Ogno—though not to Ratti's post of religious commissioner but to the more authoritative one of apostolic commissioner. The clergy could interpret this, without the Polish Government's needing to express it and thus repeat Bertram's error of implicating the Holy See, as meaning that the Breslau Cardinal had been relieved of his powers in the area and that the Vatican was directly assuming control.[64] Even Bergen feared that the new appointment might bode ill for the Reich. Vatican officials one month later were still reminding him that, although agreeing in principal to Bertram's edict, the Vatican had not meant him to use such phrases in the proclamation as "by special Papal authorization" or "the Holy See has authorized me in a special rescript drawn up on its own initiative to say. . . ." In hindsight, Bergen was of the opinion that Bertram should have issued such an edict on his own episcopal authority long before he did so that matters would not have progressed this far. Now the Cardinal Secretary was decidedly displeased with him, and because of his failure to take more drastic action earlier, he had contributed to a potentially explosive situation, had injured Germany's interests, and complicated any attempts by German diplomats at the Vatican.[65]

Ogno's presence in Upper Silesia, however, did not mean, as the French and Poles hoped and as the Germans feared, that the Vatican had lost interest in hearing Germany's side of the case. In fact, the new envoy's conduct and analysis of the problem only helped the Germans. His reports to Rome mainly supported the Reich's complaints, and his move to discipline the clergy comported with Bertram's November edict. In December 1920, Ogno was even to have informed German officials in Vienna that as a known friend of Germany he had been selected for his assignment to counter Ratti's influence and to work with the German Government in obtaining a fair and just settlement.[66] The Reich was to be assured that despite momentary displeasure and the impossibility of formal Vatican diplomatic aid Rome was still concerned with Germany's fate. The Reich indeed was to have no reason to regret Ogno's appointment.

Ogno's imposition of a ban on all political activities for the clergy somewhat pacified the troubled area in the last days before the vote. France and Poland, realizing the implications of the ban, protested to the Vatican that it was too restrictive, for it impeded Polish propaganda and gave an edge to Germany. The Vatican, however, held to the view that the clergy should not become involved in politics and hence supported its envoy's stance. England was very pleased with

---

[64] FFO, Pologne 58, Peretti de la Rocca (FFO) to Doulcet, December 14, 1920.

[65] AA, PO II, PO 24 Vat., Vol. 1, Bergen to AA, December 14, 1920.

[66] AA, PO II, PO 24 Vat., Vol. 1, Rosenberg (Vienna) to AA, December 18, 1920.

the diminution of tension and of the propaganda campaign, instructing its representative in Rome, De Salis, to support the Vatican stand.[67] In March Msgr. Ogno Serra issued a pastoral letter confirming freedom of conscience of all to vote, condemning all misuse of religion for political purposes, and declaring that any past oaths to vote a particular way were in the eyes of the Church null and void.[68]

When the vote was taken on March 20, 1921, 98 percent of the qualified voters, which also included the outvoters, cast their ballots, with 707,488 in favor of Germany and 479,369 for Poland.[69] The Silesians had voted 60 percent for Germany and 40 percent for Poland. However the northern and western areas had voted overwhelmingly for Germany and the extreme southeast for Poland, while in the critical industrial region, where the population was ethnically mixed, the vote was more evenly divided (259,000 votes for Germany and 205,000 for Poland).[70] Therefore, in accordance with the powers which Versailles had given them, the Allies opted to divide Upper Silesia into two parts and not retain the area's unity, as the Germans had hoped. In the fall, after much discussion, the League, to which the decision had ultimately been referred, awarded the larger area in the north to Germany, with 51 percent of the inhabitants and 70 percent of the territory, while Poland received the remainder, which, however, included most of the industry and the mines. Although neither side was entirely happy, the political future had at least been settled.

Germany had worked hard to remind the Curia of its legal rights and to warn the Vatican of dangers for the upcoming concordat negotiations as well as for Catholicism in Germany should the area be assigned to Poland. The Vatican, as an impartial observer, had to maintain an even hand, but undoubtedly the restrictions placed on the clergy's participation in politics worked to the Reich's advantage, and Germany's arguments taken in the larger context of general church-state relations, as well as the question of its legal position in Upper Silesia, had no doubt contributed to the Vatican's decision. In addition, the new Poland's expansionist policies which took it in all directions, including against fellow Catholics in Lithuania and Germany, embarrassed and annoyed the Vatican, causing it to reject any thought

[67] BFO, 371/5889/5308, Percival to BFO, and cover note, February 20, 1921.

[68] On March 7, for example, Polish papers published a statement by the clergy of the great Polish shrine of Częstochowa, reminding the Silesians of the oath which many of them had taken to vote for Poland. *Germania*, March 13, 1921.

[69] The Supreme Council of the Allies, meeting in November 1920-February 1921 had endorsed a plan for the plebiscite to include outvoters and to be conducted on a single day in all of Upper Silesia. Wambaugh, *Plebiscites*, Vol. 1, pp. 242-243.

[70] See Wambaugh, *Plebiscites*, Vol. 1, pp. 249-251 and Vol. 2, pp. 246-247 for the voting statistics and an analysis of their meaning.

of closely associating itself with so nationalist a policy. In 1920 the French, through their Chargé d'Affaires at the Vatican,[71] had let it be known that France would have liked the Vatican to declare its support for Poland prior to the plebiscite. But the Vatican remained firm on its stated policy of neutrality and its ban on clerical involvement in politics. Warsaw had hoped to gain support for its position by making claims of specific acts of German oppression and violence in the area and thus prove that Poles would be able to practice their religion more freely within a Polish state. However, the Vatican refused to commit itself until it studied the matter. In 1920, when an Allied Commission appointed to investigate the charges found Poland's claims groundless, it only caused the Vatican to maintain a more cautious attitude and content itself by endorsing freedom of conscience and the right to vote. An indication of the Vatican's uneasiness with Polish policy was seen in an article in the *Osservatore* of August 14, 1920 stating that since the creation of the new Polish state the Vatican had continually advised Warsaw to moderate its interest in acquiring areas whose inhabitants were neither Poles nor wished to belong to Poland.[72]

True, the Vatican had no desire to choose between parties, both of which had large populations that vowed spiritual allegiance to the Holy See, and it understandably would be inclined to maintain its declared policy of neutrality. But neutrality, together with support from Rome for the rights of the Catholic hierarchy, worked only to Germany's advantage. The Curia had first waited to see how matters would fare; but once Bertram's claim was made clear to Rome and the damages which the loss of Upper Silesia would cause Catholic Germany made evident, once Ratti was replaced by the more energetic Ogno, with more explicit instructions from the Vatican on how to remove clerical interference in a political affair, the results benefited Germany. Msgr. Ogno Serra had enforced the ban on clerical participation in politics, which was impartial but just as strong as Bertram's. After the plebiscite and the fighting, which again erupted in May, he issued a stern reprimand to Polish priests who had participated in the armed conflict, and it was not surprising to see demands in the Polish press for Ogno's recall.[73] Perhaps Germany would have gained more toward winning Vatican intervention if Bertram had not complicated affairs by his edict of November 1920. But even with the Curia's statement requiring the clergy's abstention from politics Germany had every reason to

[71] France maintained a special mission at the Vatican for a brief period (1920-1921) until full diplomatic relations were resumed in May 1921.

[72] *Osservatore*, August 14, 1920.

[73] *Bayerische Staatszeitung und Bayerischer Staatsanzeiger*, August 13, 1921.

be satisfied, for Papal neutrality silenced for the pro-German Silesians one of their greatest foes—Polish priests entering the area.

But the plebiscite did not end the contest. More battles were still to be fought, and Germany believed that it still had to remain diplomatically vigilant. Immediately after the Allied decision for partition, Poland requested that either an independent diocese be created for Polish Silesia or that the area be incorporated into one of the existing Polish dioceses. The Curia refused these petitions, stating they were too precipitous, and instead appointed an apostolic administrator for Polish Silesia, which, while being governed separately, technically still belonged to the Breslau diocese. Warsaw then asked that the administrator be drawn from the local clergy, who would be given episcopal consecration. The Poles suggested Teodor Kubina for the post. The Germans, however, still believed that someday the international situation might offer an opportunity for the return of the area to the Reich. If, however, Church officials oriented both the clergy and laity to accept a total integration into the Polish ecclesiastical structure, curtailed opportunities for religious education in the German language for those desiring it, or cut off any ties between the area and the Church in Germany, it would make it all the more difficult for the Reich to regain popular support for its cause. Berlin had evidence of Kubina's activity as a pro-Polish nationalist prior to the plebiscite, and it regarded him as an agitator. The Foreign Office therefore categorically informed Pacelli that it would regard Kubina's appointment as an unfriendly act.

Berlin was also concerned that Kubina's appointment might be construed as a Vatican preference for Poland, which, in view of the sensitivity of all parties on this issue, would in turn arouse animosity in the German press and public against the Vatican. This could not only injure concordat negotiations but also damage general relations between the two governments to such an extent that Germany could not ask nor would the Vatican be inclined to act on behalf of the Reich in other pressing diplomatic matters. Moreover, the Foreign Office feared that the German public would regard such an appointment as confirmation that the new Pontiff, Pius XI, who had once been nuncio in Warsaw, was anti-German. If politicians and journalists continued to make such accusations about the Pontiff any time that an appointment displeasing to the Germans was made, it would be difficult to maintain good working relations between Berlin and Rome. The Foreign Office therefore used every means to have Kubina's appointment blocked.[74] At the Vatican Bergen worked against the appointment of a pro-Polish

[74] AA, PO II, PO 24 Vat., Vol. 6, Haniel to Hatzfeldt, July 8, 1922.

administrator, as did Cardinals Bertram and Schulte through letters to the Curia, and Nuncio Pacelli forwarded the German wish for the appointment of a neutrally oriented prelate to the post. It was considered so important that the Foreign Office even requested the Reich Chancellor personally to write to the Curia about the matter. But all of these moves had to be conducted with a degree of circumspection since the new Pontiff, known to be strong-willed, at times even obstinate, disliked being pressured in matters where he reserved the decision for himself. Later on in 1926, when a successor for the administrator of Tütz, an area along the Polish border, was being chosen, Bergen commented that Pius seemed to regard anything to do with Eastern Europe as his exclusive domain for which his work as nuncio in Warsaw had eminently qualified him.[75]

Indeed, despite Germany's efforts, Steinmann, consultor at the German Embassy at the Vatican, wrote to Bertram on June 18 that their campaign appeared unsuccessful. The Curia itself was inclined to listen to Germany's statements, but the Pope seemingly was leaning toward the Polish suggestion. He had known Kubina from his days in Poland and Silesia and, from his own knowledge of the man, believed him to be a good candidate. The Pontiff was warned of the storm that this appointment would arouse in Germany. Under Secretary of State Giuseppe Pizzardo informed Steinmann that he had used his personal influence on the Pontiff to delay a final decision, but believed that nothing more could be done to block Kubina's appointment.[76] But when the decision was announced it was not Kubina but the Salesian father, August Hlond, who was named to the post. Apparently the Pontiff reconsidered the strong objections which Germany had made and took the advice of his staff. More important, perhaps, had been the reports and arguments of Pacelli, who was alarmed about Kubina's selection and feared that it would endanger all his negotiations for a concordat in Germany. He emphasized the strong German dislike for Kubina's candidacy and most probably spelled out explicitly in his reports the deleterious effects which his selection would have for the Vatican's German policy. He also supported the German view that a more neutral individual be named.[77]

The selection of the Salesian Hlond was significant for several reasons. He had not been identified with any political activities and was therefore believed to be more moderate and accommodating than Kubina. Normally members of religious communities were not given such

[75] AA, Geheim Vat., Pol. 24, 25, 26, Bergen to AA, March 29, 1926.
[76] AA, BRV 180, Vol. 1, Steinmann to Bertram, June 18, 1922.
[77] AA, PO II, PO 24 Vat., Vol. 5, Nuncio to German Embassy (Vatican), May 9, 1922.

assignments, and such an appointee, who was responsible to the superior of his order based in Rome and not to the local hierarchy, would give the Polish Government less ability to exert pressure on Silesian affairs than if the new administrator had been drawn from the secular clergy. Hlond's nomination, in fact, was a diplomatic victory for Germany, since it neutralized Warsaw's strategy to secure the position for one of its own candidates.[78] In making the appointment, the Vatican conceded to Polish wishes for an independent administrator of Polish background, but interestingly enough Rome had not granted the new administrator episcopal rank, as it had done for Danzig, nor had it immediately agreed to create a new diocese for the territory after the vote was taken as in Eupen-Malmédy. The usual procedure in regulating Church control was to have ecclesiastical boundaries follow the political line, and Poland had every reason to expect that this would apply here also. The position of the administrator in Silesia had a more provisional character; his authority could be expanded or diminished as circumstances required. This reflected Vatican thinking about the international situation in general. Rome still believed that the political solution reached here, as in all the border areas of the east, might be provisional and that other changes might eventually occur. The Vatican had never been pleased with the results of Versailles, and throughout the 1920's its officials, from the Pope and the Cardinal Secretary of State down to lesser dignitaries, made negative remarks about the durability of the peace.[79] It was therefore understandable for Rome to delay total separation from Breslau of part of its territories until the Curia became sufficiently convinced that the settlement was permanent.

Many other factors might have led to the Vatican's delay in transferring jurisdiction to Poland. Rome knew very well that the ecclesiastical separation in 1921 of areas that were formerly German would cause resentment not only among German Catholics but among non-Catholics, whose votes would be necessary to have the concordat negotiations, then being discussed, win the approval of the legislature. Moreover, Rome was well informed about the violence, in part inspired by the Poles, which had occurred prior to the plebiscite. In May 1921, however, there had again been a serious outbreak of insurrection in Silesia, led by Korfanty with apparent complicity from Warsaw, whose object was to gain control over the area claimed by the Poles and thus present the Allies with a *fait accompli* before their

[78] AW, 1A 250, 32, Bergen to AA, November 23, 1922; Steinmann to Bertram, November 24, 1922.

[79] AW, 1A 250, 32, Steinmann to Bertram, June 18, 1922. See Engel-Janosi, *Chaos*, p. 36ff.

announcement of partition. The fighting between the Poles and Germans, including paramilitary forces which had come in from both Germany and Poland, was put down by July, but only after much violence and bloodshed. The Vatican strongly condemned the armed disorder and blamed Poland for having supported it. An immediate transfer of ecclesiastical control, the Vatican reasoned, might lead the populace and foreign observers to conclude that Rome approved Warsaw's support for the insurgents' actions. In addition, perhaps the Curia did not wish to grant any more jurisdictional power to a hierarchy which in late 1921 had been paternally admonished by Benedict for its overzealous patriotism. The Pontiff had forwarded a letter to the Polish episcopate which, while reaffirming his support for Poland and expressing understanding for its patriotism, gently warned against using the authority of religion in the service of politics. Trying to heal wounds, he urged the Polish clergy to support their episcopal and clerical colleagues even if they differed from one another in political outlook.[80] True, Warsaw was not pleased with the Vatican's advice here, but, as a new state with a population devoted to the Holy Father, Poland deemed it imprudent to alienate the Curia by showing its great displeasure. Besides, Poland like Germany hoped for Vatican aid in future situations, and the Vatican could always use Warsaw's diplomatic need as a bargaining point in its concordat negotiations with the Poles.

The plebiscite officially settled the Upper Silesian problem; yet the ecclesiastical reorganization still demanded attention. By 1924, however, Poland was growing impatient and applied increased pressure on Rome to have the diocesan boundaries conform to the political borders and to have a separate diocese created for Polish Silesia. Moreover, since Poland was negotiating a concordat with Rome, this was a difficult request for the Vatican to refuse. In addition, French officials, both civil and ecclesiastical, naturally manifested their support for Poland. On June 19, 1923, speaking in the French Senate, Poincaré underscored French endorsement of Warsaw's position and credited the appointment of the Papal administrator for Polish Silesia and the weakening of Cardinal Bertram's authority not only to Polish pressure but also to French influence in Rome.[81] An expression of Franco-Polish ecclesiastical solidarity was also offered in 1923 when the Polish episcopate invited Cardinal Dubois of Paris to visit Poland. He promptly accepted and made the journey in 1924. The Germans interpreted this trip as an attempt to increase France's ties with its eastern allies via

---

[80] GSTA, MA 104444, Ritter to BFM, August 9, 1921.

[81] Germany, Bayerisches Hauptstaatsarchiv, Allgemeines Staatsarchiv (hereafter cited as BSTA), MK 15568, Hoesch (Paris) to AA, June 23, 1923.

the Church and to show French hierarchical support for Poland's diplomatic position.[82] But the Reich was most anxious to hinder anything which would acknowledge the finality of the division of Upper Silesia. Berlin still nurtured hopes for the reunion of both parts at some future date, if for no other reason than for the sake of the German mining and metal foundry industries which had suffered severe dislocation by the partition. The Prussian Ministry of Education and Religious Affairs had informed Cardinal Bertram several times that the government considered it important for politico-economic reasons that he now stand firm and not consent to any separation of Polish areas from the Breslau diocese.[83]

Bertram, while understanding the political reasoning, had wearied of the fight and the distress and bitterness that it had caused. Moreover, he felt that in the interests of the Church these areas, which he believed would not be returned to Germany in the near future, should have their own bishop or be attached to a Polish ordinary since Breslau's bishop could not with any ease cross the border and carry out his episcopal functions, such as confirming the children or consecrating churches in the region. It made no sense in a diocese as large as Breslau to put another impediment in the way of close contact between the population and their spiritual leader by having a political border separate them.[84] Bertram's remarks were not viewed favorably by those who saw the matter from a political standpoint. Since the ecclesiastical reorganization of Danzig had just been carried out in Germany's favor, Poland would now have greater reason in the interests of parity to press for a separation of Polish Silesia from the diocese of Breslau. Bergen felt that Bertram had also lost the will to oppose the partition which he had inadvertently encouraged by his statements that a separation would now be in the interests of religion.[85]

Despite government displeasure, Bertram's sentiments were perhaps only his practical recognition of the inevitable. Once the political decision had been made, with Germany in fact retaining a good part of Silesia, he saw that little more could be done for German interests, and his thoughts as a good pastor were for the best interest of the Catholic population. As the Polish concordat negotiations drew to a close in late 1924, even Bergen reluctantly acknowledged that, al-

---

[82] AA, PO II, PO 33 Vat., Vol. 1, Bergen to AA, July 9, 1924.

[83] There were 3 Polish areas which belonged to Breslau: (1) part of the county (*Kreis*) of Gross-Wartenburg, transferred to the Woyvoda of Posen, (2) the Polish part of Teschen, and (3) Polish Upper Silesia. Only the last of these had an apostolic administrator assigned to it.

[84] AW, 1A 25t, 9, Bertram to Steinmann, December 22, 1924.

[85] AA, PO II, PO 24 Vat., Vol. 5, Bergen to AA, May 5, 1922.

though the Reich still upheld Breslau's claims, the Vatican would have to concede to Warsaw's demand that the ecclesiastical boundaries conform to those of its political areas, since it was both logical and justifiable.[86] But the manner in which the final settlement was phrased created a great deal of unhappiness in Berlin.

On February 25, 1925, Poland formally concluded a concordat with the Holy See, announcing the expected separation of ecclesiastical areas from German episcopal jurisdiction. Several of the treaty's clauses particularly displeased Berlin. The nuncio in Warsaw was now to extend his activities to include the Free City of Danzig. Remembering the unfortunate dual role of the Warsaw envoy in Upper Silesia in 1919-1920, Berlin feared a repetition of the situation and a decline of German interests in the Free City, since events in Danzig would be reported to Rome through the eyes of Roman diplomats in Warsaw. A new diocese for Polish Upper Silesia was to be created and would carry the name of the diocese of Silesia and be attached to the Church province of Cracow. Any changes in the hierarchy or in the diocesan borders would be carried out only with the expressed approval of the Polish Government. Berlin also noted that the treaty clauses did not grant any provision for the protection of the German-speaking minority in Poland or any guarantees for the training of German-speaking priests.

In April Chancellor Wilhelm Marx wrote to Pacelli, expressing his unhappiness over the wording in some of the clauses of the concordat and his concern that the new Polish-Vatican agreement would create difficulties for German domestic policy, for it appeared to conflict with the Bull *De Salute Animarum* of 1821, which had circumscribed Prussia's diocesan borders. In 1919 Pacelli had informed Prussia that until the completion of a new agreement Rome considered the 1821 agreement still binding. The Vatican had also told Berlin of its satisfaction, even in the difficult days after the war, of Prussia's compliance with its obligations as specified in the accord, including the financial contributions specified in the Bull. Also, since the income of the diocese was based on funds from the dotations of the State and from its income properties, the reorganization of Church boundaries would cause a loss of wealth for a given diocese and consequent fiscal imbalance. Marx desired to make it clear that the German State was unprepared to assume a greater part of the financial burden for these dioceses. Now that Poland had a concordat, the Poles might be able to discuss the question of compensations for the lost properties with the German dioceses from a position of strength. This in turn might prompt

[86] AA, PO II, PO 20A Vat., Breslau, Vol. 1, Bergen to AA, December 14, 1924.

Czechoslovakia, which also had claims on some of Breslau's lands, to press for settlement of the border question before settling the financial one.[87]

After consultation with Vatican officials about the Polish concordat, however, Bergen and Ritter were convinced that the Vatican had negotiated fairly and had even protected German interests against still greater Polish demands. After further discussions the objectionable features were modified and clarified. Rome stipulated that the Warsaw nuncio would report solely concerning ecclesiastical matters in Danzig, while representatives, both lay and ecclesiastical, of the Free City could deal directly with the Vatican itself. Cracow would have only titular authority over the new diocese of Silesia, not jurisdictional rights. This clarification was important, since it then permitted the new diocese some independence and made it potentially easier for the Vatican to transfer it back to German control should the situation warrant it. Moreover, the Holy See declared itself willing to change the new diocese's name from Silesia should this offend the Reich.[88] The clause specifying consultation with the Warsaw Government before making any changes in the hierarchy or diocesan boundaries was a less serious problem than the Germans had thought. Curial officials informed Bergen and Ritter that since the Vatican had adopted the viewpoint that concordat provisions *ipso facto* became invalid if the territory to which they pertained was placed under another government's control, should these areas ever be returned to Germany, the Polish concordat immediately ceased to be valid in these territories. The Curia also assured the Germans that the rights of the German minority would be looked after by specific arrangements to be worked out. The German community living in Poland would be able to appeal to the Curia, and any decision which the Polish hierarchy made concerning the use or lack of the German language in the Church would be subject to the approval of the Holy See, thereby ensuring further guarantees for the minority. Among themselves German officials had already conceded that the diocesan borders would eventually be brought in line with those of the new state. Understandably, the Vatican would sign a concordat with the new Polish regime, and Rome would have to make some concessions to Polish desires. Despite some remaining uneasiness that the Poles might use the concordat to the Reich's disadvantage, Berlin was pleased to note, in assessing the treaty as a whole, that the Vatican made no compromises seriously jeopardizing German inter-

[87] AW, 1A 250, 33, Marx to Pacelli, April 2, 1925.
[88] The area became the new Polish diocese of Katowice.

ests and in fact had taken steps to leave the door open for change in the eventuality that circumstances would require it.[89]

Ironically, however, this settlement of a diplomatic problem between the Vatican and Poland intensified the internal difficulty of regularizing the relations of Church and State within Germany. It again raised and made more urgent the question of the legality of *De Salute Animarum* and a definition of the obligations each party now had to each other. The Vatican's settlement with the new Polish state again pointed to the value and importance for Germany of arriving at some agreement with the Curia; otherwise, treaties might be drawn up between Rome and states whose interests impinged on those of Germany and in turn weaken or curtail the Reich's bargaining power. Once more the duality of Berlin's relations to the Papacy was evident. A concordat was important for the nation's foreign policy, yet it also had serious implications for internal affairs.

The Breslau problem, however, affected not only German-Polish but also German-Czech relations. In 1922, as soon as Poland had received an apostolic administrator for Polish Silesia, Czechoslovakia requested a similar representative for the area of Teschen, ceded to the new Czech state after the war. But here Vatican officials stated that the matter could not be taken up until there was a settlement over the lands of the diocese of Breslau which were in the territory. This was a bone of contention which continued throughout the 1920's and 1930's as one of those unresolved matters left over from Versailles. Prior to 1918, although politically part of the Austro-Hungarian Empire, Teschen ecclesiastically belonged to the sprawling Breslau diocese, which owned some 300,000 hectares of valuable wooded land here. The forests were a main source of diocesan income, which if lost to Czechoslovakia would seriously impair the financial solvency of the diocese. On March 12, 1919 the Czech Government, without informing Bertram, had taken possession of the estates. There the matter rested throughout the 1920's.

Prussia and the Reich were concerned, not only because it affected the duty and honor of Germany's Government to protect the interests of its Catholic citizens but also for legal and diplomatic reasons. The diocese's boundaries and its financial support had been based on the Papal Bull of 1821. Any changes would concern not only Czechoslovakia but also the Holy See. Moreover, it was in Germany's internal interests to ensure the financial well-being of a diocese such as Breslau.[90] The German Government, rather than taking steps in Prague,

[89] GSTA, MA 104446, Ritter to BFM, March 23, 1925.

[90] In the 1920's Germany's *Grenzpolitik* continued to support the Church in the Upper Rhine area as well as in Upper Silesia and Teschen. The Reich Government showed

thought it wiser to emphasize the ecclesiastical aspect of the problem and to cooperate by supporting the Vatican position, which insisted that the Czech Government was wrong in having occupied Church lands that either had to be returned or fully compensated. But, as time wore on, the Vatican showed signs of willingness to compromise with Czechoslovakia if some equitable agreement could be reached. Although Rome still insisted that the land settlement be dealt with before problems of ecclesiastical jurisdiction were taken up, Pius was beginning to think otherwise. He had commented to aides on several occasions that the Breslau diocese, which stretched from the Baltic to Czechoslovakia, was quite large and that a reduction in its size would not be a catastrophe. Besides, the religious interests of the people, who had no fixed ecclesiastical organizational structure here yet, should not be sacrificed to the material considerations of the diocese. These statements led the German Embassy to fear that the Vatican might accept a Czech proposal without adequate compensation for the German interests. To counter any Czech arguments and to strengthen Vatican resolve, Berlin used one of its strongest weapons, which touched upon important aspects of both its internal and external policy. At that moment negotiations were in progress for a Prussian concordat, which the Vatican was most desirous of concluding. Germany informed the Nuncio that a settlement in the Teschen question with less than adequate compensation would adversely affect the current concordat negotiations.[91] The Germans, while supporting the initial Vatican position, were also reminding Rome that by standing firm the Church had something to gain not only in negotiations with Prague but also within Germany. It was again an example of the truth of Ebert's statements

---

interest in the social, charitable, and cultural activities of numerous religious organizations. The borders were not to be only protected by military and diplomatic means but also by government support for youth hostels, homes for apprentices in Catholic unions, pilgrimage organizations, pedagogic organizations, lending libraries, and other educational activities. See Schreiber, p. 63ff. In 1925 the *Reichsrat* approved a *Kulturfonds* for use by the Churches inside and outside Germany and for "related purposes." In 1925, for example, 10,000 marks were given to Breslau's diocese for the support of German institutions in Polish Silesia and Teschen. In 1926 more than 20,000 marks were sent to support German organizations, German student organizations in Prague, propagation of the German language in Polish Silesia and in Czechoslovakia, etc. In 1927, 12,000 marks was earmarked for special religious emergency needs in the Upper Silesian border area and 10,000 for pastoral work in Czechoslovakian areas; 1928, 25,000 for Upper Silesian border areas and 10,000 for the Czechoslovakian; 1929, 8,000 for Czech areas; 1930, 8,000 for Breslau's border areas; 1932, 8,500 for border areas; 1933, 3,000 for German cultural interests in Czechoslovakia. AW, see 1A 25k, 96-98 for correspondence and receipts.

[91] PGSTA, Rep. 92, Nr. 7, Trendelenburg, memorandum, "Aktenauszug über die Entwicklung der Tschechoslowakei gelegenen Breslauer Bistumsgüter," p. 10.

to Pacelli in 1919: in return for Vatican help in international problems the Reich would reciprocate with accommodations in matters which concerned the Church in Germany.

Seeking to resolve the question in the more favorable diplomatic climate of 1925, Bertram urged that consideration be given to his property rights in the negotiations at Locarno. He did not request a specific clause in the German-Czech arbitration treaty then being worked out, but suggested that perhaps a general clause could be inserted, mentioning that disagreements which affected the interests of countries, state governments, communities, and public corporations recognized under civil law (*Körperschaften des öffentlichen Rechtes*), such as the Church, would be arbitrated. When reminded by a Foreign Office official that this might then exclude an influence that the Vatican might play in the affair, the Cardinal conceded the point and contented himself with requesting Foreign Minister Gustav Stresemann to stress personally to his Czech counterpart, Eduard Beneš, the necessity of reaching an equitable settlement of a problem which both the Reich and Prussian Governments considered important and to remind the Vatican once again about the validity of Breslau's claims.[92]

But in 1926 the Vatican was doing little in the matter, for relations between Rome and Czechoslovakia were at a very low ebb. The Czechs and their government were preparing a public celebration in honor of Jan Hus, the great Czech church reformer and nationalist. In 1415, despite a safe conduct from the Holy Roman Emperor to attend the Church Council at Constance, Hus had been burned as a heretic. He was therefore an embarrassing symbol for the Curia, which now saw him so honored. The Papacy viewed him not so much as a great figure in Czech history but rather as a religious dissenter. To the Vatican the active participation of the Prague Government in celebrating Czechoslovakia's first great Protestant was seen as a provocative and insulting gesture to both Rome and the large Catholic population of that country. Under such circumstances, regulation of church-state relations or concordat negotiations were for the time being held *in suspenso*, and the Vatican recommended that the Breslau matter be handled dilatorily until some later date. Berlin could remonstrate with Prague, but the Germans could do little without Rome's active support, since the Church was the third member in this triangular situation. The Reich's tactic during the Weimar Republic and on into the Nazi era was wherever possible to support Breslau's position with diplomatic notes or messages both in Prague and at the Vatican. In

[92] AA, PO II, PO 20A Vat., Breslau, Vol. 1, memorandum of Meyer-Rodehüser, October 7, 1925.

Rome, Steinmann and other German diplomat-churchmen were constantly concerned that Rome would conclude a concordat with Prague, giving the Church lands to Czechoslovakia or transferring them to a Czech diocese—which in any case was a loss to Breslau and a diminution of German influence. The German prelate worked hard to convince Vatican officials that Church and political boundaries did not have to coincide and that no insoluble problem would arise if they did not. In fact, by keeping the ecclesiastical boundaries separate from the political ones, the Church would find it easier to retain possession of its lands, since the Czech state would have to come to terms legally with German ecclesiastical rights. Finally, Steinmann never tired of emphasizing the ultimate German argument known to be effective in Rome: that an unsatisfactory decision by the Vatican would certainly affect concordat negotiations. As if to give weight to Steinmann's arguments, upon Bergen's urging, Friedrich Trendelenburg from the Prussian Ministry of Education and Religious Affairs raised the Breslau land issue during the concordat discussions in December and in private talks with Pacelli, leaving no doubt about the seriousness with which Berlin viewed the matter.[93]

In 1928, however, the Vatican signed a *modus vivendi* with the Czech state in order to regularize church-state relations and to give the Church a legal status in that country. According to the agreement, no part of the Czech republic would be jurisdictionally subordinate to a foreign bishop. This stipulation virtually settled the border question, yet it left the door open to obtaining compensation for Breslau's diocese by making no mention of the lands. Rome had opted in favor of Czech demands for immediate ecclesiastical control of the area by leaving the Breslau lands to subsequent negotiations. In this instance Rome, mindful of its multinational obligations and pastoral concerns, found its interests not fully in conformity with those of the Reich. In answer to German inquiries about a treaty which would conflict with the Bull *De Salute Animarum*, Gasparri made the Vatican's position clear and turned the tables by using the concordat argument against Germany. There was some question, said the Cardinal, of the Bull's validity even within Prussia's existing borders, but beyond them it had none whatsoever, since Prussia had by international law recognized that the territories politically formed part of another state. Of course, if a concordat were concluded with Prussia soon, then any remaining unclear situations, such as those along Germany's eastern border, would be settled. Since there was none by 1928, the Holy See had felt itself free to regulate conditions which would be best for the Catholic pop-

[93] AA, PO II, PO 20A Vat., Breslau, Vol. 4, Bergen to AA, December 16, 1927.

ulation and had done so in the case of the *modus vivendi* with Czecho-slovakia. As if to soften this rebuke Gasparri then added that in reality Rome regarded the Czech treaty as a step forward in regulating the question of Breslau's dominial lands, since after the establishment of normal relations the Holy See would be in a strong position to bring its weight to bear on the question.[94]

What Rome had done was finally to separate the border and land issues. Being in a position to regularize its relations with the eastern states—Poland first, then Czechoslovakia—the Curia did so in order to improve its general diplomatic situation and to ensure the welfare of the Church within individual national borders. There was no value for the Church doggedly to support the German position. On matters of general policy the Vatican was prepared to see Germany strength-ened or at least retain its position. In disputes over dominial lands which might eventually be transferred to ecclesiastical authorities in the new state, and thus not lost to the Church, or which might be used as a bargaining tool to win greater concessions in other matters such as education or the rights of the clergy, the Vatican was willing to withdraw its support from Germany's claims or move from a neu-tral position to one accommodating the new states.

The question of the land continued into the 1930's with proposals and counterproposals: Breslau suggesting to agree to the nationaliza-tion of some of the lands, the Foreign Office supporting the Cardinal's claims, and the Vatican attempting to expedite the negotiations by stating that the *modus vivendi* would not be fully implemented until the difficulties over the dominial lands had been conclusively solved.[95] By this time the question became more legal than political, since the Vatican no longer chose to interfere in the matter. Berlin had more important matters with which to concern itself, and the diocese of Breslau had learned to cope with the losses that it had sustained more than a decade before. Time conferred an aura of finality on the new *status quo*, and German claims to the lands, while still maintained throughout the 1930's, disappeared, as did so many other claims in the chaos of World War II and the new situation which developed after 1945.

Although the Upper Silesian question occupied a great deal of Eu-rope's attention because of its economic significance, it was by no means the only area which Germany was striving to retain and for

[94] AA, PO II, PO 20A Vat., Breslau, Vol. 4, Gasparri to Bergen, March 21, 1928.

[95] In the *modus vivendi* between the Holy See and Czechoslovakia provisions were made to settle the question of the Breslau dominial land as well as to rectify diocesan borders, but these provisions were never carried out. Kurt Engelbert, *Adolf Kardinal Bertram* (Hildesheim, 1949), p. 12.

which it needed Vatican and Church aid. Events similar to those in Silesia were occurring simultaneously in other sectors along the eastern borders of the Reich. In early 1920 in all the plebiscite areas and in the territory already detached from the Reich by the provisions of the Versailles Treaty there were still unsettled questions concerning the fate of German Catholics and the degree of German influence to be retained. For example, the boundary of the new state of Poland encompassed most of the former West Prussian part of the diocese of Culm, including the cathedral city. In Berlin there was hope at first that the diocese would at least retain its German bishop. The Poles only requested a coadjutor with the right to succeed Bishop Rosentreter, but by late 1920 they were demanding that the seventy-seven-year-old prelate resign immediately to make way for a Pole. Now, in the Polish part of the diocese as well as in the other areas already ceded to Poland, the populace had reason to believe that German-speaking priests would be dismissed from their posts or forced to take subordinate positions. In 1919 Ernst von Simson, section leader of the Foreign Office's Justice and Peace Division, issued a memorandum to his colleagues, voicing concern over the fate of German Catholics in the areas lost to Poland and in Danzig. The Poles, who had the ear of Nuncio Ratti, were influential in Rome and were represented by such officials as the Jesuit Superior-General Vladimir Ledóchowski, who had already suggested that Curia officials place the plebiscite areas under special ecclesiastical jurisdiction. Simson acknowledged the desirability of an agreement between the two states to regulate the situation and to safeguard the rights of minorities, but the Church's position and its rights guaranteed in the agreement of 1821 made direct negotiations difficult. He therefore recommended making Rome aware of Germany's concerns and requesting the Vatican to protect the rights of German-speaking priests and religious organizations, and to support the continuance of religious services held in German.[96]

In addition to the problem of Catholics already or soon to be lost by Germany was the added difficulty of determining diocesan jurisdictions. Catholics in the new Free City of Danzig were most concerned about their situation. Up until 1920 most of the Danzig territory had belonged to Culm; now Danzig was a politically separate state and Culm was part of Poland. The German-speaking Catholics naturally desired to belong to a German diocese, i.e., to Ermland, the nearest one; the Polish Government, of course, wanted to see the territory brought under Polish jurisdiction. Moreover, the territory of

[96] AA, Botschaftsakten, Abstimmungsgebiet Ost-West Preussen, Vol. 1, memorandum of Simson (AA), September 27, 1919.

143

Memel, farther to the north, also belonged to the diocese of Ermland. Lithuania was laying claim to the area and was concurrently seeking to have ecclesiastical control here transferred to a Lithuanian ordinary. The authority of German bishops was also seriously menaced in those sections of the diocese of Ermland which lay in the plebiscite areas: in East Prussia the government district of Allenstein, in West Prussia the county (*Kreis*) of Marienwerder. The situation here in the northern plebiscite area was similar on a smaller scale to that in Silesia; Berlin's task, then, was to prevent or limit the control of Polish ordinaries over those parts of their dioceses still within the Reich and to retain German Church influence in both areas already lost in 1919 and in those yet to be decided.

Changing diocesan borders to meet new political circumstances always required careful deliberation. In the eyes of the Vatican such moves were tantamount to final recognition of the new reality, and this the Curia hesitated to do until the situation appeared stable and settled. But until such time as this occurred, Germany and its eastern neighbors took steps to strengthen their positions. The Poles as well as the Germans regarded it as a matter of prestige and good politics to have the full jurisdictional rights of their ordinaries recognized. In 1920, for example, with the approval of Warsaw, Cardinal Dalbor of Posen-Gnesen requested that he be allowed to name a delegate as his representative in those parts of his diocese which still remained politically part of the Reich, consisting of about forty parishes with more than 100,000 parishioners. He also expected the Prussian State to provide housing, office space, and financial means for the delegate's living expenses, as was allowed for the Catholic clergy in Prussia. The diocese of Culm also had approximately 15,800 communicants still living in Germany, and its bishop would eventually also want a representative across the border in the Reich.

This presented the Germans with a problem, for, as anxious as they were to retain some influence in the areas which they had lost, they were equally unwilling to see Polish influence expand within Reich territory. The Prussian Ministry of Education and Religious Affairs argued against having a representative of a Polish bishop working within Germany. If there was to be an administrator here in the German section of the dioceses of Posen-Gnesen and Culm, he should be someone to assist in keeping German culture and influence alive until the final regularization took place. Hence Berlin believed that the German not the Polish hierarchy should select him. Weighing all options, the Prussian Ministry nevertheless did not as yet wish to press for full control of German parts of Polish dioceses, since the Reich's course of action depended, in the last analysis, on the final outcome in Silesia, which was of great importance to Germany politically and ecclesiastically. If Upper Silesia or most of it were assigned to Poland, then Germany would work to keep the present diocesan borders intact so that some German influence could be retained in Silesia through the Church. This gain would be far more valuable than any control which the bishops of Posen or Culm would win in sections of Prussia. But if, on the other hand, most of Upper Silesia remained German, then the Reich would be in a position to urge the Vatican to revise the ecclesiastical borders and to transfer the German parts of the Polish dioceses to German ordinaries. If the Polish bishops immediately appointed a delegate, even a German-speaking individual, to care for their flock within the Reich, it would only weaken the argument for border changes later on should Germany desire them. Therefore Berlin decided to take dilatory action in approving delegates for the Polish bishops and to await the outcome in Silesia.[97]

In 1920 Warsaw requested, as in Upper Silesia, that since the bishop and the cathedral chapter of Ermland were German, jurisdiction for the plebiscite area should be transferred to the nuncio in Warsaw. Poland in its message to Rome as well as in its propaganda among the local inhabitants portrayed the plebiscite campaign as a struggle between good Polish Catholics and purely German Protestants. Like Bertram, the local bishop here, Augustinus Bludau, refuted Polish accusations of his unfairness and partiality for Germany in carrying out his episcopal functions and objected to any curtailment of his authority. Berlin naturally had requested Bergen to speak to officials in Rome to explain the local ordinary's problem and to obtain assurances about his administrative rights. Since the plebiscite was already to take place in July 1920, Baron Wernher Ow-Wackendorf, official on the German Commission for the East Prussian plebiscite area, suggested that after initially explaining Bludau's case, Bergen attempt to slow down the discussions, for if the appointment of the Nuncio to the area were delayed a few weeks, the plebiscite would have taken place already and the matter would have been settled without too much of a fuss.[98] But already in the spring Ratti had been appointed Papal administrator for all the Polish-German plebiscite areas. Shortly thereafter more confusion developed when some Polish Church officials let it be known that Ratti would soon appoint the Polish priest Nabrowski as general vicar for Marienwerder. Bergen, as in the case for

---

[97] AA, PO II, PO 20 Vat., Posen, Vol. 1, memorandum "Zur Einrichtung einer erzbischöflichen Delegatur . . . ," February 14, 1920. AA, BRV 352, Vol. 1, Haniel to Bergen, March 21, 1921.

[98] AA, Botschaftsakten, Abstimmungsgebiet Ost-West Preussen, Vol. 1, Ow-Wackendorf to Bergen, May 14, 1920.

Silesia, stressed the validity according to Church law of the local ordinary's jurisdictional rights. In answer to Ow's request, Bergen promised to do all he could, but desired to have as much statistical material at hand to buttress the German case, and complained that if only the Germans would bestir themselves to visit and persuade Vatican officials, as the Poles did, he would have little trouble.[99]

Berlin was also active in pursuing a diplomatic strategy to retain ecclesiastical influence in areas which had already been detached from the Reich. The Reich was most anxious to maintain Bishop Rosentreter of Culm as the ordinary as long as possible. Germany wished to prevent Danzig, which was part of the Culm diocese, from coming under Polish supervision, believing that there was a good case to be made in Rome for not transferring the Free City to Polish jurisdiction. Catholics in Danzig, ninety percent German-speaking numbered 120,000 to 140,000. In 1921, with strong German support, representatives of the Church in Danzig began negotiations in Rome. The Curia realized the logic of the German arguments and was in principle prepared to separate those parishes belonging to Danzig from the dioceses of Culm and Ermland, to which they belonged, and place them under an apostolic delegate. The plan was received with interest by the Danzig Senate, the Reich, the Curia, and the two bishops concerned, who, like their communicants, sought to preserve the German character of the area. Negotiations for this proposal went along rather rapidly, with all participants keeping watch on the health of the ailing seventy-seven-year-old Bishop Rosentreter. Most of his diocese was now part of Poland, and his successor would be a Pole who would never consent to a removal of part of the diocese from his jurisdiction. Without his approval the Curia would be less inclined to consent to the change, or would temporize and wait—all at the loss of valuable time which the Poles would use to strengthen their position in the area. It was obvious to the Foreign Office that it had to concern itself with such ecclesiastical questions in order to maintain the German character of Danzig, which in turn was crucial to the Reich for retaining its influence in the Free City.[100]

While Msgr. Franz Sander, the ranking Danzig Catholic clergyman in contact with the German Foreign Office, was pursuing conversations in Rome about an administrator for the area, the Danzig Senate in early June also formally requested the Holy See to incorporate the Free City into the diocese of Ermland. The petition was first delivered

[99] AA, PO II, PO 24 Vat., Vol. 1, Bergen to Delbrück, June 8, 1920; Botschaftsakten, Abstimmungsgebiet Ost-West Preussen, Vol. 1, Bergen to Ow, June 20, 1922.

[100] AA, BRV 356, Vol. 1, Dompropst Franz Sander of Ermland to AA, April 17, 1921.

to the Polish Commissioner for Danzig, since Poland, according to the 1919 settlement, was delegated to handle all Danzig's foreign affairs. The procedure which the Senate followed in sending its request was administratively and diplomatically correct and was taken to show Poland that the Free City intended not to violate diplomatic protocol and to inform the Poles of the wishes of Danzig's Catholics. It was also a dangerous move, since by giving the letter to the Poles to deliver to the Vatican, Danzig was asking the prosecutor to work for the defendant and was creating a case of precedent for future negotiations. Sander's discussions with Vatican officials had been aimed at securing an apostolic administrator for Danzig. His proposal was much more moderate and more likely to have an initial success at the Vatican than the Senate petition for outright incorporation into Ermland, something bound to provoke the Poles, who would naturally try to hinder a move to deprive them of control of an area which they considered rightfully theirs. Warsaw, naturally perceiving the threat to the Polish position, simply failed to pass the request on to Rome. The proposal remained in Warsaw to be "considered" by the government. In late July, annoyed by this slight, the Danzig Senate forwarded its request directly to the Holy See.[101]

Of all the areas in dispute along Germany's eastern borders, the situation in Danzig was by far the most clearcut: the Catholic population, overwhelmingly German-speaking, the territory politically a free city under the League's protection, and the government of Danzig officially requesting incorporation into a Reich diocese. Germany's representative at the Vatican therefore worked vigorously to preserve Danzig's German character and energetically supported the petition of the Danzig Senate.

On April 22, 1922, the Curia acted. Rome did not attach Danzig to Ermland, since this would lay the Vatican open either to the criticism that it was placing the Free City under a foreign ordinary—exactly the objection which Germany used to prevent Polish control here—or to the objection that the Curia was showing partiality to the Reich by ecclesiastically keeping Danzig united to Germany, something Versailles on the political level expressly sought to prevent. Instead, the Curia followed an approach worked out in collaboration with Msgr. Sander by which an apostolic administrator was appointed to the area. On his way back from Geneva in 1922, Heinrich Sahm, President of the Danzig Senate, stopped in Munich to call on Pacelli, whom he found very well informed about Danzig. The Nuncio told Sahm at

---

[101] Heinrich Sahm, *Erinnerungen aus meinen Danziger Jahren, 1919-1930* (Marburg, 1958), p. 57. AA, PO II, PO 20 Vat., Ermland, Vol. 1, memorandum of AA, May 12, 1921. AA, BRV 356, Vol. 1, Sahm to Holy See, July 29, 1921.

that time that the initiative for appointing an administrator for Danzig as a solution to the jurisdictional problem came from the Pope himself, who was also carefully watching developments here.[102] The Pontiff, perhaps seeking to dispel any remaining feelings that he had been pro-Polish during his tenure as Nuncio to Warsaw, let it be known that since he could not approve attaching Danzig to the diocese of Ermland, he had immediately agreed to grant the Free City an apostolic administrator in the hopes that that would indicate to the Germans the Vatican's goodwill toward them.[103] After consultation with Berlin to learn whether the Reich objected to the selection, the Vatican chose Count Eduard O'Rourke,[104] a Baltic German of Irish descent, as the new administrator who would carry episcopal rank, which in effect gave him all the powers of a diocesan bishop.

By the choice of a German-speaking prelate for the post, the interests of the Reich in Danzig were maintained, yet without all the difficulties that actual incorporation of the Free City into a German diocese would have involved. The Germans interpreted the appointment as signifying the Vatican's recognition of Danzig's political sovereignty, symbolically underscored by the fact that it was the Nuncio in Warsaw who communicated in a letter to the Danzig Senate O'Rourke's appointment and the Free City's separation from the diocese of Culm. It meant that in the eyes of the Vatican any Polish claims to Danzig were now put aside. The German Foreign Office was well pleased with the selection and moved to strengthen the new administrator's position almost immediately. The Danzig Senate found itself unprepared to pay the salary of its new Catholic leader, and there was danger that Poland might offer to underwrite the costs in order to gain some influence over Danzig's Catholic administrator, thereby cutting its diplomatic losses in O'Rourke's appointment. Therefore, upon the urging of Bergen and the Foreign Office, the Reich Government approved a sum of more than 50,000 marks to help to defray O'Rourke's living expenses.[105] Berlin intended to outmaneuver Warsaw in the Free City and to prevent any danger of a Polonization of the Church in Danzig. In 1923 ties between Danzig and the Reich were further strengthened by religious means. Due to shortages

[102] Sahm, p. 59.

[103] AA, PO II, PO 24 Vat., Vol. 4, memorandum of Boelitz (Pruss. Min. of Ed. and Relig. Affairs), February 27, 1922.

[104] AA, PO II, PO 24 Vat., Vol. 5, memorandum of Hüffer (AA), March 22, 1922.

[105] AA, PO II, PO 24 Vat., Vol. 5, Nuncio to Zech, May 3, 1922; Bergen to AA, May 1, 1922. The Foreign Office files do not indicate the exact sum but do state it was more than 50,000 marks.

there, Breslau, Münster, and Ermland agreed to supply Danzig with priests. Any losses which Ermland sustained were to be made up by religious from other German dioceses.

In Danzig, as in all the border areas, Berlin was careful to maintain cultural connections and German influence; therefore, any diminution in the number of the German Catholic clergy, educational instructors, or workers in charitable institutions, for example, was a matter of concern for the government.[106] One such incident occurred with the recall of the Borromean nuns from Danzig in 1923 because of shortages in the number of nuns in Germany. The announced departure of the fifty Borromeans stationed at St. Mary's Hospital caused a great commotion within the German community in the Free City. The sisters were highly respected and played a vital role in the city's social work. Already that year, Polish nuns, without the request of Bishop O'Rourke, had been arriving in the city-state to care for the sick and to teach, a move the Germans regarded as a Polish attempt to win influence in Danzig. O'Rourke thereupon wrote to German officials in Berlin and to the German Consul General in Danzig, Herbert von Dirksen, requesting the Reich Government's intervention with the Order's headquarters in Germany, stating the importance of the presence of these nuns to Germany's interests. In replying to the Bishop's request, the Consul General declared:

> The letter of the Mother-Superior of the Borromeans can only be explained by an ignorance of the ways of the world. Otherwise it is incomprehensible how the most distant [religious] communities are mechanically called home, even if they, like the one at Danzig, belong to the most important outposts of German Catholicism.[107]

[106] In order to strengthen German claims to areas along its eastern borders, especially in sections with a mixed German-Polish population, in the mid-1920's the Prussian Government encouraged a policy of resettling farmers, many of whom were Catholics from the western Rhineland area in the east and in east-Elbian Prussia. This, however, led to confessional tensions and further complications for church-state relations. The Hugenberg press, for example, complained that the majority of settlers were Catholics coming into areas traditionally Protestant. The *Deutsche Tageszeitung* (Berlin) replied that in areas along the borders menaced by Catholic Poland it was justified and advisable to use Catholic Germans. In 1927-1930 about 1,627 settlers arrived in West Prussia and a little under 50 percent were Catholics. This "invasion" by Catholics reinforced Protestant objections to any further inroads being made by Catholics in the area and increased Protestant antipathies and resistance to concordat negotiations. Wilhelm Boyens, *Die Geschichte der ländlichen Siedlung* (Berlin, 1959-1960), Vol. 1, pp. 292ff. and 308ff. Ernst Neumann, "Methoden der römischen Kolonisation in Deutschland," *Das Reich*, II (Jan.-Feb., 1932).

[107] AA, PO II, PO 24 Vat., Vol. 7, Dirksen to AA, September 18, 1923.

Berlin's energetic support for O'Rourke and its appeal to national interests were successful, for its request was honored and the nuns remained.

After O'Rourke's appointment, Berlin expressed pleasure in Rome's adherence to the jurisdictional arrangements agreed upon in 1923 and in Rome's disapproval of Polish efforts to change the situation to its advantage. In 1924, when the conference of Poland's bishops drew up administrative reforms calling for attaching Danzig to the Church province of Posen and for making Bishop O'Rourke responsible to the Archbishop of Posen, O'Rourke objected directly to Gasparri and also requested that the German Foreign Office protest against such a move. Rome sided with the Reich and Danzig and forbade the administrative change. In 1924-1925 Poland, then negotiating its concordat with the Holy See, again requested that Danzig be attached ecclesiastically to Poland, to which the Vatican again gave a negative reply. In a later stage of negotiations, Poland tried once more to gain a point by requesting that Warsaw at least have the right to represent Danzig in its diplomatic relations with the Vatican, similar to its position of representing Danzig with secular states. The Curia showed no signs of changing its mind but merely sidestepped the issue by denying that this was a question directly concerning Polish-Vatican negotiations, but was a matter involving a third party; the subject could be discussed and settled in talks between Danzig and Poland.[108] Legally Rome was correct in replying in this manner, but it also meant that the Curia was unwilling to go out of its way to side with Poland and upset the arrangements made here which had gained the support of the government of both Danzig and Germany.

Once the plebiscites (1920) had been completed, the areas of Allenstein and Marienwerder electing to remain with Germany, and once the question of Danzig had been settled, in 1923 the Vatican acted to clarify the remaining problems concerning ecclesiastical borders and jurisdictions in this region. The section of the German diocese of Culm still in East Prussia was placed under the jurisdiction of the bishop of Ermland as apostolic administrator, while another apostolic administrator with his seat at Tütz was appointed for those parts of the dioceses of Posen-Gnesen and Culm still in Prussia.[109] The latter's jurisdiction extended some 500 kilometers along the Polish border from the Baltic Sea to Silesia and in 1925 contained over 140,000 Catholics.[110] Gen-

[108] Sahm, pp. 98-99.
[109] The seat of the administrator was moved in 1926 to Schneidemühl. In 1929, as a result of the Prussian concordat, the area was raised to the rank of and became known as the Prelature *Nullius* of Schneidemühl.
[110] *Kölnische Volkszeitung*, February 21, 1926.

erally the settlement in Ermland and Culm was what the German-speaking inhabitants had desired. Although they were not joined officially to German dioceses, the appointment of apostolic administrators for all intents and purposes amounted to the same thing. Since Germany had requested the retention of jurisdiction of Upper Silesia for Breslau, any desire on Germany's part for the direct transfer of the German area of the diocese of Posen-Gnesen to a German diocese could hardly be fulfilled, but the appointment of a German-speaking administrator did ensure the retention of German interests in the area. The success in Danzig, Ermland, and in Silesia before the Allies awarded part of the area to Poland, gave Berlin no reason to be too unhappy with the compromise that it had to make in accepting the losses in the dioceses of Posen-Gnesen and Culm.

One other area in the east also required regulation of ecclesiastic jurisdictions—the port city of Memel. Politically the area was now Lithuanian, and the majority of the Catholics were German-speaking, numbering about five to six thousand communicants.[111] The Reich wanted Memel to remain attached to Ermland, but the Lithuanians sought to have this territory joined to the Lithuanian diocese of Kaunas (Kovno). In 1923 Berlin held consultations with Bishop Bludau of Ermland to learn of his willingness to retain control over German-speaking Memel, even though it belonged politically to another state, with all the added difficulties that this would entail in carrying out normal diocesan functions and in dealing with two different state systems. Since the clergy of the area favored remaining part of Ermland, Bludau declared himself prepared to counter Lithuanian demands by appealing to Rome. The only qualifications that he made were that parish costs then be paid by the Prussians, since Lithuania would certainly not do so, and that the clergy receive the same financial support as those in the rest of his diocese.[112] The benefit for the Reich of such a grant would be insurance that German influence remain alive there.

Bergen relayed to the Holy See the request of both Bludau and the German-speaking populace of Memel. Supplied with factual data, he explained to Vatican officials how the parishioners would be at a disadvantage in practicing their faith and receiving religious instruction if they were part of the Kaunas diocese, since the majority of the priests in the diocese knew little if any German and their dialect even differed from that spoken by the Memel Lithuanians. Communication between the clergy and laity would then be impeded, and religious

[111] The total population of Memel was approximately 140,000, but most of the German-speaking inhabitants were Lutheran.

[112] AA, BRV 179, Vol. 1, memorandum of Hüffer, March 16, 1923.

6. Cardinal Karl Joseph Schulte, Archbishop
of Cologne

instruction would suffer. Bergen also informed the Vatican that since
the Reich and Prussian Governments wished this area to remain part
of Ermland, if the Vatican would agree, the Prussian Government
would undertake the responsibility for paying the salaries of the Catholic clergy here as well as the costs of teaching Lithuanian to any priest
so that he might also tend to the needs of Lithuanian Catholics.[113]

Despite Germany's arguments for the the retention of Memel as
part of Ermland, its position here lacked foundation. As the Foreign
Office well knew, the Vatican by practice had not permitted any area
to be attached to a foreign diocese after final political separation.[114] It

[113] AA, BRV 179, Vol. 1, pro memoria of AA, June 7, 1923.
[114] AA, PO II, PO 24 Vat., Memel, Vol. 1, memorandum of Meyer-Rodehüser, May
12, 1926.

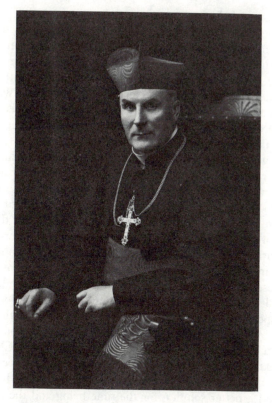

7. Cardinal Michael von Faulhaber, Archbishop
of Munich and Freising

was natural for Germany to seek to maintain the old diocesan boundaries in sections separated from Germany, but, looking at the matter
objectively, as even Bergen conceded, one could appreciate the Curia's
cogent argument for taking the position that diocesan boundaries should
conform to political ones. Rome would be hard pressed to grant the
Germans' request in view of the demands of the new states to create
a unified national hierarchy and to define ecclesiastical boundaries within
the political frontiers.[115]

[115] AA, PO II, PO 24 Vat., West Preussen, Vol. 1, Bergen to Trendelenburg, June
22, 1926. Similarly, after World War II the Vatican was under strong pressure from
the Polish Government and the hierarchy to acknowledge former German territories
acquired by Poland in 1945 as ecclesiastically integral parts of the Polish Church. In
June 1972, only after the ratification of the 1970 treaty between the German Federal
Republic and Poland provisionally recognizing the Oder-Neisse line as the boundary

The Vatican ruled in 1926 to separate Memel from Ermland. It had just concluded a concordat with Lithuania, which was now demanding to have Memel incorporated into the Lithuanian diocesan structure. However, this event only underlined to the German Foreign Office the absence of a Reich concordat to serve as a vehicle for making counterclaims. The situation left Germany in a position where parts of its territory could be bargained away as long as it lacked ecclesiastical legal protection defining its boundaries. But what the Reich did have in its favor was a historical and a pastoral argument, for Rome could not ignore the German character of Memel's Catholics. The Vatican therefore tried to do what it could for the Germans while meeting some of Lithuania's demands. Memel nominally was incorporated into the ecclesiastical structure of the hierarchy of Lithuania suffragan to the archdiocese of Kaunas, but Memel itself did not become part of any diocese; instead it was declared a prelature *nullius*, a territory with no bishop. This then allowed the region to maintain a little more independence than if it had been integrated into a Lithuanian diocese, and it permitted German traditions to be better preserved. It also gave Germany another indication of how Rome's views about the peace settlement in the east were similar to those of the Reich, for by declaring the region a prelature *nullius*, something inconsistent with the normal hierarchical structure of the Church, the Vatican acknowledged the temporary character of the ecclesiastical boundaries there. The compromise implicitly confirmed Rome's inability to find a better solution for the time being and the impermanence of the borders. Thereafter, Germany contented itself with a diplomatic campaign in Rome and Kaunas in order to make certain that the priests of Memel were allowed to receive their education in the Reich, that German-speaking clergy were allowed to be brought in from Ermland in case of need, and that the clergy of Memel have as much independent control over church affairs, without interference from the Lithuanian hierarchy, as would be ecclesiastically permitted.[116]

In surveying the situation along the eastern borders in 1926, Bergen stated that Germany had accomplished a great deal, but warned that Berlin would hurt its standing with the Curia and its objectives of seeking Vatican aid in other diplomatic matters if it too strongly criticized and protested—be it through diplomatic channels or the press—Vatican decisions not completely favorable to the Reich. Germany had to realize that Rome would officially reject any Reich interference in purely ecclesiastical matters in areas beyond Germany's borders. The

---

between German and Polish territory, did the Vatican agree to Warsaw's request. *The New York Times*, June 29, 1972, p. 2.

[116] AA, BRV 179, Vol. 1, Bergen to Gasparri, July 18, 1926.

8. Cardinal Adolf Bertram, Prince-Bishop of Breslau

Holy See had to consider what was best for the Church and its followers, regardless of nationality. Rome was extremely sensitive in this matter, lest other nations accuse the Curia of being unfair and pro-German, and the Ambassador urged that caution be exerted. Nevertheless, the Vatican had *de facto* taken into consideration German wishes and interests. In addition to the decisions made about the ecclesiastical reorganization in the east, to prove his point, Bergen mentioned the example of the Reich's concern that the sees of Posen-Gnesen and Katowice, which had been recently made vacant, might be filled by any of the anti-German candidates who had been proposed and supported by the Polish Government. In memoranda and numerous conversations with Vatican officials, Bergen had made known German views about the new appointments, without giving the impression of interfering in purely Church matters. None of the anti-German candidates was appointed to either of the two dioceses. From this fact and from the statements of Vatican officials to Bergen that one of the criteria used in the episcopal selections was the ability of the candidates to work in the interests not only of Polish but also of German Catholics, the German Ambassador was able to conclude that the Papacy was paying heed to German concerns and that German diplomatic overtures were succeeding.[117]

Although not really considered a border problem, one other place where the Foreign Office had shown concern over the ecclesiastical situation in the east was Saxony. Still unsure of the Republic's viability in 1921, the leaders of the new Germany had no desire to see foreign influences at work which could prove harmful to the integrity of the State. Suspicion was directed toward the Slavic Wends in Saxony, who were regarded as having close ties with Czechoslovakia. Though ecclesiastically Saxony was divided into two parts, a vicariate of Dresden and a prefecture of Oberlausitz, Saxon Catholics were now urging that an independent diocese be granted to them which would unite the entire area under one control. Moreover, the Germans expressed annoyance that, although the Wends numbered only 10,000-11,000 out of the entire Saxon Catholic population of approximately 200,000, this Slavic minority exerted disproportionate influence in the cathedral chapter at Bautzen in Oberlausitz, the ecclesiastical center of Catholic Saxony.[118] If the two areas were united into one diocese, Wendish strength in the cathedral chapter and Czech influence in Saxony would be reduced. Berlin strongly supported the Saxons' request for their own diocese as a means of stopping any Czech influence from coming into this state via clerical channels and causing internal difficulties within the Reich.

The Nuncio at first opposed making any changes until a full reorganization had been made for all Germany and incorporated in a concordat. He was won over, however, with German reasoning that a diminution of Wendish influence in general would prevent any possible Hussite tendencies coming into Oberlausitz from Czechoslovakia. Most of the Wendish and some German seminarians were trained in Prague, and the creation of a new diocese with its own seminary would reduce the Wends' authority and make Czech propaganda among them more difficult. Therefore the Foreign Office began negotiations with the Nuncio by requesting the closing of the Wendish seminary in Prague, placing a quota on the number of Wends in the cathedral chapter at Bautzen—a move which would allow the Germans a ma-

[117] AA, PO II, PO 24 Vat., West Preussen, Vol. 1, Bergen to Trendelenburg, June 22, 1926.
[118] There were about 34,000 Wends in Prussia, all of whom were Evangelical Lutherans. In Saxony there were about 28,000 Wends, of whom 10,000-11,000 were Catholics.

jority—and ensuring that the Wends be totally subordinate to the ordinary of the new diocese, with no allegiance to Prague. German officials informed Nuncio Pacelli that the Wends were receiving substantial funds from Prague in order to maintain and foster Slavic solidarity by contacts with the Czechs.[119] According to reports of German agents, the Czechs were expecting that as a consequence of Germany's inability to make some of its reparation payments the eastern Saxon border areas would be occupied by Czech troops, and, if events proved favorable, the area would eventually be annexed. Propaganda among the Wends would then have been of great help to the Czech cause.[120] To what extent this plan was actually considered for Czech strategy was not important, for, with considerations such as these in mind, Berlin could take no chances and was therefore most anxious to support Saxon desires for their own diocese.

In 1921 the Holy See created the diocese of Meissen, with the seat of the bishop at Bautzen. The Saxon Government had given its approval, stipulating that the bishop be a German national and that diocesan borders adhere to those of the State in order to offset any undue foreign influences. Since there was no concordat between Rome and either Germany or Saxony, much of this agreement was made verbally and informally and depended for its efficacy on the good working relations of Germany with the Curia. Final written guarantees awaited a concordat, but the Vatican with the support of the Nuncio had indicated its good faith in acceding to the wishes of the Saxon Catholics and of the Reich Government by creating this new diocese.[121]

Throughout the entire Weimar era the Foreign Office continued to protest attempts by Poland or Czechoslovakia to restrict German in-

---

[119] AA, PO II, PO 20 Vat., Meissen, Vol. 1, memorandum of Delbrück, June 2, 1921. *Deutsche Allgemeine Zeitung*, October 26, 1922. Ironically, Germany objected to Czechoslovakia's support for the Slavs beyond its borders. Yet Berlin was active in making financial contributions to cultural institutions for ethnic Germans beyond the Reich's boundaries to the east.

[120] AA, BRV 345, Bistum Meissen, memorandum of Steinmann, October 3, 1922.

[121] In 1930 the Saxon Government attempted to influence the appointment of the new bishop of Meissen. The Vatican was deeply angered by this move and communicated its displeasure in no uncertain terms. The Church had made the offer to begin negotiations for the contractual regulation of church-state affairs in Saxony, but the government had turned down this suggestion. Now it seemed to Rome that the government was trying to take advantage of the situation and unfairly interfere in ecclesiastical affairs even though the Vatican had shown its goodwill toward the Saxons by creating the new diocese in 1921. This misunderstanding, commented Bergen, only indicated once again the value and necessity of an agreement with the Holy See which would spell out clearly all the rights and obligations of both parties. AA, PO II, PO 20 Vat., Meissen, Vol. 1, Bergen to AA, July 6, 1930.

fluence among Catholics still living in territories no longer part of the Reich.[122] But these diplomatic representations no longer had the urgency or were as important in foreign policy considerations as Berlin's activities on behalf of German Catholics had been during the immediate post-war years. The situation was no longer as chaotic as it had been in 1919. During the 1920's the ecclesiastical picture in the east stabilized somewhat, diocesan lines were drawn, and independent sees were created out of administrative areas within the Reich, such as Meissen in 1921, and out of territories separated from the Reich, such as Katowice in Polish Silesia in 1925. On the whole, Germany could be satisfied with the success of its diplomatic endeavors. The Vatican, ever aware of balance and impartiality, had not been overtly pro-German, but, while conceding to the demands of the new nation-states that dioceses conform to political borders, it had tried to prop up Germany's position. It was not in the Curia's interests to see Germany made powerless in international affairs or Catholic influence within the Reich weakened by territorial and jurisdictional losses. Moreover, Gasparri had commented several times on the dangers of the Balkanization of the east, and he expressed belief that the settlement here would not last—a belief which paralleled German hopes and objectives. The legality of backing the ordinary's jurisdiction and the precedent of refusing to attach an overwhelmingly German-speaking area to a foreign diocese were points which could be justified and which helped Germany in places such as Silesia and Danzig. It was a victory for Germany that the Vatican honored the independence of Danzig and the pastoral wishes of the people and did not order the ecclesiastical incorporation of the Free City into Poland; likewise, it was beneficial to Germany that the Vatican desired impartiality and restraint against agitation in Silesia. Moreover, Germany was fortunate in being able to use the concept of historic rights and possession sanctioned by time in its case to retain its ecclesiastical borders. All the contested areas had belonged to the Reich, and it was up to the new states to show why this relationship should be altered. The reality of new political borders argued powerfully in favor of change; but, while conceding the obvious, the Vatican still frequently opted to do what it could for the German side. These diplomatic victories gave Germany cause to hope that at least its policy with regard to the Church might allow the Reich to salvage something after the defeat in 1919 at Versailles.

The eastern ecclesiastical situation in many ways paralleled the po-

[122] See, for example, AA, PO II, PO 24 Vat., Oberschlesien, Vol. 1, Brentano (Vatican) to AA, report of discussions with Polish Cardinal Hlond, August 5, 1926.

litical scene, and it was just as difficult to reach an ecclesiastical settlement there as to arrive at a political one. There was no Locarno in
the east, neither political nor ecclesiastical. Moreover, the local clergy
as well as the governments also entered into the controversy. Each
state supported by its national clergy sought to win influence at the
Vatican and to use religion to regain or maintain control of contested
areas. But the Germans had to be wary lest they overstate their case
or pressure the Vatican too strongly. Cutting off clergymen's salaries
or benefices or threatening *Kulturkampf* tactics would only create more
trouble than it was worth, and Vatican diplomatic resources on behalf
of the Reich were also needed in other areas. The only weapon that
they could use was to warn that unfavorable Curial decisions on the
eastern border could hurt the concordat negotiations. But this could
be pushed too far. In 1927 the Rumanians were to employ this threat
while discussing their concordat and were icily told that the Roman
Church had existed 1,900 years without a concordat with Rumania
and would surely be able to survive 100 years more without one.[123] In
this sense Germany was limited in its maneuverability. To anger or
threaten Rome over a little prize might cause bigger gains to slip through
Germany's fingers. This was the narrow road which the Foreign Office had to tread—deciding how much leeway it had in exerting pressure in Rome and at the same time preventing forces within Germany
which did not perceive the full diplomatic picture from criticizing Vatican actions or concordat proceedings.

In many ways, while indicating evidence of aiding Germany, the
Vatican had also demonstrated by its concessions to other states which
had regularized their affairs with the Church how beneficial it would
be for Germany to do likewise. Not only could Germany threaten the
Vatican with discontinuing concordat proceedings but Rome could
also reverse this argument and emphasize how much it would be to
Germany's advantage, even for diplomatic reasons alone, to conclude
such an agreement. Bergen therefore suggested that rather than protesting every incident unpleasant to Germany and making allusions to
dangers for the concordat negotiations it was more advantageous for
the Reich to point to the justice of its cause, the pastoral needs of
German Catholics, the injury which disturbances over jurisdictions
had on diocesan life, and the damage which these incidents had on the
Church as a whole and on the Vatican's policy of international peace.
It was such arguments, said the Ambassador, which had already convinced the Vatican to help moderate the activities of the more nation-

[123] AA, PO II, PO 20A Vat., Breslau, Vol. 4, Bergen to AA, December 27, 1927.

alist prelates and governments working against the Reich.[124] Germany therefore had every reason for satisfaction with the support that it had received from Rome and with the diplomatic successes that it enjoyed in questions of ecclesiastical jurisdictions. But this was only part of the battle and one generally waged against small powers whose own existence or stability the Vatican still questioned. In the west, Germany also had to defend its borders and here too needed Vatican support to do so. But along the Rhine the borders were more formidable as well as more permanent and the opponents more powerful and influential. It remains to be seen whether Germany's tactics here worked as effectively as in the east.

[124] AA, PO II, PO 24 Vat., Posen, Vol. 2, Bergen to AA, November 1, 1931.

CHAPTER IV

Threatened Dioceses in the West
1920-1924

Since many sections of the contested or lost territories on Germany's eastern borders contained large Catholic populations, the Vatican became an important factor in the Reich's diplomatic strategy to preserve as much influence and control in the east as possible. Here Germany faced states which, although newer and smaller than the Reich, also had large or, as in Poland's case, overwhelmingly Catholic populations, a fact which assured them a hearing in Rome, consequently creating difficulties for Germany's diplomatic campaign at the Vatican. But the situation in the west was even more serious and to some degree more critical for both German politicians and for the German Catholic Church as a whole. While the border territories in the east contained a mixed Protestant and Catholic populace, all the endangered western border areas' inhabitants were predominantly Catholic.[1] Not only was the dimension of the loss or danger to territory and population larger here than in the east, but the means and extent to which the ties with the Reich would be weakened or severed varied, thereby further complicating the matter. Some territories such as Alsace-Lorraine and Eupen-Malmédy were transferred soon after the war to the control of a western power; some, such as the Saar (Saarland), had their future placed in question; and yet still others, such as the Rhineland proper,[2] were occupied by foreign troops. The occupation of German territory, including such historically important sees as Cologne and Trier, by French troops, for example, gave France the opportunity to influence church affairs, politics, and daily life in the area by working with prelates willing to cooperate with the occupying forces.

[1] See *Lexikon für Theologie und Kirche* (Freiburg i.B., 1931), Vol. 3, Map "Kirchliche Einteilung Deutschlands bis nach dem Weltkrieg," p. 251. Krose, Vol. 9 (1919/20), section 8 "Konfessionstatistik u. Kirchliche Statistik," especially part 2 and pp. 416-456.

[2] The problem of the specific difficulties created for German dioceses because of Allied pressure either directly to detach areas from the Reich or to influence episcopal elections will be dealt with in this chapter. The more general problem of Allied influence on the Church in the occupied Rhineland will be taken up in subsequent chapters.

Moreover, the border territory in the west affected more Germans personally than did the eastern borders, since the disputed area here encompassed not only parts of Prussia but also of Bavaria, thus raising the possibility of jurisdictional and territorial loss for both of Germany's largest states and their Catholic hierarchies. The endangered areas also bordered on other German states such as Baden and Hesse, and rather than being far off in the east, away from large German urban centers, they were close to some of the most heavily populated sections of Germany, a fact which naturally made the population there more immediately aware of the struggles for control. Germany faced not the successor states but older, more established governments, including France one of the victors of the war. Belgium had a record of good relations with the Papacy and a population with a reputation of a loyal devotion to its Catholic faith. France, although still officially anti-clerical in its outlook, was a Catholic nation which could make its presence felt at the Vatican and which commanded sufficient military and political strength to implement its policies on its eastern borders. The matter was a grave one for Berlin, but the government nevertheless hoped to prevent total predominance of the Allied view of the world situation and by the force of its own arguments to convince Rome to lend the Reich its support.

Immediately after the armistice Berlin was given an example of the Church's potential for becoming involved in the political developments in the west. Even before the signing of the Versailles Treaty, reports appeared in the press stating that the German-born bishops of Metz and Strasbourg, the leading cities of Alsace-Lorraine, had resigned and were being replaced by French prelates. Berlin had not been officially informed of this and feared that the Papacy was departing from its impartiality by hastily acting to "de-Germanize" the province. The report caused even more bitterness in light of the German policy, after the absorption of Alsace-Lorraine into the Reich in 1871, of not insisting that the ordinaries be ethnic Germans. In June 1919 inquiries from German representatives to the Holy See clarified the matter. Some action had been taken, but not as stated in the newspapers. The Vatican, intent on resuming an influential position in world affairs and furthering its contacts with all the major Powers, actively sought the resumption of Vatican-French relations interrupted since 1904. Thus, anxious to strengthen its ties with France, it had begun negotiations to replace the German-speaking bishops with Frenchmen, but with the proviso that such steps could be possible only when territories in which these prelates resided had been internationally recognized as having been ceded to France. The newspapers omitted this stipulation and made it appear as though the Papacy recognized France's political rights over Alsace-Lorraine even before the official announcement of the treaty, thus giving France some propaganda advantages and Germany a potential cause for disagreement with Rome.

The Vatican had been remiss and undoubtedly should have kept Berlin closely informed of these negotiations. The Holy See, however, faced enormous pressure from French clerical and political forces to recognize the transfer, and since the Curia regarded the political cession to be a foregone conclusion and did not wish to offend France at a time when it sought to renew diplomatic relations, it actually had begun discussions before the conclusion of the treaty. This situation which proved embarrassing to Rome never would have occurred had the Curia waited several months. With the signing of the treaty neither the Vatican nor Germany could raise objections to Paris' demand for the appointment of French bishops within its borders. Thus, when in early 1920 Paris officially reintegrated Alsace-Lorraine into the French state, it appointed prelates belonging to the French hierarchy to the sees of Metz and Strasbourg and had ecclesiastical control of the provinces duly transferred from Germany to France. In analyzing the world situation in 1919-1920 Germany had believed that one point favoring its efforts to win Vatican support was that Rome would aid the Reich so that it could serve as a counterweight to French power in Europe and also because Rome would like to show Berlin its good faith in the hopes that this would lay the basis for a new church-state relationship within Germany. Berlin was, however, also aware that the loss of Austro-Hungarian and German influence in Europe might incline Rome to withhold its help and instead seek to gain concessions from the victors by acceding to their demands. The fact that the German-speaking bishops had been asked to resign in Alsace-Lorraine and that episcopal changes occurred so rapidly convinced Berlin that France had undoubtedly urged an expeditious settlement here.[3] It meant that Germany might face stiff competition in presenting its views in Rome.

The correspondence of the boundaries of these two dioceses to the political borders of an area no longer part of the Reich deprived Germany of a basis for protest. In the absence of a concordat between the Reich and the Holy See, Berlin had no legal cause even to be consulted about the changes. Along the Belgian-German border, however, in the counties (*Kreise*) of Eupen-Malmédy, which along with its population of 50,000-60,000 inhabitants formed part of the archdiocese of Cologne, the problem differed somewhat. Versailles stipulated that the tiny area should be ceded to Belgium, but provided for

---

[3] *Germania*, April 25, 1919. *Corriere d'Italia*, May 4, 1919. GSTA, MA 104452, Ritter to BFM, May 18, 1919; June 20, 1919. Krose, Vol. 9 (1919/20), pp. 79-80.

the local inhabitants to express their opinion, by a vote, about remaining within the German Reich. The League of Nations would thereupon take into consideration the wishes of the population and then render a final decision about the future of the counties. It was not properly a plebiscite, although popularly known as such, but rather a "consultation," an opportunity for the populace to protest against the cession already made, but one which had no binding legal power. Cologne, to which this territory belonged, naturally desired the perpetuation of its ecclesiastical jurisdiction. Likewise, it was also politically important for Germany that Cologne retain control, regardless of the League's decision. If Cologne maintained its authority at least until the plebiscite, the clergy might be used to influence the vote in favor of the Reich. Germany was not prepared to accept the finality of Eupen-Malmédy's loss. If Belgian sovereignty was recognized over the area, Berlin expected Brussels to request the separation of the two districts from the jurisdiction of the German hierarchy. German ecclesiastical control here, even if the area was officially transferred to Belgium, was extremely important, since through its influence the ties to the Reich would be maintained which, should a change in the international situation permit, would allow the area to be more easily reunited with the Reich. If the Vatican separated Eupen-Malmédy from Cologne and attached it to a Belgian see, this would mean diplomatically that the Vatican accepted the finality of the Versailles provision or, even worse, favored the Belgians. Such a Vatican decision would diminish German hopes of gaining support for its position and decrease its diplomatic maneuverability with the Allies. The battle for Eupen-Malmédy, therefore, began on the Vatican front almost at once.

In August 1919 the Belgian Ambassador at the Vatican began pressing Gasparri to transfer the area immediately to Belgian ecclesiastical control so that German propaganda among the clergy would not influence the populace in favor of Germany in the forthcoming plebiscite. Gasparri acted cautiously and responded: "We cannot detach these two territories from German jurisdiction by solemn act with the chance of their being returned to it [Germany] again." Instead, he promised to place the territory under apostolic administration until the final resolution of its fate.[4] Cardinal Mercier of Malines (Mechelen) joined the fray, lining up on the side of his government by writing the Curia and urging that the Pontiff should send only a Belgian to administer and supervise the area. The Belgians contended that, since the territory had been granted to their state by the treaty and was already being politically administered by that country, the vote to be taken in

---

[4] BelgFO, Eupen-Malmédy, 11.24 6B, Ursel (Vatican) to Hymans, August 16, 1919.

Eupen-Malmédy could not be considered a referendum in the ordinary sense. Consequently, Belgian ecclesiastical administration should be put in force immediately. Gasparri, a renowned legalist in his own right, presented all the reasons against such a step. The Vatican regarded any vote concerning civil matters as not relating directly to church affairs, and an argument by analogy lacked validity. Vatican policy was to remain impartial, and the nomination of a Belgian as administrator would indicate such partiality and give the German Foreign Office cause for complaint. The Cardinal Secretary of State therefore politely refused Mercier's request and stated that the final verdict about the fate of Eupen-Malmédy was yet to be made, but that the vote would be of great importance in deciding the issue in the eyes of the Church. In order to ensure that the plebiscite take place without domination from either side, he intended to name a Vatican official for the task. "Neither Belgian nor German, but representing the Holy See, he will use his power only in the exclusive interests of caring for souls without placing it at the service of either of the opposing powers."[5]

Belgium nevertheless continued to petition the Vatican with legal statements about how Brussels had already been awarded the area, with all administrative rights and powers, and with reasons why it had an obligation and duty to protect its interests against hostile propaganda from German sources. A neutral administrator, so the argument went, would not sufficiently safeguard Belgium's rights. In asking for a Belgian apostolic administrator, Brussels was not requesting a favor which would compromise Vatican impartiality, but rather a means to protect legitimate Belgian rights.[6] France also had realized the importance of ecclesiastical politics and reasoned that the Allies should make use of matters dealing with church affairs to support their own political goals. In 1920, for example, Emmanuel Peretti de la Rocca, Director of Political Affairs in the French Foreign Office, sent a memorandum to his ambassadors in Rome, Warsaw, London, Brussels, and at the Vatican in which he discussed the significance of gaining ecclesiastical jurisdiction away from the Reich as a means of weakening Germany. In both the east and west, Peretti urged that every effort be made to ensure that the ecclesiastical boundaries conform to the new political frontiers as established by the peace settlement.[7] Belgium was now in the process of following this French advice.

The Germans countered in early 1920 with legal statements. Berlin

---

[5] BelgFO, Eupen-Malmédy, 11.24 6B, Gasparri to Mercier, October 2, 1919.

[6] BelgFO, St. Siège 1919-1922, Ursel to Gasparri, October 16, 1919, Ursel to Hymans, October 18, 1919.

[7] FFO, Pologne 58, Peretti (FFO) to embassies, December 22, 1920.

objected to an apostolic administrator of any kind over part of the diocese of Cologne, since the borders and the authority of the ordinary had been defined in the Bull *De Salute Animarum* of 1821, and to which the Prussian Government had given its consent; they could now be modified only with the approval of both parties. Consent from the German side, stated Berlin, could not even be considered until the preference of the local inhabitants had been made clear by the vote. But now, having heard the opposing view from each country on how to handle the problem, Gasparri stood by a decision for compromise. He had already rejected several proposals and demands from Brussels on how to administer the area. Moreover, he had learned that Brussels, with its occupying forces, was determined and able to block contact between Cologne and Eupen-Malmédy. It would be better in the interests of the Catholic population to have a neutral administrator who could carry out his ecclesiastical responsibilities and ensure some degree of impartiality. As a counteroffer to the Belgian suggestion, the Vatican proposed that the Nuncio in Brussels, an Italian, be named provisional administrator of the area. After some further negotiation Brussels accepted this proposal, and Msgr. Sebastiano Nicotra was named administrator for six months (January 10-July 10).[8]

In March a meeting about the Vatican's new appointment between civil and church officials was held in the office of the Prussian Minister of Education and Religious Affairs. The Prussian Government, still objecting to an administrator and regarding his appointment as a violation of the 1821 agreement, did not wish to emphasize its dissatisfaction until learning what the new Archbishop, Karl Joseph Schulte, thought of the matter. After a lengthy discussion, Schulte and Prussian officials both agreed not to raise any objections to the new administrator over what, in the long run, might not be a problem for German policy. Since there had been no nationalistic tensions in the area or cases of violence, the administrator's duties, unlike the situation in Silesia, were basically to care for the spiritual well-being of the inhabitants until the political decision would allow the diocesan borders to be permanently fixed. The jurisdictional authority of Cologne's bishop was still recognized in Eupen-Malmédy, despite the new duties of the Nuncio, and both prelates had agreed to consult each other about measures to be taken for the well-being of the inhabitants. In order to safeguard Cologne's authority the Nuncio had also been di-

---

[8] Interestingly enough, the policy of appointing the nuncio accredited to the countries seeking territory from the Reich to the post of supervising the plebiscite areas was used in both east and west; in Eupen-Malmédy in January 1920 with Nicotra's appointment, and shortly thereafter with Ratti's appointment to the plebiscite areas along Germany's eastern borders.

rected by Rome to refrain from becoming involved in any matters dealing with political propaganda and to instruct the clergy to do the same.[9] The clergy in the area could still maintain contact with their Archbishop. In fact, on March 30 the entire clergy of both cantons had telegraphed their loyalty to him and to the Reich, thus indicating no erosion of the ordinary's power. Under the circumstances both clerical and political leaders felt that there was no sense in provoking the Vatican, for within the limitations of the diplomatic situation at that time the Vatican was looking out for German interests as best as could be expected.[10]

Archbishop Schulte was satisfied with this provisional solution and requested that it be retained until the League made its final decision. While Bertram had objected to any infringement upon his authority in Upper Silesia, Schulte in Cologne was more willing to cooperate, but both prelates acquiesced in an administrator only on the condition that their jurisdiction would still be recognized. Although agreeing to having a Vatican delegate in his territory, Schulte also protested to Rome about Belgian interference in parish matters in the cantons, such as requests by Belgian officials to see parish financial accounts and an official visit of the general vicar of the Liège diocese to Eupen-Malmédy, who had come without first seeking permission from Cologne. Schulte complained that these moves were made to strengthen the Belgian positions in the area. He also took the opportunity to assure the Pontiff of the loyalty of the population of the two counties to the Cologne archdiocese, to which they had belonged for 1,600 years. Moreover, he stated that, should the area be ceded to Belgium, most of his clergy would leave. No Belgian diocese was able to fill the forty-two parishes with German-speaking priests, and this changeover would cause chaos and disorder in daily church life there. The question of whether ecclesiastical jurisdiction should correspond with political boundaries, the Archbishop reasoned, should be decided from the standpoint of pastoral care. In addition, a separation of Eupen-Malmédy would not only cause distress to the inhabitants but it would also foster bitter resentment throughout Germany, which in turn would harm the cause of religion and the Church at a time when efforts were being made to reestablish a working relationship between Church and State throughout the Reich.[11]

[9] AA, IA, Preussen 2 Nr. 2b, Vol. 9, Bergen to AA, February 20, 1920.

[10] AA, IA, Preussen 2 Nr. 2b, Vol. 9, memorandum of Horstmann (AA), April 1, 1920. Letters of the clergy to Pontiff: AA, PO II, PO 24 Vat., Vol. 1, April 23, 1920 and one undated, probably early May, 1920.

[11] Germany, Cologne, Erzbischöfliches Ordinariat, CR 25,14,23, Vol. 1, Schulte to Benedict, mid-May, 1920.

The priests of the area echoed their bishop's fears that the transfer to Belgian clerical control would create numerous pastoral problems. In a letter to the Pope signed by the entire clergy, the pastors stated that their parishioners were truly distressed about the problem. During April some 8,000 people had demonstrated in Eupen against the transfer. Moreover, they mentioned that the Cologne archdiocese had over the years contributed large sums of money for religious organizations, youth clubs, laymen's societies, worker and charitable institutions, etc. The transfer might seriously threaten the work of these groups, since Belgian dioceses were not as richly endowed as that of Cologne. Should the German clergy leave, then French would be introduced into the area as the language in the schools and churches, causing disruptions in religious education and church functions. Finally, the clergy expressed their concern that the wounds of the war had not yet healed and that the Belgians, including some of the clergy, still exhibited an antipathy toward the Germans. To attach German-speaking areas to a Belgian diocese would cause problems and tensions for the local inhabitants.[12]

In order to strengthen Germany's position, Bergen, as he had done for the eastern areas, requested repeatedly that Germans from Eupen-Malmédy come to Rome to meet with Vatican officials and emphasize their loyalty to Cologne. He stressed to Berlin officials the Vatican's willingness to hear the German viewpoint and its need for more German opinions before it adopted a more active attitude in the matter. He further urged that the Vatican be kept informed of all German diplomatic moves as a sign of the candidness and goodwill of the Reich. Information which he had already given Curia officials had been appreciatively received and had, he believed, caused the Vatican to be more favorable to Germany's stand. Bergen, a strong supporter of cooperation with the Vatican, emphasized that Germany had many active friends in the Vatican and their friendship was to be fostered.[13]

Berlin looked upon any change in the ecclesiastical boundaries as a potential source of German weakness vis-à-vis its neighbors. Not only did Eupen-Malmédy have to be retained, but the government rejected any proposed divisions or reduction in size of dioceses in the west. Across the border from Eupen-Malmédy within Germany some local sentiment existed in favor of separating territory from Cologne and creating a new diocese at Aachen. If this occurred, it would diminish the authority of Cologne's archbishop and might permit France and Belgium to gain influence over the appointment of the new bishop,

[12] AA, PO II, PO 24 Vat., Vol. 1, letter of Eupen clergy to the Pope, April 23, 1920.

[13] AA, BRV 169, Vol. 1, Bergen to AA, April 14, 1920.

thereby weakening German defenses. At the time of the dispute over Eupen-Malmédy Berlin wanted no other ecclesiastical territorial revisions, especially in this region. Bergen was instructed by the Foreign Office, in line with his action taken for the two border counties, to inform the Vatican that the German Government firmly opposed any movement in favor of a new diocese. Cologne must be retained as an archdiocese in its entirety, for this thousand-year-old see, long associated with German tradition and culture, was considered a bulwark against French-Belgian influence.[14]

The controversy over Eupen-Malmédy as well as in the east had given Bergen cause to think out German strategy, and he frankly admitted his uncertainty about adopting a stance. Should he insist that the diocesan borders conform to political boundaries, or should he state that the Reich lay great store on retaining the diocesan boundaries as they were? Before going further he analyzed the advantages and disadvantages of both viewpoints. If the former line of reasoning was adhered to and the plebiscite decisions went against Germany, then Breslau's influence in Silesia and Cologne's in Eupen-Malmédy would be eliminated. If, on the other hand, Berlin chose the latter alternative, Germany's claim to Eupen-Malmédy and Upper Silesia might be strengthened, but the Reich would have to reckon with parts of Prussia, such as the German areas belonging to Posen-Gnesen, being placed under the control of a Polish ordinary. Bergen desired to know from Berlin what the best strategy would be. The Foreign Office wanted to see what could be obtained according to the circumstances, but Berlin believed that the situation at that moment was still too unclear for a final decision. Not having given up hope for changes in the treaty, the Foreign Office thereupon advised Bergen to insist on the maintenance of all jurisdictions which German dioceses formerly possessed, and to pursue the Reich's claims with the hopes that developments on the borders might further favorably clarify Germany's options. Berlin also anticipated that concordat negotiations, which had begun with Pacelli in 1919-1920, might grant Germany some of its demands.[15] This may also account to some degree for Germany's agreement, as a gesture of accommodation, to the appointment of apostolic administrators in the disputed areas, while still insisting on the rights of the ordinary. Germany had shown a willingness to compromise, yet without conceding anything that they could not later make good.

---

[14] AA, IA, Preussen 2 Nr. 2r, Vol. 1, Under Secretary of State to Bergen, February 20, 1920.

[15] AA, IA, Preussen 2 Nr. 2b, Vol. 9, Bergen to AA, February 16-17, 1920. AA, BRV 169, Vol. 1, Haniel to Bergen, March 6, 1920.

The matter of the borders and Germany's attitude toward them required a decision by the summer of 1920, when the first plebiscite seriously affecting Catholic dioceses was scheduled.[16] The "consultation" took place in Eupen-Malmédy on July 24, 1920. Belgian officials were in charge of the polling, which involved a complicated process of registration. Despite the German claim of improper procedures, few people registered their protests to the transfer. The League therefore upheld the Belgian position and declared that the opposition of the inhabitants was insufficiently strong to outweigh the reasons which had caused the framers of the treaty to cede the area to Belgium.[17] The Belgian Government thereupon announced that "now that the cantons of Eupen-Malmédy have become irrevocably Belgian, the Belgian Government requests of the Holy See that a complete rupture in the jurisdictional control of Cologne [with the two cantons] be proclaimed immediately." The situation had become more difficult for both Germany and the Vatican. Germany's justification for retaining control was now less convincing, and the Vatican was being asked to make a decision soon. The Reich contested the plebiscite and presented materials alleging illegal pressure during the election and unfair interference from Belgian authorities. It now demanded a ruling on the matter, not from the Council of the League, but from the full Assembly. In Rome Bergen received instructions once more to urge that the cantons remain with Cologne, or at least that Rome delay making a final decision. On October 10 Bergen reported that Gasparri recognized the arguments of the clergy of the area, based on historical and pastoral reasons, but legally the Belgians now had a valid right to demand transfer.[18] The Foreign Office informed Schulte of the steps that it had taken and also urged him to use his influence in Rome to support the German position.[19] Gasparri informed Bergen, however, of the impossibility of postponing the final decision for longer than several more months. Bergen then suggested, in the probable event that the League confirmed Belgium's claim, that Rome allow Schulte to appoint an administrator to represent him in Belgium and not detach the area from his control. The Cardinal listened but gave no indication of how the Vatican would ultimately decide.[20]

In late October and early November, Schulte, in Rome with a group

[16] The votes in Allenstein, Marienwerder, and Eupen-Malmédy all took place in July.
[17] For a discussion of the consultation and its procedures, see Wambaugh, *Plebiscites*, Vol. 1, pp. 518-538.
[18] AA, BRV 170, Vol. 2, Bergen to AA, October 10, 1920, Haniel to Bergen, October 16, 1920.
[19] AA, BRV 170, Vol. 2, Haniel to Schulte, October 16, 1920.
[20] AA, BRV 170, Vol. 2, Bergen to AA, October 22, 1920.

of German pilgrims, took the opportunity of conducting discussions with Vatican officials about his diocese. Calling attention to the losses his see would have to sustain in Eupen-Malmédy, he outlined the serious difficulties which any further reduction in Cologne's size would cause, should the proposal for a new diocese at Aachen be seriously considered. Given the political situation in Germany and the strong French-Belgian interest in the area, Rome agreed to put off consideration of a new diocese along Germany's western border.[21] But, in order to help Schulte administer his large diocese, the Vatican promised to name an auxiliary bishop with a seat at Aachen to govern this area as part of Cologne's archdiocese. Schulte also took the opportunity to elaborate on Bergen's suggestion to grant Eupen-Malmédy an archepiscopal delegate responsible to Cologne in the event of the transference of the area to Belgium. If that proved impossible, rather than seeing the counties attached to a Belgian diocese, the Archbishop suggested, as a last resort, that a Papal administrator be named who would be responsible directly to the Holy See. Schulte believed that the German view had good chances for success since from his conversations in Rome he thought that the Vatican did not seem fully convinced that the matter had been ultimately resolved, and before full stabilization of the political settlement Rome hesitated to make changes.[22]

Schulte's opinion of Vatican policy for the land along the German-Belgian border was consistent with Rome's general attitude toward the post-war situation, that is, a belief that the Versailles settlement was not definitive and that any weakening of Germany might unbalance Europe. This lack of confidence in the treaty's durability and the conviction that Europe needed a strong Germany might thus help to explain the Vatican's slowness in changing any boundaries which would, in addition, only disrupt the pastoral life in Eupen-Malmédy. In any event, Schulte's discussions in Rome and the answers that he had received from the Curia satisfied German officials. Likewise, the new Archbishop had favorably impressed Vatican dignitaries with his comments. The fact that his opinion was highly valued was important to the Reich. Moreover, he was, in Bergen's opinion, besides being a prelate interested in the welfare of his flock, a loyal patriot concerned with the interests of Germany. His vigorous approach in presenting the Eupen-Malmédy situation to the Pontiff and Cardinal Secretary of State underscored the importance, in the vigilant Ambassador's eyes,

---

[21] A new diocese was established for Aachen in 1929, once the problem over the borders no longer seemed critical.

[22] AA, BRV 170, Vol. 2, Bergen to AA, November 5, 1920. AA, BRV 171, Vol. 3, Schulte to Benedict, October 30, 1920.

of having German dioceses occupied by bishops who could be relied on to support the government's position.[23]

On December 13 the confirmation by the Assembly of the League of the Council's decision to transfer Eupen-Malmédy to Belgium further narrowed the room for maneuvering. Brussels thereupon again demanded the ecclesiastical separation of the area from Cologne, and now also officially requested that the cantons be immediately attached to the Belgian diocese of Liège. Despite its temporizing answer, the Curia let Belgium know that, since the League had made its decision, the Holy See was not prepared to oppose the separation. But in early 1921 Rome still had made no concrete move. The Belgians complained that because of their nation's diminutive size their wishes were not being expeditiously fulfilled, and, to indicate the gravity with which they regarded the matter, they threatened a break in diplomatic relations with the Vatican if the Eupen-Malmédy situation was not settled in their favor immediately. Germany countered in Rome, stating that Berlin did not consider the transfer of the territory as final and once more resorted to their legal tactic. The borders of the Prussian dioceses, said Berlin, had been regulated in the Bull *De Salute Animarum* and could be altered only by mutual consent of both governments, and this matter could be taken up during future concordat discussions.[24]

Despite the German maneuvers to continue the diplomatic contest, even Bergen conceded that there was little hope of the German Church's retaining control there. Legally no question now remained concerning possession of Eupen-Malmédy. The Vatican in general had adopted a policy that all diocesan borders coincide with political ones. *De Salute Animarum* dealt with altering diocesan borders within Prussian territory. Since the two cantons no longer belonged to the Reich, the Vatican could counter that the Bull was not applicable there, and since no new agreement had been worked out between Berlin and Rome, Germany had no valid legal recourse. Bergen conceded that there was little possibility of Brussels consenting to, and the Vatican granting, an administrator for the area responsible to Cologne. He asked if it might not be better for Germany to show a more conciliatory attitude, in the hopes of at least salvaging something which would be of value in retaining the German character of the area.[25] The German Embassy in Rome allowed that the temporizing attitude of the Vatican had worked so far in Germany's favor, but the Curia could not hold out

[23] AA, BRV 170, Vol. 2, Bergen to AA, November 5, 1920.

[24] AA, BRV 171, Vol. 3, Bergen to AA, January 24, 1921.

[25] Germany, Cologne, Erzbischöfliches Ordinariat, CR 25,14,23, Vol. 1, Bergen to Schulte, January 26, 1921.

any longer, and Germany had no further counterarguments to advance in order to reverse the political situation.

When the separation appeared inevitable, Germany contested every inch of diplomatic terrain in a rear-guard action even after Belgium had won the decision from the League Assembly. Berlin, while still asserting the applicability of the 1821 agreement, now requested Rome, should it not accept Berlin's interpretation of the agreement, at least to prevent the area from being attached to a Belgian diocese or divided among several Belgian dioceses. Instead, the Reich suggested that Rome create an independent diocese within Belgium for the two counties, thus possibly preserving some of the area's German identity, for, with a population of 60,000 inhabitants, taken together they were large enough to justify the creation of a new see. The Belgian demand to integrate the cantons into already existing Belgian dioceses would mean the extinguishing within a short time of the remaining German character of church life here. In separating Eupen-Malmédy from Cologne the Vatican agreed to Germany's request for an independent diocese, but provisionally placed the area under the jurisdiction of the bishop of Liège until some future redrawing of the Belgian dioceses' borders. As Under Secretary of State Cerretti declared, forming an independent diocese was very practical, for should the region someday be returned to Germany, it would not have to be severed again from a Belgian diocese but could be transfered *en toto* back to the Reich. He also stated that the Vatican had granted the provisional administration of the area to the bishop of Liège as a concession to Brussels so that later a decision to create a separate diocese would be more palatable to the Belgians, who had been insisting upon complete incorporation of the cantons into a Belgian diocese.[26]

Cerretti also informed Bergen that this was as far as Rome could go in the matter. While the Vatican recognized the *Deutschtum* of the populace, now that the decision of the League was final, further delay could only hinder Vatican relations with Belgium over Church interests in the area as well as cause disruptions in the spiritual life of the people. As Bergen had wisely predicted, Rome rejected Germany's legal arguments about the 1821 agreement. Cerretti confirmed Rome's continuing recognition of its applicability for territories and diocesan borders within Germany, but not for areas already removed from German sovereignty. The Curia noted, the Vatican official added, that, encouraged by the recent League decision, the Belgian Government was becoming more insistent in its requests. Rather than delay the

[26] AA, BRV 172, Vol. 4, Bergen to Schulte, February 2, 1921. AA, PO II, PO 24 Vat., Vol. 2, excerpt of letter of Gasparri to Schulte, January 28, 1921.

decision and risk further pressure and demands, the Vatican had acted. He was sure that Belgium would not be completely satisfied with this solution, but neither would Germany. Cerretti emphasized that, considering the spiritual welfare of the inhabitants, the Holy See had done everything within the parameters of the possible to be equitable to both sides in what was for Rome a difficult situation. The Vatican also provided a list of guarantees which it would enforce in the area to ensure that the German population would be permitted the use of the German language and ecclesiastical customs in church affairs and not be "Belgianized" by the Church. Officially the Reich stance continued to insist on the legal validity of *De Salute Animarum*, but privately Bergen conceded, and Schulte concurred, that what the Vatican offered was the maximum in concessions which could be obtained under the circumstances.[27] On June 30, 1921, the Vatican issued a bull officially announcing its intention to create a separate diocese of Eupen-Malmédy, but temporarily attaching the region to the diocese of Liège.[28]

Germany's insistence even after the League's decision of appealing to the Bull of 1821 and presenting legal arguments to show that diocesan boundaries did not have to coincide with political ones might ostensibly appear as an example of poor diplomacy or determined obstinacy supported by a very weak case. But there was a policy objective here which took into account the entire question of border rectification, which was consistent, and, from a diplomatic standpoint, logical. If Berlin could win its argument now that diocesan borders remained intact—that politically separated areas not be attached to foreign dioceses, and that they be granted some degree of administrative independence—then should the important Upper Silesian or Saarland areas pass under foreign political control, a precedent would exist for retaining some form of ecclesiastical independence for the lost areas. Germany could then be more adamant in making its demands. It was a legal position which could hold the door open for further negotiation. For the present, however, once Rome had rendered its verdict about Eupen-Malmédy, Germany could do little more than accept a decision that the Vatican had termed most beneficial to all.[29]

[27] AA, BRV 172, Vol. 4, Bergen to AA, February 2, 1921.

[28] For publication of the transfer, see *AAS*, XIII, pp. 468-469. The Bull was signed July 30, 1921 and published October 1, 1921. It is perhaps no coincidence, and in order to assuage Germany's hurt feelings, that one month later Rome proclaimed the restoration of the diocese of Meissen in Saxony, which had been urged by the German hierarchy, clergy, and laity of that *Land*. Schmidlin, Vol. 3, p. 282.

[29] AA, PO II, PO 24 Vat., Vol. 2, AA (Delbrück's office) to Prussian Minister-President, March 4, 1921. AA, IA, Preussen 2 Nr. 2h, Vol. 28, Haenisch (Prussian Ministry of Ed. and Relig. Affairs) to AA, March 5, 1920. In 1925 Eupen-Malmédy

Germany had been working against great odds in Eupen-Malmédy. The territory had been awarded by Versailles to Belgium, and Germany's only political recourse had depended on the results of the "consultation" and legal appeals to the League. This highlighted even more dramatically that, failing on the political level, the Reich hoped to retain some influence here via the Church. The crisis occurred at an inopportune time, since Cardinal Hartmann of Cologne had just died and his successor, Archbishop Schulte, was new to the complexities of the problem and could not at first bring as much pressure to bear on the matter as perhaps one could normally expect from Cologne's archbishop. Germany had based a great deal of its case on the legality of *De Salute Animarum*, the validity of which the Vatican would not recognize beyond the borders of the new Germany. Moreover, Germany faced another difficulty resulting from the situation on the western borders, for if it stressed too strongly that Church boundaries should not be made to coincide with the territorial decisions of Versailles, then Poland would also be able to demand more control over those areas still within the Reich but now under Polish prelates along Germany's eastern borders. All these problems only accentuated the fact that church-state relations were still in flux within the Reich. Had Germany had a new treaty with the Vatican, some of the problems created by this situation might have been avoided, or at least provisions might have existed which could have allowed Germany the right to make more claims on areas such as Eupen-Malmédy than it did.

The Vatican, aware of the spiritual needs of the people in Eupen-Malmédy, would probably have been inclined to leave the area in German hands, since this would also coincide with the Vatican's policy of not weakening Germany as a factor in the diplomatic balance of Europe or weakening Catholic strength in Germany by reducing the Catholic population of the Reich. The Germans had at least con-

---

was finally incorporated into the diocese of Liège. The Belgians had wanted the area divided between several dioceses, but German pressure was able to prevent this. Although provisions had been made for an independent diocese for the area, the Holy See had no funds to establish and support a new diocese. The Belgians naturally would not provide the support, and the Germans, not having regularized their own church-state relations yet, regretfully felt they were unable to do so. The solution which was reached, however, allowed the two cantons to remain together with a German-speaking vicar-general to administer the area under the authority of the Bishop of Liège. Guarantees were also given for the use of German in the schools and churches. For tactical reasons the Germans protested that the promised independent diocese had not been established but privately were pleased that, given the strength of Belgium's case, Berlin's Vatican policy had enabled them nonetheless to see some of the German character of the cantons retained. GSTA, MA 101072, Ritter to BFM, August 21, 1925. AA, BRV 174, Vol. 6, Bergen to AA, August 22, 1925.

vinced the Vatican to delay as long as possible on making a final decision and ultimately to create a separate diocese which could be someday returned to Germany should conditions so allow. This was the best that could be accomplished, and the German Foreign Office acknowledged satisfaction with the Vatican's decision, given the circumstances under which it had to work. The Reich's official position was still that control of the two cantons had not been ultimately settled and that to maintain the Vatican's decision here did not prejudice Germany's future claims.[30]

One of the important elements necessary to German foreign policy in dealings with the Vatican, especially concerning border situations, was to have the support of the local hierarchy. The bishops could play an important role by seconding government efforts and raising matters of concern to Germany in their conversations with Curia officials. The affair over the selection of Cologne's Archbishop (November 1919 to January 1920) had already demonstrated to the Foreign Office that the problem of ensuring that all border dioceses were headed by prelates loyal to the Berlin Government had indeed become serious for German foreign policy.[31] The Reich Government, with an eye to all the international and diplomatic ramifications, indicated more concern over this matter than did the Prussian Government. This may be one reason why the Reich Government was at first more anxious to conclude a concordat or reach a *modus vivendi* with the Vatican than was the Socialist-led Prussian Government, which had to concern itself with the opposition of many of its own supporters and of Prussian Protestants to a treaty with the Vatican. The Reich viewed the matter more in terms of foreign policy, Prussia more in terms of internal affairs.[32] Bergen, as representative of both the Reich and Prussia, also grasped the importance of having loyal German bishops in the border dioceses. He had discussed this matter with the new archbishop of Cologne and had won his support. Both agreed—each via his own method of relaying information—to stress to the Vatican the necessity of appointing such men to these sees should the occasion arise.[33]

Berlin soon had occasion to remind Rome of this matter. In late November 1920 the health of Georg Kirstein, Bishop of Mainz, had

---

[30] Germany, Cologne, Erzbischöfliches Ordinariat, CR 25,14,23, Vol. 1, Simons (AA) to Schulte, May 4, 1921. For Germany's later revisionist policy in the Eupen-Malmédy question, see Manfred J. Enssle, *Stresemann's territorial revisionism: Germany, Belgium, and the Eupen-Malmédy question, 1919-1929* (Wiesbaden, 1980), especially pp. 31-32, 197, 203-204.

[31] See ch. 2, p. 94ff.

[32] Dieter Golombek, *Die politische Vorgeschichte des Preussenkonkordats (1929)* (Mainz, 1970), p. 6. See also ch. 7.

[33] AA, PO II, PO 20 Vat., Trier, Vol. 1, Bergen to AA, November 6, 1920.

deteriorated to such an extent that discussions began about the choice of a successor. The dean of the cathedral and vicar general of Mainz, Ludwig Bendix, a powerful force in the diocese, was a strong candidate to succeed to the episcopal throne. So strong was his influence that the civil authority in the area, the Hessian State Government, hesitated to speak against him publicly. But Berlin, upon inquiry, had heard of Bendix's favorable statements about a Catholic Rhenish free state as the ideal solution for the area's political development. Upon further investigation the Reich concluded that it would be too dangerous to allow a man with such views to occupy the see of Mainz. One way was to bypass an episcopal election and to have Rome appoint a coadjutor bishop to the ailing Bishop Kirstein who would have the right of succession. This possibility would serve several purposes. It would please the Vatican, which alone desired the right to make episcopal selections without an election; it would do away with any need once more to debate the validity of the 1821 agreement; and by dispensing with an election it would eliminate the possibility of the French, who had occupation forces in the area, bringing pressure to bear on the cathedral chapter to vote for Bendix or someone of similar views.[34]

In Paris the question of candidates for the Rhine dioceses was also being treated as an important aspect of occupation policy, and France had let it be known in Rome that it hoped that future prelates selected for the Rhineland would have pro-French or separatist leanings. Therefore in June the Foreign Office telegraphed Bergen to see what could be done to block Bendix's election and to learn if the Vatican would be willing to appoint a coadjutor, to persuade the chapter to elect a "more suitable" candidate, or to appoint Bendix to a position in Rome and thus remove him from consideration.[35]

After negotiations in Rome between Bergen and Vatican officials and in Germany between Pacelli and Reich representatives, the Curia expressed its willingness to name a coadjutor. Although the Hessian State Government was most anxious to have a reliable man as bishop, it did not have adequate funds to pay the salary of a second bishop in the diocese. Faced with this impasse, the Foreign Office decided to intervene and allotted 2,000 marks to the new coadjutor, beginning with the month of his appointment. Pacelli was asked to handle the monthly payments since Berlin did not wish the French occupation forces to learn that the German Foreign Office was contributing to the coadjutor's income. Berlin's only request was that the person se-

[34] AA, PO II, PO 20 Vat., Mainz, Vol. 1, Delbrück to Simson, September 18, 1920 and Lerchenfeld (Darmstadt) to AA, November 23, 1920.

[35] AA, PO II, PO 20 Vat., Mainz, Vol. 1, AA to Bergen, June 13, 1920.

lected be a Rhinelander.[36] The choice fell on Msgr. Ludwig Hugo, rector of the seminary in Speyer, a choice which pleased the Germans immensely. Meanwhile, Pacelli hastened to inform the French of the selection before the official announcement appeared, and took pains to assure the French that every consideration had been made to appoint a prelate acceptable to them. The Nuncio made a favorable impression with Emile Dard, French representative in Munich, who later told his superiors of Pacelli's earnest attempt to accommodate French wishes and to dissipate beliefs in Paris of his anti-French inclinations. The Nuncio explained to Dard that the reason why French occupation officials had not been consulted about the selection of Hugo was because Rome did not even consult Paris in the choice of bishops for dioceses in France. Until French-Vatican relations were regularized, Rome would not consult French officials about episcopal appointments. Pacelli's statement was of course meant to put pressure on the French to resume diplomatic relations with the Vatican, and it also gave a logical excuse for not having the Mainz problem brought to the attention of the occupying forces. In any event, Dard accepted the Nuncio's explanation as reasonable.[37] Germany's request had been granted, and the succession in Mainz had eliminated the necessity for an episcopal election and for possible intervention from the French.

Not all French diplomats were willing to take the Nuncio's explanation at face value nor to regard him so favorably. Jean Doulcet, French Chargé d'Affaires at the Vatican,[38] who from his post in Rome could take a broader view of the situation, had a less favorable opinion of Pacelli, who he said was to be regarded with caution. Since Pacelli had already told French officials of his hopes for a German victory in Upper Silesia so that Catholic strength in the Reichstag would not be weakened by the loss of the province, Doulcet concluded that Pacelli likewise could not be counted on to support French designs to detach the territory on the Left Bank of the Rhine from Berlin or to weaken the ties between the two sections of the Reich. Moreover, Doulcet believed, specifically in regard to the question of succession in Mainz, that Pacelli had not acted in France's interest. In October 1920 the Nuncio had inquired of the French if they would object to the naming of a coadjutor. The French High Commissioner in the Rhineland, Paul Tirard, conceded the need for such a bishop and, as far as he was concerned, would be happy with the selection of Bendix, who

---

[36] AA, PO II, PO 20 Vat., Mainz, Vol. 1, memorandum of Delbrück, December 11, 1920.

[37] FFO, Rive Gauche du Rhin 103, Dard (Munich) to FFO, January 25, 1921 (erroneously dated 1920), and February 10, 1921.

[38] See ch. 3, note 71, p. 130.

took a conciliatory attitude toward the French. Pacelli, said Doulcet, at first had promised the French that he would consult them before submitting candidates to Rome, but by December he informed them he could give them the names of the candidates only after they had been submitted to Rome. Pacelli promised, however, to persuade Rome to permit him to inform the French Government of the final decision.[39] French officials naturally resented the Vatican's change of policy, and Doulcet wondered if the fact that they had not been consulted might have other explanations than those which Pacelli gave to Dard. The French Foreign Office knew that Berlin also favored the appointment of a coadjutor, but it did not know that just at that time German officials and the Nuncio were negotiating Reich subventions for a coadjutor. Although the French were unaware of the details, they suspected that some form of accommodation had been made between Berlin and Rome, and this no doubt increased their suspicion that Pacelli, though an able and influential diplomat, did not warrant Paris' trust.

The question of episcopal succession had thus taken on the aspect of importance in the diplomacy of Germany and France for control of the Rhineland. In January 1921 Pacelli informed the French Minister in Munich that attention would soon focus on another diocese along Germany's western border, since the Bishop of Trier, Michael Korum, was then eighty years old, and Rome would soon have to think of naming a successor for him. Pacelli again reminded the French envoy that, once full diplomatic relations were resumed between Paris and the Vatican, France would have a better claim to being consulted about the succession. But for the moment, in Pacelli's opinion, the French could not expect such consideration. The French regarded episcopal appointments in Trier as more important for their interests than that of Mainz, where they had been outmaneuvered. Not only was Trier geographically closer to France, and hence subject to more potential influence from Paris, but it was in Trier's seminary, where the majority of the priests for the Saarland were trained. As Doulcet commented, it was important for France to make certain that the clergy, who in fourteen years would play a significant role in the Saar plebiscite, not be educated under the guidance of a pro-German bishop.[40] Therefore, by June French officials, in discussion with Korum, had already raised the subject of consulting Paris with regard to an episcopal successor in Trier. The French representative informed the French Foreign Office that Korum did not object to Paris' request, since this

---

[39] FFO, Rive Gauche du Rhin 103, Doulcet to FFO, January 12, 1921.
[40] *Ibid.*

would be in the interests of law and order in the occupied area and would foster better relations between the occupying forces and the Rhenish population. The French had learned from what had happened in Mainz. They had taken precautions in checking with the local ordinary and in not dealing solely with the Nuncio in Munich. After hearing Korum's reply, Tirard thereupon urged Premier Briand to press the Vatican, via the newly established French embassy at the Vatican and through the Nuncio in Paris, to consult France in making any decision about Korum's successor.[41]

Diplomatic negotiations over the succession in Trier entered the critical stage by late autumn, for on December 4 Bishop Korum died. Since *De Salute Animarum*, which had regulated episcopal elections for Prussian dioceses, including Trier, had been promulgated in agreement with the Prussian Government, it was this authority rather than the Reich Government which now took action. To forestall any French interference, Prussia informed the Vatican that it regarded the situation in Trier as a purely local matter not subject to foreign interference. The privilege of the Prussian Government to be consulted and to approve episcopal candidates was not transferable. France's assertion, by virtue of administering the Saarland and by occupying area in the Rhineland, to be entitled now to participate in the selection process was inadmissible. Berlin cited a Papal *breve*, *Quod de fidelium*, dealing with a state's legal position, to prove that Prussia's rights could not be delegated to a foreign jurisdiction. The altered political situation in the Rhineland, argued Berlin, should not affect the selection of the new bishop of Trier. But, besides using legal reasoning to show its good intentions and willingness to compromise, Berlin offered a proposal. To counterbalance France's claim to consultation, Prussia would, as long as the area was occupied, forego its right to participate in the election. Berlin's suggestion conformed to its internal policy of seeking a separation of Church and State, but here it was also useful to make such a statement for diplomatic reasons, since by demanding the exclusion of French influence the Germans could now also show fairness by renouncing their rights in the election.[42]

Once Prussia had stated its case, the Prussian Minister-President urged the Holy See to make the appointment as soon as possible to forestall interference.[43] The Reich Government, finding none of the possible candidates objectionable on diplomatic or political grounds, also urged a quick selection. The Germans had seen what they re-

[41] FFO, Rive Gauche du Rhin 103, Tirard to Briand, July 6, 1921.

[42] AA, PO II, PO 20 Vat., Trier, Vol. 1, Prussian Minister-President Braun to Bergen, December 11, 1921.

[43] AA, PO II, PO 20 Vat., Trier, Vol. 1, Braun to Bergen, December 11, 1921.

garded as clear evidence of France's extreme interest in the Trier situation. The French military bishop in the Rhineland, after first stating that he could not come to Bishop Korum's funeral, on the day before the ceremonies suddenly changed his mind, most probably on orders from Paris, and insistently announced that he would come after all, despite the fact that cathedral officials had made it clear that his participation was not desired. Moreover, a French general, colonel, and adjutant were also sent. The Germans labeled these appearances as propaganda moves by the French to demonstrate both in Trier and in Rome the great interest that Paris placed in the new appointment. Berlin was indeed correct, for the French were working to obtain the selection of a candidate agreeable to them.[44] French Commissioner Tirard had analyzed a list of all the possible candidates and their attitudes toward the French. He urged the Quai d'Orsay to pressure the Vatican to confirm someone willing to work with the French and to argue that the appointee could be of great help in maintaining good relations between the civilian population and the occupation troops. Such a candidate would further peaceful conditions, which would in turn lead to reconciliation between peoples and allow the clergy to minister to the needs of the populace. Tirard believed that Rome would be more receptive if such a case were made, and even suggested that the French Ambassador tactfully stress the necessity of choosing a man favorable to, as he said, a policy of appeasement.[45] Tirard warned that France should act with great discretion for fear that official pressure would antagonize the Rhinelanders and the clergy.[46]

The Prussians had made their offer to relinquish their right to consultation precisely because of their fear that, should France be brought into the negotiations, it would seek to weaken German control over that part of the Rhineland. But their offer was neither as altruistic nor as impartial as the diplomatic language made it appear. There was the calculated risk that even without being consulted, Prussian, i.e., German, interests would still be served. If Rome reserved to itself the right of making the appointment, the Foreign Office felt confident that its arguments for a pro-German candidate in order to prevent France from extending its influence or control eastward into the Rhineland would be accorded serious consideration by the Curia. At any rate, Germany would certainly fare no worse directly at the hands of Rome than if it agreed to French involvement in the selection process. More-

[44] AA, PO II, PO 20 Vat., Trier, Vol. 1, Brügger, State Secretary for the Occupied Rhenish Territories, Reich Ministry of the Interior to AA, December 11, 1921.
[45] FFO, Rive Gauche du Rhin 103, Tirard to FFO, December 17, 1921.
[46] FFO, Rive Gauche du Rhin 103, Tirard to Briand, December 24, 1921.

over, if the electoral method were allowed here, Germany again felt confident of success.

Similar to the situation in 1919 at Cologne, at Trier the question arose of whether the chapter had a right to elect the bishop or whether, because of the still unsettled relations between Church and State in Germany, Rome could directly appoint the bishop and the chapter merely present a list of candidates for Vatican consideration. In early 1922, after much negotiation in which Cardinal Schulte actively pleaded the case for Germany, the Vatican opted for the election to be held by the cathedral chapter. Ratti had just been elected Pope. There had been much discussion that he was not particularly pro-German, especially after his work as Nuncio in Poland and Papal Commissioner in Upper Silesia. As a sign of his goodwill to Germany and in order to quash rumors that he had little sympathy for the Reich, Pius informed Schulte that Trier could choose its bishop, as it had done in the past. He stipulated, however, that the chapter would not be permitted to nominate the candidates, this being reserved to Rome, but it would nonetheless be allowed to elect its new spiritual leader. He reminded the Cardinal that, as in Cologne in 1920, this election was not to be considered a precedent for future episcopal selection. This fortuitous decision caused by circumstantial conjunction of Ratti's election to the Papacy and the vacancy in Trier was again to Germany's advantage in checking a pro-French candidate,[47] for, as even the French conceded, German influence among the canons of the chapter was very great, since six out of the ten owed their nomination to the Prussian Government.[48]

In late February the cathedral chapter of Trier met and elected Msgr. Franz Bornewasser, a prelate with whom Berlin was quite content. Bornewasser, who came from the diocese of Cologne, was not overtly pro-nationalist, yet, while trying to work with the occupying forces in order to improve the lot of his flock, he remained staunchly loyal to the new German Republic. People who knew the bishop-elect expected him to exert a moderating influence in an area troubled by innumerable tensions between the civilian population and the occupying forces, and he had been the favored candidate of most civil and Church officials, including Schulte and Pacelli. An overt pro-nationalist would have caused more difficulties by antagonizing the French, whom Schulte and Pacelli had assured of their desire for someone able to work with them to rebuild the area and maintain peace. Paris, while preferring a more pro-French prelate, raised no objection to the results

[47] AA, PO II, PO 20 Vat., Trier, Vol. 1, Brügger to AA, February 26, 1922.
[48] FFO, Rive Gauche du Rhin 103, Tirard to Briand, December 24, 1921.

of the election.[49] On the other hand, German objectives had been reasonably met. The chapter, granted the right to elect its bishop without outside influence, had elected a Rhinelander, and not one of the candidates favored by the French.[50]

For Germans the appointment of a new bishop in Trier was important not only in itself for politics in the Rhineland, but especially because within the diocese lay part of the critical Saar area. Of all the areas on the Reich's western borders, this one caused Berlin the most prolonged concern, for the Saarland—a rich mining and industrial area consisting of 991 square miles and a population of 700-800,000—lay directly on the border between France and Germany. Under the terms of Versailles this territory was separated from Germany and administered by a League of Nations commission. France received the use of the coal mines there as reparation for its wartime losses. Paris, however, hoped to incorporate the Saar completely into the French state. Yet the treaty stipulated that a plebiscite to be held in 1935 would decide whether the Saar would become permanently French or German. The area itself fell under the jurisdiction of two bishops, part of it belonging to the diocese of Trier and part to the diocese of Speyer, which in turn belonged to the Prussian and Bavarian episcopates, respectively. Now that the territory had been detached from Germany, the question of the rights of the two German bishops was governed by the applicability of agreements or understandings which the Vatican had with both the Prussian and Bavarian states. The Saarland was overwhelmingly Catholic, and its people were devoted to its clergy, who had studied either in the seminaries at Trier and Bonn in Prussia or at Speyer and Munich in Bavaria.[51]

Concerned about maintaining the Saarland's ties to Germany, Berlin saw the Church and its clergy as an important means by which to effect this. But most Catholics in the area, while considering themselves German, had few strong cultural or spiritual bonds with the Prussian State, with its Protestant Junker tradition. The French, who occupied and administered this area after the war until the Treaty of Versailles went into effect in early 1920, perceived these attitudes toward Prussia, and already in 1919 sought to capitalize on these cultural and historical differences by appealing to the populace's Catholicism. Paris tried to influence them to sever all ties with Berlin and to

---

[49] FFO, Rive Gauche du Rhin 103, Tirard to FFO, March 7, 1922.

[50] For further documents, see AA, PO II, PO 20 Vat., Trier, Vol. 1.

[51] Sarah Wambaugh, *The Saar plebiscite* (Cambridge, Mass., 1940), p. 119. The Germans also had evidence that the French were attempting to loosen the links of the Evangelical Church in the Saar with those in Germany. See AA, PO II, Bes. Geb. Saar, Kirchliche Fragen, Vol. 1.

emphasize their west German, Rhenish Catholic character in a territory which would be economically oriented westward, not eastward. In many cities and towns in the Rhineland and the Saarland, libraries and reading rooms were opened under French auspices, and the authorities immediately allowed Corpus Christi processions, hitherto permitted by the Prussian authorities only in specified places, to be held throughout the area. French officials warned pious Catholics of the dangers of Bolshevism and what they termed the Socialist policies of the Berlin Government then "engulfing" Germany, and suggested that a French administration could best preserve Church traditions. Aware of the Church's influence, and in pursuance of this policy, General Josef Andlauer, the French commander in the Saar, consciously sought to win the good opinion of the Saar clergy by taking pains among his subordinates to ensure that their conduct toward the Church and its officials was correct, if not even cordial.[52]

Already in 1919 reports from Saarbrücken reached Munich and Berlin of French activities to detach the Saarland from the dioceses of Trier and Speyer and either attach it to the French diocese of Metz or create a new diocese that would encompass the entire district under one prelate, with his seat in Saarbrücken. Such a move would encourage or parallel political separatist movements in the Saar and help to prepare the groundwork for an anti-German vote in the 1935 plebiscite. In the summer of 1919 the Abbé Coqueret, a French cleric with connections with the French Government, had visited both the bishops of Speyer and Trier, sounding them out and seeking to win them over to the French view.[53] Word that foreign powers were attempting to use the Church in the Saar as one means of attaining their goals had been already discussed in both the German press and in public speeches. The problem undoubtedly created uneasiness in the Reich, as many Germans questioned whether the Vatican would change the ecclesiastical borders and thus aid and abet Germany's enemies at a time when Germany needed all the help that it could muster to dispel these apprehensions. Segments of the Catholic-oriented press, such as the *Augsburger Postzeitung*, while acknowledging the gravity of the loss which all the threatened area in both east and west would mean for Catholic Germany, stated assuringly that the Vatican did not make such momentous decisions overnight but only after, not before, the political

[52] Maria Zenner, *Parteien und Politik im Saargebiet unter dem Völkerbundsregime 1920-1935* (Saarbrücken, 1966), pp. 153-154.

[53] GSTA, MA 106157, memorandum of State Commissioner for the Pfalz, August 14, 1919. Reports of proposals for an ecclesiastical reorganization of the Saar can be found in France, Archives Nationales (hereafter cited as AN) AJ9 3822 G 40.

problems were definitively settled.[54] But though true in principle, as the newspaper stated, that the Vatican moved very deliberately in such matters, the possibility always remained that because of negotiations over other pressing matters, it might have to make concessions to such a power as France in matters dealing with the Saarland. Any concessions, be they only provisory—such as the establishment of an impartial administrator for the area or another type of interim authority—would still decrease German influence by limiting the direct control of the German bishops.[55]

The Foreign Office had been concerned about French activities to influence the populace through the Church not only in the Saar but generally throughout the entire area west of the Rhine, and had contacted various prelates to learn of their opinion about the matter. Victor Naumann, director of the News Division of the Foreign Office, received an answer, for example, from the Bishop of Paderborn, who agreed with the Foreign Office that every effort should be made to counter French agitation in the Rhineland and the Saar; and he was certain that the other bishops felt the same way and would do everything possible to encourage their clergy to support the Reich. The Bishop, however, was confident that the population of the Left Bank of the Rhine was sufficiently loyal to the Reich not to be swayed by French propaganda. He did not favor Naumann's suggestion to send priests and religious from other parts of the Reich into the endangered areas since the local clergy were for the most part patriotic Germans.[56] But in order to bolster this loyalty of which the Bishop spoke, most prelates generally hastened to declare their support for the Berlin Government and their solidarity with the people in the endangered or separated areas. Particularly in the Saarland, now that political links had been suspended with the Reich, the Church organization was a great aid in keeping up the populace's cultural ties with Germany to the east. Immediately after the war, in 1919, Bishop Korum of Trier had declared his opposition to a separation, which he repeatedly restated in order to reassure and encourage his flock:

> We must remain true to the poor people of the Saar at any price. They should know that I am now as before still their bishop. The ecclesiastical unity must remain intact under any circumstances. This is now the firm link which binds the loyal Saar population with their German homeland. It is not to be loosened. We would stand

[54] *Augsburger Postzeitung*, March 2, 1920.

[55] GSTA, MA 101072, Ritter to BFM, August 23, 1919.

[56] Germany, Paderborn, Archivstelle beim Erzbischöflichen Generalvikariat, XXII, 1, Bishop of Paderborn to Naumann (AA), May 31, 1919.

[as] traitors before our brave Catholics in the Saar if we now left them in the lurch.[57]

Regardless of the validity of Korum's opinion or the intentions of the area's inhabitants, if Rome ordered the territory transferred to French ecclesiastical jurisdiction or even placed under neutral control, ties between the Church in the Saar and Germany would undoubtedly weaken. Germany could use propaganda in the area and even send in additional clergy, as Naumann had suggested, but this would not be enough. The crucial decision of whether the area was to remain under German control would be made in Rome, with the burden on Bergen and Ritter to present a convincing argument to counter French demands for separation. The Germans, aware of their tenuous political position in the world, took the attitude that the best defense is an offense, and made their position clear to the Vatican before French overtures in Rome began in earnest. In October 1919 the Prussian Minister of Education and Religious Affairs denounced French propaganda in the Saarland aimed toward Catholics as purely politically motivated, and he instructed Bergen to inform the Vatican that the Reich and Prussia would oppose any change here without their consent.[58] One month later Bergen wired that he had learned of France's desire for a new Saar diocese and that the British Minister, acting for France at the Vatican, had raised the matter. But, since the Prussian and Bavarian missions were still in Lugano, they felt frustrated by their inability to oppose the Allied moves directly.[59] Therefore the Reich at first counteracted French activities in Rome by voicing its displeasure to the Nuncio. He had already been informed of the Reich's position and of uneasiness over French plans. Pacelli, in discussing the situation with the Prussian Minister in Munich, seemed clearly to side with the Germans and informed the diplomat that he personally would regard it as a mistake if a provisional situation such as in the Saar were used as a basis to alter ecclesiastical borders.[60] Pacelli's opinion was important to Germany, for he would undoubtedly convey this impression to Rome.

In December, both Ritter and Bergen received information from their Vatican sources confirming that France was indeed launching a strong campaign for the creation of an independent diocese for the Saarland. This was then a serious matter for both the Bavarian and

[57] Zenner, p. 155.

[58] AA, IA, Preussen 2 Nr. 2i, Vol. 5, memorandum of Haenisch (Pruss. Min. of Ed. and Relig. Affairs), October 27, 1919.

[59] AA, BRV 151, Vol. 1, Bergen to AA, November 11, 1919.

[60] AA, BRV 151, Vol. 1, Zech to AA, November 30, 1919.

Prussian state governments as well as for the Reich. The diplomats, besides having Pacelli relay their unhappiness with French proposals, decided now to act in concert in the name of the Reich, Prussian, and Bavarian Governments, formally to protest the creation of a Saar diocese.[61] In addition Munich's Archbishop Faulhaber, who had previously been bishop of Speyer, spoke to Pacelli and stated his objections. The General Vicar of the diocese of Speyer also protested to Pacelli about any separation of the Saar, and the Bavarian bishops in a letter to the Nuncio made clear that they completely endorsed Speyer's standpoint. Moreover, Bishop Ludwig Sebastian of Speyer warned Pacelli that Reich officials would regard the creation of a new diocese as support for France's political aims in the area, and it would cause great bitterness among the German public against the Vatican.[62]

The Germans presented a strong case against any separation, even from the ecclesiastical viewpoint. Besides the historical and political argument that the separation was not final, the bishops presented a pastoral view: a separation would disrupt the religious life of the community. A small area, it could not support a seminary in the event of the creation of a new diocese. The clergy brought in from other dioceses would not desire to remain permanently there because of the unpleasant industrial nature of the entire region. The constant changes in the clergy would then disturb and disorient the laity. Moreover, a political administration set up by the Versailles Treaty and regarded as temporary should not be used as the basis of permanent diocesan changes, especially when the wishes of the populace in this matter were not even being considered.[63] The people of the Saar, said the bishops, had already given indications of where their sentiments lay. The clergy and populace had already organized several demonstrations to show the local officials that they did not wish to be separated from the cultural or daily life of Germany proper.[64] In addition, at the beginning of July 1919 a statement on behalf of the entire Saarland clergy had been issued, expressing their desire to remain with the mother dioceses or at least delay the final decision about the fate of the area until the fifteen years of League administration had expired.[65]

Having shown a united front and presented their arguments, the Germans now waited to assess the situation and learn the Vatican's

[61] AA, BRV 151, Vol. 1, Zech to AA, December 5, 1919.

[62] GSTA, Ges. Päpstl. Stuhl 970, memorandum of the State Commissioner for the Pfalz, December 9, 1919.

[63] AA, IA, Preussen 2 Nr. 2i, Vol. 5, Becker to Prussian Minister-President, November 4, 1919.

[64] *Bayerischer Kurier*, May 3, 1921.

[65] Zenner, pp. 156-157.

reaction. In January 1920 both Ritter and Bergen had an opportunity to raise the question with Gasparri and were told that no official steps had been made on the part of France for separation, but that one could expect this to occur once France resumed diplomatic relations with the Vatican. In any case, however, Gasparri assured the Germans that the French request would be met with a firm refusal, since Curial policy, as had been made clear in the case of other border situations, was to make no territorial changes in any area with a still uncertain political fate. Ritter was, of course, pleased to hear such comments from the Cardinal Secretary of State, for he sensed a distaste in Gasparri's tone for French policies and what could be regarded as overweening demands by Paris for its own political purposes. Ritter therefore advised the Germans not to push the matter further in Rome, but rather, having stated their case, respectfully to wait and see how things developed and whether the French would further antagonize the Curia by their demands. He also recommended that the bishops of Trier and Speyer keep a careful watch on the situation, for he was sure that the French would not give up easily but would also attempt to propagandize the clergy or else push for an apostolic administrator for the Saarland, similar to those in the territories along the Polish border, and an attempt would be made to relieve the local ordinaries of their authority.[66]

In March 1920, after the League commission had assumed control in the Saarland, the clergy sent a letter to the civil officials reaffirming their attachment to the German dioceses and informing them of all the technical problems and confusion that an ecclesiastical separation would cause the laity. To emphasize the importance which the matter held for the Germans, Trier's Bishop Korum, then eighty years of age, made the fatiguing trip to Rome to beg the Holy See not to divide his diocese. He had learned that Abbé Coqueret had come to Rome with the backing of Paris, to urge that the area be attached to a French ecclesiastical administrator, since, as he stated, the people were mainly pro-French anyway. At the same time Pacelli also came to the Vatican where he threw his support behind the German view that any unilateral change of diocesan boundaries in areas not permanently transferred to another power could violate agreements made between Prussia and Bavaria and the Holy See. He also stressed that any such move would also jeopardize the negotiations in Berlin and Munich, which he was then conducting for a new regulation of church-state relations.[67] The Vatican, naturally cautious, saw no reason not to assure

[66] GSTA, Ges. Berlin 1555, Ritter to BFM, January 14, 1920. Zenner, pp. 156-157.
[67] GSTA, Ges. Päpstl. Stuhl 970, Ritter to BFM, March 2, 1920.

Germany again that nothing would be done, and there was no sense in needlessly aggravating the problem and endangering the concordat negotiations.

Ritter's fears that the French had not abandoned their plan, even if the Vatican was not initially predisposed to it, proved correct. In October 1920, the French Commissioner for the Rhineland, Tirard, wrote to the French Premier about the religious situation in the Saar, expressing concern over the concordat negotiations between Germany and the Vatican since the signing of concordats could finalize church-state relations and considerably limit French attempts to change borders or jurisdictions. Since Versailles had stated nothing about the religious situation, it was the Vatican's responsibility to bring ecclesiastical administration into conformity with the new political one. The jurisdiction of Trier and Speyer, said Tirard, could be weakened if the Holy See appointed an apostolic administrator for the region. Ideally the area should be attached to a French diocese, but, failing that, the minimum that French policy required was to have Rome name an administrator. Moreover, in order to wean the Saarland clergy away from Germany Tirard advocated that French officials encourage a policy of granting the Church in the Saar as much ecclesiastical independence from their superiors as possible.[68] If the Vatican would grant the request and the local clergy were sympathetic to the idea, the possibility of success for French objectives would look very good indeed.

In December the Bavarian representative to the Reich Commission for the Occupied Rhenish Territories, Siegmund Knoch, had learned that officials, including the Saar Minister for Religious Affairs, Count Léon Albin Moltke-Huitfeldt,[69] favored separating the Saar from the dioceses of Trier and Speyer. Other signs also pointed to increased French pressure for a separation of the region from the dioceses, such as Poincaré's remark in the French Senate made specifically in connection with the discussions to resume relations with the Vatican that the fate of the Saarland would be decided neither in Paris nor Berlin but in Rome; that if Rome acceded to French wishes there, the French Government would find it easier to win legislative approval for reestablishing ties with the Holy See. Moreover, the Strasbourg Bishop, Charles Ruch, whose diocese was close to the Saar, had spoken to his clergy in very nationalistic terms about the grandeur of the French nation and its control over the Rhineland, and had publicly attended

[68] AN, AJ9 2997, Dossier 3, Tirard to Premier, October 11, 1920; AJ9 3822, Tirard to Premier, October 6, 1920.

[69] Although he was Danish by birth, he was in orientation purely French and had lived in Paris for many years.

Maurice Barrès' chauvinistic, anti-German lectures on *Le Génie du Rhin.* Speyer's Bishop Sebastian also had no doubt that France intended to reach its political aims in the area by working via the Church. Sebastian related that ever since the occupation various French *abbés* had visited him, seeking to persuade him that the region would be better cared for under French administration, and the French occupation forces had also sought to influence his clergy in a similar manner.[70] General Auguste Hirschauer, Senator from the Moselle, reinforced this feeling again in 1921 by remarking in the French Senate that

> the majority of the population there [Saar and Rhineland] is profoundly Catholic. One of the main objections which German propaganda makes against France is to represent France as an anti-religious nation. The resumption of relations with the Vatican will remove this dangerous argument from the Germans.

The French ties with the Vatican, he continued, would make a profound influence on the population in the Saarland and Rhineland, encouraging them to look more favorably on France and thereby helping French policy to win them over. Briand seconded him.[71]

Such speeches underlined German suspicion that France was resuming relations with the Vatican, not for religious reasons but for purposes of foreign policy—to further its international goals, to detach the Left Bank from the Reich, and to use the Vatican as a listening post, as Briand had stated in the Senate in December.[72] Indeed, Peretti told Tirard several years later that Paris had hoped that French priests in the Saar and the entire Rhineland had been using their influence among the clergy and the laity to help French policy: in other words, to weaken Berlin's control.[73] Moreover, the Saar Commission or Administration, set up to govern the area by the Allies, seemed in the eyes of the Saarlanders strongly dominated by French interests, and was acting in a manner which would help to wean the Saar Church away from the Reich.[74] For example, already in 1919, in order to compensate France and to emphasize that at least temporarily the Saarland was no longer part of the Reich, the victors had placed the territory under the French customs regime and provided for the free circulation of French money in the area. The Administration soon

---

[70] GSTA, MA 106157, note of Knoch, December 31, 1920.

[71] *Le Temps*, December 17 and 18, 1920, translation in GSTA, MA 106156.

[72] GSTA, MA 106157, Knoch to State Commissioner for the Saar Pfalz, January 18, 1922.

[73] AN, AJ9 4228, Cultes, Peretti to Tirard, December 31, 1923.

[74] Laing Gray Cowan, *France and the Saar, 1680-1948* (New York, 1950), p. 120 and ch. 5.

thereafter, because of the fall of the mark, began increasingly to make payments, including the salaries of the clergy, in francs, all of which some Germans feared would accustom the populace and their priests to using French currency and thereby integrate them economically into France.[75] The Commission also took pains to show consideration for the clergy's wishes—every county school board was provided with a religious counsellor to supervise religious instruction in the primary schools. This meant that the Church had a measure of control over education, a goal very dear to Rome, while in Germany the extent to which the Church would influence education still awaited the negotiation of an agreement.

The pointed statements of intent by the French, their activities among the population, as well as the pro-French attitude of the Saar Commissioners, thus made the situation especially difficult for the bishops of Speyer and Trier, who to a certain degree had to accommodate the Saar officials and not appear too nationalistic or create problems with the Administration which might prevent them from carrying out their pastoral functions. Yet, they also had to remain sufficiently resistant to French pressure and to warn their clergy of the dangers present, so that the Saar's ties with Germany and the German Church would remain intact. As one prelate from the interior of Germany stated, this was not an enviable position.

By January 1921, Bergen and Ritter, who had returned to Rome from their wartime exile in Lugano, found themselves continually inundated with work. They had to inform the Vatican about political, economic, and social conditions in Germany, as well as about problems of food shortages, difficulties with the occupation forces, and injustices in the Versailles Treaty. But, despite feeling overworked there was little time to complain, for the border problems were urgent and needed close attention. Though France had issued disturbing statements of its hopes to detach the Saarland from its German dioceses and though reports abounded of French attempts to influence the area's clergy, in Rome nothing had been done up until that time to change the diocesan structure. The Vatican continued to abide by its original position of maintaining the *status quo* along the border, and Gasparri had even instructed Pacelli to divert inquiries or discussions about establishing a diocese for the Saar. Since Bishop Korum's visit to Rome in 1920, the question of a Saar diocese had not been seriously discussed. But in 1921 events occurred in the Saarland which again aroused German fears. Early that year internal rivalries and dissension, which

---

[75] The rapid fall of the mark in 1923 caused the Administration by summer to make the franc the sole legal currency in the Saarland.

had been increasing for several months within the ranks of the Catholic Center Party of the Saarland, burst out in the open. Councillor Johann Muth and a small group of party members announced their enthusiastic support for the new Saar Administration and their sympathy for French attempts to detach the area from the Reich. To show its encouragement for this wing of the Center, the Commission adeptly appointed a member of this faction, Professor Matthias Notton, as the official to deal with school and religious affairs for the Catholic Church. Although a minority group within the party, the Muth faction was clearly in a position to assist the French in requesting an independent ecclesiastical administration for the Saar, since it could split the Center and form a political nucleus of the Catholic party which would support France.[76] Almost at the same time it appeared as if the French were stepping up their campaign. At first the Germans believed that Paris, before taking further action, would wait until Bishop Korum died to see who the new bishop might be and what his policies were. But in May Berlin learned of the imminence of further difficulties when the Saar Government requested that a French military bishop be assigned to care for the religious needs of the military personnel in the Saar as well as the entire Rhineland.[77]

Although this was a perfectly legal move, the immediate presence of another bishop in the area raised the possibility of dividing the loyalty of the clergy and laity, of influencing their attitudes, and of causing conflict with the local ordinary. In June Bishop Paul Rémond, who had been named by the French hierarchy to this post, wrote to Benedict, assuring the Pontiff that in addition to carrying out his functions as a military bishop he would like to work for a pacification of the Left Bank of the Rhine and would give the clergy all aid and support to carry out their religious work. He therefore requested the Holy Father to urge the Rhenish bishops to work with him. The German episcopate, however, looked upon him with distrust.[78] His rather broad and ill-defined duties as military bishop and his intention to work with the local clergy could cause difficulties for the local ordinaries, especially in the Saar.[79] The German bishops were unhappy about Rémond's appointment, especially when they suspected that he had been named by the French Church after having received only routine confirmation for his jurisdiction from the Consistorial Congre-

[76] AA, BRV 151, Vol. 1, AA to Bergen, April 26, 1921.

[77] AA, PO II, Bes. Geb. Saar, Kirchl. Fragen, Vol. 1, Loehrs, Prussian Minister of the Interior to AA, May 9, 1921.

[78] AN, AJ9 2997, Dossier 4, Rémond to Benedict, June 22, 1921, with note of Tirard to Briand, July 6, 1921.

[79] AA, BRV 18, Saargebiet, AA to German Embassy (Vatican), September 3, 1921.

gation, that department of the Vatican which dealt with the arrangement of ecclesiastical jurisdictions and the nomination of bishops to particular posts. The Secretariat of State had not been consulted before the announcement of his assignment was made, to which, in view of the strained political relations between the Germans and the French, Cardinal Gasparri would have had something to say.

Soon after his appointment Rémond, in conversations and speeches, began to make known what he regarded as the scope of his authority and what plans he had for the region. He declared that he had been given control not only over military and civil Frenchmen in the Rhineland and Saar but also over Germans working for the Saar Government, as well as over schools already run by the French. In the future he hoped to establish houses for members of religious orders, which in turn would permit him to import French clergy into the area. Bergen protested this rather expansive interpretation of his functions. Gasparri agreed with Bergen's argument that this would curtail the local ordinary's right and that Rémond's authorization should have gone through the Secretariat of State.[80] Gasparri, undoubtedly annoyed at the manner in which Rémond was appointed and the complications that it raised for Vatican policy, tartly remonstrated that he was not impressed with the Frenchman's diplomacy, and commented to Ritter that one should teach the French prelate a little common sense and warn him about not being so overt with his political motives.[81]

Msgr. Ludwig Kaas and Auxiliary Bishop Anton Mönch, both from Trier, in early 1922 met with Gasparri and Under Secretary of State Pizzardo. Among other questions discussed was a definition of Rémond's jurisdiction. Gasparri stated that this would be decided by the Consistorial Congregation but that the Secretariat of State would put in a word in behalf of Germany, to ensure that Rémond's powers would not conflict with that of the German bishops.[82] Pacelli had advised Kaas to broach the matter with Gasparri, who would understand the political problems involved better than the officials of the Consistorial Congregation, who had initially granted Rémond his appointment, and he suggested that Kaas be very specific in stating what the Germans requested, so that no misunderstanding would arise about what was desired.

During December Kaas and Mönch spoke to numerous officials in

[80] Germany, Trier, Bistumsarchiv, Abt. 59 Nr. 52, letter of Rémond to the President of the Saar Commission, February 13, 1926. AA, BRV 18, Saargebiet, Bergen to AA, October 27, and November 3, 1921.

[81] AA, PO II, PO 2 Vat., Vol. 1, Ritter to BFM, November 18, 1921.

[82] AA, BRV 128, Vol. 6, Bergen to AA, December 23, 1922.

the Secretariat of State as well as to the Pope himself, to explain the German belief that Rémond was extending his jurisdiction beyond French citizens, since many Germans were in the French schools over which he claimed control. They also took the opportunity of emphasizing the importance of preserving the geographical integrity of German dioceses. Through much effort and long explanations Kaas and Mönch made their point clear and won Gasparri's promise to intervene in favor of the German bishops. Moreover, the Pontiff also agreed with the German delegates and reaffirmed again his and the Vatican's objection to a separation of the Saar from Germany. A situation such as had occurred in Upper Silesia would not be repeated there, Pius promised. Ecclesiastical separation of the eastern area from German jurisdiction took place only after the political separation had been completed, and that was not the case in the Saar, for the plebiscite would not occur for another thirteen years. The Germans were reassured by the Pontiff's words and believed that their initiative had been successful, but it had been a time-consuming process to speak to so many members of the Curia and to clarify the issue.[83] Nevertheless, the time was well spent, for Vatican officials seemed to show understanding for the German complaints. Kaas had learned that Rémond had recently been in Rome again, suggesting that a separate ecclesiastical administration be set up for the Saar. As one Vatican official ironically told Kaas, Rémond raised the issue and emphatically denied any political motivation for his proposal, professing purely pastoral and religious motives. Although he was a French army bishop, Rémond hastened to add, he did not make the suggestion as a political agent of France.[84] That, said the Vatican official, rather bemused, was taken for granted.

As German representatives feared, the resumption of relations between the Vatican and France in mid-1921 had afforded Paris greater access to Vatican officials and allowed them to present their case more easily. The new link to Rome portended the increase of French influence in the Saarland via the Church.[85] Further discussions in Rome over the matter and Rémond's jurisdictional claims seemed to support this view. But in late 1921 a further difficulty for the beleaguered German bishops developed, this time arising not from France itself but from the League administration in the Saar.

In November 1921 Gasparri informed Bergen that the Saar Commission had indeed requested the appointment of an apostolic admin-

[83] AA, PO II, PO 24 Vat., Vol. 7, memorandum of German Embassy (Vatican), December 26, 1922.

[84] *Ibid.*

[85] Germany, Staatsarchiv, Speyer, R 12/223, Knoch to AA, May 10, 1921.

istrator, basing the request on the grounds that this would be more in keeping with the new civil administration and would meet Church needs. The Cardinal informed Bergen of his inclination to postpone a decision on the matter, but recommended that negotiations for Bavarian and Reich concordats be concluded as soon as possible. Should the agreements be in any way acceptable, the Curia, he said, would be prepared to authorize signing them immediately. By this means the Cardinal could then justifiably deflect any demands for an administrator. Bergen believed that the Cardinal expected more pressure from France and the Commission and desired some legal document to back him up.[86] Berlin, while eager to indicate its good faith, informed Rome that since Prussia, with its large Catholic population, would have to be consulted on any church-state agreement, they would have to wait until the appointment of a new Prussian cabinet, then being formed. Once this was accomplished, Bergen assured Gasparri that the Reich would energetically press for the conclusion of a concordat.[87]

Bergen was pleased with the Vatican's stand and did not think another trip necessary by Kaas or by representatives from the Trier diocese, since the Vatican was not ready to honor the request of the Commission. However, Bergen insisted that the Germans had to exercise great prudence in their statements and actions, even if done with the best of intentions, lest the French or the Saar Government use them against Germany. The Germans had to stand firm. To prove his point Bergen cited the example that on the occasion of Bishop Korum's visit to Rome in 1920, the Trier bishop, to show his spirit of accommodation, was ready to make some concession to the French over their demands for a separate diocese by voluntarily offering to appoint an episcopal administrator for the area. What appeared to Korum to be a step taken in the pastoral interests of the population would have nevertheless opened the door to acknowledging that the German Bishop's jurisdiction was not inviolable. Only after Bergen's strenuous objections did the Bishop refrain from this suggestion.[88] In the complicated diplomatic maneuvers in which the competing powers were engaged with the Vatican, nothing was to be given away unnecessarily. Bergen had been proved correct at that time, for any concession at that early stage in the negotiations might have raised French expectations and allowed them to increase their demands. Now, for the same reasons, Bergen again urged caution, firmness, and reliance on the Vatican to support the German position. There was every reason for Bergen's words of caution, for not only was there the problem of

[86] AA, PO II, PO 24 Vat., Vol. 3, Bergen to AA, November 3, 1921.
[87] AA, BRV 152, Vol. 2, Haniel to Bergen, November 5, 1921.
[88] AA, BRV 152, Vol. 2, Bergen to AA, November 7, 1921.

Rémond and the request of the Commission, backed by France, to have the Vatican name an administrator to the Saar, but now, with Bishop Korum's death in 1921, the Germans feared that the French would take advantage of the interim once more to raise demands for an independent Saar diocese. Berlin learned of France's preparations for such a move. Soon after the Bishop's demise, in negotiations for a French concordat Paris had hinted that in return for a separation of the Saar from German dioceses France would make an exception and not introduce into the newly reacquired provinces of Alsace-Lorraine the 1905 law for the separation of Church and State which was valid throughout the rest of France. Moreover, France asserted at that time that the Saar clergy generally supported its ecclesiastical proposals for the area.[89]

However, in early December, immediately after Korum's death, several of the clergy from the Saar met with Pacelli and repeated the ecclesiastical reasons for keeping the territory as part of the German dioceses and refuted French claims by asserting the attachment to the Reich of the Saar populace, clergy and laity. Pacelli listened with interest, but noted that the group meeting with him was only a small delegation. In order to give credence to their argument and to impress the Curia, a statement signed by the entire clergy or a majority of the Saar's priests had to be sent to Rome, reviewing the religious and social reasons for their desire to remain part of Germany. This, counseled the Nuncio, could not fail to make an impression.[90]

A letter was duly drafted, circulated, and signed in December 1921. It was sent to the Pontiff in the name of all the secular and religious clergy in the Saarland, requesting that the religious administration remain intact. After reviewing the historical background of the Church in the Saar and describing how both Trier and Speyer had been instrumental in promoting Church growth to keep up with the great industrial and economic expansion of the last sixty years, the petition explained all the administrative difficulties which would occur if the two parts of the Saar, one belonging to Prussia and the other to Bavaria, were united to form one ecclesiastical unit. First of all, such a unification would complicate church law and customs, since each area, with its own traditions, had developed independently of the other. Also, an independent diocese would require enormous financial means, a seminary, and new administrative buildings further taxing the large working-class population, which was already hard-pressed due to the post-war economic problems which Germany was facing. Because of

[89] AA, PO II, Bes. Geb. Saar, Kirchl. Fragen, Vol. 1, memorandum of AA, December 27, 1922.
[90] Zenner, pp. 156-157.

the region's rapid growth, a shortage of priests still existed, but up until then this had been made up by clergy coming in from other parts of the dioceses. This would end, should the Saarland become independent. Even if the separate diocese was not created and only an administrator named who would govern the area independently, confusion would result over the sources of ecclesiastical authority and cause distress among the laity. Attaching the area to a French diocese such as Metz also would solve nothing, since it presupposed common interests between both regions. Before World War I, continued the letter, the links to Metz and Lorraine were minimal; after the war they virtually disappeared. The ill-will between the Germans and French would cause priests from one area to be ineffectual in the other. Should the Saar be separated from the mother dioceses, a great number of priests would return to Germany proper, leaving the laity in even worse straits than before. In sum, the clergy asked that nothing be changed—that neither the French desire to have the Saar transferred to French clerical control or made a separate diocese nor the Saar Commission's request for an apostolic administrator be granted.[91]

Berlin fully endorsed sending the letter, for it lent strong support to the German Government's view that such a transfer would be against the wishes of the clergy and to the detriment of the Church and individual Catholics. Berlin believed that it needed this endorsement, especially after the Saar Government in October had made its request for an apostolic administrator. True, Gasparri at that time had informed Bergen of his preference to delay granting the request, but other factors continued to vex the Foreign Office. The Saar Administration had taken pains to indicate its goodwill to the Church and had given some measure of control over education to the clergy, while the diocese of Trier, as part of Prussia, was still in the process of working out its church-state relations, including the school question. Should negotiations for a settlement in Prussia or Germany stall on this issue, as several German officials warned, it might cause the Vatican to rethink its attitude and might even result in Germany's loss of control of the area.[92]

Soon thereafter the Germans detected signs of uneasiness among Vatican officials over the Saar situation and of their increased interest in signing a concordat with Germany in order to relieve pressure on them. As the Germans well realized, the Vatican was concerned with its relationship not only to Germany but to the opposing parties as

---

[91] Germany, Trier, Bistumsarchiv, Abt. 59 Nr. 50, letter of clergy to Holy Father, December 6, 1921. Similar arguments appeared in the *Deutsche Allgemeine Zeitung*, December 17, 1921 and *Bayerischer Kurier*, December 23, 1921.

[92] AA, BRV 153, Vol. 3, note of the Interior Ministry, December 11, 1921.

well. Rome had to maintain a neutral stance and if possible indicate its willingness to accommodate the wishes of the foreign governments. The French had argued for a separate diocese and had been rejected. But the Saar Government with French support had then suggested an apostolic administrator, stating that this would make the ecclesiastical administration neutral until the final decision in 1935. Rome did not wish to make any changes until the boundaries had been settled, nor on principle did it want to weaken the authority of the local ordinary, especially for a period as long as thirteen years, since this would inevitably weaken the Saar's ties to Germany and permit France to gain an advantage in the area. Also, Germany's arguments, supported by evidence such as the letter from the clergy, had convinced Gasparri of the wisdom of leaving the situation as it was, if this could be done without disrupting the new French-Vatican working relationship. Therefore, the Vatican had temporized over the issue in the hopes that church-state relations could be settled in Germany and provide the Curia a valid legal argument to resist French pressure. It would settle the situation within the Reich by giving the Church a new legal basis, and by recognizing Germany's borders it would help both to maintain Germany's position in Europe as it had been and to check France's growing preponderance.

Negotiations for a German concordat, however, were not running smoothly. Should the discussions fail, the Vatican ran the risk of having nothing to show for its efforts in Germany, simultaneously antagonizing France, thereby blocking possible accommodation on church-state relations in that country. Therefore, in late December 1921, when Knoch asked Pacelli if any possibilities still existed of the Vatican's appointing an apostolic administrator for the Saar, Pacelli replied that as long as the negotiations for a new concordat with Germany were progressing, the matter would be held in abeyance, but warned that the Vatican could not put off the request indefinitely. He envisioned no problems in the negotiations then underway with the Bavarian Government, although he might wish for a more rapid conclusion. He did, however, express concern that in the Prussian negotiations too many politicians emphasized party politics and individual aspects of the proposed treaty, to the detriment of concentrating on the major state issue—a general agreement with the Vatican. The failure of negotiations would impel the Holy See to consider the request of the Saar Government for a reorganization of Church administration.[93] While not a threat, Pacelli's words served as a reminder to Germany that the

---

[93] GSTA, MA 106157, Knoch to State Commissioner for the Pfalz, January 18, 1922.

Holy See was also under pressure to consider more than German interests.

As Bergen continued to urge the Vatican to support the German position, the Foreign Office sent missives to both the Prussian and Bavarian Governments to see if concordat negotiations could be expedited, and to take measures to ensure the Saar clergy's continued loyalty. Clerical salaries were extremely low, and with the ensuing financial chaos and inflation introduced by the use of French currency in 1920 the clergy found themselves in acutely strained financial circumstances. Both Prussia and Bavaria had therefore begun to allocate extra funds to assist the clergy and to pay them in marks so that they could purchase German goods as they had done before and not lose in the exchange rate. By spring of 1922 Bavaria had provided three-quarters of a million marks to the Saar clergy for this purpose, and Prussia even more.[94]

The success of German strategy also required a careful watch over statements appearing in the newspapers about the Saar question. On August 4 Bergen wired Berlin to take steps in restraining the press from provocative or polemical articles such as the one which appeared in *Germania* announcing that German Catholics expected the Pope to resist French pressure for ecclesiastical change in the Saar. Such statements, said Bergen, greatly embarrassed the Vatican, since they placed the Holy See in the position of being an arbiter between France and Germany. By making the issue so specific, an either/or, the articles emphasized that in making a decision the Vatican would be favoring one side and conversely disappointing the other. Several days before, Gasparri informed the Ambassador that reports in the German press about German demands for a clause in the proposed concordat guaranteeing the Saar's diocesan borders were making difficulties for Rome. Poincaré had remonstrated about such a provision. He informed the Vatican that France would not countenance the Holy See's undertaking anything contrary to the spirit of Versailles in a concordat—Bavarian, Reich, or other—and insisted that Rome take no steps which affected the Saar's diplomatic position without consulting France. Gasparri had had to assure Poincaré that such rumors should not be taken seriously, and that the final drafts of a concordat were still in the future. Nevertheless, these press indiscretions, which irked the Cardinal, reminded him of the leaks at the time of his 1921 *démarche* with Washington in Germany's behalf and only made both the Vatican's efforts in Germany's behalf and the concordat negotiations more

---

[94] GSTA, Ges. Berlin 1555, Goldenberger (Bavarian Ministry of Ed. and Relig. Affairs) to Schmelzle (BFM), May 12, 1922.

difficult.[95] Bergen therefore urged Berlin to exert more control over the press and prevent any disclosures that would damage Germany's position. The Vatican would keep its secret, but the openness of expression now tolerated in the new Republic could unwittingly cause major problems.[96] Bergen's strategy was to present a calm, reasoned argument favoring the German position, demonstrating the support of the Saar populace for the Reich and Berlin's good intentions to reach an accord with the Vatican as soon as possible. Thus he did not want any inflammatory public statements or press leaks to disrupt the fine rapport that he had established in Rome, nor did he deem it wise to pressure Rome unnecessarily.

The French, on the other hand, felt that they had to pursue the matter with the Vatican if they were to be successful. The Quai d'Orsay acknowledged the importance of Vatican support, and France, like the Reich, intensified its efforts to have Rome's aid for its Saar policies. After analyzing the matter, French officials conceded that the population of the Saar had remained loyal to Germany, and the plebiscite would probably prove unfavorable to France unless Paris obtained a modification of the ecclesiastical boundaries in that region.[97] Therefore, in the latter part of 1922 Paris once more took the initiative, this time not asking for a separate diocese but pressing for an administrator. The Quai d'Orsay informed Nuncio Cerretti in Paris that it fully supported the Saar Government's petition for an apostolic administrator similar to the one appointed in Upper Silesia. Since the Vatican had granted the Silesian area such an official, Paris requested that by analogy the Saar obtain one also. Gasparri, however, still steered a course which would be of help to Germany by maintaining the *status quo*. The Vatican informed Paris that it was at present considering such a step, but pointed out to French officials that the political circumstances in the Saar were different from those in Upper Silesia and no precedent should be inferred.[98]

Despite the *faux pas* in the German press and Gasparri's momentary annoyance with the Reich, the Vatican did not act on the Saar Government's request. Rémond had visited Rome and failed to persuade the Cardinal Secretary of State to change his mind. Although the German Embassy in Paris previously had feared that the Vatican might

[95] AN, AJ9 5272, FFO to Tirard, December 13, 1924; AJ9 3822, Poincaré to French Embassy (Vatican), August 1, 1922. AA, BRV 125, Vol. 3, Bergen to AA, August 4, 1922.

[96] AA, PO II, PO 20 Vat., Trier, Vol. 1, Bergen to AA, February 14, 1922.

[97] FFO, Allemagne 369, note of the FFO (Direction des Affaires politiques et commerciales), November 16, 1923.

[98] AA, PO II, PO 24 Vat., Vol. 7, Mayer (Paris) to AA, December 20, 1922.

compromise on the Saar as a concession in negotiations with Paris to obtain alterations in the French law of Separation of Church and State, Bergen did not see any signs of Gasparri's now relenting. Since Paris, due to a cabinet change, had not followed up its latest request for the Saar, Gasparri had no reason to alter his position or to make concessions.[99] In fact, the almost ironic manner in which the Cardinal spoke about the Saar Government's petition, which, as he commented, was "based on religious grounds," led German officials to believe that Gasparri lacked sympathy for the request and would continue to support the German bishops.[100]

The Vatican might have another reason for not falling in with Paris' plans. The Nuncio in Paris, in speaking to numerous French dignitaries, heard that the reason France had resumed diplomatic relations with the Vatican was not to improve church-state relations but primarily to further its foreign policy goals. France had expected to win aid from the Curia in its struggle with Germany. French opponents of establishing an embassy at the Vatican had voted for it in the belief that Rome would side more readily with "Catholic" France and its allies against "Protestant" Germany. So far France's policy objectives here had not succeeded, and the delay over the Saar was cited as a specific example of Rome's failure to assist France. Several French politicians of the Left publicly expressed doubt that France would gain much from relations with Rome. Such opinions placed a strain on French-Vatican affairs, angered the Curia, and inclined Gasparri to be less likely to rush into conceding to French demands, lest it appear as if Rome feared losing the favor of Paris.[101] Hearing of the difficulties that the Curia was encountering in France, Berlin could take satisfaction that its diplomatic campaign had increased possibilities of success, for the news confirmed Bergen's assertion of Gasparri's continued support of the *status quo*.

The tension between France and Germany, which reached crisis level over the Ruhr occupation in 1923, was also reflected in the Saar. Conflict increased between the German sentiment of the people and what they considered the pro-French attitude of the Administration. Mass meetings to protest French influence increased, and a number of strikes were called, most important of which was that of the miners, which began on February 5. Ostensibly held because of the refusal of the French Mines Administration to meet wage demands, the strike was also a demonstration of the solidarity of the Saar workers for their

[99] AA, PO II, PO 24 Vat., Vol. 7, memorandum of German Embassy (Vatican), December 2, 1922.

[100] *Ibid.*

[101] AA, PO II, PO 24 Vat., Vol. 7, Hoesch (Paris) to AA, January 17, 1923.

counterparts in the Ruhr. The strike had the support of all organized labor and quickly spread to other sectors of the work force. Faced with public disorders, the Saar Administration asked France to increase the number of troops in the territory. In March a *Notverordnung* (emergency law) was passed, which by its severity drew protests from the public and caused parallels to be made to the military controls imposed in the Ruhr. Although the ordinance was repealed in May, it did focus public attention on the Saar and on the Administration's close association with France.[102]

The precipitous fall of the mark because of the Ruhr action and the approach of the moment set by the treaty (January, 1925) for a tariff wall to be imposed between the Saar and the Reich brought new large amounts of French capital into the area. Until the franc itself began to fall in late 1923, Poincaré pursued his policy of increasing French propaganda, especially through the French Mines Administration, and encouraging separatist sentiment, a Saar for the Saarlanders, free from Germany.[103] For these purposes the Church continued to be an important consideration in French thinking. Faced with criticism from the Allies about his policies in the Ruhr, Rhineland, and the Saar, Poincaré became all the more concerned about retaining his links to the Vatican.

In June 1923 the French Senate renewed debate over the value of a French embassy at the Vatican; Poincaré laid great stress on its significance not only for domestic but also for foreign affairs. In pursuance of French policy on its eastern borders, particularly in the Rhineland and Saarland, it was essential, he insisted, for France to have good relations with the Holy See. To emphasize his point the Premier cited, as an example, Bishop Rémond's potential for helping to counter German propaganda and to present the French view either directly to the Curia or via diplomatic channels established between Rome and Paris. Almost concurrently with the debate on June 20 an article appeared in *Figaro* by the historian and member of the French Academy, Georges Goyau, who in a non-polemical manner discussed France's hope for the increase of French prominence and control in the Rhineland and the Saar via the Church. The article expressed pleasure that a Catholic separatist movement was beginning to appear in the area and called upon the French Government to support it. Three days after the Senate debate, on June 22, supporters of Poincaré's policy in the French Chamber of Deputies once more called for the establish-

[102] Cowan, pp. 131-133. Wambaugh, *Saar*, pp. 91-92.
[103] Wambaugh, *Saar*, p. 93.

ment of a Saar diocese.[104] The French Government again appeared to be making an effort to have the Vatican change its mind. Moreover, if successful it would undoubtedly be convincing proof for French skeptics at home of the value of good ties with Rome and the importance of Poincaré's decision to win the support of the Vatican for his general policy along France's eastern borders. Just as the German Foreign Office had to fight a rear-guard action at home in contending that Rome was an important factor in obtaining foreign policy objectives, the Quai d'Orsay experienced similar difficulties.

In August, Bishop Rémond, via the French Ambassador at the Vatican, returned once more to the question of a Saar diocese and at the same time requested official jurisdiction over the new schools run by French nuns then being established in the territory. The Commission had stated that schools originally maintained by French instructors would provide education only to the children of French personnel working in the army or in the mines, yet actually the French were allowing and encouraging children of the local inhabitants to enroll in them. Moreover, the French nuns who had come into the area had not even sought the local ordinaries' permission to do so. All the more irritating to the German authorities was that, while the legal status of religious schools was still in question in France, the French Government was actually encouraging their establishment and supporting them financially in the Saar.[105] When the Bishops of Speyer and Trier protested to Rome against any expansion of Rémond's control, they discovered that the matter had become enmeshed in the intricacies of Vatican interdepartmental bureaucracy. While the Curia conceded nothing to the French which would separate the Saar from Germany, the Consistorial Congregation confirmed Rémond's right to jurisdiction over the schools, since he had been already granted wide powers over French institutions, and the schools were classified as French educational institutions.

At this juncture the Secretariat of State intervened. Conceding that Rémond's moves could have political implications, Pizzardo promised the Germans that although he could do nothing about the powers already granted the French bishop, he would keep a careful watch on what the Consistorial Congregation did in the future so as not to compromise the powers of the local ordinary. Taking Pizzardo at his word, Ritter advised the bishops of Speyer and Trier to be alert, and if

[104] BSTA, MK 15568, Hoesch to AA, June 23, 1923. France, Assemblée nationale, *Débats parlementaires, Journal officiel* (Paris), Sénat, Compte rendu 1923, June 19, 1923, pp. 946-956; Chambre des Députés, Compte rendu 1923, June 22, 1923, pp. 2094-2097.
[105] *Germania*, August 28, 1923. AA, PO II, Bes. Geb. Saar, Kirchl. Fragen, Vol. 1, BFM to AA, August 31, 1923.

Rémond sought in any way to extend his jurisdiction or if other foreign religious groups or ecclesiastical organizations arrived in the dioceses without permission, they and the inhabitants of the territory should protest immediately to the Secretariat of State so that disciplinary action could be taken.[106] The Secretariat of State, although aware of the political ramifications of Rémond's activities, was conscious of the sensitivity of each Curial congregation, especially when another questioned its authority. Rémond had cleverly applied *pro forma* for authority over French schools. The Consistorial Congregation, which handled numerous similar petitions from bishops, did not see anything extraordinary in the request of a French bishop to administer French schools and had not checked with the Secretariat of State before issuing the permission. Despite Gasparri's disapproval of what had already transpired, he did not wish to present a view to the world of intra-Curial squabbling, and so he was unwilling to enter the fray unless Rémond clearly overstepped his authority. Nevertheless, Gasparri's office expressed sympathy for the local ordinaries and gave them what encouragement it could.

The French press naturally pointed to Rome's decision as proof of the Vatican's approval for Rémond's work, such as mentioned in *Le Gaulois* of August 26, 1923 and *Le Petit Parisien* of August 27, 1923. Since nothing could be done about what had occurred, Berlin sought to turn what looked like a loss to their advantage. The question of several schools was not in itself serious. Of real concern was the possibility that a pattern would develop to reduce imperceptibly the ordinaries' power. The case at hand, however, allowed Germany to bring the matter to the attention of Gasparri and to obtain a ruling to block further efforts by Rémond to gain control. Thus, in autumn, undoubtedly with urging from the Secretary of State, the Consistorial Congregation issued a statement conceding Rémond's jurisdiction over the schools established by French nuns, but expressly forbidding the establishment of any such institutions in the future without the permission of the local bishop. A detailed statement followed, explaining the rights of the ordinary within his diocese and the privileges that the military bishop had concerning school jurisdiction and who could attend them. Rémond's attempt to seek expanded jurisdiction had been stopped, and the Vatican had been alerted should it be tried again. Soon thereafter Gasparri sent Pacelli these guidelines to be applied in the event that a similar case arose.[107] The remarks were clear, the

---

[106] AA, PO II, PO 24 Vat., Vol. 7, Ritter to BFM, August 11, 1923.
[107] AA, BRV 18, Saargebiet, Meyer (Vatican) to AA, October 15, 1923.

Vatican had given preference to the ordinary and strengthened his position—in the long run a victory for Germany.

The following year Germany, secure in the knowledge that French influence had not succeeded in seriously eroding the loyalty of the Saarlanders to the Reich, was able to feel increasingly confident about the Vatican's attitude to the Saarland question.[108] In 1924, because of the crisis in the Ruhr and the separatist unrest in the Rhineland, the Vatican sent Msgr. Gustavo Testa on a fact-finding mission to the region.[109] While in Germany the envoy took the opportunity to visit the Saarland. Here he had discussions with representatives from the Catholic clergy, laity and government. His impressions were that the overwhelming majority of the inhabitants wished to remain part of the Reich and attached to the German dioceses. His report only confirmed the Vatican's policy of postponing any action on the Saar problem until the plebiscite in 1935.[110] In addition, in March Bavaria concluded a concordat regularizing relations between the Bavarian State and Rome, recognizing the boundaries of the dioceses as fixed and the jurisdictional authority of Bavarian bishops. This meant, in effect, that the provisions of the concordat would apply to all territory falling within the domain of Bavarian bishops, including that part of the Saar administered by the bishop of Speyer. The Saar Government immediately protested this new concordat as an infringement on the independence of the Saar, and the French Ambassador at the Vatican once more requested the Curia to remove the area from Speyer's control and permit the Saar Commission to enter into separate negotiations with the Holy See for a regulation of church-state relations there.[111] The Saar Commission also wrote to the Bavarian Government, stating that it could not recognize the new agreement and called to Bavaria's attention that, by the Treaty of Versailles, Germany, and thereby Bavaria, had renounced control over the Saar in favor of the League

[108] Loyalty to the Reich was visibly demonstrated at the annual Catholic convention or *Katholikentag*. In June 1923 the *Katholikentag* held in Saarbrücken drew 70,000 people. Besides dealing with religious matters, the participants heard many sermons and lectures urging them to remain loyal to the dioceses of Speyer and Trier. Bishop Bornewasser closed his speech with "Your Bishop has sworn an oath to remain true to you, and he also is sure of the loyalty of the Catholic Saarlanders to the Bishop of Trier!" The entire day was treated as a "loyalty day" and drew a protest from French authorities and a word of caution from Rome. Subsequent *Katholikentage* up until 1935 all had a national character about them, and loyalty to the dioceses of Trier and Speyer was associated with loyalty to Germany. Zenner, pp. 158-159.

[109] See ch. 5.

[110] AA, BRV 156, Vol. 6, Loehrs, Prussian Minister of the Interior, to AA, May 14, 1924.

[111] Franz-Willing, pp. 209-210.

of Nations. Bavaria could not, therefore, sign a treaty with a foreign state affecting that area.[112]

To ease the problem for the Vatican, Bavaria declared its intention not to insist on the legal application of the concordat in the Saarland during the period of the League's administration.[113] It would not oppose the Holy See if it empowered the Bishop of Speyer to grant the Saar Administration the privilege of presenting recommendations for pastoral appointments until 1935, a privilege which the concordat negotiators had granted to the Munich Government. Gasparri wrote to the Bavarian Government, thanking it for helping the Holy See to reach a formulation that would mute the legal objections and confirming that ecclesiastical jurisdictions in the Saar would remain the same as they had been, at least until the plebiscite.[114]

The conclusion of the treaty for Bavaria mutually benefited Germany and the Vatican. For Germany, it legally confirmed that the Saar would remain "intact" as part of two German dioceses and that the Vatican would refuse to negotiate a new ecclesiastical settlement for the territory until a permanent political settlement was reached in 1935. For the Vatican, it meant that the first step toward the desired regularization of church-state relations in Germany had been taken. At the same time it also provided the Vatican with a stronger hand to resist further demands from France or from the Saar Commission to separate the region from the mother dioceses until at least 1935.

The situation remained *in suspenso* throughout the Weimar era. Later on, in 1933, the signing of the Reich Concordat was interpreted in the Saar at first as a sign of the goodwill on the part of the new Berlin Government for the Holy See and helped to allay any serious doubts that the populace may have had about the Nazis' intentions toward the Church. The fact that Franz von Papen, chief German negotiator for the concordat, was a resident of the Saarland created a source of pride for many of its inhabitants and might have increased their sense of attachment to the new regime in Germany. Though the Saar was politically outside Germany and thus not affected by the concordat, the local clergy was very pleased to see it signed. But the French feared that the Nazis would capitalize on the improved church-state relations in the upcoming plebiscite. Paris therefore requested the Vatican to check on the situation in the Saarland and to keep watch lest the Reich attempt to exert undue influence via the clergy. As a consequence, the Curia sent Msgr. Testa back to the Saar as a *visitator*

---

[112] AA, PO II, Bes. Geb. Saar, Kirchl. Fragen, Vol. 2, Rault, President of Saar Commission, to the Bavarian Government, February 7, 1925.

[113] Paragraph 14 of the concordat concerns the Saar.

[114] AA, BRV 157, Vol. 7, Gasparri to Bavarian Government, December 10, 1925.

to observe the political climate and to learn if either the French or German Governments had been using undue pressure. The *Neue Saarpost* and other anti-Nazi journals attempted to have the Saar remain separate from the Reich, warning that the Germany of 1935 was no longer the democratic state that it had been in the 1920's and pointing to the dangers ahead for the Church and religion in a Nazi Germany. Nevertheless, the long years of separation had increased the Saarlanders' desire to return to the Reich, no matter which government controlled it. On January 13, 1935 the vote was taken, with more than 90 percent of the population voting for the return to Germany. The Vatican had abided by its policy of waiting until the plebiscite before making a decision. What Bergen said of the Vatican in 1935 could well be applied to the entire period of the Weimar Republic: ". . . today now that the plebiscite is over, . . . it must be stated that the *Reichsdeutsch* policy has reason to be satisfied with the position of the Vatican right up to the day of the vote on January 13."[115]

It was, however, then too late for the French to change anything, as their Ambassador to the Vatican, François Charles-Roux admitted. In 1919, when they might have been able to exert sufficient influence to obtain a separation of the region, France had no ambassador at the Vatican who could pursue the matter. The overtures of 1922-1923 were checked. In 1924, the *Cartel des Gauches* came to power and pursued a more conciliatory policy toward Germany and did not press the Reich on the matter of diocesan borders. In France itself, because of considerable political criticism of French ties with the Vatican, several politicians disputed their value, and this attitude weakened the power of the cabinet to influence the Curia. Suggestions for ecclesiastical changes in the Saarland met with no success in Rome. Paris again took up the matter with some vigor after the Nazi seizure of power—but then it was too late to change opinions before the plebiscite.[116]

All along the western border from 1919 to 1924, Germany had to face the possibility that France, and to some extent Belgium, would use the Church to increase their control over this territory. Thus this conflict again placed the Vatican in the position of arbiter between the Allies and Germany. As in the east, despite the combined influence of France and its eastern allies, the Vatican's policy considerations paralleled those of the Reich. While maintaining its "neutrality" and making concessions where deemed just and "with cause," Rome was careful not to concede too much to the Western Allies and thereby tip

[115] AA, PO II, PO 24 Vat., Saar, Vol. 2, Bergen to AA, January 14, 1935. Cowan, pp. 160-161.

[116] F. Charles-Roux, *Huit ans au Vatican, 1932-1940* (Paris, 1947), p. 101.

the international balance in favor of the west and weaken the internal stability and unity of the Reich. On the other hand, just as it had done in dealing with its eastern borders, Germany also maintained constant contact with Vatican officials about its western boundaries, keeping them well supplied with information and periodic visits from clergy and laity. Berlin relied on Bergen's activism and his ability to keep the Curia constantly aware of the Reich's position, while also expecting Nuncio Pacelli to convey the German viewpoint to Rome and hopefully to support it with his superiors. To assist in this work the Reich depended heavily on the quasi-legal argument that agreements or concordats still existed which applied to the western border dioceses, and any change would necessitate bilateral negotiations and would, by disrupting normal pastoral work, confuse and disturb the laity. In other words the Germans, revisionists when it came to political treaties, favored the *status quo* in such ecclesiastical questions, and this attitude in turn corresponded to Vatican reluctance to change any jurisdictional authority without overwhelming cause. This policy was a vehicle by which the Reich could pursue its goals and behind which the Vatican could take refuge and resist the pressure of the Western Powers to implement change. While the results in the west may not have been as dramatic as those in the east, Germany had reason to be satisfied and grateful for the Vatican's attitude, for it allowed the Reich time to settle some of its internal and external affairs after the war without undue fear that inroads would be made into the political and economic integrity of the State via ecclesiastical channels.

By 1923 many of the disputes dealing with ecclesiastical problems in the east had been or were in the process of being resolved. In contrast, in the west the crisis between Germany, France, and Belgium was yet to reach its climax in 1923-1924, when these two Allied Powers invaded and occupied German territory and when France revived and supported separatist movements. Once more both the Reich and the Allies looked to the Church for assistance in supporting or resisting the claims of the opposing side. For Germany, a statement by the Vatican against separatism and the invasion of the Ruhr would be of tremendous help to Germany's position, for it would strengthen the resolve of German Catholics to remain loyal to Berlin, condemn the morality of the French-Belgian action, and indirectly support the Reich's stand on reparations. Thus the Separatist movement and the crisis which occurred in 1923-1924 summoned the Vatican again to play a vital role in Germany's foreign policy.

CHAPTER V

The Ruhr Crisis and
Separatism in the Rhineland
1923-1924

Germany had been aware as early as 1919 of French plans to win Church support for its policies in the Rhineland. During the first few years of the post-war settlement the Reich had generally succeeded in fending off any French sorties against its territorial integrity as well as French advances in ecclesiastical politics. During the early 1920's, however, while still greatly concerned over France's designs on its western borders, Germany devoted much of its attention in dealings with Paris and the western capitals to the question of reparations. Germany continued to protest that the payments were too high and were causing a drain on its resources and hindering economic stabilization. France, however, insisted that Germany meet the agreed-upon payments. In 1923 the matter came to a head and became the crisis point of inter-war history for Germany and France. It marked the last attempt of France to collect reparations by force and the beginning of Germany's revival under Stresemann's policy of accommodation.

Because of a default in coal and timber deliveries, French and Belgian troops moved into the Ruhr valley and occupied it to ensure that the mines would continue to supply the coal due the Allied Powers. The invasion as well as the Reich's policy of resistance to it only further weakened the already shaky German economy. Moreover, during this critical period the French once more raised the question of an independent Rhenish state by supporting separatist movements in the area. Therefore the goal of Germany's diplomacy was now to convince the other Allied Powers of the injustice of the action taken by the French-Belgian move. In the view of the Foreign Office it was now all the more urgent to mobilize international public opinion through institutions such as the League of Nations, the International Labor Organization, and religious organizations. Quite naturally Berlin once more turned to the Vatican to bring pressure to bear on France and Belgium and to help to convince the other powers to do likewise. But first Berlin had to persuade the Curia not only that the invasion was unreasonable and also injurious to European stability but that it was also in the Vatican's own interest for Rome to support the Reich. Also, an even greater effort had to be made to show Rome that a separatist movement would not be to the advantage of the Church in Germany. If it were endorsed by the Papacy and succeeded in establishing an independent Rhenish state, the ecclesiastical organization of the Reich would be once more thrown into chaos and the religious balance resulting from the diminution of the Reich's size and population would certainly prove detrimental to Catholicism in that country where a new *modus vivendi* between the confessions and their relation to the State still had to be worked out. Once more Germany's foreign policy goals were connected to the internal problem of church-state relations.

The Vatican had already expressed its displeasure with foreign interference in German affairs. In March 1920, when the unrest in the immediate post-war period led to a Spartacist uprising in the Ruhr mining district, the French announced their intention to restore order by sending troops into the area. Rome reacted negatively and swiftly. Gasparri indicated that the Vatican, along with England and Italy, would urge France to permit Germany to take the responsibility for maintaining order. He also advised Reich officials to present the German case against the French action to the Italian Government, which was working closely with the British in this matter. In meetings with the Vatican Secretary of State Bergen had pointed out that in 1871 the victorious Germans had allowed the French Government to suppress the Commune in Paris and had not sent in their troops. Now, in 1920, the Germans desired to take care of their problem without French interference. Gasparri endorsed Bergen's argument not only for its logic but because it supported his belief in the necessity of sustaining the Reich in order to maintain an equilibrium in Europe and to prevent France from extending its influence within Germany.[1]

On numerous occasions in 1921-1922 the Papacy expressed concern for both Germany's plight and the unsettling conditions in Europe brought about by the reparation demands. In mid-1922 Cardinal Gasparri shared his feelings with the British representative to the Holy See, Viscount De Salis, about the worsening economic conditions in the Reich and the consequences of a default in reparations. The Curia regarded the matter as extremely serious and feared that if France took military action to ensure being paid, this could precipitate a castastrophe. Along with everyone else the Cardinal now looked to England. By conveying his appeal by diplomatic channels and by means of the

[1] AA, PO II, PO 2 Vat., Vol. 1, Bergen to AA, April 6, 1920.

English Cardinal Bourne, whom he had requested to speak to the Prime Minister, Gasparri hoped to exert pressure on Paris to avoid any hasty and ill-advised action.[2] During the latter part of 1922 the Cardinal Secretary of State consulted with Germany as well as with the other European nations in an effort to arrive at a solution to the reparations problem. Gasparri still sought support for his proposal by which Germany would pay France's and Britain's war debts to the United States in place of any direct reparation payment to those countries.[3] Thus the Vatican continued its efforts toward a permanent solution, as did the governments whose representatives met at various international economic conferences held that year.

On January 11, 1923, Gasparri's fears were actualized. Armed with the Reparations Commission's decision that the German Government was in default of payments, France and Belgium ordered troops to enter and, by the end of the month, to occupy and administer the Ruhr basin, an area sixty by twenty-eight miles in north-western Germany. In 1919, France had been blocked by its Anglo-American allies from outright annexations in the Rhineland, which also claimed that it needed for security. Soon thereafter the withdrawal of America from European affairs and the failure of Great Britain and the United States to give the French defensive guarantees against unprovoked German aggression confirmed Paris' belief that the Anglo-Saxon Powers lacked understanding of France's anxiety over its western borders. Paris believed that it needed territorial, military, and economic concessions from defeated Germany to compensate for war damages, maintain its position in Europe, guarantee its security, and prevent any move by the Reich to gain dominance, as it had tried to do in 1914. Failing to win approval for its land claims in the Rhineland, Paris increasingly had to rely on diplomatic and economic means for self-protection. It was for these reasons that France was the most demanding of the Allies in exacting reparations from the Reich.

The German Government continued to argue that the payments were destroying the German economy and currency. In 1922 Berlin declared that it could no longer meet its reparation obligations, either in cash or kind, and requested a moratorium on payments. France was also in a strained economic position because of wartime damages and

[2] BFO, 371/7517/5324, De Salis to Balfour, Forign Secretary, July 28, 1922.
[3] AA, RM 70, Vol. 1, Bergen to AA, January 3, 1923. For a general discussion of the reparations question and the European diplomatic situation including the Ruhr crisis see such works as Temperley, Arnold Toynbee, ed., *Survey of international affairs, 1920-1923, 1924* (Oxford, 1925-26); John Wheeler-Bennett, *The wreck of reparations* (New York, 1933); Maier, chs. 4, 6-8; Schuker; Artaud, chs. I-VI; Marks, *Illusion* and "Myths"; Trachtenberg; and Krüger.

saddled with war debts and was not convinced of the Reich's inability to pay but rather believed that Germany was stalling and was in fact deliberately destroying its currency by encouraging inflationary policies in order to escape reparations. Exasperated that it had not been receiving the indemnity demanded at Versailles and which the Reich had agreed to in a schedule of payments presented by the Reparations Commission in 1921, faced with what it believed was Germany's unwillingness to pay and Britain's unwillingness to apply more pressure on the Reich, Paris felt that it had no alternative but to take matters into its own hands. It feared that if a moratorium were granted, reparations might never be resumed. Paris therefore determined to present a show of strength to intimidate Berlin and obtain for France what it regarded as not only its due but also necessary for its security and economic stability; French policy was to play its dramatic last card—to secure reparations or face the possibility of eventually falling behind a larger, industrially stronger, more populous Germany.

Already accused by Britain and the United States in 1919 of making unrealistic demands on Germany, yet frustrated by the lack of support from its Anglo-Saxon allies, France, along with Belgium as a less than enthusiastic partner, now dispatched troops to the Ruhr. The occupying forces, because of a lack of cooperation from the inhabitants, soon felt themselves forced to expand their activities and control over the entire area—a region which accounted for eighty to eighty-five percent of Germany's coal and eighty percent of its steel and pig iron production, for seventy percent of the goods and mineral traffic on its railways, and ten percent of its population. No region of proportional size in any other major state played so important a role in the economic life of a country. The military forces declared a state of siege, required all German civil authorities to obey them, and demanded the surrender of all weapons in private hands. Any acts of violence, incitement to disorder, any publication or theatrical presentation that might threaten the honor or security of Franco-Belgian troops were subject to punishment. A customs barrier was erected between the area and the rest of Germany, and food became scarce. Mass arrests, heavy fines, and large confiscations of property of recalcitrants accompanied the occupation.

Berlin, appalled but not surprised by the move, halted all reparation deliveries to France and Belgium, called upon the population of the Ruhr to offer passive resistance, and encouraged the workers to strike and the local officials to withhold their help and cooperation from the invaders. The already financially impoverished government in Berlin embarked on a program of paying allowances to miners on strike, to officials relieved of their duties, and to other individuals resisting the invaders. The local inhabitants generally supported Berlin's policy and did little to help the occupying forces but rather hindered their efforts to extract reparation payments, resorting even to acts of sabotage in the factories, mines, and on the railway lines. This in turn caused Paris and Brussels to retaliate by arresting uncooperative mine owners, taking over the mines themselves, trying and punishing for acts of sabotage those Germans who tried to impede their use of the railroads, and banning all shipments of coal and iron to the rest of Germany. The Allies felt constrained to import additional technicians to operate the mines and railways and now began to expel more and more officials from the territory, and to come into conflict—both legally and physically—with the populace over their rights and duties to the new authority.

Europe's capitals were shaken by the crisis and communiqués went flying. Diplomats feared that the invasion threatened the peace of Europe, at worst by possibly leading to a renewal of the armed conflict or at best by complicating the problems of restoring normalcy to the European economy. Ironically, the French believed that Vatican policy had contributed to forcing them to take this course of action. The French had already rejected Gasparri's plans for readjusting downward Germany's reparation payments. By seeking to reduce the sum Gasparri was regarded by Paris as siding with Germany, encouraging Berlin to protest that the amount due was too high, and impeding France from receiving its rightful due. The situation did not improve when in 1923 at the New Year's reception for foreign envoys in Paris, Nuncio Cerretti was not very tactful in treating this sensitive issue. In a speech as doyen of the diplomatic corps he made reference to the reparations issue, once more advocating a reduction in the payments in tones that the French regarded as presumptuous and as an attempt to suggest how French policy should be conducted in this matter. President Alexandre Millerand flatly rejected what he regarded as interference. During the last few months the opinion among some French politicians that since Rome was not actively supporting French policies, the recent reestablishment of French-Vatican relations had not been worth the effort, had produced a marked strain between Paris and the Vatican. The Nuncio's speech at a public gathering was regarded as another sign that German influence was strong in the Curia and that France could not expect support from this quarter. In fact, some French diplomats noted that this speech, which announced publicly the Vatican's endorsement of moderation and compromise, was an important consideration in persuading Millerand to agree to Premier Poincaré's demands for occupation, and thus precipitated the crisis. As the French Minister in Vienna, P. Lefèvre-Pontalis, stated, in a future war between Germany and France, the entire blame would rest upon the Pope both for becoming involved in the matter and for his partiality for Germany and upon the United States for not becoming involved in helping to solve Europe's economic difficulties.[4] The comment, undoubtedly oversimplified and expressed in hyperbolic fashion, yet indicated the depth of Gallic anger and frustration.

Europe had yet to solve the general question of reparations and to determine to what extent Germany was capable of making the payments demanded of it. Now a second but connected problem was introduced to complicate the difficulty. The French and Belgians had invaded German territory to collect what they considered was due them: Germany stating it would not pay any more until foreign troops had withdrawn from the Ruhr, and France claiming it would not leave until it received what was owed, nor would it even discuss the matter until Berlin ceased obstructing payment and called off the passive resistence.

The reaction of the German episcopate to the invasion was to support the government's policy. The Bishop of Paderborn sent a pastoral letter denouncing the invasion, encouraging the populace to remain loyal Germans and Catholics, and ordering prayers in all the churches.[5] The Bishop of Trier and Cardinal Schulte also took the occasion to protest the "policy of violence" initiated by France. The *Trierische Landeszeitung*, a Catholic organ, for example, published articles condemning the invasion and criticized French religious policy in the Rhineland and what the newspaper termed its use of such methods as employing the military bishop to extend French control over German territory via the Church.[6]

The French remonstrated in Rome against these statements of the hierarchy and diocesan organs as unnecessary interference of the Church in political affairs. But Gasparri paid little attention to the French complaints, for he was more concerned with the consequences of the invasion for Europe as a whole. He doubted that the French realized the seriousness of their move. If Germany's economy were seriously dislocated, France would lose the possibility of ever getting reparation money. How, he asked, could one force a people of 60 million by use of military might and starvation tactics to make remuneration? Paris, he believed, was unaware of the degree of hostility that it was creating for itself. Returning to one of his favorite themes regarding European politics, the Cardinal in numerous conversations with diplomats men-

[4] AA, BRV 130, Vol. 8, Pfeiffer (Vienna) to AA, January 17, 1923.

[5] Germany, Paderborn, Archivstelle beim Erzbischöflichen Generalvikariat, XXII, 1, pastoral letter cited in *New Yorker Staatszeitung*, January 12, 1923.

[6] FFO, Allemagne 367, Tirard to Poincaré, January 18, 1923.

tioned that in ten years the political situation could be drastically changed, and Germany might not hesitate to seek revenge. Germany's action could then ignite a war of destruction without parallel in which Russia and totally heterogenous elements could unite with Germany to march against France. This dangerous prospect and the ensuing damage that it could cause to the Church's interest seemed seriously to trouble the Secretary of State,[7] and as the crisis deepened he became more disheartened. Germany had informed him that should French troops continue to advance in the Ruhr, Berlin might resist with German soldiers. Such a statement only increased the agitation of the Cardinal, who saw a resumption of the war and all its horrors. As he said to the Belgian Ambassador, Napoléon Beyens, "the French want to go to Berlin . . . as their newspapers say." Beyens, trying to calm him, explained the Franco-Belgian conviction that Germany had been procrastinating in making payment. Because moderation had not worked, the Western Powers were adopting a policy calculated to obtain satisfaction, but not intended to destroy the Reich or its economy. Nevertheless Gasparri used the conversation to sound out the Ambassador about what conditions Germany would have to meet in order to effect a withdrawal of the troops. He even expressed an idea which contained the germ of what would later be part of the Dawes plan for solving the reparations problem. The Cardinal suggested that he would like to see a committee of experts composed of neutrals and creditor nations which would determine once and for all Germany's ability to pay, since this would then shed light on the necessity and value of a Ruhr occupation.[8]

In addition, Rome was also receiving other reports that at the time looked plausible and lent credence to the Cardinal's analysis of the situation and reinforced his fears. In 1923 the Rumanians had evidence of Hungarian troop concentration on their borders. Also, rumors of increasing diplomatic and military ties between Hungary and Germany, as well as the Soviet Union and Germany, were widespread in diplomatic circles, and some observers feared that an occupation of the Ruhr would impel Germany to urge Hungary and Russia to take advantage of the circumstances in the west to create incidents in eastern Europe which would cause concern to the Great Powers and their allies, the members of the Little Entente, and thereby relieve the pressure on the Reich. Count Władysław Skrzyński, Polish Minister to the Holy See, made no secret of his government's disapproval of the Ruhr action for fear that it might precipitate a Bolshevik attack on his

[7] HHSTA, 87, Pastor to AFO, January 20, 1923.
[8] BelgFO, St. Siège 1923-28, Beyens to Jaspar, January 20, 1923.

country.[9] What wonder, then, that Gasparri urged vigilance lest a chain reaction take place across Europe which might allow the "heterogenous" group, including Germans and Russians of which he spoke, to unite someday against France.

In order to prevent an expansion of the crisis, Gasparri sought not only to moderate the French demands by having his nuncio speak to French officials in Paris but also to obtain a clarification from Germany as to its requirements for settling the crisis. In January he again made unofficial proposals to the Germans, asking Bergen whether on the condition that the Franco-Belgian forces first be withdrawn, the Reich would then permit an inter-Allied commission to supervise coal and timber deliveries or agree to a three-to-four-year moratorium on payments in order to permit the commission time to study the problem. He told the German Ambassador that these were just his own proposals, but that he desired to explore every means possible to avert open hostilities. Berlin, however, had developed a three-part strategy during this crisis: maintain the policy of supporting passive resistance, wait out the French by avoiding any revision of the 1921 reparations figure until an agreement could be reached on Germany's ability to pay as a basis, and delay negotiating until Britain and the United States, the only economic powers which could bring Poincaré into line, became involved. In the meantime, the Reich would encourage Rome to do all it could to help. Thus, not wishing to deter Gasparri in any steps that he might undertake to help, Bergen replied that, although the Reich would cooperate in reaching a solution, it would also need guarantees that an invasion of its territory would not occur again; he believed that it would want to know more specifically the duties of the control commission, and that it would urge that the matter in dispute be dealt with in cooperation with all the powers, not just Germany, France, and Belgium.[10] Germany would then fare better in a larger forum, especially with states which Germany believed more favorable to its position, than if it had to deal with France and Belgium alone. The request for the inclusion of other nations was not merely a tactical but also a logical one. Inasmuch as Germany was indebted to all the powers and had been negotiating the matter of payment at the series of reparation conferences during the last few years, it seemed understandable to include all parties concerned in the discussion of the crisis.

Gasparri considered Bergen's argument reasonable, and while awaiting Berlin's official reply to his request for information from Germany,

---

[9] *Ibid.*
[10] AA, RM 14, Vol. 1, Bergen to AA, January 21, 1923.

the next day he passed Bergen's remarks on to the British, expressing his belief that, for the moment, the Vatican could do nothing more than offer its opinion that the logical countries which could and should intervene in the matter were England and the United States. The situation, though still not clear to him, was fraught with great dangers. If France's object in the Ruhr was to retain the region or detach it from the Reich and create a buffer state, war was inevitable immediately or within ten years. If Germany, on the other hand, would allow an inter-Allied control commission, then there would no longer be an excuse for the occupation, and the crisis could be quickly diffused. In official conversations with British diplomats he linked this topic with mention once more of his uneasiness about a possible Russian move westward because of the struggle in the Ruhr.[11]

Berlin telegraphed its reply to Gasparri's suggestion on January 22. The Foreign Office went further than Bergen's informal suggestions of drawing other powers into the discussions. The Reich not only desired the number of participants expanded but the area of discussion broadened. Foreign Minister Frederic Hans von Rosenberg stated that he saw evidence of the Ruhr conflict expanding into the Rhineland proper and of France stepping up is efforts to take over transportation and industrial services in that area. Such moves, of course, if carried out, would only further jeopardize Germany's ability to meet its payments. Gasparri's idea to send in a commission, said the Foreign Minister, could only be considered once the Reich's ability to make compensation had definitely been established. This could be done only when and if the question at issue was viewed solely as an economic matter divested of all political connotations. Berlin believed that the Ruhr dispute should not be discussed or detached from the reparations question as a whole. Instead, the problem should be studied in its entirety and settled as such. Rosenberg urged the Cardinal to coordinate his efforts with other well-meaning powers, such as the United States, to bring some order and reason to bear on the entire unsettled issue.[12]

All German cabinets since the war had claimed that the territorial losses and huge amount of reparations were ruining German finances, and this the public readily believed. There was a basic unwillingness on the government's part to pay the sums demanded or at best to undertake the measures needed to honor its reparation commitments. Berlin and most Germans viewed the situation the other way around: Germany's financial or economic policy was not hindering the delivery

[11] BFO, 371/8708/5325, Dorner (Vatican) to Curzon, January 29, 1923.
[12] AA, RM 14, Vol. 1, Rosenberg (AA) to Bergen, January 22, 1923.

9. The newly appointed Chancellor Wilhelm Cuno leaving the Reichstag after the first meeting of his cabinet of "business experts" with the Chamber of Deputies, November 1922

of payments, but rather it was the payments which were injuring the German finances. The war had already produced a huge government debt and an excessive amount of currency in public hands. German officials seemed incompetent of diagnosing correctly the causes of growing inflation or incapable of balancing the budget and stopping the easy credit policy of the *Reichsbank*. Instead, the Cuno Government, backed by the industrialists, pursued an inflationary policy of increasing the paper money in circulation, allowing it to pay off at least domestic debts with depreciated marks, but causing great hardship for the middle and lower classes and only contributing to the political unrest. Moreover, by assuming the cost of the subsidies and compensations to the Ruhr populace for the passive resistance, the cabinet put an even greater strain on the treasury. German financial experts did not see the cause of German difficulties in this expansion of credit or money in circulation. Rather, the need to make cash payments for reparations and the further issuance of money to finance these only confirmed the German view about the impact of reparations on the financial situation.[13] Despite the advice of international economists in the fall of 1922 that it was within the power of government to stabilize the mark by a reform of its fiscal policy, German authorities stubbornly held to the belief that a solution could be found only with a foreign loan and a readjustment downward of reparation payments.[14] Therefore, having decided not to pay the full amount if it could be avoided, the government had no incentive to put its finances in order, for to do so would only weaken its case.

Berlin felt that the Ruhr crisis presented Germany with the possibility of settling the entire reparations question. By insisting on viewing the problem as a whole with a crisis at hand, it thought that states such as the Vatican, which were interested in averting more serious complications for Europe, would bring influence to bear on France to moderate its stand or to have the amount due reduced. Berlin, however, was not in favor of establishing a special commission to study the Ruhr predicament and supervise reparation deliveries from that area, since it feared the committee might simply order Germany to continue paying its obligations without considering Berlin's assertion that the entire economy of the Reich, the entire reparations question, and Germany's ability to pay had to be viewed as a whole, not merely in the Ruhr. Similar to 1917, when Germany declined Papal proposals to come to the conference table until conditions were more favorable to its demands, Berlin was now politely informing the Cardinal that Germany did not completely endorse his suggestions but would wait until England and possibly the United States were included in a more general discussion of the reparations issue as a whole. Upon receiving the news Gasparri indicated visible disappointment that the Reich did not initially endorse his efforts at mediation, since apparently he was then ready to begin soundings in Paris. He informed Bergen, in an injured tone, that after Germany's refusal of his suggestions he did not know of any formula at the moment for Vatican mediation.[15]

In spite of Gasparri's pessimistic opinion of the Vatican's options, Berlin did not wish to have Rome distance itself from the situation. Several days after Rosenberg's reply to Gasparri, Cardinal Schulte, at the request of the Reich Government, directed a letter to the Holy

[13] Hajo Holborn, *A history of modern Germany* (New York, 1969), Vol. 3, pp. 595-597.
[14] Trachtenberg, pp. 172-173. Maier, pp. 356-360.
[15] AA, BRV 130, Vol. 8, Bergen to AA, January 24, 1923.

Father protesting France's "brutal" actions against German civil servants in the Ruhr. The Franco-Belgian move had placed government officials in a very difficult position. Those who hesitated to cooperate with the occupying forces had been given stiff penal sentences, while any complicity with the French and Belgians was regarded as treason in Berlin. After recounting the plight of the Ruhr officials and describing instances of harsh treatment by the occupying forces against civilians, the Cologne prelate requested the Pontiff to use his influence in helping to alleviate this "state of war."[16] Berlin believed that, since the Rhineland and Ruhr area were overwhelmingly Catholic, the Vatican would be concerned with the crisis not only because of its diplomatic ramifications but also for pastoral reasons as well. Therefore, Berlin had Cologne's Cardinal make the appeal for Vatican aid, i.e., on a purely religious level. Since analysts in the Foreign Office shared Gasparri's opinion that for the moment the Vatican could do little more than it had on the international stage, Berlin thought the best strategy was to keep the matter before the Curia by letting the German episcopate take up the issue while diplomatic pressure from the government could be employed later after Germany saw how the crisis developed.[17]

Gasparri reacted to Schulte's requests[18] by replying that direct intervention was not possible at that moment, nor could Rome take sides in a political matter. While expressing sympathy for the people of the area and directing prayers to be said for relief of the suffering, the only thing that he felt he could do at present was reiterate once again his plea that the victors deal with the vanquished with justice and fraternal consideration. Although the Cardinal's reply could be interpreted as Rome's condoning the Franco-Belgian action and was received with much pleasure in Paris as a sign of Vatican passive support, it did not convey Gasparri's complete thoughts.[19] In a private conversation with the Austrian Minister, the eminent historian Ludwig Pastor, he vented his agitation and vexation over the French ac-

[16] *Kölnische Volkszeitung*, January 25, 1923.

[17] AA, BRV 130, Vol. 8, Rosenberg to German Embassy (Vatican), January 30, 1923. German bishops visiting Rome took every opportunity to inform the Pope, the Secretary of State, other members of the Sacred College, and Curial officials of Germany's problems. Although German prelates were coming to fulfill their duty of visiting the Pope every five years and to discuss with Vatican officials the situation in their dioceses (*ad limina* visit), the constant flow of German churchmen into the Holy City caused Roman wits to say that in reality the German bishops were not there to talk about the state of the Church but rather to ruin France. AA, Botschaftsakten Abstimmungsgebiet Ost-West Preussen, Vol. 2, Bergen to AA, November 26, 1923.

[18] There had been a renewed request from Schulte on January 31, 1923.

[19] FFO, Allemagne 367, Cambon to Poincaré, February 6, 1923.

tion. Looking ahead, he feared that the move was a prelude to the detachment of more land from the Reich, which would only weaken the Church in Germany after the losses already sustained in Alsace-Lorraine and along the eastern borders. Any further loss of territory by the Reich would make the Catholics in Germany a true minority. Gasparri suspected that France's explanations for the invasion were merely excuses to seize those areas whose separation from Germany had not been provided for in the Versailles Treaty.[20] Yet for the moment, until he had further evidence of his suspicions, the Cardinal believed he could do little more than he had.

Meanwhile the German episcopate was also taking further steps to support their government against the Ruhr action. In addition to asking for aid from the Vatican Schulte had also encouraged a meeting of Catholic trade unions from the Ruhr to convene in Cologne and to issue a protest about the occupation. On January 28 he circulated a pastoral letter to his flock, sharply condemning the occupation, which he presumed would destroy the last hopes for peace and plunge the German people into a new period of misery and ruin. However, the occupation, he cautioned, had also infused in the populace a new spirit of resistance and of sharing in need. Therefore he called for a greater show of cooperation and acts of charity for those afflicted by the occupation and, of course, prayers for a speedy end to the suffering. Speaking to the invaders, he warned that the occupation would imbue the Germans with a greater spirit of resistance and determination to keep their land free of foreign troops.

The French Chargé d'Affaires at the Vatican, Henri Cambon, promptly protested Schulte's letter, stating that it encouraged resistance by the populace and lent support to the laborers in the Ruhr industries then refusing to work for the French. It was, in other words, a call for passive resistance. The Cardinal's letter, Cambon maintained, directly opposed the expressed Vatican desire for a relaxation of tensions. The only method which could lead to a return of normalcy would be for the Church to encourage the inhabitants to carry on their daily tasks, which in turn would help to fulfill the demanded reparation requirements, satisfy the creditor nations, and bring an improvement in international relations. Cambon, using this line of argument, formally requested the Vatican to demonstrate some support for the occupation and to bring about a settlement to the post-war difficulties.[21] The Cardinal replied to the French on February 9, denying that Schulte's statement had been a call for passive resistance

---

[20] HHSTA, 87, Pastor to Foreign Minister Grünberger, February 2, 1923.
[21] FFO, Allemagne 367, Cambon to Gasparri, February 3, 1923.

but merely a condemnation of violent action, the sort of statement that a man of God would understandably make.[22] The dispute over Schulte's action was, in other words, a question of interpretation and illustrated once again the position that the Curia was placed in by an international crisis.

Since the Vatican had failed by the end of January to convince either side to moderate its position, France and Germany continued their attempts to win the Church's endorsement for their respective cause. The official reaction was publication of an article in the *Osservatore* on February 2, outlining the seriousness of the situation, expressing fears of a European upheaval, and emphasizing the importance of moderation at that critical moment. But the Vatican's comments could be understood and interpreted in different ways. At Bergen's urging the Foreign Office ordered the German press to give broad coverage to the Pontiff's call for moderation, and his concern over the suffering in the Ruhr, since this could be construed as meaning that Rome disapproved of the Franco-Belgian action. Also, Berlin calculated that by featuring the Vatican's interest in the plight of the Reich a favorable impression of and goodwill for the Vatican would be built up in Germany, which Bergen could then point to in dealing with the Curia and in urging the Church to greater efforts on behalf of the Reich. But here the Germans miscalculated somewhat and pursued their tactics with too heavy a hand.

The papers duly carried articles about the Pontiff's concern over the invasion and prominently featured Schulte's request, as the ranking bishop in western Germany, for Vatican help. Instead of pleasing Rome, however, it only irritated the Cardinal Secretary of State. He would have preferred to keep Schulte's request out of the public eye. He told Bergen that although the Vatican understood the reasons for the German advocacy of passive resistance and non-cooperation with French officials in the Ruhr, at present nothing warranted or justified the Curia's taking an official stand on the issue. He warned Bergen that too much publicity of Rome's actions or speculation on its motives could hinder its maneuverability. No doubt fearing a repetition of earlier incidents, Gasparri reminded the Ambassador that on other occasions his good offices on behalf of the Reich had been frustrated by ill-timed disclosures in the German press and had embarrassed the Vatican.[23] He lay emphasis on discretion and made any support for the German position contingent on secrecy. The Cardinal assured the German representative that he would continue to work behind the

[22] FFO, Allemagne 367, Gasparri to Cambon, February 9, 1923.
[23] See ch. 2, p. 66ff.

scenes and take soundings in both Paris and Brussels about what could be done. In fact, the Cardinal seemed so ready to do what he could for Germany, resolve the crisis, and avert another war that, while deeply grateful, Bergen felt the need to restrain him lest without consultation with German representatives he suggest terms that Berlin might oppose. The Ambassador tactfully reminded Gasparri that Curial efforts should be exerted with caution lest they exasperate the French and jeopardize greater and more fruitful efforts at a later time.[24]

Bergen wired Berlin that he believed the Vatican, in the interests of justice as well as of its own interests, would move to support the German view, and this appraisal was confirmed by other reports reaching Germany from Rome. Cardinal Schulte's personal representative in the Holy City, Msgr. Emmerich David, after having spoken to several Vatican officials, confirmed Bergen's analysis that the Pontiff was extremely disturbed about the consequences of the French action for the Church and that Gasparri viewed the situation most pessimistically.[25] In order to strengthen their case and prove the allegations that the Western Powers were denying, David and Bergen requested that detailed reports with documented individual cases of harsh treatment of the civilian population by the military in the Ruhr be sent to Rome to provide the Curia with substantial evidence to work with. Gasparri had informed Bergen that he could pursue fruitful conversations with the French and Belgian Governments only when he had incontestable detailed cases of oppression and inhumane acts carried out by the invasion troops. Newspaper reports were valueless for this purpose.[26] As in World War I the first steps that the Vatican took were to pursue its diplomacy on the humanitarian and pastoral level and to ascertain the truth about Germany's claims of unjust treatment of the civilian population in the Ruhr by the occupying forces.

David was also pleased to learn that the Vatican had passed off the French protest over Schulte's statement by minimizing its seriousness and backed the Cardinal by stating that the German clergy could not be expected to remain neutral in speaking up in the interests of their country. But David had hoped that the Vatican would condemn the invasion itself by taking an official stand, as had the International So-

[24] AA, RM 70, Vol. 1, Bergen to AA, February 2, 1923; RM 70, Vol. 2, Bergen to AA, February 3, 1923.

[25] On February 9 Bergen happily reported that the Jesuit newspaper and semi-official organ of the Curia, *La Civiltà Cattolica*, gave an account of the events in the Ruhr in a manner which reflected the German viewpoint, while no mention was made of French justification for invasion. AA, PO II, PO 12 Vat., Vol. 1, Bergen to AA, February 9, 1923.

[26] AA, PO II, PO 2 Vat., Vol. 1, Bergen to AA, February 10, 1923.

cial Democratic Congress and some Protestant Churches in neutral countries. This, however, was not Rome's way, as Gasparri had reminded David. The Vatican's position was especially delicate, and a public statement over the issue would serve to harden the French position and decrease Rome's options and its ability to mediate. Unlike the Lutheran Archbishop of Uppsala, Sweden, who had spoken against the move, the Catholic Church had to consider the effect of its actions on its adherents in France. Its policy was to negotiate behind the scenes. In the meantime he recommended a cooling-off period of several weeks until settlement at Lausanne of the eastern question dealing with Turkey's border revisions, when England would have more time to occupy itself with this problem. Since Gasparri doubted that England would endorse France's Ruhr policy, he hoped that London would turn its attention to moderating the effects of the Franco-Belgian move.[27]

The Secretary repeated this view to the Bavarian Minister. He had already suggested a formula for mediation in January, which Berlin had politely rejected. Gasparri had not seemed angry, merely disappointed at the Reich's refusal, since, as Ritter stated, he probably had little hope that France would accept a withdrawal so easily, but he had wanted at least to show his goodwill and intention to help. Also, feelings were running high in France about the correctness of the measures taken by Paris. Just as Cardinal Schulte had endorsed the German stance by condemning the invasion, Cardinal Louis Maurin of Lyons had praised the action against Germany's unwillingness to pay its debts. The Germans were calling for a withdrawal from their territory, and the Belgians and French, refusing to do so, were in turn requesting Germany to halt the passive resistance and to begin fulfilling its obligations under the treaty, without which, said the Allies, any discussions over the crisis were impossible. Under these circumstances Gasparri endorsed Bergen's suggestion of several days before that the Holy See wait for a better moment lest any precipitous statement on Rome's part now close all doors and prevent action at a more crucial moment.[28]

In February nothing seemed to be moving on the diplomatic level. But the local hierarchy called attention to the suffering of its flock. In addition to having visited the area, offering encouragement to the residents, and mobilizing their support for opposing the occupation, Cardinal Schulte had also been most active in personally protesting the Ruhr Franco-Belgian action. For example, he had granted an interview to an Italian journalist, Gustavo Traglia, who wrote for sev-

---

[27] Germany, Paderborn, Archivstelle beim Erzbischöflichen Generalvikariat, XXII, 1, David to Schulte, February 9, 1923.

[28] GSTA, MA 104433, Ritter to BFM, February 14, 1923.

eral newspapers of the Catholic Italian Popular Party (*Partito Popolare Italiano*). The Cardinal condemned the invasion and predicted that the populace would resist and refuse to submit to oppression. Germany, he reiterated was peaceful, and the entire populace which stood behind the opposition had no choice but to resist.[29] For his protest and encouragement of his people he was lauded by German statesmen and even by neutrals such as the Lutheran bishops of Sweden, who, as represented by the eminent Archbishop Nathan Söderblom of Uppsala, sent him a message on February 2, expressing sympathy for Germany's plight and offering his prayers for an end to the hostilities. The French press, as could be expected, castigated him for misusing his religious position for political purposes and seeking to make the Ruhr resistance movement into a sort of religious crusade.[30] On March 3, the bishops of Paderborn, Münster, and Cologne, all of whose dioceses the occupation affected, issued a joint appeal to the world-at-large and to the Vatican in particular. After deploring the sufferings caused by the war—a war, they emphasized, which the German people had not desired and for which they were not responsible—Germany had had to endure more hardship and stave off hunger and need stemming from the impositions placed on the Reich by Versailles. It was difficult, they said, to instruct their people in a spirit of forgiveness and love. In their opinion, since Germany had made every effort to meet its obligations, the recourse taken by the French and Belgians was illegal, and the actions against the civil and legal rights of the citizens were criminal. As bishops they regarded it as their duty to protest the occupation of the area, the expulsion of officials and their families because they had not cooperated with the new administration, and the incarceration of opponents to the military rule, and to ask for aid from other nations for the people of the area.[31]

The Vatican proceeded first to inquire directly through the Nuncio in Brussels and through contacts with the French Government about

[29] *Kölnische Volkszeitung*, February 11, 1923.
[30] *Kölnische Volkszeitung*, February 26, 1923.
[31] Germany, Paderborn, Archivstelle beim Erzbischöflichen Generalvikariat, XXIII, protest of Schulte of Cologne, Johannes Poggenburg of Münster, and Caspar Klein of Paderborn, March 3, 1923. The French High Command estimated that in the first twelve months of occupation "the Allies had killed 76 persons and wounded 92 (either in reply to acts of aggression or in order to exact respect for their passwords); the Germans had killed 20 Allied soldiers and wounded 66 as a result of murderous assaults and ambuscades; finally the Germans had killed 300 and wounded more than 2,000 of their compatriots in order to teach them the beauty and the necessity of passive resistance." During the first months of 1923 it was estimated that 147,000 German citizens were expelled from the Ruhr, including state officials, railway and postal workers, and their dependents. Toynbee, *Survey, 1924*, pp. 279-280.

225

the allegations. Despite the fact that Bergen told Curial officials of his readiness to submit written proof confirming Germany's case, both Brussels and Paris dismissed the accusations as prefabricated lies.[32] In meetings with Gasparri over the Ruhr crisis in February, Belgian Ambassador Beyens steadfastly maintained that the difficulties in reaching a solution lay not with the French and Belgians but with Germany. He defended the expulsion of German civil servants and their families as necessary to break the resistance of those who refused to carry out the ordinances of the new administrations. Moreover, he conveyed Belgium's extreme displeasure that a high churchman such as Schulte had interfered in the matter, making accusations against the occupying powers. Beyens warned Gasparri that Vatican intervention would only aggravate the problem by making the Germans believe that the Church endorsed their attempts to evade payment, and instead suggested that the Holy See help to calm the situation by making Germany realize that it had to honor its commitments.

The Cardinal made a facial expression conveying melancholic sadness, which he usually did not do in dealing with diplomats, and replied, "Let's hope . . . that you are not mistaken and that the European peace is not at the mercy of an unexpected incident. You see what happened in the Near East (*Orient*) after the failure of the Lausanne Conference" (November 1922 to June 1923).[33] Gasparri was referring to preparations for a resumption of hostilities, due to the failure of the conference by February 1923 to resolve the territorial dispute between Turkey and the Allies. He saw potential danger in a similar situation developing in the west because of the lack of agreement over the Ruhr problem. The Vatican, continued the prelate, certainly agreed that Germany should make reparation, but now an added dimension appeared, for in his opinion the Western Allies had linked reparations to the question of security. The Italian considered lamentable that the Anglo-American guarantee of military assistance proposed at Versailles had not been put into effect as intended so that France would

[32] AA, BRV 131, Vol. 9, Bergen to AA, February 4, 1923.

[33] European diplomats had believed they had settled the Turkish question by the Treaty of Sèvres in 1920. However, the Turks, under Mustapha Kemal (Atatürk) reopened hostilities and forced the Allies to renegotiate the treaty with their former enemy. A conference was called in 1922 at Lausanne to settle the matter and end the fighting. After heated disputes over terms, such as what Turkey could retain, the conference broke up on February 4, 1923, the political future of the area remained uncertain, and it looked as if peace was once more threatened. In February, when he made his statement to Beyens, Gasparri, like many European diplomats, was pessimistic about the outcome. The conference, however, resumed in April, and the Allies agreed to change the boundary settlements in Turkey's favor. In the end success was obtained by peaceful negotiations, but it also set a potential precedent for further treaty alterations.

have its security. The occupation of the Ruhr and the gloomy prospect of its indefinite extension now evoked in Gasparri a feeling of uneasiness.[34]

The picture, then, which the Vatican received remained cloudy. Not a day passed that the German Embassy did not fail to send reports to the Vatican about the misdeeds of the occupation forces. When inquiry was made about these allegations, the French and Belgians defended themselves by showing counterreports that the incidents had been provoked by the local populace, by arguing that the measures taken were necessary for maintaining order to run the industries in the area, and by dismissing the German accounts as highly exaggerated. Moreover, the matter was becoming more complicated for Rome, since the increasingly nationalist stance adopted by the Rhenish bishops had given the role of the Church a more political coloring than before, making it more difficult for Gasparri to brush aside Franco-Belgian protests. The Vatican watched uneasily as the climate of hostility began to unfold. European newspapers and diplomatic circles even began to speculate about the probability of war again, about France's desire for revenge on Germany, and about Germany's immoral efforts to escape its obligation that stemmed from 1914. Such speculations served to create a mood threatening to resurrect the entire issue of war guilt and only to deepen the animosity between the two nations.

The tension had developed to such an extent that it prompted René Pinon, Poincaré's successor as political commentator for *Revue des deux Mondes*, to declare, "The Ruhr is thus becoming the stakes in a formidable battle of opinions, a test of decisive strength: the conflict is economic and financial but above all it is moral and psychological."[35] Both sides continued to apply pressure on the Vatican to lend its support, Germany by seeking a condemnation of the invasion and "inhumane" actions of the occupying troops, France by seeking a statement recognizing its need to enter the area to ensure the reparations payment or, failing that, to obtain at least a tacit silence or noninterference by the Curia. Between these two attitudes the Vatican was to decide. Therefore, in March the Vatican chose to send its own observer, in the hopes of ascertaining the truth. He would travel to the Ruhr and on the way home stop in the Saarland to acquaint himself with the problems there. Msgr. Gustavo Testa, a diplomat fluent in both German and French who had already served in the Vatican legations in Munich and Vienna, was selected. Cautious in his words,

[34] BelgFO, St. Siège 1923-28, Beyens to Jaspar, February 10, and March 7, 1923.

[35] Paul Wentzcke, *Ruhrkampf* (Berlin, 1932), Vol. 1, p. 422. Editorial of René Pinon, *Revue des deux mondes*, 93rd Year, VII (1923), 718.

anxious to mediate and not offend, yet a person who showed humane interest in the problems of his fellow man, Testa seemed a good choice for the mission. A Papal observer might serve multiple purposes here; while protecting Church interests in the area, confirming the Holy See's position as a mediator, and serving as an instrument of humanitarian good, he could gather proof either for or against the allegations made by Germany so that Rome could strengthen its diplomatic hand to help the Ruhr populace and to continue its policy of seeking an equal balance among the powers of Europe.

The French and Belgian Governments made no objections to the Vatican's proposal to send Testa to the Ruhr, and London enthusiastically endorsed it. Germany also was happy to have the Vatican move along these lines and immediately set to work at the Rome Embassy by supplying Testa with large amounts of material about the events taking place in the Ruhr and lower Rhine valleys, all provided in Italian translations for the prelate's convenience. Moreover, Gasparri requested David to write Cardinal Bertram, as head of the Fulda Bishops' Conference, to ensure that the Catholic press in Germany treat Testa's appointment discreetly and without much publicity. The Cardinal Secretary authorized the publication of a simple statement that Testa was traveling to the area to learn if ecclesiastical and pastoral matters had arisen which required attention and also to inform himself about the situation in general. The Curia did not desire to have any newspaper convey the impression that Testa had been sent to aid the Germans or that his move was in response to the bishops' appeal of March 3.[36] Concurrently, the French also set about to capitalize on Testa's mission. Cambon believed that the prelate's visit could have beneficial results for French policy if the apostolic visitor were correctly shown the French side of the story and if his mission could be used to show the populace that the Vatican was supporting France and thus help in getting them to cooperate with the authorities. To do this the French would have to make every effort to convince him that the "tales" that the Reich had been spreading at the Vatican were fabrications. Aware that Testa would be bringing funds to alleviate human suffering caused by the economic dislocation, Cambon warned that it was essential for France's case that the military administration ensure that the disbursement of money did not appear as an ecclesiastical endorsement for the passive resistance. In addition, the French Foreign Office was to keep close watch and counter any attempt by the clergy or the press in unoccupied Germany from giving the envoy's mission a political coloring, that is, a pro-German coloring.[37]

[36] AW, IA 25v, 30, David to Bertram, March 19, 1923.

[37] FFO, Allemagne 367, Cambon to FFO, March 19, 1923.

While the Vatican was preparing to send its fact-finding representative to the Ruhr, Germany made certain that its views on how the
issue should be treated were also conveyed to the Pope by formal
diplomatic and political channels. A fortunate opportunity presented
itself in the spring when, worried about the worsening international
climate and concerned for its effects on Austria, Msgr. Ignaz Seipel,
Austrian Chancellor and a Catholic priest, informed Berlin that he
would be in Rome for Holy Week. He intended on his own initiative
to urge Pius to intervene in the Ruhr question or at least to make an
appeal to the conflicting parties in an allocution which he could deliver
to the Cardinals assembled in Rome for the religious rites. Seipel disclosed his plans to the Germans in order to inform them of his intentions and to ascertain what they considered a realistic foundation on
which an eventual Papal initiative could be built. In other words,
Seipel was asking for the German terms on which negotiations could
begin, which he would then relay to Rome, while assuring all parties
concerned that he was undertaking these conversations on his own
initiative. Rosenberg, Germany's Foreign Minister, was naturally pleased
with Seipel's offer. Although he personally believed that little would
come of the Austrian Chancellor's endeavors, since the time was not
ready for negotiation, he nevertheless outlined to him Germany's views
and gave an indication of what the Reich Government had in mind
about conditions for preliminary negotiations at that time.

The Reich favored a suggestion made that year by American Secretary of State Charles Evans Hughes, which called for a conference
of international financial experts to determine the extent of Germany's
ability to pay and what France and Belgium hoped to receive from the
occupation. Without in any way desiring to tell the Holy See what
course it should take, Rosenberg outlined what the Pontiff might suggest to the conflicting parties: (1) agreement to Hughes's suggestion,
(2) immediate withdrawal from all areas not allowed for in the Versailles Treaty by France and Belgium, termination of passive resistance by Germany and the resumption of deliveries of coal and coke,
and (3) amnesty for all persons whom, because of the events since
January 11, the existing authorites had punished.[38]

At the same time as Germany was making use of Seipel's good
offices, Berlin was also using another approach to win the Pontiff's
sympathy, if not his endorsement. Encouraged by Curial statements
about their willingness to assist Germany when possible and confident
that the Germans could collect sufficient proof to indict the Western
Powers of unjust and harsh behavior, Bergen wired Berlin that they

[38] AA, RM 14-1 Secr., Vol. 1, Rosenberg to Bergen, March 19, 1923.

did not have to report every incident to the Vatican but should present detailed evidence of several of the more outstanding cases at once, in the hopes of causing a stronger impact on the Vatican, evoking a realization of moral indignation, and eliciting a condemnation of the Ruhr invasion from Rome.[39] This seemed to be the best tactic for Germany to prove its point. While lamenting the Ruhr invasion, neither the United States nor England was inclined to become directly involved in the matter. Under the circumstances the odds seemed at the moment heavily in favor of France's continued occupation of the area. Surveying the situation from his vantage point in Paris, yet underestimating the economic strain which the dispute was placing on the French economy, Nuncio Cerretti even informed German diplomats that he believed France would be able to withstand a prolonged conflict, while Germany, because of its weakened position, would probably have to capitulate and terminate the passive resistance. Poincaré, sensing that the other powers would not interfere, had clearly stated France's determination. This statement, Cerretti thought, amounted to an effort to block the Vatican from undertaking a mediatory role.[40] Given these circumstances, until other events caused a change on the diplomatic scene, the time for Germany to negotiate had not yet arrived, thus leaving the Vatican little maneuverability. Germany's best tactic was not to stress the diplomatic significance of the invasion but rather to appeal to Rome's humanitarian, pastoral solicitude and to seek a disapproval of the occupation from the Pontiff on moral grounds.

Therefore, once the Vatican had dispatched Testa to the Ruhr, Germany not only had to continue to supply arguments against the occupation but now it also became necessary to ensure that Testa himself saw or directly learned about some of the activities of the occupation forces which would make him question their morality. But this would not be an easy task, for the French also intended to influence his judgment. A French Foreign Office memorandum of November 6, 1923 conceded that France had to realize that it could make no progress in the Rhine and Ruhr without support from the bishops and the Roman Curia. Testa's opinions would be very important to France and could significantly aid or hurt French policy. The Vatican observer was, continued the memorandum, "the arbiter of the situation."[41] With these considerations in mind, both sides were more than courteous when the Papal envoy arrived in March. The French admin-

[39] AA, BRV 133, Vol. 11, Bergen to AA, March 22, 1923.

[40] AA, BRV 133, Vol. 11, Hoesch (Paris) to AA, March 23, 1923.

[41] FFO, Allemagne 369, memorandum of Economic and Commercial Division of FFO to de la Croix, Belgian delegate at Rapallo, November 16, 1923.

istration placed a car at Testa's disposal in the occupied territory. A dinner was given in his honor in Koblenz, attended by leading French officers, Bishop Rémond, and other officials. In conversations with Testa, Tirard assured the Italian of France's good intentions, of his own desire to carry out his assignment in the Ruhr as smoothly as possible, and of his hopes to provide discipline for his troops so that there would be amiable relations with the civilian population. To support his statement Tirard provided documents attesting to his efforts in developing these relations with the civilians and the local clergy. The provocative statements of the Rhenish episcopate and German agents from outside the area, he asserted, had caused most of the unrest among the people.[42]

The Germans did not lag far behind the French in seeking Testa's ear. In the latter part of March the Papal diplomat paid a call on Cardinal Schulte, who provided him with written material about incidents in the Ruhr—imprisonments, finings, general harassment of the people, and the like. He recommended that Testa travel to unoccupied Germany and speak to officials there, but advised that he make his headquarters in the center of the Ruhr in Essen, so that he could fully observe the occurrences on a daily basis. Since Testa agreed to Schulte's suggestions, the Cardinal provided quarters for him in St. Elizabeth's Hospital in Essen and soon thereafter instructed the clergy in the area to visit him there regularly, informing him about their own problems and directing individuals to him who had difficulties because of the occupation. Schulte kept in close contact with Testa and had the added advantage that, after hearing Testa's observations and thoughts about events in the Ruhr, the Cardinal could send his own report directly to Rome, elaborating on or dispelling any misunderstandings which, from the German viewpoint, might have arisen. All this was done in close consultation with Reich officials.[43]

The Reich was anxious to hear what Testa and the Vatican intended to do. Not long after the envoy had had an opportunity to survey the local situation, the Germans asked what opinions he had formed about the problem. On April 1, as Testa was in Münster, meeting with local government officials, he was asked what steps Rome was planning to bring about the evacuation of the Ruhr. Testa, having heard the case from both sides, stated that under the existing circumstances, where France was not prepared to back down from any of its demands, the Curia could not work directly on France to moderate its position. Whereupon Walter Grützner, the governor (*Regierungspräsi-*

---

[42] FFO, Allemagne 367, Tirard to FFO, March 28, 1923.

[43] BA, R 43 I, Vol. 159, Brügger, State Secretary for Occupied Areas, to Reich Chancellor, April 4, 1923.

dent) of the district of Düsseldorf, asked whether the Curia might exert some pressure on England—which in turn might incline France to negotiate. Testa doubted the feasibility of this strategy, since considerable sections of the English population, largely antipathetic to the Curia, would reject any Curial initiatives which they believed were reserved to secular authorities. Rather, the most promising approach would be for the Curia to work with the United States.[44] Testa's remarks corroborated reports from other German diplomats that Gasparri had repeatedly made comments to foreign representatives that neither the reparations nor Ruhr problem could be solved without America. If necessary, perhaps the Vatican could find a way to persuade Italy to apply pressure to France if America showed absolutely no interest in using its good offices. But for the time being he preferred to wait and see what Washington would do.[45]

Not long thereafter, Austrian Chancellor Seipel, having returned from his trip to Rome, discussed his conversations in the Vatican with the German representative in Vienna. The Pontiff had reports of the conditions in the Ruhr, of shootings of civilians by occupying troops in Essen on Good Friday, and was deeply disturbed by the resulting impasse. He listened to the German suggestions which Seipel had brought with him, but again repeated that since France was unwilling to entertain discussions until the Germans first returned to work, the Vatican could do nothing but wait for an opportunity to act as intermediary in the dispute. Gasparri generally echoed Pius' sentiments, but coupled the conversation on the Ruhr issue with a concern for the growing spirit of cooperation between Germany and the Soviet Union, as witnessed by the Treaty of Rappallo (1922). Gasparri bitterly remarked that his fears were being realized, and that France's Ruhr policy was forcing Germany toward the east and Bolshevism. Exasperated, he voiced his regret about the Vatican's momentary inability to make even the slightest move to resolve the issue. As the Germans expected, Seipel's endeavors had come to naught.[46]

Meanwhile, Testa continued his fact-finding mission, visiting religious establishments in the Ruhr and meeting with both German and French functionaries. After having visited Paris to learn the government's view, he met in the Rhineland with local French officials at headquarters in Düsseldorf, with local clergy, with the German union leaders endorsing the resistance, with German officials of Westphalia, with the expelled Düsseldorf Government in Barmen, and with numerous others. While in the Ruhr he made arrangements to distribute

[44] Erdmann, *Kabinett Cuno*, report of Grützner, note 3, p. 362.
[45] AA, RM 14, Nr. 1 Secr., Vol. 1, Müller (Bern) to AA, March 31, 1923.
[46] AA, RM 14, Vol. 4, Pfeiffer to AA, April 6, 1923.

provisions to suffering families and also undertook to urge the occupying forces to permit an international commission to visit the prisons. He also took time to visit those held in custody by the occupying administration and to urge the French and Belgians to improve their lot. Both sides appreciated his efforts. The Germans emphasized the Vatican's concern for their citizens in the area and its efforts to do what it could to alleviate French "cruelty." By April the Bishop of Paderborn made public statements about the "significant improvement" in the prisoners' condition. The French, for their part, were anxious to demonstrate to the populace both their cooperation with the Vatican and Rome's active participation with French authorities. On April 24 General Jean-Marie Degoutte, Commander of the Rhine Army, announced that Vatican intervention had gained the release of the mayor of Essen, Heinrich Schäfer, then serving a three-year sentence for non-cooperation, and that other prisoners' sentences had been reduced.[47] Regardless of the reasons which both sides put forth for the deadlocked international situation, at least the Vatican's diplomacy fostered a measure of humanitarian good.

In mid-April Testa announced his intention of journeying to Berlin to confer with Reich Cabinet members as well as with prominent Center Party leaders. This trip, though not originally part of his itinerary, was initiated after Bergen repeatedly reminded Gasparri of the possibility of the impression being created that the Papal representative had come under French influence. Whether real or illusory, Bergen emphasized, French officials in the Rhineland had showered much attention on Testa, who was always accompanied by French officials on his trips throughout the occupied territory. In addition, the German Ambassador recalled Testa's previous visit to Paris, stating that impartiality dictated a similar journey to Berlin, where Reich officials could avail themselves of a similar opportunity not only to present their case to him, but to give additional documentary evidence of harsh or unjust acts inflicted on the local populace by the occupying forces and of the disruptions of German Government welfare benefits there.[48]

Bergen had reason for vigilance, as the French also believed their handling of Testa had been worthwhile. The French Bishop Rémond assessed Testa's mission as developing into a success for France, for he believed Testa was impressed with the correctness of French conduct toward the prisoners in providing for their physical and spiritual needs. Also, the Papal representative had commented favorably on the quiet and orderly atmosphere which he found then prevailing in the

[47] Wentzcke, Vol. 1, p. 421.
[48] AA, RM 70, Vol. 1, Bergen to AA, April 15, 1923. BA, R 43 I, Vol. 159, telephone conversation of Immelen (Essen) to Reich Chancellery, April 9, 1923.

Ruhr, in contrast to the widescale violence that had occurred several years before during the Spartacist uprisings. Rémond also ridiculed or minimized the importance of the large number of petitions and personal protests which the apostolic delegate had received, including one from a doctor which presented in scholastic form twenty-one arguments against the manner in which the French were applying the treaty's provisions here. Many of the petitions were irrelevant complaints or objections to the armed forces merely carrying out their duty and were not taken too seriously by Testa. Moreover, German acts of sabotage against the Franco-Belgian forces, such as destroying rolling stock, blowing up railway lines, and the like, were poor strategy psychologically and would only give Rome a negative impression of the German cause since the Vatican in general disapproved of violence. Thus Rémond assured the French Government that all was going well with Testa's visit.[49] General Degoutte, reporting in much the same words and possibly relying to some extent on Rémond's observations, supported the Bishop's assessment of the situation.[50]

Despite the encouraging news that Rémond reported, the French suspected the Germans of beginning a diplomatic offensive in Rome, since Cardinal Bertram, as well as Josef Schmitt, Bishop of Fulda, had gone to the Holy City. In addition, Bishop Norbert Klein of Brunn (Brno) and Bishop Josef Gross of Leitmeritz (Litoměřice), both German-speaking members of the Czech hierarchy, were also in the Holy City, and the French speculated that the Reich was grouping numerous prelates from "German lands" in Rome in order to persuade the Holy Father to take stronger action in resolving the Ruhr question. French information also indicated that the Germans were hoping to influence American Catholics to urge American bishops to join with their colleagues in protesting the invasion. For this purpose Cardinal Faulhaber was soon to leave for the United States.[51] Ritter in Rome confirmed that Berlin was urging churchmen to make the trip to the Vatican and that the visiting German bishops and prelates were there, emphasizing the hardships suffered by the Reich especially because of the Ruhr occupation. He was pleased to note that the Curia was now receiving this information not only from official diplomatic but also from clerical sources as well.[52] Upon returning home, all the bishops

[49] FFO, Allemagne 368, resumé of conversations between Testa and Rémond, April 11, 1923.

[50] FFO, Allemagne 368, Degoutte to Foreign Minister, April 13, 1923.

[51] FFO, Allemagne 368, note from an agent in Trier, April 12, 1923. *The New York Times*, April 20, 1923, p. 16.

[52] In their zeal to make certain the Vatican was well informed of the German position, Reich officials—from various ministries as well as from diocesan chanceries—sent too many people to Rome. The Vatican, overwhelmed by the number of visiting Germans,

informed Berlin that officials at all levels of the Curia listened sympathetically to their explanations of the situation.

Since the Pope had not spoken out strongly against the occupation, there had been concern among some Germans that the Vatican did not realize the full extent of Germany's difficult situation, and newspaper articles had already appeared, accusing the Holy See of lacking understanding for the Reich. But diplomatic reports to Berlin and the newspaper coverage of various meetings between Vatican officials and the bishops convinced German officials that these fears were groundless. The Pontiff was most concerned with the crisis as it pertained to the Church and to European peace in general. German representatives in Rome had informed Berlin that the Pope had already had the Nuncio in Paris intercede against the French policy of taking hostages, as a precaution against acts of sabotage and resistance. But the Curia had also made it clear again to the Germans that it would not help the Reich in any practical way if Rome publicly condemned France, since then all opportunities for Papal mediation would be short-lived.[53]

Reassured by the information from Rome, the Germans also had to win over Testa, who had gone to Berlin in April. Soon after the bishops had given the accounts of their successful visits to Rome, it appeared as if Testa was also listening to German arguments. In April Poincaré, frankly a little perplexed, wrote to Tirard; French Ambassador Pierre Jacquin de Margerie, in conversations with Testa in Berlin, had received a decidedly less favorable impression of the Papal envoy's attitude toward French policies than had Rémond or Degoutte. Despite Testa's compliments regarding his reception by the French in the Ruhr, he also indicated to the Ambassador that, regardless of France's justification for its move, it had set itself a task which would be impossible to carry out, given the resistance of the population. The Papal diplomat insisted on the necessity of finding a solution and finding one quickly. When de Margerie had remarked that the answer to the problem remained in the hands of Berlin, Testa countered that France also had to do its part. He too stressed the suffering of individuals in the area, citing numerous specific examples of incarceration, loss of jobs, and disruption of food supplies, which deprived children of necessary milk and caused parents to separate themselves

---

had politely reminded Bergen that it was he, the Ambassador, not the visiting dignitaries, who was responsible for transmitting communications and representing the government's position. Bergen admitted that he had requested Berlin to send secular and church officials to Rome for such purposes but by 1924 advised against having others come, lest a reaction against Germany develop within the Curia. AA, PO II, PO 2, Vol. 1, Bergen to AA, February 9, 1924.

[53] GSTA, Ges. Päpstl. Stuhl 991, Ritter to BFM, April 15, 1923.

10. Msgr. Gustavo Testa in Berlin to confer with government officials before returning to the Ruhr to continue his fact-finding mission and charitable work during the crisis, April 1923

from their youngsters by sending them off as far as Bavaria or Silesia where the living conditions were better. He ended his remarks in a reprimanding tone by stating that "these trains full of children are pitiable." There was now reason for the French to suspect that either the Vatican official had been diplomatic in his original remarks to Rémond and Degoutte about his impressions or else he had changed his mind.[54]

The Germans, for their part, were no more sure of the opinions which Testa had formed than was Paris, nor were they able to gauge

[54] FFO, Allemagne 368, Foreign Minister to Tirard, undated, probably April 1923; de Margerie to Poincaré, April 19, 1923.

the influence which the French were able to exert upon him. In spite of urging from German officials by mid-April he still had not visited Alfred Krupp to gather information and to hear first hand from a leading German industrialist about the difficulties which the occupation was causing for the Ruhr economy and its workers. Although Testa had announced his desire to visit the prisoners and to see how they were treated, without much objection he allowed himself to be accompanied by French officials and taken to the model prison at Recklinghausen. In addition, the French press reported that Testa, in stressing the religious and social character of his mission, also mentioned that he saw no objection in an autonomous Rhenish state as long as it protected Catholic interests.[55]

The Foreign Office, naturally disturbed lest Testa see things only through the eyes of French-Belgian administrators in the Ruhr, voiced this uneasiness to Vatican officials. Therefore, in order to ensure Testa's awareness of the incidents that the Germans claimed had occurred and to ensure that he be given as much opportunity as possible to pursue his inquiries, the Vatican arranged for Msgr. Rudolf Wildermann of Münster, member of the Prussian *Landtag* and expert on religious affairs, to be the liaison between the Berlin Government and the Vatican envoy. Testa was informed by Pizzardo that "by mutual agreement we have arranged that the Berlin Government relate the most serious incidents to . . . [Msgr.] Wildermann and the latter relate them to you so that you will be in the position of being exactly informed about everything *de proprio visu et auditu.*"[56] Neither side therefore was sure of the Vatican envoy's evaluation of the situation or of his recommendations to Rome. The uncertainty about Vatican policy had caused overanxious European statesmen on numerous occasions in the past to misinterpret polite or non-committal statements by Vatican diplomats desirous of being neutral or accommodating as statements of support. The Germans as well as the French were now not only listening to every word dropped by Vatican officials in Rome but were reading into every move, statement, or action taken by its representative in the Ruhr an indication of the Holy See's approval or displeasure. In any case, nothing could be assumed by either side.

In Rome, meanwhile, the Germans repeated their suggestions that the Vatican speak to other powers in Germany's behalf. In January, Berlin had requested the Vatican to coordinate its efforts with the United States and urged Washington to intervene. In February, Bergen had suggested that England might help. Now, in May, Bergen

[55] AA, BRV 133, Vol. 11, AA (Mutius) to Bergen, April 14, 1923.
[56] AA, BRV 134, Vol. 12, Steinmann to Wildermann, April 20, 1923.

again asked Gasparri to use the occasion of the visit of the King of England to Rome for the Cardinal to air his ideas for a solution to the reparations problem again and to urge England and Italy to pressure their allies to negotiate with Germany for a final settlement which would take into consideration the Reich's ability to pay. Gasparri agreed to do so. In addition, since Belgium had been less enthusiastic about the occupation and less adamant in its demands than had France, Berlin suggested that the Vatican, which also enjoyed very good relations with Brussels, might work with the Belgians and have them consider proposals for resolving the knotty problem. Again Gasparri agreed to instruct the Nuncio accordingly, since, as he noted, the information he had received from his nuncio indicated that the Belgians were now inclined to compromise.[57] Thus, by suggesting this threefold initiative, Germany hoped via Rome to work upon the smaller or less obdurate of the other states and to divide or weaken the opposing front. Bergen reasoned that the Vatican's intervention at the occasion of the British royal visit might bring England and Italy to accept Germany's proposals for settling the reparations as a basis of negotiation and not reject it out of hand, as had France. In addition, the Curia's initiative might also permit Gasparri to discuss his own suggestion for a solution with the English, something which would please the Cardinal and, if successful, would also be to Germany's advantage. If then Belgium could be convinced to take a more accommodating position, France might also be inclined to back down from its adamant stand.

The initiative undertaken by Rome as promised, however, brought no breakthrough in the stalemate. While the other powers were willing to listen to the Vatican's words, they showed no inclination to intervene actively or to break with France over the issue. Nevertheless, Gasparri had proved himself willing to try at least once more to bring Germany's message to the other governments. In spite of Rome's willingness to assist when it could, one could not push the Curia too far or too fast. At about the time that Bergen had asked the Vatican to speak to the Western Allies in May, he had also furnished various Vatican officials with a large amount of new documentation about Germany's economic plight and its inability to pay reparations. He again pressed the Holy See to make some critical comment about the French action in the Ruhr, suggesting that mention of the matter in a Papal allocution to the cardinals during the next consistory at the end of May would be an ideal time. The German Ambassador was politely but firmly rebuffed and told that the Pope would publicly speak on

[57] AA, RM 70, Vol. 1, Bergen to AA, May 4, 1923. BelgFO, St. Siège 1923-28, Beyens to Jaspar, May 4, 1923.

the subject when he considered the opportune moment and not before.[58]

Meanwhile, in May, Cardinal Schulte had arrived in Rome to make his *ad limina* visit and to tell about the situation in his diocese and the worsening conditions in the Ruhr. He stressed the growth of the Communist movement in the area and the gradual alienation of some of the workers from the Church. During the same month Testa also came to Rome to report on his findings. The seriousness of the crisis and the importance of his mission was underscored by the fact that the Pope granted him a one and a half hour private audience and asked him to confer with Gasparri and other Curial officials. Testa reported his unhappiness about the situation and about what his efforts had accomplished. He had met with German officials, French military officers, and Belgian and French diplomats. "With the extreme prudence which characterized the prelates of the Roman Curia," as the Belgian minister in Berlin described it, Testa had told them that his mission had no political overtones but was solely charitable, to study the situation and to see what could be done for any of the injured parties.[59] Yet, despite all the arguments and opinions given by the conflicting sides about the causes of the crisis, no doubt often repeated in various forms to him, Testa had been unable to change the minds of the parties involved, nor had he accomplished as much as he would have wished on a humanitarian level. He had encountered much suffering in the Ruhr and had been able to obtain some consideration for the condition of prisoners from French General Degoutte. But on the whole he did not attempt to hide his failure in ameliorating the lot of the people of the Ruhr to any significant degree.[60]

His assessment of what the future might bring was also pessimistic. Testa was impressed with the strength and degree of control which the French were exerting over the area. He informed the Pontiff and the Curia that the harsh measures taken by the occupying forces were only causing unrest and economic chaos, which might enhance the position of the Communists among the workers. Although the passive resistance of the Germans could be considered patriotic and heroic, it was in vain, since the French could eventually starve the Ruhr into submission. Resistance would only lead to a blood bath, as the French

[58] AA, RM 70, Vol. 1, Bergen to AA, May 7, 1923. The Pope nevertheless did bring up the matter in the allocution to the cardinals on May 23. *AAS*, XV (1923), pp. 245-254. AA, RM 70, Vol. 1, Bergen to AA, May 23, 1923.

[59] BelgFO, Allemagne 17, della Faille de Leverghem (Berlin) to Jaspar, April 20, 1923.

[60] Italy, Ministero degli Affari Esteri, Archivio Storico Diplomatico, Germania 1923, 1139/4298, De Bosdari (Berlin) to Italian Foreign Office, April 24, 1923.

had approximately 100,000 armed troops in the area. He also feared that the French might blockade the Ruhr's supply of food or give preference in its distribution to those inhabitants cooperating with them. While acknowledging that both sides had valid arguments for their respective positions, Testa refrained from commenting on whether either the invasion itself or the passive resistance was legal. But in his opinion only the satisfaction of the occupiers' financial demands would induce them to withdraw. He had little hope that the Italians would act as an intermediary since they stood to profit by a high reparations figure and would be disinclined to lower it. If only France would specify more clearly its long-range intentions in the area or spell out its conditions for withdrawal, perhaps negotiations could begin. Thus he too had reached the conclusion that the way to end the misery of the populace was for a general settlement on the international level. Unfortunately, with each side viewing the concept of justice and right from its own perspective and neither wishing to make concessions, for the present the Vatican's entry into the fray seemed pointless. He therefore advised the Curia that at present it could do no more than concern itself with charitable work and improving the lot of the population.[61]

Mid-May brought other incidents to public view which incensed the Germans and spurred them to further diplomatic action—the trials of German citizens before French military courts. On May 11 A. L. Schlageter,[62] Hans Sadowsky, and five others, among them a merchant, a student, and an engineer, were tried in Düsseldorf for attacks on the occupation forces and sabotage of railway lines. The verdict was swift: Schlageter was condemned to death, Sadowsky to life imprisonment, and the others received various sentences ranging from five to twenty years.[63] The trials set off an uproar in Germany about the validity of French judicial decisions for German citizens in peacetime. The newspapers were filled with journalistic and professional analyses by jurists and professors of law about the legality of the acts.[64] Germany now had concrete instances for which it could ask the Vatican to intervene on humanitarian grounds. Therefore, in May Foreign Minister Rosenberg instructed Bergen to request the Vatican to intercede for the Germans, especially for Schlageter, whose case was

[61] AA, BRV 135, Vol. 13, Bergen to AA, May 9, 1923. HHSTA, 87, Pastor to Grünberger, May 29, 1923.

[62] Schlageter was later made into a hero by the Nazis for his "patriotic resistance to foreign domination."

[63] *Vorwärts*, May 11, 1923.

[64] See, for example, *Berliner Tageblatt*, May 13, 1923 and May 17, 1923, and *Vossische Zeitung*, "Recht und Leben," May 13, 1923.

most imperative since he had been sentenced to death. The Vatican immediately had Cerretti in Paris speak to officials in several departments of the government. The French remained firm in their negative replies to Vatican overtures, enumerating the difficulties of precedent which could arise if a sentence once rendered was not carried out. The Nuncio's discussions with Poincaré also proved unsuccessful, for the Premier not only refused to change the verdict but informed Cerretti that the majority of the French Church supported a strong policy in the Ruhr question and backed the cabinet's stand. Poincaré, in other words, was telling Rome that he was aware that the Vatican on this matter did not speak for the entire Church and that at least the French episcopate supported its government's position. On May 26 Schlageter was executed by a firing squad. Clearly France was determined to break any resistance to its occupation, was prepared to go to any means, including the death penalty, to carry out its policy, and was not prepared to listen to pleas for clemency for fear that this would be interpreted as weakness and encourage further acts of sabotage.[65]

Nevertheless, the Vatican, along with several other governments, was again called upon in June to intercede on behalf of a group of local administrators and thirty-two police officials imprisoned for being uncooperative with French authorities, and for individuals such as civilian Paul Görges, condemned to death for sabotage. But perhaps the most newsworthy trials for which the Vatican was requested to help were those of Alfred Krupp and the directors of his company, who were accused of having incited the workers to resist French troops as they commandeered some trucks and cars for their use on March 31. In the ensuing melee the soldiers fired upon the employees, leaving thirteen dead and over forty wounded. Krupp along with seven of his directors and two senior officials were apprehended and tried before a military tribunal. They received sentences ranging from six months to twenty years' imprisonment and huge fines. Krupp himself was given fifteen years. Newspapers again debated the legality of the French actions. As the cases of individuals being brought to trial by French courts on charges of sabotage or carrying weapons increased, the possibility of a serious armed uprising or large-scale disorder became greater.

Cerretti went on several occasions to speak to French officials, including Poincaré, Minister of Justice Maurice Colrat, and the influential Catholic Deputy General Edouard Castelnau, and was in communication with Cardinal Louis Dubois of Paris about the fate of individual Germans. The Reich Government kept the Nuncio amply supplied with factual information and legal briefs to bolster his argu-

---

[65] AA, RM 14, Vol. 5, Hoesch to AA, May 27, 1923.

ments with the French. Berlin suggested that in Görges' case, if pardon be refused, the Nuncio should then try to obtain a suspension of the sentence of execution. In the case of Krupp and his directors, if the French insisted on carrying out the sentence, then the Nuncio should request that their incarceration take place on German soil and that they be treated as political not common criminals. Berlin sincerely hoped that France would heed the Vatican's request, reminding the Nuncio that on more than one occasion during World War I Germany had acquiesced in the Pontiff's plea for clemency for condemned prisoners, including Frenchmen.[66] When Cerretti spoke to the French Premier, he remonstrated about the strong measures being taken—Schlageter's execution, the sentencing of the Krupp directors, and the decision against Görges. Poincaré remained unmoved and firmly indicated that it was impossible for him to show moderation in this matter, which had provoked such indignation and bitter feelings among the French people, for to do so would cause them to turn against him. After these discussions the Nuncio reported to Rome that he regarded further *démarches* as hopeless and, so to speak, superfluous.[67]

Some Germans such as Carl Becker, State Secretary in the Prussian Ministry of Education and Religious Affairs, were becoming impatient with the Vatican. In a letter to the Foreign Office Becker complained that since the Vatican had not spoken out against the French and little had changed on the diplomatic scene, despite visits of German bishops, including Cardinal Schulte, to Rome to plead the case, one could draw the conclusion that Rome had little sympathy for or was indifferent to Germany's current problems in the Ruhr.[68] But those officials closer to the scene insisted that the Vatican in its usual circumspect way was doing what it could. Besides its humanitarian work and its attempts to mediate, Rome was well aware that everything hinged on ultimately settling the entire reparations question. Once the matter was settled and payments began to be made on a regular basis, there would then be no reason for the occupation, Italy would be able to stabilize itself economically and thereby be able to take a stronger counter-balancing role in world affairs, and Germany could make strides toward solving its economic and social ills and lessen the possibility of Communist success in that country.

Gasparri therefore never failed to urge his plan to connect repara-

[66] AA, BRV 140, Vol. 17, Bergen to AA, June 17 and June 22, 1923. AA, RM 14, Vol. 5, Bergen to AA, June 18 and June 23, 1923. This request may have seemed somewhat ironic to the Vatican, in view of the deportation of thousands of Belgians to Germany for war work in 1916.
[67] AA, RM 14, Vol. 5, Hoesch to AA, June 15, 1923.
[68] AA, BRV 136, Vol. 14, Becker to AA, May 31, 1923.

tions and war debts. This was a *leitmotiv* which the Cardinal repeated
with variations in discussions with European and American officials
throughout 1923. The plan, however, fell on deaf ears in France since
Paris felt itself caught on the horns of a two-pronged dilemma, menaced by both its allies and enemies. America remained firm in its
demands for debt repayment. England too, then engaged in a policy
of strengthening the pound and expanding its trade, was insisting on
payment from France, while Germany was seeking a reduction in reparations. As long as the Anglo-Saxon powers insisted on payment,
France believed it had to have the reparations in order both to pay its
debts and to rebuild its own economy to meet the foreign competition.
It would make no sense for Paris to equate debts with reparations, for
then France would lack the added funds needed to help her already
damaged economy.[69] Gasparri, however, was not fully aware of or
convinced of the seriousness of the French predicament, and he continued in his belief that a settlement of the reparations problem which
afforded the Reich the opportunity to regain some economic stability
would benefit all concerned. In numerous audiences with German delegates the Cardinal continued to suggest or advise what new steps
could be taken: German consultation with American, Italian, and
English representatives to coordinate their ideas and present a united
front at a more general international meeting; new offers or guarantees
to ensure France against another war, etc. Obviously the care with
which he had worked out some ideas showed his concern and efforts
to help by suggestion. The lack of positive results left many Vatican
officials disheartened, and reports from Germany did not give them
reason to change their mood. During the spring, Pacelli had already
sent messages confirming Schulte's comments about the spread of
Communism, especially in areas of unrest as in the Ruhr and Saxony,
and the weakening of Church influence because of the totally secular
education which, in the absence of a concordat, many young Germans
were receiving. Continuing economic difficulties, political unrest, and
secular principles would not bode well for the Church.[70]

   In June, during conversations with the Pontiff, Bavarian Minister
Ritter linked this threat of Bolshevism to the problems in the Ruhr,
as he once again urged Rome to explore new ways of helping the
Reich. Christian workers in the Ruhr were abiding by a call for pas-
sive resistance, in the belief of the moral correctness of their position.
While demanding the cessation of this resistance so that work could

[69] Trachtenberg, pp. 249-259; Schuker, p. 23; Artaud, especially chs. 3-5.
[70] GSTA, Ges. Päpstl. Stuhl 991, Ritter to BFM, June 1, 1923. Erdmann, *Kabinett Cuno*, p. 545 note 3, letter of Reich Chancellor to Pacelli, June 5, 1923. Pacelli was apparently upset by reports of Communist uprisings in Germany.

be resumed, France had shown no consideration for the suffering of the people or of Germany's problems. If Berlin now requested the workers to give up their fight without any change of attitude on the part of France, many of the men sincerely dedicated to their cause would find reason to be convinced that a deal had been struck between the two governments, and that the politicians and capitalists were manipulating the workers, thus increasing their susceptibility to the Bolshevik propaganda then being distributed in the area. Dwelling on this matter, Ritter suggested that, given the unsettled situation and the depressed mood in Germany, a success for Bolshevism in the Ruhr might even cause its spread to other parts of the Reich where it had previously been contained.

The Pontiff acknowledged that he had given much thought to the problem, but explained that what concerned him was the still unclarified question in international law of whether, and to what extent, according to the existing treaties, the French were entitled to undertake the measures in the Ruhr: could they enter the area to obtain what they stated was rightfully theirs? could they do so on their own initiative or must all the Allies act in common? what rights did they have over the citizens of the area? Since these legal and moral aspects of the issue still remained in doubt, this in turn limited the Vatican from taking action stronger than interceding for individuals on trial. The Pontiff mentioned that on May 23, in an allocution to the cardinals, he spoke of world peace, obliquely criticizing Paris' hard measures in the Ruhr, and directed a plea to France for a policy of reconciliation. Even though he had gone this far in showing his disapproval of the invasion, France had indicated no inclination to make concessions. Pius cited this as proof that a mere verbal reproach by Rome would not have a great effect and would cause the Curia to waste its diplomatic ammunition.[71] The Germans thereupon reworded their request for assistance. Both Berlin and Rome had received reports of increasing Belgian concern that the stalemate in the Ruhr might isolate Belgium, along with France, from other nations, particularly England, and increase Belgian dependence on Paris. Gasparri had heard that Belgium, never an enthusiastic partner, desired to withdraw from the Ruhr action if a reasonable way could be found. Berlin asked the Vatican to urge Brussels to moderate its attitude toward their joint Ruhr policy, a move which would then intensify the pressure on France.[72]

The Germans also requested the Pope to second their call for an-

[71] GSTA, MA 104433, Ritter to BFM, June 13, 1923; MA 104455, Ritter to BFM, June 22, 1923.

[72] AA, BRV 136, Vol. 14, Bergen to AA, June 16, 1923.

other reparations conference. The German thinking was then, as before, that if such a conference met, the Vatican could throw its entire moral weight to bear in persuading France to change its position. By urging France to change its stand and by calling for a conference Germany would be having the Vatican run some of Berlin's diplomatic errands for it. Then, together with the pressure from the United States and Great Britain on the franc, France would not be able to sustain the costs of occupation and would be forced to make concessions.[73] The German diplomats had reasons for desiring some public statement or sign of the Papal support of the German position after the six-month stalemate in the crisis. The German Ambassador as well as the Bavarian Minister on several occasions had felt obliged to explain to Vatican officials that large sections of the German population, even Catholics, were disappointed that the Pope had not denounced the French acts in the Ruhr. The German diplomats, cognizant of the Vatican's work behind the scenes, conceded that, given the circumstances, an outright condemnation would undermine further Vatican overtures. Nevertheless, statements of impatience with the Vatican, such as State Secretary Becker's in late May, became more common. Ritter, for example, feared that this mood in Germany would encourage an anti-Roman spirit which could block concordat negotiations or an improvement of church-state relations. In addition, criticism of the Curia in the German press might offend the Vatican, which in turn might weaken its inclination to aid Germany.[74]

German officials, uncomfortable with this situation, could inform the public neither of the intricacies of the problem nor of Rome's dogged efforts at mediation. Yet without this knowledge the danger of unjust, injurious anti-Vatican statements by German individuals or groups threatened the German position. In principle the diplomats did not dispute Vatican aid and were of course very grateful for its acts of charity. The Pope had sent money to assist the needy. When Testa returned to the Ruhr in June, for example, he had brought 500,000 lire to be distributed to the Ruhr inhabitants. The Vatican, moreover, had secured either the release of many men imprisoned for political causes or reduction in their sentences. It had also endeavored to have Schlageter and Görges pardoned, and had sought better conditions for Krupp and his directors. But to ensure the German public's appreciation of all its efforts and to dispel anti-Roman sentiment, German officials would have preferred an example of more visible dramatic support for Germany. However, the Pontiff consistently maintained,

---

[73] Schuker, pp. 21-27.

[74] GSTA, MA 104433, Ritter to BFM, June 13, 1923; MA 104455, Ritter to BFM, June 22, 1923.

in answer to further German inquiries, that he could take no overt steps without touching the question of the legality of France's move into the Ruhr, and this he was unwilling to do until an international court had ruled Paris' action illegal, since this would irrevocably alienate France. The Germans countered that other religious groups, including the Lutheran hierarchy of Sweden and an international congress of Methodists, had already condemned the occupation solely on moral grounds and suggested that the Catholic Church might do the same.[75] The Germans hoped he might send some sort of note, as Benedict had done in 1917, a peace message to all the nations and one that condemned the invasion.[76]

Despite Pius' replies to the Germans that Rome had to be more cautious in condemning France and Belgium than did the Swedish bishops and the Methodists whose diplomatic and pastoral responsibilities were not as great as the Vatican's, the German contentions had the desired effect. Apparently the logic of Berlin's statements that Rome had a valid right at least to speak out on moral grounds about the invasion, the danger that rising German dissatisfaction with the Vatican's stand could complicate concordat negotiations, and reports of Communism's progress in the Ruhr, prompted Rome to publish a statement which coincided with Germany's new appeal for a conference.[77]

On June 27 Pius' open letter to Gasparri dealing with reparations was published in the *Osservatore*. In it the Pontiff recalled that at the occasion of the Genoa Conference in 1922 he had directed attention to the deteriorating European situation. By 1923 the problem had considerably worsened, and, as common Father of all Christians, he felt duty-bound to plead for renewed negotiations to settle the difficulties plaguing Central Europe, most especially that of reparations. He called for settlement on the basis of Christian love, a settlement that was just but did not exact the "pound of flesh." Touching upon the question of a nation's ability to pay, he reaffirmed the debtor's obligation to pay what he owed, but added that a nation should not be taxed beyond the point of exhausting its productivity and thus creating economic and social upheaval affecting all Europe. The creditor, said Pius, had a right to guarantees of payment, but the Pontiff called upon

---

[75] Dr. Sherwood Eddy, Secretary-General of the International Committee of the Young Men's Christian Association, although a francophile, after visiting Paris, speaking to French officials, and touring the Ruhr, was also convinced that a great injustice was being done there against the populace. AA, BRV 145, Vol. 20, letter of Eddy, June 29, 1923.

[76] GSTA, Ges. Päpstl. Stuhl 995, Ritter to BFM, June 22, 1923.

[77] Erdmann, *Kabinett Cuno*, pp. 544-545, letter of Cuno to Pacelli, June 5, 1923.

the Powers to think over whether the maintenance of territorial occupation, with all the ensuing misery it entailed for the populace, was absolutely necessary for obtaining these reparations or whether other surer methods could be used. He closed his letter on the diplomatic note that if all parties concerned accepted the guidelines of Christian cooperation and ended the occupation in the Ruhr, he was certain that a general peace would eventually ensue.[78] The Vatican was risking possibly offending the Belgians and French and placing a strain on relations with these two nations. But Gasparri hoped that the moderate, non-accusatory tone of the message might bring about the desired results.

Before the publication of the letter, Gasparri discussed the text with Bergen. Although the Cardinal originally had thought of sending notes directly to all the countries concerned with reparations except Italy, which did not maintain diplomatic relations with the Vatican, he opted instead for a public statement printed in the *Osservatore*. He then spoke to the Belgian and English representatives in Rome, who raised no objections to what the Pontiff intended to say. The English advised the Cardinal to consult or at least inform the French before the actual letter appeared in the press. Gasparri, however, believed that the French would only cause difficulties if they knew of its contents beforehand. Besides, the Vatican statement, once published and supported by Belgium and England, would, he thought, make it difficult for France to disregard it. The Belgian envoy Beyens, who had opposed the invasion from the outset, now also urged his government to heed the Holy Father's advice, show some sign of compromise, and grant the German request of removing the military forces.[79] The letter, judiciously calculated not to offend either side, yet attempted again to bring the Powers to settle the issue and to help Germany in its plight. The German Foreign Office could also use it to head off anti-Roman feelings within Germany and to prove that the Vatican was aware of events taking place and acting in behalf of the Reich by spurring statesmen to action. On the question of Germany's ability to pay, the Pontiff had diplomatically refrained from commenting.

The Germans reacted gleefully to the note. Chancellor Cuno telegraphed his profound appreciation to Gasparri, but did not publish his comments, lest the appearance of his statement in the press aggravate the delicate situation by an undue show of joy on the part of the Reich. The German press, from Left to Right, while expressing ap-

---

[78] AA, BRV 137, Vol. 15, Bergen to AA, June 27, 1923. *Wolff's Telegraphisches Büro*, Nr. 1495, June 28, 1923. *Osservatore*, June 28, 1923.

[79] AA, BRV 137, Vol. 15, Bergen to AA, June 27, 1923. BFO, 371/8641/5345, Russell (Vatican) to Curzon, June 26, 1923.

proval of the Papal letter, was tactful in not exhibiting too great a satisfaction with the encouragement it gave them.[80] English and Italian newspapers generally received it sympathetically, while in French and Belgian papers, except for some Catholic and Socialist dailies, the mood was disapproving or at least reserved. The publication of the note had taken the European public and many observers by surprise, but in France the Papal statement, which offered a favorable word in support of Germany, was even less expected, since Poincaré had lately supported in the French Senate maintaining the French Embassy at the Vatican, and it was assumed that this meant that relations between the two governments were going along very smoothly. Immediately after publication of the letter French Ambassador Jonnart had a long audience with the Pope to discuss France's consternation with the Vatican's stand.[81]

The meeting with the Pope was unusual since protocol dictated that matters first be brought to the attention of the Secretary of State, but the Ambassador's insistence on speaking with Pius himself emphasized the gravity with which France viewed the Pope's comments. After expressing Paris' displeasure with the Papal letter, Jonnart warned the Pontiff that its consequences, for which he blamed Rome, might lead to the recall of the French minister from the Vatican. The Ambassador explained how anti-clerical factions in France could use this letter against the Papacy and against those interested in fostering amicable relations with Rome. Pius answered that he would seriously regret any tension developing between the two governments, but he had expressed his views after much thought and had done so with the best interests of all concerned. Nothing in the letter was directed against France. Shifting the discussion slightly, he asked again if the French really thought that their policy was succeeding and would lead to an equitable solution and if they thought Belgium would continue fully to support French policy there. In the Pontiff's opinion both points were doubtful and negotiations with Germany were immediately necessary. In answer to Jonnart's objections that the main stumbling block was Germany's passive resistance, the Pontiff stated his readiness to press Germany to give France sufficient and reasonable guarantees that its just claims would also be met.[82]

Corroboration that France was displeased with the letter and un-

[80] AA, BRV 137, Vol. 15, Cuno to Gasparri, June 29, Rosenberg to Bergen, June 29, and Stohrer (AA) to German Embassy (Vatican), June 30, 1923.

[81] HHSTA, 87, Pastor to Grünberger, June 29, 1923. BFO, 371/8641/5345, Graham (Brussels) to Curzon, June 30, 1923.

[82] AA, RM 14-1, Vol. 2, Bergen to AA, July 1, 1923. BelgFO, Allemagne 17, della Faille de Leverghem to Jaspar, July 4, 1923.

convinced by Vatican arguments was provided by other steps taken by Paris. Several days after the statement appeared, Poincaré showed his annoyance by informing French authorities in the Rhineland that Testa would no longer be allowed to visit prisoners, for, as he said, after publication of the Papal letter French public opinion would not understand the Papal envoy's continued visitations. Testa protested the Premier's action and assured Degoutte of his impartiality, as demonstrated by the care he took in his reports to represent France's position fairly. If the French Government out of pique now restricted his movements, it would aid German propaganda in portraying the French as uncharitable and petty. After several days, time and the logic of Testa's statements helped to cool tempers in Paris. On July 6 Poincaré rescinded his order and "considered the matter closed."[83] Nevertheless, during the same period he addressed the French Senate, passionately defending the course of action which the cabinet had been taking in the Ruhr. Thereafter the Senate by a unanimous vote endorsed and supported a continuation of the French policy initiated by Poincaré.[84] These incidents indicated that the Pope's statements, mild as they were, had struck a raw nerve in Paris, and they proved the wisdom of the Vatican's strategy up until then of proceeding with caution.

Rome, on the other hand, did not desire Berlin to be overly optimistic about the results of the letter, nor to forget that a long and delicate course still had to be pursued, with many opportunities for slips, before a successful conclusion could be reached. Gasparri therefore summoned Bergen on July 1 and requested that Berlin, in the interests of diplomacy, ensure that the German press continue to comment on the Papal letter in a low-key manner and be certain that, in consideration of French sensitivity, Cuno's telegram of appreciation to the Pontiff not be published. Gasparri, in his role as mediator, passed on to the Germans that Jonnart had hinted to the Pontiff of the possibility that France might be willing to discuss the entire reparations question and Germany's ability to pay, but only if German passive resistance and sabotage activities were discontinued. This was the first sign, albeit small, that the French had made indicating a willingness to negotiate and thus surmount the impasse that had developed. The Pontiff urged Bergen to stress the need for a gesture of good will from Berlin, for the cancellation of the passive resistance. Delighted with the Cardinal's efforts, Bergen politely but rather unctuously replied:

[83] FFO, Allemagne 368, Poincaré to Genoyer (Düsseldorf) and French High Commissioner in Koblenz, June 30, 1923; Allemagne 369, Degoutte to Poincaré, July 4, and Poincaré to Degoutte, July 6, 1923.

[84] See *The Times* [London], July 2-11, 1923, especially July 10, 1923.

"With us the words of the Pope never go unheard. I will fulfill your wishes immediately. . . ." Although the Ambassador doubted that the passive resistance would stop, since it was the only means available for the Germans to show their opposition, he understood that the Vatican had to request it as an indication to the French that the Curia was negotiating impartially. Bergen advised Berlin to be most careful now that it had won an advantage, so that it would not prejudice its case by acts of sabotage perpetrated by Germans in the Ruhr, especially those involving loss of life. Such acts, he said, would make a negative impression abroad on even those who had approved of the passive resistance. The Reich should in fact take measures to stop those acts in a way which would not affect the government's prestige or its diplomatic advantage but which at the same time would show the Vatican that Germany was willing to cooperate in solving the issue and to make concessions from its side.[85]

In Berlin the Papal letter seemed to signal the Vatican's success in finally surmounting the diplomatic impasse. The Pontiff's criticism of Versailles as bringing no real peace and his suggestion of seeking other means to obtain reparations besides occupying a territory were certainly comments which the Germans could use to strengthen their diplomatic hand. Berlin received word from Belgium that political circles unhappy with the occupation found encouragement in the Pontiff's statement. A recent government crisis had caused the formation of a new cabinet whose policy would bring Belgium closer to the English position and be more inclined to negotiate with Germany, thus isolating France. Catholic circles interpreted the publication of the letter as an indication that the Vatican would encourage a Belgian policy directed along these lines, and the Flemish party was particularly strong in endorsing this stand, which it viewed as a means of weakening French influence in Belgium.[86] The English press continued to argue for a compromise and to question the legality of the Franco-Belgian action in the Ruhr, while the Italian press, which generally had not paid much attention to the Ruhr problem, now prominently noted the human suffering in the area.[87]

In the Ruhr itself, despite fulminations from Paris, signs appeared of France's decreasing rigor in administering the occupation. The death sentences imposed on Ruhr citizens, including one on Görges, were commuted to prison terms. Berlin attributed this change of mood in Paris in part to the Curia's intervention and to the letter. Despite

[85] AA, BRV 137, Vol. 15, Bergen to AA, July 1, 1923.
[86] AA, RM 14-1, Vol. 2, Roediger (Brussels) to AA, June 29, 1923.
[87] *Deutsches Tageblatt*, "Die 'deutsche' Politik des Vatikans im Sommer 1923," by Freiherr Theodor von Cramer-Klett, March 6, 1924.

France's refusal to alter its course, the Vatican by virtue of its moral force and influence throughout Europe had helped to alter the thinking in some political circles and had caused Paris at least to be more cautious in its moves lest it incur further diplomatic protests from the other Powers.[88] Whether the Papal statement could have produced more pressure on France is difficult to determine, since acts of sabotage several days later halted further diplomatic momentum which could have been generated in favor of Germany in other countries and prevented the Vatican from following up the letter with appeals to England or Italy to pressure France. Suddenly the Germans, who had been well pleased with their diplomacy in Rome, were put on the defensive again, and Bergen's urging that Berlin try to curb acts of violence proved to have been well advised but perhaps came too late. It looked as if all the work for a settlement would go for naught and become entangled in misunderstandings, accusations, and counter-accusations.

On June 30 independent activists in the Ruhr blew up the Rhine bridge near Duisberg-Krefeld; a train carrying Belgian troops was destroyed and nine soldiers perished. Not only was property being destroyed by Germans protesting the occupation but lives were being lost. The authorities condemned these as gross criminal acts now widening the opposition from one of generally passive to one of serious active resistance. Testa, who had shown sympathy for the Rhenish populace, was shocked by the extent of the sabotage and loss of life. From his vantage point in the Ruhr he was well aware of the potential consequences of these new developments and immediately wired Rome to use its good offices before the crisis escalated and any initiative toward *détente* evaporated. The first step in this process was for Rome to urge Berlin to condemn the deeds just committed and to disassociate itself from violence. Operating on Testa's advice, Gasparri promptly sent a letter of protest to Bergen and Pacelli. The letter to the Nuncio was also published in the *Osservatore* on July 2-3 to emphasize the gravity with which such an act was regarded in Rome. However, while condemning such criminal actions, the wording of the text mentioned that the acts of sabotage were carried out in conjunction with the passive resistance of the general public and inadvertently seemed to imply that Rome denounced all types of resistance in the Ruhr, including non-violent ones.[89] Anger soon surfaced in the German press against the Vatican's comments. Rome, caught in the

---

[88] AA, RM 14, Vol. 5, Rosenberg to Bergen, June 29, 1923.

[89] *Osservatore*, July 2-3, 1923. Heinrich Brüning, *Memoiren 1918-1934* (Stuttgart, 1970), p. 102.

middle, with no positive results for all its efforts,[90] had to start from the beginning to clarify its intentions.

In a statement in the *Osservatore* the Vatican assured the Germans that it did not condemn passive resistance. "The Pope did not intend to pronounce against it or to invite the German Government to relinquish it, any more than he intended, by the letter addressed beforehand to the Cardinal Secretary of State, to condemn the territorial occupation of the mining district and to invite the French Government to withdraw their [sic] troops." He had merely tried to exhort both sides to seek a way to reach an agreement and had solely condemned deeds "which the German Government themselves [sic] have judged criminal."[91] After having reassured and comforted the Germans, on one hand, and emphasized its censure of violence, on the other, the Vatican in private talks with German officials stressed the seriousness of the incident and the damage which it had caused to the Vatican's efforts in helping the Reich. Rome stated explicitly its refusal to countenance or associate itself with acts which caused the loss of life. In the Curia's view there was the distinct possibility that anarchic, criminal, and radical elements were associated with or making use of the resistance movement to carry out more extreme measures, thus jeopardizing a solution for Europe as well as projecting Germany's case in a negative light. The Pope was warning Berlin to curb these activities before it was too late, lest all the good work already accomplished be for naught.

After the explosion on June 30 the French and Belgian Governments accused the Vatican of indirect responsibility for the incident. According to the conclusions drawn by the French and Belgians, the publication of the Papal letter of June 27 had evidently signaled terrorist action. Therefore, in order to disassociate itself from any connection with acts of sabotage and also to foster negotiations between the stalemated nations, the Curia formally and publicly requested Berlin to denounce such incidents.[92] Rome had wasted no time in reproving the sabotage, making clear to the world Berlin's responsibility to curb such activists. The Vatican's explicit and prompt statement of policy seemed the best possible means of preventing further misunderstandings or a worsening of the already tense, bitter situation. The German Chargé d'Affaires in Paris, Leopold von Hoesch, reported

[90] Some German newspapers carried articles expressing disappointment that the Vatican had taken the unusual step of publishing a diplomatic letter in the *Osservatore* which condemned the German resistance activities, although these acts of violence were no more than those committed by the occupying forces. *Der Tag*, July 4, 1923.

[91] BFO, 371/8642/5333, Russell to Curzon, July 4, 1923.

[92] AA, RM 14-1, Vol. 2, Bergen to AA, July 3, 1923.

that as soon as Pius' censure of the sabotage acts became known a definite moderating tone appeared in the French press with regard to the Papal letter and the Pope's proposals for a solution to the Ruhr problem. The German envoy attributed this more conciliatory attitude to the Vatican's prompt reprimand of the sabotage.[93] The Curia's insistent appeal to Berlin to restrain the saboteurs aided in calming French anger over the Papal letter and facilitating the French Government's task of silencing the opponents of maintaining the French Embassy at the Vatican.[94] The French were more willing to heed the Vatican's advice once they felt that it was not chastising them but was maintaining an even hand in its criticisms. Precisely this awareness of French thinking kept the Vatican from any public condemnation of the occupation—a step which the Vatican had warned Germany would only retard negotiations.

Even during these critical days the Vatican did not decrease its efforts at intercession on behalf of private individuals in the Ruhr. Because of the explosion on June 30, three days later, the occupying forces announced the implementation of strong measures against individuals suspected of participating in acts against the French and Belgians and a tighter control over the civilian population. At Bergen's behest Gasparri had the Curial representatives in both Paris and Brussels urge that nothing be done to perpetuate the tensions, deepen the bitterness of the inhabitants, or injure the rights of the individual. The Vatican note, though not as strong as the Germans would have desired, nevertheless was a moderating word, diplomatically phrased, and was used on Germany's behalf when the Reich itself could not appeal.[95]

In July the Holy See also took up the matter of Krupp again. With the crisis in late June, Krupp feared that he might be transferred from his place of detention in Düsseldorf and no longer be treated as a political prisoner but rather as a criminal. On July 3, Baron Ago von Maltzan, State Secretary in the Foreign Office, instructed Bergen to bring this matter to Gasparri's attention. Not only did the Vatican have Testa see Degoutte about the fate of Krupp and his directors and have Cerretti use the normal diplomatic channels in Paris, but Gasparri himself wrote a personal letter to Poincaré to discover what could be done. The French Premier offered no encouragement and bluntly replied that the entire affair was a legal proceeding in which he could not interfere. Gasparri had previously written to Poincaré on

[93] AA, BRV 137, Vol. 15, Hoesch to AA, July 3, 1923.

[94] AA, RM 70, Vol. 1, Hoesch to AA, July 7, 1923.

[95] AA, BRV 137, Vol. 15, Gasparri to Bergen, July 5, 1923; Bergen to AA, July 5, 1923. *Osservatore*, July 8, 1923.

this matter, and after this second rebuke he told Bergen he was sorry but he had "done the maximum possible."[96] Berlin, however, did not wish to see the Curia less active in employing its good offices. Early in the year Berlin had already attempted to involve Rome in the situation by recommending the establishment of a Vatican commission to investigate the alleged criminal acts of individuals in the Ruhr, but the occupying forces had rejected Berlin's suggestion. Therefore, after thanking the Cardinal for his efforts on behalf of the Ruhr industrialist, Germany now requested the Vatican to continue acting as go-between and interceding for those accused of these crimes. Bergen informed Gasparri of the Reich's deep gratitude for Rome's efforts, which had indeed been most helpful, and Gasparri reiterated his willingness to help in any way, but stated that in order to help Germany he first had to calm French and Belgian indignation over the sabotage. He stressed again that he did not condemn the passive resistance *per se*, but rather the acts of violence now endangering all hopes of a speedy settlement.[97]

To follow up Gasparri's conversations with Bergen, the Vatican sent Pacelli to Berlin to speak to Chancellor Cuno about a condemnation of the sabotage acts. The French had sought to show a connection between the Papal letter of June 27 and these criminal deeds by claiming that the letter had encouraged people to violence, and that the Papal appeal for peace and reconciliation was pro-German and oriented in a spirit of partiality to aid the Reich's diplomacy. In order to counter this reasoning the Vatican now sought to indicate its primary interest in securing peace, its impartiality to either side by exerting what influence it could on Berlin to condemn the acts. On July 4, Pacelli spoke to Cuno, who, while deploring the incident of June 30, explained that it was the act of frustration by a people who lacked other means of expressing their opposition to the injustices done them. Cuno was initially hesitant to comment on the sabotage lest it be misinterpreted by German citizens as a sign that the government would not stand by the people of the Ruhr whom it had been encouraging to continue passive resistance or that it was anxious to appease the French. But Pacelli insisted—using all the arguments at the Vatican's disposal—that a disavowal by Berlin was necessary as a first step in order to get the reparation discussions started and favorably dispose other nations toward the Reich. Most important, he said, it was necessary if Berlin expected Rome to do anything further in its behalf. After some consultation with his advisors, Cuno consented to make

---

[96] AA, BRV 139, Vol. 17a, Bergen to AA, July 4, 1923.
[97] AA, RM 70, Vol. 1, Bergen to AA, July 3, 1923.

the statement, with the wording approved and agreed upon by both the Reich and the Vatican. On July 6, Berlin issued a formal condemnation. Although they still had some misgivings about making such a declaration, the Germans bowed to the Vatican's request, since they again desired to demonstrate their willingness to cooperate and to remain in the Holy See's good graces.[98]

Gasparri's promise of support soon proved fortunate for the Reich, for it was needed at once. On June 29 a French military court in Mainz condemned to death seven Germans, ranging in age from 18 to 26, for acts of sabotage on a railroad line. The decision was upheld by a higher court on July 5. There was a strong feeling in German Government circles that since the Vatican had required Berlin expressly to condemn sabotage acts, it should exert all its skill in helping the Reich in this instance. Foreign Minister Rosenberg, in writing to Bergen, emphasized the importance of obtaining clemency for the Germans. The execution of the death penalty would evoke such bitterness among the public that the government could not declare itself ready to negotiate with the French, it might incite people to greater acts of violent resistance, and all efforts to calm the situation, notably those worked out with the aid of the Holy See in the previous months, would be negated. The Foreign Minister, once more requesting the Holy See to urge the French to change the verdict against the youths, based his petition on their age, the absence of loss of life or major loss of property, and on the argument that in German law such cases merely imposed incarceration rather than the death penalty. Bergen also reminded the Cardinal that Berlin had censured the incident of June 30 and attempted to share in calming international reactions to the violence, and he did not omit pointing to the difficulties that this had caused the government when some German citizens had construed Berlin's statements as a sign of weakness. Gasparri, appreciative of all that had been done, now promised to use his influence to help the youths.[99]

Berlin's manner of handling the crisis of June 30 pleased the Curia, which duly noted the contrast between Germany's attitude of cooperation and France's uncompromising stance. Both the Pontiff and Gasparri assured Berlin of their assistance at this difficult time. During the meeting in early July between Bergen and Gasparri to discuss the intercession for the German youths, Gasparri looked ahead to when

[98] *Il Messaggero di Roma*, July 6, 1923. AA, RM 70, Vol. 1, Ritter to BFM, July 6, 1923.

[99] AA, RM 70, Vol. 1, Rosenberg to Bergen, July 9, 1923. A brief list of cases in which the Vatican intervened and the results was published in the *Bayerischer Kurier*, May 6, 1924.

things settled a bit and inquired about the concessions Germany would then demand in order to end its passive resistance. Apparently Belgian Ambassador Beyens in conversation with the Cardinal had indicated great interest in learning the German conditions, and Gasparri, acting as the intermediary, gladly passed this information on to the Germans. Bergen recognized this as an opening for discussion, recommending to Berlin that Germany state its conditions, show a conciliatory attitude toward Belgium as a means of weaning it away from its close ties to France, and formulate these conditions in a clear and precise manner that Rome could support.[100]

The Vatican meanwhile was also taking steps to explore this avenue of approach. On July 12, Pacelli sought a meeting with Belgian Captain Aspeslagh, member of the Inter-Allied Military Control Commission stationed in Munich, and described to the Belgian his recent trip to Berlin, where he had been successful despite many difficulties in obtaining the official condemnation of the sabotage. In discussing the matter so openly the Belgians believed that the Nuncio was demonstrating the effectiveness of Vatican diplomacy and, by implication, emphasizing the value for all states, including Belgium, in working with or relying on the Curia's aid in settling the question.[101] Gasparri confirmed this to Ritter as the intent of such indirect contacts. Moreover, he informed the Bavarian that he had sent word, via a Swiss Catholic in the employ of the Holy See on secret unofficial missions, to French prelates and clerical nationalist circles in France, to warn them that, in the Vatican's opinion, Poincaré's policy was dangerous for France. For Rome, relying on what were to prove false reports, had received word of Russian military preparations, and the Holy See again feared that Poland and all Europe might be overrun should Russia see an opportune moment, such as during the turmoil in the Ruhr, for such a move. To push Germany toward Russia by a harsh policy in the west would be most unwise, and he urged these Frenchmen to help alter the Premier's policy.[102]

In July, when Ritter mentioned to Gasparri that some circles in Germany were apprehensive that the Vatican, after having issued its letter calling for peace on June 27, would be content to do no more, the Cardinal strongly denied this and cited the Vatican's recent moves. The Pacelli *démarche* in Berlin and the Papal request for moderation and clemency made in Brussels and Paris testified to the Papacy's quest for a general settlement. Also, it demonstrated the participants'

[100] AA, BRV 137, Vol. 15, Bergen to AA, July 10, 1923.
[101] BelgFO, Allemagne 17, Aspeslagh to General de Guffroy, Chief of the Belgian Delegation at the Inter-Allied Military Control Commission, July 12, 1923.
[102] AA, RM 70, Vol. 1, Müller (Bern) to AA, July 24, 1923.

attentiveness to the moral aspect of the problem which the Vatican had interjected into the diplomacy. These signs had encouraged the Curia to continue its efforts.[103]

On July 13, as requested by Gasparri, Cuno sent conditions for the cessation of passive resistance. The German Government would undertake to bring the laborers back to work, for which France and Belgium would return control of the area to Germany, release the prisoners they had incarcerated, and allow the expelled officials to return to the area. Within three weeks after the commencement of negotiations for a settlement, the legal specifications of the liens against property and the railroad would be introduced. At the same time all territory occupied since January 11, except for Essen, would be evacuated. After three more weeks the railroad monetary obligations would be handed over to a trust company in which the Reparations Commission and the German Government would be represented. With this accomplished Essen would also be evacuated, all ordinances enacted since the beginning of the Ruhr action would be abrogated, and German law and administration reinstituted. Cuno considered this as merely a working plan and subject to modification once negotiations got underway. The Chancellor, knowing full well the financial and political pressure that Poincaré's Government was under to obtain reparations, noted, however, that France seemed interested only in the cessation of passive resistance and not in a general settlement. Germany, said the Chancellor, could not discuss this issue separately nor ask its citizens to relinquish their struggles without guarantees that within a short period of time the illegal occupation would end and normal conditions would be reestablished once more. "Without such a guarantee," said Cuno, "the German Government would be just as unsuccessful as Poincaré in bringing the population back to work and getting the officials to take up their functions again." The Vatican thereupon relayed Germany's position and its willingness to negotiate some of the points to the Belgians, the English, and the Italians. The Cardinal reminded the Powers that, as requested by the Vatican, Berlin was making an effort to reach a solution by listing its conditions for negotiations. Gasparri also stated that Rome stood ready to continue its intermediary role, for, as Gasparri hoped, a fresh start had been made and the first step already taken.[104]

Meanwhile results of Vatican initiatives on behalf of individuals began to produce positive results. On July 17 Gasparri happily informed Bergen that General Degoutte had told Testa that, although the law

[103] AA, RM 70, Vol. 1, Ritter to BFM, July 13, 1923.
[104] AA, BRV 137, Vol. 15, Cuno to German Embassy (Vatican), July 13, 1923. AA, RM 70, Vol. 1, Maltzan (AA) to German Embassy (London), July 14, 1923.

mandated the transference of Krupp and his directors to France, in deference to the Holy See's wish they would be treated as political prisoners and remain in Düsseldorf, at least until the outcome of their trial.[105] Berlin was informed in the latter part of July that Papal intercession had helped secure the commutation of the death sentence against Görges to life imprisonment, and on July 30 the Nuncio in Brussels announced the Belgian Government's change of the death penalty for three Germans sentenced in Aachen, as well as for several other German prisoners, to forced labor. On July 31 the newspapers reported the news that the seven youths condemned to death in Mainz, again at the Vatican's behest, had their sentences commuted to lifelong forced labor. The Foreign Office, overjoyed with this tangible proof, hoped it would silence any skeptics who had questioned the value of the Vatican's aid to the Reich and the wisdom of Berlin's decision to bow to Curial pressure for a condemnation of the acts of sabotage.[106]

In August the court rendered the verdict against Krupp and his directors, finding them guilty of having instigated their workers to resist French troops. The Pontiff requested that France show some consideration in this case, and the Nuncio in Paris was instructed to request that they remain in Germany and not be transferred to French soil, arguing that there were legal questions about such a transfer and that it would cause much animosity against France. In reply to the Nuncio's intercession, French officials gave assurances that the prisoners would not be moved. Although the results pleased Bergen and the Foreign Office, they decided, in keeping with the Vatican's desire for discretion, to ensure that no mention of Rome's efforts appear in the newspapers.[107] The new Chancellor, Gustav Stresemann, was extremely pleased with the Vatican's success in the summer in obtaining concessions for the Germans. He praised the tireless efforts which the Holy See had made and privately thanked the Vatican in warmest tones in the name of the Reich. He also sent a personal note of appreciation to Cerretti in Paris for his aid. The Foreign Office expressed gratitude not only for the individual lives which had been saved but also for Rome's help in preventing the growth of more resentment and violence had these sentences been carried out.[108] Hostile emotions and

[105] AA, BRV 139, Vol. 17a, Bergen to AA, July 17, 1923.

[106] AA, BRV 140, Vol. 17f, Rosenberg to Bergen, July 31, 1923.

[107] AA, BRV 139, Vol. 17a, Meyer (Vatican) to AA, September 10, 1923; Gasparri to Meyer, September 19, 1923.

[108] AA, BRV 143, Vol. 19a, Stresemann to German Embassy (Vatican), September 14, 1923.

further attacks against the French and Belgians would have definitely postponed any possibility of discussing a settlement.

In spite of Germany's happiness in the concessions won, impressive and important as they were, nothing further occurred during the summer to speed the settlement of the Ruhr difficulties, as both sides held fast to their respective positions. In September Berlin asked Rome to urge Brussels and Paris to consider the Reich's conditions for calling a halt to the passive resistance or that they agree to meet with the Germans to discuss the matter. Gasparri, though ready to relay Germany's wishes, pointed out the difficulty of his position created by his recent involvement in negotiations for clemency on behalf of the prisoners found guilty of sabotage or resisting the occupying forces. Especially now that the Vatican had spoken out against the sabotage, he would have to omit requests for this type of prisoner lest the Vatican's position be compromised and Rome viewed as playing both sides of the game by pleading for the saboteurs and at the same time urging consideration of the German plan. During this meeting with Bergen the Cardinal took the opportunity to give his analysis of the overall diplomatic picture. He showed himself most concerned over the coming negotiations lest Germany find itself alone facing France and Belgium, just as it did in the Ruhr itself. He therefore advised Germany to interest England and Italy in participating in the discussions and to keep the basis of discussion as broad as possible.[109]

He expressed the same sentiments to Ritter and warned Germany not to expect too many concessions since, as he saw it, France's motives in occupying the Ruhr were not primarily economic but political. He based his pessimistic view of France's readiness to offer concessions on the fact that as yet the other Powers concerned had not tried or been able to induce France to the conference table. England's recent effort to regulate the reparation payments and aid the general economic malaise had received no cooperation from Paris. The Cardinal's suggestion that the United States save Germany by permitting war debts to be connected to the reparations problem had received no positive response from Washington, and Italy was not to be counted on since Italian policy seemed to place more value on good relations with France because of their common interests in the Mediterranean than with obtaining a solution in the Ruhr. In addition, as Gasparri thought, Italy was now indebted to France, which had not moved to prevent Italy from carrying out its military action against Greece during the recent Corfu incident. Although depressed, the Cardinal had not given up hope. True, the Curia had succeeded in obtaining clemency for

[109] AA, BRV 145, Vol. 20, Meyer to AA, September 21, 1923.

individuals and in alleviating the living conditions in the area, but the Ruhr question, with the problem of passive resistance, proved a much thornier one. He reiterated that a solution of the problem was needed in the best interests of all concerned, and it was the Vatican's task to work for international cooperation. Also cognizant of the importance of Rome's mediation for Germany, especially since none of the other Powers was actively pushing the matter, he promised to see what could be done. As Ritter said, "In him we have now as before, a true friend."[110]

But the West did not have to wait for the Nuncio to urge some concessions in return for Germany's ending the passive resistance. After Cuno's resignation in August, Gustav Stresemann formed a new cabinet drawn from his own German People's Party, the Center, the Democrats, and the Socialists, the so-called grand coalition. While only in office as chancellor for three months, Stresemann stayed on as foreign minister until his death in 1929. Bringing a pragmatic sense of the possible to his work, he shaped and set the tone for the foreign policy of the 1920's and proved himself more adept than his predecessors at convincing the Allies of Germany's willingness to cooperate, thereby gaining concessions for the Reich. The new government, perhaps influenced by Gasparri's opinion of mid-September that the French would not make any offers, acted on its own to break the impasse. The crisis had taken a heavy toll on Germany. The already shaky economy was further weakened by the dislocations brought about by the occupation, and the support for passive resistance had drained the treasury. Unemployment in other parts of Germany rose sharply because of the loss of products from the Ruhr, and the mark continued to decline steadily. Standing at 100,000 to the dollar in June, by August it already had fallen to 5,000,000. In addition to rampant inflation, political unrest coming from the Left and the Right threatened the Reich, as did the French encouragement of separatist sentiment in the Rhineland. Stresemann's government realized that it had to call a halt to inflation, stabilize the economy, and deflate the political unrest; no longer could it afford to support the passive resistance which had failed to accomplish its goal.

Stresemann with shrewd realism therefore argued that a solution had to be found by breaking the impasse with the French and by improving foreign relations to provide a better climate in which to solve the reparations question. In order to stave off disaster at home and to indicate its good intentions abroad, on September 26, without waiting for concessions from the West, Stresemann announced the end

[110] AA, BRV 145, Vol. 20, Ritter to BFM, September 22, 1923.

of passive resistance. On September 28 the order suspending reparation deliveries to France and Belgium was likewise withdrawn. Germany had abandoned the struggle unilaterally as a first step toward a general settlement. Gasparri was delighted, since one stage in the diplomatic procedure had been skipped. Instead of waiting to hear what the West would offer if Germany ended the resistance, Germany had done so on its own initiative. This fulfilled the original demand of the French and the Belgians, who had refused to discuss the Ruhr problem with the Germans unless the resistance had first ended. Now that Germany had made this concession, discussions could begin, and it was up to the West to offer something in return.

Soon thereafter Gasparri naturally asked Ambassador Beyens what the Belgian-French reaction was to Stresemann's announcement, now undoubtedly expecting a more conciliatory answer. Instead, Beyens replied that the Allies were still suspicious of Germany's motivation and had taken the attitude of "wait and see." The Allies informed Germany that the consequences of ending the resistance was not a reason to open up discussion of larger international issues but rather was a subject to be taken up and arranged by the occupying authorities and the local population. Gasparri did not try to obtain a friendlier response from the West at this time, but his irritation with the continued diplomatic stalemate began to show. Disappointed at the failure of the German initiative and the lack of Franco-Belgian reciprocation, the Cardinal expressed his sentiments in less than his usual diplomatic manner. Not only was Germany experiencing general economic difficulties and problems in the Ruhr but several areas of the Reich were considering separating themselves from the Berlin Government. Gasparri angrily made clear to diplomats in Rome that he attributed to Poincaré such centrifugal developments as the stirrings of Rhenish separatism and the tendencies for independence within the Bavarian Cabinet.[111] Despite Belgian protests that the Allies had no interest in fostering dissensions which would only weaken Germany and lessen its ability to meet its payments, the Cardinal remained unmoved. Poincaré, he declared, who was interested only in the political security of his country, had already made good use of the reparations issue and

[111] The French had been receiving reports from Rémond that the Rhenish clergy were far from hostile to the idea of a political separation from Berlin. This naturally only encouraged France to support the Separatists, with the thought that the Church would be in favor of it. FFO, Rive Gauche du Rhin 103, Rémond to Tirard, November 5, 1923. Gasparri would soon have more reason for concern over Rightist separatist tendencies in Bavaria. One month later, in November, brought about in part by the Ruhr crisis and Berlin's poor handling of the situation, the Beer-Hall *Putsch* was staged by Hilter.

was therefore now working quietly for the dismemberment of the Reich. The Cardinal did not ascribe, or was too diplomatic to ascribe, such Machiavellian motives to the Belgians. But as Beyens stated: "His conviction of a double game played by the French Government vis-à-vis Germany is ineradicable, and it had not ceased to possess him since the occupation of the Ruhr." The Belgian conceded to his superiors in Brussels that German diplomacy in Rome to a large extent had been successful. Beyens, now acknowledging the Reich's ability to convince the Vatican that what had occurred in the Rhine and Ruhr was wrong, concluded that "this conviction [of Gasparri's], fortified by the reports of numerous German prelates who have flocked to Rome this year, dominates at the Vatican, in spite of all the efforts which M. Jonnart and I have made to dispel it."[112]

The Belgians were not the only ones who heard Gasparri's opinion on the matter; in conversations with the English envoy the Cardinal pursued the same theme. After detailing his exasperation with French intransigence, he stated that Britain's and America's cancellation of war debts and renunciation of reparations would relieve Europe's agony. Gasparri conceded, in response to English protests, that this would place an unfair burden on Great Britain and the United States, but he emphasized the necessity of this sacrifice. He now had come to believe that the reparations were only a secondary objective for France, which really desired to break up Germany and establish French military hegemony in Europe. Anglo-American action now, he predicted, would spare them much trouble later and would prevent Germany, in desperation, from forming a stronger alliance with Russia.[113]

In meetings with Austrian Minister Pastor, the Cardinal had at times not hesitated to criticize Germany for its intransigence and for what he called its weak leadership. But now that the Reich had made a major concession which had been considered the main stumbling block to further negotiations, the Cardinal expressed sympathy for Germany and exasperation with France's continued obstructionary policy. Paris, he said, should display a statesmanlike attitude, as the victors had shown to France in 1815. France would only create hate for itself and would find no support from England or Italy in the future. He also was annoyed by England's failure to take a more active role in forcing France to grant some concessions. "I cannot understand England's position, which expressly declared that the Versailles Treaty has been violated by the occupation of the Ruhr area but this declaration now seems to have been completely forgotten." He also showed great con-

[112] BelgFO, St. Siège 1923-28, Beyens to Jaspar, October 4, 1923.
[113] BFO, 371/8657/5335, Russell to Curzon, October 4, 1923.

cern over the rapidly deteriorating economic situation in Germany, which seemed to confirm all his predictions. He told Pastor that it became even clearer from actions in the Ruhr that French policy was seeking to divide the Reich into little, economically weak states.[114] France, though willing to compromise on small matters, refused to budge on larger issues, even when the Germans had removed France's major objection, passive resistance. Such intransigence confirmed for Gasparri his initial inclination that France had political objectives in mind.

No doubt France conceded to many petitions for leniency so that its administration in the Ruhr would not alienate neutrals and allies alike or push the population to the breaking point. World opinion generally opposed the occupation, and France therefore deemed it worthwhile to demonstrate that, despite acts committed against its rule, it could show clemency. But there may have been other reasons. In November Rémond spoke with Testa, who acknowledged that the success of his mission to alleviate suffering in the area and to reconcile the opposing sides depended in large part on French goodwill. Rémond replied that if France had the approval of the Vatican to separate the Saar from German ecclesiastical jurisdiction,[115] most assuredly France would more readily accede to Testa's and the Vatican's request for clemency and a more conciliatory attitude in the Ruhr. Although the conversation did not go further, it indicated the desire of some French officials to cooperate—at a price. The Vatican never accepted the French bishop's suggestion of placing the Saar under an apostolic delegate separate from the German ordinaries, but, according to Rémond, the French were inclined to accede to Testa's requests in the hopes that the Vatican would then show France some consideration in a matter in which they had a very special interest, such as the Saar.[116]

On January 10, 1924 Testa left for Rome to report on conditions in the troubled region. The French were interested in his findings since, should the envoy elaborate on the negative aspects of the situation, it might increase Vatican demands in Paris for moderation. The French Foreign Office therefore wired its representative in Rome to learn Testa's impressions and "whether we are not menaced by a new Papal document about the plight of the Germans."[117] The French had reason

---

[114] HHSTA, 87, Pastor to Grünberger, October 5 and 12, 1923.

[115] See ch. 4 for France's ecclesiastical interests in the Saar.

[116] FFO, Rive Gauche du Rhin 103, transcript of conversations of Rémond with Testa, November 7-10, 1923; Allemagne 369, Rémond to Canet, Chargé des Affaires Religieuses in the FFO, November 29, 1923.

[117] FFO, Allemagne 369, Peretti to French Embassy (Vatican), January 14, 1924.

for concern, since in October the crisis over the Ruhr had widened and events gave credence to Gasparri's suspicions about Poincaré's political designs on Germany. Since the goals for which the invasion had been initially undertaken had not been reached, the French were trying another means: the use of fifth columnists. In late 1923 Separatists, with French and Belgian support, had declared a Rhineland republic and an autonomous government in the Palatinate (*Pfalz*), that section of the Rhineland west of the Rhine which belonged to Bavaria but had been occupied by the French since 1918. The Separatists seized public buildings in various cities throughout the area, including Koblenz, Bonn, Wiesbaden, and Mainz, and came into armed conflict with local citizens in most of their efforts to gain control. The French forces, while claiming that the Separatists had acted on their own, provided them aid whenever possible.[118] This political development was also of consequence for the Church. Most of the clergy of the Rhineland, for example, did not support the new Separatist governments which would naturally seek an ecclesiastical separation of the area from German dioceses, something which the clergy opposed whenever such a suggestion had been made since 1919.

The clergy of the Palatinate, on instruction from their bishop, intended to have a protest read from the pulpit in January 1924, but the commanding French general prohibited this on the grounds that it was a political issue in which the Church should not interfere. The chaotic conditions and oppressive measures taken by the new government seemed similar to those in the Ruhr, except that now it was not French or Belgian troops who were coming into conflict with the inhabitants, but Germans, disloyal to Berlin but supported by the French. The Reich and more especially Bavaria therefore felt that Testa should also investigate the situation since it was in many ways similar to and an extension of the Ruhr crisis.[119] Whereas the Separatist movement with no popular support weakened and collapsed in the central Rhineland by February 1924, the vigorous French support for the group in the Palatinate permitted the autonomous government to last longer, leaving behind a trail of anarchy, shootings, and general violence. Ritter therefore requested an apostolic visitor to come to the area, and on January 21 the Bishop of Speyer wrote to the Pontiff recounting the pillaging of the homes of Bavarian officials by Separatists and the suffering that the new administration inflicted on individuals loyal to the Bavarian Government. The Bishop recounted how people were thrown

---

[118] McDougall, ch. 8.

[119] GSTA, Ges. Päpstl. Stuhl 994, Minister-President Knilling to Bavarian legation (Vatican), January 14, 1924.

in prison, others expelled from the area, and property confiscated.[120] The Separatists, he said, possessed weapons supplied by the French, while the loyal German population had been forbidden by the French forces from carrying arms. The Bavarian Government, in a move similar to what the Reich Government had done in the Ruhr, forbade cooperation with the new government. The area plummeted into chaos, experienced acts of violence which were setting a bad example for the youth, who were encouraged to participate in looting and other criminal acts. The Rhenish prelate therefore added his voice to those of the German and Bavarian Governments, requesting the dispatch of a Vatican representative to the Rhineland, and wherever the Separatists were active, to observe the situation and hopefully lend his moral support to help in the pacification of the region.[121] The Bavarians, who urged speed, frankly suspected French diplomats in Rome of seeking to delay Testa's return to the Rhineland. Ritter pleaded that Rome was in a position to check the spread of the chaos. Already that month England had spoken disapprovingly of the events in the Rhineland and had explicitly attributed the cause of the unrest to French instigation. If now the Vatican would send its representative to inspect the area and confirm the English opinion, the Germans were convinced that the French would have to withdraw their support. Pius, who agreed on the immediate need for a Vatican observer there, accordingly ordered Testa back to the Rhineland.[122]

An indication of the Vatican's opinion about the Separatists as well as how Rome viewed the role that it could play in the Ruhr and Rhineland can be glimpsed from Testa's remarks to Beyens before he left Rome. The Vatican diplomat explained that his mission to the Rhineland would be similar to that in the Ruhr: to observe and to alleviate any human suffering. When he was in the Ruhr he had distributed money and clothing to the needy and interceded for better living conditions for the prisoners. He only hoped he could perform similar services in his new assignment. What kind of situation he would find there he could not say, but he made it clear that in the Vatican's opinion one could not really speak of a legitimate Separatist movement since the majority of Separatists were not indigenous to the region but discontents and political activists who had found a shield for their activities in the protection of the French military authorities. The Rhinelanders were passionately attached to the Reich. This was not to say that they felt themselves Prussian or Bavarian or that they would

[120] The number of people deported from just the Palatinate, with a population of less than three quarters of a million, was about 20,000. Toynbee, *Survey, 1924*, p. 310.
[121] BSTA, MK 15575, Bishop Sebastian to Pius XI, January 21, 1924.
[122] GSTA, Ges. Päpstl. Stuhl 994, Ritter to AA, January 23, 1924.

not like some local autonomy, but they eschewed autonomy granted by a foreigner—and an enemy too! Testa avoided commenting in detail about the rigor of the occupying forces' execution of their policies, but his negative opinion of Krupp's imprisonment and his statement about French support for Separatism indicate that he and the Vatican questioned the harshness and legitimacy of some of the French actions.[123]

Bavarian Minister Ritter also continued to supply Vatican officials with information about the Separatists and their activities. On February 19 he visited Msgrs. G. Pizzardo and F. Borgongini, both Under Secretaries in the Secretariat of State, to ensure rejection of the official letters from the Separatists to the Vatican seeking recognition for their government and protesting Reich claims of sovereignty over the area. The Germans feared that Rome might communicate with them, since an official reply would be interpreted in diplomatic circles and among the local populace as Vatican support for the Separatist movement as well as for the new government and a blow to German unity. If the Curia were to show any interest, it might cause Belgium, then lukewarm to the idea, to back France more actively or cause England to moderate its criticism of French support for the movement. The fact that the population of the area was overwhelmingly Catholic caused nervousness in Germany about Rome's possible susceptibility to arguments that a separate Catholic German state, either in the Rhineland or in south Germany would benefit the Church. Both Ritter and Bergen were speedily reassured, however, that Vatican policy had not changed. The Curia would pay no attention to communications from the Separatists, since the Holy See did not deem their government legitimate. As outlined immediately after the war, the Vatican still believed that the best interests of both the Church and international peace would be served by a strong and unified Germany which contained a sufficiently large Catholic population to have its opinion taken seriously in the Reichstag and which would be powerful enough to counterbalance France on the diplomatic front. Borgongini did, however, urge that Bavaria sign the pending concordat with the Vatican and stated that the French were applying pressure on the Vatican with regard to the Saar and the Palatinate. Once the concordat was signed, the Curial official emphasized, Rome would be armed with greater legal power to resist French pressure to separate the ecclesiastical organization of the area from the Reich. As the prelate diplomatically put it, "The Holy See would like Bavaria as soon

[123] BelgFO, St. Siège 1923-28, Beyens to Jaspar, February 4, 1924.

as possible to tie its [Vatican's] hand, and this will certainly not be to the disadvantage of Bavaria."[124]

The assurances which the German envoy received were confirmed by the report of a conversation between an official of the Prussian Interior Ministry and Pacelli. The prelate, who disapproved of the Separatists, believed that the movement was waning. His observations convinced him that as long as overwhelming popular support was withheld from the movement, it would eventually collapse, since the French could not maintain it permanently. Germany, he thought, would soon no longer have to concern itself seriously with this problem. He encouraged the Germans to continue to supply Rome with material presenting its view about the Separatists and volunteered to do the same himself.[125] Pacelli's opinion of the movement had no doubt been reflected in his reports to Rome and had helped in shaping the Curia's impressions. Meanwhile, Testa had arrived in the Rhineland in February, and after familiarizing himself with the problem and consulting with civil and ecclesiastical leaders, he began in March to request clemency for some of the prisoners, speeding up the trials of those detained during the bloody fighting which had broken out against the Separatist regime in towns such as Pirmasens, Kaiserslautern, and Bad Dürkheim, and permission for some of the expelled people to be allowed to return.[126]

While Testa was again performing his fact-finding and charitable duties in the Rhineland, the international situation had begun to change. Tension had increased in Franco-British relations initially over the Ruhr crisis but was exacerbated by French support for the Separatists. England was growing impatient with Poincaré's strategy, which had

[124] GSTA, Ges. Päpstl. Stuhl 988, Ritter to BFM, February 19, 1924.

[125] AA, PO II, PO 24 Vat., Vol. 8, memorandum of Elfgen (Prussian Interior Ministry), February 20, 1924. The well-known Rhenish separatist Hans Adam Dorten confirmed the Vatican's disapproval of the Separatists in his memoirs, stating that they had no chance of success since the Vatican did not support them. Vatican policy was concerned with strengthening and obtaining influence in Germany and in Prussia, which would be impossible once the Rhenish state was created and a sizable Catholic population was lost to the Reich. J. A. Dorten, *La tragédie rhénane* (Paris, 1945), p. 92. Dorten also drew some connections between the situation in the Rhineland and the rise of Nazism. The Vatican in 1923 did not endorse a Catholic Rhenish separate state but rather favored a strong unified Germany even though the philosophy of some of the Reich's leaders, the Socialists, was not to its liking. This policy then prepared the Rhenish Catholics to accept obediently the Vatican and Center support for a Nazi regime in 1933. Msgr. Kaas, leader of the Center Party and a Rhinelander, brought this thinking to bear in 1933 when the Center voted to support the Nazi Government by endorsing the Enabling Act. Dorten, p. 214.

[126] GSTA, Ges. Päpstl. Stuhl 994, Testa to de Metz, Commanding General of French troops in the Pfalz, March 1, 1924.

not produced the economic security and stability desired, and now proposed to take the entire question of the legitimacy of the Separatist government to the Permanent Court at the Hague. France was therefore becoming increasingly isolated. Passive resistance had ceased in the Ruhr, but both the French and the German economies had been weakened during the struggle. The mark and franc had fallen to dangerous lows. The German currency's value had sunk below that of the paper on which it was printed, and the franc had dropped in value by twenty-five percent. On February 28, 1924 Stresemann appealed to the world powers for a solution not only to the Ruhr crisis but to the reparations problem, which had triggered all the unrest in the first place.

The Vatican greeted Stresemann's speech with satisfaction, especially since it called for negotiations to be based on the findings of a commission of experts—the position which Rome had supported since the beginning. Gasparri, by late February, in contrast to previous months, was now guardedly optimistic and based his conclusions on several factors, such as the internal problems in France; the fall of the franc, which in turn would compel the French to compromise; and the change of governments in Belgium and England. These developments, predicted Gasparri, would force France to concede that Germany had only to pay what it could and that the occupation had been a mistake. On March 1 he informed Pastor "I am really no prophet and also no son of a prophet . . . , but I believe I can predict that the year 1924 will bring great changes for Europe." Gasparri pointed to the recent appointment of James Ramsey MacDonald as British Prime Minister, a man who for years had argued that British trade depended on the recovery of British markets, including those in Central Europe, as an indication that Britain would now vigorously push for a settlement of the reparations issue which would allow Germany to recover economically. The Cardinal also noted the fall of the Theunis Cabinet in Belgium, due in part to the failure of the Ruhr venture to secure the desired payments and to the way that Belgian foreign policy had been tied so closely to Paris, and the inability of France to create a successful Separatist movement in the Rhineland. All these things, taken together, said the Cardinal, would assist in bringing France to the conference table. All of these signs occurring at the same time as Germany's willingness to have a committee of experts investigate its economic problem and make suggestions for reparation payments were very definite causes for optimism.[127]

Meanwhile, the Curia still instructed Cerretti to continue his efforts

---

[127] AA, PO II, PO 28 Vat., Vol. 1, Ritter to BFM, February 29, 1924. HHSTA, 87, Pastor to Grünberger, March 1, 1924.

on behalf of the prisoners in the occupied areas. He had taken the opportunity to speak to President Millerand as well as to officials of the French Foreign Office. The Nuncio asked that not only pardon or clemency be granted to individual prisoners but also that any German having been convicted of crimes against the occupying forces be incarcerated on German soil or returned to Germany if he had already been taken to France. Although a general amnesty could not be allowed, Millerand told the Nuncio that he would aid in helping individual prisoners. The Vatican, besides making direct remonstrance to the French, also requested the English and Spanish Governments to urge the French to improve the lot of the German prisoners in French custody. Vatican efforts succeeded in having France grant concessions for the physical comfort of the prisoners, including permitting them to receive a small monthly allowance from their families so that they could purchase items they might need. Meanwhile the Nuncio in Brussels was able to have four Germans then in Belgian prisons for their action against the occupying forces classified as political prisoners, which meant they were allowed to wear their own clothing instead of prison garb, to write and receive letters as well as visitors, to take walks with other prisoners in the prison garden, etc.[128] In June 1924 Curial efforts had also succeeded in securing the return of 120 German prisoners from France, to which they had been transferred from the occupied territories.[129] Vatican progress was at times slow, concessions being largely won on an individual basis, but it was steady; admittedly not sensational in nature, it nonetheless succeeded in aiding the Reich and its citizens.

The optimism which Gasparri had expressed proved warranted. By the spring of 1924, seeing that the Separatist movement had failed to gain the recognition of foreign governments or the endorsement of the populace, the French withdrew their support, and the entire movement rapidly collapsed. During 1923, at Rome's suggestion, England's Prime Minister, Andrew Bonar Law, had been working to secure American cooperation to avert complete collapse of the world economy. By late 1923, increasingly concerned with the worsening situation in France and Germany and its implications for international finances, the United States had agreed to cooperate with the Europeans toward a solution. The failure of much of the French policy in the Ruhr and Rhineland and its own weakened financial condition made Paris ready now to approve the work of an international committee to

---

[128] AA, BRV 140, Vol. 17b, König (AA) to German Embassy (Vatican), March 3, 1924.

[129] AA, BRV 144, Vol. 19b, Schubert (AA) to German Embassy (Vatican), June 24, 1924.

investigate Germany's economic problem as it touched upon reparations. In April, the committee, under the chairmanship of American Charles G. Dawes, presented a proposal which ended any remaining hope that reparations could offer substantial help for the French budget. The plan provided for a reorganization of the *Reichsbank* and its currency policy, set up a schedule for reparation payments which the committee believed was within the limits of the Reich's ability to pay, and provided Germany with a foreign loan to help get the program started. The plan also intended to incorporate negotiations which had already been underway to remove most of the restrictions imposed in the Ruhr by the invasion and to reintegrate the area into the economy of the Reich.[130] In April, the Reichstag accepted the Dawes plan, while in France a new government to the Left, formed as the result of the failure of Poincaré's policy of coercing Germany, received a loan from American bankers to aid its economy. The Vatican, whose maneuverability had been severely limited during the crisis and whose position had suffered and been criticized by politicians on both sides, was pleased with the settlement and the move toward reconciliation. During the summer a conference at London officially adopted the Dawes plan. The troops began to withdraw from the Ruhr,[131] and financial provisions were worked out by which reparations could be regularly paid.

The crisis was over. Therefore, in September the Vatican announced Testa's recall from his mission in the Ruhr and Rhineland. Although both the German and French had taken pains to ensure that the prelate received information which would influence him to report positively about their policies, both countries' newspapers often voiced the suspicion that Testa had favored the other side. The Papal delegate had had to listen to both parties and to obvious exaggerations from each: the people were perhaps better off, the troops better behaved than the Germans claimed and less so than the French maintained. He was thus in a crossfire—the French stating he did too much for the Germans, the Germans accusing him of being too friendly to French officers and easily impressed by their arguments. The Vatican had had to caution Testa in early 1923 not to appear over-friendly to the French, yet Testa argued in his defense that only through good working relations with French leaders could he be effective in winning concessions.[132] It was no wonder that Borgongini, speaking to German diplomats in mid-1923, said that the Vatican's role was a hard one

---

[130] For details of the Ruhr occupation and the subsequent negotiations see Toynbee, *Survey, 1924*, p. 268ff.; Schuker, p. 35 and especially ch. 6; Trachtenberg, ch. 8; McDougall, ch. 1.

[131] The last French and Belgian troops withdrew on July 31, 1925.

[132] GSTA, Ges. Päpstl. Stuhl 994, Ritter to BFM, April 1, 1924.

since no one was ever satisfied. But the comments of officials on both sides in favor of the envoy testify to Testa's adroitness in keeping a level balance throughout the period.

Rémond had consistently maintained that Testa was generally pro-French, and in September 1924 Henri Cambon, French Chargé d'Affaires at the Vatican, believed that Testa had been passing favorable reports about French activities to Rome.[133] The French had been pleased that Testa had never condemned the occupation of the Ruhr per se nor spoken out on its legality. Paris therefore assumed that his advice had balanced the opinions of some Curial members influenced by pro-German sentiments. His reports most probably helped to convince Rome not to take a more forceful stand on the occupation itself and to have acted so cautiously before making any statement until the Papal letter of June 27. The French were also pleased that he had been successful in moderating some of the more violent anti-French statements of the clergy in the Ruhr and Rhineland and had quietly emphasized that exchange of heated words would not bring about negotiations. Testa's efforts were also instrumental in bringing about cessation of publications inspired by some of the Rhenish clergy that were propagandistic and inflammatory in nature. Finally, the French were grateful for his long discussions with Ruhr industrialists, including Krupp, and for his help in convincing them to make their feelings known in Berlin that passive resistance was not serving its intended purpose and that it would be better for Germany to begin to send the laborers back to work, since the recommencement of production would help pave the way to a settlement.[134]

The Germans, on the other hand, soon came to the realization that while the Vatican envoy had neither openly nor dramatically sided with Germany, his low-key diplomacy had in the long run helped the Reich. Though working quietly, the prelate had been able to prevent further words and actions which might have widened the breach between the two nations. By urging the Germans to return to work and to moderate their propaganda, he had pushed them to demonstrate their goodwill so that diplomacy on other levels could take up the discussions again for an eventual solution. By taking time to learn to know the French officials and to maintain good working and personal relationships, Testa was all the better prepared to ask for clemency and favors for prisoners and the population under the occupation. His diplomatic advice and work behind the scenes were known only by the diplomats and to his Curial superiors, but his pastoral and human-

---

[133] FFO, Allemagne 369, Cambon to FFO, September 9, 1924.
[134] FFO, Allemagne 369, memorandum of Canet, September 18, 1924.

itarian work on behalf of the population of the occupied areas and prisoners was known to everyone in Germany and formed the basis of expressions of gratitude to both him and the Vatican. Upon his departure, perhaps reflecting the degree to which he was liked by the Germans and the sentiments of many of the Rhineland clergy, the Bishop of Paderborn warmly thanked him for all his untiring efforts and in a personal note, unusual in business relations among north Germans, said he would like to remain in touch with and hear from him from time to time.[135]

The year 1924 marked the end of the bitter antagonism between Germany and the Western Allies and the development of a climate which fostered compromise and more understanding.[136] The long-convoluted negotiations and attempts to reach a settlement through the maze of claims and counterclaims was ending, and the sobering experiences of 1923 had not resulted in victory for either side. Throughout this period German-Vatican relations remained basically good. While wishing that the course of events had developed otherwise, the Vatican never questioned the legality of the positions taken by either side; instead it strove to speak out when it felt an injustice was done. But precisely in its role as mediator, as a neutral, it was an aid to Germany, for mediation meant compromise and that was what Germany was seeking from the victor of 1919 and that was what France was reluctant to grant. In a period when the diplomats frequently felt frustrated by the lack of accomplishments, the Germans realized that they needed all the help they could obtain. For Germany the Vatican perhaps moved too slowly and was not forceful enough, but one also had to consider the bounds within which the Pope, as "Father of all nations," could work. It was never the practice of the Holy See to speak out forcefully on political issues. Instead, the Vatican, thinking never

[135] Germany, Paderborn, Archivstelle beim Erzbischöflichen Generalvikariat, XXIII, Bishop Klein to Testa, September 12, 1924. From the French side Tirard was so pleased with Testa that he proposed to the Quai d'Orsay that, upon the completion of his mission, Testa be admitted to the Legion of Honor. FFO, Allemagne 369, memorandum of Canet, September 18, 1924. On the other hand, German politicians also conceded that Germany owed Testa a great debt of gratitude for his assistance in obtaining concessions for the Reich and for his humanitarian work in the Ruhr and the Rhineland. Schreiber, p. 92.

[136] Even relations between the French and the Rhenish clergy reflected the political détente after 1924. In 1928 Bergen reported that Rémond, for whom there had been such a dislike in the early 1920's by the German clergy for his French nationalist stance, was invited by the Bishop of Mainz to a celebration in the cathedral. There he was asked to participate in the ceremonies, and even requested to consecrate one of the new altars. When a group picture of German ecclesiastical dignitaries was taken with the Nuncio, Rémond was persuaded by them to let himself be photographed with the rest. AA, BRV 190, Vol. 1, Bergen to AA, November 8, 1928.

in years but in decades, always moved slowly, usually out of the view of the public, and was not to be rushed into making a statement or move until it judged the moment right to use its moral prestige and diplomatic contacts. The Ruhr crisis is a good example of this.

During the entire Ruhr affair the Vatican's role as middleman, as a government which viewed Europe as a whole, not from a national perspective, is clearly seen as it labored to bring the two sides together and to ensure that French military and diplomatic might did not totally overwhelm the Reich. Although the results were not dramatic, the fact remains that when other governments hesitated to intervene, the Vatican had already acted to improve conditions for the prisoners and the civilian population, whose situation without this assistance might have been much worse. When it appeared as if Rome could do nothing for the moment at the top diplomatic level to help to settle the reparations question, it concentrated further on less ambitious goals to improve the lot of individuals and relieve the human suffering. Reichstag deputy Georg Schreiber stated what many other Reich officials also believed—that Testa had done much to obtain improved conditions in the Ruhr, and the Foreign Office had no hesitancy in requesting the envoy as well as Rome to work "piecemeal" in obtaining concessions from the Belgians and the French for the population.[137] The Papal humanitarian work seemed to have had three objectives: the prevention of the implementation by the occupying forces of oppressive measures; the improvement of the lot of the individual who had been imprisoned or expelled; and the securing of clemency for those condemned for acts of passive resistance. The Holy See's intervention improved the situation of well over 300 individuals who found themselves in legal difficulties with the occupying authorities. Concurrently, the Vatican had also been working in October 1923 on a plan for general amnesty which it was urging on the Western Powers. French refusal to consider general pardons, however, doomed this project. But the idea was not without success, since in January 1924, at the Vatican's behest, Belgium began to free some of its prisoners. This in turn placed pressure on France to liberalize its policy of freeing groups and individuals, which it ultimately did month by month throughout 1924.[138]

---

[137] Schreiber, p. 92.

[138] BA, R 43 I, Vol. 159, Testa to Marx, December 2, 1923. *Kreuzzeitung*, letter of Marx to Pope, December 15, 1923. *Katholische Korrespondenz*, May 3, 1924. Lama, pp. 621-624, chronicles the work of the Vatican to ease the lot of prisoners, commute sentences, etc. A listing of Vatican efforts on behalf of prisoners of war and of the occupation, is given in the *Schlesische Volkszeitung*, "Was hat der Vatikan für die deutschen Kriegsgefangenen nach November 1918 getan," June 15, 1924.

Although the Vatican was unable to attain French withdrawal from the Ruhr, it tried to urge Paris to seek a reconciliation. It had aided Germany by being the means of transmitting Berlin's views to Paris. It had been there time and again to help to keep the diplomatic movement from ceasing altogether. By prodding, warning, and admonishing it spoke to all parties concerned in an effort to keep discussions for a solution alive. Since neither England nor Italy had made a move to aid Germany in any serious manner during the initial stages of the crisis, Germany naturally appreciated the value of the Vatican's support and was grateful that it could turn to Rome and regard it as a friend. As many times as Germany requested intervention on its behalf—and the documents list many—the Vatican readily complied.

The reasons for the Holy See's interest in the Reich were many. Undoubtedly it undertook the role for humanitarian reasons and for the sake of peace between two Christian peoples. But other factors also contributed to motivate the Curia. The Ruhr crisis was more at the heart of the diplomatic developments than even the border difficulties with which the Vatican had had to become involved during the early 1920's. The context was larger than merely a dispute involving Franco-German or Belgian-German relations, for it involved the basic question of European peace in all its aspects—political, economic, social, and military. Precisely because nothing was being done toward this goal, because Vatican overtures in 1922-1923 for solving the economic problems of Europe and contributing to "normalcy" and peace had come to naught, Gasparri indicated signs of frustration and pessimism. Germany had to be helped for the sake of Europe. Without doubt the 1922 Treaty of Rapallo between the Reich and the Soviet Union and the Bolshevik uprisings in Germany in 1923 seemed to prove Gasparri correct—that France's intransigence since 1919 was throwing the Reich into Soviet arms and menacing all of Europe. The Vatican's fear of chaos and the encroachments of Communism, which German representatives took every opportunity to play upon, strengthened its resolve to intervene in the Ruhr crisis. Another practical reason to bolster the Reich was to maintain the Catholic balance in Germany. A move by the Holy See to endorse Separatism would only have antagonized German opinion, jeopardized the newly won position of the Center Party, and certainly endangered concordat negotiations by which the Vatican stood to gain. To favor Separatism or the maintenance of French dominance in any part of the Rhineland might have allowed French authorities to introduce a separation of Church and State similar to what existed in France, which would certainly be worse than any concordat then under consideration with the Reich. In short, even in practical terms it was to the Vatican's interest to support Germany.[139]

There was also one other matter of concern which might also have influenced the Vatican to assist Germany. Coincidental with the Ruhr crisis, the Catholic Church in Russia was experiencing a particularly harsh period of persecution. The Vatican had sent the American priest Edmund Walsh as the head of a mission to Russia to determine what could be done for the disorganized and disheartened Church there. The German Embassy in Moscow was used to route messages between Walsh and Rome. In 1923 Archbishop Jan Cieplak of Petrograd and other Catholic ecclesiastics were tried for anti-revolutionary activities. Since Germany enjoyed some degree of good relations with the Soviets, especially after Rapallo, the Vatican requested Berlin to do all it could on behalf of the Catholics on trial. Throughout 1923 German diplomats in Russia were busy transmitting exchanges between Walsh and the Vatican and interceding with Soviet officials. One incident illustrates the close cooperation between Berlin and Rome. When Walsh thanked the German Ambassador, Count Ulrich von Brockdorff-Rantzau, for the support which he had given him in helping the Catholic Church, Brockdorff replied that hopefully the Vatican, with some reciprocal service, would keep in mind Germany's accommodating attitude. Walsh reported this comment to the Pontiff while in Rome in June and was told that the Ambassador should read the *Osservatore* in the coming days. Shortly thereafter the Pontiff's letter of June 27 which criticized the occupation in the Ruhr appeared in the Vatican newspaper.[140]

Thus there were moral, diplomatic, and practical reasons which permitted German-Vatican policies to work closely together and allow Rome to help Germany. Indeed Vatican support was of great value to the Reich not only in a positive sense but also in a negative manner.

---

[139] Another consideration which may have influenced the Vatican to help the Reich, in addition to humanitarian motives and a desire to strengthen Germany against France, may have been future financial expectations. One German bishop, Christian Schreiber, in a letter to Stresemann, warned about giving the outside world, including the Holy See, an over-exaggerated view of Germany's productivity and potential wealth. The prelate stated that the huge number of German pilgrims who came, and who were financially able to come, to Rome in 1925 impressed the Pontiff. Pius believed that once Germany got its currency on a firm basis again, German Catholics would be willing to make large contributions to the Church and to support all its activities. Schreiber mentioned that the Pontiff had spoken of his expectations for a prosperous Germany in various conversations with German bishops. AA, PO II, PO 2 Vat., Vol. 2, Schreiber to Stresemann, April 12, 1926.

[140] AA, RM 70, Vol. 1, Brockdorff-Rantzau (Moscow) to AA, April 24, 1923 and November 26, 1923. For discussion of German efforts on behalf of the Vatican in Russia, see AA, RM 70, Vol. 1.

By specifically not supporting French plans for the Ruhr occupation or for separating part of the Rhineland or the Saar from the local ordinaries or endorsing political separatism the Vatican strengthened not only Germany's borders and its diplomatic position but also its internal stability. Support of France or any detachment of territory would only have weakened the entire parliamentary as well as administrative structure of the Reich, caused further difficulties for the economy, and endangered the existence of the young Republic. Thus in a world where the Germans felt isolated they counted themselves fortunate that they had such a friend, for, as Ritter had mentioned, "The desire to help us is an active one and it is honorably meant."[141]

[141] GSTA, MA 103183, Ritter to Knilling, July 15, 1923.

CHAPTER VI

Diplomatic Relations, Internal Political Implications
1923-1933

In the first years of the Weimar Republic foreign policy questions took precedence over domestic issues, and this was also true in Germany's relations with Rome. Since Germany was seeking Rome's assistance in improving the Reich's diplomatic position in Europe, reparations and border changes stemming from the settlement of Versailles created numerous problems. These problems quite naturally featured prominently in the Reich's diplomacy with the Vatican. But another factor appeared in these relations which, though present in 1919, had not been given the attention accorded to the larger international questions: that is, to what degree did Rome influence or affect internal German political policy either through its diplomatic representative in Berlin, the local hierarchy, or through its political ally, the Center Party? Although this aspect of German-Vatican relations was certainly of concern and existed parallel to matters of international interest during the entire Weimar period, once the initial diplomatic crises of the first five years had subsided, it tended to take on greater significance. While Germany continued to urge the Vatican to cooperate with it abroad and to aid in such matters as the defense of German minorities in other countries, their dealings with each other increasingly involved internal Reich problems. Frequently, situations involving both governments over a diplomatic issue contained important implications for domestic German affairs, or vice versa, and only illustrated the interconnection of both fields of policy affecting German-Vatican relations. In foreign affairs the two governments cooperated, the Vatican supporting Germany not only, as German diplomats at times expressed it, because of the Pontiff's sense of justice and his concern for the German people, but also because German policy coincided with the Vatican's diplomatic goals. But in matters specifically concerning internal German affairs, even though they were often related to foreign policy questions, the two governments frequently approached the problem differently. Here the degree of cooperation was more limited to matters of concession and compromise. Rome or its representatives many times would speak out or be asked to express an opinion on matters which affected domestic issues. Thus the Vatican sought to win support for its views while the civil government and non-Catholic groups and political parties sought to restrict Rome's influence and ability to affect politics. This aspect of church-state relations was a complicated one which to many officials in both Rome and Berlin underscored the necessity to define clearly the rights and privileges of each in the areas of common interest and to provide a framework within which to operate by legally formalizing their relations with a concordat.

A. A Period of Uncertainty

The Vatican was very interested in regulating its relations with the Republic and already in 1919 had given indications of desiring contacts with the new government. By 1920 the difficulties over the levels of competency of the central and state governments had been seemingly solved, and full diplomatic relations between Berlin and Rome were established, with both a German ambassador named to the Vatican and a nuncio for the Reich. But the creation of a nunciature in the German capital brought problems. Although the Reich was represented officially in Rome, as was Bavaria, the question arose whether the nunciature itself should be maintained in Berlin. Naturally Bavaria preferred that Berlin remain without a Papal legation, for the presence of a second nunciature accredited to all Germany would only diminish the importance of the one in Bavaria. On several occasions Bavarian officials had made their unhappiness with such a plan clear to Vatican prelates. Moreover, Pacelli reported to Rome in the spring of 1920 that conservative Protestant circles in northern Germany were also unhappy about the establishment of a nunciature in Berlin. On June 1, the liberal *Frankfurter Zeitung* also carried an article about this fact, expressing the opinion that a Papal representative near the seat of the Central Government could permit the Curia to exert undue influence in matters beyond those dealing with purely ecclesiastical affairs. The Holy See was fully aware of such sentiments. Thus, with Catholic disapproval in the south and liberal and Protestant objections in the north, Gasparri informed Ritter in June 1920 that although Pacelli was now accredited to the Reich Government, the Curia was in no rush to transfer him from Munich to Berlin, but would rather wait a while.[1]

[1] GSTA, MA 100011, Ritter to BFM, June 11, 1920. *Frankfurter Zeitung*, June 1, 1920.

The position of nuncio, however, had not been created to be set apart from the center of power. As representative of the Pope the nuncio was to have the opportunity of coming into daily contact with politicians, whereby he could advise, caution, or explain the policy of the Vatican to them. At the same time a nuncio collects, filters, and analyzes information on the conditions in the country to which he is appointed, and his opinions can be one of the cornerstones upon which the Curia relies in formulating its policies. While in Munich Nuncio Pacelli had for years sent reports to Rome on matters affecting all Germany well beyond the borders of the Wittelsbach domains. German politicians had found ways to stop over in Munich to discuss matters concerning the Reich with him. The thoroughness of Pacelli's knowledge of Germany and his vigilance in safeguarding the Church's interests, while still remaining on good terms with civil officials and commanding their respect, had made Pacelli an important figure in Munich and his tenure as nuncio a most productive and influential one. It was therefore only natural that some Catholics and German politicians outside Bavaria desired to see Pacelli transferred to Berlin for the very reasons that others dreaded or feared it.

While generally endorsing the new republican government, Pacelli was ever on guard lest a too liberalizing tendency injure the Church. In 1921, no doubt in part to emphasize Rome's desire to see a strong Germany in Central Europe, he praised the work of the Berlin Government to the French Ambassador. While some of the social policies which the new Socialist-led government was advocating concerned him, he nevertheless was pleased with the cabinet's efforts to keep the country strong and united and to work out a new system of administration for its people. The Nuncio had therefore advised Catholic politicians who had sought his advice to cooperate in laying the foundations of the new German society, and he cautioned them against any division in the Center Party, lest it only weaken the Catholic cause. He warned against any close alliance with the Protestant monarchists, who, he felt, should they return to power, would be encased again in their narrow confessionalism and not really help in working for a united country or an improvement of Protestant-Catholic relations. The prelate was equally negative about the reactionary and particularist sentiments emanating from Bavaria. Pacelli did not favor pro-Catholic separatism or a coalition with the right conservatives which could topple the Central Government. Instead he supported the Berlin Government, aware of and cautious about some of its left-leaning tendencies. Nevertheless, despite his opinions on an involvement in the developments which were shaping the new Germany from Berlin, he personally showed no great haste to take up his permanent residence in the

German capital, claiming that concordat negotiations then underway in Munich required his presence there. Pacelli's attitude was of great interest to the French, who were watching closely the development of Vatican-German rapport. The French Ambassador was no doubt unaware of the Vatican's policy of not rushing to transfer the Nuncio because of its concern for the sensitivities of Bavaria, but he speculated that Pacelli's reluctance to move was also based on personal motives: fear that his success in Munich might be soon forgotten should he not cope successfully with the more complex Reich situation, which could involve him in internal Center Party quarrels, or else concern that a move to Berlin would prolong his stay in Germany and hence hurt his chances of further career advancement, since his long stay in Germany would gain for him the reputation of being a Germanophile and thus disqualify him for an important Curial post where a reputation for impartiality was necessary.[2]

Whether or not some of Pacelli's reluctance was career-motivated, he seemed genuinely glad that the Vatican had postponed his move to Berlin, for he personally was fond of Munich and the Bavarians. But by 1921, having soothed Bavaria's feelings by allowing Bavaria to retain its legation at the Vatican and expecting the concordat negotiations in Munich to be concluded soon, Rome believed the time was approaching to send Pacelli to the Reich capital. The Curia thereupon announced, but without giving a specific date, that the Nuncio intended to move his permanent residence to Berlin in the near future.

No doubt in part to assuage French fears about his impending move and its diplomatic implications, in early 1922 Pacelli again returned to the subject of his unhappiness about leaving Munich but also gave the reasons why he was needed in Berlin. He told French bishop Rémond that at least in the Bavarian capital there existed a Catholic environment, whereas in Berlin he would be placed in a Protestant milieu that was anti-clerical and in a city where the leftist, Socialist parties were very strong. Letting his thoughts run on a bit, Pacelli explained his concern that if the Bolsheviks of Russia ever allied with the Socialists of Germany it would be the end of civilization. One of the greatest dangers for the future would be an alliance between Germany and Russia—the "hordes" from the east, now organized and supplied with weapons by the west. As Rémond commented, "The Bolshevik danger seems to haunt the Nuncio, who during the weeks of the Red terror in Munich saw himself threatened in his nunciature, which had been invaded, and every night had to seek asylum in a new refuge, and his residence had been machine-gunned." What also seemed to

---

[2] FFO, Allemagne 370, Laurent (Berlin) to FFO, November 18, 1921.

distress him was the hostility of Protestant Berlin, for, as Rémond noted, he was *au courant* of the nationalist, anti-Semitic, anti-clerical articles in the Rightist newspapers, especially *Der Reichsbote*, which vehemently opposed the establishment of a nunciature or the signing of a concordat. The more extreme Protestants wanted no concessions granted to the Catholic Church in matters of education, legal guarantees for the Church, or financial support. The Nuncio expressed his opinion that the Rightist German National People's Party, or Nationalists (DNVP), the party of the Junkers, conservatives, and extreme nationalists, which backed the newspaper, was the most sectarian of parties, sought to hinder any latinizing tendencies in German culture, and regarded the Catholic Church as a propagator of Latin culture and consequently anti-German. The group lacked a leader, after the abdication of the Kaiser,[3] but militarism and nationalism had now replaced him as a rallying point. These dangerous tendencies could all become more menacing to Catholicism and therefore had to be met by the Church's launching its own counteroffensive from a nunciature directly in the heart of *Deutschtum*, in Berlin.

Moreover, Pacelli was well aware of the dangers from both Right and Left and from those created by divisions in the Center Party, torn between Left and Right tendencies within its own ranks. The Nuncio worried that Right-leaning Catholics and Center Party members who heeded the call to patriotism might make common cause with the German National People's Party, unaware of the problems that excessive nationalism, militarism, and sectarian Protestantism might create for the Church. Yet, on the other hand, to counter this challenge the avant garde of the Center might carry the party too far to the Left, toward a Marxist ideology or cooperation with the Socialists. All these political developments required the Curia to have a representative in Berlin to advise, counsel, and influence events during this crucial formative period. According to Rémond, Pacelli, in rather hyperbolic fashion, proudly announced the new nunciature in Berlin would be the new outpost of Catholic influence in the north. "Don't believe that it was Marshal Foch who has won the war! No, it is the Pope, and the test of the collapse of Germany is really not the occupation of the Left Bank of the Rhine but the presence of a nunciature in Berlin. . . ."[4]

From the first days of his accreditation to the Reich Government, Pacelli was drawn into the life of Catholic Germany and the political problems of Berlin, and he was called upon to use his skill as a dip-

---

[3] For the Kaiser's anti-Catholic attitude see Fischer, pp. 433-434.

[4] FFO, Allemagne 316, Rémond to Army General Headquarters, January 30, 1922.

lomat. For example, the debates at the *Katholikentag* of 1922, the denomination's annual convention, reflected many of the internal problems facing German Catholicism. Cardinal Faulhaber, who had supported Bavaria's royal house, condemned the League of Nations, and branded the Weimar Constitution as bearing the mark of Cain. He would have been happier had the monarchy and the pre-war political system been retained, while Konrad Adenauer, mayor of Cologne, representing the more liberal wing, hoped to carry German Catholicism toward a more democratically oriented state and society. Pacelli, however, steered a course between both viewpoints, counseling the Center Party toward moderation and at the same time taking pains in conversation with French representatives to disassociate himself from any political remarks made, such as the Munich Cardinal's disparaging remarks about the League or Adenauer's assertion that the Rhinelanders were most unhappy under foreign occupation. Although the local hierarchy had given full vent to its patriotic feelings and support for Berlin, Pacelli remained more detached, taking care to keep the diplomatic door open to the Allied Powers in order to be of use to both Rome and Berlin.[5]

The Germans correctly noted that Pacelli, on the scene in Germany, was the most important means that the Vatican had to observe conditions, especially those of the Church, in the Reich. Frequently, especially during the early years of the Republic, some issues dealing with foreign affairs also had a dimension which affected internal matters and only demonstrated how closely domestic policy depended on diplomatic considerations. Therefore, Berlin officials, in an effort to gain Vatican support for their view, took pains in explaining a problem, even if it were a diplomatic one, to show its relation or importance to the Church or to church-state relations within Germany. For example, in 1923, when German suspicions of French designs on the Rhineland and Saarland were increased by the Ruhr invasion and by French support for the Separatists, Berlin sent reports to Pacelli stressing the weakening of the Church's power should France win permanent control over these areas. During a meeting between the Reich Representative to Munich and the Nuncio in March, the German emphasized what the loss of these territories would mean for the Church, especially as it affected education. He pointed to the February 2 comments of the Prussian Minister of Education and Religious Affairs, who, after returning from a trip through the Ruhr, described how the educational system had been pitifully disrupted by the occupation. He pointed out that the headquarters of many Catholic organizations for

5 FFO, Allemagne 367, Dard (Munich) to FFO, September 4, 1922.

all Germany were located in the Rhineland—the *Volksvereinzentrale* in München-Gladbach, the Central Youth and School Organization in Düsseldorf, and the center for the Catholic public libraries (*Volksbücherei*) in Bonn, all of which were already experiencing a restriction of their activities because of the occupying forces. Pacelli, always a good listener, conveyed to all parties his interest and concern for their affairs. However, as on other occasions, while promising to pass the information on to Rome, he requested an Italian translation of official reports of curtailment of Catholic activities coupled with statistical support so that the matter would make the best impression when presented to the Holy Father.[6] Pacelli was always careful to support his reports with facts—something which impressed those with whom he came into contact and who saw him as observant, solicitous, yet prudently wise to have data to support partisan reports. Such an attitude confirmed the high regard in which Vatican officials held him and only further increased the desire of diplomats to gain his support.

One factor which always had to be kept in mind by Vatican officials formulating a policy in their dealings with Germany was the possibility of an increase in anti-Vatican sentiment. Should the Nuncio's presence in Berlin become visible too rapidly or should Rome move too far or too fast in becoming involved in German affairs, even if inadvertently or well meant, there was the danger of a reaction. In a country with a history of confessional division and the memory of the *Kulturkampf* (the Prussian State's effort to curtail Church influence) less than fifty years old, many Protestants, liberals, and Socialists were inclined to suspect the Holy See of unfriendliness to the Reich and to its secular principles, and they tended to resist any move by the Vatican which they interpreted as a step to gain more influence. Sectarian antagonism had not lessened with the changing of the old order and the departure of the Hohenzollerns. During the war the Center Party began to gain influence in the government, while the Church, through the diplomatic means at its command, continued to play an important role in Germany's foreign policy, culminating in the Papal Peace Note of 1917.[7] In the period of disorder brought about by the monarchy's collapse, the Center Party, which had gained approximately one-quarter of the seats in the last pre-war Reichstag and had held its forces largely intact, appeared as a bulwark of order and solidity that formed one of the founding cornerstones in the cabinet of the government. Finally, the passive resistance in the Rhineland, supported overwhelmingly by

---

[6] Germany, Historisches Archiv der Stadt Köln (hereafter cited as Cologne, Marx), Abt. 1070 Nr. 133, Denk (Munich) to Prussian Minister-President, March 31, 1923.

[7] See Rudolf Morsey, *Die deutsche Zentrumspartei 1917-1923* (Düsseldorf, 1966); Stehlin; Steglich.

Catholics of the Rhine and Ruhr, demonstrated the patriotism of Catholic Germans, the nationalism of their hierarchy, and the importance of this social and political group in the Weimar coalition. Catholics hoped that all these developments would calm lingering suspicions that they were *Reichsfeinde*, a group not really in sympathy with the unity that had been obtained under the auspices of Protestant Prussia. Under these circumstances it is understandable how Pacelli could mention that Catholicism had made great progress within Germany and was regarded with less suspicion, as witnessed by the recent suggestion in political circles that the government would not object to the creation of a Catholic diocese for Berlin.[8]

Nevertheless, Vatican diplomats still had to beware of antagonizing Protestant sensibilities by an all-too-rapid growth of influence or outward manifestations of strength. The privileged position which the old dynastic and military organization, in Prussia at least, had granted to the Evangelical Church had disappeared in 1918; new nations, largely Catholic, such as Poland and Czechoslovakia, had arisen on Germany's borders; a Catholic political party was now part of the ruling triumvirate within the Reich. These events were viewed by some Protestants and liberals as opportunities which the Church would now use to increase its influence. These fears caused the strengthening of old antipathies, and anti-Catholic groups accordingly sounded the warning call by condemning the Church-at-large or its most visible representative, the Nuncio, in particular. The Right-leaning Evangelical League (*Bund*), a strongly anti-Catholic group within the Evangelical Church, at all its general meetings and in newspaper articles had persistently denounced the increasing influence of Rome and its political arm, the Center Party, which aspired, the *Bund* claimed, to render Prussian Protestantism weak and ineffective. Right-leaning journals such as the *Grossdeutsche Zeitung* accused Pacelli of exerting undue influence in Munich in the post-war years, and nationalistic groups accused him of supporting Separatism.[9] Therefore Pacelli had to be all the more circumspect as he pursued his duties as Nuncio to the Reich lest anything he said be misconstrued or used to impair his functioning as Vatican emissary.

Rome then, in contrast to the domain of foreign affairs, where its aid was consistently sought and its goodwill courted by German officials, walked a tightrope in the arena of internal affairs. It could not intervene lest it be accused of seeking to control or dominate. Yet internal events were of importance to the Holy See, and it had to pay

---

[8] Lutz, "Die deutschen Katholiken," 193ff.

[9] FFO, Allemagne 368, de Margerie (Berlin) to Poincaré, June 27, 1923.

close attention to German domestic policy since a government could affect the freedom of the Church, the taxes on ecclesiastical institutions, and educational policies, not to mention its effect on the daily life of its citizens, which from a pastoral viewpoint would then also interest the Church. Thus it not only had to exert caution but had to be concerned lest any alteration in the government structure harm its interests. For example, the fact that General Ludendorff and Gustav von Kahr, two of the prominent figures in Bavaria who opposed and even defied the Central Government in 1923, were staunch Protestants, only increased the Vatican's uneasiness about the political unrest in Munich.[10] Gasparri believed for several reasons that a change in the government of Bavaria would be unfavorable to Vatican policy. As he saw it, the attempted *Putsch* led by Ludendorff and Adolf Hitler might give France an excuse to allege that the old militarists were reasserting themselves in Germany and thus afford France an opportunity to interfere in German affairs and upset the political balance in the Reich and, by extension, in Europe. Moreover, the anti-Catholic attitude of so prominent a figure as Ludendorff might provide encouragement for a growth of anti-Catholic sentiment among the general public. This, said the Cardinal, would be particularly wounding to the Holy See, since the Vatican had sent numerous sums of money, primarily through Cardinal Faulhaber, to be distributed in Bavaria for the alleviation of post-war material distress of Germans, regardless of creed. In addition Gasparri felt the General's influence should be carefully watched, since if pervasive enough it might lead to the formation of an anti-Catholic regime in Munich, a development which could possibly disrupt the concordat talks then in progress or at least be less conciliatory or understanding toward them.[11] Also, Curial officials had hoped to conclude a concordat with Bavaria as soon as possible so as to set a precedent that they could use as a model and foundation for treaties with other German states and ultimately with the Reich itself. All these plans would be endangered should Bavaria declare its independence.

The Vatican viewed ultra-nationalist movements with suspicion, undoubtedly with memories of the *Kulturkampf* still vivid in the minds of many churchmen. Thus when Lundendorff and Hitler spoke of love of the fatherland and a true nationalism that prompted them to seek to overthrow the government in a Berlin dominated by liberal democrats, Socialists, and Catholics who owed their allegiance to a foreign power, and when anti-Catholic remarks were made and the

[10] HHSTA, 87, Pastor to Grünberger, November 9, 1923.
[11] GSTA, Ges. Päpstl. Stuhl 996, Ritter to BFM, November 9, 1923.

Munich Cardinal had to be defended in the *Landtag* for his statements in favor of Christian principles as opposed to excessive nationalism,[12] the Vatican reacted with concern and indignation. Gasparri therefore in private conversations with diplomats questioned why Rome should do more for Germany on the international plane when in internal affairs segments of the German population persisted in condemning the Church.[13] Conscious of the tenuous position of church-state relations, the Vatican at first publicly refrained from making statements or specific, critical comments about political movements or internal affairs, which could only exacerbate the already overheated situation. A deterioration in these relations would not only be detrimental to the Church within Germany and impair the slow progress toward a concordat, but it would make it politically impossible for Rome to support Germany on the international level, as it had done until then, even if Rome sought to do so solely for the sake of its own European policy.

During 1923 the Curia had been content in allowing the local ordinaries to issue statements about the anti-Christian aspects of some of the political Rightists. But the prominence and support gained by people such as Hitler and Ludendorff, which had prompted them to risk seizing the government, convinced the Holy See of the urgency of expressing its opinion on the issue, at least in moral terms, lest the movement grow larger, lest Catholics be led astray into supporting such leaders without recognizing the dangers to their faith. Therefore, in early 1924 the Curia felt obliged to speak out against the proliferation of publications of the German political Right which not only criticized the Roman Catholic Church but also Christianity as a whole. Rome supported Cardinal Faulhaber, who in several speeches in Munich had soundly condemned the ultra-nationalist movement and political groups which under the cover of patriotism were attacking the Church. In an article in the *Osservatore* on February 28, 1923 the Vatican cited the work of Father Erhard Schlund, *Neugermanisches Heidentum im heutigen Deutschland* (1923), which called attention to the growth of the neo-paganism in Germany, and listed the tenets of the League for a German Church (*Bund für eine deutsche Kirche*), and articles in the review *Neues Leben* as some examples of this movement's seeking to attack the Church and to set up nationalism as the true religion of Germans. It was perhaps symptomatic, said the *Osservatore*, of the increase of anti-Christian sentiments and beliefs that the new Rightist National Socialist German Workers' Party (NSDAP) had as its sym-

---

[12] Germany, Bavaria, *Stenographische Berichte über die Verhandlungen des Landtages, 1920-1924* (Munich), Vol. 9, pp. 123ff., 217-219th Session, February 6-8, 1924. Hereafter cited as Germany, Bavaria, Landtag.

[13] GSTA, Ges. Päpstl. Stuhl 996, Ritter to BFM, January 12, 1924.

bol the *Hakenkreuz* (swastika), which, said the journal, was a visible manifestation of the attempted replacement of the cross of Christ with pagan signs.[14]

Concern over internal affairs in Germany did not diminish when, after the failure of the *Putsch*, Ludendorff, during his trial, having as his audience the entire German populace, delivered a vitriolic attack on German Catholics, the Holy See, and the deceased Benedict XV. He called them all anti-Reich in their outlook. The Pope, he said, had not been of real assistance to Germany but rather to the Allies during the war. The General condemned pre-war Catholic policies in Posen, Silesia, and Strasbourg of having made concessions to the demands of the non-German-speaking segments of the population for religious instruction in their own languages, stating that this made Germanization of the areas more difficult. He invoked the old story of French intrigue with German Catholics during and after the war to form a south German confederation, including Austria, separate from Protestant Prussia. In Germany's struggle in world affairs the Vatican, he claimed, was never neutral and he proceeded then to give examples of what he termed Vatican favoritism to France, pointing to the Jesuits' paying tribute to France's war hero, Marshal Ferdinand Foch and to former French Premier Georges Clemenceau's reception of an honorary doctoral degree from a Catholic institution. Furthermore, he continued, the Catholic clergy in Austria, no doubt upon instructions, had been making critical remarks about Germany and its wartime policy in recent years. Even Cardinal Faulhaber, stated the General, was less than a loyal German since he made "non-patriotic" statements by condemning the sinking of the *Lusitania*. Shifting to another tack, how, the former General also asked, if the Catholic clergy were true Germans could they cooperate and support the Berlin Government, filled as it was with Jews and Socialists.[15] The trial and prominence of the World War I hero publicized the incident, and the German Government feared it might prompt Rome to enter into the matter by refuting the assertions or it might prompt other nationalists to take up the accusations, further expand the controversy, and increase the confessional animosities at a time when unity was in question. The attack coincided with the Vatican's sending, in line with its charitable work, of 50,000 marks' worth of woolen goods to Germany in addition to Pius' gift of 2,000,000 lire for distribution among the needy in Mu-

[14] *Osservatore*, "Manifestazioni neopagane," February 28, 1924; see also *Osservatore*, May 5-6, 1924 and May 7, 1924. GSTA, Ges. Päpstl. Stuhl 996, Ritter to BFM, March 2, 1924. The swastika is also a type of cross, the hooked cross (*Haken*-hook, *Kreuz*-cross.

[15] BFO, 371/9831/5347, Clive (Munich) to BFO, March 12, 1924.

nich.[16] Stung no doubt by the anti-Vatican sentiments and mindful of his active diplomatic support for the Reich at a time when it appeared that Germany's economic problems were beginning to be solved, Gasparri laconically remarked, "I would not have believed, and very much regret that the Germans are such poor politicians."[17]

To soothe any hurt feelings on the part of Rome and to calm German Catholics who might react by coming to the defense of their spiritual leader, Bergen naturally wired Berlin, pleading for an official government condemnation of the General's remarks and requesting the cabinet to use its influence with the press, particularly the non-Catholic press, to denounce his irresponsible statements, which the Ambassador feared might harm inter-church relations and destroy the trust and confidence between Rome and Berlin that he had so laboriously worked to build.[18] Apologies were profuse. The German episcopate sent a letter expressing its regret about the incident and citing its confidence in the Holy See. On March 4 Chancellor Wilhelm Marx, speaking to representatives of the Catholic People's Union, censured Ludendorff's remarks as well as nationalist "*völkisch*" movements such as that of the National Socialists, since, said the Chancellor, they all preached fanaticism, hate, and un-Christian principles.[19] The Prussian Minister-President also wrote to Pacelli in March, expressing regret over the General's comments, "a regret which is all the greater inasmuch as the Prussian Government is convinced that General Ludendorff's attack has no foundation in reality. . . ."[20]

In a speech in Brunswick during March, Stresemann also repudiated the attack on Rome and lay stress on the benefits conferred on the Reich by the Vatican. To make it official, on March 6 Stresemann, speaking for the government, raised the matter in the Reichstag. Acknowledging that the government did not usually comment on the statements of a private citizen, he conceded that the General was so well known that the government felt obliged to say something. Deploring the incident, Stresemann said he could only declare the accusations as absolutely groundless. In his speech, which was directed to the Vatican, he stated his certainty that he spoke for the overwhelming majority of the German people. The Pontiff's impartiality and charitable concern were known to all Germans. The unfortunate remarks, said the Foreign Minister, were all the more unpleasant for

[16] AA, PO II, PO 2 Vat., Vol. 2, memorandum of Meyer-Rodehüser, April 15, 1924.

[17] HHSTA, 87, Pastor to Grünberger, April 4, 1924.

[18] AA, RM 70, Vol. 2, Bergen to AA, March 2, 1924.

[19] *Berliner Tageblatt*, March 4, 1924.

[20] BFO, 371/9831/5347, Russell (Vatican) to Prime Minister MacDonald, March 11, 1924.

Berlin since they were made at a time when the world had observed how the Pontiff had raised his voice and given funds to help the material suffering of the German people.[21] The Vatican then had received an official apology which satisfied the Cardinal Secretary of State and Catholics in Germany,[22] but the internal affair, which elicited an official apology in the Reichstag itself, indicated the importance which Berlin attached to maintaining its connections to the Vatican and the support of its Catholic population at home. It also again indicated to Rome that in its own interests the present Weimar Government was concerned with maintaining good relations with the Church—something which could not be said with certainty about the leaders in Berlin should the old government return or a new one from the Right or Left be established. It signified that to the Curia its best working ally was the regime then in power.

But yet another aspect of the complicated situation of 1923-1924 induced the Vatican to react to events in Germany. What had begun as, and what Rome treated as, an internal affair now began to have consequences affecting even foreign policy. The General's comments about the Vatican's pro-French bias during the war turned public attention as well as the legislators to re-examining once again the question of the Papal Peace Note of 1917. Statements made by Ludendorff had somehow to be substantiated or proved incorrect. It was not enough for the cabinet to deny the charge that the Papacy had been unfriendly to Germany during the war. Numerous newspaper articles were calling for the full story of the genesis of the peace note, and what role the Vatican did indeed play. In fact members of the Reichstag, including some Catholics, thought that publication of the documents dealing with the incident would be beneficial, and called for their public presentation. The twofold purpose would be to give a documentary account of Germany's search for peace in 1917, and secondly to substantiate the Vatican's role at that time in seeking a just peace. This would, it was hoped, silence Ludendorff's supporters and stem any anti-Vatican feeling. The problem became critical, for on March 5 Centrist Deputy Ludwig Kaas in a Reichstag speech denounced what he saw as Ludendorff's calumnious anti-Roman charges, emphasizing the damage that they had caused. Even if the documents concerning the Papal peace proposal of 1917 failed to prove that the Vatican had acted in less than good faith toward Germany, Kaas believed that the anti-Catholic remarks of the last few weeks, especially those of the General, could bring the populace to believe that the assertions were

[21] AA, RM 70, Vol. 2, Grünau (AA) to German Embassy (Vatican), March 6, 1924. Germany, Reichstag, Vol. 361, pp. 12639-640. 406th Session, March 6, 1924.

[22] AA, RM 70, Vol. 2, Bergen to AA, March 7, 1924.

true. Deputy Karl Helfferich and the German National People's Party claimed that Kaas was merely making an unsubstantiated counterassertion and demanded publication of all pertinent material. It did not help that Kaas, realizing his tactical error, declared that his purpose was not to urge the publication of the documents.[23] The matter had come to a head.

For German domestic politics this suggestion might produce a quieting effect, but for the Vatican, which had always emphasized to diplomats in all camps that it could be relied on for its discretion, this meant a non-voluntary breach in its secrecy which could expose it to charges by the West of having been overly concerned with aiding the Reich. In such a heated atmosphere as that of 1923-1924 the Curia saw no need to have the issues pursued and, what it believed to be, needlessly complicated. Nevertheless, although discussion of Papal motives had been proposed several years earlier and successfully blocked by the Foreign Office, the recent controversy had prompted the Reichstag Investigating Committee into the Causes of the World War in the second week of March to consider again permitting publication of documents from the German Foreign Office dealing with the Papal peace overtures of 1917. It appeared that what had been settled earlier would now be reopened. Pacelli, in conversations with Reich officials, was not only aghast but—rare for him—showed signs of open indignation. Such a step, he said, was contrary to all diplomatic custom, and was to be taken only with the consent of both parties in the affair—a consent which Secretary of State Gasparri would never agree to give. It would cause the Vatican to be even more apprehensive in helping Germany, since it could never be certain whether an indiscretion might occur. That afternoon he telephoned Reich officials in Berlin, including the Chancellor, requesting him to use every means at his command to avert a unilateral breach of diplomatic etiquette from which, he warned, untold consequences for foreign policy could arise. The fact that Pacelli, normally never impulsive, but always cautious and correct, had made these calls to Berlin deeply impressed the Reich Representative in Munich and emphasized for him the seriousness with which the Nuncio regarded the matter.[24]

In Rome Gasparri reacted in a similar fashion. Brushing aside the assurance that the German Foreign Office was against publication and had communicated its opinion to the Reichstag committee, Gasparri informed Bergen "The Holy See casts its formal veto against publi-

---

[23] AA, T-120, 4057H/E066578-580, Meyer-Rodehüser to Meyer (Vatican), March 18, 1924. See ch. 2, pp. 66ff. for the earlier discussion over publishing documents regarding the 1917 note.

[24] AA, PO II, PO 2 Vat., Vol. 1, Haniel (Munich) to AA, March 11, 1924.

cation of any kind of material whatsoever dealing with the Papal peace overtures of 1917. . . ." In sharp tones he stated that should the elemental rules of negotiation not be observed, there would no longer be a basis for any further communication between the two governments. Bergen, thoroughly impressed with the gravity of the situation, wired and "urgently" requested the Foreign Office to use every possible means to block publication.[25] Chancellor Marx called in Peter Spahn, a Center leader and influential member of the Reichstag, to use his influence in the matter. He called attention to Pacelli's move of personally calling the Reich Chancellery and warning that publication would make the exchange of diplomatic correspondence between the Vatican and Berlin impossible. Marx was sure that Spahn agreed with him that "by all means this request of the Vatican must be honored," and that all manner of persuasion was to be used in the Reichstag for this purpose.[26]

Before going further, because of Ludendorff's accusations, the Foreign Office, which had sponsored the publication of the multi-volume document series on the war, *Die Grosse Politik*, took the precaution of calling in its editor, Friedrich Thimme, to reassure itself that the series did not have nor would contain any embarrassing disclosures about the Vatican. Thimme replied that Series II touched on the Vatican in the period 1898-1899, but the references made only indicated the true statesmanship of Curial officials and should cause no displeasure with Rome in either French or German circles. Revealing a bit of the editorial thinking used in publishing this first series of modern diplomatic documents, Thimme assured the government that general policy for the multi-volume work was to omit any document which would be damaging to the position of a neutral power, and this, of course, included the Vatican. Thimme also emphasized that he personally checked all documents to be published.[27]

Armed with these assurances about its own publication series, Hermann Meyer-Rodehüser, representing the Foreign Office, met in mid-March with the Reichstag committee and detailed the government's position. The committee countered by requesting the Foreign Office to seek permission of the Vatican to let the documents appear. The Vatican again refused to grant it, and Meyer, armed with a Vatican statement, returned to the committee and stressed the telling argument that although perhaps desirable when viewed from the perspective of party politics and internal affairs, the publication when considered from the perspective of foreign policy was totally unacceptable. After

[25] AA, RM 70, Vol. 2, Bergen to AA, March 12, 1924.
[26] AA, PO II, PO 2 Vat., Vol. 1, Marx to Spahn, March 12, 1924.
[27] AA, PO II, PO 2 Vat., Vol. 2, Thimme to Meyer-Rodehüser, March 17, 1924.

lengthy discussion and urgent requests from the Foreign Office, the committee bowed to pressure, making its decision on the grounds of expediency, and voted definitively not to publish or to make public the material. The entire matter had been a very delicate one; it touched many sensitive issues; the committee already had a contract to publish its findings on the causes of the war; and, finally, the Foreign Office had no veto power over the matter and had had to rely on persuasion to block it. As Meyer said, "Here we are all happy that the matter which has kept us occupied and upset us so many times has finally been settled."[28]

The controversy over Ludendorff and perhaps the logical request of some politicians, journalists, and segments of the public to see all the documents and learn all the facts about the peace initiatives and the policy of their country during wartime once more indicated how an affair dealing with internal events had affected and taken on diplomatic overtones. Why, some people asked, should their government be reluctant to tell the entire story from their own documents? Why, if the Vatican had acted as it said it had, did it hesitate to allow the world a glimpse of the workings of its diplomacy? What the Foreign Office did was to convince the committee that for the sake of the Reich's present diplomatic position the past should not be made completely public; that the Vatican's success in diplomacy was largely due to its behind-the-scene negotiations and to the manner in which it observed confidences as with the seal of the confessional. Moreover, from the Vatican's viewpoint in the post-war period there were other reasons for it to continue to practice its own style of diplomacy upon which statesmen had come to rely. The Curia had been excluded from the institutions of world government which provided for open diplomacy. The Versailles Conference and the ensuing peace had not seen representatives of the Holy See invited, nor did the Vatican have a seat in the European institution dedicated to peace, the League of Nations. The Vatican naturally viewed that institution with skepticism while not opposing it in principle but rather in practice, since it was not, as Gasparri visualized it, neutral but rather dominated by and dedicated to fostering Anglo-French interests. Until the membership of the League expanded to include states such as Germany, Russia, and the United States, the Vatican reserved judgment as to the efficacy of League action and preferred to rely on its old but efficient

---

[28] AA, T-120, 4057H/E066578-580, Meyer-Rodehüser to Meyer (Vatican), March 18, 1924. Germany, Reichstag, Vol. 361, pp. 12606-607, 12620-621. 405th Session, March 5, and 406th Session, March 6, 1924. AA, RM 70, Vol. 2, Maltzan (AA) to German Embassy (Vatican), March 14, 1924. Only after 1945 were scholars able fully to utilize this material. See Steglich for example.

style of diplomacy.[29] Moreover, many critical or delicate matters necessitated that the Vatican deal with non-League members. For example, Vatican diplomacy had worked successfully on behalf of the Reich in the post-war years to ease what it considered the harshness of French punitive demands. Since it would not be done within the League framework, the Vatican preferred to deal quietly *à deux*, out of the view of the public eye. It is therefore understandable that the Foreign Office insisted that, despite internal, intra-party considerations, the Vatican's request for silence about its diplomatic activities be honored, for it benefited the policy of both governments.

Such a policy would not unilaterally help Germany but would, the Foreign Office insisted, profit both states. In 1924, exactly at the time when Rome was working for Germany to ease the problems in the west, the Curia had occasion to ask Germany, as a non-League member and one of the few states which enjoyed good contacts with the Soviet Union, quietly to act as a diplomatic intermediary. In 1923, when Moscow had taken a harsher attitude toward the Catholic community in Russia, placing restrictions on the Church, imprisoning some of the bishops and clergy, the Vatican had requested Germany to use its good influences in Moscow to secure release of Catholic clerics such as Archbishop Cieplak of Petrograd, who had been imprisoned for alleged anti-Soviet activities. Berlin took up the matter on several occasions with Soviet officials. In March 1924 Moscow informed the Vatican via German diplomatic channels of its reconsideration of Cieplak's conviction. Later in the month Gasparri requested German intervention on behalf of Ambrosius, the Orthodox Patriarch of Georgia, who was also being accused of anti-people's activities.[30] Vatican requests for intercession on behalf of priests, monks, and nuns imprisoned primarily in Moscow and Petrograd continued during the next month.[31]

Since early 1923 German Ambassador Ulrich von Brockdorff-Rantzau had used his good offices to further relations and smooth out difficulties between the Vatican and the Soviet Union. In 1923 Pacelli had met Soviet Commissar for Foreign Affairs Georgi Chicherin in

[29] BFO, 371/9935/5389, Russell to Prime Minister, May 12, 1924. *Kölnische Zeitung*, November 13, 1924.

[30] The Papacy had already made direct appeals on behalf of Orthodox prelates, the most notable case being that of the Russian Orthodox Patriarch Tikhon in 1922, but with little success. Later in 1924 Cieplak was released after Germany and later England and other nations strongly interceded for him. AA, RM 70, Vol. 2, Radowitz (Moscow) to AA, March 21, 1924; Bergen to AA, March 26, 1924. Henry L. Hull, "The Holy See and Soviet Russia, 1918-1931," unpublished dissertation, Georgetown University, Washington, D.C., 1970, p. 191. See also ch. 5, pp. 275.

[31] AA, RM 70, Vol. 2, Bergen to AA, April 22, 1924.

Brockdorff's brother's home in Berlin and had discussed possibilities for regularizing the position of the Catholic Church in the Soviet Union. The Ambassador himself on behalf of the Vatican had also taken up the matter of Soviet-Vatican relations with Chicherin, with the purpose of beginning discussions for reaching a *modus vivendi* as well as interceding for several Catholic priests and religious. He had relayed the answers from Soviet officials to Berlin via the German diplomatic service, and the Foreign Office in Berlin conveyed the information to Pacelli.[32] Apparently as Karl Radek, member of the Communist Central Committee, had told Brockdorff, after Italy's *de jure* recognition of the Soviet Government in February 1924, some officials such as Radek himself had now urged coming to an agreement with the Vatican, but the leadership had rejected it. Chicherin informed the German Ambassador that *de jure* recognition of the Soviet Union by the Vatican would have been immeasurably more important for Moscow two years before, but even if Moscow was now not as interested in diplomatic relations with the Holy See as it had been previously, it would nevertheless still like to reach some type of "religious peace with the Vatican." The Commissar warned, however, that certain matters were closed to discussion. For example, the founding of religious schools in the Soviet Union would be *a priori* a point which would neither be approved nor would it be negotiable. In addition, the Soviet leadership regarded the Papal Relief Mission, in Russia since July 1922 to perform charitable work and to stave off some of the hunger stalking the country, as an anti-Communist organization used for western and religious propaganda purposes. Now that conditions had improved somewhat by 1924 the government no longer considered its aid needed or useful and asked the mission to leave.[33] The hard line taken by Moscow made it difficult for Germany to succeed in its role as intermediary between the two states. Nevertheless, its success would have increased Berlin's influence in Moscow and Moscow's indebtedness to Berlin for opening lines to the "outside," while it also would have demonstrated to Rome Germany's use to the Vatican in return for Vatican pressure on the Western Allies. Throughout 1924 Brockdorff pursued this task, sending reports of his conversations with Chicherin and with his deputy Maxim Litvinov about the relationship with the Vatican, reducing the restrictions on the Church, and releasing some of the imprisoned clergy. Chicherin, who indicated some interest in coming to an understanding, was aware

[32] For the documents on these negotiations, see AA, Geheim Vat., Pol. 3, Russland.
[33] AA, RM 70, Vol. 2, Brockdorff to AA, March 31, 1924. For a report on the mission's purpose, organization, and work, see the memorandum "Die Vatikanische Hilfsmission in Russland," AA, PO II, PO 3 Vat., Russland, Vol. 3.

of the international implications of a working alliance with Rome. Litvinov, however, regarded matters dealing with the Church or the Vatican as a purely internal affair having no connection to him or foreign policy. There was no official interest at this time in a treaty or direct relations with the Vatican. However, Moscow still desired to maintain unofficial contact with Rome, and so the conversations went on. Brockdorff's report was now relayed directly to Pacelli in Berlin, who acted as the Vatican permanent contact in these discussions.[34]

By mid-1924 the Papal Relief Mission no longer functioned in Russia, and the last semi-official group that could represent the Curia in the Soviet Union had left. Yet the Church under no circumstances desired to lose its contacts with Russia. As an alternative means Pacelli was therefore authorized cautiously to begin discussions in Berlin with the Russian Ambassador about the possibility of sending an apostolic delegate to Moscow. According to Austrian Minister Pastor, in autumn 1924 Gasparri had favored urging full diplomatic relations with the Russians at once, but other influential cardinals who harbored strong antipathies toward Communism opposed it. A compromise was therefore reached by merely proposing that an apostolic delegate be named.[35] The Vatican viewed the delegate's role as one which would maintain contact with the government of the Soviet Union in order to deal with the problems of Catholics within that country. Should Moscow then desire formal diplomatic ties, these could be established at a later date. Moscow, however, while interested, made this proposal contingent on the Vatican's recognition of the regime before negotiations began, something which the Vatican of course refused to do, since this would give Moscow the objective that it had desired without granting any reciprocal concessions. Throughout the fall of 1924 Pacelli met with Ambassador Nicolai Krestinski in Berlin in an effort to resolve the problem and to set ground rules for the selection of a Catholic clergy in Russia, but nothing came of the talks since neither side was willing to compromise.[36]

[34] AA, RM 70, Vol. 2, Brockdorff to AA, April 16, 1924. AA, BRV 1041, Vol. 1, Brockdorff to AA, June 8, 1924.

[35] Pastor, p. 815.

[36] AA, PO II, PO 3 Vat., Russland, Vol. 1, Meyer to AA, February 10, 1924; memorandum of AA, February 28, 1925. FFO, Z Russie 124, de Margerie to FFO, February 6, 1925. In 1927 a renewed persecution in the Soviet Union of Catholics caused Catholic leaders in Germany to urge the government once more to try to mediate between Rome and Moscow, since it would also serve German interests to have both parties obligated to the Reich. AA, Geheim Vat., Pol. 3, Wallroth (AA) to Brockdorff, August 30, 1927. During the conversations which Brockdorff once more began with Chicherin over the matter, he learned that the Soviet Union might be interested in

By 1925 Pacelli had become a familiar figure in Berlin. He frequented the diplomatic round of social events and was known for his keen analysis of political events as well as his wit and use of the *bon mot*.[37] The value of his presence in the German capital for ready consultation had already been demonstrated in the preceding year or two. Nevertheless he still maintained his official residence in Munich, returning there as often as he could. The Reich's request for a full-time diplomatic representative accredited and residing in the German capital had been only partly fulfilled since 1919. But by 1925 Bavaria already had a concordat, and Poland had initialed a new one with the Vatican, the contents of which contained clauses which affected Germany's eastern borders and would be a subject for important discussion between Rome and Berlin. In other words, there now existed church-state agreements both within and without Germany's borders which could have a bearing on the Reich's conduct with the Catholic Church. There was an increasing number of questions dealing with internal affairs which could best be handled between Reich officials and the Nuncio on a personal basis and not long distance via Munich. The Nuncio's absence did not facilitate discussion of the foreign policy matters for which Berlin sought Vatican aid. Despite some Protestant resentment at seeing a Papal representative there, the Reich Government made clear that it urgently desired and needed his presence. But even after the signing of the Bavarian concordat—the ostensible reason for his remaining in Munich—Pacelli appeared reluctant to leave his beloved Bavaria and still had not moved to Berlin. In conversations with the Bavarian Minister-President in January he indicated that for the time being, although his visits to the Reich capital would be more frequent and lengthier, he still intended to reside in Munich.

On March 9, 1925, however, Stresemann wrote to Bergen asking

agreeing to issuing a unilateral circular regulating the legal position of the Church in the Soviet Union, but it would not agree to a concordat. Some time before, Chicherin, in a conversation with Pacelli in Berlin, had made a similar suggestion without much elaboration. The German Ambassador once more relayed the Russian's opinions to Pacelli, but Rome showed no desire to continue the negotiations. Brockdorff suspected that the Vatican had not thought the discussions with Moscow would result in much more. The Curia had received reports that the conditions of Catholics in the Soviet Union were so unsatisfactory and persecution was pursued with such vigor that Rome believed that the two sides were too far apart for further discussion to have any purpose at that time. AA, Geheim Vat., Pol. 3, Brockdorff to AA, August 29, 1927 and to Zech, September 8, 1927. For an opinion on Russo-Vatican relations by a close co-worker of Pacelli, see Robert Leiber's statements in Wilhelm Sandfuch's *Die Aussenminister der Päpste* (Munich, 1962), p. 116.

[37] Secretary of State and Chief of the Reich Chancellery Hermann Pünder stated that Pacelli was extremely well informed, a good conversationalist, and had become very influential in Berlin even in non-Catholic circles. Hermann Pünder, *Von Preussen nach Europa* (Stuttgart, 1968), pp. 119-120.

him to discuss the Reich's problem with Curial officials. For some time now the desirability of locating the Nuncio's permanent residence in the Reich capital had been impressed on the Curia. The Reich Government had been reasonable in 1920 when the Nuncio, while being accredited *de jure* to Berlin, explained that negotiations for a Bavarian concordat had detained him in Munich, but the ratification of the concordat no longer sustained this argument. Moreover, Pacelli, in accordance with tradition, was as Nuncio the doyen of the diplomatic corps. Edgar Vincent Viscount D'Abernon, the English Ambassador, complained that since he, the Englishman, was the "stand in" for the doyen, he never knew whether at a given moment the Nuncio would be present to carry out his duties, such as appearing at the ceremonial functions which normally the doyen was expected to fulfill. Stresemann added further that a "whole series of highly political questions" should be handled in personal discussions with the Papal envoy. The Reich Government should not have to request Pacelli to come to Berlin every time such situations arose. The Reich Government, said the Foreign Minister, considered it "very important that the Nuncio be in contact with political authorities in Berlin and not merely form his impressions in Munich."[38]

Apparently Pacelli did personally regret leaving Munich and sought to delay his official departure as long as possible. A man who liked to keep close control over all aspects of a situation, he was reluctant to forfeit supervision of the affairs in Munich and believed that he could handle both positions competently, at least for a while yet. As a diplomat who knew and was attuned to Bavarian sensibilities, he did not desire to awaken Munich's fear, by too abrupt a departure after the conclusion of concordat negotiations, that the Munich nunciature would be downgraded or that the Bavarians would lose the prestige and privileged status which they had within the Reich as the only state allowed to maintain association with a foreign power. Gasparri, however, from his position in Rome, had a larger view of political priorities and now, with the Bavarian concordat already signed, could not object to Stresemann's arguments. Accordingly the Cardinal Secretary of State informed the Foreign Minister that Pacelli had been instructed to take up residence in the German capital as soon as possible. Both sides seemed satisfied with the decision, for it finally completed the regularization of German-Vatican relations, begun in 1919, and it paralleled the normalization also occurring in Germany's relations with other governments during 1924-1925. The Reich now hoped for the establishment of better communication links so that Berlin's policies could

[38] AA, RM 70, Vol. 2, Stresemann to Bergen, March 9, 1925.

be more speedily and, hopefully, more favorably reported to Rome. The Vatican likewise now hoped that with the precedent set in Bavaria for regularizing church-state relations, Pacelli, in coming to Berlin armed with this treaty, could concentrate his efforts on promoting the long-desired Reich concordat.

Once the Nuncio announced his intention of moving to Berlin permanently, a small problem arose which, though in itself unimportant, indicated the intricacies of the relationship of state to central government and the protective attitude of the *Länder* for their particularist rights. It may also have been a belief that exactly such a situation might arise which had influenced Pacelli to delay his formal departure from Munich and to "let sleeping dogs lie." The Prussian Government informed the Foreign Office that as soon as the Nuncio officially took up residence in Berlin the Prussian Government would request the German Ambassador at the Vatican to be also officially designated as Prussian Minister to the Holy See and to have the Nuncio formally accredited not only to the Reich Government but to the Prussian Government as well. Prussia maintained that since the principal concerns in church-state relations—education, diocesan boundaries, etc.—came within the province of state governments, it believed it would be better for the Prussian Cabinet to be directly accredited to the Holy See. Despite the agreement of 1919 empowering the German Ambassador to act also in Prussia's interests without specific accreditation, Prussia now felt that diplomats instructed to deal with Germany as a whole could not properly negotiate particular or individual problems of concern to Prussia alone unless they were specifically designated to do so. Also the traditional rivalry between Prussia and Bavaria as well as the growing rivalry between Prussia and the Reich no doubt played a role in Prussia's considerations. If the Reich representative at the Vatican and the nuncio to the Reich were also designated representatives to and from the Prussian Government, this would be a matter of internal German "one upmanship" over Bavarian diplomacy.

To Gasparri's logical mind this amounted to needless formality and petty internal bickering, and his initial reaction to Prussia's request was to call it "illogical and peculiar" since "if someone represents the whole, he does not need accreditation for one's parts besides." The Foreign Office relayed the Vatican's desire to the Prussian Cabinet to leave things as they were and added its own vote in favor of the *status quo*. Nevertheless, despite this negative advice, in 1925 Prussia once more made clear its desire for this formal recognition, never failing to cite the Bavarian example. It looked as though Prussia, if it did not get its request, might try to obstruct the harmonious association between Germany and the Curia. Foreseeing some potential difficulties and trying to smooth any injured pride, Pacelli persuaded Rome to change its mind and to make the concession. Prussia's constitutional right to this representation could not be disputed. The accreditation would make little practical difference and would cost little except for added titles, plus the added care that the same diplomat would have to take in constantly considering in which capacity he was functioning at a given moment. On the other hand, Prussia's goodwill was needed if a Reich concordat were to be brought to conclusion. Failing that, Rome would then have to propose *Länder* concordats and would in any case have to deal directly with Prussia. In sum, it was better in this case to bow to Prussia's wishes.[39]

As a consequence, in June the Nuncio to Berlin and the Ambassador to the Vatican were confirmed with double accreditation from and to the Reich and Prussian Governments. Essentially it changed nothing, and Bergen did not even take time to present his new credentials in person to Gasparri but merely informed him in writing of his new position. Bavaria, which still maintained diplomatic ties with Rome, took a cynical view toward these maneuverings, regarding them as indications of Prussia's jealousy of what Bavaria already had. Ritter pointed out that in 1919 Prussia had almost succeeded in eliminating the Bavarian mission to the Vatican by transforming the Prussian mission into a Reich embassy. Now, six years later, Prussia wanted separate accreditation, claiming that its interests were not always the same as those of the Central Government, the very argument Prussia opposed when Bavaria made it in 1919 on its own behalf. To Ritter it appeared as if Prussia were falling into the hole that it had tried to dig for Bavaria in 1919 and was now trying to demand more attention for its own claims without altering the diplomatic personnel.[40] The dispute nevertheless indicated the rivalry and particularist tendencies still present within Weimar as well as the conviction of both major German states that individual representation was necessary since their interests were neither always the same nor best served by a uniform Reich policy. In any event the Vatican had sought to satisfy everyone with an eye to its overall objectives. Gasparri had pleased the Reich Government by transferring the Nuncio's residence to the German capital and had pleased the particularist sensibilities in Germany's two largest states by largely symbolic moves—retention of the nunciature in Munich and the confirmation of the nuncio in Berlin as Vatican envoy to Prussia.

[39] AA, PO II, PO 10 Vat., Vol. 1, memorandum of Meyer-Rodehüser, April 2, 1925.
[40] GSTA, MA 104455, Ritter to BFM, June 20, 1925. AA, PO II, PO 10 Vat., Vol. 1, memorandum of Meyer-Rodehüser, April 2, 1925.

B. 1925

The Church declared the year 1925 a Holy Year, a year for special prayers for peace and unity among peoples. There were grounds for Vatican optimism, since the first steps to solve the reparations question had been taken with the Dawes plan in 1924, the easing of the Franco-German antagonism over the Ruhr, and the beginning of negotiations which eventually led to Locarno. The Curia's working relationship with the Ebert Government had been advantageous to both states. The decrease in international tensions as well as the recent conclusion of the Bavarian concordat helped to focus the Vatican's attention on its policy toward Germany. In 1925, President Ebert, one of the founding fathers of the Republic and its chief executive since its inception, died, and the political uncertainties caused by this event now gave Rome another reason for reappraising the internal German situation. Always uneasy about Socialist aims, Rome nevertheless had raised no major objections in the period after the war as the Center forged what Rome considered to be a temporary coalition with the Social Democrats which had brought both of them to power in a coalition with the Democrats. Ebert, a Socialist, had understood the importance of Vatican support for Germany and had generally favored cooperation. But since many of the opposition leaders to either a *Länder* or a Reich concordat were also Social Democrats, Vatican officials wondered if they should now encourage the Center Party to cooperate as closely with the Social Democratic Party (SPD) as it had been doing in the past. The problem became more complex, for in 1925 in the second round of the campaign for the presidency, former Chancellor Wilhelm Marx, a Catholic, received the support not only of his Center Party but also that of the Social Democrats to run against the war hero General Paul von Hindenburg, candidate of the conservatives and the Right.

If the Vatican spoke out against Socialism, it would anger the Social Democrats and possibly cause them to withdraw their support from Marx. If the Vatican refused to endorse the Center policy, it might cause many conservative Catholics to bolt from the party and withhold their votes from Marx; it might even cause a rift in the party and in any event deliver the election to Hindenburg. A collapse of the Center-Social Democratic coalition would allow the parties of the Right—the German People's Party (DVP) and the National German People's Party (DNVP)—to gain in strength and place the country on a more conservative, nationalist course, a move which, as Marx believed, would certainly not be as beneficial to the Church as the results of the Center-Socialist partnership had been so far.

11. Chancellor Wilhelm Marx waiting in line at the polling place next to a Center Party (*[Z]entrum*) placard, May 1924. One month later he was able to form his second cabinet

The electoral race between Marx, supported by the democratic Left (the Democrats, the Center, and the Socialists), and Hindenburg, supported by the conservative Right (the German National People's Party and the German People's Party), also pitted a Catholic against a Protestant, in turn lending a confessional tint to the campaign. Moreover, the juxtaposition of the two men, one a leader and proclaimed supporter of Weimar, the other a former field marshal and personification of the Imperial tradition, revived the speculation about whether or not Germany's political future would lead to a continuation of the Republic or toward a return to a monarchical form of government. Should Hindenburg, an avowed monarchist, win and help to persuade the nation to accept a restoration of the Hohenzollerns, the ensuing international repercussions would certainly forestall the pacification of Europe and endanger Stresemann's efforts to end some of the Powers' mistrust of Germany by signing a security pact. The Papacy was thus vitally concerned with the internal situation. However, it also posed a problem. In return for Socialist support, if Marx won he might be forced to grant the Socialist demands for holding the line against more religious influence in educational affairs and for taking a stronger stance in working out a concordat with Rome. Yet a victory by Hindenburg posed the possibility of a monarchical restoration which could wreck Papal hopes for international stability[41] and strengthen Protestant influence within Prussia and in the Central Government, thus canceling out some of the Catholic gains made since 1919. Therefore, to prevent any negative Papal initiative and to shore up Center ties with the Holy See, Marx journeyed to Rome in April 1925 to explain to disturbed Vatican officials how his connection with the Socialists presented minimal danger to the Church and to gain Curial endorsement for his own candidacy.

Marx discussed the topic with the Pontiff during his audience on April 21. The Chancellor first outlined how, with the anarchy and deprivations caused by the war, the Center Party had had an especially difficult task in helping to establish a functioning government which would restore order in Germany. The Center's work was all the more important since the Revolution of 1918 brought socialist radicals to the fore in the workers' and soldiers' councils. Necessity as well as practical politics dictated that the Center ally with the Social Democrats. They had been the single largest party in the Reichstag in the immediate pre-war years, and the Majority Socialist wing of the party had appeared willing to set aside much of its theoretical Marxist ideals to pursue a functioning program of practical politics in the Weimar period. Protestant conservative circles, on the other hand, with which the Center cooperated before the war, refused to participate in the organization of the new governmental structure in 1919 but rather had preferred to distance themselves from the new government's policies. If the Center was to reach its goals of seeing a nation created which conformed to the Christian view of man and in which the Church would have the freedom to perform its ministry without prejudice or unfair restrictions, the Center had had to join with those willing to undertake the responsibility of government and could not abandon the political field to the Socialists. As much as Catholics might have hesitated to enter into this political alliance at other times, in 1919 it had been necessary in order to offer some influence from

[41] BelgFO, St. Siège 1923-28, Beyens to Hymans, April 3, 1925.

Christian circles upon the structure and framework of the new state and society.

Marx then pointed to the favorable results of the alliance—law and order restored in the Reich and a constitution which offered the Church even greater freedom than ever before. The Social Democrats had given up their more radical policies and allowed themselves to be influenced by the Center. Because of their cooperation with the Catholic Party, the Socialists no longer professed a radical anti-clericalism, and Christian laboring men, who in former times felt harassed by Socialists among their fellow-workers, could now meet and participate in their organizations more openly. This in turn weakened the Socialist proselytizing among the workers and in fact strengthened loyalty among the working class to the Church.

Marx, however, did not minimize the ideological differences still existing between the two parties and emphasized that the Center had to remain ever-vigilant lest its principles be compromised. Yet, to his knowledge, he said, this had not occurred in the six years in which the Center had worked with the Socialists. He warned, however, that there was still much social and economic depression in Germany, and any dangerous unrest among the workers, even Catholic workers, could cause Socialist tenets to gain increased popularity again among the laboring class. Therefore one of the functions of the Center in working with the SPD was to avert any spread of Marxism or to contain its implementation by acting as a counterweight to the more doctrinaire Socialists. Should the middle-class parties break off all contact with the Socialists, then the Socialist Party, under pressure from below, would become more radical and drift toward the Communists. Many observers, said Marx, who did not know the German political scene intimately might think it more advisable for the Center to ally with the so-called Right, or more conservative parties of the middle and upper classes, since this at least would assure the maintenance of Christian and of middle-class principles in government. Unfortunately, said Marx, the *Rechtsparteien* were not the conservative parties of former times based upon Christian principles. The membership of these parties now consisted of many people opposed to anything Catholic, willing to play upon confessional differences to disturb or discredit the Weimar Government. If the Center had to preserve its Christianity against Social Democracy, it also had to preserve its Catholicism against the Protestant *Rechtsparteien*.[42]

[42] AW, 1A 25z, 9, "Die Politik der deutschen Katholiken," Marx with cover letter to Bertram, July 21, 1925. Although the Chancellor put these thoughts in writing after the election, he mentions having presented these arguments to the Pontiff during their April meeting.

Marx had tried to show the pragmatic reasons for the cooperation, its good effects, and the dangers to German society of a radicalization if the SPD were left without Centrist support and guidance. He had had to make full use of his persuasive powers in order to convince Rome that his manner leading the party indeed accorded with the best interests of the Church. Nevertheless, after his conversations with the Curial officials Marx came away with the feeling that the Vatican, or at least the Pontiff and Gasparri, while cautious and somewhat wary, nevertheless understood the difference between more moderate Socialism in Germany and the radical, anti-clerical form that it assumed in other countries and were satisfied with the former Chancellor's explanations for a continuation of the alliance.[43]

But the mistrust for the political Left also had strong adherents in the Curia. Even if German Socialists were not as radical as those of other countries, there was always an underlying fear in Curial circles that they were irreconcilable opponents of the Church, at least over school questions, and Socialist opposition to a Reich concordat and to the recently concluded Bavarian treaty only reinforced this opinion.[44] On his April visit to Rome, Marx had been given an indication of the deep distrust of some Vatican officials for the Socialists when he met with Under Secretary Pizzardo. After dispensing with polite formalities, the German asked quite frankly what, if anything, was bothering Rome about Center Party policy. Pizzardo answered that he had received word that the Center was forcing "good Catholics to vote Social Democratic" in Center districts. Dumbfounded that such a matter could be believed in the Vatican, Marx explained that the German electoral system granted a free and secret ballot which did not allow for such voting procedures. Germany used a method of proportional representation in which voters cast their ballots according to party electoral lists. It would make no sense for the Center to concede an electoral seat to the Socialists, especially in Center territory. Later Marx men-

[43] Cologne, Marx, 1070 Nr. 66, pp. 24-30. The diocesan archives contain letters from the clergy such as that of Paul Kaletta, pastor in the diocese of Breslau, who called on his Cardinal to speak out against the Center-Socialist coalition. He cited as reasons that the Catholic voters, seeing the Center cooperate with Marxists, had now lost their fear of Socialism and were even voting Communist, while other Catholics were not voting for the Center precisely because of the alliance. The Center, said the priest, was losing votes both ways and was making it difficult for the clergy to preach against the danger of anti-Christian Marxism. Such letters no doubt also caused the hierarchy to question the Chancellor's appraisal of the situation. AW, 1A 25z, 8, letter of Kaletta to Bertram, January 1, 1924.

[44] Engel-Janosi, *Chaos*, pp. 82-83. See also Erich Matthias and Rudolf Morsey, eds., *Das Ende der Parteien, 1933* (Düsseldorf, 1960), p. 284 and Robert Leiber, "Reichskonkordat und Ende der Zentrumspartei," *Stimmen der Zeit*, CLXVII (1960/61), 213.

tioned his meeting with Pizzardo to Msgr. Steinmann, the German Embassy's religious expert, and Steinmann stated that the Embassy staff had already tried to refute these stories on numerous occasions, but they still persisted. Pizzardo's objection, only one of several to the alliance, given to Marx during the visit to Rome, illustrates the deep-seated suspicions which Curial officials still harbored against Socialism, despite both the Vatican's and the Center's good working relations with Ebert's Government.[45]

In Germany distrust of Socialism was equally prevalent in some Catholic circles. During the campaign most bishops kept a discreet silence, but the majority of church dignitaries disliked Marx's dependence on the votes of Social Democrats, which were more numerous than those of the Center Party, and disapproved of the Prussian Center's ties with the Socialist Party. In the days before the election, circulars put out by conservative local groups or the national *Ring der deutschen Katholiken* used history in appealing to the voters by evoking memories of the *Kulturkampf* and reminding them that what Catholics had suffered for their religious principles would be in vain should Marx and his Social Democratic allies win. Hopes for a school law which would provide class time for religious instruction, for constitutional guarantees of the sanctity of marriage, for protection of the economic order and the rights of private property—all these would be lost.[46] It was thus unfortunate that while the campaign was progressing, when electoral propaganda had not only concentrated on political practice and tangible results but had aroused re-examination of the ideological bases of the alliance partners, the *Osservatore* on April 21 published a lead article entitled "*Il socialismo in marcia*" (Socialism on the March), expressing the opinion that an immense gulf divided the Christian and Socialist view of life. They shared no common ground; any belief that they could work together was illusory and dangerous.[47]

The Right—the German People's Party, the Nationalists, and the National Socialists—gleefully seized upon this statement to prove that the Vatican supported their view, and that Rome tacitly preferred Hindenburg to a Catholic president, who would have to make concessions to the Socialists. It was no coincidence that the conservatives pointed out that Rome chose such a time to make its remarks. The reason could only have been the political alliance of the Center with the Social Democratic Party in the current presidential election. The Bavarian People's Party (BVP), a Catholic sister party and a traditional Center ally on many matters, had already broken with the Center over

[45] Cologne, Marx, 1070 Nr. 156, "Zwei Audienzen beim Heiligen Vater," pp. 3-4.
[46] *Die Zeit*, April 22, 1925.
[47] *Osservatore*, April 21, 1925.

this issue. Now the conservatives were appealing to all Catholics to follow the lead of the Bavarians, for if they valued the Christian education of their children, the inviolability of property, and a Christian approach to life, they should heed the warning of the Holy Father— "whosoever votes for Marx is working for the Social Democrats."[48] The repeated affirmations in the Right press that the Holy See disapproved of the Center-Socialist alliance was only reinforced and given added weight by the dramatic moves of some prominent conservative Catholics. Baron Clemens von Loë, one of the leaders of the Rhenish Farmers' League (*Rheinischer Bauernverein*) and well-known Catholic, signed a petition supporting Hindenburg, and in Trier, despite efforts of the ordinary, Bishop Bornewasser, to the contrary, Count Nayhauss-Cormans, influential Center member, defected and announced his support for the Field Marshal.[49]

The connections had thus been made in the minds of the public that the Vatican probably disapproved of the policies of the very party which had been called into existence to safeguard Catholic interests. The Center, clearly upset by the weakening of its electoral chances, requested that Rome clarify or disavow the interpretations attributed to the article. Thereupon the Vatican on April 23 published a denial of the use made of its initial article in the *Osservatore*, accusing German newspapers of citing individual sentences out of context, distortion, and complete misinterpretation of the editorial's intent. The *Osservatore* added that its comments had made no reference to the German election and that the Vatican intended to speak neither for nor against Marx's candidacy since the race was an internal affair from which the Vatican would like to remain aloof.[50]

Diplomats, however, knew that such an article would not have been written without cause. Bergen therefore sought to learn from Vatican officials the exact reason for the original column story. Apparently Rome had received reports of numerous anti-Catholic attacks by Socialist politicians and journalists in various countries of late, most notably the recent harsh criticism by the Belgian Socialist newspaper *Le Peuple* of the beloved Cardinal Mercier and the Socialist press campaign in Czechoslovakia against the hierarchy. The moment seemed propitious for the Vatican's newspaper to expound on the ideological irreconcilability of the two philosophies. Newspapers and politicians in Germany quickly picked up these statements to interpret and use during the presidential election. The Vatican, realizing the error in timing and how its remarks were being used, quickly denied any in-

48 *Die Zeit*, April 22, 1925.

49 FFO, Allemagne 371, de Margerie to FFO, April 23, 1925.

50 *Wolff's Telegraphisches Büro*, April 24, 1925, taken from *Osservatore* of April 23, 1925.

tent to have its general comments applied to Germany in particular, and Gasparri, at an interview for representatives of large Catholic newspapers, took pains to emphasize that the April 21 article was in no way directed against the Center candidate.[51] Rather, he said, in view of Socialism's worldwide policies and of its anti-Catholic activities in several countries, the Curia had felt constrained to point out the basic differences between the Church and Socialism in general and to warn Catholics of the dangers of cooperation with its adherents. One day later, on the 24th, the *Osservatore* backed up the Cardinal's statement by categorically stating that the Vatican took a neutral position toward the German election and was not against Marx.[52]

In the Rhineland, Marx's home area, the *Kölnische Zeitung*, a leading liberal journal, also condemned what it termed the misrepresentation of the Vatican's meaning in the article of April 21. The newspaper emphasized that the Vatican scrupulously avoided involvement in a nation's domestic affairs not directly pertaining to the Church, especially when its disapproval of Center policy would be tantamount to condemning the candidacy of so loyal a Catholic as Marx.[53] Marx was also quick to reaffirm that Rome had not intended to condemn the Center's policy in Germany. He maintained that no conflict existed between the Vatican and the Center. His conversations with the Holy Father and the Cardinal Secretary of State led him to believe that Rome did see the situation "correctly," that the Social Democrats in Germany were different from Socialists in many other countries, that they were not unalterably opposed to the Church, and that many clauses in the Weimar Constitution favorable to the Church had actually been written into law with SPD aid.[54] Rome's condemnation of Socialism and its rapid denial that it applied to the situation in Germany left many politicians bewildered or at least puzzled. Despite efforts by both Vatican and Center officials to stress that there was no disagreement about the party's political course, the doubt remained of how the Vatican, usually very deliberate before it acted, could not have foreseen that the article would have some negative reaction in Germany unless it was intended to do so. But, then, why did it take pains to disavow the statement?

A clue to Vatican policy here can be found in a report of one of Marx's Roman informants, which he claimed allowed him to understand the puzzling situation. It was already clear to the Germans from previous diplomatic reports that certain Curial officials admired Right-

---

[51] AA, PO II, PO 2 Vat., Vol. 2, Bergen to AA, April 22, 1925.

[52] *Osservatore*, "Fra Marx a Hindenburg," April 24, 1925.

[53] *Kölnische Zeitung*, April 22, 1925.

[54] Cologne, Marx, 1070 Nr. 66, pp. 24-30.

ist political philosophies, the most notable and vocal of whom was Under Secretary of State Pizzardo. Gasparri was in many ways more in the Christian democratic tradition, a disciple of some of the social ideas of Leo XIII, while Pizzardo was politically more reactionary and a strong Italian nationalist. The agent attributed to Pizzardo's influence many of the more politically conservative pronouncements emanating from the Vatican in the last few months which had caused diplomats to wonder about Vatican policy. While many statements dealt with the Curia's relations to Italian politics, another example was the alleged Vatican support for Hindenburg in the warning issued against Socialism. Articles in Italian newspapers questioning the Center-Socialist connection in Germany stemmed from Pizzardo, one of the key people in the Vatican then urging the Pontiff to publish an encyclical condemning Socialism as sinful. The agent claimed that a great furor and debate was taking place behind closed doors over this subject.[55]

The article of April 21 had probably been sent to press without Gasparri's knowledge of the exact contents. Once he learned and appraised the problems that it would create for the Center, he then took steps to undo as much of the damage as possible. This may, therefore, have been the reason why Gasparri, in the days after the article's publication, went out of his way to state that the Church's comments were not meant to reflect upon the German situation.[56] Apparently Gasparri had taken pains to ensure that the *Osservatore*'s article about Socialism, even if its appearance had been poorly timed, should not hurt Marx's chances of winning in Germany. On the other hand, he desired to make it clear that Rome was not exerting any pressure to have him elected as the first Catholic president of the Reich. The guideline the Vatican set for itself in this matter was to observe a strict neutrality. Ritter also relates that, in conversations in April, he noted the unusual efforts the Cardinal took to reassert that the Vatican considered the election a purely internal German affair. Gasparri remarked how careful he had been to show that the Holy See was not interfering in internal affairs. The German nationalists such as Luden-

[55] Cologne, Marx, 1070 Nr. 68, unsigned report of an agent, no date, pp. 167-168.

[56] Another incident tends to confirm the fact that Gasparri was not supervising all public statements of policy at this time. On May 2, the Belgian Ambassador Beyens asked Gasparri about an article in the *Osservatore* one day before the German election which said that during his years of military service the Field Marshal had never committed any unjust or uncivil acts. Beyens regarded the statement incorrect and pro-German. Gasparri replied that the article had not been submitted to him and that Beyens should take it up with the editor of the *Osservatore*—an odd comment for one who usually was kept well informed on what was published. BelgFO, St. Siège 1923-28, Beyens to BelgFO, May 12, 1925.

dorff, he said, should take note of Rome's keeping out of the election since they had dragged out the old shibboleth of Ultramontanism and had disturbed the confessional peace in the last year or so.[57] The Vatican had been distressed about anti-Catholic sentiments which had become visible in the press in 1924, especially after the signing of the Bavarian concordat and the announcement that the Nuncio would take up residence in Berlin. The old cry that with a Papal representative in Berlin Rome would gain undue influence and seek to receive large concessions for the Church in matters of education and State support of the Catholic clergy, as witnessed in the recently signed treaty with Bavaria, was heard once more. Ludendorff, with all of his anti-Catholic accusatory speeches at his trial in 1924, had brought all of these sentiments to the fore, and they were now being played upon by Marx's opponents in hinting that a vote for a Catholic president would inevitably help the growth of Papal influence in Berlin.[58]

Aware of the sensibilities of many Germans and the realities of the situation, the Vatican therefore took steps not to arouse any further antipathy or open itself to a charge of having used its influence to have a Catholic elected president by overtly endorsing Marx. This might, politically speaking, only weaken the chances of seeing one of Rome's prime objectives, a concordat, effectively steered through the Prussian *Landtag* or German Reichstag. Therefore two aspects of the Curia's international policy appeared to be working at cross-purposes, specifically as it affected Germany. Rome, impressed by the dangers of Socialism in several countries, had published its warning on Socialism, yet immediately disavowed its application to the German situation and stressed its neutrality in that country's elections. The situation, puzzling to outsiders trying to apprehend the direction of Vatican policy, demonstrated the differing opinions within the Curia about ideological as well as tactical priorities. But by the time the strands of this complicated situation were disentangled, explanations given, and analyses made, it already had had an effect in Germany.

In publishing the article on April 21, the Vatican wished perhaps to make a broad statement of its attitude toward Socialism, or perhaps the members of the Curia who were uneasy with the political alliance in Germany published the article to serve as a general warning, which Gasparri's explanation then clarified or modified. Whatever the varying opinions within the Curia and the exact reasons for the Vatican's actions in April 1925, the original statement in the *Osservatore* had been seized upon by the Right and anti-Marx forces, since in simple cam-

[57] GSTA, Ges. Päpstl. Stuhl 999, Ritter to BFM, May 1, 1925.
[58] Cologne, Marx, 1070 Nr. 66, pp. 26-27.

paign rhetoric it could be said that the Pope had warned against Socialism, and any party in alliance with the SPD had been tainted red by association. Despite the disclaimers of the Vatican on April 23-24, which only then appeared in the German press one day later, immediately before the election, and despite its emphasis on its neutrality, the impression that the first article had made as it was bruited about by the Rightist press was undoubtedly hard to erase from the minds of many Catholic voters. The Center press later felt that the Vatican's denial did not succeed in offsetting the original impression, and Rightists continued calmly to hand out pamphlets with the original statement at church doors up until the day of election.[59]

On April 26 the Germans went to the polls, and Marx was defeated by almost one million votes (14.6 million votes for Hindenburg and 13.7 million for Marx). Catholics comprised about 33⅓ percent of the population.[60] The combined support of the Democrats, Socialists, and Center should have made the vote at least closer than it was. Yet many electoral districts with overwhelming Catholic populations, normally Center strongholds, had defected to the more conservative candidate because of a dislike of Socialism. The Bavarian People's Party (BVP), for example, which in national parliamentary elections normally polled about one million votes, had openly endorsed the Field Marshal, and in 1925 many of its regular electors chose not to cast their ballots at all. Clearly then, not all Catholics had given the Center candidate their votes.[61] Many factors, ideological, social, and economic, had influenced Catholics to elect Hindenburg, yet Vatican support, which could have been persuasive for undecided Catholics, was not forthcoming; at best Rome issued a neutral statement, at worst a warning against Marx's allies. Officially it had indeed remained neutral, but by that very act it had exerted an influence which had grave consequences for the future of German history. The Right had now gained strength in both the Reich Government and within the Center Party itself.

[59] John K. Zeender, "The German Catholics and the presidential election of 1925," *Journal of Modern History*, LXIII (1963), 374. Zeender gives a thorough treatment of the reasons—economic, social, and ideological—for the defection of Catholics from the Center candidate.

[60] Many books (William Langer, ed., *An encyclopedia of world history*, 5th ed., Boston, 1972, p. 1007, for example) make much of the fact that if the Communists, who put up their own candidate, had given their almost two million votes to Marx he would have won. Not enough emphasis is given to the fact that the more than one million Catholic votes withheld from Marx also lost him the election.

[61] See Germany, *Statistisches Jahrbuch 1924-25*, pp. 394-395. Alfred Milatz, *Wähler und Wahlen in der Weimarer Republic* (Bonn, 1965), pp. 119-120. Zeender, "Presidential Election," 374-378. Milatz, along with other German historians, argues that the one million votes usually cast for BVP went to Hindenburg. Zeender finds, on the basis of his analysis of the electoral figures, that about 500,000 of the party's regular voters were apathetic about the election and did not go to the polls at all.

After the election, the Papacy was very much interested in learning whether the new president would set a different tone in Germany's policy than that which had characterized the general good relations between Germany and the Vatican during Ebert's tenure. Gasparri's first reaction had been negative. Shortly after the election he told Austrian Minister Pastor that he frankly wondered whether the selection of Hindenburg had been an error on the part of the German people because the fear which a former military leader as head of state would evoke in the various European capitals might upset the general diplomatic equilibrium which had been constructed with such difficulty and, secondly, because Ludendorff might exert a negative influence on his former colleague by prejudicing him against Catholics, thus disturbing domestic harmony. He noted that the Protestants had voted *en masse* for Hindenburg while the Catholics had only partially supported their co-religionist Marx. Several days later, while still of the private opinion that perhaps the election outcome had been a mistake, demonstrating the political immaturity of the Germans by "rocking the boat" at this time, he had calmed down sufficiently to tell Pastor that he was now reserving judgment and would wait and study the President's first actions and his choice of advisors.[62]

Immediately after the election, while expressing some hope for the future, Gasparri also voiced his uneasiness to the Belgian Ambassador over the potential problems that the election might cause. It was not exactly correct that Hindenburg had won only because the people had faith in him personally. Other reasons—the current surge of nationalism and monarchism due to the economic problems and the government's inability to counter successfully French demands at the conference table or in the Ruhr, the fear of Communism, and the prejudice of those who refused to vote for the Catholic Marx—all contributed to Hindenburg's victory. The selection of the Field Marshal, said the Cardinal, did nonetheless have political merit—he symbolized tradition, the old Germany, and unity around which the nation could rally after the crises of 1923-1924. Now it remained to see to whom he looked for counsel, who would urge him to act and speak out. This, said Gasparri, almost prophetically, would be important in the future for Germany.[63]

In speaking with the Germans, Gasparri's misgivings seemed less acute, his uneasiness more subdued, and he began to see the election

---

[62] HHSTA, 87, Pastor to Foreign Minister Mataja, May 8, 1925.

[63] BelgFO, St. Siège 1923-28, Beyens to BelgFO, August 2, 1925. Interestingly enough, in his analysis of the election, Gasparri, in conversation with the Belgian Ambassador, made no mention of the defections from the Center and of the *Osservatore* article of April 21 as two added reasons contributing to Hindenburg's victory. Either he did not see them as reasons or found them too embarrassing to mention to the Belgian.

in a more positive way. He now desired to emphasize Rome's good intentions to work with the new president. The Cardinal told Ritter that the Papacy sincerely wished the new head of state well and hoped that the confidence of the nation he had gained during the war would continue and help him in seeking the well-being of the German people. The Cardinal also took the opportunity to pass on to the Germans, in a spirit of friendly suggestion, his frank opinion on how the Field Marshal could avoid some of the political pitfalls which he might have to face. The Cardinal did not believe that the election result would increase confessional differences, since Hindenburg was a man of honor and above such strife. Moreover, it would make no sense for anyone in any position of responsibility to foster internal discord which could only be to the advantage of the Reich's external foes. But he did believe that, should the new President gravitate toward the circle of extreme nationalists or "saber rattlers," it could create international complications and in turn retard Germany's economic recovery, which at that moment looked more promising than it had previously. Given the recent statements made and the difficulties created by Ludendorff, the Cardinal warned Hindenburg, despite their close wartime collaboration, not to turn to his former colleague for advice. Germany had already had its share of difficulties, and Hindenburg had to be especially prudent in both statement and action since Europe frankly looked with some uneasiness upon a military man at the helm in Germany. Perhaps, suggested Gasparri, even a reassuring statement of peaceful intentions by the former Field Marshal would do not harm.[64]

By the end of April the Vatican had publicly taken an even more positive view of the new President, as if by stressing Hindenburg's good qualifications it either hoped to see them fulfilled in reality or, acknowledging the *fait accompli*, it sought to make the most of the given situation. The *Osservatore* of April 29 included an article praising Hindenburg's qualities, now calling the election a personal victory which clearly indicated that more extreme politicians of the Right would not gain the upper hand in a country with someone at the helm whose sense of law and order insured a stable internal and external policy.[65] Bergen, during his audience with Gasparri several days after the election, found the Cardinal generally calmer and more optimistic than he had been immediately after the vote. Gasparri, pleased with Hindenburg's statements that as the duly elected president he would uphold the Constitution, commented favorably on the Field Marshal's reputation for fairness and the high respect with which he was regarded in

[64] GSTA, Ges. Päpstl. Stuhl 999, Ritter to BFM, May 1, 1925.
[65] *Osservatore*, April 29, 1925.

Germany. Now as long as he remained free from chauvinistic influences, Gasparri once more reiterated, Germany could look forward to a period of consolidation and Europe to one of diplomatic relaxation.[66]

The Reich took steps soon after the election to show its regard for its Vatican connections and to dispel any lingering doubts about the Field Marshal's good intentions. During a Reichstag debate over the budget for foreign affairs on May 18 Stresemann took time to recall Germany's relations with the Holy See and what the Pontiff and his staff had done for the Reich. The indefatigable efforts of Rome to alleviate misery and uplift morale after the war and its efforts for mutual understanding among peoples would never be forgotten. German sentiments of gratitude found expression, he said, in the enormous number of pilgrims from Germany who were visiting the Eternal City during the Holy Year of 1925. By taking the opportunity of praising the Vatican, Stresemann indicated both the government's interest in strong ties with Rome and his belief that nothing had changed in their relationship. The French also interpreted the speech as significant, pointing out that Stresemann had gone out of his way in the Reichstag to use such laudatory language about the Vatican, that the speech was not delivered by a Center man, and that it came so soon after the election. It was clear to France that despite the change of the head of state, the Germans intended to maintain excellent relations with Rome, which had been of such benefit to them.[67]

Stresemann was correct in linking the German pilgrims' journey to Rome to its value for building good relations with the Holy See. An enormous number of German pilgrims had come to Rome during that year for the ceremonies, especially the canonization of Peter Canisius, the sixteenth-century German Jesuit missionary and scholar. In September, for example, the Embassy expected as many as 3,000 pilgrims in Rome at one time. The size and devotion of the German group deeply impressed all Vatican officials, and foreign diplomats were quick to observe how Pius, who was visibly pleased with the signs of loyalty to the Holy See, paid more than ordinary tribute to German Catholic piety by recalling his student days in Germany, and saying he could well understand the qualities of the German people.[68] The English Minister commented that the Holy Year had opened with German pilgrims and later closed with a pilgrimage from Germany. Although the pilgrims themselves had made the journey mostly for reasons of devotion and faith, the sheer numbers of those who came had certainly increased the diplomatic prestige of Germany at the Vatican. "There

[66] AA, PO II, PO 2 Vat., Vol. 2, Bergen to AA, May 2, 1925.

[67] FFO, Allemagne 371, Doulcet (Rome) to Briand, May 31, 1925.

[68] BFO, 371/11399/5412, annual report on the relations of the Holy See, 1925, p. 13.

is no doubt," the Englishman added, "that the Berlin Government realizes the general importance from the point of view of domestic and international policy, of strengthening its influence with the Holy See by all possible means."[69] It was such an atmosphere of mutual respect and regard which the German Government sought to foster and to make use of when it needed to seek the aid of the Holy See.

At the ceremony presenting the diplomatic corps to Hindenburg in mid-May, the President paused to converse with the Nuncio and to express his great desire to see him taking up his residence in Berlin, as Rome had promised two months earlier, reiterating that the representative of the Holy See could not continue commuting between Munich and the Reich capital. Although, as Pacelli conceded, the request might have reflected to some degree Prussian jealousy of Bavaria and uneasiness about the great influence which they believed the Nuncio could exert over Catholics if he continued to reside in the Bavarian capital, the fact that the new president took the time at the first diplomatic reception to stress the Reich's request was a significant demonstration of Hindenburg's personal interest and of the government's policy to continue the good working relationship of the last six years.[70] Pacelli further reassured the Vatican that Hindenburg had made a favorable initial impression on him, though he had not yet arrived at any firm opinions because of a lack of prolonged conversations with the President. Even Cardinal Schulte, who was in Rome in May, discussed the situation with Gasparri. The Cardinal of Cologne had been a supporter of Marx, a fellow Rhinelander, yet he did not voice any reservations about the winner, nor did he express any serious uneasiness about the outcome of the election. He assured Gasparri that the President would be a faithful guardian of the Republic's constitution and like a good soldier would honor his oath to defend it.[71] These reassurances, along with Hindenburg's own words, somewhat relieved the Vatican, which now expected the election of the new president not to alter the basic direction of German policy nor undertake any moves which would disturb the peace of Europe.

There were, however, other effects on the domestic affairs stemming from the election which involved the Vatican, namely the widening rift within the Center Party. Marx's defeat was widely attributed to his liberal leanings and his alliance with the Social Democrats,

---

[69] BFO, 371/11386/5408, Russell to Foreign Secretary Chamberlain, January 3, 1926.

[70] FFO, Allemagne 371, de Margerie to Briand, May 19, 1925. Hindenburg personally always got on well with Pacelli, and his attitude to the Vatican was cordial. Perhaps he had not forgotten that the Pope had spoken out against handing over the generals to the Allies in 1919.

[71] BelgFO, St. Siège 1923-28, Beyens to Hymans, May 16, 1925.

and the Right wing of the party now sought to sever the Socialist connection and the adoption of a more conservative policy. Religion had always held the Center together. During the *Kulturkampf* the Center received well over eighty percent of the Catholic vote. But since restrictions against the Church had been largely removed and Catholics were allowed to practice their religion freely, many Catholic voters increasingly leaned toward other parties and became divided over political and economic issues. In the 1920's the Center obtained only sixty percent of the Catholic vote.[72] The anti-Marx forces now tried to reunite the party on a more conservative basis combining the religious and politico-economic issues. They claimed that religion was in danger again, although the enemy was more subtle, attacking Christian principles and Catholic goals from within and in alliance with the Center, not from without and opposed to the Center. Moreover, the loss of Catholic votes and the open defection of the Bavarian People's Party proved that the Center's present course was interesting fewer Catholic voters than before. To regain the vote it was therefore morally and practically necessary to reject Marx and steer to the right. To aid in this drive the conservatives in the party naturally sought support from the Vatican and the hierarchy in Germany. In May, Count Anton Magnis, a leading member of the Right wing, wrote a lengthy position paper on the dangers of the Socialist connection and went to Rome with it, asking the Curia to back the position which he presented. He stressed that the cooperation between the two parties blurred the issues, confused the faithful, and fostered an uncertainty about values and what the electorate should really vote for. Since religion and the cause of the Church were in danger, Magnis requested the Pope to speak out and remind the party of its responsibilities. Gasparri replied to him equivocally, adding that although there was some truth to the Count's statement, the Vatican could not interfere in an internal affair, and that the bishops, who understood local conditions best, should clarify any questions of differences between Center and Socialist principles. Magnis, of course, was seeking to prompt the Vatican to apply pressure on the hierarchy on this matter, and he spoke to many other influential Curial officials, including the Benedictine Abbot-Primate Fidelis von Stotzingen, Pizzardo, the German Cardinal Franz Ehrle, and the Jesuit Superior-General Vladimir Ledóchowski.[73]

But Marx, after his defeat, expecting some disgruntlement with his

[72] Guenter Lewy, *The Catholic church and Nazi Germany* (New York, 1965), p. 6.

[73] AW, 1A 25z, 9, memorandum of Magnis, June 25, 1926; pro memoria of Magnis, Praschma, June 19, 1925. Günther Grünthal, *Reichsschulgesetz und Zentrumspartei in der Weimarer Republik* (Düsseldorf, 1968), pp. 163-164.

strategy and in order to counter any party revolt and support from Rome for the dissenters, also prepared a lengthy memorandum on the efficacy of his political course and the value of his alliance. The document was also brought personally to Rome and used as a basis of discussion with Church officials. Among those who made the pilgrimage to Rome were many German politicians ranging from Marx to local officials, and the point of conversation among themselves, with the German diplomats, and with the Vatican officials always concentrated on the Center Party's policy. Almost all of them were there urging the Vatican to take a stand one way or the other on the issue.[74]

The Holy See was much too politically astute to make a precise statement on such an internal question which did not directly affect the Church's interests, to cause a split among the Catholics and thereby lose influence with one segment or the other of the faithful or run the risk of being accused by Catholics of responsibility for disunity within the party and by non-Catholics of ultramontanist interference in German internal affairs. Gasparri's policy was to make no statement on behalf of either side and to withhold exerting pressure so that Vatican influence could be expended all the more effectively on an issue directly affecting the Church such as would inevitably occur during concordat negotiations. Vatican officials did, however, let it be known that the Curia did not look too favorably on further strengthening of Center ties with the Socialists. Gasparri informed Marx that he understood clearly the reasons for the electoral coalition and believed that Marx's personal prestige and capabilities were such that he could exert an influence on the Socialists. But now that the Center had gambled and lost, a strengthening of the Left orientation would not be encouraged. Nevertheless, Rome would neither openly interfere nor publicly condemn the alliance.[75]

In many ways the Vatican was practicing its customary diplomacy of not overtly interfering yet adjusting its policy to its basic principle of opposition to Socialism. As long as the Socialists remained influential in German politics and supported measures allowing Church freedom, the Curia did not oppose the coalition in Germany which in 1925 even held out the prospect of a Catholic president. Once this

---

[74] GSTA, MA 104455, Ritter to BFM, May 30, 1925.

[75] GSTA, MA 104455, Ritter to BFM, May 30, 1925. In November Steinmann, staff member of the German Embassy, heard again from the Under Secretary of State that the Vatican clearly differentiated between Socialism in Germany and in other countries, that Rome understood that the cooperation between the Center and the Socialists was not philosophical but purely tactical. Steinmann then asked specifically if the Pontiff intended to issue an official proclamation condemning cooperation with the Socialists. Whereupon the Curial official replied unequivocally, "No!" Cologne, Marx, 1070 Nr. 156, letter of Klee (Vatican) to Marx, November 27, 1925.

possibility no longer existed, once Rome perceived a pronounced conservative sentiment among the German electorate as witnessed by the recent election, once Rome verified that it could work with the new President, who was sworn to defend the Weimar Constitution which encompassed civil and political gains already won by the Church, once this was contrasted to the Socialists, who still stood opposed to any concessions being made on the school question as well as other concordat-related issues, then the Vatican gave a quiet but still clear signal of approval for a more conservative orientation in Center politics, thereby encouraging and lending support to those Centrists who desired to reorient the party's direction.

When the new President had taken office and had personally made a point of expressing his desire to see the Nuncio permanently in Berlin, there was every reason to comply and to take advantage of the friendly atmosphere in which relations seemed to be developing. In April Pacelli had already paid a visit to Bavarian Minister-President Heinrich Held to thank him officially for his services in concluding the concordat. The major work of the Nuncio in the Bavarian capital had been completed, and preparations were underway to make the move to Berlin during that summer. Pacelli had been greatly respected and widely admired in Munich, and the flood of expressions of sorrow at his departure overwhelmed him. In addition to banquets in his honor, newspaper editorials praised his activities as a churchman, statesman, and friend of Bavaria. The official farewell party took place on July 14 in the large, decorated Odeonsaal in Munich, where officials of state, church, and social and charitable organizations heaped praise on the departing prelate. On August 18 Bavarian officials headed by Minister-President Held, as well as foreign diplomats including the French, English, and Italian representatives in Munich and representatives of the Reich, Saxon, Prussian, and Württemberg Governments, saw the Nuncio off at Munich's main railway station. Seldom had there ever been such an outpouring of respect and genuine love for a foreign dignitary in the Bavarian capital as for Pacelli. The sentiments seemed reciprocal, for on August 10 the Nuncio had already sent his farewell message to the Bavarian episcopate and to the people, recalling his more than eight-year stay in Bavaria, with all the trials and crises, the joys and happiness, that it had brought him. Now with gratitude for the support and cooperation, friendship, and love that he had experienced there, he took his leave.[76] The tribute was for the man, but it also illustrated the respect and influence he had lent to the

---

[76] Germany, Munich, Erzbischöfliches Archiv, 1320, Nr. 33309, Pacelli to Bavarian bishops, August 10, 1925. *Kölnische Volkszeitung*, July 19, 1925. *Bayerischer Kurier*, August 20, 1925.

office, an office whose influence was readily appreciated by church, state, domestic, and foreign officials.

As the new Nuncio in Munich, Msgr. Alberto Vassallo di Torregrossa, presented his credentials to Held on August 22, he said, "My mission, which is to foster the excellent relations existing between the Holy See and the Bavarian State Government, has been made very easy for me with the conclusion of the concordat."[77] This was a true statement, since up until 1925 the Nuncio in Munich had conducted Vatican affairs as they related to all of Germany while settling at the same time the most pressing church-state problems in Bavaria, which in the 1920's included negotiating a concordat. Now, with no major difficulty facing Bavarian-Vatican relations, interest shifted to Berlin, where the question of diplomacy affecting both Germany and the Holy See as well as questions of church-state affairs would now be dealt with. Interconfessional relations within Germany were not good and the presence of a nuncio on a permanent basis in the Reich capital was still bound to irritate conservative Protestants. Yet if anyone could bridge the gap and get on well with the government, it was Pacelli. Most foreign diplomats and government officials believed him the ideal person for the task—universally respected, liked by the people—to whom the government would listen.[78] Countless stories abound of his solicitude for people and the respect he gained by his intimate knowledge of Germany and its people based on minute observation.[79] Once in Berlin Pacelli took an active part in the life of the city and began to form acquaintances and friends in all circles: workers, students, professors, politicians, diplomats, and the clergy. He also had to change his tactics since he went from an area fiercely loyal to Rome and more inclined to cooperate with the Vatican to one which was basically anti-Catholic and skeptical of Rome's intentions. D'Abernon said he was the best-informed man in Berlin, and Dorothy Thompson, the American journalist, stated, "in knowledge of German and European affairs and in diplomatic astuteness the Nuncio was without equal."[80] Pacelli

---

[77] Lama, p. 649. The Italian consul in Munich did not think much of the new Nuncio. He said he would be a real disappointment to the Bavarians after Pacelli, who was refined, witty, intelligent, and a brilliant conversationalist. In contrast, the Italian diplomat found Vassallo unrefined, with bad manners and a poor command of the German language. Italy, Ministero degli Affari Esteri, Archivio Storico, Germania 1929, 1182/4602, Summonte (Munich) to Italian Foreign Ministry, February 11, 1928.

[78] Pastor, p. 864.

[79] Padellaro, p. 52.

[80] Sugrue, p. 207. Robert Murphy, former U.S. Under Secretary of State was in Germany as an American diplomat in the 1920's where he had known Pacelli. Later, after Pacelli had become Pope, Murphy was granted an audience with his old colleague. They talked of old times and how they had underestimated Hitler in the mid-1920's,

literally and symbolically took the locus of diplomatic power with him to Berlin, and Munich as a center of activity, as a channel through which Vatican influence passed into Germany, and the value of maintaining a nunciature in the Bavarian capital all correspondingly diminished.

In 1925 the change of faces in the government in Berlin, both in the president's office and in the cabinet,[81] also paralleled a change of the center of Vatican influence in Germany from the south to the north. Yet one could agree with the English diplomatic report for 1925 that the shift had not harmed German-Vatican ties, that they had in fact been most cordial that year, that that they had seen some success in reaching their mutual objectives.[82] The Vatican was relieved and convinced that it could work with the new President, the Reich had shown its eagerness to continue the good relationship by stressing the desire and need of having the Nuncio reside in Berlin, and the Foreign Minister had publicly paid high tribute to Rome's efforts on Germany's behalf. By October the electoral results of the preceding April appeared to have completely satisfied Gasparri. The choice of Hindenburg, mused the Cardinal, in the long run had perhaps been for the best, since he was probably the only man among the candidates able, by force of his personal authority, to contain the ultranationalists, for no one would accuse him of not being a German patriot.

Contrary to Gasparri's original fears, Hindenburg's election had not hindered the improving international situation. In fact, several months after his assumption of duties, steps were taken toward the German-Vatican mutual goal of witnessing the Reich's total reintegration into the family of nations. The signing of the Locarno Pact, which established guarantees for Germany's western borders and provided arbitration treaties between Germany and her eastern neighbors to settle their disputes, had greatly pleased Gasparri. He believed that the first step toward treating Germany fairly had now been taken. The formulation of the Locarno Pact placed restrictions on aggression for both the victor and vanquished; Germany was being regarded as a partner that could arbitrate its disagreements with other nations, rather than as a defeated power forced to accept the dictates of the winners. The current agreement, said the Cardinal, would help to compensate for the one-sidedness of Versailles, give Germany an increased sense

---

since both Murphy and Pacelli had at first reported to their governments that Hitler would never come to power. Pacelli held up his hand for Murphy to stop, laughed and said, "In those days, you see, I wasn't infallible." *Ibid.*, p. 207.

[81] In January a cabinet formed by Hans Luther included a Nationalist for the first time in the Republic's history, signaling the shift to the political right.

[82] BFO, 371/11399/5412, annual report on the relations of the Holy See, 1925, p. 12.

12. Foreign Minister Gustav Stresemann (center) taking a walk along the lakeside after the Locarno Conference, October 1925

of security and acceptance, and contribute to European stability. The improved conditions were due in large measure to Stresemann's efforts to demonstrate Germany's good faith, to which the French and British now had responded. Locarno, he hoped, would encourage Europe to take further action toward an evenhanded approach in dealing with all nations and lead to a normalization of diplomatic affairs.[83]

In discussion with German Chargé d'Affaires Clemens von Brentano in October, Gasparri appeared optimistic. True, problems remained; as he had told diplomats of other states, he still worried about the Polish Corridor, which he considered a completely unsatisfactory solution, and about the Saar Territory, whose population did not desire to become part of France. He agreed with Berlin that France could and should make some compensation to the Germans for the use of the mines in the Saar. In the east, if the Corridor were returned to Germany, something could surely be worked out with possible guarantees for Poland to reach the sea by train and river and for harbor rights at the mouth of the Vistula. The problems, if unheeded, would encourage the extreme nationalists in Germany, who had become in-

[83] HHSTA, 87, Pastor to Mataja, October 16, 1925. BelgFO, St. Siège 1923-28, Ruzette (Vatican) to Foreign Minister Vandervelde, October 24, 1925.

creasingly visible since 1923, but this is where he hoped that the new President could play a role in restraining them. In general the Cardinal was very happy, almost exuberant, about what had been accomplished. Considering the gloomy outlook of just two years before during the Ruhr crisis, he said, it hardly seemed possible to have hoped for such progress. For the Reich it was a great moral and political success, since some of Germany's basic wishes had been fulfilled. The Cardinal's statements gratified the Germans, for they interpreted them as an indication of continued sympathy in the Curia for the Reich's problems, and Brentano suggested to Berlin that should it be needed Germany could most probably still call upon the Vatican to use its influence in the Reich's behalf.[84]

While both governments seemed generally pleased upon learning how well they were able to work with one another and with the success of some of their diplomatic objectives, within the Center Party there was still uncertainty of the role which the Curia might play in the future course of the party's politics. The continued resistance of the Socialists to the Church's concordat objectives, on the one hand, and, on the other, Rome's realization that the former Field Marshal as head of the German state would not bring the difficulties for international stability that had been originally feared, only decreased the value of the Center-Socialist alliance in the Vatican's opinion. Despite Rome's statement that it would not interfere and condemn the cooperation of the Center with the SPD, Gasparri's comments had not given any active encouragement for continuing it. This left a lingering fear among the pro-Socialist members of the party, who still controlled the Center, that Rome might still at some later date issue a condemnation of Socialism and reopen the whole issue of the Center-Socialist alliance. Marx knew of the anti-Socialist group within the Curia who had been urging the Pontiff to speak out against Socialism in a manner which would allow no exceptions for particular situations, such as Germany's. He had also learned earlier that year of the conservative and aristocratic groups within Catholic Germany which were also pressuring Rome to have the Vatican issue a formal statement condemning any cooperation with the Socialists. Indeed, Marx had heard rumors that the Pontiff was seriously considering such a statement. The importance of any Vatican pronouncement on the subject prompted Marx once more to urge moderation.

On December 6 he wrote to Pacelli about the matter. The Holy Year was drawing to a close, and an encyclical had been promised for

---

[84] AA, Botschaftsakten Sicherheitspakt Konferenz Locarno, Vol. 1, Brentano (Vatican) to AA, October 16, 1925.

the end of 1925. What Marx feared was that the Papal document might contain a statement against Socialism which could seriously affect German politics. In his long letter Marx explained how Germany was at the moment in the middle of a cabinet crisis brought on by the withdrawal of the conservative German National People's Party. This meant that Germany had the opportunity of forming a sympathetic government able to carry out the Locarno agreement and to put through economic measures necessary to curb the increasing unemployment. The old Weimar coalition of the parties most closely identified with the Republic and democratic principles (the Center, the Social Democrats, and the Democrats) had to pull together again to form a cabinet. The Socialists at the moment were not anxious to enter the government but would have to be convinced. If the encyclical contained any such anti-Socialist statement, said Marx, it would not only destroy any chances of bringing the SPD into a government committed to seeing Locarno honored, but it would irreparably cripple the Center, since then, in negotiating to form a new cabinet with the Right, the party would no longer enjoy either the power of decision or of political maneuverability; it would lose its leverage of exacting concessions from the Right by threatening that it might still form an alliance with the Left. If it entered the government, it would be in essence a prisoner of the Right. But the consequences, continued Marx, could be even worse. Having lost its bargaining power, the Center would have no means to carry out its program, and it would thus lose the confidence of the voters; it would decline in strength and no longer be sought after to help to form future cabinets. The Center would then be relegated to a perpetual opposition party.

Marx urged Pacelli to convey these considerations to the Pontiff. Remembering the rumors which had reached the ears of Vatican officials in April that Catholic voters were being urged to vote for Socialist candidates as party trade-offs in various districts, Marx tried to meet this objection to his plea for continued cooperation with the SPD by providing detailed facts and explanations about the German electoral method. He assured Rome, and called upon Pacelli to verify his statement from his own knowledge, that the system did not allow for Catholics and Socialists to trade-off votes in specific districts. Every party voted its self-contained party list. The elected representatives in party caucuses formed coalitions only after the election. The former Chancellor also mentioned his prior explanation of this to Pizzardo in Rome several months before. Although the Under Secretary of State had been informed of the true situation, Marx sadly noted that the impressions gained by the Center leader Felix Porsch, recently in Rome, indicated that not all Curial circles were clear on the issue. Marx therefore made an appeal to Pacelli who was known to have an excellent grasp of the German political situation and who realized the significance for both the Center Party and the country which a Papal statement could have, to help to explain the truth of the matter and urge no word be said about Socialism in the upcoming encyclical. Without committing himself Pacelli indicated agreement with and sympathy for Marx's argument and passed the report on to Rome.[85]

Pacelli, as already noted, was highly regarded in Rome, and undoubtedly his words were seriously considered. From other sources it appears that the Curia had already all but decided not to make a general statement against Socialism. If, however, any doubts lingered, Marx's argument and Pacelli's endorsement may have only reinforced the prevailing sentiment and silenced the proponents of such a declaration. The encyclical *Quas primas*, published on December 11, 1925, dealt primarily with the subject of establishing the feast of Christ the King and failed to mention Socialism.

C. An Era of Good Feeling

Once the Locarno Pact had been signed, the Vatican indicated its pleasure that the spirit of reconciliation was beginning to gain momentum. In a formal address delivered to the French President, Nuncio Luigi Maglione expressed the Pontiff's approval that France and Germany had been working well together during 1926.[86] There were indications that Europe was finally heading toward a degree of stability, but in order to build upon the first steps made at Locarno and settle issues still outstanding, more negotiations, more mediation, and most probably more aid from other states would be needed and appreciated. In the changed situation, Germany thought it proper to take soundings at the Vatican to determine to what degree the policies of the two states would progress in tandem in the future and to see if Germany stood as well in the eyes of the Holy See as previously, or

[85] Cologne, Marx, 1070 Nr. 156, letter of Marx to Pacelli, December 6, 1925. Cardinal Schulte also urged the Vatican to refrain from making a statement. Although personally he was not in favor of the Left orientation of the Center Party since he feared that Catholic workers might see little difference between the Center and the Socialists and consequently at times vote for the Social Democrats, he still maintained that the matter be handled as an intra-party affair. Word from Rome condemning cooperation with the Socialists would cause the immediate breakup of the Center Party, the Left and Right wings splitting apart. GSTA, Ges. Päpstl. Stuhl 1003, Ritter to BFM, November 15, 1926.

[86] *Germania*, January 3, 1927.

if its position had to any degree been altered.[87] This served two purposes: first, by learning the Vatican's attitude or its policy direction on the issues which most concerned the Reich, Berlin could wait and consider the thrust of its own policy and learn to what degree it could count on Curial support for its diplomatic forays; by hearing what information Rome had obtained from other countries, it could better assess the world situation. Secondly, it was a diplomatically accepted fact that the Vatican was an excellent clearing house for information gleaned from a variety of sources; the Curia usually could form an intelligent overview of international and domestic affairs based on information collected from the local hierarchy, its own diplomats, and representatives of other states and then distilled through a Roman prism. Opinions, analyses, and facts passed on by Vatican officials were based on the statements of officials in other countries or their envoys in Rome. Conversely, undoubtedly German attitudes were similarly transmitted to other capitals. The Vatican was thus an excellent source of communication and rightly lived up to its reputation as the listening post of Europe. Berlin hoped to learn in a wide-ranging policy discussion not only Rome's thoughts but also indirectly the thoughts of other nations such as France and Belgium. It was for this purpose that Msgr. Georg Schreiber, churchman and member of the Reichstag, at Bergen's request, met on April 8, 1926 with Cardinal Gasparri to go over the issues which concerned both governments and report the findings

---

[87] A good example of the hyper-sensitive manner in which Berlin showed concern over its standing with the Holy See occurred in November 1925. The Papal representatives in France and Brazil, recalled to Rome after completing their assignments, were to receive cardinals' hats at the next consistory, as was usual for returning nuncios. Germany, while on one hand desiring to retain Pacelli in Berlin, immediately became concerned that he, having served longer than either of the other two Vatican diplomats, was not included on the list for elevation to the Sacred College, and that this omission might reflect on Germany. Berlin feared the possibility of great disappointment in Germany and of the impression created at home and abroad that the Vatican did not regard the Berlin nunciature of equal stature with those of other first-class nations, thereby weakening the influence of the Nuncio in dealing with diplomats and politicians. Stresemann himself requested that these apprehensions be brought to the Curia's attention. Gasparri, when apprized of them, showed amazement and consternation about the gravity with which the Reich officials were treating the subject. He reminded Bergen that no nuncio received the red hat until he was recalled and no nuncio, especially Pacelli, was recalled until a specific task had been completed. The Reich concordat had yet to be negotiated, and he was essential for the task. The Cardinal assured the Ambassador that conferring the red hat on the other Nuncios in no way indicated any less respect for the Berlin post or the Reich itself. Then, trying to inject a little levity into a matter he could not take seriously, he jokingly told Bergen, of course, if the diplomat could assure him that a concordat would be signed soon, Pacelli would be named cardinal at the next possible consistory. AA, RM 70, Vol. 2, Bergen to AA, November 28, 1925; BRV 284, Vol. 1, Stresemann to Bergen, November 28, 1925.

to the pertinent ministries, such as the Foreign Office, Ministry of the Interior, and the Prussian Ministry of Education and Religious Affairs.

The conversation began with Schreiber recalling the Vatican's aid to prisoners during the war, and once more expressing Germany's appreciation. President Hindenburg had the previous month conferred the Grand Medal of Gratitude on the Cardinal Secretary of State for his aid to demonstrate that the Reich still remained grateful. While coming rather late in the day, eight years after the end of war, the award was still another example of Germany's esteem for the Vatican and the courting of its favors. The conversation turned toward the problem of Germany's western borders. On this topic Gasparri offered some advice on what he believed might help Germany's objectives here. The Cardinal knew that Germany had been negotiating with Belgium for a return of Eupen-Malmédy. Based on his knowledge of the situation, he advised the Reich to show itself accommodating in economic matters, possibly offering Belgium some tariff concessions, and then perhaps Belgium would be reciprocally more flexible with regard to the lost territory. The moment, he believed, was favorable for a new arrangement in the settlement. He knew of German inquiries about the area and of Belgium's interest in seeing a canal built from Belgium to the Rhine which would be of great economic value to that nation. Emile Vandervelde, the Socialist Belgian Foreign Minister, favored exchanging the territory for some concessions, but the Belgian public still needed time to become accustomed to the idea. If Germany made some concrete overtures, while the official Belgian press familiarized the public with the possibility of transfer, then 1927 might bring excellent results.[88]

With regard to an early return of the Saar to Germany, the Cardinal, who had already raised this question with Paris, stated that France was well aware that a plebiscite would result in a victory for the Reich. France would not risk this defeat if it could help it. Therefore, if Germany desired the speedy return of the Saar, it had to find means other than requesting the plebiscite set for 1935 to be moved up. Perhaps, he suggested, Germany could sweeten the request by offering financial compensation to France for the return of the region. He was unsure that France would accept or if Germany was in a position to make the offer. Nevertheless, he presented the idea for consideration. For his part, Schreiber took the opportunity to emphasize that under the League administration and French influence the situation of the

[88] For the complex German-Belgian negotiations covering Eupen-Malmédy in 1926, see Enssle, ch. 6.

Church in the Saar was not very good. In comparison to pre-war days, when the area was part of the Reich, in the 1920's the number of those studying for the priesthood had dropped perceptibly since the monetary exchange rate with Germany hindered candidates from pursuing their studies at Trier and Speyer, to which the area belonged, and the low clerical salaries in the Saar made assigning priests there from other parts of these dioceses less attractive. Therefore, many seminarians studied and remained either in France or in missionary orders paying the living expenses of their candidates instead of preparing to work in their own dioceses. The German added that the German Ministry of the Interior, however, was sending some funds through governmental allocations to institutions in the Saar to assist the seminarians and thereby maintaining clerical connections between the Saar and the Reich.[89] Schreiber's comments notwithstanding, the Cardinal's suggestions, though not always implemented, nevertheless gave Berlin new options to consider and demonstrated the Curia's lively interest in Germany's problem and Gasparri's willingness to offer what advice he could.

When the discussion turned to the east, however, Gasparri was more skeptical and returned to his original distrust of Versailles' accomplishments. He reiterated the Vatican's belief that the Polish Corridor would not bring a permanent solution to the border difficulties. Quick to show the connection of the Cardinal's thinking to German policy, Schreiber reminded Gasparri of Benedict XV's statement in 1920 that Curial policy, as regards Germany, was to consider all territorial changes in the east resulting from Versailles as provisional, and therefore Rome would not create any new ecclesiastical administrations which did not take the provisional nature of the boundaries into consideration.[90] What Schreiber had done, of course, while conceding a degree of permanence in the west, as evidenced by the Locarno agreement, was to remind Rome that no bilateral or final agreement in the east existed yet and that the late Pontiff had formulated the policy of awaiting such an agreement before making any ecclesiastical changes. The German was emphasizing that since Gasparri believed the situation impermanent, it would be against Rome's own logic and the statements of its leaders for the Holy See at any time to yield to Polish pressure to reorganize the ecclesiastical boundaries, thus in practice giving *de facto* recognition to the permanency of the political borders. Schreiber, indeed pleased with Gasparri's thoughts on the eastern situation, seized

---

[89] AA, PO II, PO 1 Vat., Vol. 1, Schreiber to Stresemann, April 12, 1926.
[90] *Ibid.*

the opportunity to reemphasize that here too Rome's views paralleled Germany's policy.

During the conversation Schreiber was also quick to notice that the Curia apparently no longer seemed to have as strong an aversion to the League as it had in 1918 when Gasparri viewed it as a by-product of Versailles and one dominated by the French. The Cardinal asked whether the majority of Germans, in light of the signing of the Locarno agreements, approved of Berlin's policy of requesting entry into the League; when Schreiber responded that they did, he agreed with the wisdom of the policy since he was now convinced that the League no longer served as the instrument of a particular *Weltanschauung* or as the "handmaiden" of French policy. The recent defeat of France's Ruhr policy had weakened Paris' influence and prestige in the League. The new government of Briand was more prepared to listen to other viewpoints and cooperate, so that the League could now be used more effectively as an instrument of international reconciliation. However, the Cardinal still wanted to hear why, after the noticeable failures of the Powers to solve some of the problems troubling Europe, Berlin now still desired to become a member of the League. Schreiber replied that Berlin was assured in a world forum that Germany's problems—such as the monetary, disarmament, and above all the reparation questions—had a good chance of being solved. In any event, Germany believed it harmful to remain outside the mainstream of diplomatic activity merely because of past injustices. It had to explore all possibilities of reaching a solution. The policy of reconciliation during the last few years had prompted Germany to place more faith in the League. Gasparri, who seemed pleased with Germany's position, agreed with the logic.[91] The conversation indicated that Stresemann's success at Locarno had induced Rome to view the League in a new light. The League, with Germany accepted as an equal member, could now open up new avenues for further negotiation among nations. Rome, which had looked skeptically upon League activities and tended to doubt its effectiveness, now acknowledged its potential as a valid means of promoting peace, and that the Vatican could help in a supportive role, passing information, urging moderation on particular points, and giving advice that could be used in negotiation.

The Vatican's attitude toward the League raised further questions. Now that the hostility of the war years had diminished and progress was being made toward diplomatic cooperation, could not the Vatican assist and serve its own policy by also becoming a member of the League? Italy had prevented its participation at the Peace Conference,

[91] *Ibid.*

but since 1922 Mussolini's government increasingly had indirect contacts with the Curia, and many diplomats did not expect Italy to voice as strong objections as it had in 1919 to seating the Vatican at an international meeting. When Germany entered the League in September 1926, rumors spread in diplomatic circles that Germany might then push for Vatican admission to that body. This did not turn out to be so, but Berlin did explore the possibility of having the Holy See take a more active part in League work. Up until then the Vatican had continually disclaimed interest in becoming a member. Its position had been that the League did not include all nations and hence was not a valid place to make international decisions since important states such as Germany and the United States were not represented. Rather, it was an institution founded by the victors at Versailles, with a definite goal and outlook: the maintenance of the 1919 settlement. As late as April 1926 Curial Cardinal Frühwirth had confirmed that this viewpoint represented the official position of the Papacy. "The Holy See," said the Cardinal, "has never taken any steps to be represented in the League of Nations since its membership in the latter—at least in its present form—would not be in its interests nor would it correspond to its character or to its lofty mission. . . ."[92]

But there had begun to be a change by 1926. The League had just settled a Greco-Bulgarian border dispute that had threatened the peace and had helped to delimit the contested Turco-Iraqi boundary which had also involved Britain as mandatory power in Iraq. The League Council was now meeting in quarterly sessions with most European foreign ministers in attendance, thus drawing further attention to the importance of the Geneva meetings. With Germany's entry into the League in that year, except for the Soviet Union, all European powers of consequence now belonged to the organization. After Locarno it thus appeared as if this world body might provide an effective vehicle in speeding the work of international conciliation, and this possibility was not lost on Curial officials. As 1926 progressed, foreign representatives in Rome found Vatican statements less negative about the League than previously. Frühwirth, in his comments in April, while disclaiming Vatican interest in membership, paid tribute to League efforts for peace and reconciliation, and Gasparri, meeting with Schreiber, had expressed hope that now France and Germany could begin talking to one another in Geneva. This shift in attitude was confirmed when Schreiber, after meeting with the Secretary of State, took up the matter of the League in discussions with Pizzardo. Noting

[92] Angelus Walz, *Andreas Kardinal Frühwirth* (Vienna, 1950), p. 442. *Neue Züricher Nachrichten*, April 26, 1926.

328

the more favorable view which the Vatican was now taking to the work of the international body, he urged the Curia to increase its ties with the League by perhaps sending an observer to Geneva who could develop contact with League officials. Pizzardo, who agreed that possibly the Nuncio in Bern could take on this work, seemed interested in Vatican participation in the scientific and cultural work of the sundry League commissions. Undoubtedly Berlin, now that it had entered the League and shifted a considerable amount of its diplomacy into this theater of operations, sought to have the Vatican move closer to this organization, where it could also exert its influence on the international scene. Schreiber and Pizzardo had discussed at length means in which the Vatican could join in some of the League activities, such as work dealing with the minority question.[93] Since the Vatican had frequently spoken out and indicated its concern for minorities in various lands, such humanitarian work would be a logical field in which Rome could participate as befitted its calling.[94] If Rome assumed such a task, it would also serve Germany's purposes, since Rome would then be the advocate for the German minorities, especially along the eastern border, and in this international forum could considerably influence world leaders, and Catholic Poland in particular.[95]

Germany, on several occasions, did raise the issue and suggested that the Vatican become a member. Despite the Curia's more favorable attitude toward the League, it nonetheless still remained outside its circle. Rome cooperated from time to time in independent commissions and used the good offices of its Nuncio in Bern to make contact with League delegates, but it did not join. The Curia, after weighing the issue, decided that it could best work by using its influence outside the League. At first the Reich was disappointed that the Holy See was not at Geneva to second some of Germany's views. But in many ways, as some Germans came to realize, Rome was right that it still could work best from outside. It now enjoyed the advantage of cooperating in some League work, maintaining contact should discussions be necessary with its delegates via the Bern nunciature, and still keeping its position of neutrality by not participating in the actual voting of the League. By remaining outside, the Holy See ironically was of aid to Germany's policy to revise its eastern boundaries. By

[93] AA, PO II, PO 1 Vat., Vol. 1, Schreiber to Stresemann, April 20, 1926.

[94] The *Osservatore* carried numerous articles during the 1920's expressing the Pontiff's concern over the legal, economic, and civil rights and welfare of minorities in general or, on a specific occasion, of one group in particular.

[95] For example, in 1921 German sources stated that there were at least one million Germans living in Poland. *Der Grosse Brockhaus*, 15th ed. (Leipzig, 1928-1935), Vol. 12, p. 575.

accepting membership in the League, the Vatican would have appeared to be acknowledging the settlement of Versailles, which, according to the logic of diplomatic progression, would then have meant that greater pressure could and would have been applied by France, Poland, and Czechoslovakia on Rome to be consistent in her position and recognize the new political boundaries and reorganize the ecclesiastical structure of the territories to conform with the realities created by Versailles. Thus away from the deliberations in Geneva the Vatican was better able to maintain an air of impartiality and have more freedom to decide the correct moment to adjust ecclesiastical boundaries in the Church's interest. When this would occur depended on when the political situation became clearer and when Rome became assured that the changes were final, but for the moment this temporizing was a boon for Germany.[96]

As was indicated in Schreiber's discussions with Pizzardo, an objective of German policy which began to take a more prominent place in dealing with the Vatican after 1925 was the problem of German minorities outside the Reich. Up until that time the question had dealt essentially with the German population of the lost areas along the eastern border, especially Upper Silesia, with some mention made of the situation of Germans in other areas such as the South Tyrol and the Balkans. During the first years of the post-war era, while speaking out against human suffering and the plight of ethnic groups in specific cases, the Vatican had not taken any specific position on German minorities in other countries and had acted cautiously, listening attentively but not overtly supporting the German view that these Germans in other states were frequently deprived of their legal or civil rights and through a government policy of education and cultural pressure were being de-Germanized. Many ethical, legal, and political aspects of the minority problem were emphasized only as a result of the World War. The new political situation in Europe had created to a large degree an increased feeling of ethnic solidarity among Germans within and without the territorial boundaries of the Reich, as a sort of reaction to what the Germans considered the political and moral deprivation of their rights. The Curia, while noting a growing solidarity among Germans, as a conservative institution, adopted an attitude of waiting and observing to see how this feeling of *Deutschtum* would develop lest it turn revolutionary. Another factor which caused the Vatican to act in a restrained manner was the new elements of political power in the post-war era. The Curia had to consider its relations with the victorious and newly created states where there were German minorities,

96 GSTA, Ges. Päpstl. Stuhl 1003, Ritter to BFM, November 21, 1926.

such as Poland or Czechoslovakia. In addition, just as the Vatican could use the protection of a legal concordat with Bavaria to resist French demands for ecclesiastical jurisdiction changes in the Palatinate, so also could the Vatican use the lack of Germany's legal authority to speak on behalf of these minorities to justify Rome's hesitancy to support Germany's minority policy.[97]

Now that the Austro-Hungarian Empire was no more, the major German-speaking state felt itself responsible for watching over the interests of not only Germans who had once been part of the Reich but all those, especially in southeastern Europe, who still spoke or felt themselves part of the German cultural group. There was here not only a moral and ethnic reason for Berlin's policy but also a practical one. By aiding the minorities directly beyond the borders Berlin maintained and strengthened the cultural identity of *Auslandsdeutschen* and their ties to the Reich, which helped Berlin in its fight to have these territories returned by either having the ethnic Germans agitate within these areas or allowing Berlin to represent them before the other Powers.[98] In aiding the German minorities more distantly located, Berlin hoped to strengthen German cultural ties with these groups which could be used as a means of acquiring influence with the states in which these people were situated.[99]

The new era of good feeling and Germany's entrance into the League gave the Reich an international forum in which to represent the Germans living in other lands. In addition, Berlin believed that the Curia could also be of aid here. Now Berlin could not only remonstrate about the injustices of the Reich's territorial losses and the need for a strong Germany in Central Europe, but while promoting the rights of German minorities, it could appeal again for regaining some of the lost areas and strengthening German cultural ties with these German-speaking groups. In approaching the Vatican, Bergen naturally stressed

[97] For the minority question see Kurt Düwell, *Deutschlands auswärtige Kulturpolitik; 1918-1932* (Cologne, 1976); *Das Auslandsdeutschtum in Osteuropa einst und jetzt*, edited by der Arbeits-und Sozialminister des Landes Nordrhein-Westfalen (1963); Richard Bahr, *Volk jenseits der Grenzen*, 2nd ed. (Hamburg, 1935); Carole K. Fink, "The Weimar Republic as the defender of minorities, 1919-1933," unpublished dissertation, Yale University (New Haven, Conn., 1969), especially ch. 1; Carole K. Fink, "Defender of minorities: Germany in the League of Nations, 1926-1933," *Central European History*, V (1972), 330-357.

[98] Fink, "Weimar Republic," ch. 1.

[99] Although mere approximations, according to varying census dates in the 1920's, the population of the German-speaking minority in the following countries was: Belgium 100,000; Czechoslovakia 3,200,000; Denmark 30,000-40,000; Estonia 20,000; Finland 2,400; France 1,370,000; Hungary 560,000; Italy 212,000; Latvia 70,000; Lithuania 37,000 (without Memel); Poland 1,128,000; Rumania 725,000; and Yugoslavia 600,000. *Der Grosse Brockhaus*, Vol. 12, p. 575.

the Catholic and religious dimensions of the question since Pius had made it clear that Rome should concern itself with purely religious problems and, where possible, not meddle in the political affairs of the world powers. But the close connection of the political and religious aspects of the problem hindered the Vatican from disentangling the two and thus made Rome even more wary of speaking out in favor of the minorities lest it be interpreted as a political move.

Germany's efforts to enlist Vatican aid for this issue were only partly successful. Germany desired Rome clearly to speak out about minority rights—civil, legal, and economic—or actively to take up the matter of German minorities with the individual states concerned. This Gasparri steadfastly declined to do. When Germany mentioned difficulties pertaining to religious affairs, Rome was more attentive. For example, in 1925-1926 Bergen several times protested that German-speaking Catholics, particularly in Polish Silesia, were again being prevented from using their mother tongue in worship and religious instruction. These attempts at Polonization were strongly protested, and the Curia immediately took it up with Polish officials, since the Holy See stood firmly behind the principle that worship and religious education must reach the faithful in a language they could understand and in which they could feel comfortable. By December 1926 the Consul General in Katowice reported that, thanks to Vatican intervention, the use of the German language was again allowed more freedom. Reports from other sections of Poland and Danzig corroborated this impression. In view of the concordat negotiations going on with such states as Yugoslavia and Rumania, Germany sought to have minority rights worked into these negotiations. Gasparri agreed, and kept in mind the rights of the faithful to use their mother tongue in worship. But when Bergen pressed for a statement in principle about minority rights or asked the Holy See to support the South Tyroleans in their fight to use German in all areas of daily life, the Cardinal always deftly shifted the conversation, saying that such problems should be addressed to the League, the acknowledged guardian of minorities.[100] True, the Vatican had been able to help by guaranteeing the use of German in religious affairs and in that sense had helped the Reich to maintain links with *Auslandsdeutschen*. It had worked to correct the problem as the opportunity arose in countries such as Poland and Czechoslovakia and had inserted guarantees into concordat clauses, but it was not willing to make a categorical statement which could be interpreted by other states as meddling in political affairs and thus limit its own sphere of action and its relations with such states. Over the next few years

[100] AA, PO II, PO 35 Vat., Vol. 1, Bergen to AA, December 12, 1926.

Berlin worked hard to draw the Curia out of its reserve and have it issue a strong statement of support. But Rome generally remained circumspect, issuing a mild protest about South Tyrolean rights at one time or speaking in broad terms about minorities at another. In general, however, true to Pius' policy it acted and was of assistance when the issue dealt with Church affairs, leaving politically sensitive or general problems to the lay diplomats and statesmen.

The first month of 1927 saw a new cabinet formed to head the Reich Government. In itself this was not extraordinary since Weimar had long grown used to periodic cabinet shifts, but what marked a notable change was that the Catholic Centrist Marx formed a new cabinet by including the Rightist German National People's Party, signaling formally that he had broken with his allies of the early 1920's, the Social Democrats. Some newspapers, unhappy with Marx's decision to go so far to the right in building his cabinet and keeping in mind the Left-Right split already existing in the Center Party, drew the conclusion that Rome or its respresentative had played an important role in Marx's decision. Other more moderate journalists, in analyzing the Center's strategy, simply asked to what degree Rome had influenced the move. During January statements had circulated in the German press accusing Nuncio Pacelli of having had a hand in the formation of the new cabinet. Aware of the sensitivity of the issue of Vatican interference in internal affairs and the Protestant distrust of him when he had arrived in Berlin, the Nuncio heatedly protested and denied these accusations. The Foreign Minister sought to calm his distress and even had a statement placed in the influential *Deutsche Allgemeine Zeitung* citing the government's regret that individual diplomats accredited to the Reich had had their names brought into discussion of internal affairs in various newspapers.[101] Foreign journals, especially in the French-speaking world, also speculated on the Vatican's influence in Berlin. The well-known liberal Paris weekly *L'Europe Nouvelle* characterized the Center, and by implication the Vatican, as the arbiter of political coalitions. According to the journal, during the Christmas holidays in 1926, Heinrich Brauns, Reich Minister of Labor and close associate of Pacelli, had met with other politicians, including Heinrich Held, Minister-President of Bavaria, and Msgr. Johann Leicht, a Reichstag deputy, to decide on a strategy for collaborative action by the German and Bavarian Catholic parties to press for a concordat between the Vatican and the Reich and more Church control of educational policy. Since this had been hard to achieve with anti-clerical

---

[101] AA, PO II, PO 2 Vat., Vol. 3, news draft for the *Deutsche Allgemeine Zeitung*, Köpke (AA), January 28, 1927. Interestingly enough, the Center-Socialist alliance continued on the state level in areas such as Prussia and Baden.

allies on the Left, they now turned to the Right and persuaded Marx, then experiencing difficulty forming his cabinet, also to look to the Nationalists. The switch of allies, or *mariage de raison*, without compromising party or religious principles, was seen by the newspaper as a master stroke for Vatican diplomacy.[102] *La Tribune de Genève* by February noted the new cabinet's denial of rumors that it had initiated moves to sign a concordat. Why, asked the paper, should this matter be so carefully brought to public attention and denied? It was because the Center, plagued by a bad conscience, feared that if such a story continued to be spread the party would be accused of pursuing a policy of "Romanizing" Germany. Nevertheless, maintained the paper, this was exactly the reason that the Center, probably with Pacelli's prompting, had taken Nationalists into the cabinet. The Center Party had clearly broken with the Socialists, given up the idea of forming a cabinet including the more democratically oriented parties, and accepted the collaboration of the Nationalists since it wanted above all assurance that the German school system would be organized as it desired with guaranteed rights for religious instruction in the classes.

> The attitude taken by the Center, arbiter of German internal politics, corresponds exactly with that which the Vatican must desire to see it adopt since collaboration with the Socialists supposed, on the other hand, the complete laicization of the State.[103]

Nothing was proved, but the speculation prompted further investigation. The Quai d'Orsay, for example, requested its representative in Rome to see if he could learn if indeed the Vatican had pressured the Center to make such a decision, but even he could find no substantiation for the accusations. Moreover, he personally doubted that the Vatican had given any directives. Too many Germans, he reasoned, as well as Frenchmen, required little to convince them that the Vatican was directly influencing politics by directing the Center in its policies. The Ambassador found nothing to the rumors, which had been denied by Berlin in an official statement on February 8 and by the Vatican in conversations with diplomats, and by the German episcopate. In fact, continued Ambassador Doulcet, if one thought about it, one would understand that it was counter to Rome's interest to issue any directive, simply because it did not have to. The demand of the Center for a Reich concordat had been in the party platform for sometime and was known to all. The Curia could rely on the Center to work things out on its own without Rome laying itself open to the

[102] AA, PO II, PO 2 Vat., Vol. 3, abstract from *L'Europe Nouvelle*, February 5, 1927.
[103] *La Tribune de Genève*, February 10, 1927.

charge of mixing in Germany's internal politics. Moreover, at the beginning of the ministerial crisis in late 1926, the Center had first approached the Left, but when no agreement had been reached on the matter of a concordat, the party turned to the Right. The essential point confronting the Center was the consolidation with a concordat of the gains made for Catholics. Some Catholic leaders, said Doulcet, would like to justify their seesaw tactics to their Catholic constituencies by hiding behind the authority of the Vatican. But the Curia was run by statesmen too astute to risk censure when its goals could be reached by allowing German Catholics to act on their own—their goals were compatible with Rome's, and there was no need for suspecting Vatican pressure.[104]

As more and more of the facts of the cabinet formation became known—the strong opposition of the SPD to the concordat, the refusal of the German People's Party (DVP) to enter a government with the Socialists, Hindenburg's pressure on Marx to move to the right in an effort to break the impasse—more and more of Doulcet's logic seemed apparent. The Vatican indeed did not have to interfere in order to secure its objective. But the fact that the suspicion of implication came so readily to mind, and that people did not look for less sensational, more domestic and intra-party political reasons, indicated the Vatican's vulnerability in the Reich capital and how such a rumor could damage the fine rapport built by Pacelli. It also explains why he reacted out of character and protested so vehemently.

Although there was no proof to allegations of any pressure brought to bear on the Center by the Nuncio, once the newly formed cabinet began to function, Curial officials concurred that the move to the right had indeed not proved harmful to the Church, which gave further weight to indications of Vatican satisfaction with the election of the conservative Hindenburg two years earlier. In conversations with Ritter in February, the Cardinal Secretary of State commented that he was content that the Center no longer stood in close contact with the SPD. Close cooperation with the Social Democrats, he said, always contained great dangers for the maintenance of Catholic principles, and there was no question that the Center's former ties had injured its image in the eyes of many Catholics. Hindenburg had in earnest tone—with a hint almost of a field marshal's command—asked the Center to

---

[104] FFO, Allemagne 371, Doulcet to FFO, March 7, 1927. Hans Gatzke's comment on Russo-German military collaborations could also by analogy apply very well here. "But the Reichswehr's military involvement with Russia was not as far-reaching as many people suspected. The twilight of secrecy had a way of magnifying things." Hans Gatzke, "Russo-German military collaboration during the Weimar Republic," *American Historical Review*, LXIII (1957-1958), 595.

13. Nuncio Eugenio Pacelli leaving the presidential palace in Berlin after congratulating Hindenburg on the occasion of his eightieth birthday, October 1927

seek the formation of a viable coalition to the right, and this invitation had pleased Gasparri.[105] He only hoped that now the Nationalists would prove intelligent enough to take a moderating tone in international affairs and not be so stridently nationalistic that the new coalition would run into difficulties and be of short duration.[106]

Despite Vatican expressions of general satisfaction with Reich policies, the attitude of the President or a particular minister, or with the policies of the Center, it was one thing to express satisfaction and it was another for the Vatican to become involved in Germany's internal affairs. Especially since the establishment of the nunciature in Berlin, accusations or suspicions continually arose about Rome's influence on various political matters; at times they dealt with a dramatic issue such as the 1927 cabinet formation, at other times they dealt with a specific

[105] In October Bergen again reported that Gasparri had spoken of his warm sympathy for Hindenburg and his satisfaction with the manner in which the German President was carrying out his duties. AA, PO II, PO 2 Vat., Vol. 3, memorandum of Meyer-Rodehüser, October 10, 1927.

[106] GSTA, Ges. Päpstl. Stuhl 1009, Ritter to BFM, February 11, 1927.

piece of legislation. French Ambassador Pierre Jacquin de Margerie in Berlin noticed the difficulty in analyzing the relations of the Vatican, local Church leaders, and the Center during this period. In 1927, he said, Cardinal Schulte along with Nuncio Pacelli were accused of having a hand in the formation of the Marx Cabinet and cooperating with the Nationalists. One year later the Cardinal was reproached for being too republican, too liberal. This example, lamented de Margerie, sufficed to indicate how difficult it was to be aware of all the issues which divided German Catholics and the role which Church leaders and the Vatican played in these dissensions and political discussions.[107]

Rome's influence, then, on the Center was rather indirect. The overall objectives to protect the interests of the Church were common to both, though their attitude toward tactics at times varied. That Center Party members as well as other politicians consulted Pacelli there can be no doubt. That Rome voiced its opinion or preferences through the Nuncio or the diplomatic staff just as other diplomatic representatives did and were expected to do so in the interests of their state can be assumed. Although Rome let it be known what it thought, there appeared to be no documentary evidence, despite the attractiveness of a sensational story of Rome's sending directives, exerting pressure, or intensively lobbying for the shift to the right. True, directives could have been delivered orally and protestations of non-involvement could have been for appearance sake. But by interfering directly in internal affairs the Vatican simply had too much to lose. As Doulcet stated, it would have been of no advantage to become actively involved, for Rome's basic goals were already covered in the Center platform, and the party on its own and for its own reasons could steer a course to the right and reach these objectives. At best its opinion could have been one of the many factors which would have influenced a Center Party decision. In dealings with German diplomats Vatican officials repeatedly went out of their way to stress their reluctance to becoming involved in any situation dealing with internal affairs not directly of concern to the Church, no matter how advantageous such an involvement might be. One such instance illustrating this policy occurred before the Reichstag elections in 1928, when Pacelli left for Rome and remained there until after the vote had been taken so that he could not be accused again of having interfered in the campaign. The Vatican did not receive visiting German dignitaries during this time. Bergen advised former Chancellor Joseph Wirth, in Rome in May, not to seek an audience. In answer to the suggestion of the *Tägliche Rundschau* that he was there for consultations about Center electoral policy, Ber-

---

[107] FFO, Allemagne 369, de Margerie to Briand, May 29, 1928.

gen verified that Wirth had not even been received at the Vatican and that he had not met with Pacelli or any German bishops in Rome at this time.[108]

A more complicated example of how Rome refused to be drawn into internal affairs concerned the perennial problem of centralization versus federalism. For some time critical minds in Germany had come to think that the Weimar Constitution, which was based on a compromise that created a state neither completely centralized nor completely federal, was too complicated to meet the demands of the times. The 1919 solution satisfied neither federalist nor centralist. Particularly since 1924, there had been proposals for constitutional revisions which differed widely except to agree that the situation was unsatisfactory. But in 1926 the Reich Government had again made some attempts at administrative centralization in order to streamline the bureaucracy and to allow Berlin more effective control in areas that touched the *Länder*, such as the apportionment of state tax subsidies and the Central Government's control of education. Bavaria, always jealous of its rights and suspicious of Berlin's motives, looked for arguments and allies to oppose the Central Government and believed to have found both in Rome.

In 1926 Ritter already was vigorously pointing out to the Curia the dangers of centralization. The 1925 election, Ritter emphasized, also highlighted this problem. Bavarians abandoned Marx not only because of his electoral alliance with Socialism but also for his advocacy of increases in the Central Government's powers. If, he continued, Berlin decreased the share of the taxes which the *Länder* received, as Berlin proposed, to help to pay its bills and reparation debts, then states such as Bavaria would have to cut their cultural and social programs. If the centralizing tendency prevailed and an anti-clerical government came to power, the Church would then be the loser. To appreciate the damage of an anti-clerical policy, the Bavarian cautioned, one had only to look across the border at France. The more highly centralized the state, the less influence the individual *Länder* would have. In a centralized Germany Rome could never have been able to obtain the favorable conditions which it had been able to do in the treaty with Bavaria. He assured Gasparri that Munich in no way desired to injure German unity. Ritter stressed this point since he was aware of the Vatican's concern about Germany's strength on the international scene. Nevertheless, in internal affairs the Bavarian hoped to win the Curia's support for federalism by appealing to the Vatican's other great concerns: the rights and privileges of the Church within the individual states. He asked Gasparri, Borgongini, and Pizzardo to speak to Cen-

[108] AA, PO II, PO 2 Vat., Vol. 3, Bergen to AA, May 4, 1928.

ter Party members to urge them not to support centralizing legislation. If, said Ritter, the financial allotment to Bavaria were decreased, Munich would find it difficult to carry out its obligations to the Church, such as payment of clerical salaries as specified in the concordat. While he found them ready listeners, especially Pizzardo, who already had expressed his disapproval of the Center's alliance with the pro-centralizing Socialists, they did not feel themselves in a position to intervene.[109]

In 1927 Ritter again renewed his efforts to enlist Vatican support for the federalist principle. In October he prepared a memorandum for the Curia explaining the value to the Church of Bavaria's autonomy. If centralization were adopted, the old *Länder* would become mere provinces. This in turn could harm the religious and ecclesiastical interests of Catholic Germany. In the census of 1925 Catholics numbered slightly under one-third of the population.[110] Should a unified centralized form of government be adopted for all Germany, the anti-clerical Social Democrats and Protestants could outvote the Catholics in matters such as education. Under a federal system, wherever Catholics were in a majority, as in Bavaria, legislation favorable to the Church could be enacted, and pro-Catholic state governments represented in the federal upper house, the *Reichsrat*, could help Catholic politicians in the Reichstag exert influence on the central administration. Should Bavaria, the largest Catholic state in Germany, lose its autonomy, the Church would lose one of its strongest supports in

---

[109] GSTA, Ges. Päpstl. Stuhl 1003, Ritter to Held, October 22, 1926.
[110] Statistics for the Catholic Church included:

	1910 Including the Territories Lost in 1919	1925	1933
Members	*19,322,041*	*20,193,334*	*21,172,087*

Germany, *Statistisches Jahrbuch 1926*, p. 4; *1934*, p. 14.

		1917-18	1925	1931
Conversions		4,600	7,511	10,366
Religious Establishments	male	320	559	640
Members		6,677	10,458	13,206
	female	5,741	6,619	7,147
		61,236	73,880	77,525
Clergy	Secular	18,412	19,015	19,360
	Religious	2,269	3,092	3,008

Krose, Vol. 8 (1918/19), pp. 394, 417; Vol. 9 (1919/20), pp. 374-376; Vol. 14 (1926/27), pp. 255, 302-303, 313; Vol. 18 (1933/34), pp. 222, 273-274, 282.

Germany and church-state relations could be altered for the entire Reich.

The Bavarian Minister-President Held had instructed Ritter, unbeknownst to German Ambassador Bergen, to present this long report to the Curia in the hopes that Rome would then speak out more strongly in favor of Bavaria's autonomy. Aware of Berlin's regard for Rome's opinion, Held sought to utilize its influence in behalf of the south German state. Gasparri found many of the Bavarian arguments persuasive, and he acknowledged the dangers which centralization might have for the Church, the importance of Bavaria's autonomy for the Vatican, and the problem of Center-Socialist cooperation, but he restated his former position, this time explicitly and with some finality that although Church interests were indirectly concerned in the situation, the question basically was one of states rights, an internal German affair in which the Vatican would not and could not intervene.

Gasparri on various other occasions had explained to other German politicians the danger for the Holy See to become involved when it did not directly or explicitly affect the Church. Since the war the Vatican had worked laboriously to gain international respect and had reached a high level of influence. Many times the Church's adherents, impatient with Rome's caution, silence, and secrecy, grew annoyed and asked why it did not take a stand and speak to the issue. Keeping in mind the dictum "states think in years, the Church in centuries," Gasparri reminded his listeners that the Church had to consider long-range consequences. Rome had time on its side and was not given to impetuous acts. The Cardinal knew that many politicians and anti-Church factions were waiting for Rome to make a false step, to take a step affecting internal politics of a country which could then be interpreted as willful intervention. Such an error could make the Church subject to the politicians' wrath and result in more harm than good. The most he would do in behalf of Bavaria's request was have Pacelli select a suitable opportunity to inform the Reich Chancellor verbally of the reasons why the Vatican deemed the federalist principle of government best suited to the interests of the Church.[111]

The results of the May 1928 Reichstag election brought a mixed reaction from Rome. The Socialists and Communists had gained, while the Center and especially the Nationalists had lost. The Center losses in the Rhineland were attributed to the dissatisfaction of the populace with the occupation there, where, despite promises, foreign troops still remained on German soil. Many people believed that the Left, with

---

[111] GSTA, Ges. Päpstl. Stuhl 1009, Ritter to Held, October 28, 1927; memorandum to Pizzardo, November 9, 1927; Ritter to Held, November 18, 1927; Ritter to Held, December 27, 1927.

its ties to Marxist leaders in western countries, would be more interested in pursuing the move toward reconciliation and would best be able to gain some concessions, and thus gave their votes to the Left parties. While Rome was pleased that parties committed to the policy of speedy reconciliation had gained, it was unhappy that the Left had improved its position at the Center's expense. If a significant number of voters went over to the Socialists, believing especially the SPD to be most effective in working toward international reconciliation, then, said some Curial analysts, the Vatican had to redouble its own efforts to bring about this reconciliation between nations so that when international conditions had once been improved, the defecting voters would return to the Center. The fact that the electorate was interested in seeing a speedy settlement to Germany's diplomatic difficulties, Gasparri pointed out, proved the wisdom of the Curia's policy of strenuously working for international reconciliation during the 1920's. The loss of Center votes in the Reichstag, to some degree over a foreign issue, once more could influence the Church position in internal matters, since a loss of votes might influence the outcome of the school issue and the concordat negotiations.

Within the Center itself there were also explanations for the losses. Members of the Right wing of the party claimed that the years of cooperation between the Center and the Social Democrats had so confused the mass of Catholic voters that by 1928 many discerned no essential difference between Centrist and Socialist principles. The Left wing claimed that the party had not been sufficiently outspoken in its support for reconciliation and therefore lost votes to the SPD. Theodor von Guerard, chairman of the Center Reichstag caucus, on a visit to Rome in June, told Vatican officials that the defeat was attributed to the disunity in the party and the fact that it had become too concerned with economic matters, to the detriment and expense of paying heed to its constituents' interests. The Curia observed the election results with its usual reserve. While regretting the Center's losses, it seemed pleased that in the arena of foreign affairs policy lines would remain the same, with Stresemann as Foreign Minister and a continuation of the efforts toward cooperation between France and Germany. Nevertheless, Vatican officials commented that although the German Socialists were by no means as radical as those in other countries, still in religious questions their newly acquired strength in Germany might prove problematical for the Church and bore close watching.[112]

But while in Rome Guerard was not permitted to discuss politics

---

[112] HHSTA, 88, Pastor to Seipel, May 26, 1928. GSTA, MA 104455, Ritter to BFM, May 25, 1928; MA 104469, Ritter to BFM, July 3, 1928. See also Ellen Lovell Evans, *The German Center Party, 1870-1933* (Carbondale, Ill., 1981), pp. 337ff.

with the Pontiff. Even after the election, until the formation of the new cabinet, Pius declined to see or receive Guerard in all but a very short courtesy call, although the Pope let him know that on another visit to the Eternal City, he, Pius, would welcome a detailed discussion of the political situation in Germany. The Vatican was still taking pains to avoid accusations of involvement in Germany's internal affairs. The Pope maintained a personal belief that because of the Socialists' basic position on religion, their materialistic philosophy of life, and their secular approach to the school question, no Catholic party could have a satisfactory working relationship with them for long in a governmental coalition since the Socialists would use the opportunity to beat back and eventually try to defeat the Catholic parties. The Pope had also held this view in 1920, when the Popular Party in Italy desired to unite with the Social Democrats against the Fascists. Nevertheless, in order not to prejudice the Church's interests in Germany by speaking out on an internal affair, the Pontiff had resolved under no circumstances to give any evidence of interfering, no matter how painful this reticence was for him.[113]

The formation of the new cabinet once more gave Bavarians the chance to express their wariness that Berlin might try to curtail the federalist privileges of the southern German state. Ritter mentioned to his Munich superiors and to Rome that the new Socialist Chancellor Hermann Müller might seek to abolish the Bavarian legation. Might the SPD leaders in Berlin not work with their fellow Socialists in Munich to have it closed? In 1919 Müller had indeed supported its closing.[114] The Curia had already given its final word about the federalism issue and had by many statements and signs indicated that it would not intervene unless the legation were indeed in jeopardy. Apparently Rome had decided to put the best face on the matter and to look at the good which the cabinet formation had brought, for matters were not as bad as many who disliked the Socialists would have preferred to think. During the summer Gasparri seemed optimistic, commenting to Ritter that Bavaria's rights still seemed intact, for which he was grateful. He praised Bavaria for its loyalty to Rome and to Catholic teaching. Turning to a discussion of the new Reich cabinet, he also gave the impression of not being displeased with the Socialists in it for they would probably be a pacifying force in foreign policy,

---

[113] GSTA, Ges. Päpstl. Stuhl 1014, Ritter to BFM, June 2, 1928. See also Morsey, *Zentrumspartei 1917-1923*, "Zentrumspartei," and *Der Untergang des politischen Katholizismus* (Stuttgart, 1977) for background as well as Leiber, "Reichskonkordat." Leiber insists that the Center had no official word on what the Vatican would have liked it to do.

[114] GSTA, Ges. Päpstl. Stuhl 1014, Ritter to Stengel (BFM), June 12, 1928.

especially in relations with France which in turn would serve the cause of general peace. Here Ritter again found another indication that Rome would not speak out for Bavaria in Berlin. The Cardinal, aware of the difficulties which Socialists in the government could have for the Church's attempts to win concessions from the State, had decided to play down any potential problems, not to speak out openly against the Center-Socialist cooperation, but rather to concentrate on the more optimistic international implications of the cabinet's formation.[115]

Gasparri's failure to show undue distress about German internal affairs and the formation of a Socialist-led coalition in 1928 had much to do with the world vision of both the Cardinal and the Pontiff, who viewed the solution of diplomatic problems as a prerequisite for internal stability. In other words, while not approving Socialist domestic policies, the Cardinal looked favorably on some of their views about world issues. Both the Socialists and the Curia were working to encourage international cooperation and solve some of the world's economic and diplomatic difficulties upon which internal conditions and the harmonious workings of church-state relations also depended. Therefore, Rome hoped to see some of its own objectives pursued by the policies of the new cabinet. Despite the optimism resulting from the progress made on the international scene in 1925, Rome believed there were still grounds for caution and still much to be done in order to restore Europe's equilibrium.

In conversation with a series of foreign diplomats in 1927, Gasparri conceded that Briand was on the right track but did not conceal his belief that France still had to make determined efforts to remove the remaining serious obstacles to a lasting peace and then be prepared to act upon these principles. He again designated the Rhineland and Saar territory as the greatest obstacles to peace, with the Polish Corridor and Upper Silesia close behind. Military occupation of Germany's western territories had been tried and had accomplished little since the population of the areas had indicated by innumerable examples its desire to remain German. France, continued Gasparri, had even contributed to this feeling of the local inhabitants with its poor policy. It lost the sympathy of many Rhinelanders who desired to break with Prussia after the war, of whom there had been a considerable number, and caused them to reject France as an alternative. By 1927 there was no longer any possibility that France could successfully carry out a meaningful policy there, and in his opinion a prolongation of the occupation was resented not only in the Rhineland but in all Germany and would, as a consequence, continue to poison European relations.

[115] GSTA, MA 104449, Ritter to BFM, August 3, 1928.

Likewise, repeated Gasparri, other conditions of the Versailles settlement such as the decisions made in the Corridor and Upper Silesia also had to be abandoned or altered or else, sooner or later, they would lead to another war.[116] What the Cardinal had done here was once more exhibit his distrust for the efficacy of the Versailles Treaty which the Vatican considered a poor blueprint for world peace. It also indicated that, despite the progress made by the European diplomats, Gasparri's greatest concern in naming key areas of international tension amounted in sum to stating that Germany's borders were not sufficiently equitable to ensure world peace, and that France was the major power that had to be prepared to concede more in the interests of this peace. Even if the Germans could have prompted the Cardinal's remarks, they still could not have given a better statement of their position.

Despite Gasparri's expression of concern about some diplomatically unsolved problems, by 1928 the Vatican's principle of non-intervention in German internal matters had now generally extended to foreign affairs as well. Once the opponents had been brought together for direct discussion as at Locarno and in the League, Rome was content to let negotiations take their course. The Foreign Office would have preferred the Curia to express an opinion in favor of revising the Dawes plan downward or to speak against Germany's state of disarmament, and other matters with which it was dissatisfied, and at times it showed impatience and disappointment that Rome had not taken a stronger stand. But as long as some progress was being made, the Vatican did not speak out as vigorously as it had before. The French, of course, gleefully expressed the belief that a pro-German policy at the Vatican was at an end or that the Pope had never really been convinced of Germany's arguments and claims.[117] Rome's policy, however, of saying less now was in no way contradictory, for in keeping with its plan of intervening only to redress a balance, the Vatican refrained from speaking out since there were now diplomatic methods established again for mediation and conciliation between the opponents. There was no need to intervene further; rather, the Vatican could now turn greater attention to other difficulties.

An example of this attitude taken by the Vatican occurred in 1928. The Anschluss question, the problem of German-Austrian unification into a single state, had not been acute in the last few years. Since the Reich's admission into the League, Stresemann had concentrated his energies on increasing cordial relations with France, and the issue had not received any prominence lest it disturb the détente with the West.

---

[116] HHSTA, 88, Pastor to Seipel, January 8, 1927.
[117] FFO, Allemagne 371, Doulcet to FFO, February 10, 1928.

But in 1928 discussion of this subject increased in the newspapers once again, the large Schubert musical festival in Vienna in the summer occasioned demonstrations for Anschluss, and the topic was again raised by diplomats. The French press took fright and envisioned this as the prelude by Germany, having won some diplomatic concessions from Paris, to make another demand for the union. Moreover, the rumor circulated in the French press, similar to that in 1919-1922, that Rome favored a south German Catholic state uniting Bavaria with Austria, that Rome supported and was encouraging the Anschluss. The French were so concerned about possible German-Austrian moves toward union that Cardinal Louis Dubois, Archbishop of Paris, came to Vienna in October to try to persuade the Austrian hierarchy to oppose Anschluss.

In December, in the French Chamber, Leftist Deputy François Albert made the same assertion, which Foreign Minister Briand promptly contradicted, stating that it would hardly be to Rome's interests to see such a bulwark of Catholicism as Austria disappear from the map. On the basis of the remarks in the French press, which continued on into December, and considering it important enough to reply, the Vatican published a disclaimer in the *Osservatore*. Paris also instructed its representative at the Vatican himself to verify if there was any truth to the rumors. After intensive discussions with numerous clerics and talks with his colleagues, the French envoy reported his satisfaction that the story had no foundation, and was based on supposition and speculation, then picked up by journalists who sought to discredit the Vatican or to injure French-Vatican relations. On the contrary, he said, the Curia displayed studious neutrality. In conversations at the Vatican, officials made a point to inform diplomats that the Holy See had made no official pronouncement which could be interpreted either for or against the Anschluss. In the opinion of the English legation at the Vatican, the Curia was well aware of the delicate international aspects of the problem and knew full well that union of the two countries could have important benefits for the Church, such as strengthening the Catholic populace and increasing Church influence in the larger German state, but it also could have very many disadvantages, especially if it took place against the express wishes of neighboring countries, particularly France. An Anschluss would upset the balance, stability, and the atmosphere of good feeling which had been increasing in Europe during the last few years.[118] In the opinion of the English, Rome had acted very wisely.

In fact the Vatican felt it very unpleasant to be drawn into this issue

[118] BFO, 371/13692/5421, annual report on the relations of the Holy See, 1928, pp. 12-13.

by rumors of its complicity. Gasparri called in the German representatives and conveyed to them the same thoughts that he had mentioned
to the western diplomats. The Vatican and he personally had gone to
the greatest pains not to express any opinion about the formation of a
south German Danubian federation or about the Anschluss question
so that no one could accuse the Holy See of having assisted, or influenced the matter. This was a difficult situation since the war had truly
left Austria in an untenable condition. But he nonetheless said that
the Vatican had to put aside any thought of advantage that this development might bring to the Church and let the methods for understanding and arbitration, set up and working so well since 1925, work
out a solution.[119] Once more the policy of the Vatican was to deem-
phasize any interest that it might have in the matter and stress world
peace as of primary importance.

Although Rome was now more reluctant to become involved in many
issues and possibly damage the improved French-German cooperation, Germany nonetheless still actively sought Rome's aid and in some
cases believed its help absolutely warranted and essential because of
the intricacy and delicate nature of the problems. Berlin therefore at
times had to use indirect methods or more elaborate justification for
requesting the Holy See to intervene. One example which illustrates
the complexity and interrelation of many aspects of internal and external policy and the Reich's diplomatic handling of the Vatican in
order to secure its cooperation took place in 1929.

Germany at Locarno had declared its acceptance of the political
border with France and had renounced interest in regaining Alsace-
Lorraine. In order to concentrate on sustaining the good working relationship so that the two governments could discuss important problems still outstanding, such as the Rhineland occupation, the least
desirable thing for Berlin, was to have a political party or interest
group in Germany raise the issue of possible discrimination by the
French Government against its German-speaking populace. Germany
well knew that in a period of transition and final settlement some cases
of misunderstanding between the French and German population in
Alsace-Lorraine would inevitably appear. If the alleged cases of discrimination were given sufficient publicity in Germany, popular opinion on such a sensitive issue would force the government to act. To
do nothing might make the public forget that the border had been
definitively settled, cause them to expect action to be taken, as had
been done over incidents in the east where the border was still not
finalized, incite the press to increase attacks on the government, and

[119] GSTA, Ges. Päpstl. Stuhl 1014, Ritter to BFM, December 8, 1928.

arouse the ire of nationalist groups in Germany. To protest to Paris directly about any discrimination could be misconstrued as intervention in French internal affairs and injure the growing sense of accord between the two nations. Similarly, such an official protest could also provide French nationalists with grounds to suspect that Berlin had been playing falsely and was secretly encouraging a separatist movement in the former German territory. Yet something akin to all this which Germany feared was exactly what happened.

After the finalization of the borders, some Alsatians, especially among the German population, tried to maintain as much of their own cultural identity as possible and spoke of working to have Alsace granted autonomous status within France. But Bishop Charles Ruch of Strasbourg, sensing that the movement was gaining strength and might create difficulties, made a series of ultra-patriotic statements. What he feared was that the talk of autonomy would cause the government in Paris to take note of this agitation in heavily Catholic Alsace and prompt it to pass legislation that might restrict the rights of the Alsatians as well as their Church there. To prevent this, he veered in the other direction and made his nationalistic comments. He openly opposed retention of any German-Alsatian identity and encouraged a Gallicization of the populace. Many of the clergy were involved in the autonomist agitation, and the Bishop countered by issuing a pastoral letter on September 2, forbidding his clergy from participating in the movement, condemning any thoughts of autonomy for the area, and asserting that it was a religious duty to retain an unrestricted love for France itself. Later that month Ruch made speeches linking autonomists with Communists, and spoke in his public prayers of the God of France and Alsace—all statements sure to arouse resentment in Germany, where the prelate's action was regarded as a high-handed attempt to suppress German culture.

Despite Berlin's sympathy for the Alsatians, it refrained from any political statement over the matter and tried to curb the press from making any derogatory remarks about Paris' policy toward Alsace, even though the German press printed rumors that France was seeking Curial approval or at least tacit support for Ruch. This placed Berlin in a very difficult position. If the Vatican were to endorse Ruch's actions, which would appear as a suppression of a national minority's fight for its language and ethnic identity, it would have repercussions beyond Alsace, especially when Berlin was seeking Vatican aid for German minorities in the east, where everything was still in flux. Yet if the Foreign Office sent a direct *démarche* to the Vatican about this, Berlin ran the risk that it might be interpreted by the sensitive and at times mercurial Pius as criticism of the hierarchy, whose members as a rule the Vatican usually supported.

Rome had always heeded Germany's appeals not to change ecclesiastical boundaries until the political issues were made final, at which time the full authority of the ordinary within the national borders would be recognized. To request the Pontiff directly to reprimand a French bishop after the border had become permanent might seem to Rome as if the Reich desired the advantages both ways. Berlin had no desire to lose endorsement of the Vatican for its policy along the eastern borders by making demands in the west. Yet it feared that internal pressure within Germany would force it to take action. Therefore, after intensive consultation with Berlin, Bergen conferred with Gasparri on an informal basis. No official protest was lodged, and no personal condemnation of Bishop Ruch was made. Instead, Bergen explained the difficulties which the situation created for the Reich. The point was emphasized that any sign of support by Rome for nationalistic sentiment in Alsace could only place more stress upon Franco-German relations, which were of such great importance for the peace of Europe. In addition, as Bergen deftly pointed out, any sign of Vatican disapproval of the German minority's activities could harm negotiations for the Prussian concordat, then in a crucial stage and soon to be concluded. The point was well taken. While supporting the Bishop's right to prevent his clergy from becoming involved in the autonomy movement, Rome made no statement nor gave any sign of encouragement to the prelate which could be interpreted as support for France.[120] Instead, perceiving all the international ramifications of the problem, Rome undoubtedly cautioned Ruch to moderate his language, since he had already proved his loyalty to the *patrie*.

Shortly after completing the work of negotiating the Lateran Accords with Italy in 1929, Cardinal Gasparri announced his retirement. He had had a long and distinguished career, first as one of the Church's foremost legal authorities, who before World War I had been responsible for the new codification of cannon law and then for the last fifteen years as Secretary of State. As the Church's foreign minister he had worked to establish diplomatic relations with many countries and to secure treaties with lay governments which would ensure the Church's rights and regularize church-state cooperation. He had guided Vatican policy which spoke out for neutrality and impartiality during and after the war. The added prestige and importance which the Papacy had acquired was affirmed by the increase of representation at

---

[120] AA, Geheim Vat., Pol 3 Frankreich, Bülow (AA) to Bergen, January 9, 1929 and Bergen to Bülow, January 20, 1929.

the Vatican. Whereas before World War I there were only two embassies and twelve legations to the Holy See, by 1928 there were ten embassies and eighteen legations. Before the war there were six nuncios and seven diplomatic missions abroad; by 1928 there were twenty-two nunciatures and six inter-nunciatures. Much of the credit for this increase could go to Gasparri, who worked closely with and carried out this policy under the direction of two popes. He had worked well with his pontifical superiors; they had formed a fine working relationship. While the Pontiff was usually more reserved in his public statements and spoke to general issues, Gasparri was garrulous, affable, and handled more of the daily, practical diplomatic affairs after close consultation with the Pope. Diplomats viewed Gasparri, in many ways the Pontiff's alter-ego, as the person who directed and explained Papal policy on an everyday basis.

Although it had been a long and difficult negotiation, Gasparri's crowning achievement was the completion of the concordat and treaty with Italy by which the Vatican's position as a sovereign state was both legally and diplomatically assured, thereby ending the Roman Question which had plagued Italy and Europe since 1870. German officials, as well as those of many other nations, considered the Lateran Accords a success for the Papacy and an indication of the rising importance of the Vatican in world affairs. They were, however, also quick to discover a possible advantage for Germany in the signing of the accords. Both Konstantin von Neurath, German Ambassador at the Quirinal, and Bergen confirmed that the accords might be interpreted as a Papal endorsement or at least acceptance of Fascism and that the Papacy might now be more inclined to see Italy pursue some of its foreign policy goals, particularly its bid to take over France's role of protector of Catholics in the Orient and leader of the Latin states. This could strain relations between the Vatican and France, which in turn could cause the Curia to draw closer to Germany.[121]

Another interesting effect of the Lateran Accords was that it raised a problem for German domestic affairs since it again brought into question the validity of the Bavarian concordat and Munich's representation at the Vatican. Bavaria had concluded its concordat in 1924 when the Vatican was solely a spiritual power, but after 1929 with the creation of the Vatican State it had become recognized as a temporal power as well. Article 78 of the Weimar Constitution expressly stated that the Reich Government had sole competence in matters with foreign states. Could Bavaria, which had concluded a concordat

---

[121] AA, RM 70, Vol. 2, Neurath (Rome-Quirinal) to AA, February 13, 1929 and Bergen to AA, February 13, 1929.

with the head of a religious organization, still consider this treaty valid, even though this religious leader was now also a temporal ruler and head of a state? Once more the old particularist-centralist conflict surfaced. Centralists, including many members of the German People's Party (DVP) in Berlin, now claimed that the concordat was no longer compatible with the Constitution. For many secularists and anti-Church politicians the Lateran Accords and the creation of the Vatican State presented an opportunity for Reich law to invalidate the Bavarian treaty and to cancel the favorable position which had been granted the Church there in terms of salaries, privileges, and religious instruction. For several weeks the controversy continued. Berlin newspapers demanded that the Reichstag renew the entire debate and be allowed to vote on the validity of the concordat. Bavarian papers refuted these claims and made the distinction that the treaty had not been concluded with the sovereign of the Papal state but with the spiritual head of the Catholic Church. The cabinet wisely left things as they were, for any changes would only further widen the rift between supporters of the federal and centralized theory of government and antagonize Bavaria and Rome. Instead, Berlin announced its adherence to the decision of 1920, which allowed Bavaria to retain its Minister at the Vatican, and it was able to muster enough support within the Reichstag so that the issue was not pursued further.[122]

Gasparri, pleased with the Lateran Accords, recognized that it was the most important single work of his career. He had gained the Secretariat during a war and a period of great upheaval and turmoil; he had served the Holy See and served it well. Now at age seventy-seven he believed it time to turn over the tasks of conducting the Church's foreign policy to younger people. The choice fell on fifty-three-year-old Eugenio Pacelli, the Nuncio to Germany. He also had had a long career in his post, having served in Germany since 1917, first in Mu-

[122] FFO, Allemagne 371, Ormesson (Munich) to FFO, February 18, 1929. Bavarian diplomats never tired of reminding Vatican officials of its special status within Catholic Germany, its constant struggle against the centralists since Bismarck's days, and how necessary Vatican support was for Bavaria. See, for example, Ritter's audience with Pius XI on February 17, 1930 and Minister-President Held's congratulatory letter to Pacelli on his appointment as Secretary of State, February 12, 1930. In 1930 Pacelli expressed to Ritter his great sympathy for Bavaria's position but mentioned that it was difficult to exert any real pressure on German domestic affairs in order to assist Bavaria to maintain its autonomy. Rome could not make any direct overture about the matter to the Reich Government or to the Center Party lest it give the opponents of the Church the opportunity to protest Vatican interference in matters not directly within the Church's province. But he assured Ritter that if indirectly, without overstepping boundaries, he could put in a good word, he would do so. GSTA, Ges. Päpstl. Stuhl 1027, letter of Held to Pacelli, February 12, 1930; Ritter to BFM, February 17, 1930; Ritter to Held, February 21, 1930.

14. Cardinal Pietro Gasparri in 1929, nine
months before he retired after having served as
Cardinal Secretary of State from 1914 to 1930

nich and later in Berlin. He had successfully negotiated a concordat
with the Bavarian State, another one with the Prussian State, and was
in the midst of preliminary discussions over yet another one for Baden.
Known for his intense loyalty to the Church, his skill as a negotiator,
and his wide grasp of diplomacy, Pacelli was informed of the Pontiff's
decision to elevate him to the cardinalate and appoint him Secretary
of State. The Nuncio was apparently not anxious to leave the country
where he had served so long, especially since there were still matters
dealing with church-state relations in Germany yet to be attended to.
Despite the arguments which he personally made to the Pontiff to put
off this appointment, Pius was not one to reverse a decision; he duly
named the Nuncio as Gasparri's successor.[123]

In the Reich capital there was almost a repetition of what had occurred in 1925 when Pacelli had left Munich for Berlin. Expressions
of genuine sadness were voiced in both government circles and by the
populace of Catholic Berlin as Cardinal-elect Pacelli left Berlin for the
last time in December 1929. The Germans remembered the prelate

[123] AA, PO II, PO 11 Vat. Nr. 3, Vol. 5, Bergen to AA, December 16, 1929.

for his humanitarian work in 1917, his delivery of the Papal peace appeal, his efforts to alleviate suffering after the war, and for the successful conclusion of two concordats which brought peace in the area of church-state relations. He had personally won the respect and even affection of colleagues and had dispelled the suspicions of all but the most recalcitrant Protestants about a Papal representative in the Reich capital.[124] In his place, the Curia named Msgr. Cesare Orsenigo to the Berlin nunciature. An era was ending; the two key members of the Vatican diplomatic staff who worked so closely with German officials were no longer in their accustomed posts, and the Reich wondered if the changes would in any way now affect policies.

D. THE INCREASING DANGER FROM THE RIGHT

The change of personnel in the Vatican Secretariat roughly coincided with increasing economic difficulties throughout Europe caused by the crash of 1929, the death of Stresemann, and the development of Right-wing groups such as the National Socialists (NSDAP), or Nazis, in Germany. Pacelli had observed this Rightist movement at first hand during his years in the Reich. The Reich's economic recovery in the period 1924 to 1929, based on financial loans made to Germany largely by the United States, had been more apparent than real. Similarly the growth of the Nazis seemed to indicate that Germany's commitment to a stable democracy was less than the supporters of the Republic would have wished. The Church was always concerned about groups purporting to be indifferent to established religion, and Pius XI in the 1920's had been deeply disturbed with what he considered godless movements which negated the very basic Christian principles. But in 1930 the Nazis, whose platform placed party loyalty above religious loyalty, racial purity above human dignity, were already an important political force in Germany, occupying close to one-fifth of all the Reichstag seats after the September election. They had not hesitated to criticize the Church for its activities. Hitherto Berlin had been able to control or at least influence the leading parties as well as the press in restraining disparaging remarks about the Church. In general this had been done in the interests of national policy. The most notable example of criticism—the case of General Ludendorff—had been soundly condemned by the government, and the Vatican had been assured of Berlin's good intentions. But by 1929-1930, with the enormous growth of a party which showed no inclination to cooperate and heed a government call for moderation, which openly contained

[124] *Germania*, December 11, 1929.

elements contrary to Catholic teaching, and which protested against what it called political Catholicism, the Church, believing this party to pose a serious threat to its vital interests, now began to express itself, at first through the local hierarchy, on aspects of the internal political situation.

In 1930 Cardinal Bertram had sounded a warning note, citing as a grave error the glorification of race, the contempt for revealed religion, and the Nazi call for a more "positive Christianity," which he said, "for us Catholics cannot have a satisfactory meaning since everyone interprets it in the way he pleases." Fanatical nationalism, which led to mutual hatred and racism, would not be recognized by the Church. "Here we are no longer dealing with political questions but with a religious delusion which has to be fought with all possible vigor."[125] Several months earlier the Chancery of the Mainz diocese had issued a statement declaring that, just as it was impossible for Catholics to belong to the Socialist Party because its principles ran contrary to Catholic teaching, so also was it incompatible with the Church's beliefs for its adherents to become members of the Nazi Party. In anger, Nazi journals increased their attacks on Church dogmas which emphasized the Jewishness of the Old Testament, urging the deletion of "distortions" from the New Testament, and accusing the Church of political oppression and forcing all believers to adhere to the Center Party. The Nazi press even cited some pronouncements of Leo XIII about the relations of practicing Catholics to political parties, in order to bolster its argument that Catholics in good conscience could join the NSDAP. These statements by the National Socialists struck at Church teaching and, as Bertram noted, no longer remained purely political questions. The Nuncio therefore urged the dioceses and the Catholic press to refute these attacks. While still maintaining its intention not to interfere in internal struggles, the Vatican gave what support it could to the bishops. Pacelli ordered the insertion of a lengthy article in the *Osservatore* defending the Center Party, correcting the distortion made of Leo's directives, and restating the duties of a Christian not to belong to a political party which worked against Christian ideals. The article was picked up by pro-Catholic German papers such as the *Augsburger Postzeitung* and the *Bayerischer Kurier* and given circulation within Germany. Although the Catholic episcopate issued no formal prohibition to becoming a member of any party, the Vatican had taken the opportunity of issuing a supportive statement about the Center Party and, more significantly, while still couched in general terms, of speaking about Catholics and their adherence to political

[125] Lewy, p. 8.

parties. It had decided, realizing the danger of Nazism and considering it serious enough not to remain silent, discreetly to back the local ordinaries on an issue which could have been considered a matter of internal politics.[126]

Debate over political orientation and coalition policy had been going on within the Center between 1924 and 1926. As mentioned, in January 1927 a shift to the right had become clear when Marx formed a coalition that included the Nationalists. Party leaders hoped that this combination would help to facilitate the signing of a Reich concordat and the passage of school legislation favorable to the Church. In 1930 the tendency to the right became more pronounced under the Chancellor and Center Party member Heinrich Brüning.[127] The new Chancellor and Msgr. Ludwig Kaas, the chairman of the Center Party since December 1928, an associate of Brüning, along with Pacelli, definitely believed that the Church was in a critical position since it was not only now being opposed by the Left but also was receiving attacks from the extreme Right. In order to retrench and strengthen its political position the Center had to draw nearer to its sister Catholic party, the Bavarian People's Party, by becoming more conservative, less inclined to support political centralizing proposals or cooperation with the SPD and more inclined to work with at least the non-radical Rightist parties—to concentrate, as a primary objective, on the defense of Church teaching and prerogatives, under attack from both sides of the political spectrum. In September 1930 Pacelli journeyed incognito to Innsbruck to meet with Kaas to discuss the situation within Germany, and both German and foreign newspapers reported that they particularly discussed what action the Center should take with regard to the Nazi Party. There was no question but that Rome was carefully watching the rapidly changing political developments. Bergen also confirmed the Vatican's uneasiness about the anti-religious attitude of this new political power. In a speech to German pilgrims in September, the Pope spoke of a nationalist reawakening in Germany and called the period a critical moment in time for the German people and for religion, a speech which was interpreted as expressing his concern over recent political developments. The Vatican took no official stance nor made express reference to the Nazi Party, but exerted its usual restraint, speaking in broad, general terms, expressing its misgivings privately to diplomats or political officials. For Rome to issue an offi-

---

[126] *Osservatore*, October 11, 1930 and November 3, 4, 1920. *Augsburger Postzeitung*, November 6, 1930. GSTA, MA 104455, Ritter to BFM, November 8, 1930. William M. Harrigan, "Nazi Germany and the Holy See, 1933-1936," *Catholic Historical Review*, XLVII (1961), 165ff.

[127] See ch. 7 and Evans, chs. 16-18.

cial objection without specific given cause at that moment would be regarded by many as interference and might motivate many hitherto impartial citizens, in a surge of patriotic loyalty against foreign meddling, to look more favorably on the Nazis, or it might weaken Rome's ability diplomatically to contain, restrain, or deal with the National Socialists. Official statements for the present would be left to the local ordinaries to make. But that the Vatican was concerned, there was no doubt.[128]

To most diplomatic observers the new Secretary of State appeared a very cautious man, given to careful consideration of every word he let drop, whether it be officially or in private conversation, as opposed to his predecessor, who had given the impression of being more open, even garrulous. Nor was Pacelli prone to making official protests or direct appeals to another state; he preferred to work quietly and indirectly toward his goals. Nevertheless, after several months in office he appeared to be continuing the policy which had characterized Pius XI's pontificate and Gasparri's work.

Since the Locarno Pact and the acceptance of Germany in the League, the Vatican had been more content to let Germany work bilaterally with France in the interests of peace, for it saw no great need to intervene, and conversely Germany saw new avenues of diplomacy opening and pressed the Vatican less actively to speak in its favor. Moreover, the Vatican was aware that conditions were also changing in world affairs. The great economic depression which almost ruined world trade and pushed many states almost to bankruptcy was bringing the era of good feeling to a close. France, unable to solve its financial woes now exacerbated by the worldwide economic slump, showed no inclination to alter its basic opposition during this insecure period to any treaty revision which might endanger its own shaky economic or political position. The time was inappropriate for Rome to advocate further changes in the Versailles settlement, which the Curia still deemed unjust and unnecessary. To undertake such a task on Germany's behalf might bring about results contrary to those desired, undo the efforts toward peace, and even create more difficulties for the Church in France. In many ways the dimensions of Rome's diplomatic maneuverability had narrowed since 1930. Therefore in 1931, when the economic situation had become serious enough for Germany and Austria to suggest a customs union between the two nations and to try to gain Vatican support for it, the Curia seemed interested but noncommittal. At first, despite the negative reaction which the announcement

[128] *Le Temps*, December 6, 1930. AA, PO II, PO 2 Vat., Vol. 4, Bergen to AA, December 17, 1930.

of the intended union caused in other nations, neither the Vatican's press nor its officials made mention of it. On March 28 Bergen presented a copy of the proposed treaty to Pacelli. After discussions with the Secretary, the German, Austrian, and Bavarian diplomats all had the impression that he was pleased with the idea that the two nations might get the sluggish pace of movement toward economic recovery and international understanding in Europe going again by first settling their own economic difficulties and establishing a regional agreement, inasmuch as the international conference had done so little.[129]

German foreign policy had also experienced a shift of emphasis in 1930. The new Chancellor, Brüning, was an old-time conservative nationalist who sought to see the Reich restored to the position that it had held prior to 1914. While still wedded to Stresemann's policy of peaceful revision, he and officials in the Foreign Office like State Secretary Bernhard von Bülow believed that Stresemann's methods had been too cautious, too conciliatory, and had not properly realized the potential for Germany's policy abroad. In the hopes of satisfying the Right and thereby halting further growth of its political strength, Brüning showed a greater determination than Stresemann to pursue a more nationalist policy on such matters as reparations and armaments, and to oppose Briand's proposal of 1929 for a European union. Such a union would only make revision of the German borders virtually impossible. The economic crisis had incited popular pressure on German leaders to adopt more assertive methods toward solving the nation's problems—such as by extending its influence and control in Eastern Europe through economic means.

In contrast to Stresemann's method of consultation with the League or other Powers before undertaking important diplomatic initiatives, in 1931 the Reich and Austria had negotiated in great secrecy, which, with some justification, only aroused suspicion among the other European states that this was a prelude to political Anschluss or at least a plan to make *Mitteleuropa* economically stronger than other areas and possibly force the smaller states of Eastern Europe into their economic orbit. The announcement of the treaty raised a storm of protest. France and Czechoslovakia, among others, cited their belief that the agreement would violate existing treaties, increase international mistrust, and hinder the cause of European cooperation. Both the Austrians and the Germans gave their version of the purpose and terms of union to the Curia and hoped for its endorsement. The envoys of both countries felt that, despite French pressure to have the Vatican show its disapproval of the union and to advise the two states against it, Pacelli

---

[129] GSTA, Ges. Päpstl. Stuhl 1031, Ritter to BFM, March 28, 1931.

seemed friendly, well intentioned, and had decided to maintain a neutral stand without making any statement on the issue. The feeling of the German and Austrian representatives was that they would now have to persuade the European secular powers of the importance of the union by their own arguments, but at least they would not have to fear disapproval from the Vatican.[130] Austria and Germany, however, were unable to win over the other states to their plan. The failure in May of the Credit Anstalt, one of Europe's most prestigious financial institutions, allowed France to exert financial pressure on Austria to withdraw from the agreement. By September Paris' objective was secured, for the Austrian Foreign Minister announced the abandonment of the project.

The Germans had believed that the Customs Union had provided an excellent opportunity to solve some of their economic difficulties. Although disappointed, even if the European Powers had blocked the plan, Berlin decided that in any case it would not go back to the period of 1923, would not set German economic planning on a collision course with France, a method which had already proved disastrous. Instead the Germans reasserted their intention to continue to seek a solution in cooperation with other European states. This was in essence the message which Brüning and Foreign Minister Julius Curtius brought to Vatican officials during a visit to Rome in August. The Chancellor assured Pacelli that Germany was earnestly trying to cement relations with France in the spirit of the 1925 agreement, to which the Vatican expressed its satisfaction and encouraged the Germans to continue to work along these lines.[131]

The Germans had probably hoped that their original plan for the Customs Union would have helped first their own and, by extension, international economic stability, causing the Vatican to support such a regional agreement and perhaps persuading France and her allies to soften their opposition to the Reich's proposals. While not taking sides over the issue, the Vatican, however, seemed satisfied that Germany was at least taking some action toward resolving the crisis and restoring economic stability and could do so on its own initiative. In a personal letter to Curtius after his visit to the Vatican, Bergen told him not to be too surprised by the traditional reluctance of the Vatican

---

[130] HHSTA, 89, Kohlruss (Vatican) to Foreign Minister Schober, March 31, 1931. See also F. G. Stambrook, "The German-Austrian Customs Union project of 1931: a study of German methods and motives," *Journal of Central European Affairs*, XXI (1961), 15-41, and Anne Orde, "The origins of the German-Austrian Customs Union affair of 1931," *Central European History*, XIII (1980), 34-59.

[131] BelgFO, St. Siège 1928-31, Ypersele de Strihou (Vatican) to Hymans, August 20, 1931.

15. Pius XI at his desk in the Vatican

actively to mix in secular affairs which had become more pronounced in the last few years. Only Gasparri, he said, who was particularly interested in the reparation questions and whom Bergen had supplied with a great deal of material to study, might have taken a more active part in the discussions over the matter. The old Cardinal had frequently spoken out about the economic ills of Europe and had made suggestions and plans which even involved the Americans in order to help the nations solve the problem. Such overt tactics, however, did not seem to be the methods of the new Secretary of State.[132]

As the economic crisis deepened in the early 1930's, Vatican officials privately voiced their concern over European affairs and their fears that the League system was no longer capable of solving the world's problems as it seemed to have been doing after 1925. In November the German Government announced that any further payment of reparations at that time would seriously endanger the economic life of the country. An international committee was set up to study the matter, and a conference was arranged for June 1932 to meet in Lausanne. Once more the reparations problem reemerged to plague the statesmen. By the end of 1931 the seventy-four-year-old Pontiff spoke in a wearied, saddened manner to Ritter. The economic and financial situation had once more unleashed an insecurity affecting

[132] AA, PO II, PO 2 Vat., Vol. 4, letter of Bergen to Curtius, August 15, 1931.

every phase of life. It could not go on in this way, for very few rays of hope appeared on the horizon. Instead, the world seemed to be reverting to the chaos and unhappy days immediately after the war. The politicians occupied themselves in useless conferences and endless speeches, accomplishing very little. In addition to high unemployment there was loss of desire to work, and the capitalists did little enough to combat the problem. The Pontiff seemed to spend an extraordinary amount of time occupied with such thoughts of social and economic unrest, which he connected with the specter of Bolshevism that was prospering in times of uncertainty. Should the German dam break and the political system collapse, he held to his old fear that Communism would inundate Europe. Yet, on the other hand, he was now also tormented by his worries about the radical Right in Germany—the Nazis. He saw the latter like the former, as a movement with beliefs running counter to Church teachings, against which some German bishops had already warned the faithful. It would probably be impossible, he believed, for the parties favorable to the Church even to form a coalition with the NSDAP. The Catholics would be able to cooperate with the Nazis only for temporary or specific goals or when some great crisis necessitated that they work together. Ritter believed that, although the Pope was very reserved in his comments, allowing his thoughts to range over the diplomatic situation and events in Germany, he had let his opinion slip out about how he thought Catholics and the Center should act if the Nazis became strong enough to form a government. Rumors were also afoot that Kaas, who was in Rome at the time, was there to consult with Pacelli, who knew Germany so well, for his opinion of what the Center should do if circumstances offered it the possibility of entering a coalition with the Nazis, just as it had done with the Social Democrats.[133]

The Vatican's concern over Germany was echoed in reports of the

[133] GSTA, Ges. Päpstl. Stuhl 1031, Ritter to BFM, December 20, 1931. See also ch. 7, note 148. Pius XI became increasingly disturbed about the events in both Italy and Germany during the 1930's and the infractions of the concordats in both countries. In 1939, on the tenth anniversary of the Lateran Accords, when civil and ecclesiastical officials were assembled in Rome for the occasion, the Pontiff was scheduled to make an important speech. It was rumored that it would be a fierce protest against the policies of both Fascism and Nazism. He died only forty-eight hours before the scheduled speech. Binchy, p. 98. Cardinal Eugène Tisserant in his diary is to have asserted that Mussolini, knowing what the Pontiff intended, had him poisoned to prevent the speech. Virtually all Vatican experts discount the statement as lacking in credibility. The old Pope had been ailing for some time, and the celebration for the anniversary of the Lateran Accords had been scheduled long before the condition of Pius XI worsened. A possible explanation for the assertion is that Tisserant, known to have kept voluminous diaries, had simply recorded in his entries this story as well as other hearsay and gossip about the Pontiff's death. *The New York Times*, June 12, 1972, p. 13.

representatives of other nations at the Holy See. Austria's replacement for Pastor, Minister Rudolf Kohlruss, commented in late 1931 that the problem of the Nazis was very much on the minds of the entire Curia those days. Speaking in grave terms, one Curial Cardinal informed the Austrian that the Vatican believed 1932 to be a very decisive year for the Reich, for most probably Hitler's party would win a majority in the upcoming Prussian elections, and this would have a vast impact on the entire Reich. Having won in Prussia, the largest state, the Nazis would certainly raise the question of whether or not Germany should continue to make further reparation payments, just as they had promised in the campaign. This provocative attitude by one of Germany's major parties would further complicate and darken the diplomatic scene. As regards the party's relations to the Church, the Cardinal was skeptical; if the Nazis won in Prussia, there would undoubtedly be a clash with the Church over such issues as racial theories, the glorification of the state, their advocacy of non-dogmatic Christianity, etc. For the Cardinal the future did not look favorable, and he saw nothing on the horizon that might bring any improvement.[134] The Belgian representative noted that whereas on the left bank of the Tiber at the Quirinal, a victory of Hitler in the upcoming April presidential elections was sincerely hoped for and seen as an expansion of world Fascism and a triumph and justification for Italy's policies, on the right bank, at the Vatican, Hitler was visualized as an Attila sending out his hordes to assault world peace and religious truth. A Nazi success, in the Curia's opinion, would bring more chaos to an already confused world order; it would foster a recrudescence of materialist nationalism and provide a triumph for a concept of the state, viewed as Moloch, on whose altar the liberties of the citizens and the rights of the Church would be sacrificed.[135]

During January, Pius had indicated his uneasiness to Bergen. He had known and dealt with both Ritter and Bergen for almost ten years and had discussed with them all the trials and crises that had characterized the 1920's. He trusted and respected both men and could not hide his sadness and uncertainty about the world situation and about Germany in particular. He told Bergen of his anxiety over the stalled talks with regard to reparations and disarmament which were making world peace so elusive and about the rumors he had heard that Germany was secretly rearming. Bergen answered that, in view of the world disorder, Germany, now as before, was ready to cooperate with France at international conferences, but unfortunately the statesmen

---

[134] HHSTA, 89, Kohlruss to Schober, January 20, 1932.
[135] BelgFO, St. Siège 1931-34, Ypersele de Strihou to Hymans, March 15, 1932.

had not yet found the proper formula for final agreement on the reparation payments or for limiting armaments. Here was a case where Germany and France were no longer able to negotiate on their own initiative, and the Vatican again had been thinking of mediating or making suggestions in order to help them. But the problem was that Germany was demanding equality in armament with other nations and removal of the restrictions imposed at Versailles, while France insisted it must first consider its national security needs before it consented to talk of general disarmament. The French still feared another attack by Germany. This meant that if the Papacy intervened and appealed for a reduction in armaments, it could seem as if the Vatican were favoring the German position and condoning a weakening of French security. This dilemma formed part of the anguish, impatience, and frustration which the Pontiff was experiencing.[136] The Pontiff nevertheless urged Germany to seek means of breaking the impasse with France, for, as he stated, the key to a fundamental peace in Europe was a Franco-German understanding. While on that subject he also voiced his fears about the Nazis, who were not ready to compromise but who, he believed, were bent on war. The German Ambassador then suggested that perhaps a statement from the Vatican exhorting the nations to renew the effort to find peace would be beneficial, but Pius replied that he prayed daily for peace and was ready to make some move but at present thought his words might be misinterpreted. When reminded by Bergen that Benedict's peace initiatives were at first condemned but with time were truly appreciated, the Pontiff politely replied that he would think over the suggestion.[137]

The Vatican now found itself in a difficult position; the Pontiff, no longer as active as formerly, had as his new Secretary of State a man less inclined to speak out on world issues than his predecessor, and the growing strength of the National Socialists gave every indication that they might form the next government or at least enter into a ruling coalition. The Vatican saw neither need nor even wisdom in encouraging other powers to grant concessions to Germany, which had already attained success on its own in achieving diplomatic gains in the last few years but which was causing the Vatican grave misgivings about the belligerent tendencies coming especially from its political, radical Right. Rome had taken Germany's part on many occasions in the early 1920's when the Reich had been the underdog and

[136] In June in a letter to a Catholic congress in Lille, the Vatican did appeal to France to respect the justifiable interests of other lands and to practice justice and brotherly love within the family of nations and not devote itself solely to purposes of self-interest. GSTA, MA 104455, Ritter to BFM, July 31, 1932.

[137] AA, RM 70, Vol. 3, Bergen to AA, January 25, 1932.

the European equilibrium was in imbalance and tilting in favor of France. While still believing that some injustices remained in the Versailles settlement, Rome had no desire to perpetuate the imbalance, only reversed, with Germany now the stronger power, to see its efforts for peace undone, or to watch a party come into power in the Reich which would cause difficulties for peace and for the Church. Rome therefore chose a course of watchful waiting and speaking in general conciliatory terms. The Vatican kept watch on the financial negotiations at the Lausanne Conference in June-July 1932, still believing that some formula could be worked out to aid the world's ailing economy and to prevent extremist groups from gaining power in individual countries. In early July a settlement was announced which seemed to offer help to Germany, among other states, and hope that now Europe was on the way to resolving its difficulties. The terms of the agreement called for setting aside the German reparations debt and substituting five percent bonds for 3,000,000,000 marks to be issued over the next fifteen years when and if it became possible to market them at ninety percent or better. This was made conditional on an agreement worked out between the Europeans and their creditors. This meant that the European powers would at last come to an agreement on reparations, in return for a reduction of their debts to the United States.[138]

The Vatican indicated undisguised satisfaction that Europe's statesmen had apparently finally settled the reparations question according to the guidelines suggested by Benedict XV shortly after the signing of the Versailles Treaty and again by Pius XI and Gasparri. Curial officials in 1932 reminded diplomats of Benedict's letter to the Archbishop of Genoa before the opening of the conference in that city in 1922 when he recommended that the victors facilitate the defeated nations' discharge of their financial obligations. They also recalled the letter of Pius XI to Gasparri in June of 1923, in which he stated that if the debtor showed goodwill in earnestly trying to pay his obligation, the creditors should not demand more of him than what he could pay without exhausting his resources and productivity. Both Pontiffs had warned of dire consequences and acceleration of economic crises should statesmen ignore this advice. Perhaps, then, only after many years and

---

[138] The treaty never became actual since Washington refused to allow any reduction or cancellation of the amount owed. America remained firm in the position that it had taken in the early 1920's, that there was no connection between German reparations and Allied war debts. Germany never made any further payments, and the next year the National Socialist Government repudiated the "interest slavery." But all this development was unknown to the Holy See in mid-1932, when it appeared as if the Europeans were solving the problem.

after many conferences, the results of which would not always conform to the nations' original desires, would the situation be finally rectified.[139] The events of the last thirteen years seemed to corroborate the Vatican's analysis. Now Vatican officials, with a certain degree of smug satisfaction, were in any case glad to see that Europe was finally coming around to their view, and that the advice which the Holy See, especially Cardinal Gasparri, had never tired of giving was at last being heeded.

Even now Rome sincerely hoped that it was not too late to avert the crisis, that peace and stability would be restored on the international level, and that the extremist groups which had increased their political strength since 1929 because of these economic difficulties would now begin to decline. But Rome's hopes were too optimistic. The crisis left many wounds, causing much dislocation, and the solution had been delayed too long to halt political momentum at once. With regard to Germany the Curia had anticipated that a speedy solution would prevent Catholic votes from being deflected to the Right and to the Nazis. Since 1930 Brüning had been governing largely by emergency presidential decree and had instituted stringent "belt-tightening" legislation to balance the budget. Both the Communists and the Nazis periodically challenged the emergency rule, which was able to be sustained with the implicit support of the Socialists, who saw Brüning as the means to block Nazi accession to power. Brüning's economic policies and his support from the Socialists alienated many conservative members in the Center as well as aristocratic elements in the party and the rural electorate. Some politicians accused him of leading a veiled "grand coalition" with the Socialists again. Recalling the defections in the election of 1925, the Vatican feared that some of these Catholics might give their votes to Hitler. Though Hindenburg, supported by the Center and SPD, won the April 1932 election, the Nazi threat was still great. The *Osservatore* had not published any opinions about political issues in Germany of late. In 1932, however, in order to keep the balance even and dispel any lingering belief that Rome had officially condemned cooperation with the Socialists, Pacelli without taking issue on the merits of the parties, directed the printing of a newspaper article on the subject. On April 20 the *Osservatore* carried a commentary on the work of the Center and emphasized that, despite its cooperation with the SPD, the Center had been effective in carrying out its program and had remained loyal to Catholic principles.[140] What the Vatican was doing was reminding any wavering Catholics

[139] GSTA, MA 101072, Informatorische Aufzeichnung Nr. 7, August 3, 1932, pp. 11-12.

[140] *Osservatore*, April 20, 1932. GSTA, MA 104455, Ritter to BFM, April 20, 1932.

that the Center was still a true Christian party and that tactical co-operation with the SPD was not necessarily a reason for withdrawing support from this party. In this indirect manner at least the Vatican had voiced its concern and tried to stem the Nazi wave threatening to envelop Germany, without directly intervening or taking a stand on issues.

Throughout the fast-moving events after Hindenburg's re-election, with the resignation of Brüning, the Reichstag dissolutions, further growth of Nazi power, and martial law in Prussia, the Vatican nerv-ously watched the unfolding of events. Despite urging from laymen and the Church leaders for Rome to comment on the deteriorating parliamentary situation in Germany, the Secretariat steadfastly main-tained that internal political issues, while causing the Curia much anx-iety, were not something to which Rome should publicly address it-self. Matters of conflict between Christian and Nazi principles it left to the national hierarchy to comment on. Any direct statement from Rome at that moment would receive international attention, would be seen by the Church's opponents as outside interference, and only prove detrimental to the Church, especially in its efforts toward obtaining a concordat with Germany.

Roman officials were as puzzled and uncertain over the rapid change of events as were other statesmen. After the July Reichstag election Pacelli informed Ritter that almost all his suspicions and fears had materialized with the growth of the extremist parties. The only thing which really surprised him was the extent to which the Communists had gained, polling 14.3 percent of the vote. True, their progress had fallen short of the Nazis, who gained 37.2 percent of the vote, but he feared that the Communists had laid a basis for future expansion which would then endanger Christian culture. Since the Nazi vote had shown only slight improvement since the presidential election, he believed their growth had peaked and they would have to work with other parties if they wished to enter the government. Knowing Hinden-burg's dislike for the Nazis and for Hitler personally, he probably did not expect the Führer to be invited to form a government. Thinking ahead, Pacelli wondered if under these circumstances, all parties de-siring to stem Communist growth should not unite to stop the increase of Bolshevism in Germany. Since the Socialists' philosophy was sim-ilar to the Communists in opposing Christian culture, he asked if it might not be wiser for the Center and the Bavarian People's Party, for the moment, to orient themselves more to the Right and form a working relationship with the parties of the Right. The Catholic par-ties had gained in the election and therefore were in a strong position to help form a coalition and press for a concordat, and they had sufficient strength to carry through their insistence on Christian principles in politics and thus contain the more radical Right.[141] This was not a fixed policy declaration on Pacelli's part, merely his thinking out loud and a point for discussion. The Cardinal, certainly still very wary of the Nazis, thought that perhaps having reached their height in popularity they might be more willing to cooperate and eliminate some of their anti-Christian rhetoric. Knowing the Communists' avowed hostility toward religion, exemplified by their policies in Russia, Pacelli seemed, given the present condition in Germany, ready to suggest exploring the possibility of at least a *modus vivendi* with all the Right, including the Nazis, in order first to combat the danger from the Left.

But in the next four months events continued to change rapidly, and the situation which Pius had dreaded and Pacelli feared occurred. Upon Hindenburg's request, Hitler forged a working government which excluded the Center. From then on the Vatican had a new Germany to deal with—with new internal and external objectives—and Rome had to reevaluate its policy of how to react to the new events and what they would bring for the Church, the Reich, and for Europe.

During the nine-year period since the end of the Ruhr conflict and the easing of international tensions, German-Vatican relations had undergone some modification. While the German Government experienced frequent changes and shifted generally to the right, the Vatican instituted personnel changes in the highest levels of administration. More important, however, was the subtle shift in policy. Germany had always been intent on mustering as much support as possible and convincing the Vatican of the validity of its position. But, with the failure of the Ruhr invasion, and the ensuing *détente* ushering in the "Era of Good Feeling," Germany had gained some of the aims for which it had been fighting since 1919—reductions in reparations and promises of eventual evacuation of the occupied territories. With its acceptance into the League in 1926, the Reich could now pursue its own policy more directly and work with its former opponents through the personal diplomacy of men such as Stresemann. As a consequence, there was no longer the urgency, no longer the need, to pressure the Vatican as strongly as it had previously done to take its part. The communiqués between Berlin/Munich and their Vatican representatives no longer conveyed the obsessive insecurity of previous years. The Vatican, on the other hand, also visualized its role somewhat differently. Rome saw its own interests best served by a power balance in Europe, which had been tipped in 1919 in favor of the Allies, especially France. For the sake of justice as well as for its own foreign

[141] GSTA, MA 104455, Ritter to BFM, August 2, 1932.

policy the Vatican had spoken out against some of the Versailles provisions and, through the vigorous personality of Cardinal Gasparri,
had at times intervened when it thought that Germany had been dealt
with unfairly. By 1925, with Germany's position improving and Europe embarking on what appeared to be a more balanced course, the
Vatican, in accordance with its customary policy of reserve, was now
content to husband its diplomatic credit and let Germany undertake
many of the initiatives.

In the early years of Weimar, when a united Germany was seen as
necessary for maintaining the international balance, the Curia appeared content in refraining from strong condemnation of the Center-
Socialist alliance. Although basically suspicious of Socialism and its
anti-clerical tenets, the Vatican also saw the SPD's endorsement of
peace and its efforts for international harmony as parallel to those of
the Vatican. The Socialists' participation in the Reich Cabinet only
strengthened Germany's efforts for cooperation with other European
powers. By the mid-1920's however, once the Reich as well as the
world situation appeared to have attained some stability, once the
presidency of Hindenburg, although to the Right, proved not to be a
threat to peace but was an administration with which the Vatican
could work, Rome seemed to look more approvingly on a Center alliance with political groups to the Right in the hopes that they might
prove more cooperative in helping the Catholic parties carry through
the legislation needed for a Reich concordat.

Since the international situation no longer appeared as imminently
critical as in the early post-Versailles period, questions of internal affairs interjected themselves more and more frequently into the relations between the two governments and, while always having been
present and frequently interconnected with foreign policy issues, now
seemed to acquire added importance of their own. The question of
church-state relations, which had not been solved in the first years of
the Republic, became a perennially nagging problem which was settled by stages in a series of concordats between 1924 and 1933. But
while making its wishes known about church matters, during concordat negotiations, the Vatican exercised discretion in voicing its opinions about other aspects of Germany's domestic affairs. Rome nevertheless observed events with close attention. The specter of Bolshevism,
against which Germany claimed to serve as Europe's bulwark, was a
fact that Rome always considered, and Communist electoral gains in
Germany always caused uneasiness. But in the late 1920's the rise of
an equally radical and materialist or secularist alternative on the Right
supplied the Vatican with further cause for concern. Since the growth
of either extreme would be antithetical to Church interests, the Vati-

can was less inclined to lend Germany support on the diplomatic level, an action which in turn might only strengthen the Nazis. Yet for fear of making official pronouncements indicating disapproval of the NSDAP, and thereby allowing the Nazis to gain sympathy at home from Germans who would see the Vatican's statements as unnecessary interference in the Reich's politics, it contented itself with waiting, watching, and letting the German episcopate speak out about the non-Christian aspects of National Socialism. By 1933, however, no hope remained that the NSDAP would grow weaker rapidly from natural causes, for the party had captured the chancellorship and the instruments of government. The Curia now faced the choice of adopting a stand of non-cooperation or of continuing the efforts, which had characterized German-Vatican relations since the Republic's inception, for a concordat as the best method at least to insure some safeguards for the Church. Pius XI had on one occasion stated his readiness to employ any possible means, even dealing with the Devil himself, if it would accomplish some good.[142] The Vatican chose the latter policy.

[142] Hansjakob Stehle, "Motive des Reichskonkordats," *Aussenpolitik*, VII (1956), 564. Engel-Janosi, *Chaos*, p. 103.

CHAPTER VII

The Question of Concordats
1919-1933

A. General Negotiations

Throughout the course of the Weimar Republic there was no question but that the foreign policies of the Vatican and Germany in many ways had worked in tandem. True, the Curia had acted out of a sense that justice had not been fully done at Versailles and in line with its own policy of maintaining a healthy balance in international affairs. But for all the mediation and the support for Germany's position on border revision or for the unity of the Reich, the Vatican also hoped for, and perhaps reasonably expected, something in return, especially in the area of church-state relations. Here the two governments did not cooperate as they had in the field of diplomacy, for they sat at opposite ends of the bargaining table, defining their areas of competence while trying to limit that of the other. The degree of compromise and cooperation was more limited as both sought to gain as much and concede as little as circumstances permitted in negotiations to regularize their relations with a concordat.

Despite its influence and work in the diplomatic affairs of the secular world, the Vatican represented a church and its religious concerns. Its foremost duty and the primary purpose of all its diplomatic activities was to uphold, preserve, and, if possible, strengthen the interests of the Church against secular forces, be it the state or civil government per se or particular interest groups or political parties, which many times worked through the normal parliamentary channels to incorporate their opinions or beliefs into law. The secular states, on the other hand, responsible for the framework, laws, and institutions by which society maintains its daily existence, were not always inclined to have the power of another authority such as the Church exist in what was at times competition to their control. As in other centuries, the extent of allegiance of one population to two authorities, both secular and religious, had posed a thorny problem throughout the 2,000 years of Christian history. The alternatives open to each power in dealing with the other were to risk outright confrontation, as during the *Kulturkampf* in Germany or at the time of the Laic Laws in France, to ignore one another, or to seek an accommodation. The limits of control on such areas as education, clerical appointments, and the taxation of Church lands were many times blurry or ill-defined and led to problems and conflict.

In the nineteenth century, as the powers and authority of the secular nation-state grew and the rights and responsibilities of the individual to that state were specified in constitutions and legal enactments, there was also a correspondingly increasing interest in legally specifying the relationship of Church and State. To define the area of competence for each power—the clerical seeking to expand, the secular seeking to limit, the Church's control—was the goal set by both sides if they chose to work out a *modus vivendi* or concordat to interpret church-state relations within a given country. Much of the Vatican's dealings with foreign powers was therefore devoted to matters of these relations, and all of Rome's activities in international affairs were certainly colored by concern for what it deemed its interests and those of its adherents.

In the twentieth century several factors made accommodation and negotiation increasingly attractive to Rome. The Church had revised its canon law in the first decade of the century. The new code, worked out by Cardinal Gasparri, specified what the Church regarded as its area of legislative competence, clarified its vocabulary, and defined its rights and prerogatives. Such a code made it simpler and now more desirable to bring church law into conformity with the civil law of the new states as they related to one another.[1] A settlement in the area of church-state relations, thus ensuring the legal status of the Church as well as of other religions, would contribute to the support of civil order. The Vatican readily perceived that the new governments needed as much support as they could obtain, and it realized the moral value which its support could contribute to these governments by signing treaties with them.[2] On the other hand, the Church increasingly saw the need to have its own rights and privileges legally outlined in order to counter the civil authorities, which it regarded as encroaching on its prerogatives.

The confusion in government and society which occurred after the political collapse in 1918 in many countries gave the Vatican still further reason legally to clarify its relationship to the civil order by means of a treaty. Versailles had created states which had no formal agreements with the Holy See and cast doubt on the validity of already

[1] For a summary of the new canon law see Krose, Vol. 8 (1918/1919), pp. 29-50.
[2] François Dissard, "Les concordats de Pie XI," *Revue des sciences politiques*, LVIII (1935), 555-557.

existing accords, due to the many political and territorial changes. During the period of transition in 1919 Rome naturally urged the populace to remain calm and to obey the law and the established authorities, but the Church did not disguise its concern that the earth had been shaken, frightening radical forces unleashed, and that a different, uncertain world was being born out of the chaos. For the Church this new world held many dangers. Agnostic liberals and materialistic socialists, who had come to power or had increased their influence in many states, spoke of creating a secularized society, instituting a total separation of Church and State, dissolving the confessional schools, and abolishing State support for the Churches.[3] It is little wonder that two years later Benedict XV, in the General Consistory of November 21, 1921, called upon the world governments, in the interests of internal harmony within a state, to enter into new contractual agreements with the Church. At the same time he underlined his concern and determination to defend the Church's principles by stating that in all future concordats the Vatican intended to insist, for example, on its right and duty to teach Catholic religious and moral principles in the schools and to resist the secularizing ideas current in lay or neutral schools.[4] Clearly the Curia believed that much work remained to be done in regularizing these church-state relations in the new world of 1919.

The Reich as well as the various German states also realized that in order to bring full order to the internal affairs of their country the important question of church-state relations first had to be settled, and that one step in accomplishing this goal was establishing a rapport between the Reich and the Holy See. Moreover, a contractual guarantee of the status of the Church and recognition of the diocesan boundaries as they had existed prior to 1914 would strengthen the government's claims to the political boundaries in dispute with its neighbors, such as Belgium and Poland. The Reich was also aware of the Church's strong desire to conclude a treaty, one which would be applicable to the entire Reich. Berlin readily perceived that a trade-off might be effected; by signing such a treaty and making some concessions on internal issues it could win the goodwill of the Vatican and hopefully gain Curial support in international affairs, which were, especially immediately after the war, uppermost in the minds of the German leaders. Thus Berlin, like the Vatican, was also prepared to investigate the possibility of a treaty.

After the war, in keeping with the centralizing tendencies of the

---

[3] Krose, Vol. 8 (1918/1919), pp. 29-31.

[4] *Osservatore*, November 21-22, 1921. *AAS*, XIII (1921), 521ff. John Brown Mason, "The concordat with the Third Reich," *Catholic Historical Review*, XX (1934), 25.

new Republic, more attention began to be paid to the idea of having a policy to deal with education and religious and church affairs (*Kultus*) for the entire nation. Up until this time the individual states had retained the right to treat with religious bodies and to regulate church-state relations within their borders. The framers of the new German state, however, desired Berlin to speak for all Germans in dealing with religious institutions such as the Catholic Church. The *Länder* wanted to retain their particularist prerogatives and be able both to regulate church-state relations for themselves and to sign agreements and treaties with religious bodies.[5] There had been no concordat for all Germany since 1447-1448, when representatives of the Holy Roman Empire worked out such a treaty with the Papacy. In the early nineteenth century Church and secular officials raised the idea of a Reich concordat, but Napoleon had vetoed it since he feared that such a treaty would strengthen the Reich's prestige and fan the fires of German nationalism. Under the Constitution of 1871 a concordat for the entire Empire was not possible since religious affairs were a matter left solely to the *Länder*. Article 10 of the Weimar Constitution now permitted the Reich Government by way of legislation to prescribe fundamental principles concerning the rights and duties of religious bodies and concerning the educational system, and the government's prerogative to end State support for the churches.[6] Even though the individual *Länder* still retained much control over church-state relations and over education by determining exactly how these general principles were to be implemented in specific legislation or, as in the case of Bavaria, by maintaining the right to sign concordats, now with the powers and areas of competence relegated to the new Reich Government considerably expanded, a concordat for all Germany was theoretically legally possible and in fact even desirable.

Even without a concordat the Weimar Constitution provided much more favorable conditions for the Church than did the laws and institutions of the Imperial period, due in large part to the important participatory role of the Center Party in both the government and in writing the document. Since prior to Weimar religious and educational matters had been administered by the *Länder*, the Church had benefitted largely only in those areas where Catholics were in the majority. In 1919 the Center, representing Church interests, argued both for and against states rights, supporting national legislation where the party believed it would help the Church and endorsing the states' position where that was deemed best. The Constitution as it affected the Church

[5] Schreiber, p. 58.

[6] Mason, p. 24. Dieter Kakies, ed., *Deutsche Verfassungen* (Munich, 1965). For the Weimar Constitution, see pp. 77-109, especially Articles 10, 138, and 146.

and religion then was, as in many other matters, a compromise between the centralist and federalist theory of government. The Center and especially the Bavarian People's Party were committed to the retention of states rights; yet, mindful of anti-clerical laws that had been enacted in such *Länder* as Saxony, Brunswick, and at one time in Prussia, it argued for a national religious and school law. Despite Socialist and Democratic pressure to have a declaration of the separation of Church and State written into the document, it was not stated specifically. Instead, the rights of the State to interfere in Church affairs were curtailed, the automatic right of the civil government to approve Church appointments was abolished, and the Protestant Evangelical Church was disestablished in all *Länder*. On the other hand, the Church, along with other religious bodies, was permitted to become a public corporation which could then receive financial support from the State. The Central Government was also to provide general principles for the commutation of any financial agreement between the Church and the states (Section III, Articles 135-141). Until such time as guidelines were issued, however, the Church could continue under whatever arrangements it had made with the individual states.

In educational matters (Section IV, Articles 142-150) the provisions of the Constitution were left vague. The coalition partners agreed to provide a national public school system. The Democrats and the German People's Party wanted a basic common school (*Volksschule*) which was non-denominational, but with religion as part of the curriculum, like any other subject. The Socialists favored a completely secular system or at least one with non-compulsory religious instruction. The Church, however, sought recognition and State support for the public confessional schools, where a Catholic environment could be given to the pupils. Since no agreement was reached on this matter, the decision was put off until later, when a national school law (*Reichsschulgesetz*) would be written. For the present, the Constitution provided for the inclusion of religion in the curriculum in all but secular schools, and the right of the State to supervise religious instruction. Participation in religion classes was voluntary and left to the parents or guardians to decide. Article 146 specified that the *Volksschule* be designated as the basis of a "new organically planned" national school system, but denominational or secular schools could be set up if sufficient demand warranted this. But until the passage of a *Reichsschulgesetz* the existing laws would continue to be enforced, that is, the statutes of the individual *Länder*. In sum, although not having won everything it desired, the Church's position according to law looked very good and needed only to be confirmed by concordat or made more specific, as for example by the future school law. Secure in its rights as specified in the Constitution, the Church now had to deal with the secular government on both the Reich and state levels to secure its aims in the form of a treaty or school legislation. Circumstances varied, of course, on the state level from *Land* to *Land*. In Bavaria the hierarchy was generally satisfied, where a conservative Catholic party dominated political life after 1920; was less satisfied in Prussia, where the Catholic Center was the junior partner of the Social Democrats; and was not pleased at all with the difficulties it was encountering with anti-clerical legislation in states such as Socialist-run Saxony.[7]

The new Constitution was not anti-clerical but had attempted to be neutral. It had guaranteed the right of association and organization to all religions, made some general statements about the relations of Church and State, and provided for further definition of this relationship. But by its omissions it also created problems about the legality of previously existing agreements. Was the Papal bull of circumscription, *De Salute Animarum* of 1821, promulgated by Rome for territories of the Kingdom of Prussia, or was the Bavarian concordat of 1817 still valid, or did the change in the form of government automatically invalidate them?[8] Could or should either or both of these agreements be retained, or should they significantly be altered, or entirely new arrangements be worked out to conform to the new politico-social situation after 1919? Should the *Länder* negotiate individual treaties or should the Reich Government undertake the task? What would be the guidelines for negotiations, and, until such accords were put into effect, what would be the status of church-state relations?

The importance and necessity of having a concordat became apparent immediately after the founding of the Republic. The Foreign Office made other ministries aware of its significance for foreign affairs. In May 1920, for example, the Reich Government reiterated to the Prussian Minister of Religious Affairs[9] the importance of the diocesan boundary question for German policy and how valuable a concordat would be. In the future the Foreign Office asked to be consulted on any steps taken by German officials that would deal with this problem, especially in any negotiations with foreign prelates.[10] The state

---

[7] Evans, pp. 230-240. Grünthal, chs. 2-30.

[8] For text of this and other agreements and concordats with Rome, see Lothar Schöppe, ed., *Konkordate seit 1800* (Frankfurt a.M., 1964). For agreements dealing with Prussian territory prior to 1929 see pp. 51-63.

[9] Although *Kultusminister* carries the meaning of Minister of Education and Religious Affairs, for brevity's sake, in this chapter it has been rendered as Minister of Religious Affairs.

[10] AA, PO II, PO 24 Vat., Vol. 1, Reich Minister of the Interior Köster to Prussian Minister of Religious Affairs Haenisch, May 1920, *sine dato*.

ministries of religious affairs also let it be known how difficult it was to operate without a formal treaty. Without further clarification of the relation of the Church to the State the civil government constantly had to consult Church officials. Did secular authorities have the right, for example, to approve or to veto non-German clerics from being assigned to parishes within the Reich, or was this purely an ecclesiastical matter? Prussian officials bitterly decried the difficulties. Given the sensitive political nature which ethnicity played in the border areas, they asked Bertram and the episcopate to support the government's right to oppose the appointment of non-German pastors.[11] The problems were simply becoming too numerous and protracted unless something was done to simplify the matter. Already in December 1919 officials on both sides realized that steps had to be taken, and Pacelli journeyed to Berlin to discuss the situation with Prussian and Reich representatives. As a temporary measure the Prussian and Reich Governments issued a memorandum, stating that all formerly existing agreements would remain in force, for the present, but in order to bring the *Länder* treaties in line with the new political situation, negotiations between Rome and German officials for a Reich treaty should begin as soon as possible.[12]

Several months later Richard Delbrück, who manned the Vatican desk at the Foreign Office, traveled to Munich to discuss the basis of a treaty with Pacelli. The Reich counsellor explained that Berlin favored negotiating a Reich concordat for all Germany rather than having Rome work out separate agreements with the individual states. The Nuncio stated that the Prussian bishops had already been confidentially informed that the Curia also intended to seek a concordat for all Germany rather than revise the former agreements. The two men proceeded to enumerate some priority issues that would have to be considered in the negotiations. Berlin demanded that German nationality be a prerequisite for exercising any religious duties within the Reich. The government feared that foreign clergy, especially the Poles,

[11] AW, 1A 25k, 154, Haenisch to Bertram, July 16, 1920. The Vatican's objective of showing support for the Reich in diplomatic affairs in exchange for concessions on matters dealing with church-state relations was clearly indicated in mid-1920. Cardinal Bertram had written to Pacelli, inquiring what the Vatican's attitude would be to Berlin's request that it be granted the right to approve any non-German who occupied a clerical position in the Reich. Pacelli replied on July 30 that basically he had no objections to the State's demands, but for tactical purposes the Church should not at that moment grant final approval since this would give away the Nuncio's bargaining power to gain concessions in important matters such as education. AW, 1A 25k, 154, Pacelli to Bertram, July 30, 1920. Padellaro, p. 49.

[12] AA, PO II, PO 2 Nr. 1 Vat., Vol. 1, memorandum of Niermann (Prus. Ministry of Relig. Affairs), January 9, 1920.

might use their pastoral office to spread anti-Reich propaganda among the faithful, particularly in such politically sensitive areas as Silesia. The Reich also requested that the German clergy be trained in German institutions. Pacelli agreed, but said that exceptions would have to be made for some seminarians to pursue their studies in Rome. While on the subject of higher education, the Nuncio stated that although the universities were state run, Rome had great interest in maintaining the Catholic character of Catholic theological faculties at German institutions. Rome believed that the Church should have some influence in the selection of the faculty and a right to remove professors who by their teaching or example would give offense to Catholic doctrine. Pacelli pointed out that the Weimar Constitution had granted the Church full control over its internal affairs, which included the selection of cathedral chapters and the election of bishops, but since Rome was requesting some influence over the selection of university professors, who were state employees, Rome would not be averse at least to discussing the question of government rights in ecclesiastical appointments. Delbrück informed the Nuncio that a concordat would have to incorporate the idea that diocesan boundaries could be adjusted only to the political ones, once all political treaties and plebiscites had been completed, lest any government concession on this point lead the public into believing that it had abdicated total control over the disputed areas. Pacelli agreed. The Nuncio also clearly remarked that the school question—the right to have public confessional schools, and the problem of providing for teaching religion in the public schools—would have to be fully treated in a concordat, but agreed that negotiations might wait on this matter to see first what the laws dealing with public education, then being written, would say on the subject. Rome also wanted to see a clause inserted in any concordat specifically granting complete freedom to the Church to found religious orders in Germany. Both men agreed that the problem of State financial support for Catholic institutions was an area where much work would have to be done.[13] Once the two officials in principle seemed willing to begin negotiations, they decided that each side should prepare an agenda of topics to be discussed during the negotiations, and that the Foreign Office should seek to dispel any objections at home to the Reich's signing such an agreement and should convince the states that a Reich concordat would be better than a series of *Länder* treaties.

But Bavaria had already taken the lead in January 1920 and had

---

[13] AA, PO II, PO 2 Nr. 1 Vat., Vol. 1, report of Delbrück to AA, July 12, 1920; memorandum of Delbrück, July 16, 1920.

started negotiating with the Vatican. It was shortly after these negotiations with Bavaria had begun that Pacelli let Berlin know that the
Vatican would also like to conclude a concordat for all Germany. He
had then been assured by Foreign Minister Walter Simons that a Bavarian treaty would not hinder the conclusion of a Reich concordat
later. However Pacelli's comment that the Bavarian concordat might
not only be signed first but also serve as a model for future treaties
caused Prussian officials, ever anxious of their own state's prerogatives, to call for consultation among all concerned. In August the Prussian Minister of Religious Affairs stressed his need to be kept current
about any concordat negotiations and about Rome's attitude to the
form it should take for Germany. He suggested that he consult with
his Bavarian counterpart before any binding treaty be signed with the
Vatican, since it was evident that should a concordat with Bavaria be
signed before a treaty with Prussia or the Reich, its contents would
certainly influence ensuing negotiations, especially in the matter of
episcopal nomination.[14]

Virtually all of the old special privileges granted to Bavaria at the
time of unification—its own army, postal system, etc.—had been swept
away by the Constitution of 1919. Still what remained was the right
of that state to make an agreement with religious bodies such as the
Catholic Church. For Bavarians, a concordat, like its legation at the
Vatican, was a symbol of their state's unique status. Since the entire
area of church-state relations had to be once more legally worked out,
Bavaria desired its own concordat again. The concordat question reflected an aspect of the long-standing conflict between Bavaria's federalist philosophy of state government and the unitarist, centralist policies of the Reich.[15] But Bavaria, true to its particularist spirit, showed
no inclination to coordinate or seek approval for its negotiations with
other states of the Reich. Nor were the Bavarians at all favorable to
having their work subsumed under a general Reich concordat. Instead,
Munich insisted on negotiating its own treaty, which it desired to have
signed before Reich-Vatican discussions were completed. The only
thing the Bavarians conceded was to assure Berlin that they were proceeding legally and in accordance with the new Constitution and that
before any final draft was signed they would submit the document to
the Reich Government for its comments and approval. Naturally Bavaria, as well as the Reich and Prussia, had been anxious to learn what
the Vatican would ask of Munich, and they had not been surprised to
learn that the negotiating points consisted of broad demands in pas-

[14] PGSTA, Rep. 90, P.11.1.1., Vol. 10, Minister of Religious Affairs Fleischer to
Prussian Minister-President, August 18, 1920.
[15] Franz-Willing, pp. 206-207.

toral and school control, the naming of Catholic university professors, and the general elimination of State participation in all Church affairs. In early 1920 the Bavarians, however, had reacted negatively to Pacelli's opening position, and Berlin was of the opinion that the discussions in Munich would continue for some months before any understanding would be reached.[16] Berlin was skeptical about Pacelli's remark that a Bavarian concordat would soon be signed, and therefore now made preparations to negotiate a Reich concordat.

Apparently the Vatican had anticipated a rapid and advantageous conclusion first of the Bavarian treaty and soon thereafter the signing of a Reich concordat. It either believed that Germany would cooperate in consideration of what the Vatican was endeavoring to do for Germany by means of Curial diplomacy or it hoped that the Germans, anxious to ensure civil and internal peace as rapidly as possible, would grant Rome favorable terms in an effort to bring the negotiations to a speedy conclusion. Pacelli expressed his disappointment to German officials that no treaties were near completion by the fall of 1920. He assured Germany that the Vatican asked for nothing which would run counter to the Constitution, but looked only for preferences on the basis of *praeter legem*, on the basis of what it already had been granted under previous law. Deleterious and endless bickering, he warned, would result in a concordat-less situation, which meant that the Curia, for example, would not be in a position to refute the demands of Germany's neighbors for the abolition of German ecclesiastical jurisdictions in the lost territories. Should the new states created by Versailles sign treaties with Rome soon, then their rights in the areas might even have to be conceded.[17]

Berlin also remembered how, one year before in 1919, the Vatican and Prussia had been at loggerheads over the method of selecting the new archbishop of Cologne. The canons of the chapter claimed their right to elect the new archbishop; Rome, applying the new canon law, expected to appoint the new incumbent. The government claimed the right to instruct the canons as to its preference, and Rome claimed that the Bull of 1821 was no longer valid and that the new Weimar Constitution had guaranteed the Church freedom to select its own administrators.[18] Negotiations had been intense and led finally to a solution suggested by Pacelli whereby the chapter could elect the new

---

[16] Germany, Nachlass Carl Becker, located at the Institut für Bildungsforschung, Berlin (herafter cited as Germany, Becker), Folder 33, Delbrück to Simson (AA), September 18, 1920.

[17] *Ibid.*

[18] See ch. 4. For a good discussion of the problem, see Norbert Trippen, *Das Domkapitel und die Erzbischofswahlen in Köln 1821-1929* (Cologne, 1972), pp. 468-469ff.

archbishop and Berlin express its preference, but settlement would not serve as a precedent. Speed had been needed in replacing the spiritual leader of western Germany's Catholics before the French could influence the election. In this sense Pacelli had demonstrated the value of Berlin's concluding a legal treaty with Rome as soon as possible for diplomatic interests and in order to bring a measure of stability to German society.[19] But it also illustrated to Berlin that Rome intended to retain the power of episcopal selection in its own hands and to concede less to local authorities and to the civil government than before. It served as a warning of future hard bargaining over a concordat and an indication that all aspects of the problem had to be first carefully considered. True, Pacelli and the Curia seemed most interested in obtaining Bavarian and Reich concordats and had urged that work on them be completed as rapidly as possible. But the haste and demands made by Rome did not please the Germans, who presumed that the pace would have to be somewhat slower.

By January 1921 the Reich Government had decided to open formal negotiations with Rome. Since several state governments might desire their own treaties and cause difficulties when it came to final legislative approval of a Reich concordat, the Central Government sent memoranda to the *Länder*, inquiring if they had any objections to a general concordat and appealing to them to support the cabinet's decision to conclude such a general treaty soon. The Minister of the Interior, Erich Koch, urged that these negotiations begin, stressing the connection between domestic and foreign considerations in advocating this step, "since lasting good relations between the [German] State and the Catholic Church is a prerequisite for the orderly development of political relations between the Reich and the Curia."[20] The government then circulated a list of general points on which it proposed to negotiate and included the following demands: (1) all Catholic clergy working on German soil would have German citizenship; (2) all Catholic clergy would have a certificate of education specifying that they had studied for a specific number of years in German schools; (3) the right of the State to influence or participate in episcopal appointments, wherever that pertained, would be transferred to the cathedral chapter; (4) episcopal election would be made by the cathedral chapters; (5) any diocesan border change would be taken up in special negotiations at a later time; (6) confessional schools and religious education would be permitted; (7) the possibility and degree of the State's contribution to the Church would be approved only by mutual agree-

[19] Ludwig Volk, *Das Reichskonkordat vom 20. Juli 1933* (Mainz, 1972), pp. xxvi-xxvii.
[20] AA, BRV 265, Vol. 1/3, Reich Minister of the Interior to the governments of the *Länder*, January 6, 1921.

ment; (8) the Church would have complete freedom to establish religious orders if they in no way conflicted with the Constitution's clauses regarding the rights and duties of religious bodies; (9) the Curia would allow no reduction in the number of the German-supervised religious missions in other countries. If for diplomatic reasons this was not possible, then it would still permit German missionaries to continue their work under superiors of other nationalities.[21]

When the intentions of the Reich Government were circulated, some disagreement arose about exactly what level of administration would do the negotiating. On January 19 Prussia informed the Central Government that it did not fully agree with the idea of a Reich concordat generally valid for all Germany. Prussian Minister-President Otto Braun called attention to Article 78 of the Constitution, which allowed individual states to maintain relations with the Vatican and stated that Prussia had relinquished its envoy at the Vatican, with the specific understanding that the German Ambassador to the Holy See would also undertake the responsibility of representing the concerns of that state. A general treaty might not take Prussia's specific needs into consideration and might invalidate the very reasons for which the north German state had given up its legation at the Vatican. A Reich concordat was possible only by the voluntary renunciation of the states to deal with this matter. Prussia was not prepared to give an immediate final answer but would do so only if all German states with large Catholic populations were also prepared to do so.[22]

Bavaria also sent word to the Reich Government that it also opposed a general treaty and was then at the point of concluding one of its own with Rome. The replies which arrived from most of the other states were also negative, the opposition centering on the fear that an all-German concordat would remove the religious and educational questions from the competency of the individual states, which, by negotiating their own treaties, could maintain tighter supervision over these affairs and take into account local circumstances which might not be considered in a more general accord. By the end of the month, Saxony, the last of the states with a sizable Catholic population to send word to Berlin, requested the Reich Government not to undertake negotiations since the Dresden Government also desired to settle the Church question without Central interference.[23]

Despite further discussions with the states, the Reich Cabinet had suffered a defeat. Bavaria would not consider abandoning the negoti-

---

[21] Germany, Becker, 33, guidelines for the *Reichskonkordat*, attached to memorandum of Reich Interior Minister, January 6, 1921.
[22] AA, BRV 284, Vol. 1, Braun to Reich Interior Minister, January 19, 1921.
[23] BFO, 371/6178/5283, Kilmarnock (Berlin) to Curzon, January 28, 1921.

ations that it was conducting and, notwithstanding all the foreign policy arguments about safeguarding its borders by a speedy conclusion of a treaty, Prussia could not be swayed to modify its particularist standpoint. Citing the Bavarian precedent, Prussia declared itself interested in a treaty which would be an updated but little altered version of the agreement it had with Rome since 1821. Prussia would at some future date be amenable to seeing the concordats of the individual states collected under a kind of general, but basically substanceless, Reich concordat. Saxony and Hesse with Prussia, and Württemberg also leaned in that direction, although it acknowledged the diplomatic value of a treaty for the entire nation.[24]

The Interior Minister tried to modify the states' views by reasserting that the Reich in no way desired to invalidate their prerogatives in dealing with the Vatican. On the other hand, he also wanted to emphasize that the Constitution in no way hindered the Reich from negotiating a concordat which would form a framework for further agreements between the Vatican and the individual states. Should the negotiations begin, they would be directed toward emphasizing the unity of the Reich. In a time when the unity of Germany had been expressed in the new Constitution and demonstrated at the Vatican by the presence of an ambassador representing the entire Reich and by a nuncio accredited to the Berlin Government, there could be no better way, the Reich Minister urged, to underline this unity than to let the Central Government now negotiate a treaty with Rome in matters common to all the states. Thereafter the individual states could conclude supplemental treaties which would deal with their specific problems and individual needs. He attempted to strengthen his argument by emphasizing how Rome also very much desired a Reich concordat. Should the Curia be confronted with a series of drafts for *Länder* treaties, it could justly conclude that the commitment of the states to a unified Reich Government was very weak indeed. Moreover, foreign powers would also soon notice these divisive tendencies. The Minister therefore cautioned that a united front always had to be presented to the outside world, especially in those troubled times. Berlin believed the state governments were well aware of this and expected them to make allowances for the important international and external considerations involved in this issue.[25]

The problem, however, was not as simple as perhaps Minister Koch

[24] AA, PO II, PO 2 Nr. 1 Vat., Vol. 2, memorandum of Delbrück, February 4, 1921.
[25] AA, PO II, PO 2 Nr. 1 Vat., Vol. 2, memorandum of Reich Minister of the Interior to AA, Prussian, Saxon, Baden, Hessian, and Württemberg Cabinets, February 25, 1921.

had presented it. A Reich concordat could in theory be formulated in such general terms that it would allow for individual states later to sign their own treaties with Rome. But if any of the *Länder* concluded an agreement with Rome first, then the provisions in that treaty would influence the subsequent Reich negotiations, and perhaps clauses dealing only with conditions in one state would have to be provided for in the general concordat, much against the wishes of the other states. This was exactly the dilemma that had to be faced in 1921, for Bavaria was busy with its own negotiations and had flatly stated that it did not intend to allow any changes in its treaty with the Curia, once signed, because of anything subsequently worked out between Rome and Berlin. Concordat legislation dealing with school and church affairs in Bavaria, where the Church was very influential and the government under more pressure to grant concessions than in other parts of the Reich, would never be approved in a general concordat by Germany's legislative upper house, the *Reichsrat*, which represented all the states. Difficulties would also arise over how to make allowance for financial, material, and political assistance to the Church, since this could vary from state to state, and already the Constitution had provided for the elimination of State responsibilities to the Catholic Church. At best, then, nothing more than general guidelines could be put into a Reich concordat. Yet Bavaria was already hard at work making specific recommendations as to amount and degree of support. Any specific provisions on the school question would encounter various parliamentary difficulties in most states. Prussian Minister-President Adam Stegerwald pointed out at a meeting called in Berlin in September that to bind school affairs by an international law would never pass the Prussian *Landtag*, given its composition of large numbers of Social Democrats and parties dominated by conservative Protestants. If Bavaria proceeded to sign a separate treaty, this would cause further difficulties since Prussia had more Catholics than did Bavaria, and such a treaty with provisions regulating conditions for only one of the two large segments of the German Catholic population would cause even greater chaos, disunity, and overall dissatisfaction with the new social and political structure that Berlin was trying to weld together.[26]

In spite of the negative reaction that the proposal had received during 1921, the Reich Government continued trying to persuade its constituent member states of the necessity and value of a general concordat. The greatest opposition and difficulty, as to be expected, arose from the two largest states, Bavaria and Prussia. The Bavarian Gov-

[26] AW, 1A 25k, 154, memorandum of meeting in Berlin between Bertram, Schulte, and Prussian ministers, September 15, 1921.

ernment bluntly stated that it did not favor a Reich concordat even in the form of a general framework treaty, and it would not entertain any suggestion to renounce its treaty in favor of a Reich concordat. In Prussia, State Secretary for Religious Affairs Carl Becker discussed the matter with Reich Foreign Minister Simons. After assuring Becker that a Reich concordat automatically assumed that the individual states would later also negotiate treaties, the Reich Minister was apprized of some of Prussia's objections to a concordat. Becker expressed his sympathy for all the diplomatic arguments for such a treaty, but he also knew that the Reich hoped to define its role in cultural and church-state matters and to unify and extend its applicability to the entire Reich by means of such a treaty; that the new Nuncio, as the first Papal representative to all Germany, would like to conclude a treaty for the entire country and thereby secure the influence of the Church by international accord; and that certain circles within Germany would also like to see the rights of the Church established by the Constitution now secured by international law. Nevertheless, Prussia believed that the Reich could in no way extend its competence in church-state affairs by diplomatic means and by negotiating with other governments. It was understandable that the Nuncio would find the Central Government a desirable partner since, as opposed to the individual states, it was not familiar with the problems of each local area and lacked experience in bargaining and making counter proposals in church-state matters. Although Becker fully understood the arguments for granting concessions in internal affairs in exchange for Vatican support in diplomatic situations, Prussia was not ready to see her sovereignty impinged upon. For example, simply because of the Reich's international needs, he said, Prussia was not prepared to define and verify by international treaty the character of the state's school policy for the next few centuries. Becker then went on to enumerate a whole series of difficulties that such an agreement would cause for Prussia. The Prussian finally declared that perhaps the best solution would be for Prussia, Bavaria, and all concerned states to begin discussions separately with the Holy See, and only when all negotiating parties agreed on the basic points should the subject of an "umbrella-like" Reich concordat be pursued.[27]

In March Delbrück reported to the Foreign Office that little progress had been made and that the Bavarians were still negotiating for their own concordat and that the Prussians, in consultation with the Bavarians, had been strengthened in their opinion to sign a Prussian

[27] PGSTA, Rep. 90, P.11.1.1., Vol. 10, note to Becker, February 11, 1921, accompanying Haenisch's note to Prussian Minister-President, February 15, 1921.

treaty before considering a Reich concordat. Apparently, added Delbrück sadly, the Prussian Cabinet had determined to pursue its course without considering the needs of Germany's foreign policy.[28] In April, the Bavarian Minister for Religious Affairs, Franz Matt, gave a similar reply to the Reich Interior Minister, as had his Prussian counterpart to the Foreign Minister. He insisted on Bavaria's right to negotiate a concordat in full freedom. In the opinion of the Munich Cabinet the arguments based on internal and foreign policy made in favor of a Reich concordat were still insufficient reasons for Bavaria to renounce its intention of regulating its affairs with the Catholic Church by itself. Since the Vatican had not objected to a Bavarian treaty, Munich intended to continue negotiations. To buttress his argument for Bavaria's action, Matt proceeded to raise objections to Berlin's circulated guidelines for the Reich concordat, saying that they did not satisfactorily take into account the religious situation existing in the individual states.[29] The replies from Bavaria and Prussia, so remarkably similar, once more highlighted the extreme jealousy with which the states defended their rights against the encroachment of the Central Government and their fears lest they lose prestige or influence by the actions of another state. It also portrayed the virtual cross-purposes with which the two levels of government approached the question—the Reich Cabinet giving primacy to foreign affairs, the state governments to internal matters—a division of purpose frequently characteristic of Weimar history which ultimately proved injurious to both.

The Vatican did not completely share the Reich Government's view. Although it most definitely desired to conclude a Reich concordat, it had no objection to signing a treaty with Bavaria before completing the work on any others. In fact, as early as July, when he thought a concordat with Munich imminent, Pacelli asked Delbrück if it might not be better to await its completion, since it would contain important clauses that could have a bearing on a Reich treaty. There were several reasons for Rome's attitude. Bavaria, unlike the other states, had already had a concordat with the Holy See, and even after German unity in 1871 tradition and the Imperial Constitution had permitted this state to maintain its diplomatic relations with Rome and to continue to conduct its own policies with the Vatican. Moreover, Munich had served well as the center for Catholicism in Germany from which the voice of the Pontiff had been heard throughout all of the Reich. In fact the pervasive Catholic influence in the southern German city

[28] AA, PO II, PO 2 Nr. 1 Vat., Vol. 2, Delbrück to Simson (AA), arrival date March 16, 1921.

[29] GSTA, Ges. Päpstl. Stuhl 972, Matt (Bav. Min. of Relig. Affairs) to Reich Interior Minister, April 22, 1921.

was so great that friends frequently referred to it jokingly, enemies denounced it peevishly, as the "secret Rome." Rome had no desire nor saw reason to bypass its old ally or to insult it by negotiating solely for a Reich concordat, especially when Munich clung so tenaciously to its particularist rights. Rome really lost nothing and had everything to gain by dealing with Munich. Even if little came of the negotiations or if Bavaria agreed to permit its interests to be served by a Reich concordat, the fact that the Vatican was dealing with the Bavarians or could always resume such discussions could prod Berlin to speed up the work for a general treaty. If, on the other hand, the Curia could conclude an agreement with the south German state it would also have won a diplomatic victory. In view of the overwhelming Catholic population in Bavaria[30] and the legendary piety and loyalty of its rural population to the Church, there was every reason to hope in Curial circles that a concordat which would please the Vatican could be concluded in a short time. Besides, as Pacelli had already made clear, this treaty could then serve as a precedent and model for the impending negotiations with the Reich. It was therefore not surprising that Rome entered discussions with Munich and had remained diplomatically discreet, raising no objections to its independent stand and disagreement with Berlin.

Rome, however, did not take the same attitude toward Prussia, as was indicated in the spring, when Prussian officials discussed with Pacelli the possibility of opening negotiations similar to those with the Bavarians. In this *Land* there had never been an international treaty or a concordat, merely a bull of circumscription delimiting diocesan borders and regulating ecclesiastical affairs which had been issued by Rome with royal sanction that recognized it as having the validity of civil law.[31] Here the population was not overwhelmingly Catholic nor were the legislators, many of them conservative Protestants and liberal-minded Socialists, greatly disposed to such an accord. Prussia which had stated its opposition to settling the school question in a treaty with Rome preferred to deal with it separately as an internal matter. Since, however, one of the most important objectives of Vatican policy was the definition of the Church's rights in educational matters, a concordat without such a clause would be of much less value to the Curia. Pa-

[30] In 1925 Bavaria's population consisted of 5,163,106 Catholics and of 2,126,438 Lutherans. *Der Grosse Brockhaus*, Vol. 2, p. 417.

[31] Besides *De Salute Animarum* (1821), which dealt with the basic old Prussian lands, there were other bulls promulgated (1821, 1824) dealing with such territories as the Upper Rhineland and the area of Hanover annexed in 1866, etc. Volk, *Reichskonkordat*, p. 1. For purposes of simplification in this work, *De Salute Animarum*, the most important of these bulls, will be used to refer to all of them.

celli, therefore, clearly stated that if the Prussian Government maintained its position, the Curia would prefer a "concordat-less" situation
in Prussia and would concentrate its efforts on obtaining an agreement
with the Reich.[32]

There was much to be said for a Vatican policy in favor of a Reich
treaty, of which the Prussians were well aware. On the national level,
with the assured support of the Center Party, some political lobbying
among other parties, and pressure from the Foreign Office, there was
a better chance for the approval of a concordat than in several states
where political parties opposed to the concordat held power. A Reich
treaty would be beneficial to Rome not only because it dealt with all
Germany in one accord, but if it contained clauses dealing with the
school question it would be valid for all states, including Prussia, where
the Socialists were in control and stood opposed to religion in the
schools. If this were to occur, Prussia would have failed in maintaining
its opposition to Vatican demands, yet would have gained nothing in
the bargaining that would have occurred had it negotiated its own
treaty with Rome. Pacelli also reminded the Prussians that without a
concordat they, particularly, stood to lose much along their borders,
for many of the disputed territories were or had been part of Prussia.
Basically what Rome desired, and appeared to be in a favorable position to obtain, was a treaty; its tactic was to request Prussia to be
more accommodating or it would negotiate with the Reich and at the
same time indirectly to apply pressure on the Reich to speed up negotiations, or it would have no objections to concluding a treaty with
Bavaria first. The circle had gone full swing, and the Reich was still
confronted with the basic problem of how to get its component parts,
the states, to renounce their particularist outlook and, for the sake of
national welfare, let Reich policy take precedence.[33]

The states were not arbitrarily making things difficult for the Central Government, but they carefully guarded their rights against what
they visualized as an attempt by the Reich to weaken their historical
basis of power and turn them into mere provinces. Moreover, legally
the Constitution gave them grounds for assuming the position that
they did. While Articles 10 and 135 defined the relations of the State
to religion and religious bodies, and provided for the Reich to issue
federal legislation at some later date to define by way of general principles the education system of the country and the rights and duties
of religious bodies, Articles 137-138 and 143-144 left the implementation of much of these principles, as for example the question of State

[32] GSTA, MA 104493, Ritter to BFM, May 11, 1921. AA, PO II, PO 2 Nr. 1 Vat.,
Vol. 2, Delbrück to Reich Minister for Foreign Affairs, May 4, 1921.
[33] *Ibid.*

support for the Church, to the *Länder*.[34] In other words, the competence of the two levels of government remained unclear. Until the Reich legislated these general principles to which the Constitution referred, the *Länder* understandably believed that church-state relations could and should still best be handled at the state level. In order to have the states change their stand during the spring of 1921 the Central Government repeated in an infinite number of variations the argument for the primacy of foreign policy needs.

The diplomatic isolation of Germany after the war made Berlin place greater importance on its relations with the Holy See, especially since Rome appeared willing to act as intermediary between Germany and the Allied Powers. Foreign relations with the Vatican were very good and would continue so as long as there was a cooperative relationship between the German Catholics and the Reich and state governments; this could be ensured and institutionalized with a Reich concordat. Moreover, the states' approval of a Reich concordat would demonstrate the Central Government's ability to represent all Germans. The greater part of Germany's Catholic population was located in the western, southern, and eastern border areas in which there was some separatist activity or upon which neighboring governments were casting covetous eyes. The Curia constantly reevaluated the problem of how seriously it had to take these efforts to separate territory from Germany. In dealing with Rome Berlin felt the need to stress the unity of the Reich, the loyalty of the states, their confidence in the Central Government, as well as to call attention to the fact that the Reich had taken into account the justifiable needs and aspirations of the Catholic population, especially after the Imperial period, when Catholics lacked the political influence in the Central Government to which their numbers normally would have entitled them. Moreover, a Reich concordat could serve as a check on any anti-clerical legislation which a particular state government might at some point seek to initiate or any anti-Church attitude it might adopt, which in turn would threaten the good working relationship between Berlin and Rome.

For all these reasons then, the Foreign Office found it imperative to conclude a Reich concordat before any local one was signed. Should Catholics in Germany be in a less favorable position than their coreligionists in the neighboring states, the Vatican could justifiably ask whether it was to the Church's interests to leave the disputed territories as part of Germany. The Church's attitude to questions such as the Separatist movement in the Rhineland, the creation of an independent Saar diocese as urged by the French, the union of Bavaria

[34] See Kakies, pp. 77-109.

and Austria to form a purely Catholic South German state, and the Polish activities in Upper Silesia would be crucial. A Reich concordat, on one hand, would demonstrate Berlin's willingness to comply with Rome's desire for a treaty and, on the other, would indicate Vatican confidence in the Central Government and discourage the separatists, especially in the Rhineland, and the foreign powers eager to gain territory at Germany's expense. Lastly, the Foreign Office argued, as an added benefit, if Berlin could have the Vatican agree to support by a concordat clause Germany's request to have its missionaries abroad remain at their posts, the possibility emerged that these German priests and nuns, particularly in the territories to the east, could help the Foreign Office to increase its influence in the new states.[35]

The repeated reasons did have some effect, but unfortunately not on the most important states. Hesse and Saxony in general approved of the Reich policy; Württemberg agreed to Berlin's argument on the basis of diplomatic necessity, while still protesting that Bavaria should have no special privileges; Baden, seeing no reason for any concordat whatsoever, nevertheless gave its assent; but Bavaria and Prussia still remained unconvinced.[36] In June 1921 the Prussian Cabinet met again to discuss the matter and relayed to the Reich Interior Ministry that since Bavaria continued to negotiate its own treaty without regard for a Reich concordat, the question of Prussia's yielding to the Reich was not open to discussion. A special position for Bavaria, said the Prussian note, would weaken the idea of a unified Reich, and any foreign policy gain of the moment would lose significance in comparison with the damage to internal harmony that would occur. Prussia's particularism came out most pointedly in the argumentation. "Should an attempt be made to justify Bavaria's special position of precedence before Prussia in the concordat question on historical grounds, such an attempt must be contradicted at once. The fact that Bavaria had a Catholic and Prussia an Evangelical monarch belongs to the past." In Prussia's opinion Bavaria had to be included in a Reich concordat if there were to be one.[37]

In spite of continued opposition to the Central Government's proposals Prussia did not want the Vatican to think it was creating needless difficulties and blame the north German state for delays in concordat negotiations. Therefore on June 20 the Prussian Cabinet wrote to Pacelli diplomatically assuring him that Prussia was not, in princi-

---

[35] Germany, Becker, 33, memorandum, "Zur Frage eines preussischen und eines Reichskonkordates," zu G II 616/21.

[36] *Ibid.*

[37] AA, PO II, PO 2 Nr. 1 Vat., Vol. 2, Minister-President Stegerwald and Becker to Reich Interior Minister, June 15, 1921.

ple, protesting Bavaria's intention to sign its own treaty with Rome but merely desired to call to the Vatican's attention the problems that it would cause for completing a Reich treaty. If Bavaria concluded its treaty first, then a Reich concordat would be possible only when the contents of the Bavarian treaty were taken up and incorporated into the general treaty and became not only state but also Reich law. If, on the other hand, a Bavarian treaty were signed granting broad concessions to the Church, these provisions would not be approved by representatives from other parts of Germany, and the Reich concordat would once more be delayed by intra-German disagreements.[38] Prussia undoubtedly expected that such a letter would blunt any Vatican criticism of that north German state as the main obstacle to a concordat. Specifying the difficulties which the Bavarian concordat might cause, Prussia was also implying that Rome might have to make a choice of which treaty was more important, for by winning Bavaria it might lose all of Germany. Even if Bavaria and Rome continued to negotiate, Prussia presumed that by issuing this veiled warning at least it might cause Rome to mitigate its demands or cause Bavaria to take a harder line in the negotiations.

Matters came to a standstill with internal bickering, lack of unity, and foreign and domestic interests at cross-purposes. Given this frustrating situation, Delbrück believed that the Vatican might break what was an intra-German deadlock. In June he wrote to the Reich legation in Munich, laying out the problem. Prussia, he stated, could only be won over for a Reich concordat if it included Bavaria, and the other German states, which were of the same opinion, would no doubt support Prussia if it held out. Bavaria had to be convinced to concede that some matters which it now claimed for itself could be dealt with in a Reich concordat. Only the Curia had a chance of persuading Bavaria to become more flexible. Since Rome maintained contact with both Munich and Berlin over the matter, it had to be prevailed upon to tell Munich that it would appreciate a speedy conclusion of a Reich concordat.[39]

The matter became even more urgent for Berlin when in July it learned that the Government of Württemberg was coming under considerable pressure from the Social Democratic Party in that *Land* to announce a formal separation of Church and State. Should this be officially enacted into law, it would weaken further the chances for a Reich concordat by placing further legal obstacles it its way. Berlin therefore urged Stuttgart to delay on this question as long as possible,

[38] PGSTA, Rep. 90, P.11.1.1., Vol. 10, Becker to Pacelli, June 20, 1921.
[39] AA, PO II, PO 2 Nr. 1 Vat., Vol. 2, Delbrück to Reich representative in Munich, June 1921, *sine dato.*

while on July 15 the Reich Cabinet and Prussian officials debated Delbrück's suggestion of appealing to Rome.[40] After much discussion, Germany's diplomatic situation was such that the cabinet reluctantly decided against approaching the Vatican on this domestic issue. Berlin believed it inadvisable to irritate the Vatican or Bavaria by requesting some concessions from Munich in favor of a Reich concordat until the fate of Upper Silesia was decided. The Reich needed to show a united front in the crisis, and Germany needed the full support of the Vatican. The Cabinet therefore voted to refrain from requesting the Nuncio or the Vatican itself to intervene with the Bavarian Government.[41] The Holy See probably was just as happy that it had not been asked, for it would not have been overanxious to apply pressure on Bavaria to make concessions. Indeed, as Pacelli confided to Cardinal Bertram, Rome regretted that negotiations for the Bavarian treaty were taking so long and thereby allowing the whole problem of which government level should take precedence to be discussed and to expand. Since the Bavarian negotiations were so far advanced, the Vatican now wanted to have this treaty concluded first.[42]

Although both Rome and the Reich Government were anxious for a treaty, they disagreed on its type and timing. Rome desired a Bavarian concordat, which it expected to be favorable to the Church, to be signed rapidly, setting a precedent in all future negotiations. Berlin desired a Reich concordat signed quickly for diplomatic reasons and sought to delay negotiations for a Bavarian treaty on the presumption that partisans of a Reich treaty could overcome any objections, or at least have the Bavarian treaty become part of or be subsumed under the broader all-German accord. In either case it looked as if Rome was in a favorable position to obtain some type of concordat and that two German governments were competing for the Curia's favor.

By autumn 1921 several things had occurred which Berlin assumed might work to its benefit in solving this problem. The decision about Upper Silesia had already been made, and Berlin had no reason to wait any longer before urging the Vatican to prevail upon Bavaria to concede to the Reich's needs. Second, the Bavarian negotiations were taking longer than even the Vatican wished, and Pacelli had already expressed his annoyance. No doubt out of conviction but probably also to prod Munich, the Nuncio had taken the opportunity in September at the *Katholikentag* meetings in Frankfurt once more publicly to express his expectations that a Reich concordat would be signed

[40] AA, PO II, PO 2 Nr. 1 Vat., Vol. 2, Zech to Reich Chancellery, July 18, 1921.
[41] AA, PO II, PO 2 Nr. 1 Vat., Vol. 2, memorandum of a meeting in the Reich Chancellery, July 16, 1921.
[42] AW, 1A 25k, 154, Pacelli to Bertram, August 20, 1921.

soon. Third, the new Bavarian Government of Count Hugo von Lerchenfeld (nephew of the Bavarian diplomat of the same name) which
assumed office in September, was not as adamant in upholding all of
Bavarian particularist prerogatives as had the administration of his
predecessor, Gustav von Kahr; instead, Lerchenfeld sought to reach
an accommodation with the Reich Government.[43] Events had also progressed so that Rome too began to modify its position. The Vatican,
which made its impatience with Bavaria and the Reich known, now
desired swift conclusion of both concordats.

In 1921 a nuncio had arrived in Paris to resume relations with France
and to help to regulate church-state affairs in that country. It was
important for the Vatican in the interests of international balance and
prestige to have an envoy in Berlin begin negotiations there also. Indeed, Rome could use one country to prod the other, Germany versus
France, into signing a treaty, lest on border matters one state gain an
advantage over the other. In November Gasparri put increased pressure on the Reich to find a solution by informing the Chancellor that
the Saar Administration had requested Rome to grant an apostolic
administrator for the territory—someone who in conformity with the
new political situation would more readily understand the religious
needs of the populace than a German bishop located some distance
away. The Cardinal intended to defer making a decision, but again
urged conclusion of both German concordats; since once diocesan jurisdictions had been delimited in the concordats, Rome could more
easily resist French and Saar Administration pressure. Bergen also
thought that a rapid conclusion of negotiations with Germany would
be helpful to the Vatican in arranging accords with other states, even
France, and so the Curia had added reason to advocate their completion.[44] Rome then, rather than persuading Munich to be more flexible,
as the Reich Government had hoped, was urging Bavaria and the Reich
toward speed for their own sakes as well as for the Vatican's.

The Vatican was applying pressure to both Munich and Berlin to
resolve their problems, lest territory be separated from Bavarian and
other German ecclesiastical jurisdictions. The Reich Government
understood this danger very well, yet the internal problems, especially
for the Reich Government, were exactly what made speed impossible.
The Reich needed time to sort and settle the multitude of varied difficulties confronting it at once. Prussia and Bavaria had hardened their
positions, both maintaining opposite views of a concordat. Prussia would
approve a Reich treaty only if it were valid for all Germany, which
then would supersede any state concordat and cancel any of its clauses

[43] AA, PO II, PO 2 Nr. 1 Vat., Vol. 2, Reich Interior Minister to AA, October 3,
1921.
[44] PGSTA, Rep. 90, P.11.1.1., Vol. 10, Bergen to AA, November 3, 1921.

which conflicted with the Reich concordat. Bavaria insisted that its concordat would be an international, bilateral treaty, constitutionally valid, which could neither be superseded nor invalidated should a Reich concordat be signed. The technicalities of these interpretations were a matter that jurists might have to study before reaching a legal decision. Another serious matter touching on this crisis was the school question, which everyone knew would have to be discussed and some resolution arrived at before Rome would agree to any concordat. The Constitution in 1919, however, had provided for the formulation of a Reich educational law code at some later date, but this provision presented serious problems for concordat negotiations because of the difficulty of making stipulations in an international treaty about schools when the federal law on the matter had not yet been written. This too was a subject for which no rapid solution existed, since a basic disagreement had arisen between the Center Party and the Social Democrats as to what the law should contain. Internal political reasons and fears for the durability of the ruling coalition had caused the government to delay introducing a *Reichsschulgesetz*. Yet foreign policy urgently necessitated it, since the lack of such a law was one of the major obstacles to a speedy conclusion to a concordat, which in turn was viewed by the Foreign Office as important in securing Vatican diplomatic aid.[45] Again the inextricable interaction of internal and foreign relations caused difficulties, and many observers were curious to see how government officials would extricate themselves from this dichotomous position.

The matter of having a concordat concluded was sufficiently serious to have a meeting called for November 11 in Berlin, attended by both the Reich Chancellor and the Bavarian Minister-President, which sought to reach some sort of formulation for a treaty to which all—the Vatican, the Reich, and Bavaria—could agree. Delbrück began by emphasizing the diplomatic necessity of the treaty. For a long time to come, he said, the Curia would be the intermediary through which Germany could maintain contact with former enemy governments. No doubt reflecting his agitation and frustration, Chancellor Wirth interrupted Delbrück and explained to the group the gravity of the situation in his own words: "If we now add church-state difficulties to the present enormous problems, we might as well allow ourselves to be buried." The concordat had to be considered from the view of serving the fatherland. If Germany began its contacts with the world powers once again and took a policy antagonistic to the Holy See, then, in the opinion of the Reich Government, that policy would be doomed. It

45 PGSTA, Rep. 90, P.11.1.1., Vol. 10, Zech to the Prussian Cabinet, November 11, 1921.

was absolutely necessary to live peacefully with Rome, and any type of internal church-state disturbances could upset this peace. The Reich concordat was a political necessity, and he, the Reich Chancellor, was ready to make any arrangement with Bavaria to obtain it.

Delbrück was then allowed to spell out what consequences such a treaty might have. As Pacelli and Gasparri had told the Germans, a concordat could help Rome to resist pressure to have diocesan borders changed. The Saar, for example, was also important to Bavaria he reminded the Munich officials, since part of the territory was considered part of the Bavarian Palatinate and was administered by the Bavarian episcopate. To separate the area from German ecclesiastical control, which included educational institutions, charitable organizations, and a parochial structure administered by German priests, would mean the disappearance of the German character of the area. In the east the problem was similar if not more critical, where, without the finalization of diocesan boundaries in favor of Germany and without a German-speaking clergy, some areas would be de-Germanized within a generation. Moreover, a treaty speedily agreed upon by the Reich could also persuade Rome to decide favorably on such other issues as appointing a German rather than a Polish administrator in Danzig. Without Bavaria's agreement to let a Reich concordat take precedence, Prussia would not agree to an all-German treaty, and this would mean that the border dioceses with some two million Germans could be lost to the Reich and their German character disappear within a generation. Once more the argument was made with appeals to patriotic sentiments for sacrifices for the good of the whole, for national over state concerns, for diplomatic over internal interests.

While less impressed with Delbrück's remarks about the Saar, stating that existing agreements were still valid and sufficient to allow the Vatican to resist change here, the Bavarian Minister-President Lerchenfeld did agree that the condition in the east was serious. Having been the German representative in the Silesian plebiscite area, he was well acquainted with the troubles there and with the importance of maintaining the diocesan boundaries. Also having heard Delbrück's detailed analysis and having exchanged views, the representatives at the meeting left with a slightly optimistic feeling, since Lerchenfeld promised to convey Berlin's arguments to Munich, to consult with Bavarian politicians, and to use his influence to see if some accommodation could be reached. After officials from both governments had been assigned to work on the problem,[46] Wirth informed Pacelli that he also would become involved in the discussions in an attempt to

---

[46] GSTA, MA 104493, memorandum of meeting in Berlin, November 11, 1921, signed Goldenberger, Counsellor in Bavarian Ministry of Religious Affairs.

speed them along. To expedite things even further the *Reichskanzler* requested that the Vatican present him with a list of points which it would most especially like to have incorporated into a Reich concordat and promised to mention them immediately in negotiations with the minister-presidents of the individual German states, adding that he hoped he had shown the Nuncio how serious the Reich Government was in heeding Rome's advice about speed.[47]

After talks with Lerchenfeld and Pacelli in November, the Reich Government was hopeful of success. In asking Pacelli what the Vatican expected from a Reich concordat Wirth already knew what general topics were to be dealt with and that the Foreign Office had a series of objectives which it specifically wanted incorporated into the treaty: confirmation of the already existing diocesan borders in the west, redrawing diocesan jurisdictions in the east; Papal delegates, not Polish ordinaries, for Danzig and Polish Silesia; and guarantees for the Germans in the separated areas against Polonization by the clergy. Bavarian and Reich officials were working on a formulation for a Reich concordat so that a Bavarian treaty could be incorporated into a general one with an addendum dealing with matters of special concern to the Bavarian situation. Wirth hoped that such a draft, along with the Bavarian Minister-President's support, would win the endorsement of the Bavarians and the Prussians as well. Yet another problem arose; this time the difficulties came from the northern rather than the southern *Land*. In the November discussion with Pacelli over Vatican objectives the Chancellor had noted the importance that Rome placed on having the school question incorporated into the treaty. Yet Prussia had also let the Central Government know that it did not want to see this question included. Education was a matter still within the competence of the states, which had no guidelines from the Central Government, since the *Reichsschulgesetz* had not been yet written. While it looked as if Prussia's objections to Bavaria's position might be met, on the school issue Prussia remained adamant. Since Wirth had requested Rome's negotiating list and had expressed his desire to be accommodating, the Nuncio asked the Chancellor to give him privately a general promise that the school question would be included in the concordat. Wirth could not comply, but assured the prelate that the Reich was laboring to have its own officials as well as the Center Party members prevail on the Prussian Cabinet to acquiesce, and he, Wirth, promised, upon receiving a copy of the Vatican's specific requests, to give them every consideration possible.[48] Pacelli countered by stating

---

[47] Germany, Cologne, Erzbischöfliches Ordinariat, C.R. 1, 17a, Vol. 1, Wirth to Pacelli, November 14, 1921; Pacelli to Wirth, November 15, 1921. Eighteen points for discussion were enclosed.

[48] AA, BRV 265, Vol. 1/3, Delbrück to Bergen, November 15, 1921.

that while he understood the problem, the Holy See would never agree to the desired concordat without the inclusion of this provision. The government would then have to take the consequences of not having a concordat, for which it alone would be responsible.[49]

Meanwhile Rome continued to urge Munich to persevere in its efforts to reach a settlement. Although Lerchenfeld had apprized Wirth of his intention to use his influence to convince the parties in the *Landtag* to accommodate their treaty to an all-German one, once back in Munich he nonetheless insisted on the importance of Bavaria's signing a legally separate one based on its own interests. Knowing how anxious the Reich was to have its concordat and hoping to pressure Berlin into asking fewer concessions of the Bavarians, Lerchenfeld had Ritter request Rome to remind Berlin of the high regard the Pontiff had for Bavaria's Catholicism and loyalty to the Holy See and his wish to see Bavaria have its own treaty. But this Rome would not do. Just as it indicated no inclination to speak to Munich in Berlin's behalf, now it would not speak to Berlin in Munich's. The Curia had no intention of intervening in internal German affairs and intra-governmental differences at a point when there was no need to irritate unduly the Reich Cabinet and when instead the situation could be utilized advantageously by the Curia in pursuit of its own goals. Gasparri replied neither positively nor negatively to Ritter. Instead he voiced his belief that the key to solving the problem lay not in Berlin but in Munich, since a speedy conclusion of a Bavarian concordat was the best way for the Bavarians to secure their particularist rights in church-state matters, to counter further pressure from Berlin, and to end the debate over which concordat would come first.

After further discussions with Vatican officials, Ritter now believed he saw clearly what policy Rome was adopting. Rome still preferred a separate Bavarian treaty and would like to have this concluded as the first of the two treaties since it assumed the Bavarian Government, rather than the Reich or Prussian, would better understand its views on such matters as the school question and State support of the Church. Apparently Rome was confident that once Bavaria had signed, despite Prussian objections, the diplomatic as well as internal advantages of a Reich concordat would surmount the problems. Armed with the Bavarian treaty whose clauses it expected to be favorable to the Church, Rome could then negotiate from a position of strength for any further treaties. But should the Bavarian negotiations take longer than planned, Munich prove too difficult a negotiating partner, or the Reich make some appealing concessions, the Curia might be inclined to conclude

49 AW, 1A 25k, 154, Pacelli to Bertram, November 23, 1921.

an agreement with the Central Government rather than with Munich. A Reich concordat, after all, also proved very attractive to the Holy See, for it would regulate church-state concerns for all Germany, including Prussia, with its large Catholic population, at a time when the possibility of a separate Prussian concordat appeared very dim. Even Ritter believed that Munich's bargaining position was weakening because of the alternatives which Rome seemed to possess. "*Faites vite et tout s'arrangera*," said Ritter, was the constant refrain that he heard in all his conversations with Gasparri and his assistant Pizzardo. The Curia now held the trump cards.[50]

The Vatican did not fail, however, to keep up its pressure on all concerned. On December 31, Pacelli, without prior arrangement, "dropped in" to visit Otto Boelitz, Prussian Minister of Religious Affairs, a rare procedural step for the Nuncio. During a wide-ranging conversation, when Boelitz asked Pacelli's assistance in having Rome name someone who strongly supported the Berlin Government to the vacant border see of Trier, Pacelli answered that this would depend on Prussia's willingness to see the school question taken up in *Reichskonkordat* negotiations. The matter was the *punctum saliens* of a concordat for the Vatican. Should it be omitted, then the Church had no interest in a treaty, and the Vatican would under these circumstances be better off in making its decisions without the binding limitations of a treaty. All other questions dealing with the rights and privileges for the Church and its members were, said the Nuncio, basically guaranteed in the new Constitution. The Prussian explained that his government would be prepared to discuss the issue, but one could not, nor should not, tie the issue of Trier, where speed was essential, to a larger and more complex problem, where more time was needed to consult various people and political parties. Both sides agreed to continue the discussions, but in general Boelitz felt that Pacelli was viewing the problem solely from the Church's perspective and had no grasp of the complexities and difficulties of German internal affairs, particularly the relations of the Reich to the individual states with regard to church-state concerns.[51]

The Prussian Minister's interpretation of Pacelli's action did not give the envoy due credit. He certainly did understand the complexities and interrelations of Germany's governmental levels. Precisely because of multi-leveled competencies, he was applying urgency to hasten matters. Although the Germans did not like the Nuncio's tactics in this instance and the Chancellor believed such statements as his

[50] GSTA, Ges. Päpstl. Stuhl 972, Ritter to Lerchenfeld, November 27, 1921.

[51] Germany, Becker, 33, memorandum of meeting between Pacelli and Boelitz, December 31, 1921.

might complicate the negotiations, the Prussian need to indicate good faith and prove they were not being obstructionary did seem to bring results. A conversation which Pacelli had in late December with Boelitz proved Prussia's willingness at least to make some tactical concession. The Prussian assured the Nuncio that in principle Prussia would not refuse to talk about the school question and would thoroughly study the Vatican's proposals. He nevertheless warned that a treaty which dealt with that issue would be impossible to obtain approval from the *Landtag*.[52] On January 6, in a letter to Pacelli Boelitz made even more concessions by stating that Prussia would not insist on retaining the privilege of naming candidates for the vacant see of Trier, as had been the case in former elections, and would rely on the Vatican's making a good choice, which Berlin expected would be very soon. In addition, in the same letter the Prussian Minister now specifically announced that upon the Reich Government's urging, his cabinet was ready to explore the problem of regulating the religious aspects of the school question by means of a concordat.[53] Pacelli's compelling persuasion, the Reich's need, and the danger of a long vacancy in the critical border diocese of Trier, all prompted the Prussian Cabinet to indicate some willingness to compromise. Without conceding any points, it at least had promised to consider the matter— a crucial step in removing the obstacles to a Reich concordat.[54]

During the latter part of 1921 both German and Bavarian diplomats in Rome had detected in Cardinal Gasparri's remarks an increasing interest in a Reich concordat. Reparations and the territorial demands on Germany had convinced the Cardinal Secretary of State that in order to maintain Rome's policy of balance in Europe, and in the interests of future peace, Germany had to be strengthened. During the last few months separatist movements had threatened the integral unity of the Reich, and the Saar Administration had requested the Vatican to detach that area from Trier and Speyer and give it a separate administrator. The new prelate would probably be in a weaker position to oppose the wishes of France or the French dominated Saar Government than would the bishops of Trier and Speyer, who resided in Germany. This would mean an increase of French predominance among the clergy which could cost Germany victory in a future plebiscite. In Upper Silesia in the same year the area which fell to Poland

---

[52] AA, BRV 265, Vol. 1/3 Mutius (AA) to Bergen, January 3, 1922.

[53] Germany, Cologne, Erzbischöfliches Ordinariat, C.R. 1, 17a, Vol. 1, Boelitz to Pacelli, January 6, 1922.

[54] In a letter to Schulte, Pacelli acknowledged credit for having broken the stalemate, that his firm stand had not been without results. Germany, Cologne, Erzbischöfliches Ordinariat, C.R. 1, 17a, Vol. 1, Pacelli to Schulte, January 10, 1922.

by the plebiscite was still being administered by a delegate of the Bishop of Breslau, but Berlin doubted if this situation could be maintained for long. Poland would demand that this area be attached to a Polish diocese, and this would have serious implications for the German population there. To gain time in the anticipation of political changes, Germany desired to have an apostolic administrator named for at least the duration of the transition period.[55]

Gasparri considered a concordat one way to maintain the balance in Europe and to support German unity. Increasingly Gasparri reminded the German representatives that Rome would be content to leave the still disputed areas under German jurisdiction if a satisfactory concordat were signed. He reminded them frequently that a Reich treaty would be to their benefit, for it would permit Rome to resist French or Polish demands since neither of these states currently had concordats with the Holy See. He warmed to the idea of such a general treaty for all Germany. It would strengthen Germany's unity, a fact of interest to both Rome and Berlin, by showing the Vatican's opposition to separatist sentiment. It would be beneficial to Catholic minorities in German states such as Mecklenburg and Saxony, whose governments up until then had indicated little interest in cooperating with the Church. While the German representative in Rome was delighted with Gasparri's remarks, the Bavarian minister viewed them as an indication that the Curia was beginning to lean toward signing a Reich concordat before the Bavarian one. The only way, said Ritter, to block this danger for Bavaria was to complete its negotiations as soon as possible. He feared that the longer the delay, the more inclined the Vatican would be to sign a Reich treaty.[56] Time, believed Ritter, was on the Reich's side in the race with Bavaria to win the Vatican as a negotiating partner. The events of the year and the Vatican's adroit diplomacy had convinced the Bavarian representative that Gasparri's idea that Munich held the key to winning the competition and Pacelli's suggestion that speed was essential were correct.

On December 7, Wirth telegraphed Bergen to inform Gasparri that the Reich shared the Cardinal's views about the importance and scope of a Reich concordat. In reply to Gasparri's question about how the rest of Germany would regard it if Rome did sign a treaty with Bavaria first, the Chancellor answered that it would be unfortunate, for the German public as well as foreign states might interpret it as Curial endorsement for separatist tendencies within the Reich. Unfortunately at the moment he had no progress to report from his side, for Prussia

---

[55] AA, BRV 265, Vol. 1/3, memorandum of Delbrück, December 23, 1921.
[56] GSTA, Ges. Päpstl. Stuhl 972, Ritter to Lerchenfeld, December 2, 6, 1921.

could not be persuaded to agree to a Reich concordat unless it were valid for all *Länder*, including Bavaria, and Reich and Bavarian officials had as yet been unable to agree on a formula. Wirth once more proposed that Rome help in the situation. In conversations with the Nuncio, Berlin officials had noted with some annoyance how Pacelli, by way of explaining the Vatican's side in the argument for a Reich concordat, also defended Bavaria's right to a separate treaty in order to safeguard against any future *Kulturkampf*. Berlin thought that Pacelli, whose sympathy for the Bavarians was well known, had no great desire to press Munich to take a more conciliatory attitude. The Chancellor therefore appealed directly to Gasparri, who had now spoken with greater enthusiasm for a Reich concordat, to have his Nuncio urge Munich to compromise. In addition, so that the Papal representative not be unduly influenced by the Bavarian position, Wirth suggested that Pacelli transfer his permanent residence to Berlin and leave further negotiations for a Bavarian treaty to his successor. His presence in Berlin would help both sides to meet and to clarify the points of discussion and perhaps prompt the slowed negotiations to proceed more rapidly. This in itself, said Wirth, was reason enough to grant the Reich's request to have the Nuncio permanently installed in the Reich capital.[57] Several weeks later, Berlin had Cardinal Schulte speak to Cardinal Faulhaber, one of Bavaria's most outspoken opponents of a Reich concordat, who viewed it as a threat to Bavaria's special status and its independence. The Cardinal of Cologne was asked to reassure his Munich colleague, and persuade him to appreciate the need for a *Reichskonkordat*.[58]

The Reich's moves were well timed. Some recent events had given the Vatican reason to reexamine its policy, for it had already experienced delays in obtaining a Bavarian concordat, observed the internal dissensions which the issue was causing among the individual states and between the states and the Central Government, and was well aware that any move to weaken an already shaken Germany could only strengthen French influence on the continent and increase the imbalance in European affairs. By mid-December even Ritter was now assured that the Curia was giving serious consideration to the idea that a comprehensive and independent concordat for Bavaria might increase separatist activities within the Reich and embolden France and its Allies, fresh from their victory in Upper Silesia, to place further demands on both the Holy See and Germany for concessions. The Munich Cabinet was naturally very distressed when it learned what

[57] AA, BRV 283, Vol. 1, Wirth to German Embassy (Vatican), December 7, 1921.
[58] AA, BRV 265, Vol. 1/3, Bergen to Schulte, January 3, 1922.

the Curia was thinking. There were still problems which had to be negotiated before a treaty agreeable to Rome and to the political parties in the *Landtag* could be approved. The Bavarians were very concerned that they would be outmaneuvered by Berlin and that all their efforts would be in vain. Pacelli confirmed that the Vatican Secretariat had increasingly begun to view the Reich treaty as an article of prime importance, but tried to reassure them by telling them that he had sought to allay Gasparri's fears and had underscored the fact that separatism was not as strong in Munich as the Cardinal had imagined. Pacelli explained that the attraction of a Reich treaty for the Holy See was that it would provide a legal agreement that would include and be binding on those states with which individual concordats could not be envisioned. He promised once more to present energetically the Bavarians' position to Gasparri and explain again their arguments for a separate treaty.[59]

A difference of opinion seemed to have developed among Church officials on how to approach the problem. Pacelli, as he originally stated, preferred to conclude the Bavarian concordat before any other treaty was signed and use it as a model for further treaties. He had the full confidence of the Bavarian Government, which believed he was willing to present the Bavarian standpoint in the best possible light in arguing this point with his superiors. But in Rome Gasparri had a greater opportunity to view the international scene and to grasp the importance and significance of the varied diplomatic developments as a whole. If it could be worked out, he would have no objections to Bavaria's treaty preceding the Reich concordat or being subsumed in it. But during the latter part of 1921 the Cardinal Secretary's interest in a Reich treaty seemed to have increased, for he perceived the treaty as another diplomatic instrument which he could use to fend off any further French demands on Germany. Bergen reported that scarcely an interview went by without the Cardinal's urgently recommending that negotiations for a Reich treaty be speeded up "in Germany's interests."[60] In fact a difference of opinion was also found among the leading German prelates. Schulte of Cologne argued for an all-inclusive Reich treaty, Bertram of Breslau was inclined to have the Bavarian treaty signed first and to wait and discuss later the relationship of that agreement to a Reich concordat, and he encouraged Pacelli to support the Bavarians. Faulhaber of Munich, needless to say, favored the Bavarian standpoint.[61] But despite the encouragement and prefer-

[59] GSTA, Ges. Päpstl. Stuhl 972, BFM to Ritter, December 19, 1921.

[60] PGSTA, Rep. 90, P.11.1.1., Vol. 10, Bergen to Prussian Cabinet, January 16, 1922.

[61] AA, BRV 266, Vol. 4/5, Bergen to Delbrück, February 3, 1922.

ences of the Church's leaders the decision still rested with the civil authority; could Munich reach a final agreement with Rome on such matters as education or State support for the Church, matters which were holding up the conclusion of the Bavarian treaty, or could the Reich win the support of the states to negotiate for all Germany? Which would come first?

In 1922 the Reich Cabinet, encouraged by Rome's interest in a treaty, began serious discussions with Pacelli about matters to be dealt with in the Reich concordat. The subjects covered ranged over items such as episcopal nomination, diocesan borders, and seminaries, with each side stating its viewpoint and modifying the suggestions of the other. These proposals, which basically dealt with subjects that Delbrück and Pacelli had covered in their preliminary talks in early 1920, were then sent on to Rome for study. The problem was that these talks were conducted only between Vatican representatives and the Reich Government. The state governments had not been included in the consultations. Despite all the conferences which the Reich had held with Bavaria, Munich still continued its own negotiations, maintaining that its treaty could not be invalidated by a Reich treaty later on. Prussia, while having agreed to discuss the school question, still gave no indication that it would agree to what Rome wanted included in the treaty, maintaining, however, the necessity of a Reich concordat that would have validity for all Germany, even if it would invalidate parts of Bavaria's treaty. The Reich Government then was moving ahead, probing for a basis of agreement with Rome in the expectation of being able to persuade the two states to moderate their stands along the way. The Reich Government argued that the talks between Reich officials, the Curia, and the Nuncio should first continue and that once there was a general agreement about its contents and some degree of assurance that it could be approved by the Reichstag, then the states could be asked to join the talks. The treaty, in this way, would stand a better chance of being accepted by the states and their representatives in the *Reichsrat*.[62] Some churchmen, however, were not certain if it was wise to continue these talks without the *Länder*. They argued that, despite the confidential nature of the discussions, the states would surely learn of their existence. Then it would appear as though the Central Government were negotiating behind the backs of the state governments, even if the Reich later assured them of their merely preliminary and non-binding nature. Such feelings of distrust and suspicion would further complicate any agreement.[63]

[62] AA, BRV 266, Vol. 4/5, memorandum of Meyer-Rodehüser, June 26, 1926.
[63] AW, 1A 250, 32, Steinmann to Bertram, June 18, 1922.

Almost three years after the idea of a Reich concordat had been raised, by mid-1922 matters were still at the early negotiating stages, while Pacelli continued to work diligently for the completion of the Bavarian treaty. Berlin was also unable to obtain Prussia's consent to any concrete agreement on the school question. Although by no means giving up hope, by mutual consent Rome and Berlin agreed on postponing further intensive negotiations indefinitely until the solution of internal difficulties with which the Reich Government had to contend.

Initially the failure of negotiations occurred primarily because Bavaria had already begun and had made some progress toward its own treaty.[64] Anticipating that negotiations would be short, Pacelli spent much of his time in Munich, concentrating on finishing the work there. But even while occupied in the Bavarian capital Pacelli did not rest but looked beyond his current task to further diplomatic initiatives. Since Prussia in 1921 had conceded or at least was willing to reconsider its total opposition to having the school question discussed in a concordat, Pacelli also began preliminary discussion about the contents of a similar treaty with that state. Perceiving no progress at that time toward a Reich treaty, the Vatican, in spite of Gasparri's reservations but with Pacelli's urging, aimed on completing the agreement with Bavaria where at least something tangible promised to be obtained in the not too distant future and also on extending discussions now on the *Länder* level either to obtain a Prussian concordat or to help remove Prussia's objections to a Reich treaty. Attack from the flank rather than a direct assault now seemed to the Vatican a more prudent tactic. Fortunately for Germany, while waiting for the results of all these negotiations, Rome appeared willing to make no preemptory moves to change the diocesan boundaries or to yield to foreign pressure. Even Bavaria, realizing a little later that its concordat would probably be signed soon, assumed a more conciliatory tone and informed Berlin that it would endeavor to formulate the treaty in a language that would offer no problems or conflicts for a subsequent Reich concordat. But the fact remained that it was with Bavaria and not the Reich that the Holy See was signing the first German concordat after the war, and diplomats abroad and German politicians all across the political spectrum and in all levels of government had been closely observing the progress of negotiations to learn what the concordat portended for the future and how it would affect both the domestic and foreign policy problems of the German states.[65]

[64] Rudolf Morsey, "Zur Vorgeschichte des Reichskonkordats aus den Jahren 1920 und 1921," *Zeitschrift der Savigny-Stiftung für Rechtsgeschichte*, LXXV (1958), 267.

[65] AA, Geheim Vat., Pol. 2 Nr. 2-1, memorandum of Meyer-Rodehüser, July 17, 1926.

B. The Bavarian Concordat (1924)

Discussions had begun in 1919 over a new Bavarian concordat; although Bavaria had had one since 1817, the new situation demanded clarification of the church-state relationship. The Vatican desired to strengthen its position by renegotiating some of the clauses of the old concordat and allowing more power to Rome in matters such as episcopal selection and education. The new government had originally announced that the old concordat was still in force but relegated to itself the rights previously assigned to the monarch, such as the right to approve clerical appointments, something which Rome was not prepared to accept. Moreover, the new Weimar Constitution provided for a separation of Church and State, specifying that religious bodies had a right to select their own leaders without State interference. Bavaria as well as other German states, however, felt that the civil authorities still had to have some voice in ecclesiastical selections, particularly when they concerned crucial border dioceses. The Church was an international organization, and should Allied pressure in Rome succeed in having non-nationalist prelates appointed, it could cause complications for Germany's or Bavaria's unity and internal peace. This question, one of many which was raised by the new governmental structure, made the Bavarians realize that discussions to legalize and regulate church-state relations by means of an international treaty should begin.[66] Pacelli, having lived through the rapid changes that had taken place in Munich in the last year, went to Rome in early 1920 to brief the Curia on Munich's viewpoint. He had the confidence of many Bavarian officials, who believed he would do the best he could for them and would expedite the necessary preparations for negotiation. In fact, in Rome Ritter was so impressed with Pacelli's grasp of conditions in the Bavarian situation that he urged his government to request the Curia to delay Pacelli's transfer to Berlin until all was settled in Munich.[67]

During the next few months the Nuncio made good use of his time, undertaking intensive discussion with the Bavarian hierarchy and members of the Catholic Bavarian People's Party so that when he came to the conference table he would be well armed with facts, figures, and an excellent grasp of the problem.[68] Already in January 1920, Minister-President Johannes Hoffmann had stated in the *Landtag* the necessity for a new formula for church-state relations in Bavaria, and a majority of parliamentarians had voted to open negotiations for a

[66] GSTA, MA 104492, Ritter to BFM, November 17, 1919.
[67] GSTA, Ges. Päpstl. Stuhl 976, Ritter to BFM, April 6, 1920.
[68] AA, PO II, PO 2 Nr. 1 Vat., Vol. 1, Zech to AA, May 29, 1920.

new accord. Although the Nuncio presented a list of points which the Vatican desired to have discussed, intensive talks did not begin at once, and there were still many obstacles to a quick solution. The urgency of organizing the new government and creating some stability after the war, the dissolutions of the *Landtag* and new elections, and the pressure of ministerial meetings all gave the cabinet little time to consider which points it desired to discuss. In addition, several matters had to be clarified with Berlin. Would all the proposed clauses in the treaty conform to the new Weimar Constitution? If, for example, the State insisted, as Munich did, on the right to approve episcopal selection or to negotiate an international treaty that Reich law would not supersede, would not the possibility still exist that the constitutionality of these provisions might be questioned?[69] In any event, the one thing all parties in the legislature and cabinet were sure about was that they intended to sign their own treaty and not relinquish it in favor of an all-German treaty.

In answer to a query from Berlin asking to be informed of what Rome wanted in the treaty and requesting to be kept abreast of the negotiations, Munich politely but firmly apologized that Bavaria could not forward a copy of the Vatican proposals, since negotiations were to remain secret. The Bavarian Government assured Berlin that it was doing nothing extraordinary, negotiating only on the basis of what the Constitution permitted, and that immediately before the conclusion of the agreement a copy would be submitted to Berlin for comments. But so that the attitude of the Bavarians did not appear too high-handed and only increase the strained relations between the capitals, Councillor Franz Xaver Goldenberger of the Ministry of Religious Affairs gave some verbal indication of the Vatican's suggestions to Delbrück, who was in Munich to discuss the matter. In general the points dealt with the usual demands, such as more Church control over education and government financial support of the Church.

The number of suggestions made and the areas covered contained nothing surprising and, as Delbrück noted, were similar to topics mentioned in conversations he had had with members of the Prussian episcopate when he had raised the issue of a Reich or a Prussian concordat. But of significance was the size of the demands the Church was making, the amount of control to be granted the Church, and the amount of support the State would grant. No doubt, said the visitor from Berlin, the Vatican's tactic was to keep its demands high so that it still would be in an advantageous position when it compromised for less. The previous expectation of a speedy conclusion of the treaty

---

[69] AA, PO II, PO 2 Nr. 1 Vat., Vol. 1, Zech to Prussian Cabinet, July 30, 1920.

now appeared overly optismistic and illusory. Goldenberger agreed with Delbrück and gloomily predicted that the proceedings would necessitate long deliberations, many drafts and counterproposals.[70] This disclosure no doubt encouraged Delbrück at this early stage to believe that Bavaria did not necessarily have all the advantages on its side and that perhaps the Reich could sign an agreement with Rome before Munich did.

Nevertheless, the Rome-Munich discussions continued, and by October 20 Pacelli was able to wire the Holy See that preliminary agreement had been reached on several issues proposed by Rome and that negotiations were then concentrating on specifically difficult problems, such as the school question. At that moment an incident occurred which illustrated the inter-connection of the Central and state governments' involvement in this matter and the many interests which had to be considered in these discussions. Just then a first draft of the Reich school legislation was sent for comment to Munich. The Bavarians were very upset about it and totally disapproved with its formulation which, if it were not changed, would lead to sharp disagreements between Bavaria and the Reich Government. As a consequence, Munich regretfully requested Rome to postpone further work on the concordat until this legislative matter was settled. Internal affairs had to be regulated before dealing with a foreign power. The draft had proposed a strongly centralized educational system that would unify the schools throughout the Reich. Neither of the two negotiating parties were happy to see this introduced, for it would remove control out of the hands of the *Länder* and perhaps not provide sufficient consideration for the circumstances prevailing in each of the individual states. Bavaria, as in other controversies with the Central Government, feared domination by Berlin and was willing to resist it. The Vatican, of course, feared that a general public law, enacted without prior discussions to consider the special interests of the Holy See, would surely not be as beneficial as a treaty with a government representing a predominantly Catholic population. In addition, ever mindful of wider considerations, Rome worried that the internal discord and animosity which could result between the states and the new Central Government at this critical time might be viewed in the eyes of the world only as a weakening of German national unity. Gasparri told Schulte that a fight over the schools could only strengthen separatism, the very thing neither Rome nor Berlin wanted to see occur.[71]

---

[70] AA, PO II, PO 2 Nr. 1 Vat., Vol. 1, Delbrück to Simson (AA), September 18, 1920.

[71] AA, PO II, PO 2 Nr. 1 Vat., Vol. 1, Bergen to AA, October 25, 1920. GSTA, Ges. Päpstl. Stuhl 972, Ritter to BFM, October 26, 1920.

Fortunately for Bavaria, the objections to the draft from the *Länder* and the politicians who opposed the centralizing tendencies coming from Berlin were such that the Reich Cabinet did not present the proposal to the Reichstag but withdrew it for reworking. Rome was very relieved, but the incident only reinforced Rome's desire to have at least the Bavarian treaty signed. Gasparri informed Ritter that besides being pleased with the outcome of the school draft he politely recommended that, especially in the area of church-state relations, the Reich not raise any further issues which could cause internal dissension at a time when Germany should be stressing unity. Pacelli, while in Berlin in November, spoke with both Wirth and Simons of the importance of the Bavarian concordat, how far both sides had progressed in their talks, and the Vatican's present desire to conclude it as soon as possible before a Reich concordat. Conceding that Munich had advanced far more rapidly in its negotiations with Rome than had Berlin, and realizing that the Reich still had much to do before it could push through its school legislation, the Reich Government virtually agreed that it would not sign a treaty or raise any objections about the competence of Munich to sign one with a foreign power.[72]

This gesture of goodwill by Berlin was a sign of its eagerness to maintain good relations with Rome, for it expected it would pay dividends in the Reich concordat negotiations later on. It also removed the impediments or hesitations on the part of Bavaria in continuing talks with Rome, for now at least the constitutionality of its actions would not be questioned by the Reich, and this meant a great deal to Bavaria, which had suspected Berlin in 1919 of desiring the closing of Munich's legation at the Vatican. It was an attempt by the Reich Cabinet to heed Gasparri's advice that Berlin soothe the sensitive feelings of the Bavarians, who were necessary to maintaining a united Germany, and it was a way for Berlin to show the Vatican the Reich's seriousness in seeking to remove all obstacles in the way of better church-state relations. Once having indicated what it was prepared to do, Berlin on the other hand now sought to persuade Bavaria to coordinate the content of the treaty, wherever possible even verbatim, with that of the intended Reich concordat and in some way stress the integral connection between the two. For Bavaria this was looked upon with suspicion, since it again was viewed as an attempt to erode Bavaria's independence by eventually decreasing the significance of its own treaty in favor of the Reich concordat. Nevertheless, Ritter warned his government that although Rome did not object to Bavaria's wish for its own treaty, should Munich prove a difficult negotiator with

[72] GSTA, Ges. Päpstl. Stuhl 972, Ritter to BFM, November 28, 1920.

405

Rome or resist granting concessions to Curial demands, the Vatican might become disappointed and lend more support to an immediate Reich concordat.[73] This dilemma placed Bavaria in a position of trying to please all parties, maintain its independent position, and yet still hurry with negotiations.

As Goldenberger had said, the matter would not be concluded quickly. The Ministry of Religious Affairs had needed time to work out its answers to the proposals made by the Vatican. Once agreement had been reached among ministry officials, the terms of the treaty would have to be approved by the Nuncio and then placed before the entire cabinet for its consent. Thereafter, the entire concordat would have to be studied by Reich officials to ensure that the document was in conformity with the Constitution. All of this would be accomplished, if not with bureaucratic thoroughness, at least with bureaucratic slowness. Pacelli had done his best to inform the Pontiff of the necessary administrative procedures, and the Pope showed understanding for them, though the Curia still urged a rapid conclusion of the negotiations. In addition to the previously mentioned reasons for speed, the Curia was troubled by the fear that the longer the delay, the greater the possibility of a change in the Bavarian Government, which might bring in a less cooperative cabinet or one which might even undo the work already accomplished. Finally, another reason remained for Rome's sense of urgency. The Danubian successor states had laid claim to privileges which had applied to the Austro-Hungarian Monarchy as stated in the old Austrian concordat. The Curia refused to recognize these demands or the validity of the old treaty because of the changed political situation in the area and insisted on having entirely new treaties worked out. If the Bavarian treaty, which had already made such progress, could be speedily signed, it would strengthen Rome's position in dealing with the successor states and serve as an example for the rapid regularization of church-state relations in the new political situation. To show its concern in expediting matters, the Vatican made a conciliatory gesture by suggesting that should Bavaria lack funds to settle the question of State support for the Church, Rome would willingly postpone specifying the details of the compensation and would be satisfied if only the principle of support were recognized in the treaty.[74]

At the beginning of 1922, after a year of informal discussions and delays, Bavaria finished its list of counterproposals to those of the Vatican. Ritter learned, however, that Pacelli officially had not yet

---

[73] GSTA, MA 104493, Ritter to BFM, July 24, 1921.
[74] GSTA, Ges. Päpstl. Stuhl 972, Ritter to AA, January 14, 1922.

communicated Gasparri's offer to defer the question of State support for a later accord. Always suspicious, the Bavarians speculated that Zech, the Reich representative in Munich, might have been influencing him to delay mentioning this, for as long as negotiations were slowed down, the chances for signing a Reich concordat increased. The more pertinent reason, however, was that Pacelli, a hard bargainer, saw no reason to procrastinate on a matter when he could obtain it at that moment. In other words he was, as Ritter stated, more "Papal than the Pope."[75] Upon Ritter's remonstrance in Rome that Pacelli had not informed Munich of Rome's concession, Gasparri told the Nuncio expressly to so inform Munich. Previously the State Secretary had suggested that the Nuncio do so; now he ordered it.[76]

After this impasse had been circumvented, by March all the Bavarian counterproposals in Latin translation and their accompanying documents were in Rome for study by experts in all the appropriate Curial congregations. The major areas of discussion were still the rights of the State in Church affairs, the question of finance, and the school question, a major stumbling block in Bavaria just as in Prussia or other parts of the Reich without an overwhelming Catholic population. Rome felt that Munich's demands for some influence over clerical appointments was an attempt to resurrect the old State Church as it had existed before the war. The Holy See declared that the Weimar Constitution granted religious bodies the right to select their own officials. Thereupon Munich countered that if it was to give up important rights and privileges it could not be expected to be generous in its financial support of the Church. Pacelli knew of the government's eagerness to have its treaty and of the pressure created by the difficulties with the Reich. He therefore thought that if he held firm, Munich would concede, and since in his opinion the *Landtag*, with its present composition, would not be dissolved for at least two more years, the concordat should pass in the legislature. But the Nuncio's strategy also presented dangers to both negotiating partners. If the concordat were not signed soon, the Cardinal Secretary might be willing to push for the Reich treaty first. Rome would win either way, but Munich and Pacelli, who had advocated the signing of the Bavarian treaty first and who looked for a diplomatic success, would lose. Ritter therefore persuaded Munich to make some concession on the State's demands in order to show Bavaria's desire for the continuation of the talks. For its part, in order to bring the treaty to a close, Pacelli, speaking for the Curia, was then willing to make some concessions on financial matters.[77]

[75] GSTA, MA 104494, Ritter to Lerchenfeld, March 14, 1922.

[76] GSTA, Ges. Päpstl. Stuhl 972, Ritter to BFM, March 17, 1922.

[77] GSTA, Ges. Päpstl. Stuhl 972, Ritter to Lerchenfeld, April 24, 1922.

A final draft was hammered out by early 1923 after the various Bavarian ministries had injected minor alterations in the text. Pacelli passed these comments on to Rome, with the recommendation that they be accepted. Pius XI, however, demanded all the details be worked out to his personal satisfaction, and he scrutinized every clause, many times summoning advisors from the various congregations to clarify specific points.[78] Because this was to be a model for future concordats and especially for the one with the Reich, great care was taken. Negotiations dragged on into the fall of 1923, with much of the work and discussion centered on the thorny problem of specifying the exact nature of episcopal selection. Under the old treaty the monarch selected the bishops, who were then approved by Rome. Since the monarchy no longer existed, the Curia desired the selection of bishops to be made solely by the Pope. Bavaria, however, argued that the right of selection belonged to the government not to the person of the king, and the new Bavarian Government, as legitimate successor of the monarchy, could also expect to receive that right. The Vatican countered that it could not make such a concession lest other new states, Rumania and Czechoslovakia, for example, claim the same right, and this would be against the principles formulated in the new canon law. Instead it offered to allow the State to raise an objection of a "political nature" against the candidate. Bavaria wanted to have the bishop elected by the cathedral chapter or at least have the cathedral chapter participate in some way in the Papal appointment of the bishop. This would allow for some Bavarian influence over the selection process and not let it totally pass into the hands of "foreign prelates."[79]

After rewordings and minor concessions, by December most of the major hurdles had been circumvented. Only during December did Munich try to have one more provision inserted in the treaty. The recent attempt by Hitler and Ludendorff at a *Putsch* had sparked some demonstrations in its aftermath which protested the Church's lack of Bavarian nationalist spirit. Supporters of the treaty feared that any vote on the concordat in such an environment might cause some legislators to vote against it. To counter any rumor that the Curia did not show sufficient concern for Bavaria's interests and to ensure that Berlin did not outmaneuver Munich at some later date, the cabinet proposed inserting a most-favored-state clause, indicating that the Vatican promised not to grant in future discussions any privileges or concessions to the Reich not given to Bavaria. But Rome would not be bound in advance by any promise that would limit its future options. Pacelli informed the Bavarians that the concordat would have

[78] GSTA, Ges. Päpstl. Stuhl 973, Ritter to BFM, March 25, 1923.
[79] AA, PO II, PO 2 Nr. 1 Vat., Vol. 5, Meyer (Vatican) to AA, September 14, 1923.

to pass as it was. Not until February 8, 1924, however, did all sides reach final agreement on the details so that the concordat could be signed on March 29. During the last days of negotiation there was an increasing opinion among Vatican officials that although Pacelli wanted to complete work on a Bavarian treaty before starting on one for the Reich, his strong stand to gain acceptance for all the Vatican proposals and to concede as little as possible was a major reason for the delay in reaching final agreement. His overanxious approach, while obtaining a great deal, had needlessly delayed the proceedings when Gasparri and other Curial officials had been inclined to make concessions for the sake of speed. Pacelli had assured them that his strategy in the final analysis would bear results, since at that moment a Reich concordat did not look promising and the difficulties were even greater than those for a Bavarian treaty. Some diplomats suspected that Pacelli's obvious love for Munich and his reluctance to move to Berlin were psychologically and unconsciously influencing him to proceed so carefully and deliberately with Bavarian negotiations.[80]

The text had, as agreed, been submitted in February to the Reich to determine whether any sections conflicted with the Constitution, the Vatican requesting that Berlin pass on it as soon as possible and proceed in strictest secrecy lest the text be published before final approval. One month later Chancellor Marx informed Munich that the Reich found no objection with the concordat, and it could be sent to the *Landtag*.[81]

Before presenting the treaty, the Munich Cabinet had also been negotiating an agreement with the Evangelical Church in Bavaria so that no charge of favoritism toward the Catholic Church could be made and to ensure less opposition from the Protestants when it came to a vote. After several months of debate, in January 1925 the treaty was approved by a vote of 73 to 52, the main support coming from the Bavarian People's Party and its opposition from Social Democrats, Communists, Democrats, and the new National Socialist Party.[82] For many Bavarians it not only provided the necessary regulation of church-state relations but gave expression to Bavaria's uniqueness. Georg Wohlmuth, a Bavarian People's Party deputy, expressed it well during the *Landtag* debate:

> The concordat . . . has obviously a significance for church-state relations; but viewed more closely we find that the concordat goes far

[80] GSTA, Ges. Päpstl. Stuhl 973, Ritter to BFM, February 8, 1924.

[81] AA, PO II, PO 2 Nr. 1 Vat., Vol. 5, Marx to BFM, March 18, 1924. Germany Reichstag, Vol. 386, p. 2368ff. 76th Session, June 17, 1925.

[82] For debate on the concordat in the *Landtag*, see for example, Germany, Bavaria, Landtag 1924-1925, Vol. 1, pp. 746-67, 769-820, 823-872. 27th Session, January 13, 1925.

beyond this and extends into the area of political affairs. It may even be said actually that it extends in many ways into the area of world affairs. With the conclusion of the concordat on March 29, 1924, the Bavarian Government has executed an act of sovereignty which loudly proclaims Bavarian sovereign rights. In this age of tedious centralization this alone for a patriotic Bavarian is something comforting, a ray of light. With the conclusion of this document today's Bavaria was recognized by the major powers of the world as equal to all other states, as empowered to have a concordat made with it. . . ."[83]

The Munich Government had succeeded in having the agreement ratified, and six years after the founding of the Republic, Bavaria became the first German state to have a new concordat with Rome. The liberal and secular press had regarded the concordat as having too many concessions to the Church, as having placed canon law above Bavarian state law, and having given too many privileges to the Church in educational matters.[84] But the powerful Catholic Bavarian People's Party had vigorously worked to attain this accord, and with the simultaneous presentation of an agreement between the Bavarian State and the Evangelical Church for ratification many Protestant deputies also were inclined to go along with the concordat. Foreign diplomats regarded the treaty with Rome as a victory for the Vatican and a personal one for Pacelli. Bishops were to be appointed by the Holy See from a list of candidates drawn up by ecclesiastical authorities to whom the State raised no objections of a political nature. Full and complete liberty was granted to institutions such as religious orders, and their juridical personality was recognized so as to enable them to acquire and own property. The only qualification here was that religious superiors had to be of German nationality. The State agreed to a generous settlement providing financial support for the clergy and for the upkeep of Church institutions. Religious education not only was required in primary schools but formed part of the secondary school curriculum. The ecclesiastical authorities were to be consulted on the conduct of general public education. Catholic theological faculties were to be maintained at Bavarian universities, and appointments to these faculties were subject to the approval of the local bishops. In addition, at least one professor of philosophy and one of history at Munich and Würzburg had to be appointed who had had a thorough Catholic educational training.[85]

[83] Germany, Bavaria, Landtag 1924-1925, Vol. 1, p. 749. 27th Session, January 13, 1925.

[84] *Neue Tägliche Rundschau*, December 2, 1924.

[85] FFO, Allemagne 371, Doulcet to Premier Herriot, November 30, 1924. Padellaro,

Gasparri was jubilant. For Rome the concordat was considered a masterpiece of hard bargaining, skill, and patience. The fact that there had been objections in the *Landtag* during the debate and that the vote had not been overwhelming did not matter to the Cardinal: the treaty had passed. He reminded Pastor, the Austrian Minister, that Italian Prime Minister Francesco Nitti once got a bill passed by two votes and said at that time that "it was still one vote too many."[86]

The Bavarian Cabinet also had reason to realize the wisdom of having signed an agreement with Rome, for soon after the ratification of the treaty the Saar Administration, supported by France, announced that the concordat was not binding in its territory. The Saar Administration considered the prior concordat of 1817 still in force and arrogated to itself, as the legal government, the right of consultation on clerical appointments. Diplomats viewed this as a move to increase pressure on Rome to appoint an independent ecclesiastical administrator and eventually to create a separate diocese for the area. Several months of further correspondence between Rome, Munich, and Saarbrücken ensued on this point, but the value of the new concordat's legal status proved its worth. The Vatican conceded that until final determination of the political status for the Saar, the Bavarian concordat was technically *in suspenso* for the area, but it also cited Article 12 of the new treaty, which stated that Bavarian Church provinces would not be altered unless a change of political boundaries had been definitely confirmed. Rome furthermore assured Munich and Berlin in writing that now that it had this internationally recognized legal document on which to base its decisions, it would be able justifiably to reject the Administration's assertion. In other words, the Saar would not be separated from the German dioceses, the clergy would still be under the control of German bishops, and French influence would not be able to increase so readily in the territory by means of the Church.[87]

The concordat was then satisfactory to both governments involved. For Bavaria it settled and regulated a very important issue which af-

---

pp. 49-50. For the text of the concordat, see Schöppe, pp. 46-51. For a comparison of the concordats of 1817 and 1924 and discussion of negotiations, see Franz-Willing, pp. 181-227.

[86] HHSTA, 87, Pastor to Mataja (AFO), January 19, 1925. Not all of the Bavarian episcopate were as pleased as the Curia. Several bishops were apprehensive that the debate on the school question and the opposition of the Bavarian Teachers' Association (*Lehrerverein*) and the Evangelical League to the treaty had aroused some bad feeling among the populace toward the concordat and to the Church. They also believed that the negotiations with the Protestants had given them too much in comparison with what the concordat provided the Catholics. AW, 1A 25k, 155, Faulhaber to Bertram, February 3, 1925.

[87] AA, PO II, PO 2 Nr. 1 Vat., Vol. 7, Bergen to Köpke (AA), December 22, 1925. GSTA, MA 104501, Ritter to BFM, March 5, 1926.

fected the internal affairs of the State where the Church was still an important influence, and it provided Bavaria with the psychological and diplomatic support for its particularist claims both within and without the Reich. Concessions, it is true, had been made, and the government had relinquished the right to help in episcopal selection and had accepted the Church's influence in education. But in such a predominantly Catholic *Land*, where the Catholic philosophy toward the schools and where the belief that education should be grounded in orthodox Church teaching was widely accepted by people and Catholic political parties alike, and in a *Land* already accustomed to a concordat, the advantages outweighed the concessions. For both Bavaria and the Reich the guarantees of maintaining the present diocesan borders in the west was tangible proof of the wisdom of agreeing to a treaty that the Curia wished to see completed. In return and in conformity with their foreign policy goals, the government had won the promise that no diocesan borders would be altered without its consent and that all bishops would have to possess German citizenship.

For the Vatican the treaty granted the Church a legal status guaranteed by international law. Rome had obtained most of its demands by keeping control over clerical selection and education in Bavaria and now also had a concordat which could serve as a framework for future referral in bargaining with other states. The Vatican in the 1920's had adopted a policy of obtaining legal confirmation of its association with as many states as possible, and several treaties were then in the critical negotiating stage. Even within Germany the existence of a concordat with one of the *Länder* could not be ignored and would certainly induce any and all other *Länder* to reconsider signing one in the future. The Vatican was satisfied that the first one had so successfully met many of the Church's aims. Even the Reich, although still without its own concordat, could derive some satisfaction. The ambiguous situation of having Berlin and Munich competing to sign a treaty with Rome had been clarified. Once Berlin knew what had been specified in the Bavarian agreement, it could concentrate its efforts on accommodating its provisions to a more general treaty and removing any obstacles which this created. It meant, as Berlin hoped, that the Holy See and the Reich Government were now one step closer to a Reich concordat, that the Nuncio could now come to Berlin, and that negotiations, stalled at a low level since 1922, could once more be intensively resumed.

C. The Prussian Concordat (1929)

The major causes for delay in negotiating a Reich concordat had been the progress already made toward the Bavarian treaty and the lack of legal competence of the Reich in church-state affairs and in the administration of the educational system, which had been left largely in the hands of the *Länder*. In addition, the states ultimately had to approve the Reich concordat.[88] The first of these difficulties had now been overcome, and in 1925 Pacelli officially transferred his residence to Berlin to continue the negotiations there. In spite of the goodwill of the Central Government in Berlin, he was faced with different conditions than those in Munich—a negotiating field that had to encompass a much greater number of varied components and circumstances than in Bavaria, a government that was not expressly pro-Church, a territory consisting of a majority of Protestants where no concordat had previously existed, and an area with some state governments controlled by the Socialists, such as in Prussia. Moreover, since Prussia contained the greatest number of Catholics of any *Land*,[89] Rome was particularly interested in having a treaty which regularized the Church's status for its adherents in this state. But the school question had been a stumbling block for discussions with the Prussian Government, which also had reservations about the nature of a *Reichskonkordat*. In spite of the successful conclusion of an agreement in Bavaria, it had taken four to five years to complete, and there was no reason to believe that further concordats would follow in rapid succession.

On November 27, 1924, Prussian Minister-President Otto Braun informed the Reich Government that since discussions for a Reich concordat were once again being talked about, he wanted to remind the Reich that Prussia's position, stated on January 9, 1921, had not changed; that is, since no constitutional provision for a concordat had been provided, one could be negotiated only by the voluntary agreement of the German *Länder* charged with regulating church-state relations. Prussia was willing to agree to such a Reich treaty if all other states did so. These conditions would now be difficult to fulfill since Bavaria already had proceeded to sign its own concordat. Prussia would therefore have to insist on her own treaty, since it would not be consistent with Prussia's dignity as a state to have provided less for its own specific church-state needs than did another *Land*. The memorandum ended with the terse retort: "A Reich concordat without Bavaria would no longer be a Reich concordat but would simply mean the recognition by the Reich of further special rights . . . for individual states."[90]

[88] Golombek, p. 9. See also Hömig, p. 184ff.

[89] In the mid-1920's Prussia had slightly less than 12,000,000 Catholics while Bavaria, the second largest state, had more than 5,000,000. *Der Grosse Brockhaus*, Vol. 2, p. 417; Vol. 15, p. 89.

[90] PGSTA, Rep. 90, P.11.1.1., Vol. 10, Prussian Minister-President to Reich Minister of Interior, Foreign Office, Reich Chancellor, November 27, 1924.

Prussia had not shown great urgency to negotiate a treaty of its own in the early 1920's and indeed had expressed reservations about a Reich treaty because of Bavaria's actions and the Vatican's stand on education. There had been informal discussions with the Nuncio as early as 1920, and the Prussian episcopate had been consulted by Rome about what it deemed the minimal demands to be made by the Church, but the talks had not gone much further.[91] But by 1925, now that Bavaria had its own treaty, the intra-German rivalry caused Prussia to become anxious to assert and maintain its sovereignty and to show increased interest in opening discussions with the Church. Prussia, as much as the Reich, was aware of the value of a treaty in securing the diocesan boundaries. While rejecting the contents of Bavaria's concordat, Prussia began to understand the wisdom of Bavaria's example of settling with Rome lest in a general treaty the specific conditions of the *Land* not receive the attention they should. The Prussian Cabinet, still rather piqued that the south German state had concluded its own treaty, now felt, if only for reasons of prestige, it should do likewise. Where Bavaria led, Prussia was to follow. But some thorny problems still had to be solved before an agreement could be reached. Prussia was not interested in an all-encompassing treaty but rather in one which primarily settled the problems of diocesan borders and the question of State subsidies, for the Prussian Cabinet viewed such matters as of great political importance. At first the cabinet envisaged a short concordat covering general principles and several specific subjects, but not including the broad coverage found in the Bavarian agreement. The Vatican, of course, was also interested specifically in the educational question and the extension of Church control of episcopal selection, issues which Prussia would not like to see raised. Because of the differences in the confessional makeup of Prussia and Bavaria, observers in both Curial circles and in Berlin presumed that concessions from the Social Democratic dominated Prussian Government would be difficult to obtain.[92]

During the 1920's the Vatican, besides waiting to complete the Bavarian concordat, had not urged discussions with Prussia, since the possibility of a Reich concordat still loomed and Rome was prepared to wait in anticipation that a cabinet change might bring to power a more accommodating government. Neither of these conjectures materialized, and by 1925 the Vatican was now prepared to tackle the next problem: Prussia. The Holy See was quick to pick upon the renewed interest of the Prussian Cabinet by letting it be known in

[91] AA, PO II, PO 2 Nr. 2 Vat., Vol. 1, Bertram to Pacelli, January 24, 1922.

[92] BA, Nachlass Pünder, 27, pp. 52-54, May 1, 1926. AA, PO II, PO 2 Nr. 2 Vat., Vol. 1, memorandum of Meyer-Rodehüser, March 22, 1926.

December 1924 that Rome was not averse to negotiating with other German states besides Bavaria. The Nuncio hinted that Rome would specifically like to open talks with two other German *Länder*, Prussia and Baden, which also had sizable Catholic populations. On the other hand, this would not preclude further discussions about a Reich concordat.[93] Soon after the Bavarian concordat had been signed, Pacelli returned to the matter of a Reich concordat. In December he had urged Reich officials to reassess the situation and see if such a treaty could not now be completed. The Vatican was thus making overtures on two fronts, either to conclude a treaty for all Germany at once or, if this proved too difficult at first, then to take it in stages by dealing with the leading states.[94] In either case, official representatives now seemed interested in negotiating.

There was an added reason in the beginning of 1925 for both Prussia and the Reich to consider the Vatican's offer to negotiate. A Polish concordat had been signed in February. When the treaty's clauses became known, they greatly disturbed the Germans, for they provided for placing Danzig under the authority of the nuncio in Warsaw, allowing no part of Poland to come under the jurisdiction of a non-Polish bishop, permitting disciplinary action against priests "where activities endangered the security of the state," and guaranteeing that ecclesiastical boundaries conform to political ones. All of these provisions, if observed, would be a serious setback to the German claims. Even if these clauses were placed *in suspenso* until all boundaries were finally settled, the existence of such terms would weaken German demands for compensation of property losses in areas that Berlin had already relinquished.[95] Reich, Prussian, and German Church officials sent their protests about the treaty to Rome, and Bergen was active in seeking some modification of its terms.[96] The Prussian Government specifically requested Pacelli to remind Rome of the consequences of the concordat for Prussian dioceses. Pacelli promised to do what he could before the concordat was finalized, but reminded the Prussians, almost admonishingly, that they were in a weaker position than the Poles since they had no legal treaty with the Vatican. He also stated

[93] PGSTA, Rep. 90, P.11.1.1., Vol. 10, Denk (Munich) to Prussian Minister-President, December 2, 1924.

[94] AA, RM 70, Vol. 2, Bergen to AA, December 23, 1924. Hermann Pünder, State Secretary of the Reich Chancellery, stated that Pacelli was interested in a Reich concordat and seemed to be more concerned in being able to complete an agreement as such than in the actual content. Pünder, *Von Preussen*, pp. 119-120.

[95] AA, PO II, PO 3 Vat., Polen, Vol. 2, memorandum of Meyer-Rodehüser, March 25, 1925.

[96] PGSTA, Rep. 90, P.11.1.1., Vol. 11, Marx to Pacelli, April 2, 1925; Braun to Pacelli, December 29, 1925.

that their case would be much stronger if the Prussian concordat negotiations were further along. If Germany or Prussia had a treaty of its own, the Polish concordat might not have contained as many problems for Germany as it did.[97]

The Germans succeeded in obtaining changes providing for such items as property compensation and guarantees for German-speaking Catholics to use their mother tongue in worship and religious instruction and in satisfactorily clarifying the situation over Danzig.[98] Nevertheless, the fact that Poland now had a legally binding treaty with the Vatican only demonstrated to both governments in Berlin the dangers inherent in the situation unless either or both administrations, as Pacelli had said, countered with concordats of their own.

Already on January 29, 1925 a meeting had been held between Reich and Prussian officials about what could be done. After extended discussions and the now familiar plea that Germany's foreign policy goals required such a treaty, Prussia announced its willingness in principle to agree to the Reich's resumption of negotiations with Rome that had all but lapsed since 1922, but only if nothing was included in the discussions which exceeded the constitutional limits of the Reich's competence and only if these negotiations took place in close consultation with Prussia. In turn the Reich made a concession to Prussia's wounded dignity; it agreed that the *Land* had the constitutional right to be specifically represented at the Vatican and that Bergen would also carry the title of Prussian Minister to the Vatican and likewise the Nuncio in Berlin would be doubly accredited, i.e., to both governments.[99]

The Reich Government also busied itself during much of 1925 in preparing a list of topics for inclusion in a Reich concordat and in making overtures to the Evangelical Church for a similar treaty. In that way, similar to the Bavarian experience, the cabinet anticipated reducing Protestant opposition to the treaty with Rome. On January 20 the Center Party in the Reichstag had also requested the government to resume negotiations. The cabinet thereupon named specialists from the Ministries of the Interior, Justice, and Foreign Affairs to begin work on a draft. But the idea of a Reich concordat again ran into trouble, especially after the signing of the Bavarian treaty in 1924. Once this treaty's clauses were made known, they evoked lively criticism, particularly from conservative Protestants and from the Left.

[97] PGSTA, Rep. 90, P.11.1.1., Vol. 11, memorandum of Trendelenburg, May 6, 1925.
[98] AA, PO II, PO 3 Vat., Polen, Vol. 2, Meyer-Rodehüser to Bergen, April 3, 1925.
[99] AA, RM 70, Vol. 2, memorandum of Meyer-Rodehüser, January 29, 1925. See also ch. 6, p. 298f.

Both groups objected to the concessions in education made to the Church, and some organizations such as the anti-Catholic Evangelical League warned in sharply worded statements against a Reich concordat. The German Democratic Party and the German People's Party both announced in advance that they would not support a treaty with such wide-ranging concessions as had been granted in Bavaria. The Prussian Government also warned the Reich that it did not wish to have the Bavarian treaty serve as a precedent, and was prepared to oppose any attempt to formulate sections of a Reich agreement to conform to and incorporate into it certain objectionable parts of the Bavarian agreement. It stood by its original intention of endorsing a Reich concordat only if a formulation were reached that was acceptable to and endorsed by all states.[100]

By 1926 the experts had generally agreed that a Reich treaty should deal with the legal status of the Church, diocesan boundaries, school affairs, and army and institutional chaplaincies, realizing of course that it had to be formulated in such a manner as not to conflict with any concordat already signed. Yet on the crucial school question Prussia and Bavaria disagreed on what should be included, and the Reich had not formulated its own school law which would spell out general guidelines for the common school (*Volksschule*) and the public confessional schools. Until the formulation of such a law, the legal situation remained unchanged, and each state was free to supervise its own educational system. The Reich might then have difficulty in working out a plan that would be acceptable to Bavaria as well as to the other states.[101]

On July 19, 1926, a meeting of Reich officials was held to discuss how to proceed. Noting the difficulties that would be faced, aware of the frustrations that the government had already experienced, Chancellor Marx posed the question of whether the concordat should be negotiated first or a Reich school bill passed—both considered difficult matters to get through the Reichstag. Since one of the principal points of controversy dealt with education, a school bill might help to clarify the situation. After much debate and regrets that the treaty might again be delayed, the Reich Government agreed that a school bill had to be passed first, giving the Reich a legal basis in dealing with Rome about a matter in which it was specially interested and helping to remove some of the *Länder*'s objections to the Reich treaty.[102]

[100] AA, Geheim Vat., Pol. 2 Nr. 2, Vol. 1, Trendelenburg to Zech, June 10, 1926.

[101] AA, PO II, PO 2 Nr. 1 Vat., Vol. 7, memorandum of Meyer-Rodehüser, June 17, 1926.

[102] AA, PO II, PO 2 Nr. 1 Vat., Vol. 7, excerpts from the meeting of Reich officials, July 19, 1926.

Prussia meanwhile took one step further in following the Bavarian example. Since March, the State of Prussia had officially opened discussions with the Vatican about a concordat. Now, in October, Prussian Minister-President Braun formally requested the Reich Chancellor to delay further negotiations for a Reich treaty until the conclusion of a Prussian concordat. Braun understood the reasons for a diplomatically united front in dealing with Rome and for a general treaty. Nevertheless Prussia, which had begun to work for a concordat, had made, in Braun's opinion, some progress and had all the material at hand for carrying through the negotiations. He requested the Reich to wait until Prussia completed its treaty, just as the Reich had done for Bavaria. Moreover, since Bavaria now had an internationally valid treaty which had not taken into consideration conditions pertaining to the entire Reich, out of self-respect Prussia could not permit the Central Government to make a treaty binding on it before it too worked out an agreement suitable to its own particular needs.[103]

At a meeting on October 13 between Reich and Prussian representatives, Prussia gave all its reasons for negotiating first. Its relations with Rome had not been regulated by a concordat but merely a Papal bull, *De Salute Animarum*, circumscribing the Prussian dioceses, to which the government had agreed. Lawyers had argued for the State that the bull remained in effect until a new law replaced it. However, the more time elapsed until this new law was passed, the weaker Prussia's position became, as witnessed when the clauses of the Polish concordat had been announced. A new treaty was urgently needed to guarantee the borders and to ensure that the State had some word in the selection of bishops and over the nationality of the clergy. In addition, Prussia desired to clarify the usual questions concerning the subsidies to the Church and the degree of influence that it should be afforded over the administration of the educational system on both the school and university level. Prussia was now requesting the Reich to allow it to take precedence in negotiating, for its discussions were more advanced and the *Land* was more experienced in drawing up laws dealing with the rights of religious bodies than was the Reich, and much of the substance of a concordat's stipulations fell within the competence of the *Länder*. In addition, argued Prussian representatives, since many of the objectives of both governments for such a treaty were identical, simultaneous negotiations could only complicate matters further.

Friedrich Trendelenburg, the representative from the Prussian Ministry of Religious Affairs, argued the state's case politely but uncompromisingly. Since the Reich Cabinet had already stated its desire to

[103] GSTA, MA 104455, Braun to Reich Chancellor, October 26, 1926.

have the *Reichsschulgesetz* passed before its concordat was signed—and this would probably take some time before it could be satisfactorily worked out and presented for a vote in the Reichstag—Prussia believed that its request should not cause the Reich Cabinet any problem. Prussia saw no difficulty from the Vatican since Pacelli was officially accredited to Prussia and could deal with this state separately from the Reich Government, and success with Prussia, as with the Reich, would mean a victory for the Vatican. The Prussian position was very strong since legally Prussia could negotiate and proceed on its own, and the Bavarian precedent had only strengthened its case. Although Reich officials from both the Ministry of the Interior and the Foreign Office stated that a "united front" of Prussia and the Reich was necessary and that the two governments should work this out in close cooperation, Prussia, while ready to continue discussions with the Reich, like Bavaria beforehand, had now resolved to carry on its own negotiations.[104]

The Reich Government, faced again with what seemed to be perpetual obstacles to its plans, nevertheless did not entirely oppose Prussia's pursuing of its own negotiations. Since one of the primary concerns of the Reich's Vatican policy was to secure diocesan borders, most of which were situated within Prussia, an agreement between that *Land* and the Vatican would not negate but only postpone the Reich's plans for its own treaty. If Prussia reached an accord with Rome, it would secure many of the Reich's objectives and in the long run possibly save time and long negotiations by removing some of Prussian objections and easing the way for a final general treaty.[105]

Since Prussia was not prepared to compromise, and the Reich did not have a *Reichsschulgesetz* near completion, and since many of Germany's foreign policy objectives could be dealt with in a Prussian concordat, in November Chancellor Marx wrote to the Prussian Minister-President, officially announcing that the Reich would not undertake negotiations for a Reich concordat immediately. It reserved the privilege, should the opportunity or conditions be suitable, to continue discussions with the Nuncio, if for no other reason than to indicate good faith and the continuing interest of the Reich in such a treaty. Already on October 8 Councillor Richard Wienstein of the Reich Chancellery had informed Prussian officials that the Central Government still considered it important to have a Reich concordat and that its completion in itself was far more significant than its contents. The Chancellery also considered it important to sign the treaty specifically

---

[104] PGSTA, Rep. 90, P.11.1.5., Vol. 1, memorandum of meeting in the Reich Ministry of the Interior, signed Conring, October 13, 1926.

[105] *Neue Tägliche Rundschau*, April 16, 1926.

with Pacelli since the Foreign Office was certain that the Nuncio's influence in the Vatican's inner circle would grow after he successfully negotiated a Reich treaty immediately after having brought the Bavarian concordat to its conclusion. Berlin's willingness to cooperate and work with him could yield dividends for Germany later on when he became more powerful in the Curia.[106] In deferring to Prussia's arguments, the Central Government only asked to be kept very closely informed of all Prussian-Vatican discussions. Once more the Reich had postponed its objective because of the strong legal case, the uncompromising attitude, and the progress already made in negotiations by one of its constituent member states. Once more the Vatican would negotiate with Germany piecemeal, proceeding by stages toward its goal of coverage for all Germany. Once more both would wait to see how these negotiations would affect future plans for a Reich concordat.

Discussions had begun officially in March 1926 between Prussia and the Vatican. Before the war the anti-Catholic sentiment of the Court and conservative Protestants had made official Vatican representation in Berlin impossible. After centuries of tradition and prejudice, the political change of 1919 served as a liberating force for Catholicism and caused the Reich and Prussian Governments to allow a nunciature to be opened in Berlin and even to encourage discussion with Rome of their mutual concerns. During the Empire the governments of the Reich and Prussia were chiefly in the hands of Protestants. There had been only one case of a Catholic's being promoted to the command of an army corps between 1870-1914, and even General Hans von Seeckt, despite his brilliant military service, received no independent command during the war because of his religion. Until 1917 no Catholic had headed either the Reich or Prussian Governments. Among the lower bureaucrats Catholics were also sadly underrepresented, although Catholics constituted about one-third of the population of the Reich as well as approximately one-third of Prussia's population.

Since the war the situation had changed dramatically. By 1927 Germany already had had three Catholic Chancellors (Fehrenbach, Wirth, and Marx). The cabinets generally contained at least one-third Catholics and many times more. The chief of the army command in the early 1920's had been Catholic, as well as most officials in the Reich Chancellery and the Ministry for Occupied Territories. In 1914, of the total Prussian county councillors (*Landräte*) 67 were Catholic and 421 were Protestant; in 1926-1927, 116 were Catholic and 271 Prot-

---

[106] PGSTA, Rep. 90, P.11.1.5., Vol. 1, memorandum of meeting in the Reich Ministry of the Interior, signed Conring, October 13, 1926; Marx to Braun, November 28, 1926.

estant. In 1905 all governors (*Oberpräsidenten*) of Prussian provinces were Protestant; in 1926 three out of twelve were Catholic. Much of the cause for this dramatic change was due to the dismissal of the Hohenzollerns, the removal of control of the Reich and Prussian Governments from the hands of generally anti-Catholic Junker or National Liberal politicians, and the crucial role which the Center now played in Weimar politics.

As its name implied, the Center marked the middle ground between political extremes, and no government existed without its support or at least its benevolent neutrality. The Party contained within it a miniature parliament and political shadings from Right to Left, including feudal landlords who thought like Junkers, such as Prince Aloys Löwenstein-Wertheim; industrialists sympathetic to the German People's Party, like Rudolf Henckel; agriculturally oriented men like August Crone-Münzebrock, and representatives of the trade unions like Adam Stegerwald and Josef Joos, who had many interests similar to the Socialists. Compromise was possible on all issues except one—the interests of the Church. This unity of purpose allowed the Church via the Center to exercise some influence over other parties. In the Prussian *Landtag* the power of the Center as well as the votes of some Catholics for the Socialists prevented the SPD from being anti-Christian, while in the Reichstag it prevented the German Nationalists from adopting an overtly anti-Catholic stance.[107]

The political transformation which took place after 1919 also emboldened Catholics to become more visible in areas such as Prussia, where they were in the minority. The number of Catholic social and professional associations increased, and their conferences took place with more publicity and press coverage than ever before. Religious celebrations and processions were held in public, often in predominantly non-Catholic cities where ten years before these processions would have been unthinkable. Marx, while he was Chancellor, for example, marched along with his fellow Catholics in the Corpus Christi day procession in Berlin. Pacelli himself repeatedly expressed to foreign diplomats in the 1920's his surprise and pleasure at witnessing a renaissance of Catholic life in Germany.[108] The Church by the end of the 1920's was to have twenty-four dioceses and one prelature *nullius* with 22,000 priests for 20 million Catholics as compared with 16,000

---

[107] See also Evans, especially chs. 12-13. For Center-Socialist cooperation in Prussia which continued virtually throughout Weimar, see Hömig.

[108] Material about the Catholics in Imperial and Weimar Germany in the preceding paragraphs was drawn from Philipp Funk, "Kritisches zum neuen Katholischen Selbstgefühl: Die Jungen und die Alten," *Hochland*, XXII (1924-1925), 233. BFO, 371/12147/5412, Lindsay (Berlin) to A. Chamberlain, February 16, 1927.

pastors for 40 million Protestants. There was also an increase of religious orders and the number of their members.[109] In 1931 politician and historian Karl Bachem commented that "never yet has a Catholic country possessed such a developed system of all conceivable Catholic associations as today's Catholic Church [in Germany.]"[110] All of these manifestations of a Catholic presence were particularly evident in Prussia, the largest German state and one in which Catholicism had not appeared as powerful and influential as it did in the 1920's.

The wide gains won by the Church in Bavaria and its increasing prosperity in Prussia rendered the question of a concordat extremely sensitive in the north German state. Even more than in Bavaria it aroused the concern of Protestants and some liberals that Rome was now seeking to gain a preferred position for itself and to impose its religious and philosophical views on all Prussia. The Protestants believed that such a treaty would endanger Protestantism by giving Catholicism a more favored position, with an internationally legal treaty, while the liberals feared a clericalization of the Republic, especially should the Church be granted its demands in the school question, and a weakening of modern secular culture and the sovereignty of the State. Among the Protestant groups which stood opposed to a concordat was the Evangelical League, which organized a propaganda campaign and vehemently remonstrated to the Ministry of Religious Affairs about the dangers of such a treaty. The liberal views were represented, for example, by the *Frankfurter Zeitung*, which carried articles warning that what Germany had gained in the Republic was now being seriously threatened.[111]

Despite the arguments of the concordat's opponents, negotiations continued during 1926-1927. Most of the discussions took place in Berlin between the Nuncio, assisted by Msgr. Kaas, and members of the Prussian Ministry of Religious Affairs, Minister Becker and his assistant, Trendelenburg.[112] Since the negotiations were secret, regardless of the frequent inquiries in the *Landtag*, the Minister for Religious Affairs made only general statements concerning the progress being made. By early 1928, after some twenty-five meetings, the negotiators were working particularly on redefining diocesan borders, the procedure of episcopal appointment, and settling financial matters.

---

[109] See ch. 6, note 110.

[110] Lewy, pp. 4-5.

[111] HHSTA, 88, Pastor to Seipel, September 30, 1927. *Germania*, October 8, 1927. *Deutsch-Evangelische Korrespondenz*, June 24, 1929. *Kölnische Volkszeitung*, June 25, 1929.

[112] The Nachlass Becker (Germany, Becker), supplemented by that of Trendelenburg (PGSTA, Rep. 92) contains virtually all the pertinent documents and transcripts of the concordat negotiations.

Prussia contended that as in Cologne in 1919 or in Trier in 1921 it was crucial to have a loyal patriot appointed. Someone elected by the cathedral chapter, which as a rule was more conscious of national interests, would be of more benefit to the Reich than a selection procedure conducted, as the Nuncio suggested, solely by Rome. The border question was of course of paramount interest, and the *Land* desired guarantees that no one would have ecclesiastical jurisdiction without German citizenship, even if it were a case of the appointment of an administrator for parts of Polish dioceses remaining in Prussia. When the Nuncio at first objected to a blanket guarantee, the Prussians warned that this might jeopardize the negotiations since one of Prussia's main objectives in seeking a concordat was to gain concessions that would help to secure the borders. Prussia also wanted assurances that the clergy would be trained in Germany or, with some exceptions, in Rome, lest they receive some of their training in a country unfriendly to Germany. In return, the Vatican raised the question of what the State was willing to contribute to support the Church and to aid clerical education. Discussions also were held about increasing the number of dioceses and raising Breslau to the rank of archdiocese and metropolitan see, a move which would lend prestige to the Church and also strengthen Germany's position in the area of Upper Silesia. Prussia wanted the Vatican to press Breslau's claims to compensation for property lost in Czechoslovakia. More than once Becker and Trendelenburg reminded Pacelli that representation of Prussia/Breslau's interests here could help to preserve a favorable atmosphere for the concordat negotiations, or, in other words, Prussia would be more amenable to concessions in other areas, such as State subsidies, in return for foreign policy aid.[113]

Meanwhile, on the national level, the entrance of the Nationalists into Marx's Cabinet in January 1927 gave the Center reason to hope that a school bill could be drafted and carried into law. The Constitution had provided for the common school (*Volksschule*)—one which would permit religious instruction to all denominations—to be the norm for a future national school system. Deviations were made possible by a provision which allowed, upon petition of the parents of the students, for separate local confessional or secular schools. The Center, representing the Church, wanted the confessional school to be given parity with the common school. Without such an endorsement the Center would not support a school bill. On the other hand, liberals and Socialists, those in favor of either the common or secular school,

[113] Germany, Becker, 32, transcript of Trendelenburg and Pacelli conversations, December 15, 1927.

423

were not willing to agree to the Center's demands. In 1927 Interior Minister Walter von Keudall tried to solve the dilemma by providing for five possible public schools: Catholic, Lutheran, and Reformed confessional schools; common schools, offering instruction in more than one faith; and secular, non-denominational schools. This proposal in turn effectively negated the concept of a nation-wide common school which the framers of the Constitution had envisioned. In addition although the bill declared five types of schools equal, it in actuality favored the confessional schools and basically granted what the Center had wanted. The Minister's draft, however, met strong opposition in the *Reichsrat*, in the Reichstag committee, and among the general public, and caused bitter disagreements among the coalition partners, some of whose members accused the Center of exerting undue pressure to get the bill passed. The matter came to a head over the specific problem of the common schools in Baden. No compromise could be reached; not only was Keudall's plan scrapped, but the coalition itself collapsed over the issue in February 1928. Objections to the plan not only in the Reichstag but among the parties in a government whose composition made passage more likely than before was still too great. The defeat of the bill only further dimmed the Reich's chances to carry through its own concordat and made the negotiations going on in Prussia more critical than ever.[114]

During 1928 general agreement dealing with diocesan borders, episcopal appointments, and financial problems had been virtually reached between the Holy See and Prussia. The school question and the education of the clergy still remained in dispute. The sessions on these issues had been frequently heated and bluntly forthright. Pacelli still insisted on Rome's demand for separate public confessional schools and warned that without agreement on this Rome would prefer a treaty-less situation. Becker countered that there were also limits to which the state was willing to compromise and a treaty-less condition was preferable to an oppressive concordat—apart from even considering that a treaty with such a clause could ever pass the *Landtag*. Becker also reminded the Nuncio that Prussia was compromising by basically agreeing to Rome's right to appoint the bishops and now expected some sign of concession from the Holy See. Pacelli stated that the German Nationalists (DNVP) would probably favor the school clause since they too desired confessional schools. He was thereby implying that the Center might unite with that party over this issue and thus possibly topple the present government. Becker refused to be frightened. He politely informed the Nuncio that he had to disagree, for he had reliable word that though the Nationalists were interested in

---

[114] Evans, pp. 321-322, 324-329. Grünthal, ch. 8. See also Hömig, p. 204ff.

confessional schools, their official position was still to oppose the extension of Catholic influence, and hence the concordat.[115]

Ultimately, when this impasse was reached, Pacelli despite his threats of preferring no treaty, reluctantly agreed to the omission of the school question from the draft and its deferral to a later time. The Holy See agreed to drop the school clause only after Pacelli realized that the SPD and Democratic opposition to the concordat could be overcome, but only with this omission.[116] Becker and the Prussian officials had consistently emphasized that, even it they agreed to the Vatican's wishes, the opposition of the Socialists and the secular-minded Democrats and German People's Party would never permit it to pass the legislature. What probably convinced Pacelli of the wisdom of their arguments was that the Reich Government's attempts to formulate a compromise plan on the school issue agreeable to both those for and against ecclesiastical influence on public education had caused such a controversy that it precipitated the fall of the cabinet in February. At such a time it seemed most unwise to suggest and unrealistic to expect that Catholic demands in the field of education could win acceptance. The opponents would be only all the more determined to prevent the Church from gaining its wishes by means of an international treaty. Since forcing the issue risked defeat of the concordat itself, which, after all, did provide the Church with other benefits, the Holy See was practical enough to accept what the situation allowed.

All negotiations were completed in the spring of 1929, and the treaty formally signed on June 14. Journalistic comments, except those from the Communist and Rightist press, were on the whole favorable. The liberal *Berliner Tageblatt* compared the treaty with the Bavarian concordat, which had conceded more to Rome, and concluded that the Prussian treaty, in that sense, was a success. It also stated that Prussian Catholics were entitled to be guaranteed the religious rights which their numbers and influence warranted. The Socialist newspaper *Vorwärts* endorsed the treaty and pointed out that everything really controversial had been eliminated from the agreement.[117]

The Prussian concordat granted freedom to profess and practice the Catholic faith but did not extend the protection of the State to its ministers in carrying out their pastoral duties, as did the Bavarian treaty. Diocesan borders were fixed and legally formalized, new dioceses were created in Aachen and Berlin, and Breslau and Paderborn were raised to the rank of archdiocese. Bishops were to be chosen from lists of candidates prepared by the Prussian episcopate from which the

[115] PGSTA, Rep. 92, Nr. 8, Trendelenburg, note of Becker, December 27, 1928.

[116] AA, PO II, PO 2 Nr. 2 Vat., Vol. 2, Bergen to AA, June 18, 1929.

[117] BFO, 371/1364/5414, Rumbold (Berlin) to Foreign Secretary Henderson, June 16, 1929.

Holy See chose three names to be sent to the cathedral chapter, which would in turn consult the government to learn if there were any political objections. The chapter then elected the bishop, and the Holy See confirmed the appointment. In this manner the government maintained influence in the selection so that no alien or politically undesirable candidate, especially in border sees, would be selected, and the Papacy maintained the selection of the three final candidates. This provision left more of the selection process in Prussian hands than did the Bavarian treaty to its state officials. The Prussian government agreed to provide a fixed sum for support of the Church and to hand over buildings for its use. The right of the Church and its institutions to be recognized as legal corporations was verified. Provisions were also made to ensure that the clergy were German citizens and had received their training at German institutions.[118]

The education system and the degree to which the Church could influence it were not even mentioned in the accord, and the Prussian Government was left technically independently free to administer the schools. In addition, the question of Catholic professorships at universities was not touched upon. But Pacelli exhibited his skill in this difficult situation in order still to gain something for the Church by leaving the door open for future discussions. Several weeks prior to the signing of the agreement, he sent a letter to the Prussian Cabinet, stating that should nothing be said about the schools in the treaty, the State could not conclude that the Holy See had no interest in Catholic religious education in the schools. The letter also cited a former statement by the Prussian Government to Pacelli recognizing the Holy See's right to continue seeking a settlement of the issue in an eventual Reich concordat. While no reference was made to the educational question in the treaty, two letters were appended to it; the first, from the Holy See to the Prussian Cabinet, declared its approval of the concordat but regretted the absence of a provision about the schools; the second, from Braun, replied that discussion in the press about the presumed contents of the treaty had become so heated that the concordat would probably fail in the *Landtag* if the school issue were included. This exchange put in writing Rome's lack of total satisfaction with the situation, and Pacelli had safeguarded the principle of further negotiation.[119]

Not everyone of course was pleased with the treaty. Some protest meetings were held, and letters were written by various Evangelical

[118] Schöppe, pp. 63-70.

[119] FFO, Allemagne 371, de Margerie to Briand, June 14, 1929. PGSTA, Rep. 92, Nr. 8, Trendelenburg, Pacelli to Braun, August 5, 1929; Braun to Pacelli, August 6, 1929. Padellaro, p. 59. *Deutsche Allgemeine Zeitung*, September 25, 1929.

Lutheran groups objecting to a treaty with the Church.[120] Bavaria was also annoyed since it appeared that the Vatican had not made as many demands on Prussia as it had on the southern German state.[121] Prussian Minister-President Braun, not completely happy about the concessions yielded by the State, knew of the Vatican's relative dissatisfaction with what it had received in comparison with what it had obtained in Bavaria. Within Prussia he was also aware that he personally and his Socialist Party were criticized by the Communists (KPD) and by the liberals in the old *Kulturkampf* tradition (*Kulturkampfpolitiker*) for having "gone to Canossa" and having signed the agreement. But on the whole the negotiating sides were reasonably satisfied. They had obtained an agreement that was the best that the situation would allow.[122]

The new treaty permitted the Church to strengthen its administration with two new dioceses and two new archdioceses and to have a bishop finally installed in the Reich capital. Moreover, it gave the Vatican a great deal of satisfaction to have the rights, prerogatives, and legal existence of the Church and its institutions in Prussia internationally guaranteed and to have arrived at some agreement with a predominantly Socialist government ruling a Protestant state. The treaty also included satisfactory provisions for State financial support for the

---

[120] *Deutsche Tageszeitung*, January 5, 1929.

[121] GSTA, Ges. Päpstl. Stuhl 1008, letter of Stengel (BFM) to Ritter, July 4, 1929.

[122] The Church had already made great gains in 1919-1920. The State had been financially supporting the Church in the 1920's, since Article 173 of the Reich Constitution specified that until a new Reich law was passed dealing with this subject, all laws and treaties concerning the states' contribution to religious groups were still binding. As long as the Center was a member of the ruling coalition in the Reich and Prussian Governments, the Church did not have to worry about a law detrimental to its interests. Prussia, for example, in 1927, gave 1.8 million marks toward support of the dioceses and their institutions and 21 million for the salaries of the Catholic clergy. Thus, with the more liberal republican Constitution which restricted State interference in religious affairs, the Church had a much freer and more independent position and yet was economically more secure than before. Otto Braun, *Von Weimar zu Hitler* (New York, 1940), p. 274. On the other hand, as early as 1920 Zech noted that perhaps the new Republic would cause itself problems later on. In the democratic euphoria of 1919 the framers of the Constitution had granted the principle of a separation of Church and State and non-interference by the State in Church affairs. In the interests of liberal philosophy, the State had been deprived of one of its bargaining points since the Church had already gained a great deal by Weimar's fiat. The State, however, still had concessions it desired from Rome—guarantees about diocesan borders, the German citizenship of the clergy, the education of the clergy in German institutions, etc. Naturally, in granting Berlin's wishes, Rome would require something in return. Zech predicted that Rome would make demands in the field of education, exactly in the area sure to elicit strong opposition from liberals and republicans. This, he said, the Constitution by being so democratic would put the government in this dilemma. AA, PO II, PO 2 Nr. 1 Vat., Vol. 1, Zech to AA, July 20, 1920.

Church and provided for an increase in the number of diocesan seminaries. This could serve as a precedent for the Vatican in its dealings
with other countries, especially since current Curial policy sought to
extend the number of these concordats. The conclusion of the treaty
proved that an agreement could be reached with a state which was not
predominantly Catholic. For, had it failed, it would have established
only a negative example which could have worked adversely in Rome's
negotiations with other countries, and the objections which had caused
its failure would still have had to be overcome in later discussions
about a Reich concordat.

On the Prussian side Braun also thought his government had acted
wisely, and later, in his memoirs, he defended the decision, first mentioning the political and diplomatic advantages gained by defining the
diocesan boundaries. Moreover, he added, until Prussia had a new
settlement with Rome regarding State support, constitutionally Prussia had been liable to payments under existing law, the Bull of 1821.
The new treaty had now made adjustments more in keeping with the
realities of the current situation. Without any legal agreement which
provided for the needs and took into account the conditions in Prussia,
the danger always existed that a Reich concordat similar to the Bavarian model would bind Prussia and would be signed over its head.
Under these circumstances a Prussian concordat which met some of
the state's specific needs was the lesser of two evils. Also, the treaty's
conclusion ended a great deal of the tensions within the ruling coalition in both the Reich and Prussian Cabinets between Socialists and
the Center.[123] Despite some Socialists' opposition to the concordat, the
party leadership had gone along with it in order to keep the coalition
together lest the Center withdraw from the government, for only with
the help of the Center could the Socialists fend off the Right.[124] For
Braun, then, despite the importance of a concordat for Germany's
foreign policy, internal considerations basically convinced him to advocate it.[125]

On July 9, 1929, after a short period of debate, the *Landtag* approved the treaty, 243 to 172, supported by the government parties—
the Socialists, the Center, and the Democrats; and opposed by the
Communists and the Rightist parties—the Nationalists, the German
People's Party, and the Nazis.[126] Once the *Landtag* had ratified the
treaty, public discussion of the matter ceased. Trendelenburg even

---

[123] Braun, p. 279.

[124] HHSTA, 88, Pastor to Seipel, September 30, 1927.

[125] Schreiber, p. 80.

[126] Germany, Prussia, *Sitzungsberichte des preussischen Landtages 1928/29* (Berlin, 1930),
Vol. 6, columns 7564-752, 7956-989, 8117, 8135. 92nd Session, July 1, 1929; 93rd
Session, July 5, 1929; 96th Session, July 9, 1929.

commented that after the vote the public seemed to lose interest, even though the "ominous" words "*Prussian* concordat" began to appear in official Vatican publications.[127]

The possibility of a Reich concordat had been continually postponed. Frequent government crises and changes as well as disagreements among the coalition partners had not helped the cabinet to agree upon and sustain a continuous policy on the subject. Other matters of urgency dealing with foreign and domestic problems took time away from settling the objections of both political parties and individual states.[128] After the collapse of negotiations on the *Reichsschulgesetz* in the latter part of 1927, Reich officials were not inclined to enter into battle on the concordat issue immediately, as it was regarded as "too hot an iron." Pacelli therefore had had to redirect and concentrate his efforts on obtaining something in Prussia.[129] By 1929 he had completed his work well. Few nuncios could boast of having negotiated two different concordats and laid the groundwork for possibly one or two more. Having brought his diplomatic work to a satisfactory conclusion, Pacelli was rewarded with the red hat, a little more than five months after ratification of the treaty, and left Berlin to take up his new duties as Secretary of State.

D. The Baden Concordat (1932)

The Baden concordat did not play an important role in foreign policy considerations of the Reich, for no borders were threatened here. It could then only add to the cumulative impression that Germany was settling its differences with Rome. The treaty was basically concluded for internal reasons, and as long as the prospects for a Reich

[127] AA, BRV 280, Vol. 2/3, Trendelenburg to Bergen, December 31, 1929.

[128] In April 1927 Stresemann gave a speech before his party (DVP) in Hanover in which he mentioned a treaty with the Vatican, the need to examine its importance for both internal and external reasons, and whether a Reich concordat should be signed at that moment now that the negotiations were taking place with the *Länder*. His speech caused much confusion among the politicians and at the Vatican about what he meant exactly. The Foreign Minister assured Rome that he was, in fact, still in favor of a Reich concordat and had made his remarks on tactical grounds to head off any outright rejection of negotiations by his party and other segments of the population. Nevertheless, in speaking to Stresemann about the matter, Pacelli received the impression that the Reich Government seemed less inclined to press for a concordat at the moment and that negotiations on the Prussian level held more promise for the Vatican than dealing directly with the Reich. BFO, 371/12147/5412, Lindsay to Chamberlain, April 7, 1927. Germany, Reichstag, Vol. 393, p. 10505-508. 306th Session, April 5, 1927. AA, RM 70, Vol. 2, Stresemann to Bergen, April 4, 1927. FFO, Allemagne 371, de Margerie to FFO, April 6, 1927.

[129] PGSTA, Rep. 92, D 90, letter of Braun to Adolf Arndt, SPD Party leader in the *Bundestag*, January 27, 1950.

concordat were not encouraging, Rome was also interested in negotiating. The fact that Germany's two largest states had already signed treaties with the Vatican and had been able to reach agreements weakened resistance to negotiation in this southwestern state. Baden had a large Catholic population (60 percent) centered mainly in the archdiocese of Freiburg in the Black Forest. In November 1929, immediately after conclusion of Prussia's treaty, Baden's Minister-President Joseph Schmitt announced his government's readiness to discuss the concordat question with Rome.[130] The government contained SPD, Center, and (after 1931) DVP members. Buoyed by results in the other two states, the Center was pressing hard for the concordat and threatening to disrupt the coalition should one not be signed. Negotiations which lasted but two and a half years were completed in the summer of 1932, and the treaty was signed in October, a few short months before the end of the Republic.[131]

Although discussions were progressing during 1930-1931, the political events of 1932 compelled the negotiations to be accelerated. In the Reichstag elections of July 31, 1932 the Nazis received 37.2 percent of the popular vote and with 230 seats had become the largest party in the legislature. Catholic leaders feared that should Hitler's party, with all the anti-Christian aspects of its ideology, come into power, it might impose legislation inimical to the Church.[132] To try and guard against such a danger with legal safeguards, Baden's Center Party prevailed upon the government to make an extra effort to wind up negotiations. In early August the Baden officials, accompanied by the head of the Baden Center Party and the Archbishop of Freiburg, Conrad Gröber, went to Rome. With a virtual *tour de force* in eight days the treaty was hammered out. The concordat, modeled after Prussia's, repeated certain passages almost verbatim. Differences were slight, merely rewordings in some clauses to make them more explicit. The one new element was the provision stating that the Catholic religion was a standard subject to be taught in both primary and secondary Baden public schools.[133] The treaty was signed on October 12 and

[130] Germany, Badisches General Landesarchiv, 48 (233/27 775), Pacelli to Schmitt, November 29, 1929.

[131] Horst Rehberger, *Die Gleichschaltung des Landes Baden 1932/33* (Heidelberg, 1966), p. 41; for a full discussion of the interparty strife over the issue and the SPD's reasons, such as fear of Communist inroads among its membership, for leaving the coalition rather than supporting the concordat, see pp. 41-49. For the treaty clauses, see *Osservatore*, December 12/13, 1932; Schöppe, pp. 38-43.

[132] *Osservatore*, November 3/4, 1930.

[133] Germany, Baden, *Stenographische Berichte über die Verhandlungen des badischen Landtages 1931-32* (Stuttgart, 1933). See especially Vol. 570a, Protokoll Heft 2, columns 54-191, 202-239, 249-298, 306-354. IV Wahlperiode, March 11, 1932.

ratified immediately by a special proclamation, for on the same day, some three hours later, Schmitt's Cabinet handed over the government to the Nazis. The Belgian minister in Rome, who found this speed important, commented: "It reveals to us the impression which the swastika produces among certain state officials and among the Catholic hierarchy, that is, that according to their belief, Hitler in short time could well become effectively the master of Germany."[134] Archbishop Gröber wrote to Pacelli in March 1933 expressing his relief that the concordat had been completed, for he felt that they were living, at least temporarily, in what was then beginning to look like another *Kulturkampf* with all the violent attacks being made by the Nazis on the Church.[135] He assumed, of course, that this was only a passing phase.

E. The Reich Concordat (1933)

By 1930, once Bavaria and Prussia had concluded concordats and Baden had declared an interest in discussing the matter, there remained, except for possible treaties with other states such as Württemberg and Saxony, only a general Reich concordat for the Vatican to have signed, because it was only on this level that the school question could now be regulated to its satisfaction. But from the German side things looked somewhat different. Germany's pressing needs of the early 1920's were no longer critical, or had been met or in part satisfied by the *Länder* concordats. Moreover, by the late 1920's Germany's position had improved in diplomatic affairs; it was no longer the pariah but could now deal with many nations directly or through the League. That is not to say that the diplomatic problems which had motivated the Reich to pursue concordat negotiations in the early 1920's were not still present or that advantages could not still be obtained by such a treaty. It meant that now the issue was no longer acute and that Germany's improved financial and international position offered it other possibilities for solving its problems and allowed it to turn its attention to matters of greater priority. Under Ebert the government had been favorably inclined to a treaty and had made efforts to convince the states to agree to it for the welfare of the Reich. After 1925 the arguments of a foreign policy need became less convincing, the need less actual as *Länder* concordats were signed, and less possible as

---

[134] BelgFO, St. Siège 1931-34, Ypersele de Strihou (Vatican) to Hymans, August 26, 1932. Charles-Roux, p. 93. Ernst Föhr, *Geschichte des badischen Konkordats* (Freiburg i.B., 1958), pp. 10-40.

[135] Bernhard Stasiewski, ed., *Akten deutscher Bischöfe über die Lage der Kirche, 1933-1934* (Mainz, 1968), Vol. 1, pp. 9-10. Letter of Gröber to Pacelli, March 18, 1933.

issues such as the *Reichsschulgesetz* continued to complicate the situation.[136]

Postponements and delays had constantly plagued discussions for a *Reichskonkordat*. Intensive negotiations lapsed in 1922, when both German and Vatican officials agreed to wait until Bavaria had completed its treaty and the Nuncio had moved to Berlin. But in 1925 Prussia's insistence on its rights to a separate treaty, and the continued lack of a school law caused the Reich to postpone matters once more. During the protracted discussions on the formation of the new government in 1927 and the crucial role of the Center Party in it, rumors circulated that the Center had exacted guarantees from its coalition partners for concordat negotiations as the price of its participation. The new government felt itself obliged to deny this on February 7, 1927 and categorically stated that no mention of negotiations over a concordat had been made in the discussions over the new cabinet's formation. Quite naturally in the months thereafter neither inclination nor purpose existed to pick up the subject, especially since the debate over the *Reichsschulgesetz* was still continuing without results.[137] As a result in 1927-1928 the Reich Government contented itself with keeping watch over the negotiations between Prussia and Rome. By 1929, once Bavaria and Prussia had both obtained their own treaties, it became increasingly more difficult to envision a Reich concordat. The objections to school questions persisted, while the need for a concordat had decreased, and it would now be more difficult to conclude since its formulation had to take into consideration provisions already included in both the former treaties.

The *Länder* feared that a Reich concordat might preempt their own treaties or impose new ones or alter conditions already so laboriously worked out and agreed upon. In Prussia, Braun foresaw difficulties for such an agreement, mindful that the Prussian treaty, even without a school clause, had been supported by the Socialists only after he used his personal prestige and influence to get his own party to endorse it.[138] In Bavaria the cabinet and the episcopate opposed it since it would weaken Bavaria's unique position and, from the hierarchy's viewpoint, endanger some of the concessions already won.[139]

One of the issues that had not and could not be dealt with in the

[136] Schreiber, p. 139.

[137] AA, RM 70, Vol. 2, memorandum of the AA, August 17, 1928.

[138] Germany, Nachlass Robert Leiber, S.J., located at the Pontifical Gregorian University, Rome (hereafter cited as Germany, Nachlass Leiber). Taped recording of a speech by Fr. Leiber, *sine dato* (probably mid-1960's), p. 2.

[139] Ludwig Volk, *Der bayerische Episkopat und der Nationalsozialismus, 1930-1934* (Mainz, 1965), p. 9.

Länder concordats was the regulation of pastoral care for the military (*Reichswehr*). Shortly after the signing of the Prussian concordat the Reich Government approached the Vatican about establishing a military chaplaincy. The problem had plagued the Weimar Government thoughout the 1920's. Berlin wanted the creation of a military diocese with a bishop and priests responsible to him and not to the local ordinaries. The regular hierarchy opposed this since it would then exercise no control over the chaplains. In 1929 Minister of Defense Otto Groener insisted that the matter be taken up with the Holy See, for it needed a rapid solution since the military chaplains did not have regular parishes and could not administer baptisms or perform marriages without permission from the local clergy or bishop. Pacelli, now Secretary of State, who had never given up the idea of a Reich concordat, saw an opportunity here to reopen talks for such a treaty and wanted to tie the chaplaincy issue to concessions in matters of civil versus church marriages, the school issue, State contributions to the Church, and to guarantees that new legislation would not impair already existing concordats. There had been discussions in government circles of an eventual reform of the Weimar Constitution, and Pacelli desired to ensure that the Church's interests were protected if the independence of the states and the validity of their concordats were called into question.[140] After all, a Reich concordat, besides providing further benefits, would serve as insurance to back up the *Länder* concordats and extend the basic points they contained to all Germany. The Curia was willing to grant Berlin's request for a military chaplaincy in return for compensations in other areas. Berlin, however, insisted on keeping the issues separate since it knew that the cabinet would never win the approval of either the Reichstag or the states for the treaty if it contained provisions such as Rome sought.[141]

Matters had come to a standstill in July 1931. On a visit to Rome in August, Chancellor Hermann Brüning also assured Pacelli that a concordat would not survive a Reichstag vote. The Communists would be against it, as well as some Socialists, the liberals, and the extreme Right.[142] During the years 1931-1933 discussions continued between Rome and Berlin as well as between political parties to explore possibilities of ensuring a majority for some form of a concordat. Kaas, now leader of the Center Party, sought contact with various politicians from other parties who would be willing to find a way out of this dilemma and he even approached the National Socialists for assist-

---

[140] GSTA, MA 104455, Ritter to BFM, March 9, 1930.
[141] Lewy, pp. 58-59.
[142] Brüning, pp. 358-359. See also note 148.

16. Dinner at the Villa Bonaparte (German Embassy at the Vatican), Rome, August 1931. From left to right: Cardinal Secretary of State Eugenio Pacelli, German Ambassador Diego von Bergen, German Chancellor Heinrich Brüning, Frau Vera von Bergen, and, on the extreme right, Msgr. Giovanni Battista Montini, the future Pope Paul VI

ance.[143] But as 1932 drew to an end and in spite of slight concessions by both governments on basic issues, nothing had changed, and Berlin had to reiterate to the Holy See that a majority could not be mustered for the passage of a concordat containing Rome's demands.

The coming of the Nazis to power in 1933, however, brought a dramatic transformation in conditions in Germany which also had significant implications for negotiations with Rome. The Vatican made no official statement about its attitude toward the new government, and the *Osservatore* restricted itself to reporting the events of the government change in Berlin. It was known, however, that both Pacelli and Pius XI had expressed very uneasy feelings about the Nazi anti-Christian stance.[144] The episcopate had at first expressed concern over

[143] Germany, Nachlass Leiber, taped recording of a speech by Fr. Leiber, *sine dato* (probably mid-1960's), p. 4.

[144] Germany, Nachlass Leiber, taped recording about the Vatican's uneasy feelings in a speech by Fr. Leiber, *sine dato* (probably mid-1960's), p. 5. For further information, see Engel-Janosi, *Chaos*, ch. 4 and Volk, *Reichskonkordat*, ch. 5.

what the attitude of the new government toward the Church might be, and Bertram wrote to Hindenburg and Hitler about the matter. Now in office, Hitler sought to present himself as a statesman of moderation in order to win the Church's support for his government. He gave assurances that the Catholic Church's freedom of action would not be interfered with. During the spring of 1933 Vice-Chancellor Franz von Papen, a Catholic, met many times with representatives of the hierarchy to assure them that it was Hitler's wish to unite the country, and he would not engage in any *Kulturkampf* which would divide the *Volk*.[145] Moreover, Hitler's anti-Bolshevist stance and his promise to make Christianity the basis of German morality and the family the basic unit for the nation and State were bound to please the Holy See.[146] In the first meeting of the new Reichstag, in a speech which the French journal *Le Temps* noted was fashioned almost exactly like Mussolini's first address as Prime Minister in the Italian Chamber of Deputies, Hitler expressed the government's commitment to Christian principles and looked forward to developing amicable relations with the Holy See.[147] Before taking power the Nazis had made many anti-Church statements. Now the Führer was offering the olive branch and undoubtedly confirming the idea in the minds of some politicians that Hitler only spoke radically, but once in power would act moderately.

In March internal upheavals and unrest, in large part instigated by the Nazis themselves, prompted Hitler to request an Enabling Act which granted the Government power to set aside the Constitution and govern without the Reichstag. After much soul-searching the Center Party voted for the bill on March 23, thereby eliminating itself as a political force and receiving only gurantees from the Government that Catholic rights would be respected.[148]

[145] AW, 1A 25k, 124, minutes of a conference of diocesan representatives in Berlin, April 25-26, 1933, p. 18.

[146] AA, PO II, PO 2 Vat., Vol. 4, Bergen to AA, February 8, 1933.

[147] *Le Temps*, March 29, 1933.

[148] The topic of how much pressure the Vatican put on the Center in the early 1930's to cooperate with the Nazis is still hotly debated. Kaas, the intimate friend of Pacelli, frequently traveled to Rome to discuss German political affairs. Brüning, however, in his memoirs (the reliability of which are also contested, see for example Rudolf Morsey, *Zur Entstehung, Authentizität und Kritik von Brünings "Memoiren 1918-1934*," Opladen, 1975) claims that Pacelli pressured him in the fall of 1931 to form a Rightist coalition including the Nazis for the purpose of paving the way for a concordat. Klaus Scholder claims that the Center Party, under Kaas's leadership, voted for the Enabling Act at the request of the Vatican so that a concordat could be concluded with the Nazi regime. Konrad Repgen argues that there is insufficient explicit documentary evidence to support Scholder's position. See Brüning, p. 358ff.; Klaus Scholder, *Die Kirchen und das Dritte Reich* (Berlin, 1977), Vol. 1, especially Part 2, chs. 2, 8 and "Altes and Neues zur Vorgeschichte des Reichskonkordats," *Vierteljahrshefte für Zeitgeschichte*, XXV (1978), 535-

Hitler's Government was still an unknown quantity, his methods and ideology were viewed at best with suspicion and at worst with condemnation by foreign governments and many people within Germany. He needed recognition for his regime as soon as possible, particularly from such a symbol of moral authority as the Holy See. Such recognition could remove the last bit of reluctance on the part of Catholics at home to endorse his regime and could bolster the diplomatic standing of his government by trading on the moral prestige of the Papacy, which by negotiating with Germany would recognize the new government, by implication show that it was worthy of trust. A treaty which could accomplish this quickly was worth large concessions. As a memorandum of the Foreign Office aptly put it, circumstances had changed overnight with regard to the Reich's ability to negotiate with Rome.

> The situation has been completely altered by the new composition of the Reichstag and especially by the passage of the Enabling Act. There now exists the possibility to comply fully with the wishes of the Holy See without also involving the Reichstag. Above all it is now possible to conclude a *Reichskonkordat*, the realization of which until now had always failed because of the objection of the Reichstag.[149]

On April 7, Vice-Chancellor von Papen prepared to go to Rome to discuss a concordat.[150] The first day's visits contained protocol meetings by Papen and Nazi leader Hermann Göring, who had accompanied him to Rome, to win the confidence of the Curia about the seriousness of Germany's intent to negotiate. Upon meeting the German envoys, the Pontiff "remarked how pleased he was that the German Government now had at its head a man uncompromisingly opposed to Communism and Russian nihilism in all its forms."[151]

570, especially 559-567; and Konrad Repgen, "Über die Entstehung des Reichskonkordats Offerte im Frühjahr 1933 und die Bedeutung des Reichskonkordats," *Vierteljahrshefte für Zeitgeschichte*, XXV (1978), 499-534.

[149] AA, Geheim Vat., Pol. 2 Nr. 1, Vol. 1, memorandum of Menshausen (AA), April 5, 1933. Lewy, p. 62.

[150] There is an excellent summary of the literature on the *Reichskonkordat* question in Volk, *Reichskonkordat*, pp. xxi-xxvii. Of some of the major authors Bracher argues for discontinuity in the history of concordat relations between the Weimar period and the Nazi era, Deuerlein for the continuity. Morsey deals with its connection to the last days of the Center Party and the history of political Catholicism. For an updating of the interpretations of this subject see John Jay Hughes, "The Reich Concordat 1933: capitulation or compromise?" *Australian Journal of Politics and History*, XX (1974), 164-175; the articles in *Vierteljahrshefte für Zeitgeschichte*, XXV (1978) by Repgen and Scholder; and Jedin, p. 63ff.

[151] Franz von Papen, *Memoirs*, trans. B. Connell (London, 1952), p. 279.

Discussions were held frequently between Papen and Kaas, who had also come to Rome, and Curial officials during the next ten days. At first the Reich Chancellery took charge of the negotiations, and the Foreign Office and Bergen were relegated to the sidelines. On April 18 Papen returned to Berlin while Kaas remained to continue the talks, keeping in close touch with the Vice-Chancellor in Berlin and with Bergen in Rome.[152] The Foreign Office now began to participate more in the negotiations.[153] On June 29 Papen was once more in Rome for final discussions. Bergen praised the Vice-Chancellor's skill in handling the talks and Kaas for all the preparatory work. The Ambassador believed, in fact, that the negotiations had set a record for brevity.[154] After further changes made in Rome and Berlin the treaty was then signed on July 20.[155]

One of the major difficulties in the negotiations had been Berlin's important demand to have the Church removed from politics, to have the hierarchy forbid the clergy from registering or being active in any political party. The withdrawal of priests from the Center, where many held important positions (such as Kaas himself), would severely cripple that party. Hitler sought one-party rule for his Third Reich and to weaken seriously the Center, one of the pillars of Weimar; negotiating over its head would considerably strengthen his power in the State and remove a potential center of opposition to that control. There was also the belief among Center leaders that Rome would pay this price to obtain the concessions it desired from the Reich and that, under present circumstances, a concordat was a better means to ensure the Church's position than was a political party. Moreover, with the Enabling Act in force, virtually making political parties useless, the concessions that Hitler desired were in reality not so great.[156] Nazi criticism of the Center was continued, and other parties had been already outlawed, such as the Socialists, or had dissolved themselves, such as the Democrats and Nationalists. By the end of June Nazi officials were calling for the dissolution of the Center too. Torn be-

---

[152] Karl Dietrich Bracher, "Nationalsozialistische Machtergreifung und Reichskonkordat," in *Der Konkordatsprozess*, ed. Friedrich Giese and Friedrich August Freiherr von der Heydte (Munich, 1958), Vol. 3, pp. 984-985. The fact that Bergen was not doing the negotiating was evident from the reports he was sending home. See AA, Geheim Vat., Pol. 20.

[153] The Ministry of the Interior was only brought into the discussions on July 4 despite the fact that much of the material covered fell within the competence of that department.

[154] AA, Geheim Vat., Pol. 2 Nr. 2, Vol. 1, Bergen to AA, July 3, 1933.

[155] For a detailed account of the negotiations see Volk, *Reichskonkordat*; Deuerlein, *Reichskonkordat*; and Lewy, ch. 3.

[156] Lewy, p. 69.

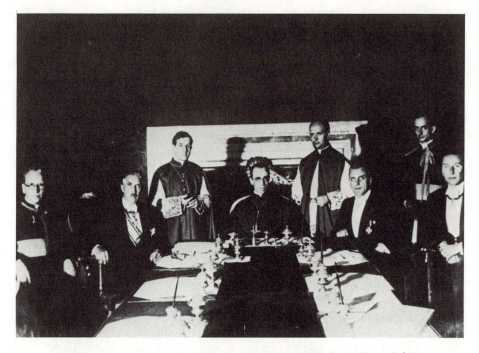

17. The signing of the Reich Concordat, Rome, July 1933. From left to right: Msgr. Ludwig Kaas, German Vice Chancellor Franz von Papen, Under Secretary of State Giuseppe Pizzardo, Cardinal Secretary of State Eugenio Pacelli, Substitute Secretary of State Alfredo Ottaviani, Rudolf Buttmann, German negotiator from the Reich Ministry of the Interior, Msgr. Giovanni Battista Montini (the future Pope Paul VI), and Eugen Klee, Counselor at the German Embassy to the Holy See

tween those members of the party willing and those unwilling to co-operate with the Nazis, experiencing large numbers of defections from the party already, and learning of the Vatican's agreement to the Reich's demands, the Center Party voted on July 5 to dissolve itself.[157] Rome

[157] Leiber contends that Pacelli would have preferred the Center to wait several more days before dissolving. When he heard the news, one of his co-workers reported him as saying, "Too bad that it happened at this moment. Of course the party couldn't have held out much longer. But if it only had put off its dissolution at least until after the conclusion of the concordat, the simple fact of its existence would have still been useful in the negotiations." Robert Leiber, "Pius XII," *Stimmen der Zeit*, CLXIII (1958-1959), 97. Leiber also takes issue with the argument that pressure was applied by the Vatican on the Center to vote for dissolution. Leiber, *"Reichskonkordat,"* 215-216.

did not need to pressure the Center leaders; they themselves realized that a failure to dissolve would have endangered the concordat and would have led to major clashes with the Nazis, who during June had continued their agitation and acts of violence against Catholic political organizations, with physical abuse of individuals, breaking up Church meetings, arrests, dismissals from office, and the like.[158]

The new concordat guaranteed full freedom to the Holy See, bishops, clergy, and laity in the exercise of their religion, and the government further granted protection to Church institutions and the clergy. The *Länder* concordats were reaffirmed, as were the diplomatic representatives of both governments. Catholic parishes, dioceses, and religious orders were juridically recognized and had the same rights as other legal corporations. Bishops were appointed by Rome on the condition that the Reich Government had no political objection to them. The bishops had the right to appoint the clergy, the only requirement being they had to be German nationals.

The State, for its part, recognized its obligation to continue with Church subsidies, which could only be discontinued after mutual agreement with Rome. The Holy See also obtained its long-desired goal in educational matters. The Church received the right to maintain theological faculties at state institutions and to establish seminaries. In addition the State acknowledged that Catholic religious education would be taught in public primary, secondary, vocational, and high schools as a regular subject and that the Church had the privilege of approving the selection of the religious instructors even though they were state employees. The Church also obtained guarantees for the maintenance and establishment of public, Catholic confessional schools. Rome's demand for a revision of the matrimonial law which gave more recognition to Church weddings was also conceded. Thus, more than a decade after it had made these demands, the Vatican's wishes were generally fulfilled and not just in one section of the Reich but in the entire country. In return Rome had to agree to the dissolution of all political and some social and professional organizations of German

[158] Lewy, pp. 74-76. Volk, *Reichskonkordat*, pp. 181-186. Harrigan, 169-172. Karl Buchheim, "Warum das Zentrum unterging," *Hochland*, LIII (1960-1961), 15-25. Karl Otmar Freiherr von Aretin, "Das Ende der Zentrumspartei und der Abschluss des Reichskonkordats am 20. Juli 1933," *Frankfurter Hefte*, XVII (1962), 237-243. Josef Becker, "Das Ende der Zentrumspartei . . . ," *Die Welt als Geschichte*, XXIII (1963), 149-172. Rudolf Morsey, "Die deutsche Zentrumspartei," in *Das Ende der Parteien, 1933*, ed., Erich Matthias and Rudolf Morsey (Düsseldorf, 1960), pp. 279-453. Morsey, *Untergang*. Evans, ch. 19. The Belgian Ambassador in Rome reported that the party had not even consulted Rome about its decision to dissolve, and Pacelli was rather piqued over the manner in which it was done, believing it had disappeared without dignity. BelgFO, St. Siège 1931-34, Ypersele de Strihou to Hymans, July 4, 1933. Charles-Roux, p. 94.

Catholicism, accede to the Reich's demand for an army chaplaincy, and, by signing the treaty, accord recognition to the new regime.

Many of the terms of the treaty were vaguely worded and broad enough to be subject to several interpretations, as soon became apparent when Rome protested that its rights were not being observed and its clergy not being protected. For the Holy See the concordat looked on paper like a great victory, for it granted Rome many of the concessions that had evaded the Church in other treaties. But Hitler was not interested in the details of what had been granted, and he dismissed any objection that the accord had been too generous. What he desired was to use the document for its political effect at home and abroad; the rest was unimportant and could be disregarded, reinterpreted, or changed later.[159]

The agreement signed on July 20, 1933 was ratified September 10. The long years of negotiation between Germany and the Vatican had finally ended in a Reich concordat. It was one of many concordats and treaties which the Vatican had signed since 1919[160] and which by their clauses introduced many aspects of Church law into the legal systems of a growing number of states. Statutes of canon law pertaining to episcopal selection, seminaries, and education were now influential or had to be considered as factors in the formulation of civil laws in view of the concluded treaties. The Vatican by its legal diplomacy had turned back the linear progress of laicism and, in many ways, of nineteenth-century liberalism, which appeared by 1919 as the victor. Instead of total separation of Church and State, an ostensible preference appeared for cooperation or accommodation in church-state relations.

World opinion was surprised at how rapidly Hitler had been able to eliminate political Catholicism as a force and sign a treaty with Rome. It wondered how Rome could enter into an alliance with a government which was based on an anti-Christian ideology, with a party which had stated its opposition to a concordat and which had opposed all the *Länder* treaties. But the Curia's consistent policy had been to sign concordats with civil governments, even with those with which it was not in agreement.[161] Pius' State Secretary believed firmly in the concordat system and, possessing a strongly legalistic mind, saw the greatest safeguards for the Church in statutory gurantees which

[159] Schöppe, pp. 29-36; Lewy, pp. 79-86. Philip Hughes, *Pope Pius XI* (New York, 1937), pp. 176-186. For complete texts and a comparison of all four concordats, see Joseph Wenner, *Reichskonkordat und Länderkonkordate* (Paderborn, 1934), pp. 13-72.

[160] Between 1919-1933 approximately thirty-eight concordats, treaties, and agreements were signed with foreign states.

[161] Stehle, "Motive," 564. This is also the rationale of the Holy See today in signing agreements with totalitarian states.

would give Rome the right to concern itself with Hitler's religious policies against any Nazi counterclaim that these were purely domestic affairs.[162] Pacelli was also aware of what was occurring in Germany and of Nazi efforts to concentrate and centralize power under their control in Berlin. If this were to happen and Germany were reorganized, he feared that the *Länder*'s rights might be reduced, consequently jeopardizing their concordats and all the work that he, as Nuncio, had accomplished since 1919. Several Catholic politicians, including former Chancellor Wirth, were in Rome at Easter 1933 and stressed the point that the freedoms of German Catholics and the *Länder* treaties were indeed in danger and that only a Reich concordat, something legally agreed upon with the new government, would help in remedying the situation.[163] The Catholic Center Party was already non-existent, and Catholic organizations were in the process of being dissolved. Pacelli had been most distressed during the negotiations about the continued acts of terrorism against Catholic organizations and individuals.[164] A concordat, as he visualized it, was a means of stopping a further erosion of the Church's position, a means of guaranteeing in writing the rights that it and its members still possessed. Foreign observers had also commented on how uneasy the Curia nevertheless felt about the new Nazi regime even after signing the concordat.[165] The choice as the Curia saw it then was to risk endangering all that the Church had won so far or to sign another treaty with the Reich which offered such good terms. The French Ambassador at the Vatican, François Charles-Roux, believed that neither Pacelli nor the Pope were under any illusions about Hitler's word, but, as Pacelli stated to him, "I do not regret our concordat with Germany. If we did not have it, we would not have a foundation on which to base our protests."[166]

---

[162] John Jay Hughes argues that the Vatican's thinking about the future of the Church in Nazi Germany was more realistic than usually believed, but in the period after 1933 Rome relied too heavily on diplomatic protests against infractions of the treaty instead of immediately informing the clergy and laity of its efforts to help the local Church, and of mobilizing German Catholics to support Church rights. John Jay Hughes, 174. Brüning states that Hitler readily perceived how the idea of a *Reichskonkordat* fascinated Church leaders and how they were prepared to make concessions to obtain it. Brüning, p. 656.

[163] Leiber, "Pius XII," 97.

[164] Volk, *Reichskonkordat*, pp. 135-139.

[165] BFO, 371/16749/5457, Clive (Vatican) to Foreign Secretary Simon, July 13, 1933.

[166] Charles-Roux, pp. 94-95. In August 1933, speaking to a British diplomat in Rome, Pacelli deplored Hitler's recent action in Germany against the Jews and against political opponents by creating a reign of terror. He saw no grounds for the easy optimism which said that, once Hitler gained full power, he would moderate his actions. BFO, 371/16727/5452, Kirkpatrick (Vatican) to Simon, August 19, 1933.

In August British Chargé d'Affaires Ivone Kirkpatrick passed on to London the reasons Pacelli gave for having signed the concordat.

The German Government had offered him [said Pacelli] concessions—concessions, it must be admitted, wider than any previous German Government would have agreed to, and he had to choose between an agreement on their lines and the virtual elimination of the Catholic Church in the Reich. Not only that, but he was given no more than a week to make up his mind. In a matter of such importance he would have liked more time but it was a case of then or never. . . . The Church, he continued, had no political axe to grind for they [sic] were outside the political arena. But the spiritual welfare of 20 million Catholic souls in Germany was at stake and that was the first, and, indeed, the only consideration. If the German Government violated the concordat—and they were certain to do so—the Vatican would have a treaty on which to base a protest. In any case, the Cardinal added with a smile, the Germans would probably not violate all the articles of the concordat at the same time.[167]

Even as the treaty was being signed, there were indications that the agreement was being disregarded, that Catholic meetings were being broken up and the clergy harassed. German officials passed this off as the exuberance of the revolutionary spirit and the ardor of the adherents. But for the Curia it was perhaps all the more reason for speed and proved the fact that a concordat as a legal defense was necessary.[168]

Mussolini congratulated Hitler on his new agreement with the Vatican and stated that together with the Four Power Pact, then being signed at that time in Rome, and to which the Reich along with Great Britain, France, and Italy was a signatory, the concordat had made Germany's diplomatic position look considerably brighter.[169] Hitler agreed. In the cabinet meeting of July 14 he had rejected debate on any of the particulars in the treaty and insisted that one should only see the gains. He designated the concordat as a great victory for his foreign policy, for its conclusion signified the Vatican's recognition of the National Socialist regime, and he anticipated that the Vatican by its example and its moral position would now influence other powers to do likewise.[170] Moreover, the agreement had great tactical value, for

---

[167] BFO, 371/16727/5452, Kirkpatrick to Simon, August 19, 1933.

[168] William Teeling, *The pope in politics* (London, 1937), p. 207.

[169] AA, RM 70, Vol. 3, Hassell (Rome-Quirinal) to AA, July 15, 1933.

[170] Germany, Auswärtiges Amt, *Documents on German foreign policy, 1918-1945*, Series C (Washington, D.C., 1957), Vol. 1, pp. 651-653. Minutes of the cabinet meeting, July 14, 1933. Aretin, "Ende," 242-243.

it deflected world attention from the actual *Machtergreifung* to the prompt recognition by a religious body of the Nazi Government.[171] Hitler had obtained his first success in diplomatic affairs.

By 1933 the long-drawn-out negotiations for a general concordat were completed. Looking foreward, we can see it as heralding a new relationship between Church and State for all Germany and between the Vatican and the Nazis, but looking backward we can also see it as the culmination of a complex series of negotiations fraught with frustrations for Rome and Berlin which had lasted as long as had the Republic. Over the years since 1919 the concordat issue had highlighted the divergent attitudes of the political and geographic regions of Germany and the political parties on religion and educational issues, the extent and limits of control granted to the Central Government by the Constitution, and the particularist sentiment in the *Länder*, each of which was reluctant to relinquish any of its individual privileges. This failure to reach an agreement within Germany on a common policy placed the Vatican in an enviable bargaining position, having several options to obtain its goals: it could negotiate directly with the Reich, separately with the *Länder*, or with both. At worst it could negotiate with at least one state, at best with all Germany. While securing concessions from one negotiation partner it could still play them off one against the other.

Since Bavaria, a predominantly Catholic state, was likely to be accommodating, to present fewer difficulties to Rome, and to be more inclined to make concessions to the Church than other states, it was natural for the Nuncio to urge the Bavarians to sign their treaty. Here negotiations had proceeded more rapidly than with any other German government, and, as the Vatican correctly perceived, the conclusion of a treaty with this *Land* would then serve as an example for either the Reich or other German states to do likewise. By 1929 the Vatican had scored notable successes in Bavaria and Prussia, where the majority of German Catholics resided, and the Church was in a more favorable position than ever before as regards its legal and financial rights. Its successes were impressive; only the crucial school question, outside of Bavaria, eluded Rome and was sensed, with clear perception in 1933 by Hitler, to be the necessary concession to obtain the Vatican's speedy signing of the concordat, which he so desired at that time.

[171] Karl Dietrich Bracher, *Die deutsche Diktatur* (Cologne, 1969), p. 420. The concordat was also significant for general European diplomatic affairs, for soon after its signing in 1933 Nazi violation of its clauses already provided European statesmen with ample opportunity to see what little value Hitler placed in his commitments to international treaties. Nevertheless, Europe's leaders chose to disregard this lesson and instead followed a policy of appeasement based on a totally different assessment of Hitler's character. John Jay Hughes, 175.

The difficulties and obstacles in obtaining a treaty during the Weimar era, however, only underscored the divergent viewpoints within Germany since 1871 and the narrowness of regional and particular interests which considered local concerns more important than the overall welfare of the Reich. The concordat problem paralleled many other issues of a factional nature that caused difficulties for the political life of Weimar that were settled in 1933 not by compromise or negotiation but by fiat. The Republic had expected to settle with Rome in order to secure Vatican aid for Germany's foreign policy objectives and to strengthen unity more effectively and integrate Germany's Catholics into the Reich by meeting their Church's demands and legally specifying the rights and duties of both Church and State toward one another. But religious and philosophical differences on such matters as the role of the Church in society and in educational affairs prevented the political parties from agreeing on a mutually acceptable treaty. More than once harmony between the parties was disrupted in a system where political cooperation was a prerequisite. The fragility of coalition politics, in turn, only illustrated the evasive nature of stability during the Weimar period. In the early years of the Weimar era the Center and the Social Democrats, two pillars of the democratic system with broad support among the electorate, failed to agree on a concerted policy to support a Reich concordat, considered so necessary by the Foreign Office. A long-lasting alliance between them would certainly have helped to maintain the democratic system in time of crisis. The Socialists were, however, unwilling to make concessions on the Church's rights and on the school issue desired by the Center, while the Center was unprepared to relinquish demands considered so basic to its philosophical outlook. Toward the end of the Weimar period the Social Democrats were frequently in the opposition, and the Center cooperated more frequently with Rightist parties. The government, existing with minority cabinets or support from the Right, which because of its Protestant or secular liberal adherents was then also disinclined to negotiating a concordat.[172]

The policy of Germany in 1920 had been to have a Reich concordat signed first, with addenda later taking into consideration the individual regional and historical differences. Instead, the process for a treaty went in reverse—step by step or block by block; the treaties proceeded from the particular to the general, from local treaties to a general one. The Reich undoubtedly felt itself beleaguered. In its attempts to maintain unity it had to fight foreign states abroad and now particularism at home. Just as it feared dismemberment by forces from abroad, it

[172] Buchheim, 15-16.

also feared any move by the *Länder* to go their own way and by forming their own policies cut the link to the Central Government. Just as the Vatican played an important role in Germany's foreign policy, it could thus also be of significant importance for internal developments by contributing to centrifugal or centripetal political developments. While in no way wishing to see a diminution of Germany's unity, Rome was also anxious to have some sort of treaty concluded. The issue became at times triangular, with the Reich believing in the necessity of a general treaty; the states, first Bavaria and then Prussia, placing obstacles in the way of a Reich treaty and desiring to conclude an agreement which dealt specifically with the situation of their particular areas; and the Vatican in between, wishing to respect the *Länder*'s desire to see their unique or particularist traditions guaranteed, but at the same time desiring to have common guarantees for the Church legally applicable to the entire Reich.

The Reich was most anxious to begin negotiations in the early years, but was stymied by its own member states and by its failure to gain enough support from the political parties on either the Reich or state level to have the concordat approved. Prussia or Bavaria or the parties did not view the problem from a national perspective and realize the seriousness of the diplomatic situation, which required a general treaty. Again and again Prussia and Bavaria answered that church-state relations were an internal question which could not be regulated by an international treaty, and they expressed doubt that there even existed a constitutional basis for a Reich concordat. The triangle made for some complicated and frequently competitive negotiations. The Reich tried to convince the Curia that a Reich treaty should come first and thus strengthen German unity. Gasparri, who in Rome had a better grasp of international affairs, inclined toward this view. Bavaria, ever conscious of its tradition, sought to prevent the Vatican from favoring the Reich position. Pacelli, in Munich, tended to favor the Bavarian position when there was every reason to believe that a treaty with Munich would be concluded in the not-too-distant future. But the Reich was asked to settled this question almost immediately after the founding of the Republic. The timing for the Central Government was not the best. Germany was beset by many other problems, and the concordat question was in many ways contingent upon other constitutional and legal issues which ideally should have been settled first, and the Reich Government was simply not prepared or able to do so in 1919-1920. The Reich then was handicapped in pressing its case because of the constitutional questions of competence still to be clarified, its need to win the endorsement of the states to carry the agreement through the legislature, and the lack of a *Reichsschulgesetz*. Without a school law, as provided for in the new Constitution, and without support from its constituent parts, Berlin could not negotiate from a position of strength and had to permit the *Länder* to negotiate first.

But delay and legalistic bickering took a toll. With every year, as Germany won back some of its prestige and self-respect, the urgency for the Reich concordat for foreign policy purposes diminished, and the Foreign Office, which still believed it important, had to exert even greater efforts to convince parliamentary opponents of the measure to vote for it. Internally, events also weakened the Reich's arguments, for the *Länder* concordats could also meet some of the needs of Catholics. Those states which had or considered having their own treaties were apprehensive lest some clauses of a Reich concordat supersede the agreements they had or would have with Rome. But while the Reich viewed it as an important foreign policy objective, the states continued to view it from the perspective of internal affairs. They were the level of administrative competence, so to speak, that had to live with the concordat, to supervise much of how its provisions were carried out. After 1922 the chances for a Reich concordat had increasingly dimmed; there were too many people against it, either because they opposed a treaty with the Vatican, because they believed *Länder* concordats more practical, or increasingly after 1926 because they had or were soon to have most of their objectives satisfied.

Thus, by the end of 1932, the negotiations begun early after the war were still dragging on long after other nations had their own treaties. With the new regime of 1933 and a new political order, however, the deadlock was broken. What had been taking so long was then concluded with incredible speed. An authoritarian leader, having overrun his opponents and knowing what he desired, could now use the basic formula already hammered out during Weimar to offer Rome conditions that it could not refuse. Hitler offered the Holy See simply what it basically had desired since 1919, with the added inducement that a refusal might endanger any progress already made in church-state relations and subject German Catholics to a situation far worse than before.

For his part, Hitler in his reasons for making the offer ironically still continued the basic line of German policy which Weimar had adopted—to obtain the Vatican's aid for Germany by thinking in terms of the external ramifications of an internal situation.[173] Germany needed

---

[173] The "continuity-discontinuity" question in German historiography has been discussed by many well-known scholars such as Fritz Fischer, Klaus Hildebrand, and A.J.P. Taylor. Deuerlein and Bracher have also dealt with it as it regards the Reich concordat (see note 150). Interestingly enough, even a recent popular impressionistic work entitled *Germans* (New York, 1972, p. 360), by George Bailey, a journalist and

recognition for the regime by the greatest moral force in Europe, and for this the Führer was willing to offer advantages without much quibbling. Once signed, the concordat bestowed that recognition. How the terms were to be carried out—that could be left for later discussions. Hitler also incorporated another concern of Weimar German policy in his objectives for a concordat. Just as the Weimar Government desired unity against divisive elements and saw the Vatican assisting them, Hitler also saw the concordat as providing unity by disarming any residual Catholic resistance within Germany to his new regime and strengthening his drive toward *Gleichschaltung*. The form was in many ways similar; the objectives were different. Weimar had delayed too long in reaching an agreement which ironically the government really wanted. Had Weimar signed a concordat with Rome, it would have deprived Hitler of making some political capital within and outside Germany. Tragically what democracy was unable to provide because of its own internal difficulties, a dictator was able to offer.

---

former army intelligence officer, touches on this theme by seeing a continuity in the problem between Church and State in Germany running from the medieval Holy Roman Empire to the concordat of 1933.

CONCLUSION

The search for security is a major theme in post World War I history—security, for example, through treaties, accords, and alliances. This need to buttress their respective diplomatic positions also characterizes much of the motivation of both Germany and the Vatican in their relations with one another. In general, by 1933 each state had reason for satisfaction with what it had gained by cooperating with the other in international affairs, while each came away with less than it had originally hoped for in negotiating with the other over church-state or domestic issues.

In the nineteenth century Germany and Italy, with their disruptive wars of unification, had helped to make the Pope a prisoner in the Vatican, greatly diminishing his role in world affairs. After 1919, however, the reorganization of Europe offered the Holy See an opportunity to regain its position as an important influence in diplomacy. A balance, with no country exerting hegemonic control, was necessary for Rome to maneuver. Germany was the linchpin in this policy. After having witnessed France's moves to influence the newly created states of Central Europe, its plans for the south German states and the Rhine, and having experienced the anti-clerical attitudes of its government, the Papacy became convinced that it did not want a French-controlled Europe and doubted very much that a French-dominated League could bring about a lasting peace. In addition, well aware of the danger emanating from Russia, the Curia did not need German diplomats to remind it of the threat which Bolshevism posed to the Church. It had already grown impatient with what it deemed the lack of attention of the Western Powers to the Soviet anti-religious policies. In order to help to ward off what it regarded as a potential catastrophe in Europe, Rome was convinced of the necessity for diplomatic intervention. It feared the world might be turning either to atheistic or to secular solutions for its problems, solutions in which political interests alone would predominate, which would end the Church's opportunity to speak for justice or humanitarian concerns as well as permanently eclipse the Papacy's position in the world. Instead a balance had to be maintained among the Powers of Europe. Moreover, the Pontiff also believed that a great wrong had been done the Germans by the Allies, who had placed a heavy financial burden on them as reparation for the war. Thus prompted by moral considerations and with an eye to diplomatic necessity, Rome readied itself, when Berlin requested aid.

The Vatican needed Germany to offset France in the west and Russia in the east. The Curia, especially Cardinal Gasparri, worked tirelessly, suggesting and mediating, in order to restore a more equitable climate in European diplomatic relations and to get the stalled economic negotiations going once more. Germany was fortunate to have had this support when it had few friends to whom to turn. In this sense, then, Rome was not so much pro-German as anti-Versailles and anti-Bolshevik, objecting to the solutions offered by their leaders, for in the eyes of the Curia they were unjust, immoral, and impermanent.

Rome's position was always very difficult and perhaps paradoxical—a universal Church which had to deal with a particular need of national groups, a church-state which had to be aware of the role it played in both religious and secular affairs, a strong moral force in international affairs which maintained a very conservative stand on many political, social, and educational issues. It was subject to pressures from all sides and from factions within the Church which represented various national interests. The problem in aiding Germany illustrated the particular danger the Church faced in any political or diplomatic situation of pushing its case too far and being accused of being less than impartial, thereby risking losing everything or exposing the Holy See to allegations of meddling in matters not of concern to it. It also helps to explain the deliberateness with which Rome moved.

The Holy See after World War I attempted in its diplomacy to blend moral vision with political realism; to speak out against war, the causes of social unrest, or ill-advised world economic policies, while at the same time making concessions to and displaying understanding for the sensibilities of national governments and the complexities of practical issues facing them. Rome's view of Europe, however, was a unified one. If Germany were allowed to collapse or to remain prostrate, this would precipitate a chain of events which would have dire political, economic, and social effects on both the continent and the world. Precisely because it did not consider matters from a national perspective—as did France or England, with their concerns for reparations, or the United States, which chose to withdraw, demand debt repayment, and concentrate on its own affairs—it could with its supranational orientation offer its advice in identifying and remedying the malfunctions in the European system. Time and again the information sent into the Vatican and the assessment made by Gasparri, with his long years of experience, proved remarkably accurate. Today, in a world shaped by World War II and its ramifications, such as the Cold War, many aspects of Rome's unheeded advice now seem to have been perceptive and forward-looking at a time when most states were bogged down in nationalistic particularism.

The consultation and mediation in which the Holy See was involved in its efforts to satisfy all parties, seek peace, and call special attention to the spiritual needs of Catholics, demonstrates Rome's re-emergence after World War I as a diplomatic force—a fact even more apparent after World War II, with diplomats and statesmen continually stopping at the Vatican to consult on world affairs and the cause of peace. The Vatican perceived it could best function diplomatically in a stable, balanced, international situation. True, at other times and under other governments, Germany's drive for power had disturbed the European equilibrium and had contributed to and even precipitated events in 1914 and 1939, causing states in both the east and west to draw together against what they perceived as a common threat. Such treaties as the Franco-Russian Alliance of 1894 and the Franco-Soviet Pact of 1935, both largely defensive in nature, are examples of agreements made to block these German designs. But in the period after World War I the situation was reversed; the Vatican believed it was now France and Russia that had to be contained and prevented from gaining predominance in Europe. For Rome, aiding Weimar Germany was essential in order to maintain the diplomatic equilibrium it sought. By 1926 Germany had become a member of the family of nations again, and its political and economic difficulties appeared destined for solution. Rome had reason to be pleased with its efforts to help effect this stability. Within Germany too the Vatican had helped bring about a balance between the states and the Central Government. By aiding Berlin in diplomatic affairs, by refusing to endorse separatist movements, the Papacy had helped to preserve a unified state. While endorsing some of Bavaria's demands for an independent policy and its own legation at the Vatican, by negotiating with the individual *Länder* for a concordat, Rome lent some support to the federalist forces within Germany. The Holy See, then, was in the enviable position of negotiating with two levels of the administration within the Reich, giving precedence to whichever offered Rome the greatest advantages.

The Holy See also pursued a policy seeking security for the Church within Germany. It was not without some justification that the postwar period had been labeled the new era of concordats in Vatican policy. Just as the secular states of Europe entered into a host of treaties, alliances, and accords, so did the Vatican effectuate a series of concordats, *modi vivendi*, and conventions.[1] It was only sensible, then,

[1] For example, the Vatican signed agreements with Latvia—concordat (1922), Bavaria—concordat (1924), Poland—concordat (1925), Lithuania—concordat (1929), Italy—concordat (1929), Prussia—concordat (1929), Czechoslovakia—*modus vivendi* (1927),

for Rome to want to guarantee its rights, obtain legal status for the Church, and clarify its relations to the German secular state. More than once, Curial representatives reminded German officials of the close connection between German foreign and domestic problems and that a concordat would only strengthen Rome's ability to be of more assistance to Germany. True, Rome had hoped at first for an all-Reich treaty. When opposition from the *Länder* eliminated this possibility, the Vatican had to shift its tactics, adjust to the peculiarities of German Central and state governmental competencies and negotiate treaties directly with the individual *Länder*. By 1929 it had obtained many of its objectives—legal status and State subsidies for the Church, new guidelines for episcopal selection in the two largest states of the Reich, where the majority of Catholics lived. Catholics during the Weimar period had less restrictions on the practice of their religion, and participated more in public life than they had under the Empire, while the Church had gained a more secure position within society. Although the Vatican had an authoritarian form of government, Rome by no means looked disapprovingly on Weimar, for Rome was favored and enjoyed better relations and the Church more freedom than they had under the previous or would under the succeeding German government. Vatican policy sought to have a strong Germany in Central Europe, and this was best pursued at that time by supporting its democratic, republican administration.

The only goals which continued to elude Rome were those in the field of education (except for Bavaria) and those for a treaty to cover all Germany. Given the frustrations of thirteen years of negotiations, the Nazi offer in 1933 greatly tempted Rome. The Vatican entertained no illusions about the nature of the Nazi leadership, but since it had been unable to obtain an agreement with the Weimar Government, since its policy was to seek treaties with all states, it was not inconsonant for the Curia to view this concordat pragmatically as one of many, as one which would at least give a modicum of legal assurance that the Church could maintain some of its rights. Most probably aware of and weighing the moral consequences of signing a pact with the Nazi regime, it opted, in Pius XI's words, for dealing with the Devil. It was not that the Curia wanted to negotiate with Hitler, but since Rome was willing to enter discussions with all nations which expressed an interest, in view of the failures it had encountered in dealing with the Weimar Government, and given the favorable conditions that the Nazis offered, it was difficult for the Vatican to refuse.

Rumania—convention (1927), as well as pursuing negotiations with many other states including France and Yugoslavia.

It saw no recourse but to seek to secure its position by contractual agreements. Unfortunately for the Vatican, the new government which brought the Weimar Republic to an end was soon to disregard the concordat, treating it as a mere scrap of paper.

Germany also had reason for satisfaction with its diplomatic cooperation with the Holy See during the Weimar period. Despite Socialists in the government, relations with Rome were generally cordial in comparison with the difficulties the Vatican was experiencing with some other states such as France or Czechoslovakia. Germany's leaders in 1919, like Hitler in 1933, realized the value of having Rome's moral authority on their side. Their reasons and motivations were different from Hitler's later on, but their objective—Vatican aid for the Reich at a crucial time—was the same and forms a continuous thread in German foreign policy through Weimar and into the Third Reich. In a more stable period perhaps the Vatican would not have loomed so important in Berlin's strategy. During the chaos after the war, however, Germany looked about for an impartial judge who would appreciate the validity of its complaints and who would mediate with the Allies with whom Germany had no formal contacts. The experience of the *Kulturkampf*, when even the Iron Chancellor had to admit defeat in his effort to bring Rome to heel, was a lesson which impressed Germany's new rulers in 1919 and made them value the Papacy's strength and influence. Berlin, then, was very grateful when Rome undertook to intercede for the Reich with the Western Powers and to urge moderation in reparation demands and clemency for German civilians arrested by the occupation forces.

In 1919 Berlin clearly perceived the Vatican as an important factor in Germany's foreign policy. It had to be. The demography of confessional geography showed that in the areas lost or contested after the war the majority of the population was Catholic. The Vatican had to be considered in any move to maintain or regain this territory. Germany was fortunate that the Vatican moved slowly and was inclined to alter ecclesiastical administrations only after all political changes had been finalized, for this extended time to Germany to secure the recognition of its diocesan borders against the claims of other states, such as Poland, and in turn strengthened its claim to political control over the area.[2]

In the early 1920's Rome had already shown its goodwill by its appointments to the sees of Cologne and Trier. Had pro-French candidates been selected, enormous consequences for the unity of the

---

[2] The Vatican's position and the Federal Republic's reaction to it were similar after World War II.

Reich might have developed. To counter French moves in the Rhineland and to defeat separatist tendencies, Germany understood it as absolutely essential to have pro-Berlin prelates in both sees. The Bavarian concordat of 1924 helped Germany to secure its western borders and to prevent France from detaching the Saarland from German ecclesiastical administration, and made it easier to reincorporate the territory politically into the Reich in 1935, since at least cultural and religious ties had remained unbroken. In the east, Germany was also successful. For example, Breslau was elevated to an archdiocese, a political necessity along its eastern borders, where Poland already had archdioceses in Cracow and Posen-Gnesen, and Czechoslovakia had those of Prague and Olmütz, while Germany had none. The diocese of Ermland, which had not been connected to any archdiocesan metropolitan see, was attached in 1929 to Breslau, and East Prussia, which was geographically separated from the Reich, at least by means of church administration and international law, was bound more closely to the Reich. Similarly, the prelature of Schneidemühl, running along the border area of Posen and West Prussia, was also placed as a suffragan district under Breslau. By acknowledging in the concordat of 1929 that the area in West Prussia was only an administered territory and not an independent diocese, the transitory nature of the political settlement in the east was underscored in legal form.[3]

The results of Rome's efforts to moderate some of the Allies' harsher demands and Germany's success in keeping many of its diocesan borders intact confirmed the Reich Cabinet's belief that Rome could and would be of help. Many documents indicate an almost obsessive desire or anxiety on the part of the Reich Government to explain its policies to Rome, and to win Vatican approval. The Holy See was a sort of confessional for German officials, a place to explain their policies, discuss their problems, and hope for diplomatic absolution. Germany was ready to grant concessions in return for the Vatican's aid in foreign affairs. In this sense Eckart Kehr's assertion of *der Primat der Innenpolitk*[4] does not seem to be readily applicable here, for *Aussenpolitik* was foremost in the minds of the Reich Cabinet, which continually argued that foreign policy considerations had to take precedence over internal policy for the sake of preserving the State and German unity. Favorable developments in international affairs would eventually help to solve internal problems as well.

The Reich also hoped that cooperating with the Vatican and reaching an agreement over church-state affairs would lend stability to the

[3] AA, PO II, PO 2 Nr. 2 Vat., Vol. 1, memorandum of Meyer-Rodehüser, June 12, 1929.

[4] See Eckart Kehr, *Economic interests, militarism and foreign policy* (Berkeley, 1977).

Republic by meeting the demands of its Catholic population and of one of the coalition partners in the government, the Center Party. Although the Catholics and the Church did win some of their objectives in the concordats signed during Weimar, it was not the Reich Government which provided these gains. True, some stability was obtained by the *Länder* concordats, and the state governments received privileges such as the right to express their objections to politically undesirable candidates for the hierarchy, a provision which also benefited the Reich Government. But the failure of the Reich to reach a general settlement with the Church, as had been done in countries which had not worked as closely with the Holy See or had as many similar diplomatic policy objectives as had Germany, only demonstrated that the structural weaknesses apparent in the Reich of 1871 had not been surmounted in 1919. The old strife over particularism versus centralism, north versus south, Catholic versus Protestant, was again highlighted in the fight over the nunciatures and legations, over the concordats, over the competencies of the various governmental levels. The mistrust, the tendency to view problems from a limited perspective, prevented a general solution to the problem of church-state relations and caused many Center adherents to despair of ever reaching an agreement on this matter with the other parties in Weimar. Unfortunately, the Reich Government perceived the solution to many of its woes in combatting the "enemy from without" and concentrating on diplomatic objectives. The authorities considered the country as "fortress Germany" which had to be defended with aid from the Holy See. Seen from this perspective, they were successful during the Weimar era. But the delay in formulating and defining laws such as the basic school law, the wrangling over the competencies of various levels of government, the insistence of the *Länder* on preserving their rights, even at the cost of a unified German policy, allowed little room to deal successfully with important domestic issues critical to internal stability. While concentrating on foreign issues, which were indeed important, the Germans forgot or perhaps did not sufficiently heed the fact that a country cannot only be menaced from abroad but can also be taken by the enemy from within.

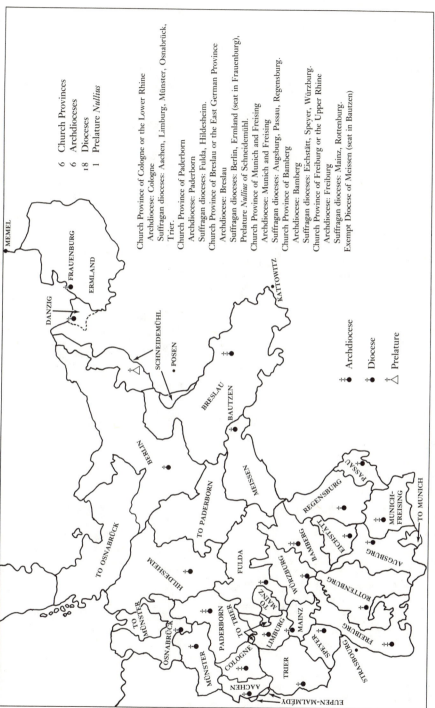

Ecclesiastical Map of Catholic Germany (1930)

Church Provinces 6
Archdioceses 6
Dioceses 18
Prelature *Nullius* 1

Church Province of Cologne or the Lower Rhine
Archdiocese: Cologne
Suffragan dioceses: Aachen, Limburg, Münster, Osnabrück, Trier.
Church Province of Paderborn
Archdiocese: Paderborn
Suffragan dioceses: Fulda, Hildesheim.
Church Province of Breslau or the East German Province
Archdiocese: Breslau
Suffragan dioceses: Berlin, Ermland (seat in Frauenburg), Prelature *Nullius* of Schneidemühl.
Church Province of Munich and Freising
Archdiocese: Munich and Freising
Suffragan dioceses: Augsburg, Passau, Regensburg.
Church Province of Bamberg
Archdiocese: Bamberg
Suffragan dioceses: Eichstätt, Speyer, Würzburg.
Church Province of Freiburg or the Upper Rhine
Archdiocese: Freiburg
Suffragan dioceses: Mainz, Rottenburg.
Exempt Diocese of Meissen (seat in Bautzen)

Archdiocese
Diocese
Prelature

BIBLIOGRAPHY

The following list is restricted to material cited in footnotes in this book or which has been of especial value to this work. It therefore omits numerous books and sources which were useful in providing background information.

PRIMARY SOURCES

I. Unpublished Materials

No detailed information about the contents of document volumes or files have been cited here because of the large number of documents studied. Only a listing of document file reference numbers has been provided. For a detailed explanation of German Foreign Office records, one of the main sources for this work, see George Kent, ed., *A catalog of files and microfilms of the German foreign ministry archives, 1920-1945*, 4 Vols. Stanford, 1962-1972.

Austria
> Oesterreichisches Staatsarchiv, Abt. Haus-Hof-und Staatsarchiv, Vienna.
>> Fasz. 116, 153, 709, 712, 713; NPA, Karton 8-11, 57, 87-89.

Belgium
> Ministère des Affaires Étrangères, Service des Archives, Brussels.
>> Allemagne 1919-1934
>> Allemagne 2, 17
>> Eupen-Malmédy
>> St. Siège 1919-1934.

France
> Archives Nationales, Paris.
>> AJ9, Papiers de la Haute Commission Interalliée en Rhénanie
>> 94 AP 205-208, 226, Allemagne
>> 149 AP 21-23, Papiers du Général Mangin.
> Ministère des Affaires Étrangères, Archives et Documentation, Paris.
>> Allemagne 316-318, 367-371
>> Paix, 17-22
>> Rive Gauche du Rhin 103
>> Ruhr 28-30
>> Pologne 58

Papiers d'Agents: Canet 18, Doulcet 33-38
Z Russie 124.
Germany
Auswärtiges Amt (AA), Politisches Archiv, Bonn.
File: IA Bayern 50, 53, 58-60; IA Deutschland 125 Nr. 1, 162; IA Päpstl. Stuhl 1-15, 17, 24; IA Preussen 2 Nr. 2, 5; IA Preussen 6i; IA Vereinigte Staaten v. Nordamerika 13a; Weltkrieg (WK) Nr. 2; RM: 5, 9, 14, 15, 17, 39, 68, 70, 82, 87; Geheimakten Vatikan: PO 2 Nr. 2, PO 3, 8, 10, 12, 20, 24-36; Russland; Besetzte Gebiete: Saargebiet; W Rep: FV Allgemeines 14A; Inland: Deutschland PO 5, 16; PO II: Vatikan PO 1-3, 7-12, 16-24, 28, 32-35, 38-39; Referat D: PO 16; Nachlass Stresemann; Nachlass Maltzan; Botschaftsakten* Rom-Vatikan: Lfd. Nr. 15, 18, 25, 60, 63-70, 76, 78, 87, 90, 93, 95-98, 101, 103-106, 122-140, 143-157, 168-192, 198, 243, 265-266, 279-284, 324, 344-346, 352-358, 370-377, 402-406, 462, 738-739, 982, 989, 1041-1042, 1047-1049; Abstimmungsgebiet Ost-West Preussen; Sicherheitspakt Konferenz Locarno. Microfilm (in the U.S. National Archives), series T-120, roll 1999, serial 4057H (Relations with the Vatican).
Bundesarchiv, Koblenz.
R 43 I Reichskanzlei; Nachlass: Kaas, Maltzan, Pünder.
Church Archives
Bamberg, Archiv des Erzbistums Bamberg.
    Akten der Erzbischöfe (Hauck).
Cologne, Erzbischöfliches Ordinariat.
    File: CR 1, 2, 14, 16, 25, 27, 30; Gen. 1B, 22-33, 28, 32.
Freiburg, Erzbischöfliches Ordinariat.
    Nachlass Gröber.
Munich, Erzbischöfliches Archiv.
    Folio: 1200, 1250, 1261, 1300, 1320, 1352, 2051, 2063, 2069, 3220, 7222, 7231, 7238, 7404, 7601, 9356.
Paderborn, Archivstelle beim Erzbischöflichen Generalvikariat.
    File: II, 5b, 6d; XIII, 11d; XXII, 1, 2, 3; XXIII.
Speyer, Bischöfliches Hausarchiv.
    File: A XV 21, 67, 68.
Trier, Bistumsarchiv.
    File: BIII 3, 4; Abt. 59, 108.
Private Papers

* Since the research for this work was done, the Politisches Archiv, Bonn has given the *Botschaftsakten* new *Atkenzeichen*. To correlate old and new document signatures see, for example, Kent, IV, p. 699ff., and information in the Politisches Archiv.

Nachlass Carl Becker, located at the Institut für Bildungsforschung, Berlin and in the possession of his son Prof. Helmut Becker.

Nachlass Robert Leiber S.J., located at the Pontifical Gregorian University, Rome and in the possession of Rev. Burkhart Schneider, S.J.

State and Local Archives

Badisches General Landesarchiv, Karlsruhe.
File: 7(233/27), 48(233/27), 15(235/31)—Concordats, Nunciature Berlin, Pope, etc.

Bayerisches Hauptstaatsarchiv, Allgemeines Staatsarchiv, Munich.
File: MK 15507-515, 15518-528, 15560-563, 15568-576, 19122-128, 19792, 19803 (Occupied territories, French activities in the Rhineland).

Bayerisches Hauptstaatsarchiv, Geheimes Staatsarchiv, Munich.
File: Gesandtschaft, Berlin 1408, 1555, 1740; Gesandtschaft Päpstlicher Stuhl 947, 949-954, 958-960, 962-965, 967, 969-970, 972-980, 982, 988-989, 991, 994-1001, 1003, 1008-010, 1012-014, 1021-024, 1027, 1031, 1038, 1044-046; MA 976, 989, 1009, 2362, 2567, 3072-073, 99-359, -365, -373, -375, -377, -380-383, -385, -410, -443-498, -512-524, -535-541, -874, -877-879, -883, -885, -936, -962, -974, 100-002, -009-012, -018, -104, -150, 101-060, -072, 102-156, -163, -379, -387-389, -627, 103-007-010, -098-100, -170-171, -183, -186-187, -505, 104-064-067, -090, -092-093, -095-096, -156, -322, -432-433, -435-436, -439-442, -444, -446, -449-450, -452, -455, -457-458, -467, -469-470, -472, -474-484, -492-499, -501, -510, -520, -532, 106-156-158, 107-258, -635.

Geheimes Staatsarchiv Preussischer Kulturbesitz, Berlin.
Rep. 90 Religions-und Kirchensachen; Rep. 92 Trendelenburg; Nachlass Otto Braun.

Hauptstaatsarchiv, Düsseldorf.
Nachlass Lammers.

Historisches Archiv der Stadt Köln, Cologne.
Nachlass Marx, Abt. 1070.

Landesarchiv, Saarbrücken.
Nachlass Hoffmann.

Staatsarchiv, Koblenz.
Abt. 403, 441-442 (Occupied territories, French activities in the Rhineland).

Staatsarchiv, Speyer.

File: R 12/223 (Occupied territories, French activities in the Rhineland).
Great Britain
Foreign Office, Public Record Office, London.
FO files 1919-1934, especially file FO 371.
Italy
Ministero degli Affari Esteri, Archivio Storico Diplomatico, Rome.
Germania, 1919-1934.
Poland
Archiwun Archidiecezjalne, Wrocław (Breslau).
File 1A 25 a-e, i, k, l-p, r-v, z (Church affairs, relations with Rome, church-state relations, etc.).

II. Published Documentary Material

Erdmann, Karl Dietrich, *et al.*, eds. *Akten der Reichskanzlei.* 13 Vols. Boppard a.R., 1968- .
France, Assemblée nationale: Sénat, Chambre des Députés. *Débats parlementaires, Journal officiel.* Paris.
Germany, Auswärtiges Amt, *Documents on German foreign policy, 1918-1945*, Series C, Vol. 1. Washington, D.C., 1957.
Germany, Baden. *Stenographische Berichte über die Verhandlungen des badischen Landtages.* Karlsruhe.
Germany, Bavaria. *Stenographische Berichte über die Verhandlungen des Landtages.* Munich.
Germany, Prussia. *Sitzungsberichte des preussischen Landtages.* Berlin.
Germany, Reichstag. *Stenographische Berichte über die Verhandlungen des Reichstages.* Berlin.
Germany, Statistisches Amt. *Statistisches Jahrbuch für das Deutsche Reich.* Berlin.
Germany, Zentrumspartei. *Flugschriften.* 1924.
Giese, Friedrich und v.d.Heydte, Friedrich, eds. *Der Konkordats-prozess.* Vol. 3. Munich, 1958.
Kakies, Dieter, ed. *Deutsche Verfassungen.* Munich, 1965.
Krose, H. A., ed. *Kirchliches Handbuch für das Katholische Deutschland.* Vols. 3-18. Freiburg i.B., 1919-1934.
Kupper, Alfons. *Staatliche Akten über die Reichskonkordatsverhandlungen 1933.* Mainz, 1969.
Mercati, Angelo, ed. *Raccolta di concordati su materie ecclesiastiche tra la Santa Sede e le autorità civili.* Vol. 2. Vatican City, 1954.
Morsey, Rudolf, ed. *Die Protokolle der Reichstagsfraktion und des Fraktionsvorstands der deutschen Zentrumspartei, 1926-33.* Mainz, 1969.
Schöppe, Lothar, ed. *Konkordate seit 1800.* Frankfurt a.M., 1964.

Schulthess, H. *Europäischer Geschichtskalender*. Vols. 60-74. Nördlingen, 1919-1934.

Stasiewski, Bernhard, ed. *Akten deutscher Bischöfe über die Lage der Kirche, 1933-1934*. Vol. 1. Mainz, 1968.

Steglich, Wolfgang, ed. *Der Friedensappell Papst Benedikts XV. . . .* Wiesbaden, 1970.

United States, Dept. of State. *Papers relating to the foreign relations of the United States, 1921*. Vol 2. Washington, D.C., 1936.

Vatican, *Acta Apostolicae Sedis*. Vols. 7-8, 11-25. Vatican City, 1915-1935.

Volk, Ludwig, ed. *Akten Kardinal Michael von Faulhabers 1917-1945*. Vol. 1. Mainz, 1975.

III. Memoirs, Diaries, and Personal Accounts

Bergmann, Carl. *Der Weg der Reparationen*. Frankfurt a.M., 1926.

Beyens, Napoléon Eugène. *Quatre ans à Rome, 1921-1926*. Paris, 1934.

Bismarck, Otto von. *Die politischen Reden des Fürsten Bismarck*. Ed. by Horst Kohl. Vol. 5. Stuttgart, 1893.

Braun, Otto. *Von Weimar zu Hitler*. New York, 1940.

Brüning, Heinrich. *Memoiren 1918-1934*. Stuttgart, 1970.

Bülow, Bernhard von. *Denkwürdigkeiten*. Vol. 2. Berlin, 1930-1931.

Charles-Roux, F. *Huit ans au Vatican, 1932-1940*. Paris, 1947.

D'Abernon, Edgar Vincent Viscount. *An ambassador of peace*. 3 Vols. London, 1929-1930.

Dorten, J. A. *La tragédie rhénane*. Paris, 1945.

Faulhaber, Michael von. *Deutsches Ehrgefühl und Katholisches Gewissen*. Munich, 1925.

———. *Rufende Stimmen in der Wüste*. Freiburg i.B., 1931.

———. *Zeitfragen und Zeitaufgaben*. Freiburg i.B., 1935.

François-Poncet, André. *The fateful years*. Trans. by J. LeClercq. New York, 1949.

Hertling, Georg. *Erinnerungen aus meinem Leben*. 2 Vols. Munich, 1920.

Heuvel, J. van den. "Benoît XV," *Revue Générale*, CVII (1922), 248-275.

Kanzler, Rudolf. *Bayerns Kampf gegen den Bolschewismus*. Munich, 1931.

Meissner, Otto. *Staatssekretär unter Ebert, Hindenburg, Hitler*. Hamburg, 1950.

Papen, Franz von. *Memoirs*. Trans. by B. Connell. London, 1952.

Pastor, Ludwig von. *Tagebücher, Briefe, Erinnerungen*. Ed. by Wilhelm Wühr. Heidelberg, 1950.

Pünder, Hermann. *Politik in der Reichskanzlei*. Stuttgart, 1961.

———. *Von Preussen nach Europa*. Stuttgart, 1968.

Riezler, Kurt. *Tagebücher, Aufsätze, Dokumente.* Ed. by Karl Erdmann. Göttingen, 1972.

Sahm, Heinrich. *Erinnerungen aus meinen Danziger Jahren, 1919-1930.* Marburg, 1958.

Scheidemann, Philipp. *Memoiren.* 2 Vols. Dresden, 1928.

————. *Papst, Kaiser, und Sozialdemokratie in ihren Friedensbemühungen im Sommer 1917.* Berlin, 1921.

Schreiber, Georg. "Der erste Entwurf des Reichskonkordats (1920/ 21)," *Gegenwartsprobleme des Rechts.* N.F.1., II (1950), 159-196.

————. *Zwischen Demokratie und Diktatur.* Münster, 1949.

Severing, Carl. *Mein Lebensweg.* 2 Vols. Cologne, 1950.

Tirard, Paul. *La France sur le Rhin.* Paris, 1930.

Tumulty, Joseph P. *Woodrow Wilson as I know him.* New York, 1921.

IV. Newspapers

Augsburger Postzeitung (Augsburg)
Bayerischer Kurier (Munich)
Bayerische Staatszeitung und Bayerischer Staatsanzeiger (Munich)
Berliner Tageblatt (Berlin)
La Civiltà Cattolica (Rome)
Corriere d'Italia (Rome)
The Daily Telegraph (London)
Deutsche Allgemeine Zeitung (Berlin)
Deutsche Tageszeitung (Berlin)
Deutsch-Evangelische Korrespondenz (Berlin)
Deutsches Tageblatt (Berlin)
Frankfurter Zeitung (Frankfurt)
Germania (Berlin)
L'Italia (Milan)
Katholische Korrespondenz (Berlin)
Kölnische Volkszeitung (Cologne)
Kölnische Zeitung (Cologne)
Kreuzzeitung (Berlin)
Il Messaggero di Roma (Rome)
The Milwaukee Sentinel (Milwaukee)
Münchner Neueste Nachrichten (Munich)
Neue Preussische Zeitung (Berlin)
Neue Tägliche Rundschau (Berlin)
Neue Züricher Nachrichten (Zurich)
Neue Züricher Zeitung (Zurich)
The New York Times (New York)
New Yorker Staatszeitung (New York)

L'Osservatore Romano (Vatican City)
Rhein-Echo (Düsseldorf)
Schlesische Volkszeitung (Breslau)
Der Tag (Berlin)
Il Tempo (Rome)
Le Temps (Paris)
The Times (London)
La Tribune de Genève (Geneva)
Vorwärts (Berlin)
Vossiche Zeitung (Berlin)
WTB, Wolff's Telegraphisches Büro (Berlin)
Weser Zeitung (Bremen)
Die Zeit (Berlin)

V. Interviews

Msgr. Walter Adolf (Berlin)
Cardinal Carlo Confaloniere—secretary to Pius XI (Vatican City)
Dr. Dieter Golombek (Bonn)
Marie Elizabeth Klee (Bonn)
Prof. Wilhelm Klein, S.J. (Bonn)
Mother Pascalina Lehnert—Pius XII's housekeeper (Rome)
Dr. Angelo Martini, S.J. (Rome)
Dr. Walter Münch—last secretary of Cardinal Bertram (Munich)
Dr. Hermann Pünder (Cologne)
Theda Freifrau von Ritter (Rottach, Bavaria)
Dr. Johannes Schauff (Bonn)
Prof. Burkhart Schneider, S.J. (Rome)
Johannes Waxenberger—last secretary of Cardinal Faulhaber (Munich)
John Wheeler-Bennett (London)

SECONDARY SOURCES

Books and Articles

Aretin, Karl Otmar Freiherr von. "Der deutsche Katholizismus und die Politik, 1914-1935," *Neue Politische Literatur*, IX (1964), 41-48.
———. "Das Ende der Zentrumspartei und der Abschluss des Reichskonkordats am 20. Juli 1933," *Frankfurter Hefte*, XVII (1962), 237-243.
———. *The papacy and the modern world.* Trans. by Roland Hill. New York, 1970.

————. "Prälat Kaas, Franz von Papen, und das Reichskonkordat von 1933," *Vierteljahrshefte für Zeitgeschichte*, XIV (1966), 252-279.

Artaud, Denise. *La question des dettes interalliées et la reconstruction de l'Europe (1917-1929)*. 2 Vols. Paris/Lille, 1978.

Das Auslandsdeutschtum in Osteuropa einst und jetzt. Edited by der Arbeits-und Sozialminister des Landes Nordrhein-Westfalen. 1963.

Bahr, Richard. *Volk jenseits der Grenzen*. 2nd edition. Hamburg, 1935.

Bailey, George. *Germans*. New York, 1972.

Bauer, C. *Deutscher Katholizismus, Entwicklungslinien und Profile*. Frankfurt a.M., 1964.

Becker, Josef. "Das Ende der Zentrumspartei und die Problematik des politischen Katholizismus in Deutschland," *Die Welt als Geschichte*, XXIII (1963), 149-172.

Beyhl, Jakob. *Deutschland und das Konkordat mit Rom*. Würzburg, 1925.

Binchy, Daniel A. *Church and state in fascist Italy*. London, 1941.

Boyens, Wilhelm. *Die Geschichte der ländlichen Siedlung*. 2 Vols. Berlin, 1959-1960.

Bracher, Karl Dietrich. *Die deutsche Diktatur*. Cologne, 1969.

————. "Nationalsozialistische Machtergreifung und Reichskonkordat," *Der Konkordatsprozess*. Ed. by Friedrich Giese and Friedrich August Freiherr von der Heydte. Vol. 3. Munich, 1958, pp. 947-1021.

Breuning, Klaus. *Die Vision des Reiches*. Munich, 1969.

Brüggemann, Fritz. *Die rheinische Republik*. Bonn, 1919.

Buchheim, Karl. "Warum das Zentrum unterging," *Hochland*, LIII (1960/61), 15-27.

Calisse, Carlo. "Il Cardinale Pietro Gasparri," *Nuova Antologia*, Anno 68, CCCLXVI (1933), 225-236.

Campbell, Gregory. "The struggle for Upper Silesia, 1919-1922," *Journal of Modern History*, XLII (1970), 361-385.

Carr, Edward H. *The twenty years' crisis, 1919-1939*. 2nd edition. London, 1948.

Churchill, Winston S. *The gathering storm*. Cambridge, Mass., 1948.

Cianfarra, Camille. *The Vatican and the Kremlin*. New York, 1950.

Claar, Maximilian. "Die Aussenpolitik des Vatikans seit den Lateranverträgen," *Zeitschrift für Politik*, XXI (1930-1931), 801-810.

Conway, John S. *The Nazi persecution of the church, 1933-45*. London, 1968.

Cowan, Laing Gray. *France and the Saar, 1680-1948*. New York, 1950.

Deuerlein, Ernst. "Bismarck und die Reichsvertretung beim Heiligen Stuhl," *Stimmen der Zeit*, CLXIV (1958/59), 203-219, 256-266.

————. "Die erste Begegnung zwischen Reichspräsident Ebert und

Nuntius Pacelli," *Münchener Theologische Zeitschrift*, XVIII (1966-1967), 157-159.

———. *Das Reichskonkordat*. Düsseldorf, 1956.

Dissard, François. "Les concordats de Pie XI," *Revue des sciences politiques*, LVIII (1935), 554-576.

Doepgen, Heinz. *Die Abtretung des Gebietes von Eupen-Malmedy*. Bonn, 1966.

Doerries, Reinhard R. "Imperial Berlin and Washington: new light on Germany's foreign policy and America's entry into World War I," *Central European History*, XI (1978), 23-49.

Doyle, Charles Hugo. *The life of Pope Pius XII*. New York, 1945.

Düwell, Kurt. *Deutschlands auswärtige Kulturpolitik; 1918-1932*. Cologne, 1976.

Ehrle, Franz. *Neu-Deutschland und der Vatikan*. Freiburg i.B., 1919.

Eimers, Enno. *Das Verhältnis von Preussen und Reich in den ersten Jahren der Weimarer Republik (1918-1923)*. Berlin, 1969.

Engel-Janosi, Friedrich. *Österreich und der Vatikan, 1846-1918*. 2 Vols. Graz, 1958.

———. *Vom Chaos zur Katastrophe*. Vienna, 1971.

Engelbert, Kurt. *Adolf Kardinal Bertram*. Hildesheim, 1949.

Enssle, Manfred J. *Stresemann's territorial revisionism: Germany, Belgium, and the Eupen-Malmédy question, 1919-1929*. Wiesbaden, 1980.

Epstein, Klaus. *Matthias Erzberger and the dilemma of German democracy*. Princeton, 1959.

Eschenburg, Theodor. *Matthias Erzberger*. Munich, 1973.

Euler, Heinrich. *Die Aussenpolitik der Weimarer Republik*. Aschaffenburg, 1957.

Evans, Ellen Lovell. *The German Center Party, 1870-1933*. Carbondale, Ill., 1981.

Fabrègues, J. de. "The reestablishment of relations between France and the Vatican in 1921," *Journal of Contemporary History*, II (1967), 163-182.

Falconi, Carlo. *The popes in the twentieth century*. Trans. by Muriel Grindrod. Boston, 1967.

Fink, Carole K. "Defender of minorities: Germany in the League of Nations, 1926-1933," *Central European History*, V (1972), 330-357.

———. "The Weimar Republic as the defender of minorities, 1919-1933," unpublished dissertation, Yale University, New Haven, 1969.

Fischer, Fritz. *Germany's aims in the First World War*. New York, 1967.

Föhr, Ernst. *Geschichte des badischen Konkordats*. Freiburg i.B., 1958.

Franz-Willing, Georg. *Die bayerische Vatikangesandtschaft, 1803-1934*. Munich, 1965.

Friedländer, Saul. *Pius XII and the Third Reich.* Trans. by Charles Fullman. New York, 1966.

Funk, Philipp. "Kritisches zum neuen Katholischen Selbstgefühl: Die Jungen und die Alten," *Hochland,* XXII (1924-1925), 587-597.

Galeazzi-Lisi, Riccardo. *Dans l'ombre et dans la lumière de Pie XII.* Paris, 1960.

Gathorne-Hardy, Geoffrey. *A short history of international affairs, 1920-1939.* 4th edition. New York, 1969.

Gatzke, Hans. *Germany's drive to the West.* Baltimore, 1950.

————. "Russo-German military collaboration during the Weimar Republic," *American Historical Review,* LXIII (1957-1958), 565-597.

————, ed. *European diplomacy between two wars, 1919-1939.* Chicago, 1972.

Golombek, Dieter. *Die politische Vorgeschichte des Preussenkonkordats (1929).* Mainz, 1970.

Gottlieb, W. W. *Studies in secret diplomacy during the First World War.* London, 1957.

Goyau, Georges. "Sur l'horizon du Vatican," *Revue des deux mondes,* Année 92 (1922), Part 1, 753-781.

Graham, Robert. *Vatican diplomacy.* Princeton, 1959.

Der Grosse Brockhaus, 15th ed. Leipzig, 1928-1935.

Grünthal, Günther. *Reichsschulgesetz und Zentrumspartei in der Weimarer Republik.* Düsseldorf, 1968.

Halecki, Oscar and Murray, James F. J. *Eugenio Pacelli, pope of peace.* New York, 1951.

Hanus, Franciscus. *Die preussische Vatikangesandtschaft, 1747-1920.* Munich, 1954.

Harrigan, William M. "Nazi Germany and the Holy See, 1933-1936," *Catholic Historical Review,* XLVII (1961), 164-198.

Hirsch, Helmut. *Die Saar von Genf.* Bonn, 1954.

Hömig, Herbert. *Das preussische Zentrum in der Weimarer Republik.* Mainz, 1979.

Holborn, Hajo. *A history of modern Germany.* Vol. 3. New York, 1969.

Huddleston, Sisley. *Those Europeans.* New York, 1924.

Hughes, John Jay. "The Reich Concordat 1933: capitulation or compromise?," *Australian Journal of Politics and History,* XX (1974), 164-175.

Hughes, Philip. *Pope Pius XI.* New York, 1937.

Hull, Henry L. "The Holy See and Soviet Russia, 1918-1930," unpublished diss., Georgetown University, Washington, D.C., 1970.

Jedin, Hubert and Dolan, John P., eds. *The Church in the modern world.* New York, 1981.

Johnson, Humphrey. *Vatican diplomacy in the World War.* Oxford, 1933.

Jurkiewicz, Jarosław. *Nuncjatura Achillesa Ratti w Polsce.* Warsaw, 1953.

———. "Watykan i Plebiscyt na Górnym Śląsku," *Sprawy Międzynarodowe,* V (1952), 28-51.

Kehr, Eckart. *Economic interests, militarism, and foreign policy.* Berkeley, 1977.

Kent, Peter C. *The pope and the duce.* New York, 1981.

Kimmich, Christoph. *The free city.* New Haven, 1968.

Koeniger, A. M. *Die neuen deutschen Konkordate und Kirchenverträge mit der preussischen Zirkumskriptionsbulle.* Bonn, 1932.

Koszyk, Kurt. *Deutsche Presse, 1914-1945.* Berlin, 1972.

Krüger, Peter. "Das Reparationsproblem der Weimarer Republik in fragwürdiger Sicht," *Vierteljahrshefte für Zeitgeschichte,* XXIX (1981), 21-47.

Kupper, Alfons. "Zur Geschichte des Reichskonkordats," *Stimmen der Zeit,* CLXIII (1958-1959), 278-302, 354-375; CLXXI (1962-1963), 25-50.

Lama, Friedrich Ritter von. *Papst und Kurie in ihrer Politik nach dem Weltkrieg.* Illertissen, 1925.

Lange-Ronneberg, Erwin. *Die Konkordate.* Paderborn, 1929.

Langer, William, ed. *An encyclopedia of world history.* 5th edition. Boston, 1972.

La Piana, George. "The political heritage of Pius XII," *Foreign Affairs,* XVIII (1940), 486-506.

Leiber, Robert. "Pius XII," *Stimmen der Zeit,* CLXIII (1958-1959), 81-100.

———. "Reichskonkordat und Ende der Zentrumspartei," *Stimmen der Zeit,* CLXVII (1960-1961), 213-223.

Lewy, Guenter. *The Catholic church and Nazi Germany.* New York, 1965.

Lexikon für Theologie und Kirche. Vol. 3. Freiburg i.B., 1931.

Loiseau, Charles. "La politique du S. Siège en Europe centrale (1919-1936)," *Le monde slave,* XIII (1936), 181-199; XIV, 1 (1937), 98-121; XIV, 2 (1937), 57-86, 218-249.

Lulvès, J. "Papst Benedikt XV und die Friedenskonferenz," *Die Grenzboten,* LXXVIII (1919), 129-131.

———. "Papst Benedikts XV. Verhalten gegenüber Deutschland seit dem Erlöschen des Weltkrieges," *Deutsche Revue,* XLV (1920), 97-108.

Lutz, Heinrich. *Demokratie im Zwielicht.* Munich, 1963.

———. "Die deutschen Katholiken in und nach dem ersten Weltkrieg," *Hochland,* LV (1962-1963), 193-216.

MacCormick, Anne. *Vatican journal.* New York, 1957.

McDougall, Walter A. *France's Rhineland diplomacy, 1914-1924.* Princeton, 1978.

Maier, Charles S. *Recasting bourgeois Europe*. Princeton, 1975.

Marks, Sally. *The illusion of peace*. New York, 1976.

————. "The myths of reparations," *Central European History*, XI (1978), 231-255.

Mason, John Brown. "The concordat with the Third Reich," *Catholic Historical Review*, XX (1934), 23-37.

Matthias, Erich and Morsey, Rudolf, eds. *Das Ende der Parteien, 1933*. Düsseldorf, 1960.

Mayer, Arno J. *Political origins of the new diplomacy*. New Haven, 1959.

————. *Politics and diplomacy of peacemaking*. New York, 1967.

Mehnert, Gottfried. *Evangelische Kirchen und Politik 1917-1919*. Düsseldorf, 1959.

Micklem, Nathaniel. *National Socialism and the Roman Catholic Church*. New York, 1939.

Milatz, Alfred. *Wähler und Wahlen in der Weimarer Republik*. Bonn, 1965.

Mirbt, Karl. *Das Konkordatsproblem der Gegenwart*. Berlin, 1927.

Moody, Joseph, ed. *Church and society*. New York, 1953.

Morsey, Rudolf. "Die deutsche Zentrumspartei," in *Das End der Parteien, 1933*. Ed. by Erich Matthias and Rudolf Morsey. Düsseldorf, 1960, pp. 279-453.

————. *Die deutsche Zentrumspartei 1917-1923*. Düsseldorf, 1966.

————. *Der Untergang des politischen Katholizismus*. Stuttgart, 1977.

————. *Zur Entstehung, Authentizität und Kritik von Brünings 'Memoiren 1918-1934'*. Opladen, 1975.

————. "Zur Geschichte des Preussischen Konkordats und der Errichtung des Bistums Berlin," *Wichmann-Jahrbuch*, XIX/XX (1965-1966), 64-89.

————. "Zur Vorgeschichte des Reichskonkordats aus den Jahren 1920 und 1921," *Zeitschrift der Savigny-Stiftung für Rechtsgeschichte*, LXXV (1958), 237-267.

Mourin, Maxime. *Le Vatican et L'U.R.S.S.* Paris, 1965.

Muckermann, Friedrich. *Im Kampf zwischen zwei Epochen*. Mainz, 1973.

Müller, Hans. "Der deutsche Katholizismus 1918/19," *Geschichte in Wissenschaft und Unterricht*, XVII (1966), 521-536.

Murphy, Paul I. with Arlington, R. René. *La popessa*. New York, 1983.

Neumann, Ernst. "Methoden der römischen Kolonisation in Deutschland," *Das Reich*, II (Jan.-Feb., 1932).

Nitzschke, Volker. *Die Auseinandersetzungen um die Bekenntnisschule. . . .* Berlin, 1964.

Orde, Anne. "The origins of the German-Austrian Customs Union affair of 1931," *Central European History*, XIII (1980), 34-59.

Padellaro, Nazareno. *Portrait of Pius XII.* Trans. by Michael Derrick. New York, 1957.

Patin, Wilhelm. *Beiträge zur Geschichte der deutsch-vatikanischen Beziehungen in den letzten Jahrzehnten.* Berlin, 1942.

Peters, Walter H. *The life of Benedict XV.* Milwaukee, 1959.

Pinon, Paul. Editorial review in the *Revue des deux mondes.* 93 Année, VII (1923), 718.

Rehberger, Horst. *Die Gleichschaltung des Landes Baden 1932/33.* Heidelberg, 1966.

Repgen, Konrad. "Über die Entstehung der Reichskonkordats Offerte im Frühjahr 1933 und die Bedeutung des Reichskonkordats," *Vierteljahrshefte für Zeitgeschichte,* XXV (1978), 499-534.

Rhodes, Anthony. *The Vatican in the age of the dictators 1920-1945.* New York, 1973.

Roth, Joseph. "Zur Vorgeschichte der Berliner Nuntiatur," in *Reich und Reichsfeinde.* Vol. 4. Hamburg, 1943, pp. 215-236.

Ruppel, Edith. "Zur Tätigkeit des Eugenio Pacelli als Nuntius in Deutschland," *Zeitschrift für Geschichtswissenschaft,* VII (1959), 297-317.

Sandfuchs, Wilhelm. *Die Aussenminister der Päpste.* Munich, 1962.

Schauff, Johannes. *Das Wahlverhalten der deutschen Katholiken im Kaiserreich und in der Weimarer Republik.* Mainz, 1975.

Schmidlin, Josef. *Papstgeschichte der neuesten Zeit.* Vols. 3-4. Munich, 1936-1939.

Schneider, Egon. "Die heutige Rechtskraft der Bulle de Salute Animarum," *Theologie und Glaube,* VI (1926), 805-828.

Scholder, Klaus. "Altes und Neues zur Vorgeschichte des Reichskonkordats," *Vierteljahrshefte für Zeitgeschichte,* XXV (1978), 535-570.

―――. *Die Kirchen und das Dritte Reich.* Vol. 1. Berlin, 1977.

Schuker, Stephen. *The end of French predominance in Europe.* Chapel Hill, 1976.

Schwend, Karl. *Bayern zwischen Monarchie und Diktatur.* Munich, 1954.

Solzbacher, Wilhelm. *Pius XI. als Verteidiger der menschlichen Persönlichkeit.* Lucerne, 1939.

Spadolini, Giovanni. *Il Cardinale Gasparri e la Questione Romana.* Florence, 1972.

Stambrook, F. G. "The German-Austrian Customs Union project of 1931: a study of German methods and motives," *Journal of Central European Affairs,* XXI (1961), 15-41.

Stehle, Hansjakob. "Motive des Reichskonkordats," *Aussenpolitik,* VII (1956), 558-564.

―――. *Die Ostpolitik des Vatikans: 1917-1975.* Munich, 1975.

Stehlin, Stewart A. "Germany and a proposed Vatican state, 1915-1917," *Catholic Historical Review*, LX (1974), 402-426.

Stump, Wolfgang. *Geschichte und Organisation der Zentrumspartei in Düsseldorf 1917-1933*. Düsseldorf, 1971.

Sugrue, Francis. *Popes in the modern world*. New York, 1961.

Taliani, Francesco. *Vita del Cardinal Gasparri*. Milan, 1938.

Teeling, William. *The pope in politics*. London, 1937.

Temperley, H.W.V., ed. *A history of the Peace Conference of Paris*. 6 Vols. London, 1920-1924.

Töpner, Kurt. "Der deutsche Katholizismus zwischen 1918 und 1933," in Hans Joachim Schoeps, ed., *Zeitgeist im Wandel*. Vol. 20. Stuttgart, 1968, 176-202.

Toynbee, Arnold, ed. *Survey of international affairs, 1920-1923, 1924*. Oxford, 1925-1926.

Trachtenberg, Marc. *Reparation in world politics*. New York, 1980.

Trippen, Norbert. *Das Domkapitel und die Erzbischofswahlen in Köln 1821-1929*. Cologne, 1972.

Volk, Ludwig. *Der bayerische Episkopat und der Nationalsozialismus, 1930-1934*. Mainz, 1965.

———. "Kardinal Faulhabers Stellung zur Weimarer Republik und zum NS-Staat," *Stimmen der Zeit*, CLXXVII (1966-1967), 173-195.

———. *Das Reichskonkordat vom 20. Juli 1933*. Mainz, 1972.

Walz, Angelus. *Andreas Kardinal Frühwirth*. Vienna, 1950.

Wambaugh, Sarah. *Plebiscites since the World War*. 2 Vols. Washington, D.C., 1933.

———. *The Saar plebiscite*. Cambridge, Mass., 1940.

Weber, Werner, ed. *Die deutsche Konkordate und Kirchenverträge der Gegenwart*. Göttingen, 1962.

Weinberg, Gerhard L. "The defeat of Germany in 1918 and the European balance of power," *Central European History*, II (1969), 248-260.

Weinzierl-Fischer, Erika. *Die österreichischen Konkordate von 1855 und 1933*. Vienna, 1960.

Wende, Erich. *C.H. Becker, Mensch und Politiker*. Stuttgart, 1959.

Wenner, Joseph. *Reichskonkordat und Länderkonkordate*. Paderborn, 1934.

Wentzcke, Paul. *Ruhrkampf*. 2 Vols. Berlin, 1932.

Wheeler-Bennett, John. *The wreck of reparations*. New York, 1933.

Wirth, Günter. "Zum vatikanischen Einfluss auf die Politik des Zentrums," *Jenaer Beiträge zur Parteiengeschichte*, XXIII (1968), 89-92.

Zeender, John K. "The German Catholics and the presidential election of 1925," *Journal of Modern History*, LXIII (1963), 366-381.

—————. "The German Center Party during World War I: an internal study," *Catholic Historical Review*, XLII (1957), 441-468.

Zenner, Maria. *Parteien und Politik im Saargebiet unter dem Völkerbundsregime 1920-1935*. Saarbrücken, 1966.

Zimmermann, Ludwig. *Deutsche Aussenpolitik in der Ära der Weimarer Republik*. Göttingen, 1958.

Zittel, Bernard. "Die Vertretung des Heiligen Stuhles in München 1785-1934," in *Der Mönch im Wappen*. Munich, 1960, pp. 419-494.

ADDENDUM

The following book arrived too late to be utilized in this work.

May, Georg. *Ludwig Kaas; der Priester, der Politiker und der Gelehrte aus der Schule von Ulrich Stutz*. 3 Vols. Amsterdam, 1981-1982.

INDEX

The italic numbers indicate pages on which pictures are to be found.

LIBRARY OF CONGRESS CATALOGING IN PUBLICATION DATA

Stehlin, Stewart A., 1936-
    Weimar and the Vatican, 1919-1933.

    Bibliography: p.
    Includes index.
    1. Catholic Church—Relations (diplomatic)—Germany. 2. Germany—Foreign relations—Catholic Church. 3. Germany—History—1918-1933. 4. Church and state—Germany—History—20th century. I. Title.
BX1536.S73   1983   327.45'634'043   83-42544
ISBN 0-691-05399-5